*Baby Boomers
and Popular Culture*

Baby Boomers
and Popular Culture

An Inquiry into America's
Most Powerful Generation

Brian Cogan and Thom Gencarelli, Editors

 PRAEGER

AN IMPRINT OF ABC-CLIO, LLC
Santa Barbara, California • Denver, Colorado • Oxford, England

Library of Congress Cataloging-in-Publication Data

Baby boomers and popular culture : an inquiry into America's most powerful generation / Brian Cogan and Thom Gencarelli, editors.

     pages cm
  Includes index.
  ISBN 978-0-313-39886-5 (alk. paper) — ISBN 978-0-313-39887-2 (ebook)
  1. Popular culture—United States—History—20th century.   2. Baby boom generation—United States—History.   3. United States—Civilization—1945-   4. United States—History—1945-   I. Cogan, Brian, 1967-   II. Gencarelli, Thom.
  E169.12.B245   2015
  306.097309'04—dc23   2014024866

ISBN: 978-0-313-39886-5
EISBN: 978-0-313-39887-2

19 18 17 16 15   1 2 3 4 5

This book is also available on the World Wide Web as an eBook.
Visit www.abc-clio.com for details.

Praeger
An Imprint of ABC-CLIO, LLC

ABC-CLIO, LLC
130 Cremona Drive, P.O. Box 1911
Santa Barbara, California 93116-1911

This book is printed on acid-free paper ∞

Manufactured in the United States of America

Contents

PART 4: LITERATURE

Introduction

Brian Cogan and Thom Gencarelli

We wonder how people will react to this book. Will their interest be based on the expectation that we have put forth the latest celebration of Dylan, drugs, and debauchery that epitomizes so many popular culture celebrations of the baby boomers? Will they read it as another celebration of all things Clinton—Bill *and* Hillary—who symbolize the baby boomer generation to so many? Or will they have a genuine interest in examining the lives and the social, cultural, and political movements that have shaped our national landscape for the past half century?

Or will they simply pick up this book and roll their eyes. Not *another* book about the baby boomers. Really? Haven't we had enough of that self-conscious, narcissistic proto-me generation by now? Do we really need another book about the generation that made navel-gazing, self-importance, and self-promotion the new norm?

Well, these are two possibilities—especially if we stick to the simple binary notion that Tom Brokaw was wrong and Leonard Steinhorn was right in calling the boomers the greater generation,[1] or if we simply dismiss them as narcissistic and self-obsessed. But of course nothing in our world can ever be accurately and fairly summed up according to such an oversimplified, black-versus-white set of assumptions—and especially not the baby boomers. The baby boomers are the generation that not only defined the 1960s—a period in which we lived through the Vietnam War, the civil rights movement, the rise of feminism and gay rights, and the counterculture movement—but who have also continued to make cultural, social, political, and economic contri-butions long after the sixties heyday: for the better, sometimes for the worse, and certainly in ways in which both the immediate and the lasting value remain open to question and debate.

Our ultimate purpose with this book is to make the case that, up to the present day and the presidency of Barack Obama, the boomer generation has been *enormously* influential, literally changing the landscape of social, political, and mediated life in the United States in ways that led to radical shifts from the practices and ways of life in the decades of the 20th century preceding their arrival and ascendancy. In other words, they are a revolutionary generation. At the same time, they have been the subject of sustained criticisms as the result of their apparent narcissism, their desire for material possessions, and their gradual abandonment of the very same principles they themselves established and stood for and that defined them during the 1960s. Although both of these views—that the boomers were a revolutionary vanguard and that they turned into crass yuppies—are, again, binary exaggerations, both do contain some grain of truth.

In addition, though the initial wave of boomers has now reached retirement age, they have not left the American cultural and political scene. And though it is important to gauge this continued presence against the fact that one of the defining aspects of the boomer generation is their apparent eternal youthfulness—derided by some critics as simply another facet of their narcissism—it is certainly the case that they continue to be influential figures in the media, the arts, and political and civic life. Like it or not, the boomers aren't going anywhere soon. We therefore seek in this collection to examine the long run of the boomers on the stage of U.S. politics, on the television screen, in the movies, and in popular music and literature—as well as to catalog and analyze the undeniable impact they have had from the 1960s up to the present day. Warts and all.

The boomers are most easily defined as the postwar generation born during the years that stretched roughly from 1946 to 1964.[2] This is the demographic point of view, anyway. The boomer generation—or perhaps we should more accurately say "generations"—are a complex and heterogeneous group with no real or strong sense of connection other than the fact that they are lumped into this historical place and time. The origin of the term as it relates to "*the* baby boom" as opposed to "*a* baby boom," is also not entirely clear. However, Meyers et al. credit *New York Post* financial columnist Sylvia Porter with one of the earliest, if not the first, references to a "boom" in the annual birthrate during the postwar years, in an article she wrote in 1951: "Take the 3,548,000 babies born in 1950," she wrote. "Bundle them into a batch, bounce them all over the bountiful land that is America. What do you get? Boom. The biggest boomiest boomy boom ever known in history."[3]

Wade Clark Roof, in his book about boomers and religion, cites the Canadian philosopher François Ricard and his point that it was during the boomers' formative years that Western modernity truly and finally triumphed. In both Roof's and Ricard's view, it was during this time that "[o]lder definitions of the world and how it operated gave way to new ones including . . . a growing preoccupation with the 'new,' whether as the latest material gadget, the remaking of a person's self-image, or the most promising vision of salvation."[4] Roof is, however, careful not to give the boomers all of the credit. He points out how "nuclear warfare, the birth control pill, advances in communications technology, the expansion of multinational corporations, and changing global patterns of political and economic alliances coalesced to remake the world"[5] during this time. And he emphasizes how this was also the age in which the mass culture gained an unprecedented influence over human affairs.

Despite all of this, however, the demographic birth curve is more of a simplification than any kind of accurate categorization. In a recent *New York Times* article, Richard Perez-Pena acknowledged that his date of birth situated him at the tail end of the boomer generation. He took pains, however, to explain the dissimilarities of the boomers as opposed to any overarching sense of connection. He acknowledged that although there was a substantial enough growth in births to validate the term "baby boomer," the phrase itself does not adequately describe the differences inherent in a population that is much too easily categorized together. As he articulated it: "the kind of broadly shaped cultural experiences that could bind people together across that vast span? That just didn't happen."[6] He emphasized the distinction between the boomers born in the immediate postwar years and those born during the late 1950s and early 1960s. In his view, the extent of "political content, darkness and skepticism"[7] was not something the earlier boomers experienced as they grew up. For later boomers like him, however, "they were part of the landscape. The early boomers were born into a world without rock 'n' roll, swearing in the media or even much in the way of really harsh satire. A lot of us late boomers can't remember a time before the British invasion, Hunter S. Thompson and George Carlin."[8]

This is not a particularly new argument. As far back as 1993, in an article entitled "The Boomlet Generation," Alexander Abrams and David Lipsky argued that those who attempted to market to the tail end of the boomer generation as though they had anything in common with boomers born during the late 1940s were inevitably doomed to failure. In defining their "boomlet," they mistakenly marked the end of the baby boom at 1961. But as they wrote about their own cohort: "The members of the Boomlet generation are like middle children: The people ahead of us, the Boomers, got the inheritance; and now our noisy, younger siblings are getting all the attention. We're getting passed over, with all of our easily identifiable tastes and our irresistible purchasing power."[9]

Steve Gillon makes a similar distinction in his introduction to his book, *Boomer Nation: The Largest and Richest Generation Ever and How It Changed America.* He divides the "roughly 76 million babies"[10] born during the period into two groups: the boomers themselves, born between 1946 and 1957, and what he refers to as the "Shadow Boomers," born between 1958 and 1964. As he writes:

The early generation of Baby Boomers grew up with rock and roll, the Mickey Mouse Club, prosperity, crewcuts, the idealism of John F. Kennedy, and the social struggles of the 1960s. A child born in 1964 confronted a world of oil embargos, stagflation, Watergate, sideburns, and disco balls. Older Baby Boomers spent much of their lives trying to reconcile their youthful idealism with social reality. Younger Boomers, raised in an age of cynicism, had less idealism to compromise.[11]

What all of this points to is the fact that the assumptions we make in simply grouping people into categories lead us not only to ignore differences in race, gender, class, sexuality, and ideology but also, in this particular case, to make the assumption that an entire generation can be defined by their representations in our popular culture and our understanding of them via such representations. We would also add that, despite such demographic quibbling, Perez-Pena's, Abrams and Lipsky's, and Gillon's second-wave boomers, who struggled for their own identity, are now in their fifties and as prominent and formidable a presence in American culture as the earlier boomers who are now well beyond traditional retirement age.

Indeed, one frequent complaint about the boomers, at least in the popular culture, is that they are, to put it bluntly, *still here*. The normal assumption is that once a generation has had its time in the spotlight it gradually moves aside and lets the next generation boldly march forth to put its mark on the world. The boomers, however, have proven too déclassé to simply walk off the stage and into retirement. And although this is of course a generalization and an exaggeration, there is some truth to it. It is a fact that Americans now live longer and have greater access to sophisticated diet and nutrition information (whether or not they take advantage of it) and that boomer icons are still highly visible, actively and publicly working in entertainment, literature, the arts, sports (at least as coaches or spokespeople), and, most importantly, politics. The editors of this volume probably see images of former President Bill Clinton as often as they see similar coverage for any currently serving politician. Thus, though some of this can be attributed to better health and health care and some to new conceptions and/or perceptions of aging, the result seems clear: 60 is the new 40, and 80 may now be the new 60.

In a recent article in the *New Yorker*, Patricia Marx noted a preference among many in the baby boomer generation to forestall retirement and in some cases not even consider retirement as an option. As she wrote: "Baby boomers are not simply delaying retirement; they are retiring retirement altogether by starting new careers. The fifty-five-year-old-and-up crowd is the only age group that is growing as a share of the workforce."[12] She added that this is not a by-product of necessity or of austerity measures. It is the result of a pervasive attitude that "spending days in full-time leisure and repose no longer connotes a sense of privilege and deservingness; it means you are unemployed."[13] It is the result of the fact that for many boomers, and especially for those over 65, the assumption of a job and career as a finite marker in one's life is no longer the case, and many simply do not see the point in slowing down or leaving public life.

Let's face it, then: the boomers do not seem to be going anywhere soon, which makes this book timelier than ever. And although quite a number of books have examined the boomers and their legacy, most have either lauded or derided them. We, however, have no interest in passing such judgments. Our task with this collection is to examine the boomer generation in terms of critical theory using an array of approaches from a multidisciplinary point of view that seeks to examine them in all of their contradictions and complexity.

What interests us in the subject and in the first place is not the fact that we are boomers ourselves (albeit one of us is). What interests us comes down to three factors, and we offer these here to the reader in ascending order with respect to our priorities and concerns.

The first is that the sheer size of the boomer population taken as a whole enabled them, as they rose to adulthood and prominence, to become a cultural force that has obviously and overpoweringly shaped events, trends, values, and the overarching gestalt of our life's world over the past half century. The same presumably can be argued for any generation, regardless of its size and the life and times in which it arose. However, we would argue that size matters: that it matters with respect to the number of boomers as consumers and tastemakers, to the number of boomers in the workforce, to the number of boomers as citizens and as a voting bloc, etc. We would further argue that the particular age into which the boomers were born, grew up, matured, and took their seat at the head of the table also matters a *great* deal—which leads us to our second concern.

The second factor that interests us is the era that is the latter half of the 20th century. To us, it matters a great deal that the boomers at the leading edge of this population explosion—those who were born in 1946—turned 18 years old in 1964. That is to say, they were no longer minors but became adult "majors" in the very year after John F. Kennedy was assassinated and the idealism of the days of Camelot ended abruptly and tragically. They became adults the year after the Beatles first appeared on the *Ed Sullivan Show* and set off the cataclysm in popular music and the popular culture that exploded during the 1960s. (It also bears mentioning that they turned 10 years old in 1956: the year that Elvis Presley scored five Top 40 hit records and ushered in the era of rock and roll.) They became adults in the year President Lyndon Baines Johnson signed into law the Civil Rights Act of 1964—some of them after participating in the Freedom Rides and civil rights marches that included the 1963 March on Washington for Jobs and Freedom—and a year before Malcolm X was assassinated. They became adults in the year the Gulf of Tonkin incident led the United States Congress to pass the Gulf of Tonkin Resolution, which President Johnson cited in escalating our military involvement in Vietnam. They protested the war as students in colleges and universities all across the United States.

They were adults when Martin Luther King Jr. and Robert F. Kennedy were assassinated in 1968. They were adults when Apollo 11 landed on the moon and the Woodstock Music and Art Fair took place during the summer of 1969. They were adults when the 1960s ended—not literally, on January 1, 1970, but depending on the cultural event one recognizes as the figurative end of the 1960s: the stabbing death of an audience member at the Rolling Stones' free concert at the Altamont Speedway in San Francisco in December 1969; the shooting deaths of four Kent State University students at the hands of the Ohio National Guard on May 4, 1970; the resignation of President Richard Nixon in the aftermath of the Watergate scandal in August 1974; or the final, closing chapter of U.S. involvement in Vietnam in April 1975, just one year short of the year the oldest boomers reached their 30th birthday.

Our point isn't that no significant, earth-shattering, or catastrophic events have taken place in the United States or in the world before or since the 1960s. Certainly, Tom Brokaw was right in defining what he called the "greatest generation" based on the extent to which their lives were affected by the years of the Great Depression, into which they were born, and World War II, in which they fought and lost their lives and the lives of loved ones— and in which the entire country lost the lives of so many young men. We do argue, however, that the 1960s were an intense, compressed period in which a great deal of social, cultural, and political upheaval took place, which resulted in extraordinary change—change we continue to negotiate and seek to further realize and bring to fruition.

We also continue to be surprised by the utter lack of serious protest in the United States in response to any serious political, civic, and social issues since that time; about the fact that no cohort since—generation X, generation Y, the millennials, etc.—has started and grown a movement. Of course, we could point out that the Tea Party constitutes a protest movement. We also recognize the Occupy movement as a legitimate protest, albeit one that never sustained its momentum and that largely came to an end as the result of a change of seasons. We would also remind our reader that many prominent members of both of these movements, as well as other, lesser movements, came from the ranks of the boomers. In the meantime, no matter how far the boomers have come since the 1960s, how much their original idealism may have been co-opted, or how much their involvement in those heady times in which they were swept up may have been immature, superficial, misguided, and/or impractically romantic in the first place, they undoubtedly continue to be affected and shaped by those times.

Finally, we approach the subject that is the culture and legacy of the boomers from the perspective of media studies. And we argue that it is not merely appropriate to examine the subject from this perspective. We argue that this is *the* only and best means to frame such an examination: that this is what sets *this* book apart from any other works on the subject, and that this is therefore our book's critical contribution. We say this because the very means by which people recognize and distinguish a baby boom and everything about it in the first place is through the culture-wide discourse that, at one point, seized upon Sylvia Porter's realization, gave it a name, and effectively reified the concept, evolving and exploding it into existence and into the zeitgeist. In addition, such discourse comes about and is mainly carried out through the various vehicles of our mass media—in particular books and the news and information media of print, radio, television, and the Internet. In other words, there is not and never has been a truly connected cohort of people in the world known as boomers, and certainly not any self-defining group of people. Nor have there ever been the two groups Perez-Pena, Abrams and Lipsky, and Gillon have argued. All of this is simply the by-product of a *construct* that has enabled us to carry out and carry on a coherent and significant discourse about a group of people in a specific time and place.

In sum, although many of the authors in this collection come from a media studies background, we as editors work from a set of assumptions about media that is often collectively referred to as "media ecology." The term's origins hark back to the work of Marshall McLuhan, as well as others before and contemporary to him, including Walter Ong, Harold Innis, and especially Neil Postman, but the term today refers to an approach to the study of media institutions and representations that looks at media as environments in which we live and in which our culture takes its shape, as opposed to a direct causal agents.

Moreover, we have chosen, and have had the pleasure to bring aboard, a wide array of contributors not just from media studies and media ecology but also from all over the broader field of the humanities. We have challenged them to use their own critical lenses to examine myriad facets of the boomer experience from their perspective. We have also encouraged a contrarian tendency and made it clear that we did not want a dispassionate, clinical examination of the boomers but a spirited debate. Some contributors clearly disagree with one another, and others express similarities that give due credence to nuance and subtlety. The common mission, however, is to look at the boomers not as a set of common missions and causes (e.g., civil rights, the women's movement, gay rights, anti-war protests, the student movement) but as a contradictory and often downright confusing set of what Benedict Andersen would call "imagined communities."[14]

Because of the fact that the boomers present us with a dissimilar set of contradictory impulses rather than a coherent whole, we therefore cannot *but* leave room, with this volume, for debate. That is to say, though no one can write the definitive tale of a generation as complex, puzzling, and fascinating as the boomers, we seek to blend multiple compelling, and sometimes competing, narratives that illustrate what we hope are all-encompassing parts of the boomer experience. Whether our authors are examining boomer movements, politics, television, film, music, or literature, they try not to enshrine the boomers as legends nor take them to task for excessive hubris. Rather, we have together sought to foster and further a conversation about the baby boomers that will not end with this book but that we hope will continue afterward.

This book, then, seeks to analyze the baby boomers in terms of all their apparent contradictions and take a deep and extensive look into their impact on American culture, politics, film, television, music, and literature.

NOTES

1. Leonard Steinhorn, *The Greater Generation: In Defense of the Baby Boom Legacy* (New York: St. Martin's, 2006).

2. Cheryl Russell, *The Baby Boom: Americans Born 1946 to 1964* (Ithaca, NY: New Strategist, 2004), 1–3.

3. David Meyers, Beverly Meyers, and Elise Meyers Walker, *Look to Lazarus: The Big Store* (Charleston, SC: History Press, 2011), 93.

4. Wade Clark Roof, *Spiritual Marketplace: Baby Boomers and the Remaking of American Religion* (Princeton, NJ: Princeton University Press, 1999), 49.

5. Ibid., 49.

6. Richard Perez-Pena, "I May Be 50, but Don't Call Me a Boomer," *New York Times*, January 6, 2014, http://www.nytimes.com/2014/06/booming.

7. Ibid.

8. Ibid.

9. Alexander Abrams and David Lipsky, "The Boomlet Generation," *New York Times*, January 4, 1993, http://www.nytimes.com/1993/01/04/opinion/the-boomlet-generation.html.

10. Steve Gillon, *Boomer Nation: The Largest and Richest Generation Ever and How It Changed America* (New York: Free Press, 2004), 13.

11. Ibid., 14.

12. Patricia Marx, "Golden Years: How Will the Boomers Handle Retirement? Hire an Expert," *The New Yorker*, October 8, 2012, 72.

13. Ibid.

14. Benedict Andersen, *Imagined Communities: Reflections on the Origin and Spread of Nationalism* (New York: Verso Press, 2006).

REFERENCES

Abrams, Alexander, and David Lipsky. "The Boomlet Generation." *New York Times*, January 4, 1993. http://www.nytimes.com/1993/01/04/opinion/the-boomlet-generation.html.

Andersen, Benedict. *Imagined Communities: Reflections on the Origin and Spread of Nationalism*. Rev. ed. New York: Verso Press, 2006.

Gillon, Steve. *Boomer Nation: The Largest and Richest Generation Ever and How It Changed America*. New York: Free Press, 2004.

Marx, Patricia. "Golden Years: How Will the Boomers Handle Retirement? Hire an Expert." *The New Yorker*, October 8, 2012, 72.

Meyers, David, Beverly Meyers, and Elise Meyers Walker. *Look to Lazarus: The Big Store*. Charleston, SC: History Press, 2011.

Perez-Pena, Richard. "I May be 50, but Don't Call Me a Boomer." *New York Times*, January 6, 2014. http://www.nytimes.com/2014/06/booming.

Roof, Wade Clark. *Spiritual Marketplace: Baby Boomers and the Remaking of American Religion*. Princeton, NJ: Princeton University Press, 1999.

Russell, Cheryl. *The Baby Boom: Americans Born 1946 to 1964*. 4th ed. Ithaca, NY: New Strategist, 2004.

Steinhorn, Leonard. *The Greater Generation: In Defense of the Baby Boom Legacy*. New York: St. Martin's, 2006.

Part 1

Politics

From Camelot to Watergate: Ten Years That Changed the Politics of Boomer Culture

William M. Knoblauch

For the baby boom generation, 1963 to 1973 proved to be a transformative period in postwar politics. When the 1960s began, Americans had faith in their government. They were optimistic and hopeful about changing their country, and even the world. Civil rights campaigns inspired their activism, while television and popular music promoted their politics. President John Fitzgerald Kennedy appealed to boomers. He exuded youthful vitality, and the press treated him, and his family, like royalty. When his wife dubbed the Kennedy White House "Camelot," the sobriquet stuck. In three short years, however, optimism faded. In November 1963, Kennedy's assassination traumatized a nation. As Camelot fell, Kennedy's successor, Lyndon B. Johnson, escalated U.S. involvement in Vietnam. In response, the antiwar movement grew, race riots erupted, and politics became more contentious. By 1968, a conservative backlash fractured the country, and the 1973 Watergate scandal shook boomers' faith in their government. By the 1977 Jimmy Carter administration, idealism and optimism of the 1960s seemed distant memories. But in 1961, Kennedy's call to each and every American to "ask not what your country can do for you—ask what you can do for your country" resonated with a generation ready to break with 1950s political complacency (Winkler 2011, 80).

EISENHOWER'S AMERICA: 1953–1961

President Dwight D. Eisenhower (1953–1961) was a lifelong military man and supreme allied commander of the European forces in World War II. Eisenhower's predecessor, Harry S. Truman (1944–1953), adopted a foreign policy of containment, which aimed to stop the spread of communism by bolstering capitalist economies abroad, building defensive arsenals at home, and, when necessary, waging proxy wars, which he did in North Korea. Once elected, Eisenhower reassessed these policies. He supported containment, but his "New Look" approach sought to constrain growing costs. A growing thermonuclear arsenal reduced America's need for a large army and left an imprint on many young boomers. Schoolchildren learned, through the advice of cartoon character Bert the Turtle, to "duck and cover" (Winkler 1999, 115-116). Despite growing nuclear fears, 1950s' Cold War consensus—that America was right in its anticommunist cause—held, in part because Eisenhower seemed to scale back U.S. military commitments. A July 27, 1953, compromise ended the Korean War at the 38th parallel, while covert operations in the third world of Africa, Latin America, and the Middle East minimized public scrutiny of U.S. Cold War activities. All told, Ike's New Look produced short-term geopolitical gains but also set the stage for future foreign policy quagmires that shaped boomer politics (Pach and Richardson 1991, 80-98).

The 1950s witnessed the birth of the modern civil rights movement. The 1954 Supreme Court case *Brown v. Board of Education* made "separate but equal" practices unconstitutional. Refusing to relinquish Jim Crow segregation practices, southern racists responded violently. In August 1955, an African American teenager, Emmett Till, whistled at a white woman in Mississippi; he was abducted and murdered, only to be found three days later in the Tallahatchie River. His mother shipped the body back to Chicago for a four-day open-casket funeral, and the gruesome corpse made national headlines. After a sympathetic southern jury quickly acquitted Till's assailants, the National Association for the Advancement of Colored People (NAACP) redoubled its desegregation efforts (Patterson 1996, 395-396). On December 1, 1955, NAACP member Rosa Parks refused to relinquish her bus seat for a white passenger in Montgomery, Alabama. African Americans boycotted the bus system and demanded that the city discontinue its discriminatory policies. A 26-year-old pastor named Martin Luther King Jr. traveled to Montgomery to stress nonviolence. A year later, a Supreme Court order outlawed discriminatory practices. Activists also sought to integrate southern schools. In Little Rock, Arkansas, Governor Orval Faubus pledged to maintain segregation. Television cameras captured southern whites taunting, and turning back, nine black students. When a federal court ordered the guardsmen removed, local police failed to protect African American students. Eisenhower intervened, federalizing troops and forcing integration. Montgomery and Little Rock marked two major victories, but the civil rights movement was just getting started (Patterson 1996, 411-416).

CAMELOT: 1960-1963

In 1960, Americans had to choose between Republican vice president Richard M. Nixon and Democrat John F. Kennedy. Politically, the two men weren't dissimilar. Both were World War II vets and members of the 80th Congress. They were only four years apart in age, and both preferred foreign policy over domestic politics (Perlstein 2008, 51). For many Americans, the choice came down to image; in this arena, there was no contest. Kennedy spoke of a young, vibrant America moving forward, and he looked the part. Once voted the most handsome man in Congress, the Massachusetts senator seemed all the more confident next to a pale and dour Nixon. Not even black-and-white television could hide the contrast. In one of the closest elections in American history, the first-ever televised presidential debate helped the photogenic Kennedy win (Watson 1994, 14–17).

Kennedy's White House reflected his faith in young, bright, and energetic Americans. Breaking with Eisenhower's cabinet of Washington insiders, JKF surrounded himself with a bipartisan collection of successful men from the fields of academe and business—a group David Halberstam later deemed (with more than a touch of irony) the "best and the brightest" (Rorabaugh 2002, 19–21). He secured Harvard professors Arthur Schlesinger Jr. and McGeorge Bundy as high-ranking advisers; handpicked Ford Motor Company president Robert S. McNamara for secretary of defense; and perhaps most brazenly, appointed his brother Robert to be attorney general and his brother-in-law R. Sargent Shriver to head the Peace Corps. His young wife, Jacqueline, was no less important. She courted the press and cultivated an aura of high culture, creating the Camelot image (Patterson 1996, 459–460). These figures, all of them under the age of 50, implemented Kennedy's "New Frontier" agenda, which challenged communism and sought to spread goodwill throughout the third world (Cobbs Hoffman 2000, 39–72). Kennedy's pledge to put an American on the moon by decade's end reflected the country's high ambitions.

Kennedy relied heavily on the CIA to gain an advantage in the Cold War, but these efforts had uneven, and sometimes disastrous, results. First, Kennedy aimed to oust Cuba's leader, Fidel Castro. Less than 100 miles from Florida, communist Cuba was a thorn in America's side. Kennedy supported an Eisenhower-era plan for a coup led by Cuban nationalists. This botched Bay of Pigs invasion led Castro to strengthen ties with Soviet premier Nikita Khrushchev, who had first antagonized Kennedy in a 1961 standoff over divided Berlin. Seeking to cut off the outflow of East Berliners flowing to the West, Khrushchev ordered the construction of a wall to keep them in. Some advisers sought action, but Kennedy let the wall be built. The Berlin standoff set the stage for a far more dangerous showdown (Patterson 1996, 492–497).

The Cuban Missile Crisis began on October 14, 1962, when U-2 reconnaissance airplanes captured images of Soviet intercontinental ballistic missile (ICBM) silos on Cuban soil. Kennedy went on national television and warned the Soviets that failure to remove the missiles might lead to war. For

13 tense days, Kennedy's Executive Committee debated how to respond. Hawks called for an invasion of Cuba, while doves cautioned restraint. A combination of tense nerves, imperfect information, and reconnaissance blunders all threatened to turn the Cold War hot. In the end cooler heads prevailed. Kennedy's blockade of Cuba forced Khrushchev's hand. Soviet ships turned back—in return for the secret removal of U.S. Jupiter missiles from Turkey. Kennedy avoided apocalypse, but by the narrowest of margins (Herring 2008, 719–723).

At home, civil rights struggles continued. In 1961, two groups—the Committee on Racial Equality (CORE) and the Student Nonviolent Coordinating Committee (SNCC, or "snick")—embarked on Freedom Rides, integrated buses that would travel through the South to challenge segregation. Southern racists responded with violence. Freedom Rider (and later U.S. Congressman) John Lewis was clubbed unconscious in South Carolina. In Alabama, Ku Klux Klan members destroyed one bus and severely beat occupants of another. In September 1961, Robert Kennedy finally forced the Interstate Commerce Commission to desegregate bus terminals (Patterson 1996, 467–470). A year later, James Meredith became the first black student to enroll at the University of Mississippi. Claiming the sovereignty of states' rights over federal power, Governor Ross Barnett challenged Kennedy to enforce desegregation. When a 3,000-plus crowd attacked marshals with bricks and bombs, and after two innocent bystanders died, Kennedy sent in troops and Meredith was admitted (Patterson 1996, 477–478).

By 1963, activists entered one of the most dangerous cities in America. Birmingham, Alabama, witnessed more than 50 racially targeted bombings, and local public safety commissioner Eugene "Bull" Connor was determined to keep "Bombingham" segregated. In April he arrested King, who penned the nonviolent manifesto "Letter from Birmingham Jail" (Branch 1988, 673–845). When police opened fire hoses and unleashed attack dogs on protestors, it later led some activists to break with their nonviolent pledge (Patterson 1996, 479–480). In Jackson, Mississippi, the murder of NAACP activist Medgar Evers shifted focus from the South to Washington, DC. On August 28, 1963, King led a procession of 250,000 protestors to the Lincoln Memorial, where he delivered his famous "I Have a Dream" speech. Hoping that his "children will one day live in a nation where they will not be judged by the color of their skin but by the content of their character," King struck one of the most memorable chords of the decade (Weisbrot 1991, 45–85).

Americans will never know the extent to which Kennedy would have supported civil rights. On November 22, 1963, in Dallas, Texas, assassin Lee Harvey Oswald shot and killed the president. Official investigations, forensic evidence, and the realities of physics all suggested that Oswald acted alone (Posner 1993). Yet a combination of grief, disbelief, and in time a growing distrust of the federal government made Kennedy assassination conspiracy theories one odd legacy of the New Frontier. By November 23, 1963, as the country mourned, Vice President Lyndon Baines Johnson assumed the presidency.

A GREAT SOCIETY AT HOME: 1964–1967

A lifelong New Deal Democrat from Texas and a highly persuasive legislator, LBJ capitalized on national sympathy for a fallen president and asked Americans to "carry forward the plans and programs of John Fitzgerald Kennedy." In reality, Johnson was more committed to racial equality than his predecessor: "We have talked long enough in this country about equal rights. We have talked for one hundred years or more. It is time now to write the next chapter, and to write it in the books of law" (Schulman 2006, 67–70). After conferring with King and other civil rights leaders, Johnson pushed the 1964 Civil Rights Act through Congress. It guaranteed equal employment opportunities regardless of race and withdrew federal funds from segregated institutions (Schulman 2006, 89). Then, in the 1964 presidential election, Johnson routed his challenger, Arizona senator Barry Goldwater, winning a record 61.1 percent of the vote, while Democrats maintained a strong presence in Congress. Johnson had a rare window of opportunity, and he knew it.

Speaking at the University of Michigan in May 1964, LBJ introduced his vision of a "Great Society." This "War on Poverty" would address issues of lagging elementary education, economic inequalities (especially in the rural south and Appalachia), and the growing plight of America's sick and aging. With most of the 89th Congress behind him, LBJ acted fast, passing 60 Great Society legislative programs, including the 1965 Elementary and Secondary Education Act, which provided educational funds for schools in need, and the Medicare Act, which promised federal health care for an increasing elderly population. He raised Social Security levels as well as funding for heart disease, stroke, cancer, child nutrition, and mental health research. Johnson also raised the national minimum wage and, with the help of his wife, Lady Bird Johnson, started a national highway beautification program, increased the number of national parks, and created new wildlife refuges. According to historian Bruce Schulman, in only two years LBJ "left behind the most productive law-making record in American history" (Schulman 2006, 91–93)

Great Society legislation was bold, but for many African Americans it failed to address political inequalities. Voting rights remained a key issue, especially in places like Selma, Alabama, where blacks made up 58 percent of the population but only 2 percent of the registered voters (Schulman 2006, 107). When activists embarked on a 50-mile symbolic march to the state capital in Montgomery, local troops attacked the nonviolent protestors and beat them bloody. News cameras captured "Bloody Sunday" and shocked the nation. According to John Lewis, "the images were stunning—scene after scene of policemen on foot and on horseback beating defenseless American citizens." King agreed, noting that after Selma "people all across the country were with us" (Lewis and D'Orso 1998, 327–345). When a defiant Governor George Wallace pledged to keep Alabama segregated, Johnson responded with a rare, prime-time joint session of Congress. He praised African Americans' attempts to "secure for themselves the full blessings of American life" and pleaded that Americans "overcome the crippling legacy of bigotry and injustice." He closed by reciting the spiritual slogan of the civil rights movement: "We shall overcome." On August 6, 1965, LBJ signed the Voting Rights Act into law, ending voting barriers for blacks, and sent federal troops to enforce it (Schulman 2006, 108–110).

Legislation helped but economic inequalities remained; by the mid-1960s, urban poverty pushed black communities to the breaking point. On August 12, 1965, police officers in the Watts neighborhood of Los Angeles arrested a young black man for drunk driving. A crowd gathered in protest, and soon riots erupted. For six days and nights, thousands of frustrated residents looted and burned the city. In 1966 alone, 38 riots led to seven deaths, hundreds of injuries, and thousands of arrests throughout the United States. The next year, even more rioting—most notably in Detroit and Newark—killed 66. Vandalism and looting became rampant, leaving thousands homeless (Patterson 1996, 662–663). Violence begat violence, and in trying to contain the chaos, National Guardsmen killed unarmed women and teenagers. The attacks fractured the civil rights movement. Some joined the emerging black power movement. Led by Stokely Carmichael, the Black Panthers vowed to protect themselves with force if necessary. As 1967 came to a close, violence in American cities could not be ignored, but for many it was overshadowed by growing casualties in Vietnam (Schulman 2006, 111–113).

The inescapable issue for the boomers, America's involvement in Vietnam began with Eisenhower. In 1954, the Vietnamese were about to overthrow their French colonial overseers. Vietnamese communist leader Ho Chi Minh accepted a temporary partition plan that allowed him to control the north but let Catholic president Ngo Dinh Diem rule the south, with the provision that planned elections set for 1956 would determine Vietnam's fate. When polls predicted a communist victory—and convinced of the domino theory, in which communism might spread throughout all of Southeast Asia—Eisenhower sent U.S. military advisers to bolster South Vietnamese forces. Kennedy raised these troop levels from 948 in 1961 to more than 16,000 in 1963. But in August 1964, when the U.S. destroyer *Maddox* reported shots fired, Johnson requested congressional authority to take "all necessary measures to protect American troops and prevent further aggression." The Gulf of Tonkin Resolution had near unanimous support. LBJ could now raise troop levels without any formal declaration of war (Schulman 2006, 131–134).

As more troops went to Vietnam, protests grew, especially on college campuses. Many students initially supported Great Society initiatives and civil rights activism. Others were influenced by the social critiques of Marxist professors, or writers like sociologist C. Wright Mills. At the University of Michigan, former SNCC member Tom Hayden drafted the Port Huron statement, which reflected these influences. It spoke of American problems couched in "systems" and preached "New Left" politics. New Left groups, like the Students for a Democratic Society (SDS), renounced traditional politics and favored sit-ins or mass demonstrations. Soon, New Left ideas turned college campuses like UC-Berkeley and New York's Columbia University into political staging grounds (Patterson 1996, 623–625). The SDS initially focused on free speech, but draft-age students quickly focused their energies on the war effort (Schulman 2006, 143). Some even idolized Ho Chi Minh or Cuban revolutionary Che Guevara, revealing a new acceptance of communism and signaling the end of the Cold War consensus.

They may have thought themselves radical, but many SDS chapters adhered to 1950s gender norms. By 1964, women made up one-third of SDS membership, but held only six percent of the seats on its executive council. Sick of filing papers or fetching coffee, women sought greater responsibility. The modern women's movement drew its inspiration from civil rights heroism and its organizing acumen from SDS, but its ideas came from the 1963 book *The Feminine Mystique,* which warned of the "problem that has no name." Author Betty Friedan explained that child rearing and domestic chores left many American women unfulfilled; soon, a "second wave" of feminism emerged. By 1966, the National Organization for Women (NOW), seeking equal pay and opportunities, pushed for an Equal Rights Amendment (ERA) to the Constitution (Patterson 1996, 645–647)

For those not participating in college campus protests, American mass media and popular culture captured activists' spirit. In the early 1960s, folk artists like Bob Dylan supported the civil rights movement. Dylan's song "A Pawn in Their Game" eulogized fallen activist Medgar Evers. P. F. Sloan's antiwar anthem "Eve of Destruction," as sung by a raspy-voiced Barry McGuire, reminded draft-age students that they were "old enough to kill but not for voting." As the 1960s progressed, folk merged with rock and roll. By 1967, long-haired groups from the Haight-Ashbury neighborhood of San Francisco, such as the Jefferson Airplane and the Grateful Dead, wore tie-dyed T-shirts and sang about drug use. Hippies represented the emerging counterculture. By the 1967 Summer of Love, even the Beatles promoted peace and love. For boomers, drug use and dress reflected personal politics.

By decade's end, and for decades to come, rock music and politics went hand in hand (Patterson 1996).

Mass media and popular music so effectively captured youthful activism that the 1960s are often remembered as a decade of protests. In truth, Vietnam politically divided the nation. Conscription rules meant that college and graduate students could get draft deferments, and well-connected families found ways around conscription (perhaps notes from a sympathetic doctor). Unlike World War II draftees, Vietnam-era soldiers largely comprised the underprivileged or minorities. The media's persistent coverage of long-haired, college protestors led many Americans to see students as ungrateful kids shirking responsibility. Even LBJ complained that the "thickness of daddy's wallet" protected rich students from serving. As the war dragged on, political divisions deepened. The SDS-ers made up only a vocal minority on college campuses; nevertheless, Americans soon equated elites and the highly educated with peaceniks and considered working classes to be patriotic (Patterson 1996, 631–633). These assumptions obfuscated the boomers' increasingly diverse political beliefs (Klatch 1999).

The turbulent year of the decade proved to be 1968. In January, at the onset of the Vietnamese holiday Tet, surprising new attacks on the U.S. embassy in Saigon shocked Americans. For months, General William Westmoreland had been promoting the success of his "strategic hamlet" strategy, but the Tet Offensive suggested that Westmoreland, Defense Secretary McNamara, and much of Johnson's administration had been lying to reporters. Wary of the growing credibility gap between the government and the media, America's most trusted newsman, Walter Cronkite, headed to Vietnam to appraise the situation firsthand. In February, he reported that the Johnson administration was misleading the public; at best, America might achieve stalemate in Vietnam. Having lost the support of the American people, and worn down from waging simultaneous wars against poverty at home and communism abroad, on March 31 President Johnson took to television and announced that he would not run for reelection (Pach 1994, 107–111).

Any illusions that LBJ's refusal to run might calm the nation were quickly shattered. On April 4, Martin Luther King was assassinated at a Memphis motel. In New York, Columbia University students staged a sit-in that closed campus for six days; it only ended after police violently removed protestors. In Mexico City, two African American Olympic medal winners raised clenched black-gloved fists—a symbolic black power salute reaffirming racial divisions at home. Disillusioned Democrats scrambled to fill the void Johnson left. In California, just as Robert Kennedy's presidential campaign was building momentum, he too was assassinated. Frustrated, demonstrators flocked to Chicago to protest the Democratic National Convention. The radical Youth International Party ("yippies" for short) nominated a pig, "Pigasus," for president. An already tense situation deteriorated when city police attacked yippies, demonstrators, and even reporters. Inside the convention walls things fared little better. While candidates George McGovern and Hubert H. Humphrey battled over the nomination, on the raucous convention floor, reporter Dan Rather was punched by a security guard (Perlstein 2008, 315–327). The television cameras caught it all, reminding Americans that the once mighty Democratic Party was in tatters.

In 1968, the persistence of violence, misconduct, and incivility that plagued America allowed for one of the most miraculous political comebacks in modern history. Richard M. Nixon, who lost to Kennedy in 1960, suffered a second loss two years later when he ran for governor of California. Nixon blamed the loss on the media. In his concession speech, he fumed to astonished reporters, "just think . . . you won't have Nixon to kick around anymore" (Perlstein 2008, 61). But by 1968, Nixon was back. In those six years he had campaigned for numerous Republican candidates, built his war chest, made political alliances, and bolstered his foreign policy credentials. By 1968, Nixon ran on a platform that pledged peace with honor in Vietnam and a return of law and order at home. Nixon courted former Southern Democrats (i.e., Dixiecrats), while nationwide he appealed to a "silent majority" of voters who supported the war—and who hated the ongoing protests. It was a close election, but Alabama governor Wallace's third-party ticket helpfully split the vote. Nixon's narrow victory capped a year of disorder, disaster, and disunion. But Nixon's promise to reestablish normalcy never materialized. America soon became even more divided (Patterson 1996, 700–709).

NIXON AND THE POLITICS OF BACKLASH: 1969–1973

In the summer of 1969, nearly half a million boomers flocked to a three-day music festival in upstate New York. Woodstock featured counterculture icons Jimi Hendrix and Janis Joplin and promoted three days of "peace, love, and music." A generation's hopes for peace were soon dashed. Four months later, at California's Altamont festival, bouncers from the Hell's Angels motorcycle club killed an attendee. More violence followed. The Weathermen, a radical group of former SDS-ers, began bombing political targets. In New York City's Greenwich Village, long-harassed homosexuals rebelled against antagonistic police officers outside the Stonewall Club. The Stonewall riots marked the beginning of a new civil rights campaign for the lesbian-gay-bisexual-transsexual (LGBT) community. As 1970 approached, many boomers became disillusioned with politics, opting instead to focus on improving their mental, physical, and spiritual health. This new self-focus was so sweeping that it led journalist Tom Wolfe to christen the 1970s the "Me Decade" (Patterson 1996, 710–711, 786).

The women's movement similarly fractured over disagreements about sexual and gender politics, yet one issue overshadowed these divisions. In 1973, the Supreme Court's ruling in *Roe v. Wade* upheld the constitutionality of abortion and further polarized the nation (Rosen 2000, 158–159). Pro-choice proponents argued that legal, safe abortions gave women equal rights to govern their own bodies. A vociferous opposition to abortion saw pregnancy termination as murder. Phyllis Schlafly led a conservative backlash against ERA ratification. Her STOP-ERA campaign ignored economic inequalities, choosing instead to argue that ERA might lead to unisex bathrooms or fully integrated armed forces. In the years that followed, ERA ratification failed, and the politics of abortion grew increasingly heated, at times even violent (Rosen 2000, 39–40).

The early 1970s also brought modern environmentalism. In 1962, Rachel Carson's *Silent Spring* had warned of the dangers of pesticides. By 1968, pollution, usually relegated to the poor South and the industrial Midwest, made headlines. *Time* magazine's coverage of Ohio's Cuyahoga River on fire alarmed Americans, as did a 1969 oil spill off Santa Barbara's coast. In 1969, the National Environmental Policy Act established the need for "environmental impact statements" for future federal projects. By 1970, Wisconsin Democratic senator Gaylord Nelson promoted the first Earth Day. Congressional acts, including the Clean Air Act, the Clean Water Act, and the Endangered Species Act, reflected Americans' increasing environmental concerns. Recognizing environmentalism's popularity, Nixon shrewdly supported most of these regulations, if only half-heartedly (Schulman 2001, 30–32).

Regarding race relations, Nixon was less liberal. He agreed with adviser Daniel Patrick Moynihan that a period of "benign neglect" would benefit the black community. Nixon thought the government had attempted to legislate integration for too long. Busing was the most prescient issue. In the early 1970s, forced busing aimed to integrate black and white schools. Nixon never agreed with the practice, and in cities like Boston and Detroit the backlash to busing was palpable. In the 1974 case *Milliken v. Bradley*, the Supreme Court ruled that local school districts had not actively pursued segregation and did not need to bus students to integrate schools. Schools remained racially segregated, and white flight out of inner cities continued (Patterson 1996, 730–733).

Nixon was especially ideologically flexible in the realm of foreign policy. Alongside his adviser, the German émigré Henry Kissinger, Nixon pursued a policy of détente (a relaxation of Cold War tensions) that opened relations with communist China and led to a historic nuclear arms limitation treaty with the Soviet Union. Nixon hoped these new relations might advance diplomacy with Hanoi; they didn't, and Vietnam plagued his presidency. Nixon campaigned on promises of peace with honor and de-escalation. Yet he secretly escalated bombing without congressional approval. He even began bombing nearby Cambodia, attacking the Vietcong's Ho Chi Minh Trail supply lines. Nixon's policy of "Vietnamization" aimed to bring American troops home after training South Vietnamese to defend themselves. Still, antidraft demonstrations continued, especially after the public learned about American involvement in Cambodia. On May 4, 1970, protests at Kent State (Ohio) turned deadly when National Guardsmen shot and killed four students. Soon after, the leak of classified documents—the so-called "Pentagon Papers"—alarmed citizens about U.S. conduct in Vietnam. The leak enraged Nixon, who became obsessed with controlling government information (Patterson 1996, 750–756).

Nixon tasked assistant John Ehrlichman to form a secret group, the "Plumbers," to stop the leaks and engage in burglary to dig up incriminating information about political enemies. With the 1972 reelection campaign underway, ex-Plumbers joined the Committee to Re-elect the President (CREEP) but were caught breaking and entering into Democratic National Committee offices at the Watergate Hotel. The story might have been buried if not for investigations by *Washington Post* reporters Carl Bernstein and Robert Woodward, who benefited from a secret informant known as "Deep Throat" (later revealed to be Mark Felt, an ex-agent of the Federal Bureau of Investigation [FBI]). As press speculation continued, America became obsessed with Watergate, and Nixon scrambled to kill the story. When a grand jury ordered that White House tapes be turned over, Nixon instead released redacted transcripts of conversations. Later subpoenas ordered that all tapes be turned over—tapes that revealed Nixon ordering the CIA to halt the FBI's investigation, a clear obstruction of justice. Impeachment loomed, and on August 8, Nixon resigned. The next day, Vice President Gerald Ford took over; he later pardoned Nixon (Patterson 1996, 771–779). Whether or not Nixon ordered the Watergate break-in remains unknown, but such secret actions seemed unnecessary; Nixon handily won against George McGovern in 1972, overshadowing Johnson's electoral landslide eight years earlier (Perlstein 2008, xi).

LEGACIES

In many ways, political issues have varied little since Nixon resigned. Abortion continues to divide the electorate, as do issues of gender inequality. The Stonewall riots started a struggle that continues with calls for gay marriage equality. Barack Obama's presidency suggests that racial tensions have eased some, but income and educational inequality remain inescapable legacies of the period. Many American cities remain racially gentrified. The boomers' methods of politics, especially mass public demonstrations that court media coverage, continue even in the Internet age (Patterson

1996, 482–485). But in a broader sense, another important legacy is distrust in our government. Kennedy-era optimism seemed almost impossible after Watergate. Revelations about Nixon's wrangling continue to fuel modern conspiracy theories. Some are far-fetched, such as falsified presidential birth certificates and moon landings; others are far more important, such as government invasions into personal privacy. In 1976, this distrust in government influenced the election of a relative political outsider, James E. Carter, to the presidency. Carter's outsider status may have helped his campaign, but it also plagued his presidency. After Carter, it was the conservatives who capitalized on this skepticism of government.

Many 1960s pundits, distracted by media coverage of antiwar demonstrations and the counterculture's ascent, miscalculated the growing popularity of conservatism. In 1964, Johnson's landslide victory suggested the assured, continued dominance of American liberalism (Perlstein 2008, 3–7). But one Goldwater campaigner, former actor Ronald Reagan, offered something his candidate could not: a softer conservatism with populist appeal. Reagan believed that government legislation was going too far, that Americans could better control their individual destinies than bureaucrats (Bimes 2003, 61–84). As the decades progressed, more and more Americans agreed, and demographic data reflected shifting political allegiances. Angry with civil rights, former southern Dixiecrats turned Republican. A more extreme New Right touted economic libertarianism. Upset with the counterculture's seeming amorality, religious evangelism grew. Third-party fringe candidates became more common, and compromise became a dirty word (Schulman 2006, 72–79). By 1980, conservatives shifted political discourse so far right that 1960s-era leftist stances seemed unthinkable. In short, politicians learned to embrace the backlash. They continue to court voters by vilifying their opposition, have become increasingly caustic in their rhetoric, and frame political problems in dire dichotomies. In this way, the battle lines drawn in the 1960s continue to divide the nation.

REFERENCES

Bimes, Terri. 2003. "Reagan: The Soft-Sell Populist." In *The Reagan Presidency: Pragmatic Conservatism and its Legacies*, edited by W. Elliot Brownlee and Hugh David Graham, 61–81. Lawrence: University Press of Kansas.

Branch, Taylor. 1988. *Parting the Waters: America in the King Years, 1954–63.* New York: Simon & Schuster, 1988.

Cobbs Hoffman, Elizabeth. 2000. *All You Need Is Love: The Peace Corps and the Spirit of the 1960s.* Cambridge, MA: Harvard University Press.

Gaddis, John Lewis. 2005. *Strategies of Containment: A Critical Appraisal of American National Security Policy during the Cold War.* Rev ed. Oxford: Oxford University Press.

Herring, George. 2008. *From Colony to Superpower: U.S. Foreign Relations since 1776*. New York: Oxford University Press.

Horowitz, Daniel. 2000. *Betty Friedan and the Making of "The Feminine Mystique": The American Life, the Cold War, and Modern Feminism*. Amherst: University of Massachusetts Press.

Klatch, Rebecca. 1999. *A Generation Divided: The New Left, the New Right, and the 1960s*. Berkeley: University of California Press.

Lewis, John, and Michael D'Orso. 1998. *Walking with the Wind: A Memoir of the Movement*. New York: Simon & Schuster.

Pach, Chester J., Jr. 1994. "And That's the Way It Was: The Vietnam War on the Network Nightly News." In *The Sixties: From Memory to History*, edited by David Farber, 90–118. Chapel Hill: University of North Carolina Press.

Pach, Chester J. Jr., and Elmo Richardson. 1991. *The Presidency of Dwight D. Eisenhower*. Lawrence: University Press of Kansas.

Patterson, James T. 1996. *Grand Expectations: The United States, 1945–1974*. New York: Oxford University Press.

Perlstein, Rick. 2008. *Nixonland: The Rise of a President and the Fracturing of America*. New York: Scribner Press.

Posner, Gerald. 1993. *Case Closed: Lee Harvey Oswald and the Assassination of JFK*. New York: Doubleday.

Rorabaugh, W. J. 2002. *Kennedy and the Promise of the Sixties*. Cambridge: Cambridge University Press.

Schulman, Bruce J. 2001. *The Seventies: The Great Shift in American Culture, Society, and Politics*. Cambridge, MA: Da Capo Press.

Schulman, Bruce J. 2006. *Lyndon B. Johnson and American Liberalism*. New York: Bedford/St. Martin's.

Watson, Mary Ann. 1994. *The Expanding Vista: American Television in the Kennedy Years*. Durham, NC: Duke University Press.

Weisbrot, Robert. 1991. *Freedom Bound: A History of America's Civil Rights Movement*. New York: Penguin Group.

Winkler, Allan M. 1999. *Life Under a Cloud: American Anxiety about the Atom*. Urbana: University of Illinois Press.

Winkler, Allan M. 2011. *The Cold War: A History in Documents*. New York: Oxford University Press.

2

The Whole World Is Watching: The SDS and Student Movement of the 1960s

Ed Tywoniak

The year is 2012 and Muhammad Ali, arguably the world's most beloved living athlete, feebly yet proudly stands in front of hundreds of thousands of adoring fans at the opening-day ceremony of the 30th Olympiad held in London, England. His face is still handsome, sitting stoically atop a frail body ravaged by Parkinson's disease, the result of years of brutal pounding endured over a lifetime of professional boxing. Muhammad Ali, born Cassius Clay in 1942, became the international darling of fans and media alike during the post–World War II years; standing tall and proud, he became the spokesperson of a generation struggling to make sense of a world they were destined to change with profound depth, breadth, and scope in the 50 years to follow.

Watching a replay of Ali on the Olympic broadcast can still bring an unexpected welling of a tear—Muhammad Ali, the 1960 Olympic gold medal winner, three-time world champion, captivating orator, Sunni Muslim convert, and antiwar activist who defiantly declared in 1966, while being arrested for draft evasion: "I ain't got no quarrel with the Viet Cong . . . no Viet Cong ever called me nigger."[1] That was the Ali that was—strong, virile, filled with the optimism of youth, and seemingly invincible—ready to take on all challengers and challenges. Ali looks much older now, certainly more tired—like all of his generation. And like most of his contemporaries there is no doubt a more purposeful reflection about the future generations waiting in the wings to inherit their collective cultural legacy. But isn't this natural for all those born of any era—a final reflection at journey's end?

Official census statistics generally refer to the demographic birth range of the post–World War II generation as spanning the years 1946 through 1964; 79 million children were born during that period, and by 1964, 40 percent of the U.S. population was under the age of 19. For decades, cultural scholars have placed different labels on this group, but "baby boomer" is the one that seems to have stuck. Under this general boomer moniker are two subgroups categorized by age. The first boomer wave is commonly thought to span the years 1946 through 1955 and is the predominant referent when one thinks of the 1960s countercultural revolution in all its psychedelic manifestations.

Those within this demographic intimately relate to the shared cultural memes littering their memories and cocktail party banter—telephone party lines, the marvels of color television, the first moon walk, draft card lottery numbers, and the stark immediacy of recalling John F. Kennedy's assassination. And there are similar influences from those who immediately preceded them—Lenny Bruce (b. 1925), Allen Ginsberg (b. 1926), Martin Luther King Jr. (b. 1929), Elvis Presley (b. 1935), John Lennon (b. 1940), Bob Dylan (b. 1941), Jerry Garcia (b. 1942), and Keith Richards (b. 1943) to name but a few.

The years 1956 through 1964 represent the second wave of boomers. The dark shroud of Nixon's Watergate, out-of-control inflation, and the weight of Cold War pressures placed a pall over this age group's formative years in the 1970s. This resulted in a cynicism that is in direct contrast to the starry-eyed Aquarian optimism of the Woodstock-era hippies who came of age a decade earlier in the 1960s. It didn't take long for the second-wave boomers to morph into the consumer-driven yuppies of the 1980s, who created a worldview based on the accumulation of contrivances and contraptions. Consumerism became the new battle cry for second-wave boomers—a symbolic warning of the nascent technological culture being constructed.

It's become fashionable these days to speculate on the elite representatives of the boomer generation with names like George W. Bush (b. 1946), Bill Clinton (b. 1946), Hillary Clinton (b. 1947), Jay Leno (b. 1950), and Rush Limbaugh (b. 1951) often representing first-wave boomers, and the likes of Joe Montana (b. 1956), Barack Obama (b. 1961), Sally Ride (b. 1961), Michael Jordan (b. 1963), and Quentin Tarantino (b. 1963) appearing on many second-wave lists. Such lists are, of course, ubiquitous and ultimately meaningless; which is not to say that debating the most influential album, greatest rock guitarist, or Ginger versus Mary Ann can't be a fun way to spend an afternoon. However, it is not inconsequential to speculate on who might be the most influential member of the post-World War II generation, and for the purpose of this chapter the answer is—Steve Jobs.

Jobs quite simply revolutionized the world. As *Time* magazine editor Richard Stengel stated: "Steve Jobs engineered his dreams—and ours."[2] His singularly unique vision and uncompromising passion for the way things should be led him not only to completely remake the personal computer, music, telephone, animated film, and retail industries but also challenged us all to think differently about ourselves and the world we create around us. Like Apple's 1997 commercial stated, Jobs was a constant reminder that "the people who are crazy enough to think they can change the world are the ones who do."[3]

Jobs was born in San Francisco in 1955, squarely on the transitional cusp of the two baby boomer waves. Shortly after his birth, Jobs's adoptive family moved a few miles south of the city to the suburb of Menlo Park in the heart of what was to become known as Silicon Valley and the budding young computer industry. Both the year and location of birth were important to who he was and who he became.

The year, 1955, was important because of its pivotal juncture between generational waves and what this represented in terms of his ability to bridge the optimism of the hippies and the consumerism of the yuppies into a coherent worldview. The place, San Francisco, was important because of the region's preeminent status as ground zero for both the 1960s cultural revolution and the post–World War II technology explosion that set into motion Marshall McLuhan's prescient vision of a "global village"[4] that was to forever change the way we live, work, and play. Because of the confluence of Jobs's unorthodox approach to life, the humanistic influence found in first-wave boomers, and the technological preoccupation found in second-wave boomers, it seems almost like preordained destiny that Jobs would be the one to bring together these disparate elements into a cohesive vision that was to transform the lives of millions of people around the world. This was most aptly evident at the January 27, 2010, Apple press conference at the Yerba Buena Center for the Arts in San Francisco for the worldwide unveiling of the first iPad. Framing Jobs's slight frame as he characteristically paced the stage was a giant projected image of a San Francisco street sign showing the intersection of "Technology Street" and "Liberal Arts Street"—an image that provided a poignant and profound visual insight into how Jobs saw himself, Apple in general, and the iPad in particular—"the place where creativity met tools for living."[5]

Jobs's shadow extends, completely and absolutely, across the collective consciousness of those born in the 20th century and the digital natives of the 21st century, and in that sense we all have a bit of Steve within us. And of course, for Jobs, as for many of us, it was always about the music. And it is with the music where our story now truly begins.

A DIFFERENCE THAT MADE A DIFFERENCE

Looking at a person's iPod music playlist is like having a window into his or her soul. Or, as Steven Levy wrote: "All somebody needs to do is scroll through your library on that click wheel, and, musically speaking, you're naked. It's not just what you like—it's *who you are*."[6] The music on Steve Jobs's personal iPod could pass as the soundtrack for his entire generation with Bob Dylan and the Beatles making up most of the songs— songs often-times about change and revolution. Jobs himself said: "I was very lucky to grow up in a time when music really mattered. It really changed the world."[7]

It's no surprise that the songs of Dylan, Lennon, and McCartney became the musical backdrop for the iconoclastic Jobs, for these musicians, like Jobs, stood tall in support of their convictions despite the seemingly insur-mountable obstacles that stood in their path. Like the biblical tale of the trumpet's blare that leveled the walls of Jericho, music was thought to be the mystical force that would change the course of human destiny, knocking down the walls of societal ills that had insidiously seeped into the cultural fabric over decades of war, hatred, bigotry, and mistrust.

The music of the 1960s brought focus to the worldwide hegemonic forces that had fostered two world wars decades apart, and whose Cold War ten-sions were now boiling over in the tempest pot of Vietnam. The bards of the time echoed loudly the rising voice of unrest from the large group of increasingly disenfranchised youth who had found a new trumpet of Jericho to wield in their revolution—the electric guitar. Now their words of protest had amplified voices that could project the message of unrest to one and all—culminating in Jimi Hendrix ripping the early morning air on the last day of Woodstock with feedback shards for notes as he shredded the melody of the "Star Spangled Banner" in a burst of creative anarchy.

Wars and conflict are not unique to the human condition. The parents of the boomers were called the "greatest generation" for a reason. But it seems reasonable to state that the boomers saw themselves as something special, as if there was something unique about who they were and the times they lived in—a collective gestalt that somehow resonated as different from all generations that came before. And so, in retrospect, it's fair to ask about the ways in which the boomers were different and the reasons. It's also fair to speculate about the extent to which they succeeded in planting the seeds of their utopian ideals of peace and love into the consciousness of future generations. And I suppose it's even fair to ponder the consequences if the answer is no to any of these questions. In other words, it's fair to ask if these were differences that made a difference.

YOU SAY YOU WANT A REVOLUTION?

One way of analyzing the cultural milieu that was collectively beginning to take shape in the years immediately following 1945 is through the com-posite lens of five overarching cultural themes—civil rights, technology, spir-ituality, drugs, and music. Undergirding these themes, of course, was the antiwar movement and its role as the primary impetus for radical change. However, before we begin exploring these five cause-and-effect topics, it may be helpful to provide some deeper historical context to better understand the issues leading to the mass social protests of the 1960s.

The introduction of the printing press in the mid-15th century created a shift from an engagement with the world using all our senses to a paradigm that favored the visual and with it cultural uniformity, alienation of the individual, a tendency to nationalism, and the rise of colonial expansion—what Marshall McLuhan referred to as the Gutenberg effect.[8] By the 19th century, the newly crafted machines of the Industrial Revolution became the dominant focus of our technical inventiveness, providing the capacity for vast changes in design, manufacturing, transportation, and the shift in human labor to a system of assembly lines and human capital in which line workers were treated with machinelike indifference. The dawning of the 20th century and the clash of World War I exposed an unsuspecting world to the full destructive capabilities of the new century's mechanized weapons. By the end of World War II 30 years later, an unprecedented number of consumer products based on scientific advancements from the war effort were infused into an emerging postwar American culture—inventions that included transistors, television, radar, x-rays, plastic, rocket propulsion, and early computers. Coupled with the newfound electronic reach of a newly introduced television technology in the early 1950s, it became easy for corporations and media companies to create the illusion of a budding technical utopia with humanity watched over by "machines of loving grace."[9] Besides having an immediate and profound impact on postwar America, these technologies also rapidly coalesced into a singular dream that would, 50 years later, be commonly referred to as the "digital age." Again, it was McLuhan's prescient insights developed in the 1960s that forewarned us of the new age that was being birthed that represented "the final phase of the extensions of man—the technological simulation of consciousness, when the creative process of knowing will be collectively and corporately extended to the whole of human society."[10]

By the end of the 1950s, the century's steady rise of technical inventiveness, coupled with the international industrial war effort of World War II, resulted in what President Eisenhower called the "military-industrial complex."[11] This explicit merging of interests of private corporations and the government's public trust became the immediate target of protest by aging pacifists from the first half of the century and other Beat-era radicals. In the years that immediately followed, the last vestiges of the industrial age bumped headlong into the rapid coming-of-age of the boomers until, by the beginning of the sixties, the old paradigm began crumbling under the weight of half a century of warfare and mounting international tensions.

The 1960s counterculture movement was fueled primarily by white, middle-class, college-educated youth who sympathized with the plight of those marginalized at the societal fringe of racial segregation, gender bias, socioeconomic opportunity, and lifestyle choice. This generational empathy might be partially explained by the fact that, during World War II, large numbers of African American families relocated from the southern states to cities like San Francisco and San Diego to pursue work in the shipbuilding industry. This migration pattern provided postwar youth with opportunities for racial integration that previously hadn't existed in prior generations. Elsewhere on the East Coast, the heritage of oppression understood by Jewish youth resonated with the early strains of racial tensions felt by the black community. As Frank Zappa observed: "The people who came to see us at the Garrick mostly had short hair, they came from middle-class white Jewish environments, mostly suburban. They came to see our show because we were something weird that was on that street."[12]

Cold War concerns and escalating military incursions into Vietnam fueled the engines of the weapons industry during the 1950s that, along with large investments into peacetime manufacturing efforts in newly formed industries such as aerospace, plastics, and microelectronics, created a sense of seemingly unending economic prosperity for postwar families. Simultaneously, the mass introduction of television to millions of American homes in the 1950s brought about a wave of broadcast entertainment propaganda, such as *Ozzie and Harriet* and *Father Knows Best*, that created an illusion of a wholesome America that subtly reinforced misogynistic and bigoted behaviors by celebrating a patriarchal worldview that excluded people of color and shunted women to support roles in the plastic world of suburbia. The rising tide of unrest that culminated in the social protest movement of the sixties initially began as a rejection of these propaganda efforts to portray a postwar America that was a combination of *The Jetsons* and *Leave It to Beaver*—a high-tech suburban world in which white families in white homes with white picket fences solve all of life's messy travails in 30-minute televised morality plays replete with a laugh track. Given all of this, it was only a matter of time before the dream, for some, of a white, middle-class America whose hegemonic dominance and superiority would recapture the perceived power and glory of prior decades would crash headlong with an angry generation of young people who understood that the broadcast images of a utopian America were not the lived realities of most people. It was time for the awakening youth of the nation to realize that the revolution was not going to be a televised infomercial but was live in the streets of America.

The Students for a Democratic Society (SDS) were the first to take up the challenge in the early years of the 1960s. The SDS started from the Student League for Industrial Democracy, the youth branch of the League for Industrial Democracy, a socialist educational organization. Tom Hayden, who was married for a time to Jane Fonda and went on to become a leading figure in the counterculture movement and a California state assemblyman, was the primary drafter of the Port Huron statement, an SDS manifesto advocating for nonviolent civil disobedience, participatory democracy, and, in a move that was considered radical even in the New Left movement, openly supportive of communist ideologies. Of equal importance in the early stages of the revolution was the Free Speech Movement begun in 1964 by student leaders at the University of California–Berkeley. With early beginnings in the student political movement of the late fifties, the Berkeley Free Speech Movement culminated in a passionate speech from student activist Mario Savio in December 1969 where, in front of 3,000 students, he advocated passive protest, student sit-ins, and a shutdown of the Berkeley campus. The 32-hour event eventually led to a confrontation between students and Berkeley police during which 800 arrests were made.

Another student group, the Youth International Party (known more popularly as "yippies"), led an oftentimes more humorous counterculture movement. Founded in 1967, the yippies used guerilla theater strategies to spread their protest message, including gaining access to the New York Stock Exchange to throw fake money from the balcony, applying for a permit to levitate the Pentagon, and nominating a pig as candidate for president in 1968. Primarily a New York–based organization, the group's membership included such noted radicals as Jerry Rubin, Abbie Hoffman, Phil Ochs, Allen Ginsberg, William Kunstler, Ed Sanders, and Paul Krassner.

The year 1968 also saw Lyndon Johnson announce that he would not seek reelection for a second presidential term. This put added pressure on the Democratic National Convention that would be held in Chicago that August, at a time in which the nation already had to deal with the growing unpopularity of the Vietnam War, the assassinations of Robert F. Kennedy and Martin Luther King, and civil rights riots in more than 100 U.S. cities. Added to this political maelstrom was a youth festival that was going to be held in Chicago at the same time as the convention. Sponsored by the yippies, the SDS, and other radical groups, 10,000 demonstrators descended on the Windy City only to be met by 23,000 police and National Guard troops. Mace, pepper spray, and tear gas were sprayed in waves of toxic smoke while police batons pummeled the protesting crowd under the glare of television lights, further polarizing the country and the world.

Pushing the envelope even further were radical groups like the Weather Underground and the Symbionese Liberation Army (SLA)—the latter group's name referencing the universal symbiosis of cultural identities. The Weather Underground organized in 1969 as a splinter group from the SDS, taking its name from the Bob Dylan song "Subterranean Homesick Blues" and the line "You don't need a weatherman to know which way the wind blows."[13] Taken from the playbook of the black liberation movement, the goal of the Weather Underground was the violent overthrow of the U.S. government that featured a declaration of a state of war and a campaign of public bombings that lasted through the mid-1970s. Like the Weathermen, the SLA was another reactionary group that espoused violent action. The group gained international notoriety when they kidnapped media heiress Patty Hearst in 1974 and then coerced her to participate in a series of armed bank robberies. Most of the group, excluding Hearst, was killed in a violent shootout with police in Los Angeles in the same year.

Just five months after Mario Savio's student demonstration at UC-Berkeley, violence erupted again on a college campus—this time Kent State University in Ohio. On May 4, 1970, student activists showed up on the Kent State campus to protest the My Lai massacre by American troops in Vietnam in which more than 500 Vietnamese women and children were brutally murdered. The Kent State student protesters were met by Ohio National Guard troops who, in a chaotic 13-second period, fired 67 shots that killed four students and wounded nine others, one who suffered permanent paralysis. Also during that same period, students at San Francisco State College (now San Francisco State University) clashed with college officials over the founding of an ethnic studies program. The event captured a large amount of media attention because federal troops were mobilized and then-college president S. I. Hayakawa pulled the plug on the student protestors' sound system.

The defining moment for the civil rights movement took place early in the epoch's history on August 28 1963, with the March on Washington for Jobs and Freedom, during which an estimated crowd of 400,000 people from every racial group came together in solidarity to witness Martin Luther King deliver his legendary "I Have a Dream" speech. Of course, King's dream was soon to be shattered by continued racial violence and the eventual assassinations of John F. Kennedy in 1963 and Dr. King himself and Robert Kennedy in April and June of 1968, respectively, tearing asunder the heart and soul of the country through the continued strains of internal tension. By the time of King's assassination, the country's disenfranchised had coalesced into a powerful coalition that found an iconic image for its struggle in the raised-fist black power salute at the 1968 Olympic games in Mexico City by black athletes Tommie Smith and John Carlos at their medal ceremony. Reflecting the multidimensional coalition of support that was growing throughout the country, Smith suggested in his autobiography that the defiantly raised fist was not a black power salute, but in fact a human rights salute.[14]

The quest for human rights, of course, was not restricted to black America, even though by the mid-sixties the rising black power movement had eclipsed other factions of the struggle with the rise to power of the Black Panther Party, founded by Huey Newton and Bobby Seale at Merritt College in Oakland, California, in 1966. Even so, Mexican Americans, Native Americans, gays, and lesbians all found their voice during the civil rights struggles of the 1960s. The Chicano movement held mass student walkouts in Denver and East Los Angeles in 1968 and founded MECHA (Movimiento Estudiantil Chicano de Aztlán), an organization of youth groups in colleges throughout the country whose mission was to promote Chicano studies programs and an ethno-nationalist agenda. Members of the American Indian Movement (AIM), which was patterned after the Black Panthers, defiantly occupied Alcatraz Island in San Francisco Bay in 1969, and by the early 1970s had occupied a military base in Minnesota, the Bureau of Indian Affairs headquarters in Washington, DC, and the Custer County courthouse in South Dakota; in addition, in 1973, 200 members of the Lakota tribe heroically stood ground against federal marshals at the site of the original 1890 Wounded Knee massacre. Similarly, the struggle for civil rights for gays and lesbians found traction in the Stonewall riots of 1969 in New York's Greenwich Village, resulting in the founding of openly gay communities in New York and San Francisco and the first gay-pride marches in New York, Los Angeles, and Chicago in 1970 to commemorate the one-year anniversary of the riots.

And, of course, perhaps the counterculture movement that had the most impact on the eventual course of human history was the founding of the women's liberation movement and the ushering in of what is now known as second-wave Feminism (in contrast to the women's suffrage movement in the first half of the 20th century). Simone de Beauvoir's 1940s examination of women as "other" in patriarchal society, coupled with the objectification of women in postwar America as exemplified by Robert Young's portrayal of real and symbolic paternal dominance in the CBS television series *Father Knows Best*, helped to focus the frustration of millions of women across the country who were no longer willing to accept their role as the "second sex." By the time John F. Kennedy commissioned the Presidential Commission on the Status of Women in 1963, the discontent felt by American women had finally begun to be assuaged when legislation like the Equal Pay Act of 1963, Title VII of the 1964 Civil Rights Act, and the *Griswold v. Connecticut* decision of 1964 granting permission for the use of contraception in the state of Connecticut, began to right decades of discriminatory wrongs against women. Helen Reddy's[15] musical refrain of "I am woman, hear me roar!" was finally a voice with teeth—an equal countermeasure to the dominant misogyny celebrated in the pages of Hugh Hefner's *Playboy*. Although the struggle for women's equality continues to this day, the seeds of change that were planted in the sixties has blossomed 50 years later into a cultural gestalt that has women respected as equals and valued for their talents and skills as opposed to their objectified status as sex toys. This has resulted in women like Hillary Clinton and Maya Angelou taking center stage in the nation's discourse about the future direction of our country and planet and the women's perspective now standing as equal to that of their male counterparts. Finally, young girls can realistically aspire to the White House.

OHM, OM ON THE RANGE

While the civil rights movement attempted to confront the societal ills perpetuated over centuries of bigotry and hatred, the seemingly disparate influences of technology and spirituality were also powerful change agents in the development of the boomers' psyche. The watershed shift in our scientific inventiveness was never more dramatically evident than in the horrific carnage brought about by the nuclear devastation leveled on the populations of Hiroshima and Nagasaki in the closing chapter of World War II. The devastating potential of these weapons of mass destruction engendered a paranoid fear throughout the general public and created a palsied stalemate for superpower nations during the Cold War era. Conversely, it wasn't too long after the war's end before consumer products based on these same military scientific advancements began to creep into the public sector. Transistor radios, jet airplanes, space exploration, and the nascent computer industry all seemed like real manifestations of speculative technologies only hinted at by the science fiction writers of the 1930s and 1940s. By the time *The Jetsons* appeared on primetime television in 1962, the country had already settled into a suburban mind-set that shared a vision of a utopic existence made possible by an ever-increasing reliance on technical solutions and consumer contrivances. Our human dependence on technology—so called technological determinism—has always been a part of our evolutionary trajectory, including the gracile anatomical features of modern humans brought about by our earliest use of and dependence on tools. But by the 1960s, the technical worldview had established such a powerful foothold in the public consciousness that any notions of reversal immediately became moot.

Of all the postwar inventions, it was probably television that had the most impact on the boomer generation. Seemingly overnight, the world was shrunk into a 4×3 aspect ratio that brought every corner of the globe into the flat-screened reality of the American living room. Black-and-white television was first introduced in the early 1950s, and by the decade's end color TV was developed along with the remote control and the replacement of vacuum tubes with new transistor technology. As McLuhan noted in 1961: "Today, television is the most significant of the electric media because it permeates nearly every home in the country, extending the central nervous system of every viewer as it works over and molds the entire sensorium with the ultimate message."[16]

Inspiration for television programming in the sixties was culled from the major themes of the times. Shows like *Get Smart*, *Mission Impossible*, and *The Man from U.N.C.L.E.* reflected the Cold War tensions that had begun to intensify. Suburban culture was well represented by shows like *Father Knows Best*, *Leave It to Beaver*, *Ozzie and Harriet*, *The Donna Reed Show*, and *The Brady Bunch*. America's newfound interest in popular music was reflected in shows like Dick Clark's *American Bandstand*, Don Cornelius's *Soul Train*, *Where the Action Is* featuring Paul Revere and the Raiders, and *The Monkees*, America's lame attempt to replicate the success of the Beatles. And newfound gold was discovered by television executives in the late night hours with a plethora of variety shows that included *Tomorrow Coast to Coast* hosted by Tom Snyder, *The Merv Griffin Show*, *The Smothers Brothers Show*, and of course *The Tonight Show* featuring the legendary Johnny Carson. On the *Steve Allen Show*, an unsuspecting television audience was introduced to a young Frank Zappa in 1963. Dick Cavett hosted his show from New York during the Woodstock Festival of 1969 with a featured interview and performance by Stephen Stills with Joan Baez, Joni Mitchell, Grace Slick, Paul Kantner, Jorma Kaukonen, and other music luminaries sitting cross-legged on the audience floor. *Rowan & Martin's Laugh-In* became the laugh track for a generation, sprinkling the popular vernacular of the age with such memorable phrases as "Sock it to me" and "Here comes da judge." And by 1975, one of television's greatest success stories was introduced to the American television audience, *Saturday Night Live*, featuring a mix of sketch comedy, political satire, and musical performance that is still going strong 40 years after its inception.

And of course science was not going to take a backseat in the world of sixties television. Gene Roddenberry's *Star Trek* became the quintessential boomer television series by taking note of the unfolding technical paradigm that was rapidly reshaping the imaginations of individuals and industries alike while also borrowing liberally from the humanistic tales of the Great Books and the utopian idealism of the hippie movement. *Star Trek* was a space opera for the masses that shepherded the imagination of the country into the far distant reaches of space. Although the lessons of a 23rd-century universal peace found in the *Star Trek* narratives never found traction in the real-world troubles of planet Earth, the *Star Trek* franchise did succeed in creating an immediate techno-lust for all things flashing and shiny.

While the conquering of outer space and other technical pursuits became a general preoccupation for the postwar generation, on an individual level people began a deep exploration of inner space by answering the call for a greater spiritual fulfillment than was being offered by the world's mainstream religions. The "ohm" of the new world of electronics was merging with the "Om" of new-age spiritualism, opening the floodgates for young seekers eager to find their neo-primitive mandala center of spiritual grounding in a rapidly technologizing age. A variety of spiritual practices were pursued, including Zen Buddhism, Transcendental Meditation, Hare Krishna, and a variety of other yogic and meditative practices from India, Tibet, and Native American traditions. Tarot and astrological readings saw a resurgence in popularity during the 1960s as the musical *Hair* proudly proclaimed the "dawning of the age of Aquarius" in 1967. Religions like the Unification

Church of Rev. Sun Myung Moon (better known as the "Moonies"), L. Ron
Hubbard's Scientology, and the Order of Rosicrucian found a new lease
on life along with a broad array of alternative religions like the Saint John
Coltrane African Orthodox Church in San Francisco.

The boomer generation's search for inner peace was obviously being
driven by, among other things, the revolutionary tensions of repression
and anarchy coursing through America's cities as well as the sense of won-
derment and promise that the new age of science afforded. It was also an
antiestablishment rejection of the world's dominant religions and their
authoritarian hierarchical structures. But it was also obvious in the sixties
that the new spiritualities and modern technologies were only part of the
answer. The other part lay in something much more primal—sex, drugs, and
rock and roll!

TURN ON, TUNE IN, DROP OUT

"It was 20 years ago today, Sgt. Pepper taught the band to play."[17] All right,
it was more like 48 years ago from today, but it seems like it was just yesterday when the Beatles released their epic album *Sgt. Pepper's Lonely Hearts
Club Band* in 1967. Better known as "the Summer of Love," 1967 became
the historical magic moment during which the combination of the various
elements of the boomers' quest for enlightenment—political rebellion, new
technologies, and spiritual enlightenment—exploded into a brilliantly kalei-
doscopic rainbow of creative energy the likes of which the world had never
seen. But the powder keg for this cultural explosion still needed a fuse and
a match to be ignited, and these were supplied in large doses in 1967 by the
last two pieces of the sixties cultural experiment—drugs and music.

Probably the most recognizable pop-culture aphorism from the 1960s is
"sex, drugs, and rock and roll." Although there certainly was a so-called
"sexual revolution" during that decade, it wasn't nearly as important to the
making of the counterculture as the antiwar and civil rights movements
for two primary reasons. The first is that young people of any generation
have a certain amount of sexual promiscuity as part of their rite of passage
during their hormonal coming of age. Second, sexual liberation seemed
to be important to the boomers' worldview as demonstrated by the overt
nudity and sexually charged themes found in the radical-for-its-day theatrical
production of *Hair: The Tribal Love-Rock Musical*, which opened in 1967. But
in reality, there was a much greater concern for liberating those at the fringe
of sexual mores and norms during that period—namely homosexuals and
women. Far more than mere pubescent promiscuity in free-love communes,
the acceptance of same-sex partnerships and the empowerment of women
to control their own sexual affairs was an essential step in the overall move

toward erasing the bigotries, prejudices and oppressions levied toward those at the cultural edges.

The ushering in of the Summer of Love took place on January 14, 1967, with an event called the Human Be-In at Golden Gate Park in San Francisco. Following the sit-in model of nonviolent protest, the Be-In became a critical coming together of the more radical Berkeley Free Speech Movement faction of the Bay Area's youth movement with the more passive and spiritually oriented hippie movement in San Francisco. The defining moment of the event was the galvanizing phrase pronounced by Timothy Leary that was destined to become the rallying cry for the entire sixties—"turn on, tune in, and drop out"—a phrase that Leary, interestingly enough, credited to Marshall McLuhan. But this wasn't just rhetoric, thanks to the psychedelic prophet Owsley Stanley, who distributed enough "White Lightning" LSD to turn on the entire 20,000 people in attendance. Richard Alpert, better known as Baba Ram Dass, who assisted Leary in the early LSD experiments at Harvard, was also there along with Beat-era heroes of the underground like Allen Ginsberg, Gary Snyder, Lawrence Ferlinghetti, Jerry Rubin, and Dick Gregory. Music was supplied by the Grateful Dead, Quicksilver Messenger Service, and the Jefferson Airplane who, along with other up-and-coming San Francisco bands like Big Brother and the Holding Co. featuring Janis Joplin, had been cutting their musical teeth at such venues as the Fillmore Auditorium and Avalon Ballroom—living laboratories for cultural experimentation that had sprung up the prior year in 1966. It was at these clubs that the early seeds of the scene germinated in the swirling vortex of psychedelic drugs, colorful light shows, amplified feedback, outrageous clothing, and, of course, the ubiquitous smell of marijuana adding to the stoned reverie.

Almost overnight San Francisco's Haight-Ashbury district became the national magnet for the new hippie movement. The Haight benefited from its geographic adjacency to the Fillmore district, a black community on the western side of the city that was a jazz and blues mecca in the 1950s—which meant it already had a reputation as having a copious supply of creative artists, cheap housing, and readily available drugs. By the spring of 1967, thousands of young students on spring break flocked to the area, sowing the seeds of the hippie movement, which by the fabled summer of '67 flowered with Day-Glo intensity at the free concerts and spontaneous "happenings" at Speedway Meadows and Hippie Hill in scenic Golden Gate Park. The Haight soon became the center of public attention with tour buses of bemused and bewildered tourists gawking at the "freaks" while being reminded by Scott McKenzie "to wear some flowers in your hair."[18] Even George Harrison visited the Haight in August of that summer.

On June 10 and 11, five months after the Human Be-In, a San Francisco radio station, KFRC-AM, sponsored the Fantasy Fair and Magic Mountain

Music Festival at a scenic mountaintop amphitheater overlooking San Francisco from across the Golden Gate Bridge in Marin County. The festival is
considered the first large rock concert event and featured bands like Canned
Heat, Country Joe and the Fish, the Jefferson Airplane, 5th Dimension,
and the Byrds with exiled South African trumpeter Hugh Masekela playing in front of 36,000 fans. It was also the Doors' first large concert performance and coincided with the release of the group's bestselling single,
"Light My Fire." One week later, the three-day Monterey International Pop
Music Festival took place during which close to 90,000 people witnessed
a blazing performance by Janis Joplin followed by the inaugural American
appearances of the Who and Ravi Shankar, and a reputation-making set by
Jimi Hendrix. Hendrix's performance in particular is remembered because
he lit his Stratocaster guitar on fire while writhing sensually over its flaming
body during the song "Wild Thing."

The music industry at that time was much more reliant on the older media
formats of radio and print journalism, which fortunately could provide many
more opportunities for social experimentation than the more traditionally
conservative media format of television. America's first alternative free-form
radio station was San Francisco's KMPX, founded by Tom "Big Daddy" Donahue, the legendary disc jockey, record producer, artist manager, and concert
promoter who staged the Beatles' last concert performance in San Francisco
in 1966. Music programming at KMPX, and later at KSAN, was totally free
form, meaning each DJ was allowed to choose his or her playlists, resulting in
set lists that could include everything from Tower of Power to Miles Davis, the
Who, and the Grateful Dead. Donahue also bucked the radio industry trend
of excluding women announcers and engineers by hiring female staff members for on-air and technical positions. The SLA also used KSAN to broadcast
their public demands after the kidnapping of Patty Hearst.

College radio stations also rose in number during the sixties because the
Federal Communications Commission (FCC) made available new low-power
class D licenses on the FM band. College radio became one of the first places
to broadcast controversial album cuts from radio comedy troupes like the
Firesign Theatre and the Credibility Gap, which specialized in political satire.
Also popular with the radical left in the sixties were the five stations of the
Pacifica radio network. Founded in Berkeley in 1949, the Pacifica network is
where George Carlin's then-scandalous monologue "Seven Words You Can
Never Say On Television"[19] was first aired, and for which the network was
brought to trial by the U.S. government. Eventually, Pacifica lost the case in
1978 in a landmark Supreme Court decision that broadened and affirmed
the government's ability to regulate indecent material on public airwaves.

The granddaddy of alternative print publications is the *Village Voice*.
Founded in New York's Greenwich Village district in 1955, the *Voice* has
maintained a reputation to this day of supporting new and underground

movements in the arts and letters as well as investigative probes into political and social issues of concern. Two other publications of note found their roots in San Francisco. The first—lesser known but of greater historical importance—was *The San Francisco Oracle*, a psychedelically inspired view of the newly emerging drug-fueled music scene that only managed to produce 12 issues between 1966 and 1968. Of much greater national renown is *Rolling Stone* magazine, which featured John Lennon on the cover of the inaugural issue in 1967. Founded by Jann Wenner and beloved music critic Ralph J. Gleason, *Rolling Stone* became the print voice of the boomer generation and still maintains an annual circulation of close to 1.5 million readers.

Film also played a critical role in defining the decade of the sixties, including such seminal films as the three original James Bond movies featuring Sean Connery, *Dr. No* (1962), *From Russia with Love* (1963), and *Goldfinger* (1964); the brilliant Cold War satire *Dr. Strangelove* (1964); Dustin Hoffman's early career performance in *The Graduate* (1967); the Stanley Kubrick masterpiece *2001: A Space Odyssey* (1968); Jane Fonda's sexy sci-fi spoof *Barbarella* (1968); and the memorable American road tragedy, *Easy Rider* (1969), featuring Peter Fonda, Dennis Hopper, and Jack Nicholson, the latter of whom received an Academy Award nomination for Best Actor in a Supporting Role.

But the real defining work of the decade has to go to the extensive body of work of Martin Scorsese. His chronicling of the significant musical artists of the boomer generation includes such documentaries as *The Last Waltz* (1978), featuring the last concert performance of the Band, Bob Dylan's famous group of backing musicians. The film was shot in San Francisco at the Winterland Ballroom and featured an all-star lineup including Dylan, Eric Clapton, Neil Young, Paul Butterfield, EmmyLou Harris, Neil Diamond, Ringo Starr, and Van Morrison. Scorsese went on to produce a seven-part documentary series called *The Blues* in 2003, a Bob Dylan documentary called *No Direction Home* (2005), a Rolling Stones concert film titled *Shine a Light* (2008), and *George Harrison: Living in the Material World* (2011) about the life and music of the former Beatle. But perhaps Scorsese's greatest influence came in his work as an editorial assistant on the 1970 film *Woodstock*. In particular, Scorsese is credited for suggesting the split-screen technique featured during Santana's incendiary set, a cinematic technique that would become synonymous with other rock films to follow.

Woodstock the actual concert became the defining event of the sixties revolution. Formally called the Woodstock Music and Art Fair: An Aquarian Exposition of 3 Days of Love and Music, the rain-soaked event in upstate New York drew more than 500,000 attendees, most of whom did not pay, to hear the best of the decade's musicians, including only the second public performance of Crosby, Stills, Nash & Young and a fired-up Country Joe McDonald greeting the assembled masses with a modified "Fish Cheer" screaming "Give me an F-U-C-K!"

The Rolling Stones would attempt to replicate the Woodstock festival several months later in San Francisco. Because of initial problems with city officials, the original Golden Gate Park site adjacent to Haight-Ashbury was not chosen; instead, they selected Altamont Speedway, a remote race-car track about an hour's drive from San Francisco. The joyous expression of "peace, love, and tie-dye" that was so much a part of the Woodstock festival was nowhere in evidence at the Altamont concert; fans and musicians alike complained of a variety of technical and scheduling snafus, and an increasingly unruly crowd threatened the safety of some of the performers. When the Rolling Stones finally arrived on the stage several hours late, the already anxious crowd quickly worked itself into an uncontrollable frenzy that resulted in a clash between audience members and members of the Hell's Angels motorcycle club who were hired as security for the event. Before the concert ended, a young black man in the audience, Meredith Hunter, lay stabbed to death in front of the stage. The concert was filmed and later made into a 1970 documentary, *Gimme Shelter*,[20] which showed close-up shots of the horrified faces of Mick Jagger and Charlie Watts as they watch the replay of the stabbings, graphically underscoring the sorrowful moment. The tragic events of the Altamont concert in late 1969 signified the official end of the short-lived social experiment of the age of Aquarius and the dream for a utopian world built on universal peace and harmony.

WHAT A LONG STRANGE TRIP IT'S BEEN

Perhaps the eventual demise of the Woodstock generation's technicolor dream can be attributed to three overarching factors: the end of the need for a radical revolt when the Vietnam War ground to a halt in 1973, the dead-end hedonism of drug-fueled excess, and the shift of generational focus toward the development of the technologies and lifestyle that would soon power the digital age. The last factor, in particular, can most likely be attributed to the shift in temperament by the second-wave boomers away from radicalism and toward consumerism.

So did the boomer generation prove to be a difference that made a difference? Individually, for the members of the generation, the results are probably mixed. Many boomers have gone on to become civic leaders; others have chosen quieter yet satisfying lives. These are signs of generational success by any standard. But many baby boomers did not fare so well, dying prematurely due to excessive living or simply fading away into the private hell of Vietnam War post-traumatic stress disorder.

And what of those dreams of a better world for all? Perhaps we fared a little better there. First and foremost, the Vietnam War was put to an end, which was always the primary goal for the revolution. The collapse of many racial, gender, and lifestyle barriers has been another significant contribution by the boomers to our contemporary society; opportunities are now available for large numbers of the American population who had very little hope before the cultural revolution. The environmental, recycling, alternative energy, and organic farming movements have strong footholds in public awareness and should continue to build momentum in subsequent generations. And the technologies that this generation developed, thanks to the groundbreaking work of Steve Jobs, Bill Gates, Tim Berners-Lee, and others, continue to amaze as we marvel at the future possibilities afforded by our technical inventiveness.

It has been a "long strange trip"[21] as those of us who were around in the sixties can attest. The initial problem facing the boomers—an unpopular war—still persists in the contemporary age. The players are different, but the song remains the same. So in that sense one can suppose that nothing much has really changed. Yet, somehow it seems that something unique actually did happen 50 years ago that set in motion a series of events that has given us keener insights, heightened awareness, and newfound hope. Full eradication of war and prejudice is probably only a pipe dream given the nature of our human condition. But if nothing else, the 1960s taught us that things seem a little better if you have the right music soundtrack.

NOTES

1. Muhammad Ali, Interview with Ian Woolridge, BBC, 1969.

2. *Time* magazine, Steve Jobs special commemorative issue, October 17, 2011, 6.

3. Walter Isaacson, *Steve Jobs* (New York: Simon & Schuster, 2011), vii.

4. Marshall McLuhan, *Understanding Media: The Extensions of Man* (1964; repr., Cambridge, MA: MIT Press).

5. Isaacson, *Steve Jobs*, 494.

6. Steven Levy, "The Perfect Thing: How the iPod Shuffles Commerce, Culture and Coolness" (New York: Simon & Schuster, 2007), quoted in Isaacson, *Steve Jobs*, 412.

7. Steve Jobs, Steve Jobs Quotes website, 2006, http://stevejobsdailyquote.com/.

8. Marshall McLuhan, *The Guttenberg Galaxy: The Making of Typographic Man* (Toronto: University of Toronto Press, 1962).

9. Richard Brautigan, *The Pill Versus the Springhill Mine Disaster* (New York: Dell Publishing, 1968), 1.

10. McLuhan, *Understanding Media* (New York: Signet, 1964), 19.

11. Dwight D. Eisenhower, section four, farewell address, January 17, 1961.

12. Barry Miles, *Hippie* (New York: Sterling Publishing, 2004), 226.

13. Bob Dylan, "Subterranean Homesick Blues," Columbia Records, 1965.

14. Tommie Smith, Delois Smith, and David Steele, *Silent Gesture: The Autobiography of Tommie Smith* (Philadelphia: Temple University Press, 2007).

15. Helen Reddy, "I Am Woman," Capitol Records, 1971.

16. Marshall McLuhan, "The Playboy Interview: Marshall McLuhan, *Playboy*, March 1969," in *The Essential McLuhan*, edited by Marshall McLuhan, Eric Mcluhan, and Frank Zingrone (New York: Basic Books, 1996), 233.

17. The Beatles, "Sgt. Pepper's Lonely Hearts Club Band," Capitol Records, 1967.

18. Scott McKenzie, "San Francisco (Be Sure to Wear Some Flowers in Your Hair)," MCA Records, 1967.

19. George Carlin, "Seven Dirty Words," Atlantic Records, 1972.

20. *Gimme Shelter*, directed by Albert Maysles, David Maysles, and Charlotte Zwerin, independent film produced by Porter Bibb and Ronald Schneider, distributed by Maysles Films, 1969.

21. Jerry Garcia, Robert Weir, Phil Lesh, and Hunter S. Thompson, "Truckin'," Warner Brothers Records, 1970.

3

Breaking Down Doors: The Stonewall Riots and LGBT Rights

Anastacia Kurylo

The Stonewall riots did not begin the gay rights movement.* Instead, it solidified a latent cultural shift within the gay community that boiled over into an overt divide between that community and American culture at large. At the center of this shift is the group now known as the Stonewall generation, a subsection of the baby boomer generation. The Stonewall generation marks "a huge expansion . . . in the number of lesbian, gay, bisexual and transgender older adults who are open about their sexual orientation and/ or gender identity."[1] This openness was characteristic of a new homophile movement, as it was referred to at the time, that manifested as a result of the Stonewall riots.

In 1969, the year of the riots, Stonewall Inn, located at 53 Christopher Street, was a popular Greenwich Village nightspot in New York City that "could not possibly have been more centrally located."[2] The laws at the time restricted homosexuals from congregating, dancing, and being served alcohol. In violation of these laws, the Mafia-owned bar catered to a mostly male gay clientele, served alcohol, and was "the only gay male bar in New York where dancing was permitted."[3] Stonewall Inn became "the largest gay club in the 1960's"[4] and "the most popular gay bar in Greenwich Village."[5] In these ways, the bar was a friend to gays. In many other ways, Stonewall Inn was not a friend. As a result, the Stonewall riots occurred, thereby enabling baby boomers to redefine homosexual identity, and created a visible gay community by fighting against American cultural norms and more privileged groups.

---

* During the 1960s gay was considered a generic term suitable to be used in reference to both gay males and lesbians. Today, gay is still used in this way, but the usage is viewed as androcentric and, thus, problematic in its reference to lesbians.

CULTURAL NORMS ABOUT HOMOSEXUALITY

Before the Stonewall riots, laws prevented homosexuals from joining the military, congregating in public places, being served alcohol, and physically touching in public, such as through displays of affection and dancing. For example, in 1953, President Eisenhower signed Executive Order 10450 which legalized "sexual perversion" as a rationale for dismissal from employment. Perhaps unbelievably, "by 1961 the laws in America were harsher on homosexuals than those in Cuba, Russia, or East Germany, countries that the United States criticized for their despotic ways."[6] Law enforcement thrived on enforcing these laws, sometimes adding police brutality to an already terrifying arrest. Police and others enforced heterosexual societal norms through brutality and other victimization. Aside from the potential for physical consequences, there were financial consequences to acting on homosexual desires as well.

Entrapment was de rigueur. This occurred when police officers, regardless of their own sexual orientation, would make advances to someone they suspected was gay. Once in a compromising situation, sometimes after sexual acts had taken place, the police officer could threaten the victim with arrest. Bribes helped to prevent those arrests from taking place, but not always. Those who had not been entrapped by the police did not escape harassment. Anyone could, given the desire, threaten to expose someone as homosexual. Indeed, this could occur regardless of whether the person being threatened was actually gay at all.

In addition to the harassment faced by gays, the American Psychiatric Association had classified homosexuality as a mental disorder. The field of "psychiatry was united behind the notion that homosexuality was diseased, pathological behavior that . . . could be cured."[7] Suspected or confirmed homosexual activity could result in parents or even the legal system requiring psychiatric intervention. Even organizations that had formed to help the homophile movement had "internalized the view of that era's prime experts, the psychiatrists, that their 'condition' was pathological."[8]

Religion raised the stakes further by suggesting that homosexuality was an affront to God and posed a threat to one's access to the afterlife. As a result, homosexuals "found almost universal moral condemnation from religions, whether mainstream or obscure."[9] The position on homosexuality within the psychological industry served as a tangible and seemingly scientific reinforcement for the religious view of homosexuality as an aberration that departed from God's plan.

Many gays internalized these psychological and religious perspectives and suffered from self-hatred.[10] They thought that there was something wrong with their thoughts and behavior and that they should be ashamed of who they were. The fear of losing everything was real and weighed heavily on the minds of many homosexuals at the time. Therefore, a successful gay lifestyle required a life of secrecy. Homosexuals could act on their inclinations only when safety and secrecy were a certainty.

The risk associated with exposed homosexual sexual activity did not deter gays from finding companions for short- and long-term relationships. Even in places like the 1960s Actors Studio in New York City, "homosexuality was commonplace . . . [but] no one talked openly of it, or ever publicly declared his or her orientation."[11] Liquor laws that prohibited the sale of alcohol to homosexuals made gathering in bars difficult because persons suspected of being homosexual would not be served. There were "not more than thirty exclusively lesbian clubs in the whole country in late 1963."[12] As a result, the homosexual dating scene did not often include bars. Instead, trysts and more serious relationships were often initiated in casual and subtle ways. The following story demonstrates the subtlety of the dating scene for homosexuals in the 1950s and 1960s.

> One night, after he had been living with his mother for about a month, he went out to Howard Street to get the evening paper. It was raining lightly; as Craig headed back home, a man suddenly started to walk next to him and then said something about how it was too wet even for the ducks. Craig instinctively knew the guy was coming on to him, and he wanted him to, but he was scared—he guessed the man was at least twenty-three years old. Yet he gave him his home phone number and told him to call from three to six in the afternoon, when his mother would still be at work.[13]

The prominent pickup scene was on the street. In suburbs and urban centers throughout the United States certain streets were known to be places to idly chat and strike up a conversation with a potential partner strolling by. With cruising at select known locations commonplace, entrapment was often hard to avoid. There were few other places to pick up partners. However, these spots were also known outside local homosexual circles and could be dangerous as some locals perpetrated violent homophobic crimes. Such spots were less likely to be frequented by lesbians than by gay men; lesbianism during this time was often depicted in lesbian-themed novels as "centrally characterized by confined options and negative consequences" with "many of the books portray[ing] loneliness, alcoholism and suicide as the common lesbian lot."[14]

CLASS, AGE, AND PRIVILEGE

In the 1960s in the United States, some gays did have privileged lives. To the extent that gay men or lesbians had a wealth of resources, they could use those resources to maintain a lifestyle against cultural norms. Rumors circulated about suspected closeted homosexuals, including J. Edgar Hoover, yet their names were kept out of the media, which instead teased readers by ambiguous statements like "a motion-picture actor" or "a much-admired television personality"[15] was caught in a police raid. Wealth was needed to provide bribes and respond to blackmail threats of being outed that were common at the time. To be outed meant that a man's homosexuality would be revealed to friends, family, employers, and others at great cost—the possibility of losing jobs, income, and family bonds and the risk of eviction, ostracism, and physical violence. Nonfamous homosexuals in the upper class were often able to slip relatively unscathed by America's rigid homophobic culture. Upper-class status afforded homosexuals freedom. For example, two upper-class lesbians who married men and had children could still retain their romantic relationship with each other and be considered "a special category of 'upper-class lesbianism'—no labels, no apologies, no guilt, no remorse."[16]

Often class privilege intersected with age. For wealthy gays, their resources provided them a way to respond to threats while being able to live with less fear of retribution. For the middle class, life involved the fear of being revealed lest there be a cost for their families, their jobs, their status, or their freedom. However, the generation of young gays that began to emerge during the sixties had a different perspective. This group distinguished themselves from older gays whose "suits and ties presented an image rejected by young gay hippies in the Village."[17]

Additionally, a lower-class gay subculture was being fostered within American culture. This group involved younger gays who had voluntarily—or not—left the security of their homes, had few tangible or emotional ties that bound them to middle-class morality, and often had nothing to lose except their lives. This group included the homeless, prostitutes, gamblers, drug users or dealers, and those who engaged in other criminal activities to survive. This group was willing to hustle or sell sexual experiences because they needed to in order to make money, chose to in order to own their identity, or a combination of both. A poem titled "The Hustler" demonstrates this isolation and fait accompli, noting that the protagonist considers himself "just a whore" who without the ability to sell his love would simply find himself alone.[18]

As early as the 1940s, places like Times Square in New York City were popular locations for homosexuals to prostitute themselves. Transvestites and other gays who led this lifestyle were visible about their homosexuality and more willing to take the risk of dissenting from cultural norms. The scene was dangerous. It was not uncommon to be robbed, overdose from drugs, or be a victim of a violent predator. Additionally, frequent arrests were commonplace; "the police would hold the queens overnight . . . and release them the next morning to return again to Times Square."[19]

The intersection of class and age within the homophile movement set the scene in which the Stonewall riots emerged in 1969:

> The pre-Stonewall generation lived most of their lives in a society where the expression of their sexual orientation was criminalized by the government and pathologized by the medical community. This elderly generation of LGBT persons is much more likely to keep their sexual orientation hidden. In contrast to the pre-Stonewall generation, the Stonewall generation of LGBT baby boomers, those currently in their 50s or 60s, came of age during the social unrest of the 1960s, a time of rising social acceptance of LGBT people. LGBT baby boomers are more likely to be at least partly open about their sexual orientation (i.e., open to certain people but perhaps not to others).[20]

Conservative, typically over-40 older gays sought to protect their normative lives legitimized by the dominant mainstream culture. In contrast, younger emerging and visible gays, baby boomers who would later be called the Stonewall generation, had little to lose and were motivated toward embracing their gay identity, being visible about it, and engaging in activism.

CAPITALISM

In addition to the generational split that emerged in the 1960s, capitalism and those who profited from it set the stage for the Stonewall riots. This capitalistic system that was endemic of the Stonewall Inn involved two key figures, the Mafia and the police. Both were able to protect and serve gays while profiting immensely from them.

The Mafia ran the Stonewall Inn because it was a profitable business. There was no other reason. The four partners who opened the bar recovered their entire $3,500 investment and $300 monthly rent on the first night they were open.[21] Homosexuals provided an equal opportunity for profit despite the Mafia's contempt for their homosexual clientele, whom they referred to with the term "faggot scumbags."[22] That they had "little or no concern for their clientele's welfare"[23] was obvious during a hepatitis outbreak in 1969. Because of a lack of running water in the bar, employees washed barware with stored water that was reused throughout the night.[24] Patrons suffered in other ways as well. They were fodder for blackmail by Mafia owners. This provided substantial side revenue that supplemented the money the Mafia gained by selling watered-down drinks and charging admission.

Because Stonewall Inn violated laws in order to service its homosexual clientele, the Mafia enlisted law enforcement to secure their business by paying off police officers. Because the bar was a known gay bar serving alcohol illegally, the police were required to raid the bar to keep up appearances. The bar would be notified in advance of when the raids would occur; most took place before midnight, which was beneficial because prime time was after midnight and could proceed as normal after the raid had taken place. In this way, the police were able to provide the appearance of law enforcement while taking kickbacks, and the bar owners were able to easily manage the raids while making a large profit. However, the system required sacrificial lambs to go to slaughter in order to satisfy this police routine. Therefore, the biggest cost of this system was to the patrons. During the raids, random patrons would be taken into police custody, arrested, potentially beaten by police, and risk having their identity revealed.

On the surface, the Stonewall Inn was a haven for gays to congregate, drink, and dance without fear of being outed, unless they were the target of blackmail by the owners. Inasmuch as there was profit for the Mafia and the police, there was reason to protect homosexuals. However, the role they played as pawns in a lucrative capitalistic system for the Mafia and police did not go unnoticed.

CIVIL RIGHTS AND HOMOSEXUALITY

The 1960s was a time of considerable public protest. White men with access to wealth were in dominant societal positions and reaped the benefits. Nonwhite men and women generally did not. The relatively neat alignment between race, gender, and class meant the less visible characteristic of class was made visible through the characteristics of race and gender. Cultural icons like Malcolm X and Martin Luther King Jr. inspired blacks to engage in civil rights protests. An antiwar movement, wherein the wealthiest Americans were viewed as being able to maneuver themselves out of the military, was taking hold of the middle and lower classes. The introduction of the birth control pill to mainstream society after approval by the Food and Drug Administration on May 9, 1960, empowered women to embrace a feminist mind-set. The divided groups were mostly visible and easy to identify. The result was a visible distinction between the "in groups" who had access to resources and privilege within American culture and "out groups" who were marginalized. Unlike these other civil rights issues of the time, the homophile movement crossed class, racial, and gender divides, and the Stonewall Inn would "draw all kinds of gay people."[25]

Despite or more likely because of this, the homophile movement was slow to gain momentum. In great part this was because the costs of being a visible homosexual were punitive given American culture in the 1960s. Moreover, because there is no visible consistent marker of homosexual identity people could pass as heterosexual if they desired rather than risk the severe cost of being visibly homosexual at the time. Making matters worse was the rampant homophobia that ran through each of the more prominent civil rights movements of the sixties. Unfortunately, "the barriers of race, class, and gender that centrally characterized mainstream American culture in the fifties were also decidedly in place, though perhaps marginally less noticeable, in the gay subculture."[26] The black political movement of the 1960s was characterized by endemic homophobia, as were the political left and the feminist movement.[27] As a result, identification with a cohesive group bound by their gay identity, upon which solidarity might be built—even among the most activist—remained elusive.

The homophile movement in San Francisco took root earlier and more firmly than in New York. By 1966, the Society for Individual rights in San Francisco had become the "largest homophile organization in the country"[28] with 1,000 members. However, homosexual advocacy groups had emerged in other areas and in such seemingly unlikely places as Columbus, Ohio.[29] Typically, however, the homophile movement was most active in large cities where the melting-pot philosophy of the United States had deep roots in immigration. Adding diversity related to sexual orientation seemed a natural extension of this melting-pot philosophy. San Francisco and New York provided prime locations for homosexual communities to emerge in the Castro District and Greenwich Village, respectively.

In this way, the Stonewall riots did not create a gay identity. Rather, they transformed the old identity. Homosexuals in the 1960s had a cultural way of life in which isolation and secrecy served as the safest form of expressing that identity. The riots at Stonewall Inn provided a symbol through which otherwise disparate gay Americans could make themselves visible through a new cohesive community.

BABY BOOMERS AND A VISIBLE HOMOSEXUAL COMMUNITY

Before the Stonewall Inn riots, a new identity had begun to form for younger homosexuals throughout the United States. This was the case particularly in New York and San Francisco where protests and becoming vocal and visible were emerging as a civil rights resistance strategy. Being vocal and visible was far from the mind-set of older, more conservative homosexuals who were entrenched and invested in a dominant American culture proud of its homophobia. For older homosexuals, an aggressive and visible youth-oriented counterculture threatened to do more harm than good for the homophile movement.

Many older homosexuals had internalized their position as a subclass within American culture with an abnormal problematic identity. Homophobic laws and illegal victimization aside, the psychological component of

American homophobia generated considerable self-hate and fear. Even gays who were active in the homophile movement used pseudonyms because taking a more active role in activism came with considerable risks and "a fair chance that [activists] would be summarily arrested, carted off to jail, and possibly beaten."[30]

Resistance techniques were often responsive to the current state of homosexual rights that assumed any visibility of homosexuality to be socially, psychologically, spiritually, or legally inappropriate. The Mattachine Society was a leading homophile organization that worked actively to secure homosexual civil rights. It was led by older homosexuals who argued that the way into a mainstream American culture was by demonstrating that homosexuals were no different than heterosexuals. They argued for "gradualism and quietism in modifying gay comportment so that it would better coincide with middle-class notions of proper behavior."[31] Their dress code for protests required suits for men and no same-sex displays of affection because "it was important to look ordinary, to get bystanders to hear the message rather than be prematurely turned off by appearances."[32] The intent was to shatter stereotypes that depicted homosexuals as counter to mainstream American norms.

Younger gays, predominantly baby boomers, were enamored of and often involved with the highly visible civil rights movements being undertaken across the country that were pro-black, were antiwar, and encouraged equal rights for women. For example, "by the fall of 1968, . . . black students [had taken] over the administration buildings at Cornell . . . the black Panthers and the Oakland police had a shoot-out; a contingent of feminists invaded the hitherto sacrosanct Miss America pageant; and incidents of arson and bombings [were] commonplace."[33] Young gays viewed their experiences with disenfranchisement through the same lenses they looked to understand and empathize with these other groups.

Younger gays and more liberal older gays argued that the restrictions placed on protests sponsored by the Mattachine Society were internalizations of dominant cultural norms about homosexuality. The Mattachine Society's position was viewed as being too slow to yield success. Moreover, it was viewed as a step in the wrong direction because it legitimized homophobic attitudes by arguing that mainstream culture had the right to expect homosexuals to meet heterosexual norms. Younger homosexuals rejected this position and argued that working within a heterosexual normative system would marginalize homosexuals who wanted to live outside the artificial and often seemingly irrelevant constraints imposed upon them by mainstream America.

Indeed, there was increased visibility of gays in mainstream American culture, at least urban mainstream culture, as evidenced by an article in *The New York Times* titled "Growth of Overt Homosexuality in City Provokes

Wide Concern."[34] Although not a cohesive community before the Stonewall riots, characteristics that had developed in younger homosexuals provided the seeds for what would later grow into a more visible homophile movement. The 1960s provided a unique moment in which baby boomers had more freedoms—including access to drugs, sex, and dialogue about civil rights issues—than their older counterparts.

Baby boomers had either witnessed first-hand or took part in the civil rights protests occurring around them. They had an increasing awareness of the role capitalism played in their rights and freedom. This realization—that there was a system that benefited from their *lack* of organizing—resulted in increasing frustration over their own lack of control over their life circumstances. This developing homophile movement was counter to the dominant culture and the mind-set of many older gays. For younger gays, the homophile movement was not about the right to be homosexual; it was about the right to be *visibly* homosexual.

Eventually, the mantra for this younger generation of homosexual activists was simply, "gay is good," which first appeared in a *Village Voice* advertisement for the Oscar Wilde Memorial Bookshop in 1967.[35] This became a rallying call for change in how dominant American culture, as well as older gays, understood the homophile movement. The new, more visible homophile movement was unapologetic and embraced rather than tried to thwart associated stereotypes. The catchphrase later used by San Francisco's first openly gay politician resonated with this visible and unapologetic homophile mantra: "My name is *Harvey Milk*, and I'm here to *recruit* you."

Those involved in the emergent homophile movement were, at first, united in their characteristics more than their practices. Older homosexuals held firmly to their hegemonized agenda to be accepted into American mainstream culture organically. Younger homosexuals were of a different mind-set. The country would need to accept homosexuals on their terms—not as part of the dominant culture but as a legitimate counterculture. Given the dynamics of the homophile movement in the 1960s—older homosexuals at conflict with younger homosexuals, a capitalist system of Mafia and law enforcement profiting from homosexual oppression, and ubiquitous civil rights activism—the Stonewall riots were inevitable.

THE STONEWALL RIOTS

A police raid on the Stonewall Inn on June 28, 1969, garnered an unexpected response from the crowd that gathered outside. Historically, the police raids that were commonplace at Stonewall Inn and other locations were met with acquiescence. No single identifiable prompt sparked the riots that day. Rather, rioters fought back this time because of a unique combination of circumstances. The raid comprised innumerable small acts of aggression interpreted through the lens of a broader homophile movement.

The specific details of the Stonewall riots need not be recounted here. They are available elsewhere in explicit historical detail. One of the most enduring images of the night, however, occurred when "About twenty queens . . . put their arms around one another and started forming a kick line, and the cops just charged with the [nightsticks] and started smacking them in the heads, hitting people, pulling them into cars."[36] The homophile movement was asking for the same thing other civil rights–oriented groups were asking for at the time: to be treated as people with the same enduring rights as others in American culture. The response to this basic request, palpable in this image from the riots, was anger and violence.

In the aftermath of the Stonewall riots, there was fractioning as the baby boomer mind-set conflicted further with the older mind-set about how the homophile movement should proceed. Activist groups such as the Gay Liberation Front and later the Gay Activists Alliance emerged as a "new kind of gay organization, imbued with the militant spirit of the riots that engendered them"[37] and empowered by a baby boomer contingent who demanded visibility and respect rather than acceptance. In contrast, "many of the older homophile[s] were more inclined than ever to view anything other than moderation as destructive extremism."[38] The moderate Gay Activists Alliance eventually gained credibility after being able to demonstrate productive activism for the emergent homophile community.

With a new in-group created, other groups were marginalized. The Mattachine Society "remained overwhelmingly male (and white)."[39] Lesbian organizations emerged but struggled in their fight to end "the profound isolation and invisibility of lesbians."[40] Although transvestites had been by some accounts the most vocal instigators during the early moments of the Stonewall riots,[41] they were not empowered to be a part of the emergent visible homophile movement, though one of the most active transvestites, a Times Square hustler named Sylvia Rivera, worked to organize the short-lived Street Transvestite Action Revolutionaries (later changed to Street Transgender Action Revolutionaries).

CONCLUSION

The homophile movement is marked in history as one of the prominent civil rights movements of the 1960s.[42] The fight for marriage rights has been a much longer battle than other initiatives of the homophile movement.[43] Currently, "[n]ineteen states plus Washington, D.C. have the freedom to marry for same-sex couples."[44] Even the two states most welcoming to the homophile movement have only recently made any progress on the issue of same-sex marriage. California briefly legalized same-sex marriage in 2008 then did not now allow same sex marriage until June 2013. New York legalized same-sex marriage on June 24, 2011.

The list of rights still denied to same-sex couples is extensive. Access to information about patients; visitation rights; partner health care benefits; medical, family, and bereavement leave; immigration, parental, and adoption rights; insurance; Social Security benefits, and so forth represent issues with tangible costs for homosexuals. Employment discrimination still exists[45] as does fear of discrimination:[46] "While laws, beliefs, and attitudes have changed over the past 40+ years, a recent study . . . found that only 22% of LGBT respondents would feel comfortable revealing their sexual orientation or gender identity in a long term care setting."[47] Meaningful diversity initiatives that foster inclusion[48]—not as an afterthought but as an integral foundation—are necessary to realize the full potential of LGBT equality.

Today, Stonewall Inn has a different meaning than the oppression that the bar symbolized for rioters in 1969. President Obama invoked that meaning in his second inaugural address delivered on January 22, 2013. He did so despite naysayers who argued that expressing sympathy with LGBT rights issues was a risky political move.[49] The speech indisputably and unapologetically placed the Stonewall riots alongside other iconic civil rights moments when he stated, "We, the people, declare today that the most evident of truths—that all of us are created equal—is the star that guides us still; just as it guided our forebears through Seneca Falls, and Selma, and Stonewall."[50]

Today Stonewall Inn provides a powerful symbol of LGBT pride. The baby boomers of the Stonewall generation created the path for a united, visible, and activist LGBT community.

NOTES

1. David Godfrey, "Key Legal Issues Faced by Older LGBT Adults," National Resource Center on LGBT Aging, November 2011, http://www.lgbtagingcenter .org/resources/resource.cfm?r=423.

2. David Carter, *Stonewall: The Riots That Sparked the Gay Revolution* (New York: St. Martin's Griffin, 2005), 11.

3. Martin Duberman, *Stonewall* (New York: Penguin, 1993), 182.

4. Carter, *Riots*, 13.

5. Duberman, *Stonewall*, 182.

6. Carter, *Riots*, 15.

7. Duberman, *Stonewall*, 48.

8. Duberman, *Stonewall*, 77.

9. Carter, *Riots*, 16.

10. Carter, *Riots*, 113.

11. Duberman, *Stonewall*, 59.

12. Duberman, *Stonewall*, 40.

13. Duberman, *Stonewall*, 45.

14. Duberman, *Stonewall*, 52.

15. Carter, *Riots*, 91.

16. Duberman, *Stonewall*, 52.

17. Carter, *Riots*, 113.

18. Carter, *Riots*, 113.

19. Duberman, *Stonewall*, 69.

20. Mark J. Simone and Jonathon S. Appelbaum, "Addressing the Needs of Older Lesbian, Gay, Bisexual, and Transgender Adults," *Clinical Geriatrics* 19 (2011): 38–45.

21. Carter, *Riots*, 113.

22. Duberman, *Stonewall*, 181.

23. Carter, *Riots*, 79.

24. Duberman, *Stonewall*, 181.

25. Carter, *Riots*, 73.

26. Duberman, *Stonewall*, 41.

27. Duberman, *Stonewall*, 41.

28. Duberman, *Stonewall*, 99.

29. Ann Bremner, "Stonewall Days in Columbus," Wexblog (Wexler Center for the Arts), September 29, 2010, http://wexarts.org/wexblog/?p=4645.

30. Duberman, *Stonewall*, 81.

31. Duberman, *Stonewall*, 108.

32. Duberman, *Stonewall*, 111.

33. Duberman, *Stonewall*, 170.

34. Robert C. Doty, "Growth of Overt Homosexuality in City Provokes Wide Concern," *New York Times*, December 17, 1963.

35. Duberman, *Stonewall*, x41.

36. Carter, *Riots*, 178.

37. Carter, *Riots*, 2.

38. Duberman, *Stonewall*, 227.

39. Duberman, *Stonewall*, 77.

40. Duberman, *Stonewall*, 77.

41. Carter, *Riots*, 113.

42. David Farber, *The Age of Great Dreams: America in the 1960s*, American Century Series (New York: Hill and Wang, 1994); Jeff Goodwin, *The Social Movements Reader: Cases and Concepts*, 2nd ed. (Hoboken, NJ: Wiley-Blackwell, 2009).

43. Marriage Equality: A Retrospective. Now Is the Time website, March 1, 2012, http://box8661.blogspot.com/2012/04/marriage-equality-retrospective.html; Congressional Budget Office, "The Potential Budgetary Impact of Recognizing Same-Sex Marriages," Washington, DC: Congressional Budget Office, June 21, 2014.

44. Freedom to Marry, "States," August 4, 2014, http://www.freedomtomarry.org/states/.

45. Patrice M. Buzzanelli, "Employment Interviewing Research: Ways We Can Study Underrepresented Group Members' Experiences as Applicants," *Journal*

of Business Communication 39 (2002): 257–275; David Godfrey, "Key Legal Issues Faced by Older LGBT Adults," National Resource Center on LGBT Aging, November 2011, http://www.lgbtagingcenter.org/resources/resource.cfm?r=423.

46. Burton Bollag, "Gay Professors Face Less Discrimination, But Many Still Fight for Benefits," *Chronicle of Higher Education*, September 28, 2007.

47. David Godfrey, "Key Legal Issues Faced by Older LGBT Adults," National Resource Center on LGBT Aging, November 2011, http://www.lgbtagingcenter .org/resources/resource.cfm?r=423.

48. Jennifer Delton, "Why Diversity for Diversity's Sake Won't Work," *Chronicle of Higher Education*, September 28, 2007; Jacky Lumby, and Marlene Morrison, "Leadership and Diversity: Theory and Research," *School Leadership and Management* 30 (2010): 3–17.

49. Christina Ballantoni, and Terrance Burlij, "Obama: Support for Gay Marriage 'May Hurt' Politically," *PBS Newshour*, May 10, 2012, http://www.pbs.org/ newshour/rundown/2012/05/obama-support-for-gay-marriage-may-hurt-politically .html.

50. Barack Obama, "Obama's Second Inaugural Speech," *New York Times*, January 21, 2013.

REFERENCES

Ballantoni, Christina, and Terrance Burlij. "Obama: Support for Gay Marriage 'May Hurt' Politically." *PBS Newshour*. May 10, 2012. http://www.pbs.org/ newshour/rundown/2012/05/obama-support-for-gay-marriage-may-hurt -politically.html.

Bollag, Burton. "Gay Professors Face Less Discrimination, But Many Still Fight for Benefits." *Chronicle of Higher Education*, September 28, 2007.

Bremner, Ann. "Stonewall Days in Columbus." Wexblog (Wexler Center for the Arts). September 29, 2010. http://wexarts.org/wexblog/?p=4645.

Buzzanelli, Patrice M. "Employment Interviewing Research: Ways We Can Study Underrepresented Group Members' Experiences as Applicants." *Journal of Business Communication* 39 (2002): 257–275.

Carter, David. *Stonewall: The Riots That Sparked the Gay Revolution*. New York: St. Martin's Griffin, 2005.

Congressional Budget Office. "The Potential Budgetary Impact of Recognizing Same-Sex Marriages." Washington, DC: Congressional Budget Office, June 21, 2004. http://www.cbo.gov/sites/default/files/cbofiles/ftpdocs/55xx/ doc5559/06-21-samesexmarriage.pdf.

Delton, Jennifer. "Why Diversity for Diversity's Sake Won't Work." *Chronicle of Higher Education*, September 28, 2007.

Doty, Robert C. "Growth of Overt Homosexuality in City Provokes Wide Concern." *New York Times*, December 17, 1963.

Duberman, Martin. *Stonewall*. New York: Penguin, 1993.

Farber, David. *The Age of Great Dreams: America in the 1960s*. American Century Series. New York: Hill and Wang, 1994.

Freedom to Marry. "States." August 4, 2014 http://www.freedomtomarry.org/states/.

Godfrey, David. "Key Legal Issues Faced by Older LGBT Adults." National Resource Center on LGBT Aging. November 2011, http://www.lgbtagingcenter.org/resources/resource.cfm?r=423.

Goodwin, Jeff. *The Social Movements Reader: Cases and Concepts.* 2nd ed. Hoboken, NJ: Wiley-Blackwell, 2009.

Lumby, Jacky, and Marlene Morrison. "Leadership and Diversity: Theory and Research." *School Leadership and Management* 30 (2010): 3–17.

Marriage Equality: A Retrospective. Now Is the Time website, March 1, 2012, http://box8661.blogspot.com/2012/04/marriage-equality-retrospective.html.

Obama, Barack. "Obama's Second Inaugural Speech." *New York Times*, January 21, 2013. http://www.nytimes.com/2013/01/21/us/politics/obamas-second-inaugural-speech.html?pagewanted=all&_r=0.

Simone, Mark J., and Jonathon S. Appelbaum. "Addressing the Needs of Older Lesbian, Gay, Bisexual, and Transgender Adults." *Clinical Geriatrics* 19 (2011): 38–45.

4

Wearing Members Only Jackets: Baby Boomers and the Shift from *Sharing in* to *Buying into* Community

Todd Kelshaw

The popular imagination of the generational cohort known as the "baby boomers"—Americans born approximately between 1946 and 1964—is confused. On one hand, we have the rebelliously progressive and community-oriented champions of rock and roll, social justice, and environmentalism; on the other, we have socially and fiscally conservative and self-concerned accumulators of personal excess. The moment of rupture between the "hippie" and "yuppie" manifestations of baby boomerism is typically dated to the first presidential term of Ronald Reagan—or, even more specifically, to the moment when Reagan (a bastion of the older "greatest generation") was shot by John Hinckley (a baby boomer) (Casale and Lerman 2002, 128). Of course, it was not the character, rhetoric, policies, or victimhood of Reagan that singularly effected this transformation; rather, it was the gradual tide-turning confluence of myriad historical, cultural, technological, and political currents before and during that period, as American society reflected on the Vietnam War, reimagined the Cold War, suffered the surge of AIDS, brought computers into the home, channel-surfed through post-network television offerings, and so on.

This chapter does not attempt to explore the complicated totality of factors that coincide with the baby boomers' bipolar generational character. Instead, it focuses on just one facet: how baby boomers, as the socially and politically ascendant generational cohort of the early 1980s, shifted their espoused concern from social capital to physical capital and, in so doing, established new normative understandings of what it means to belong in a community. In addressing this transformation, this chapter argues that, as baby boomers shifted from declarative preference for *sharing in* to *buying into* affiliations with others, they advanced the liberal-individualistic fragmentation of the United States' civic and political culture. More specifically, this chapter recognizes how the baby boomers' adolescent emphasis on social capital and their middle-aged preference for physical capital coincided, respectively, with their espoused eschewal and, then, overt embracing of communication technologies—media that were becoming increasingly geared to personalization and the marking of social status. These media were ideologically saturated with ideals of liberal-individualism and advanced capitalism, and the sociopolitically ascendant baby boomers, in their new conspicuous consumption, legitimated for the broader populace not just a technetronic culture but also a new understanding of what it means to belong in a democratic society.

THE NASCENT BABY BOOMERS: SHARING IN COMMUNITY

One way of understanding community is informed by the word's etymological basis in the Latin word for "sharing." A community in this sense is less about people existing *side-by-side* among *distributed* resources and more about people existing *together* among *integrated* resources. As a cohort of youthful baby boomers began to question the assumptions of post-World War II suburbanization—as such assumptions are connected to what Ritzer (2012) called the "McDonaldization of society," replete with the trappings of depersonalizing bureaucracy—they established social enclaves that were at once subcultural and countercultural with respect to the broader American public sphere. To understand how these enclaves reflected a particular conception of community that was tenuously yet consequentially connected with the broader American public sphere—a simultaneous "dropping out" and "being in"—it is helpful to consider the young baby boomers' appreciation and functional application of social capital.

Social Capital for Bridging

Social capital is a concept that has multiple meanings, spanning individual concerns (e.g., the use of social networks for professional advancement), collective concerns (e.g., grassroots community empowerment), and socially beneficial and detrimental implications related to, respectively, inclusion and exclusion (Putnam 2000, 19–22). The mode of social capital that, in the popular imagination, is most associated with the youthful baby boomers during the Beat era of the 1950s and the hippie era of the 1960s is complex, as it entailed rejection of "the man," "the system," and "the Establishment" (MacFarlane 2010, 123) at the same time that it embraced the ideal of interpersonal connection (Elkins 2013). A good inroad for considering this dualistic mode of social capital and how it affected popular understandings of community and democratic life during the 1960s and 1970s is the commune.

Baby-boom era communes, which originated in urban settings and began a migration to rural areas around 1966 (Carden 1976), captured the public imagination by being "media attention-grabbers, full of photo opportunities, wild anecdotes, and the weirdest-looking people most Americans had even seen" (Miller 1992, 73). Heralded as such, they bore potential for affecting the general public's ideas about organizational life, even as they were situated outside of mainstream culture. A commune, by definition, is a "group of people who have chosen to live together with a common purpose, working cooperatively to create a lifestyle that reflects their shared core values" (Fellowship for Intentional Community 2009). As the communes of the 1960s took shape, they did so according to two general approaches. The first, termed an "anarchistic" or "retreat" commune (Fitzgerald 1971), modeled an egalitarian social ideal and manifested outright rejection of the bureaucratic (control-oriented) structures attributed to mainstream American society. In this kind of commune, "usually anyone is welcome, members are transient, and there are no rules or regulations. This type of commune, for obvious reasons of disorganization, usually doesn't last long" (Meunier 1994). The second form of commune—a "service" or "intentional" commune—entailed members who "pool resources and agree to live a certain way with a motivating philosophy" (Meunier 1994). As Fitzgerald (1971) and Kanter (1972) described it, membership is relatively restrictive and adherence to an explicitly defined shared purpose is required; vertical position-based structures and formal rules establish social order and enable productivity.

For the baby boomers of the 1960s, the anarchic/retreat type of commune enabled disaffected youth to not just "drop out" of society but also, through their purposeful avoidance of positional structure and formal rules, to (dis)organizationally articulate their rejection of what they viewed as a bureaucratic, dehumanizing society. As Miller (1991) noted:

> Withdrawal often meant heading for a hip commune. The [retreat] communes . . . were not aimed at cultural confrontation, but simply were turning away to build a new society apart from the old. Down on the commune, a hipster wrote in 1969, "We are Amerika, but we are no longer a part of it." (xviii)

Focusing on equality (i.e., lack of hierarchical positions), they practiced mutuality in their relational structures, focusing on affiliations and relational experiences rather than the coordinated and efficient accomplishment of tasks.

The second type of commune—the service/intentional type—went a bit further in manifesting countercultural ideals, even as it embraced some of the vertical organizational forms of the outside world. With primary concern for adherence to moral codes rather than capital gain, such communes distinguished themselves from their organizational counterparts (e.g., corporations) in industrialized society in terms of both purpose and methods. In using formal organizational structures toward cooperative—rather than competitive—achievement, they provided a counter-model of organizational life and thus advanced ideas among the general populace about what is wrong with the dominant template and what an alternative might look like. As well, unlike the anarchic/retreat communes that provided places for disaffected youth to simply drop out of society, service/intentional communes often had connections with broader social movements.

The kind of social capital that baby-boom commune members of the 1960s and 1970s privileged is what Putnam (2000), drawing on Gittell and Vidal (1998), described as "bridging." The bridging form of social capital is about inclusive relationship-making, with emphases on mutuality and reciprocity that benefit all interdependent members in a social network. The bridging form of social capital, exemplified by civil rights and social justice movements, ecumenical religious organizations, youth service groups, and service/intentional communes, "can generate [broad] identities and reciprocity" (Putnam 2000, 22–23). In this sense, a bridging conception of social capital has both internal benefits (on relational and substantive levels) and outward reaching efficacy.

Internally, the bridging form of social capital emphasizes inclusiveness, interdependence, mutual benefit, and esprit de corps. As Miller (1992) noted about the baby boomers' communes:

> While it is hazardous to generalize too extensively about hip communal styles (the communes were a diverse lot, with a wide variety of purposes and attitudes), a few features tended to define the genre. For example, many communes, unlike most of their predecessors, subscribed to the concept of open membership. Openness was basic to the hip ethos; hippies tended to have a naive optimism about human nature, a belief that if one could simply be rescued from the nightmare of American culture and placed in a supportive setting, one would respond in kind and contribute to group harmony and achievement. So anyone willing to reject mainstream culture—to drop out, as the argot had it—was welcome. (79)

This kind of sharing-in is seen in other images of 1960s countercultural life:

> The hippies are clearly a contact species. They huddle together, like walruses, and the typical hippie crash pad is comparable in many ways

to the crowded, all-purpose communal room of the Middle Ages. Something like 400,000 young people attended the now-famous Woodstock Music and Art Fair. . . . They were packed together for three days and nights in a sea of mud, and the policemen who were assigned to the event were utterly astonished. Said one: "I've never seen that many people in so small an area who acted so peacefully." Said another: "This was the nicest bunch of kids I've ever dealt with." Apparently there was not so much as a single fight; the young people shared their food and their shelter and related to each other in what appeared to be perfect harmony. (Braden 1970, 243–244)

This kind of openness and interpersonal concern manifested itself in many ways, one of which was, in Miller's terms, "the hippie belief in abolishing all restrictions on sexual behavior. The standard hip theory was one of total sexual freedom: multiple partners, multilateral relationships or no commitment at all, homosexuality—there were no boundaries" (1992, 80). At first glance, this sexual freedom might seem to be chiefly about hedonistic personal gratification rather than a relational kind of social capital. But consider an example from the Weather Underground Organization (WUO), which, although not a commune, was a militant political organization with communal characteristics. The WUO's "smash monogamy" initiative celebrated group sex not just to challenge dominant social codes but, more importantly, to galvanize members. "The purpose was not pleasure so much as welding together an enforced unity of the body," reflected Collier and Horowitz (1989, 86). As one organizational member quoted by Collier and Horowitz summarized the initiative, "People who fuck together, fight together" (86). Accordingly, the physical melding of community members and the "smashing" of monogamy's exclusivity-related ideals manifested social capital. This social capital had some bonding characteristics (in that it advanced solidarity) but also bridging characteristics that emphasized familiarity, cooperation, and mutual respect.

Just as a bridging form of social capital fostered affiliations within collectives, it also functioned externally by bearing consequences for issue-management beyond a community's formal membership. Whereas members of anarchic/retreat communes did not directly work to affect the world beyond—they were escapists, after all, striving to live apart rather than within the broader society—the narratives of their egalitarian relational systems modeled for the outside world an alternative mode of citizenship and fueled broader questioning of the era's industrial order and related power structures. Depending on the organizational mission, a given service/intentional commune had more potential for engaging with and directly affecting the broader world. This was especially true of organizations affiliated with social movements. It is certainly true that a bridging form of social capital motivated the efforts for racial and gender empowerment as well as environmental conservation, which were all crucial advents of the era (Evans 2002; Morris 2002; Shabecoff 2002; Eversole 2010; Monhollon 2010b; Voss 2010). A critical mass was crucial for legal and cultural change, and such strength in numbers required a bridging form of social capital. In this sense, insofar as the young baby boomers of the 1960s and 1970s were the champions of social and environmental justice, social capital toward relational bridging was the generational cohort's essential value. Life for the disaffected baby boomers was not simply about *dropping out*; it was much more about *sharing in*, engaging with each other as relational affiliates and engaging with the society that they at once rejected and sought to transform.

A Humanistic Basis for Community

In 1956—as the first baby boomers were about to emerge as socially and politically disaffected teenagers—the British scientist and novelist C. P. Snow (2013) identified an ideological rift between the "two cultures" of science and humanities. Although he did not necessarily have American youth in mind (being more concerned with professional intellectuals), he recognized that the bifurcation of scientific and humanistic orientations was an enormous impediment for social problem solving throughout Western society. Fourteen years later, as the baby boomers' countercultural age of Aquarius was in full swing, Braden (1970) saw in America's generational culture clash an important manifestation of Snow's dichotomy. For Braden:

> [T]he Two Cultures conflict can be seen as a basic factor in the Black Power movement; in the protest of the New Left; in the supposed confusion of sexual roles; in the development of an LSD subculture; in the so-called Leap to the East by many drugstore disciples of Hinduism and Zen Buddhism; in the current faddish enthusiasm for astrology, witchcraft, and sensitivity training; in anti-scientism; in the newly emerging emphasis on ecology, environmental control, and the often mystical worship of mature; in the reassertion of ethnicity; in the now-defunct Death of God theology as well as the newer attraction referred to as the Theology of Hope. (7)

In this conflict, as Braden understood it, the baby boomers were radical humanists, revolting against the scientific/technetronic older generation that held civic and political control.

Before proceeding with consideration of this humanistic/technetronic framework, it is important to note that there is often a distance between what one (whether an individual, organization, or social movement) espouses and what one does; and that often the discursive (rather than the enacted) is more consequential for shaping understandings as it is passed along and concretized through narratives. Accordingly, as a preface for addressing some prominent countercultural, antimaterialistic ideals pronounced by a visible segment of baby boomers during the 1960s and 1970s, it should be noted that "consumerism was perhaps the defining characteristic of the baby boom era" (Monhollon 2010a, xvii). More specifically:

> Freed of economic responsibility to the family by postwar prosperity, teenagers—especially the white middle class—became significant consumers. One industry estimate put the youth market at $10 billion annually, on such products as cosmetics, cars, telephones, televisions, radios, movies, and music. . . . Advertising targeted teens, especially through the relatively new medium of television. Hollywood churned out movies to appeal to their tastes. Radio stations did the same by playing rock and roll music, which provided—in many ways—the first stirrings of rebellion among the baby boom generation. (Monhollon 2010a, xviii)

So, at the same time that the disaffected, countercultural members of the baby boom generational cohort (such as the hippie contingent) denounced technologies and consumerism, they, as a general demographic category, continued to consume media, albeit often in veiled or unacknowledged ways. Sometimes, though, their media consumption was more obvious but, somehow, seen as coherent with their ideals and thus not hypocritical. A case in point is the manner in which rock and roll music provided a soundtrack for countercultural movements during the 1950s, 1960s, and 1970s, enabling solidarity among baby boomers (and distinction from older generations) as well as revolutionary rallying cries. What is often overlooked when thinking about rock and roll as a dimension of the baby boomers' countercultural penchant, though, is that much of the music was a corporately produced commodity—strategically conceived and marketed and heavily consumed. If American society's ideological formations have always been somehow bound up in its technologies (as the advent of the early 1980s eventually illustrated), then it is important to briefly note here that, as much as the countercultural baby boomers derided technocratic ideology, they could not actually step outside of it.

With that said, thinking about the disaffected baby boomers as humanists who were diametrically opposed to the technetronic older (and sociopolitically dominant) generational cohorts is helpful for understanding their rejection of "the system" or the Establishment as a bureaucratically mechanistic social structure manifested in the Levittowns of their youth. In repudiating what many of this generation's members considered the dehumanizing apparatuses of their parents' post–World War II life, the youthful baby boomers were in essence devaluing and casting away much of the era's emerging technology. Of course, as noted earlier, there were important exceptions as, for instance, this was the first generation to be raised with television, and that medium was extremely consequential (Light 2002). But the baby boomers' heightening appreciation of agrarianism and spiritualism, the neo-Luddite movement, and other anti-materialist concerns during the 1960s and 1970s makes sense as a humanistic response to the dehumanizing ramifications of new technologies.

"[O]ne day the nation woke from its American dream to find that its alabaster cities were in flames," wrote Braden (1970, 7). He continued:

> Now in the streets and on the campuses was heard the sound of angry voices. . . . "*I am a human being. Do not fold, spindle, or mutilate.*" That was the rallying cry during the Free Speech Movement in 1964 in Berkeley—a shout of protest against our apparent acceleration toward a wholly computerized, IBM civilization. (7)

The generation's antipathy for emerging technologies is not cut and dried, though, for there was a thriving community of hackers who embraced computers but wished to seize their control from corporate interests.

> In the early 1960s, the hackers got their hands on the tool that would wrest computing from the priests forever—the minicomputer. Though they were as big as refrigerators at first, these machines were revolutionary: unlike huge room-size mainframes, they were accessible, nimble, and inspiring to those who didn't want to put on white shirts and ties and join IBM's army of bureaucrats. (Gross 2002, 153)

The consistent understanding was that, as tools of American industrialized society, technologies limited human potential. As science and technology manifested a quantitative approach to the world they provided a basis for the uniformity, efficiency, isolation, and class stratification seen in facets of mainstream life like suburban developments (Monhollon 2010c) and the military. It was the disaffected baby boomers of the 1960s and 1970s who strove to resuscitate a qualitative approach to democratic society, and they did so by embracing a bridging form of social capital (while rejecting materialism) and celebrating art (while denouncing science and technology as corporate tools). In this sense, Colorado's Drop City, a "full-blown hippie commune" founded in 1965, "brought together most of the themes of its predecessor communities—anarchy, pacifism, sexual freedom, drugs, open membership, art—and wrapped them in an exuberance and an architecture that trumpeted the coming of a new communal era" (Miller 1992, 87). It was the humanistic answer to the technetronic Levittown.

THE ASCENDANT BABY BOOMERS: BUYING INTO COMMUNITY

Any social system experiences tensions between individual and collective emphases. The coming-of-age baby boomers of the late 1950s through 1970s modeled a form of social capital that celebrated interdependence and collective empowerment as a way of differentiating themselves from and challenging the dominant "greatest" and "silent" generational cohorts and their technetronic, industrial ideology. As the baby boomers began to take society's leadership mantle in the early 1980s, though, they found themselves in a position to benefit from the ideological formations they formerly railed against. Thus, as they bought into the emerging technologies of the era, their concerns shifted from interdependence and collectivity to independence and individuality—ideological features promoted by the new communication media. The essence of this shift was a supplanting of social capital with physical capital as a means for defining one's membership in a community. Instead of *bridging* through *sharing in* community, the new paradigm—advanced through newly embraced technological developments and the rise of advanced capitalism—celebrated the importance of *bonding* through *buying into* community.

Physical Capital for Bonding

Social capital was an appropriate currency for the young, disaffected baby boomers who saw the United States' dominant technetronic culture—with its dehumanizing corporate and military industrialization—as rooted in the evils of money. This is not to say that the generation was not born of affluence—"The baby-boom kids had kicked off in America a buccaneering orgy of buying and selling that carried all things before it" (Jones 2002, 33)—but, as they entered adolescence, baby boomers endeavored to distinguish themselves generationally from their parents. This entailed, in part, a minimization (at least discursively) of physical capital and a prioritization of social capital.

But in the early 1980s the ascendant baby boomers began to take the mantle from the greatest and silent generations, and something changed. Whereas once they saw fit to challenge societally dominant ideologies—those ethical and discursive formations that had benefited the senior generational cohorts—now they themselves were poised to be the recipients of ideological benefits. There was retrospective regret from many who had participated in "the inchoate attack against authority [that had] weakened our culture's immune system, making it vulnerable to opportunistic diseases," including metaphoric ones (e.g., crime and drugs) and actual ones (e.g., AIDS) (Collier and Horowitz 1989, 16). Such regret was stimulated by real social problems and a legitimate sense that, in the preceding decades, "It was a time when innocence quickly became cynical, when American mischief fermented into American mayhem" (Collier and Horowitz 1989, 15). What is important to note is that many baby boomers realized that the stable, industrialized social order they previously opposed (and its hierarchical authority, both formal/ legal and cultural) was, at this point in their lives, somehow beneficial. One former commune dweller, interviewed in the 1980s by Casale and Lerman (2002), explained his transformation: "Well, after a while, after I went back and took a shower and put on some clothes, I felt really good. It does get a little bit old and you get tired of freedom. It's too much work. It's human nature: when you get tired you want to rest" (136).

Social capital remained important for this cohort, but now, in many ways, it was geared more toward bonding than bridging. According to Putnam (2000), bonding social forms of capital are "inward looking and tend to reinforce exclusive identities and homogenous groups. Examples of bonding social capital include ethnic fraternal organizations, church-based women's reading groups, and fashionable country clubs" (22). Certainly, a great degree of bonding was occurring with the younger baby boomers as they distinguished themselves from mainstream American culture and, in so doing, formed and maintained solidarity (as was crucial for the anarchic/ retreat commune members, for instance, who wished to distance themselves from mainstream American society, or the WUO members who wished to "fight together"). But the general openness and egalitarianism—rather than exclusivity—that characterized the communes and social movements of the 1960s and 1970s placed an emphasis on bridging, at least as a complement to whatever bonding was needed for social cohesion. As the baby boomers moved into the early 1980s, though, inclusiveness gave way to exclusiveness, and bonding became more prevalent than bridging.

Bonding is a mode of social capital but, for the baby boomers of the early 1980s, social capital was secondary to—that is, a product of—*physical* capital. In other words, membership in communities was increasingly seen as something to be *bought into*. Community, in this sense, does not require much active participation (per traditional expectations of citizenship) but rather the capacity (currency) for entrance; and, upon admission, one's membership reflects a particular social status corresponding to societal authority and privilege. The exclusive country club, for example, requires certain currency for entrance, and this requirement ensures the community's socioeconomic homogeneity as well as a clear division between "us" and "them."

Inherent in this newly emphasized conception of community membership is commodification, or "the way that market values can replace other social values, or the way a market can replace a communal system" (Rushkoff 2005). Whereas communicative artifacts such as attire and accoutrements have always articulated group/cultural membership—and there was nothing new about the socioeconomic connotations of clothing styles—increasingly during this period emphasis was placed on the economic values of things. "Money, money, money is the incantation of today," wrote Magnet (1987), continuing:

> Bewitched by an epidemic of money enchantment, Americans in the Eighties wriggle in a St. Vitus's dance of materialism unseen since the Gilded Age or the Roaring Twenties. . . . And the M&A [mergers and acquisitions] decade acclaims but one breed of hero: He's the honcho with the condo and the limo and the Miro and lots and lots of dough.

It is appropriate, then, to consider the Members Only jacket as a telling emblem of this period. The article of clothing hit the American market in 1980, advertised with the tagline, "When you put it on, something happens" (Members Only, 1982). The jacket itself was not exorbitantly expensive, so it was within reach of middle-class Americans; but the product's name and marketing revealed much about the emerging ideology of consumerism as bonding. In the prior decade, discourses surrounding the baby boomers highlighted the inclusiveness of bridging forms of social capital—consider how the Coca-Cola Company, targeting baby boomers in 1971, wanted to "teach the world to sing in perfect harmony [and] to buy the world a Coke and keep it company" (Coca-Cola Company, 1971). Now, though, the emphasis was increasingly on exclusiveness and bonding forms of social capital.

A Technetronic Basis for Community

Braden (1970) attributed the social unrest of the 1960s fundamentally to a clash between the disaffected baby boomers' humanistic worldview and their seniors' scientific/technetronic worldview. As the 1980s dawned, certain important technological and industrial developments coincided with the baby boomers' newfound appreciation of physical capital. As these developments supported and encouraged consumerism, the middle-aged baby boomers' heightening consumption of technology and media further solidified an ideology of commodification—spurring the generational cohort to supplant its humanistic approach for a technetronic one. Specifically, the technological/media trends of the period advanced two primary and related themes that bear consequences for how members of a democratic society may view their membership: liberal-individualism and advanced capitalism.

The ideology of liberal-individualism

An ideology of liberal-individualism favors personal (rather than collective) empowerment. Community membership from a liberal-individualistic

orientation is conceived in terms of benefits for the individuals, with particular celebration of merit as justification for socioeconomic and other kinds
of social distinctions. Accordingly, egalitarianism and inclusion are not as
valued as hierarchical order and exclusion. Community members are conceived as distinct actors rather than conjoined interactants. Isolation and
disengagement—as described notably in Putnam's *Bowling Alone* (2000)—are
consequences of liberal-individualism. In the early 1980s, technologies supported such an ideology in two primary ways.

First, new communication technologies emphasized individualized experience. Sony's Walkman portable audiocassette player with headphones, for
example, hit the American market in 1980 and enabled a listening experience that was portable and private—a white, suburban response, in ways, to
the mid-1970s' urban, community-oriented boombox (also called a "ghetto
blaster"). This instance of privatized media mirrored what was already on the
rise with television viewing. Not only were televisions increasingly common
in American households but, further, they were increasingly common in
multiple rooms of a given house. Whereas very early television viewing was
often a community experience (with neighbors converging, food offerings
in hand, to view a program on the neighborhood's only set), now audiences
were increasingly socially isolated. As well, the early 1980s' rise of cable television's HBO and other film-oriented subscriber channels (and, of course,
the 1981 invention of microwave popcorn) resituated audiences from the
communal theaters to their private homes for movie viewing. The falling
price point for home videocassette recorders in the late 1970s and early
1980s also contributed to the emptying of public theaters. And, as a final
example of individualizing media, the fax machine—as it became smaller
and less expensive for personal use in the early 1980s—increasingly enabled
people to send textual materials without intermediary postal workers. Kurt
Vonnegut, for one, pointed out how his fax machine took away his purpose
for visiting and developing interpersonal relationships with employees at his
local post office, thus fostering a regrettable kind of social isolation (*Augusta
Chronicle* 1997).

Second, emerging communication technologies of the early 1980s
emphasized personalization and, relatedly, the creation of niche publics.
At issue is personal empowerment through consumer choice. The upsurge
of cable (post-network) television in the early 1980s—and, by necessity, the
establishment of the remote control as a standard household tool—gave rise
to the practice of channel surfing. As American households moved from
approximately four channels to (depending on one's subscription) numerous specialized channels (CNN for news, ESPN for sports, HBO for movies,
etc.), viewers developed greater choice and opportunity for media tailoring.
With this increased diversity and personal empowerment came the beginnings of what Gitlin (1998) described as the fracturing of the American

public sphere into "public sphericules." The heightened tailoring of media content to niche audiences, Gitlin posited, has prohibited an ideal of a common discursive environment in which citizens may deliberate together about shared information; instead it has created multiple cultural enclaves in which audiences access different content and, in a sense, do not come into deliberative contact.

The ideology of advanced capitalism

In association with an ideology of liberal-individualism, the emerging media of the early 1980s fostered an ideology of advanced capitalism. The communication technologies that were being produced and consumed increasingly became the means of their own marketing, as their values—along the lines of what Marx (1990) described as "commodity fetishism" (165)—gained more connection to connotative understandings of consumers' identities and sociopolitical relationships than to material costs of production. In this sense, the consumption of technologies propagated further consumption in an upward spiral, fueling a social climate in which consumption was a desirable marker of status.

One example of the connection between technology and perceived status during the early 1980s was the rise of the car phone. Whereas the car phone dates to the mid-1940s, it was not until 1983, when America's first cellular network was implemented, that it became prevalent in noncommercial applications. Although Motorola's DynaTAC phone—launched in 1985 and affectionately called "the brick" (Vintage Mobile Phones 2013)—was, compared with household phones of the era, clunky, the portability enabled individualization (as discussed earlier) and convenience; the expense made it a signifier of socioeconomic status and membership within a supposed professional elite. What is most telling about the fetishism of the car phone during the mid-1980s was not the increasing prevalence of car phones themselves but of *fake* car phones and antennae. From a 1988 article in the *New York Times*:

> Heaven knows, it's hard to keep up. On your last trip to Paris, you dropped into Chichen Itza for a custom-made pigskin briefcase, only to arrive back at work and find some 26-year-old with a new $2,500 alligator model he snapped up in San Francisco while his Ferrari was being serviced. But help has arrived. . . . A tiny company . . . called Faux Systems has created the Cellular Phoney, an inexpensive replica car phone that looks just like the real thing. The company motto: "It's not what you own, it's what people think you own." (Bishop 1988)

This commodity fetishism pertains to one's ability to literally buy into what is called in marketing parlance an "aspirational reference group." The car phone, beyond the functional utilities of the product itself, became more valued for its connotative value pertaining to consumers' perceived identities and relationships around socioeconomic status. "We are a status-driven city—there's no doubt about it," said Michelle Stein, the president of a Dallas high-tech accessory store in an Associated Press interview (1988). The article continued:

> The Cellular Phoney is a realistic copy of the devices that have become standard fixtures in the BMWs and Mercedes of big-city dealmakers. At $15.95 for the handset and a fake, stick-on antenna, the fake phones live up to the advertising slogan of "status without the static," Stein said. She said she sold hundreds of the fake phones in the last year.

In addition to the commodity fetishism advanced by emerging technologies of the 1980s, there was a great rise in the quantity and sophistication of advertising. This is because as people consumed new technologies they were not simply buying mechanical things; they were creating new avenues for marketing in which they themselves were the willing targets. In terms of advanced capitalism, the consumed products were means for the consumption of further products. There was nothing necessarily new about this concept, as radio advertising, for example, had existed almost since the very first radio was purchased and turned on. But the proliferation of media in the early 1980s—spanning videocassettes, personal/home computers, video game systems, cable television, etc.—enabled heightened quantity, diversity, and sophistication of advertising because the recipients of marketing messages were increasingly *willing* recipients. Liberal-individualistic consumers now thought of themselves as active agents who were participating, by choice and by virtue of their sense of self, in the marketing process; the given medium was, as a consumed product, somehow connected to their identity, so extended consumption of advertisements as products as well as the things they promoted was wholly consistent with their sense of who they were as members of society. Thus, the ideology of advanced capitalism partnered with the ideology of liberal individualism to establish a cultural climate of conspicuous consumption.

MEMBERS ONLY: BABY BOOMERS, THE EARLY 1980s, AND THE FRAGMENTATION OF AMERICAN CIVIL SOCIETY

In *Bowling Alone*, Putnam (2000) considered data from the archives of the General Social Survey, the Roper Social and Political Trends survey, and the DDB Needham Life Style survey. He understood from these data that, across the prior two decades, Americans were becoming less participatory in communities and, by extension, in their broader democratic society. Although this chapter's discussion is very much simpler and narrower in scope than Putnam's, it shares concern for American society's fragmentation and civic/political lethargy. What has happened since the often-boisterous activities of the 1960s to transform civic/political insurgence into relative complacency? There is no specific answer to this question, but one thing to consider is the period of time when the social capital–oriented hippies became physical capital–oriented yuppies in the public imagination. How did the sociopolitically ascendant baby boomers of the early 1980s help to propagate newly embraced ideologies of liberal individualism and advanced capitalism, and how did these ideologies coincide with a more fragmented and apathetic democratic society?

Of course, this discussion of the baby boomers as a generational cohort does not presume that the age-related category is homogeneous or objectifiable in any simplistic way. Not by a long shot were most baby boomers commune-dwelling hippies during the 1960s and 1970s, for instance, and not by a long shot were most of them yuppies during the 1980s—as though "hippie" and "yuppie" are themselves cleanly definable social categories to begin with. But there is something important and telling about the historical period when a youthful celebration of social capital for inclusive bridging transformed into middle-aged appreciation of physical capital for exclusive bonding. This chapter does not pretend that the United States suddenly became, for instance, a capitalist society at the dawn of the 1980s. However, that marketers urged us to "buy the world a Coke and keep it company" in 1971 and to wear "Members Only" jackets in 1980 says something about a discursive trend away from inclusive bridging toward exclusive bonding. Surely there have been consequences for Americans' collective understandings of democratic community and citizenship.

The ideology of liberal-individualism that was advanced through the consumption of new communication technologies in the early 1980s stimulated flight from the public sphere to the private sphere or at least contributed to the fragmentation of the public sphere into what Gitlin (1998) called public sphericules. In one sense, there was a newly placed emphasis on individual empowerment rather than collective empowerment. In another sense, there were new restrictions on Americans' opportunities to talk deliberatively across sociocultural difference and hierarchical strata.

As the baby boomers became the United States' dominant sociopolitical generational cohort, the manners in which they embraced this ideology were consequential for the broader American society. It is important to recognize how the discursive shift from a celebration of bridging social capital to that of bonding social capital (established through the generation and application of physical capital) coincided with this ideological embrace. Likewise, the ideology of advanced capitalism fueled a sense that we *buy* our way into sociopolitical identities and affiliations rather than *participate* (or, further, *collaborate*) our way into them. There are indeed ramifications stemming from this historical point of cultural transformation—consequences for how we conceive community membership and citizenship in a democratic society.

REFERENCES

Associated Press. 1988. "The Cellular Phoney Is a Big Hit with Not-So-Rich Yuppies." *The Telegraph*. June 12. http://news.google.com/newspapers?nid=2209&dat =19880612&id=1w4mAAAAIBAJ&sjid=vPwFAAAAIBAJ&pg=5101, 3696529.

Augusta Chronicle. 1997. "Vonnegut Advocates Human Company." September 24. chronicle.augusta.com/stories/1997/09/24/met_215087.shtml.

Bishop, Katherine. 1988. "A Car Phone That Links People and Their Desires." *New York Times*. April 24. http://www.nytimes.com/1988/04/24/us/a-car-phone -that-links-people-and-their-desires.html.

Braden, William. 1970. *The Age of Aquarius: Technology and the Cultural Revolution*. Chicago: Quadrangle Books.

Carden, Maren Lockwood. 1976. "Communes and Protest Movements in the U.S., 1960–1974: An analysis of Intellectual Roots." *International Review of Modern Sociology* 6 (Spring): 16.

Casale, Anthony M., and Philip Lerman. 2002. "From Hippies to Yuppies." In *The Baby Boom*, edited by Stuart. A. Kallen, 127–141. San Diego: Greenhaven Press.

Coca Cola Company 1971. Untitled advertisement. Video file. http://www.you tube.com/watch?v=ib-Qiyklq-Q.

Collier, Peter, and David Horowitz. 1989. *Destructive Generation: Second Thoughts about the '60s*. New York: Summit Books.

Elkins, Jason. 2013. "5 Ways Thinking Like a Hippie Can Help You with Social Media Marketing." Weblog post. https://transparentsocialmedia.com/5-ways-thinking-like-a-hippie-can-help-you-with-social-media-marketing-jason-elkins./.

Evans, Sara. M. 2002. "The Growth of the Women's Liberation Movement." In *The Baby Boom*, edited by Stuart. A. Kallen, 98–109. San Diego: Greenhaven Press.

Eversole, Theodore W. 2010. "Hispanic Americans." In *Baby Boom: People and Perspectives*, edited by Rusty Monhollon, 73–90. Santa Barbara, CA: ABC-CLIO.

Fellowship for Intentional Community. 2009. Intentional communities. April 29. http://wiki.ic.org/wiki/Intentional_Communities.

Fitzgerald, George R. 1971. *Communes: Their Goals, Hopes, Problems*. New York: Paulist Press.

Gitlin, Todd. 1998. "Public Sphere or Public Sphericules?" In *Media, Ritual and Identity*, edited by Tamar Liebes and James Curran, 168–174. London: Routledge Press.

Gittell, Ross J., and Avis Vidal. 1998. *Community Organizing: Building Social Capital as a Development Strategy*. Thousand Oaks, CA: Sage.

Gross, Michael. 2002. "Computers: Another Kind of Revolution." In *The Baby Boom*, edited by Stuart A. Kallen, 152–158. San Diego: Greenhaven Press.

Jones, Landon Y. 2002. "A Booming Baby Explosion." In *The Baby Boom*, edited by Stuart A. Kallen, 31–40. San Diego: Greenhaven Press.

Kanter, Rosabeth. 1972. *Commitment and Community: Communes and Utopias in Sociological Perspective*. Cambridge, MA: Harvard University Press.

Light, Paul C. 2002. "The First TV Generation." In *The Baby Boom*, edited by Stuart A. Kallen, 41–49. San Diego: Greenhaven Press.

MacFarlane, Scott. 2010. "The Counterculture." In *Baby Boom: People and Perspectives*, edited by Rusty Monhollon, 117–131. Santa Barbara, CA: ABC-CLIO.

Magnet, Myron. 1987. "The Money Society." July 6. http://money.cnn.com/magazines/fortune/fortune_archive/1987/07/06/69235/index.htm.

Marx, Karl. 1990. *Capital*. London: Penguin Classics.

Members Only. 1982. Untitled advertisement. Video file. http://videosift.com/video/When-you-put-it-onsomething-happens-Members-Only-Ad.

Meunier, Rachel. 1994. "Communal Living in the late 60s and early 70s." December 17. http://www.thefarm.org/lifestyle/cmnl.html.

Miller, Timothy S. 1991. *The Hippies and American Values*. Knoxville: University of Tennessee Press.

Miller, Timothy S. 1992. "The Roots of the 1960s Communal Revival." *American Studies* 33 (2): 73–93.

Monhollon, Rusty. 2010a. "Introduction." In *Baby Boom: People and Perspectives*, edited by Rusty Monhollon, xiii–xxxi. Santa Barbara, CA: ABC-CLIO.

Monhollon, Rusty. 2010b. "African Americans." In *Baby Boom: People and Perspectives*, edited by Rusty. Monhollon, 55–71. Santa Barbara, CA: ABC-CLIO.

Monhollon, Rusty. 2010c. "Suburbanites and Suburbia." In *Baby Boom: People and Perspectives*, edited by Rusty Monhollon, 149–163. Santa Barbara, CA: ABC-CLIO.

Morris, Aldon D. 2002. "A Decade of Black Protest." In *The Baby Boom*, edited by Stuart. A. Kallen, 62–68. San Diego: Greenhaven Press.

Putnam, Robert. D. 2000. *Bowling Alone: The Collapse and Revival of American Community*. New York: Simon & Schuster.

Ritzer, George. 2012. *The McDonaldization of Society*. 20th anniversary ed. Los Angeles: Sage.

Rushkoff, Douglas. 2005. "Commodified vs. Commoditized." Weblog post. September 4. http://www.rushkoff.com/blog/2005/9/4/commodified-vs-commoditized.html.

Shabecoff, Philip. 2002. "Birth of the Environmental Movement." In *The Baby Boom*, edited by Stuart A. Kallen, 110–119. San Diego: Greenhaven Press.

Snow, C. P. 2013. "The Two Cultures." January 2. http://www.newstatesman.com/cultural-capital/2013/01/c-p-snow-two-cultures.

Vintage Mobile Phones. 2013. Untitled content. Weblog message. http://www.vintagemobilephones.com/.

Voss, Kimberly Wilmot. 2010. "Women and the Baby Boom." *Baby Boom: People and Perspectives*, edited by Rusty Monhollon, 19–36. Santa Barbara, CA: ABC-CLIO.

Chapter 5

Boomers in the Global Village

Michael Grabowski

As the *Apollo 8* spacecraft maneuvered to a lunar orbit on December 24, 1968, NASA astronaut William Anders snapped a photograph of the Earth rising into view. Born in 1933, Anders was not a boomer, but as one of the first three men to see the Earth from the moon, he produced a picture that became a symbol for the boomer generation. For the first time, a generation grew up with an image of the Earth as a unified whole, a fragile oasis spinning through the hostile darkness of space. This iconic image, known as "Earthrise," became a symbol of the burgeoning environmental movement. Activists reminded the public that we are all citizens of spaceship Earth, and our stewardship of our fragile planet will determine our own survival.

The paradox this image conjures reflects the generation of boomers themselves. As historian Robert Poole notes, "Apollo 8 set out to discover a new world, the moon, and ended up discovering its home."[1] Likewise, as boomers grew and left home to explore their world, they in turn made the entire world their home. As they came of age, the boomer generation transformed the world into a global village, not only collapsing distances between geographies and cultures but also setting up new conflicts in their reimagined home.

Of course, boomers were not the first generation to think and act in global terms. Empires have risen and fallen on the ideal of a unified world under one power. In fact, the parents of boomers themselves fought to repel the advances of a totalitarian empire seeking to remake the world in an Aryan image. The Nazi occupation of Europe was met first with distant concern in America. Isolationists considered the war a European problem and resisted involvement, fearing that intervention would contribute to American imperialism.[2] However, the Japanese attack on the American naval base at Pearl Harbor on the Hawaiian island of Oahu on December 7, 1941, compelled the nation to war. The next day, President Franklin D. Roosevelt addressed a Joint Session of Congress, where he warned: "There is no blinking at the fact that our people, our territory, and our interests are in grave danger."[3] Partisan bickering gave way to national unity, and Congress voted to declare war that same day. As American soldiers traveled to battlefields in Europe, Africa, Asia, and the waters of the Pacific and Atlantic, they became a global army engaged in a conflict that touched virtually every corner of civilization. Though hostilities in Europe ended via a conventional invasion of Berlin, war with Japan concluded with the detonation of two atomic bombs, a weapon that marked the introduction of an era in which humankind had achieved the means to render the entire planet uninhabitable.[4]

However, American soldiers had little desire to participate in the establishment of an empire of their own at the conclusion of the war. Instead, millions of men came home to begin the life they were deprived of during the Great Depression and overseas military service. As they started families, the "greatest generation" facilitated the first wave of the baby boom in 1946. Government funding of higher education opportunities for veterans, housing prospects that favored young families, and a policy that encouraged working women to leave the workforce so that men could fill those jobs to support their families all contributed to the sharp spike in births associated with the boom.[5] Thus, parents of boomers, along with a taxpayer-supported free public education through high school, provided their children with the stability and support necessary to experience a prolonged period of adolescence, allowing boomers to forge a youth culture and generational identity distinct from that of their parents.

The childhood life of boomers was vastly different from that of their parents. Instead of worrying about survival against the immediate threats of starvation, financial insolvency, and adequate housing, boomer children looked out into their world with wonder. Where Manifest Destiny drove previous generations to settle the frontier, boomers lived in a country whose borders were set by 1959, when Hawaiians voted to become the 50th state of the Union. The frontier became mythologized in westerns, which played out for boomer children imagined hostilities that good cowboys faced from lawless black-hatted gunfighters and heathen Indians who sought to disrupt or destroy American civilization.[6] This narrative possessed moral clarity: the rule of law and order would always triumph and provide a foundation and justification for an individualized, Eurocentric American culture.

These fabled conflicts were congruent with the dominant clash of the boomer generation, a fight between American interests and the Soviet Union.[7] Anticommunist propaganda battled over the hearts and minds of citizens, reinforcing the ideology of moral superiority that consumer capitalism within a largely Christian nation provided. President Dwight D. Eisenhower equated communism with slavery and predicted that the "Godless doctrine of Communism" would end up destroying itself if Americans stood resolute against it wherever it appeared.[8]

This Cold War shaped the conflicts of the boomer generation. Although total war between the United States and the Soviet Union never materialized, the fear of war was ever present. Though the United States has been the only country to use an atomic bomb in war, the security of being the only nation in possession of such a powerful weapon was short-lived. The Soviet Union developed and detonated an atomic weapon during the summer of 1949, leading President Harry S. Truman to authorize the development of the much more powerful hydrogen bomb, which was completed in 1952. However, the Soviets developed their own hydrogen bomb in 1955, pitting the two nations in a nuclear standoff by the time the first boomers were only nine years old.[9]

During their childhood years, boomers faced the global threat of nuclear war at home and school. Civil defense organizations identified fallout shelters and conducted drills to prepare for a possible nuclear surprise attack from the Soviets. Boy and Girl Scout troops volunteered as patients and first responders during national exercises to prepare America for global thermonuclear war.[10] Educational films like *Duck and Cover* attempted to replace panic with a reassuring plan in case of attack. The animated character of Bert the Turtle, who tucks his head and limbs inside his shell when he hears an air-raid siren, provided a comic character for children, as officials sought to make atomic drills as banal as fire drills.[11] Civil defense authorities had to publically reassure one European immigrant high school student who worried that plans for students to use school hallways as a shelter would lead to "mass murder" in case of attack.[12] For many civil defense and school authorities, the fear of attack was a worse enemy than the Soviets.[13]

Boomer children did not leave these fears at school. Newspapers encouraged families to prepare civil defense first-aid kits at home and set up basement shelters to prepare for nuclear attack.[14] Some homeowners built more elaborate bomb shelters,[15] and New York governor Thomas Dewey clamored for more federal funding of public shelters.[16] The *Daily Boston Globe* featured a story about a schoolboy who decided to dig his own shelter while on vacation. The teen told the newspaper: "You never know when an A-bomb will hit Boston, and we want to be ready."[17]

These amorphous fears solidified during the 13 days of the Cuban Missile Crisis in October 1962, when the oldest boomers were only 16. Soviets installed nuclear warheads in Cuba, giving them the capability to strike the U.S. mainland with no warning. The failed CIA-backed invasion of Cuba at the Bay of Pigs and other attempts to assassinate its leader, Fidel Castro, convinced Soviet premier Nikita Khrushchev to install medium-range ballistic missiles to protect Cuba from further U.S. aggression. President John F. Kennedy responded with a naval blockade of Cuba and addressed the nation over live television on October 22.[18] Newspapers and broadcast commentators argued over the proper solution to the crisis: should the United

States negotiate a truce with the Soviets or orchestrate a surprise attack, which surely would result in massive U.S. civilian casualties?

Further desperate negotiations resulted in an agreement, but not before the nation prepared for the possibility of global war. Residents flooded civil defense offices with phone calls seeking information about bomb shelters and medical supplies in case of nuclear attack,[19] and grocery stores reported runs on items like bottled water and canned goods.[20] These concerns were not unfounded. In his memoir of the crisis, President Kennedy's brother Robert, who was attorney general at the time, wrote, "The American Joint Chiefs of Staff . . . had been all-out for invasion. Had their advice prevailed, as [U.S. Defense Secretary] McNamara later said, nuclear war would have begun on the beaches of Cuba and might have ended in a global holocaust."[21]

While the world was transfixed by the threat of nuclear war, a more lasting revolution was taking place almost without notice. AT&T tested its new Telstar satellite to send and receive business transactions across the country and overseas. Launched on July 10, 1962, the satellite made instantaneous global communication possible by receiving and transmitting back to Earth data, text, images, and audio and video broadcasts. Less than 17 years before, Arthur C. Clarke envisioned the possibility of telecommunications satellites orbiting in geostationary orbit that could blanket the earth with electromagnetic radio signals.[22] Though Clarke imagined a massive manned space station that would require continuous maintenance, the invention of the transistor allowed AT&T to launch a satellite that measured less than three feet across. Several companies, including television networks and IBM, employed the new technology to connect the planet with electronic communication. Telstar carried Kennedy's address to the nation informing the world about the nuclear showdown, and while the Americans and Soviets negotiated a way out of the crisis, AT&T simulated financial transactions over the satellite and demonstrated its ability to connect computers over vast distances.[23]

Five years earlier, the Soviets had launched the world's first orbiting artificial satellite, Sputnik, creating a national panic that communism would dominate space and enslave the world from above.[24] The satellite orbited 560 miles above the Earth's surface and circled the planet in about 95 minutes, emboldening the Soviets to announce, as reported in the *New York Times*, that "'the new socialist society' had turned the boldest dreams of mankind into reality."[25] A central concern of the space race was the question of which superpower would dominate the skies enveloping the planet, but Telstar demonstrated a seemingly more pedestrian but certainly farther-reaching upheaval: the global reach of instant communication, one that eradicated the distance between the superpowers and the countries in between.

Advances in electronic media and satellite communication led literature professor and media theorist Marshall McLuhan to conclude that the world was remaking itself into a global village that had "recreated the simultaneous 'field' in all human affairs."[26] McLuhan compared electromagnetic signals to the beating of tribal drums, where a holistic, acoustic environment displaced the sequential ordering of print in a visual space. He astutely observed that the generation growing up with television thought and ordered their world differently from their predecessors, extending senses across the world while "retribalizing" into new groups disconnected from geography. Telstar not only provided a means for global connectivity but also served as a symbol for cultural connectedness.

The most overt example of that symbolism was the popular instrumental song "Telstar," written and produced by Joe Meek and performed by his band the Tornados. Inspired by the space race, Meek innovated with electronic sounds and distortion to create an otherworldly sound so different that "Telstar" became the first song by a British band to top both the British and American pop music charts, paving the way for other British bands to cross the Atlantic and become integral to American popular culture.[27] Often only consisting of four or five members, these bands were smaller and more manageable than the big bands popular with boomers' parents, and the proliferation of the portable record player and transistor radio provided a platform for boomers to share the music these groups created. Their songs were short, limited by the length of sound the 45 rpm record could hold, and supported the development of the pop song, with catchy melodies and musical hooks that demanded multiple plays on the radio and the jukebox. The dance halls may have been empty, but the record stores were full of teens listening to, trading, and talking about the music that unified their generation.[28]

The Tornados were the front edge of a wave that changed popular music in America. Coined "the British Invasion," bands like the Rolling Stones, the Animals, the Kinks, and the Yardbirds all dominated American radio during the mid-1960s. The band that paved the way and enjoyed the most success was the Beatles, who first came to Americans' attention as the nation reeled from the assassination of President Kennedy late in 1963.[29] Formed in Liverpool, the group developed their style and sound while playing gigs in Hamburg, West Germany, where it was cheaper to book British imitators to play rock and roll cover songs than fly in original American bands.[30] The Beatles combined the American R&B, folk, and country sounds with an American beatnik sensibility and created a popular moment that they exported back to America. Beatlemania invaded the United States in 1964 when the foursome of John, Paul, George, and Ringo landed at the recently renamed JFK Airport and played on CBS's *The Ed Sullivan Show* in February that year.[31] Transatlantic communication enabled transatlantic cultural influence, as American movements were consumed and remade in Europe and then brought back to America as something new, further transforming American culture. Regional sounds induced global change.

Soon, American producers sought to capitalize on the excitement surrounding the Beatles by creating a television show featuring a fictional band.
The Monkees combined three Americans with English actor and musician
Davy Jones, who himself appeared on the same episode of *The Ed Sullivan
Show* as the Beatles when he performed the role of the Artful Dodger from
the hit Broadway musical *Oliver!* The program itself, premiering in 1966,
combined a slapstick vaudeville style of comedy with performance footage,
but fans recognized the musical talent that members Peter, Mickey, Michael,
and Davy possessed, who began to negotiate more control over the band.
Soon, the Monkees were touring and performing their own music, even
after their program was canceled in 1968.[32]

Television's role in introducing boomers to the world beyond their shores
extended beyond the British invasion. The seemingly innocuous comedy
variety program became a dissemination point for a generational expression of global engagement. Programs like NBC's *Rowan & Martin's Laugh-In*
(1967–1973) peppered observations of generational change in the global
village among the usual vaudeville-styled comedy and musical numbers:
hunger strikes, the Vietnam draft, and the Cold War were regular subjects
for jokes.[33] However, a CBS variety program, *The Smothers Brothers Comedy
Hour* (1967–1969), challenged the conventions of the commercial television
status quo to provide boomers with a window on the global scene of music,
politics, and social unrest. Israeli-born folk singer Esther Ofarim introduced
viewers to what would later become known as world music, and one week
after Tom and Dick Smothers, along with George Segal, sang the Phil Ochs
song "Draft Dodger Rag," the brothers opened their show with footage of
student riots occurring throughout the world. Despite confrontations with
CBS censors, the program articulated the expanded worldview and political
consciousness of boomers during its brief two-and-a-half-year run.[34]

Boomers' protests over Vietnam and the draft conflicted with the larger
narrative of the fight against communism. The specter of nuclear Armageddon suppressed the impetus toward total war, but the war of words peri-
odically heated up in countries undergoing civil wars, coups d'état, and
invasions from neighboring powers. The United States and Soviet Union
placed their bets and offered financial and military support in order to
gain allies in the larger global conflict. Proxy wars in Korea and Vietnam
required American support but not total mobilization. Though less than 10
percent of boomers volunteered or were drafted for service in Vietnam, the
growing resistance to the undeclared war became a defining experience for
the boomer generation and propelled many youth to become aware of the
global context of war.[35]

The way boomers experienced these wars changed as they grew. Newspapers reported on the hidden war in Korea, and a few groundbreaking
news programs like Edward R. Murrow's *See It Now* (1951–1958) showed

filmed interviews with soldiers spending Christmas halfway around the world. By the mid-1960s, television, transmitting broadcasts in vivid color, had evolved to providing evening news footage and interviews from Vietnam, and more boomers watched the war than read about it.[36] As the war dragged on, television reported on American causalities nightly, and American support of the fight against communism morphed into despair over sending more Americans to be killed there. Boomers led this resistance, but the news media and the entire American public soon followed. CBS news anchor Walter Cronkite traveled to Vietnam in 1968 to report on the war, and when he returned, he concluded at the end of a special broadcast that the United States was "mired in stalemate."[37] By the time the last of the troops left Vietnam, about 3.4 million American service members had been deployed to Southeast Asia, and more than 58,000 had died in the undeclared war.[38]

Despite witnessing the growing quagmire in Vietnam play out on their television sets, boomers coming of age in the 1960s were exposed to more positive representations of the conflict with communism in the fiction programs they watched. Throughout the decade, boomers saw many popular depictions of heroes winning smaller battles in the Cold War while keeping hostilities to a minimum. American spy shows like *The Man from U.N.C.L.E.* (1964–1968), *I Spy* (1965–1968), and *Mission: Impossible* (1966–1973) presented the ingenuity of American agents battling Soviet-bloc nemeses. These characters used teamwork, cunning, and superior technology to outwit criminal masterminds attempting to undermine the American way of life. However, the 1950s overreach of the House Committee on Un-American Activities, the corresponding Senate committee led by Joseph McCarthy, and the Hollywood blacklist sowed disillusion about anticommunist rhetoric among boomers and contributed to the exhaustion of spy genre tropes, leading to parody shows like *Get Smart* (1965–1970) and the animated *The Rocky and Bullwinkle Show* (1959–1964).[39]

Another front in the Cold War sought to win the hearts and minds of the global community. Urging young boomers to look beyond "an economic advantage in the life struggle," President Kennedy established the Peace Corps, an alternative to military service that placed American youth in African and Asian countries, prime sites in the fight for postcolonial alliances.[40] During his campaign for the presidency, Kennedy asked college students at the University of Michigan to travel the world and contribute to a "greater purpose."[41] Set up by Kennedy's brother-in-law Sargent Shriver, the Peace Corps was designed to counter the stereotype of the "ugly American" prevalent in African countries and deflect global attention from the embarrassment of American segregation and race relations at home. Shriver promoted an antiauthoritarian environment that empowered volunteers and produced a democratic, if chaotic, ethos. The same participatory culture would take root in the civil rights movement at home, and many Peace Corps volunteers returned after their service to take part in that struggle.[42]

While some boomers served overseas, either for peace or war, more affluent boomers traveled the world for leisure. Pan American World Airways, commonly referred to as Pan Am, introduced regularly scheduled passenger jet airplane service with the Boeing 707 in 1958.[43] Soon, those who could afford the ticket price hopped on jets to cross oceans for weekend trips. The "jet set" would become known through publicity accounts of high-end parties held in Paris, London, Milan, and other international destinations. In 1964, Pan Am partnered with IBM to create PANAMAC, which allowed travel agents to book reservations within minutes.[44] The communication revolution of networked computers paired with transportation innovations provided boomers with the ability to reach just about any corner of the world within hours instead of weeks. Within a decade, jet travel became a regular experience for the boomer generation; by the 1970s, more than half of adult Americans had traveled by jet.[45]

Even as the deployment of communication satellites and PANAMAC provided opportunities to collapse symbolic and physical distance, a larger communications network was taking shape in the 1960s that would transform the global connectivity of boomers and every generation thereafter. The Advanced Research Projects Agency (ARPA) funded research to create a decentralized "internetwork" of computers. Initially intended to establish a common protocol for connecting research computer systems, ARPANET provided an infrastructure to allow communication between anyone connected to the network, regardless of location. Though the first two computers using this protocol were housed within UCLA and Stanford University, ARPANET moved over the next 40 years to provide connection points between businesses, organizations, governing bodies, and individuals.[46]

The Internet became more useful through the efforts of engineers who developed such applications as e-mail and Tim Berners-Lee's hyperlink protocol called the World Wide Web.[47] However, a precondition for sharing information over the Internet was the need to encode that data into packets of digital bits. Pictures, videos, music, spoken words, text—virtually any symbolic communication—could be shared globally, as long as that information was digitized. Like the Industrial Revolution, in which the production of interchangeable parts led to the assembly-line model of production, the digitization of information has enabled an Internet revolution that is still playing out.

If ARPANET provided a means to connect global communities, Ravi Shankar introduced boomers to musical influences beyond Britain and Western Europe. The Indian sitar player performed in Paris at the celebration of the 10th anniversary of the United Nations in 1958, and he later toured Europe and the United States. Shankar introduced Western audiences to raga, a traditional Indian music that is meant to color mood with its tones. Performers like the Byrds and George Harrison from the Beatles adopted elements from Shankar's music into their own work, and Harrison invited Shankar to tour with him. By 1969, Shankar had performed at the Monterey Pop and Woodstock festivals.[48] Despite his complaints that American youth had defiled his sacred music by associating it with drug use, boomers incorporated Eastern music, yoga, and other cultural products of the East into their own culture.

Boomers also became more acquainted with the East through President Richard M. Nixon's tour of China in 1972. Nixon and Secretary of State Henry Kissinger pursued a strategy of establishing relations with communist China to drive a wedge in the Soviet bloc. In his 1969 inaugural address, Nixon referred to the ideal of a world open to trade and ideas. Mao Zedong, chairman of the Communist Party and leader of the People's Republic of China, used that reference as an opening to create a strategic relationship. An alliance with the United States would buttress China's defense in its skirmishes with the Soviet Union over their shared border and decrease the isolation the country experienced during the Cultural Revolution.[49] Long steeped in the rhetoric that communist nations were the enemy of freedom, Americans watched television images of President Nixon and the First Lady sitting with Chinese leaders at a grand banquet while a band played the national anthems of both countries.[50] The China visit improved relations between the two countries and paved the way for an economic relationship that would reshape boomers' experience with global trade.

As they grew into adulthood, boomers witnessed a transformation of the U.S. economy from a manufacturing powerhouse to one powered by consumer purchasing, service sectors, and information industries. Emergent economies in postwar Asia began to supply the United States with consumer products, like Sony's (slightly larger than) pocket-sized, inexpensive transistor radio. Though the transistor was developed at Bell Labs, and the first transistor radio was produced by Texas Instruments, Sony engineer Kazuo Iwama created an inexpensive process for producing the tiny replacement for the bulky and fragile vacuum tubes, which had been the heart of broadcast technologies.[51]

Later, other Japanese companies, like Toyota and Honda, competed with American automobile manufacturers by producing relatively inexpensive, fuel-efficient vehicles. The second oil crisis combined with economic recessions in the 1980s to persuade Americans to buy Japanese cars. American manufacturers complained about unfair trade practices and having to go up against a cheaper Japanese labor force but failed to address the more efficient Japanese style of manufacturing. Just-in-time inventory, streamlined production, and shared responsibility between management and labor gave

Asian companies an advantage.[52] Meanwhile, American companies that had promised generous pension and health benefits to their workforce in lieu of increased wages began to feel the weight of these costs. Newfound Japanese wealth found its way to American shores, and Japanese investors purchased companies, real estate, and cultural institutions. By the end of the 1980s, Sony had bought Columbia Pictures, a major movie studio,[53] and Mitsubishi had closed a deal for Rockefeller Center.[54]

Asian investment in the United States generated anxiety and sometimes hostility in American popular culture. The film *Rising Sun* (1993), starring Sean Connery and Wesley Snipes and based on Michael Crichton's 1992 novel, presented a condescending portrayal of Japanese corporate culture.[55] Though Bruce Willis battled German criminals in *Die Hard* (1988), the Los Angeles–based action film was set in the fictional Nakatomi skyscraper, reflecting an apprehension over the Japanification of Hollywood. Concern over "Japan-bashing" spilled over to a more general fear of Asian economies taking American jobs, and "buy American" became a slogan for politicians and marketers.[56]

Despite these fears, the United States adapted by integrating a global production process. As China opened its economy to international trade, American companies moved more production facilities overseas, outsourcing jobs and services beyond America's shores. Annual imports from China increased from $3.9 billion in 1985 to $440 billion in 2013.[57] National borders increasingly became irrelevant as businesses determined where to manufacture products. Adopting the just-in-time inventory practices of Asian companies, American businesses relied on global suppliers and services, and contract labor replaced employees. The integration flowed in both directions, as Asian automakers built assembly plants in the United States to reduce shipping costs and diffuse antipathy.[58]

The decreasing costs of telecommunication services allowed more service jobs to enter the global marketplace. International call centers blossomed in countries with English-speaking populations, such as the special economic zones in India. Scholar Reena Patel has argued that these centers do more than offer higher-paying jobs to local populations: "transnational call center employment represents a shift from exporting the *production* of material goods or culture to a full-scale *reproduction* of identity and culture."[59] Taking on American accents and Americanized names, and often inventing a back story that includes American customs, Indian call-center workers sell back to Americans an image of themselves shaped through consumer ritual. Well into their adulthood, boomers participate on a regular basis in a transnational global conversation simply by dialing customer service or answering a telemarketer's call.

Connected by communication and transportation networks that provided a global perspective, baby boomers became aware of the environmental impact of the modern world. The consumption of fossil fuels and chemical pollution of the environment concerned the boomer generation and fostered the birth of environmental groups. Rachel Carson's *Silent Spring* (1962) warned about the ecological damage from the widespread use of pesticides, including DDT.[60] Her book generated a groundswell of opposition to environmental pollution, and she testified before Congress the next year. The Clean Water Act (1963) and the Clean Air Act (1972) followed, and in 1970 President Nixon established the Environmental Protection Agency.[61] Countercultural icon Stewart Brand published *The Whole Earth Catalog*, which in 1968 featured NASA's satellite image of the planet on its cover. Brand wrote, "We are as gods and might as well get used to it."[62] He offered the environmentally-friendly products and books advertised inside as a set of tools for boomers to take control of their relationship to the land and act as stewards, rather than exploiters, of it.

However, some have begun to question the boomer stance toward environmental causes. Naomi Klein argues against an "astronaut's eye worldview" of the planet because it disregards negative effects on the local level in favor of a distant and dispassionate approach. She cites the issue of fracking, which well-funded environmental groups have promoted as a method to provide a bridge fuel but grassroots activists have protested because of the risk of poisoning local water supplies.[63] Brand himself has reversed his position on nuclear power and now promotes it as a green energy source, in opposition to many environmental groups.[64] More recently, the issue of climate change has devolved into a political battle, with liberal and conservative boomers arguing not just over policy but also over whether global warming is occurring at all. From the environmentally conscious counterculture that had seemed to define the boomer generation, Nixon's "silent majority" of conservatives have reasserted themselves to produce a seeming political stalemate.

Boomers have begun to reflect on their experience in the global village as they enter their senior years. Reminiscing about the moon landing, the sexual revolution, and rock music, and remembering where they were when they heard about JFK's assassination, the generation that defined themselves by their difference from their parents is now changing definitions of aging itself.[65] That outward projection of definition extends temporally, as expressed humorously by P. J. O'Rourke:

> The American Baby Boom is the future. We'll all turn into us eventually, as soon as families get excessively happy and start feeling too much affection for their kids. Unless, of course, extravagant freedom, scant responsibility, plenty of money, and a modicum of peace lead to such a high rate of carbon emissions that we all fry or drown. But you can't have everything.[66]

Boomers even defined their children in relation to themselves, calling them "echo boomers." And as that generation escapes their parents' shadow and rebrands themselves as millennials, they enter an environment transformed into a global marketplace, global culture, and global village. They must grapple with the consequences laid out by Adlai Stevenson in his 1965 speech to the United Nations, in which he stated, "We travel together, passengers on a little space ship, dependent on its vulnerable reserves of air and soil . . . preserved from annihilation only by the care, the work, and I will say, the love we give our fragile craft."[67] Thanks to the baby-boomer generation, we will henceforth view our journey from this perspective, as members of a global community who are responsible to each other and to our home.

NOTES

1. Robert Poole, *Earthrise: How Man First Saw the Earth* (New Haven, CT: Yale University Press, 2008).

2. Justus D. Doenecke, *Storm on the Horizon: The Challenge to American Intervention, 1939–1941* (Lanham, MD; Rowman & Littlefield, 2003); Frank A. Ninkovich, *The United States and Imperialism* (Malden, MA: Blackwell Publishers, 2001).

3. Franklin Roosevelt, "Pearl Harbor: FDR's Day of Infamy Speech," December 8, 1941, http://library.umkc.edu/spec-col/ww2/pearlharbor/fdr-speech.htm.

4. Gar Alperovitz, *Decision to Use Atomic Bomb*, RHVP-Remainder Series (New York: Random House Value Publishing, 1999).

5. Robert Beuka, *SuburbiaNation: Reading Suburban Landscape in Twentieth-Century American Fiction and Film* (New York: Palgrave Macmillan, 2004).

6. Richard Aquila, *Wanted Dead or Alive: The American West in Popular Culture* (Urbana: University of Illinois Press, 1996).

7. Bob Herzberg, *Savages and Saints: The Changing Image of American Indians in Westerns* (Jefferson, NC: McFarland & Co., 2008).

8. Robert R. Bowie and Richard H. Immerman, *Waging Peace: How Eisenhower Shaped an Enduring Cold War Strategy* (Oxford: Oxford University Press, 2000).

9. Joseph Cirincione, *Bomb Scare: The History, Theory and Future of Nuclear Weapons* (New York: Columbia University Press, 2007).

10. Guy Oakes, *The Imaginary War: Civil Defense and American Cold War Culture* (New York: Oxford University Press, 1994).

11. Joanne Brown, "'A Is for Atom, B Is for Bomb': Civil Defense in American Public Education, 1948–1963." *Journal of American History* 75, no. 1 (1988): 68. doi:10.2307/1889655.

12. "Boy Bomb Survivor Fears Our Shelters," *New York Times*, May 6, 1952, 17.

13. Brown, *Journal of American History*, 77–78.

14. Glendy Culligan, "Your Civil Defense Job Begins at Home," *Washington Post*, January 13, 1952, S1.

15. "Bomb Shelter Built Under Home," *New York Times*, March 23, 1951, 3; "Cleveland Man Builds Home With Bomb Shelter;" *Washington Post*, April 15, 1952, B1; Thomas Carvlin, "He's Ready for A-to-Z Bomb with His Homemade Shelter," *Chicago Daily Tribune*, August 25, 1955, S2-3.

16. "Bomb Shelter Lag Decried by Dewey," *New York Times*, April 2, 1952, 17.

17. "Roxbury Boy Uses Vacation to Build A-Bomb Shelter," *Daily Boston Globe*, April 18, 1951, 9.

18. Robert F. Kennedy, and Arthur M Schlesinger, *Thirteen Days: A Memoir of the Cuban Missile Crisis* (New York: W.W. Norton, 1999); Sheldon M. Stern, *The Week the World Stood Still: Inside the Secret Cuban Missile Crisis* (Stanford, CA: Stanford University Press, 2005); Michael Dobbs, *One Minute to Midnight: Kennedy, Khrushchev, and Castro on the Brink of Nuclear War* (New York: Vintage Books, 2009).

19. "Inquiries Flood C.D. Offices," *Los Angeles Times*, October 25, 1962, I1; Howard James, "Calls Deluge Civil Defense Offices Here," *Chicago Daily Tribune*, October 24, 1962, 10.

20. "War Fears Bring Run on Market Supplies," *Los Angeles Times*, October 28, 1962, OC1.

21. Kennedy and Schlesinger, *Thirteen Days*, 9.

22. Arthur C. Clarke, "Extra-Terrestrial Relays," *Wireless World*, October 1945, 305–308.

23. David R. Francis, "Telstar Passes Business Test," *Christian Science Monitor*, October 26, 1962, 10; Louis Solomon, *Telstar: Communication Break-through by Satellite* (New York: McGraw-Hill, 1962).

24. Everett C. Dolman, *Astropolitik: Classical Geopolitics in the Space Age* (Portland, OR: Frank Cass, 2002).

25. William J. Jorden, "Soviet Fires Earth Satellite Into Space; It is Circling the Globe at 18,000 M.P.H.: Sphere Tracked in 4 Crossings Over U.S.," *New York Times*, October 5, 1957, 1.

26. Marshall McLuhan, *The Gutenberg Galaxy : The Making of the Typographic Man* (Toronto: University of Toronto Press, 2011), 31.

27. James E. Perone, *Mods, Rockers, and the Music of the British Invasion* (Westport, CT: Praeger Publishers, 2009), 72.

28. Paul Friedlander and Peter Miller, *Rock & Roll: A Social History* (Boulder, CO: Westview Press, 2006).

29. Steven Stark, *Meet the Beatles : A Cultural History of the Band That Shook Youth, Gender, and the World* (New York: Harper, 2006), 33.

30. Stark, *Meet the Beatles*, 75–77.

31. Bill Harry, *The British Invasion How the Beatles and Other UK Bands Conquered America* (New Malden, Surrey: Chrome Dreams, 2004).

32. Andrew Sandoval, *The Monkees: The Day-by-Day Story of the '60s TV Pop Sensation* (San Diego: Thunder Bay Press, 2005).

33. Hal Erickson, *"From Beautiful Downtown Burbank": A Critical History of Rowan and Martin's Laugh-In, 1968–1973* (Jefferson, NC: McFarland, 2000).

34. David Bianculli, *Dangerously Funny: The Uncensored Story of "The Smothers Brothers Comedy Hour"* (New York: Simon & Schuster, 2010).

35. Christian G. Appy, *Working-Class War: American Combat Soldiers and Vietnam* (Chapel Hill: University of North Carolina Press, 1993), 365.

36. Eugene Secunda and Terence P Moran, *Selling War to America: From the Spanish American War to the Global War on Terror* (Westport, CT: Praeger Security International, 2007), 101.

37. Daniel C. Hallin, *The Uncensored War: The Media and Vietnam* (Berkeley: University of California Press, 1989).

38. Department of Veterans Affairs, "America's Wars," Office of Public Affairs, November 2011. http://www1.va.gov/opa/publications/factsheets/fs_americas _wars.pdf.

39. Cynthia Hendershot, *Anti-Communism and Popular Culture in Mid-Century America* (Jefferson, NC: McFarland, 2003); Michael Kackman, *Citizen Spy: Television, Espionage, and Cold War Culture* (Minneapolis: University of Minnesota Press, 2005).

40. John F. Kennedy, "Remarks of Senator John F. Kennedy," October 14, 1960, http://www.peacecorps.gov/about/history/speech/.

41. Ibid.

42. Elizabeth Cobbs Hoffman, *All You Need Is Love: The Peace Corps and the Spirit of the 1960s* (Cambridge, MA: Harvard University Press, 2000).

43. Robert Daley, *An American Saga: Juan Trippe and His Pan Am Empire* (New York: Random House, 1980), 529.

44. Sam Howe Verhovek, *Jet Age: The Comet, the 707, and the Race to Shrink the World* (New York: Avery, 2010).

45. Ibid.

46. Katie Hafner and Matthew Lyon, *Where Wizards Stay up Late: The Origins of the Internet* (New York: Touchstone, 2001).

47. Janet Abbate, *Inventing the Internet* (Cambridge, MA: MIT Press, 2000).

48. Ravi Shankar, *Raga Mala: The Autobiography of Ravi Shankar* (New York: Welcome Rain Publishers, 1999), 336.

49. Henry Kissinger, *On China* (New York: Penguin Books, 2012).

50. Margaret MacMillan, *Nixon and Mao: The Week That Changed the World* (New York: Random House, 2008), 147.

51. John Nathan, *Sony: The Private Life* (Boston: Houghton Mifflin, 1999).

52. Kōichi Shimokawa, *Japan and the Global Automotive Industry* (New York: Cambridge University Press, 2010), 327.

53. Paul Richter, "Sony to Pay $3.4 Billion for Columbia Pictures: Japanese Firm Willing to Offer High Price to Get Film, TV Software for Video Equipment It Makes," *Los Angeles Times*, September 28, 1989, http://articles.latimes .com/1989-09-28/news/mn-361_1_columbia-pictures.

54. Robert J. Cole, "Japanese Buy New York Cachet with Deal for Rockefeller Center," *New York Times*, October 31, 1989, Business section, http://www.nytimes .com/1989/10/31/business/japanese-buy-new-york-cachet-with-deal-for-rockefeller -center.html.

55. David Ferrell and K. Connie Kang, "Charges of Racism Mar 'Rising Sun' Opening: Entertainment: Protesters Fear the Film Will Contribute to Hate Crimes against Asian-Americans. However, Viewers Differ on Whether It Is Offensive,"

Los Angeles Times, July 31, 1993, http://articles.latimes.com/1993-07-31/local/me-18850_1_asians-film-american.

56. Narrelle Morris, "Destructive Discourse: 'Japan-Bashing' in the United States, Australia and Japan in the 1980s and 1990s" (PhD thesis, Murdoch University, 2006). http://books.google.com/books?id=YjG_SgAACAAJ.

57. U.S. Census Bureau, "Foreign Trade: Data," 2014, http://www.census.gov/foreign-trade/balance/c5700.html.

58. Kōichi Shimokawa, *Japan and the Global Automotive Industry* (New York: Cambridge University Press, 2010), 327.

59. Reena Patel, *Working the Night Shift: Women in India's Call Center Industry* (Stanford, CA: Stanford University Press, 2010), 27–28, emphasis in original.

60. Rachel Carson, *Silent Spring*, 40th anniversary ed. (Boston: Houghton Mifflin, 2002).

61. Eliza Griswold, "How 'Silent Spring' Ignited the Environmental Movement," *New York Times Magazine*, September 21, 2012, http://www.nytimes.com/2012/09/23/magazine/how-silent-spring-ignited-the-environmental-movement.html.

62. "Whole Earth Catalog Fall 1968," http://www.wholeearth.com/issue/1010/.

63. Jason Mark. "Naomi Klein: Green Groups May Be More Damaging than Climate Change Deniers," *Salon.com*, September 5, 2013, http://www.salon.com/2013/09/05/naomi_klein_big_green_groups_are_crippling_the_environmental_movement_partner/.

64. Todd Woody, "Stewart Brand's Strange Trip: Whole Earth to Nuclear Power," *Environment 360*, December 22, 2009. http://e360.yale.edu/feature/stewart_brands_strange_trip_whole_earth_to_nuclear_power/2227/.

65. Emanuella Grinberg, "Boomers Will Redefine Notions of Age," *CNN*, May 9, 2011, http://www.cnn.com/2011/LIVING/05/09/baby.boomers.retirement.legacy/.

66. P. J. O'Rourke, *The Baby Boom: How It Got That Way and It Wasn't My Fault and I'll Never Do It Again* (New York: Atlantic Monthly Press, 2014), 249.

67. Adlai Stevenson, Speech to the UN Economic and Social Council, Geneva, Switzerland, July 9, 1965. http://www.adlaitoday.org/articles/connect2_geneva_07-09-65.pdf.

Part 2

Television and Film

6

Let the Games Begin: Baby Boomers, Capitalist Ideology, and the Containment of Gender in Sports Television

Cheryl A. Casey

INTRODUCTION

This chapter applies a critical cultural studies framework to an examination of the emergence of the sports/media complex and its subsequent implications. As the baby boomer generation came of age in the 1960s and 1970s, so did the relationship between sports and mass media. The resulting sports television revolution brought athletics to a dominant position in popular culture, and the boomers were right in the middle of this cultural shift as both producers and consumers. The following analysis details the links between the conditions of production of sports media texts and the meanings they reinforce, identifying sports television as a powerful tool to the baby boomers in safeguarding capitalist ideology and containing notions of gender along traditional patriarchal lines.

Contemporary culture is saturated with sports-related imagery and information. From live sporting events to classic reruns, sports programming is nearly ubiquitous. In June 1985, *ABC Evening News* quoted a kidnapper involved in the Shiite kidnapping crises as remarking: "Americans don't care about politics, they are only interested in sports" (quoted in McChesney 1989, 67). All kinds of contexts in daily life provide an outlet for sports-related discourse, and each context spirals into the next; some people are paid to play sports, some are paid to write and talk about sports, while still others—indeed, the vast majority—spend a good deal of time talking about the players and what has been written or said about them. According to Real's (2005) survey of television and sports, "Today's many dedicated satellite and cable sports channels combine with regular sports telecasting on broadcast networks and stations to make sporting events, stars, and controversies a constant feature of daily life and a frequent topic across all communications media" (338).

As the baby boom generation came of age in the 1960s and 1970s, so did the relationship between sports and mass media, resulting in the hyper-commodification of professional sports (Giulianotti 2005) and a sports television revolution (McChesney 1989), deemed by some as "the greatest revolution in sports history, as football and other sports increased their following by millions" (Falk 2005, 64). Since the first telecasts of baseball and tennis, in May and June 1937, respectively, and of professional football in October 1939, television has been central to the emergence of the sports/media complex (Jhally 1989; Real 2005) that has come to occupy such a significant portion of the pop culture terrain. And the baby boomers seemed to be right in the middle of it all.

The Boomers' Cultural Influence

For the baby boom generation (those born 1946-1964), television represents the core of their mediated experience (Guttman 1986). The television industry found early on how to speak to this generation, about 78 million strong, and remained attentive to its interests in the ensuing decades (Puente 2011). The goal of this chapter is to trace the emergence of the sports/media complex by examining key themes in the literature about sports television and the sports-media relationship more generally. This literature details the links between the conditions of production of sports media texts and the meanings they reinforce. Specifically, the following discussion uses a cultural studies framework outlined by Sut Jhally (1989) to evaluate sports television as a powerful tool to the baby boomers in safeguarding capitalist ideology and containing notions of gender along traditional patriarchal lines.

Discussions of baby boomers' influence on culture have tended to paint a stark contrast between the boomers and their parents, reinforcing a dichotomy whereby the boomer generation broke with the stuffy conformity of their parents and marched to a completely new tune altogether. Rhetoric surrounding the boomer youth culture has popularly characterized the boomers as hostile to established tastes, hungry for authenticity, suspicious of tradition, thirsty for immediate gratification, and averse to the conformity of their parents' mass society ideals. Thomas Frank (1997), however, has rejected this dichotomization in favor of understanding how the baby boomers entered a major cultural shift—in business, in politics, and in popular culture—that was already gaining steam. Out of this cultural shift, in which the boomers were producers and consumers of popular culture by the late 1970s (Gitlin 2000), roared the sports television revolution.

May (1988) also outlined the continuities amid the tensions between baby boomers and their parents. She argued that for parents of the baby boom, "containment" served as the buzzword of the day, fostering a therapeutic approach to the Cold War that sought to keep the tone of postwar life apolitical. The domestic version of containment took trends of consumerism, women's liberation, and technological advances into the fold of the family ideology; contained within the home, these worrisome yet simultaneously liberating trends could be tamed. At the same time they were tamed, however, these trends could also be harnessed as a means to achieving personal well-being and happiness, most especially through the expertise of scientific and psychological experts. Containment equaled security in postwar life. As the boomers grew up, they embraced many of their parents' values and embarked on similar quests for meanings; the difference, May argued, was that when the boomers came of age, they abandoned the rhetoric of domestic containment and "substituted risk for security as they carried sex, consumerism, and political activity outside the established institutions" (15), that is, outside the home.

Nevertheless, institutions and gender roles remained resistant to change, and when the powerful political force of the New Right emerged in the late 1970s and early 1980s, Cold War militancy and containment rhetoric returned (May 1988). This analysis suggests that the sports television revolution emerging in the same period provides clues to how the baby boomers practiced containment *outside* the home, through other kinds of institutions, as they navigated the countercultural currents that had marked their generation. In *The Conquest of Cool* (1997), Frank suggested that, like their parents, the boomers were cautious to keep order amid the chaos, yet did so in revolutionary ways: "The sixties . . . are a commercial template for our times, a historical prototype for the construction of cultural machines that transform alienation and despair into consent" (235).

Theoretical Framework

Jhally (1989) argued that "sports/media complex" is the most fitting terminology relevant to a discussion of sports in a capitalist society because the cultural experience of sport is hugely mediated, and the organizational structures of sports are dependent on media dollars. David Rowe (1999) tweaked Jhally's terminology, describing the "media sports *cultural* complex" [italics added] as better able to emphasize "both the primacy of symbols in contemporary sport and the two-way relationship between the sports media and the great cultural formation of which it is a part" (4). In the sports/media complex (a term that from here forward takes into account Rowe's point about symbols while maintaining Jhally's core arguments), television plays a central role; the "seemingly innocent" (Rowe 1999, 8) televised sporting event manifests the economic, social, cultural, and ideological power that is central to the process of media sports production and consumption. Michael Real (2005) has suggested that Jhally's (1989) cultural studies approach to the sports/media complex is effective because it combines attention to representational power, interpretive cultural analysis, social theory, political economy, and history. Modern sport is more than just an industry, as pointed out rather obviously by Horne (2006): if sport could be reduced to its political economy, consumers would not keep consuming at such high levels regardless of whether price and/or quality fluctuate.

The cultural studies approach, as explicated by Jhally (1989), rejects the notion that spectator sport is merely the latest "opiate of the masses," channeling potentially political activity into a safer realm. It likewise discards arguments for sport as compensation for the unfulfilling experiences of capitalist society. Rather, cultural studies maps out the complex relationship among production of media texts, the texts themselves, how texts are read by ordinary people, and the lived cultures in which people use texts and contribute to further cultural production. Jhally argued that sport lies at the tension of social relations and emotion, or consciousness and subjectivity. As such, sport operates as one of the resources for establishing hegemony, which, in Gramsci's terms, refers to a form of consciousness, or lived system of meanings, that come to predominate over other possible systems of meaning (Jhally 1989). The dominant classes' hegemonic structures for seeing the world gain their position not only from political and economic power but also from their presentation as "common sense." When operating at the level of common sense, a system of meaning is more easily naturalized in the subordinate groups' sense of reality. Sage (1998) placed mass media as central to this process of naturalization: "Basic to hegemonic theory is the premise that access to the means of mass public communication is access to the minds of the public—to public attitudes, values, and beliefs" (163). The mass media help to build consensus about systems of meaning surrounding such structures as capitalism and gender relations, but the project of consensus is always an ongoing struggle.

In his attempt to "sketch an approach to the hegemonic thrust of some TV forms" (577), Todd Gitlin (2000) argued that the routine formal devices of television work in combination to contain, divert, and express social conflict and possibilities. Similarly, sports provide "occasions for discourse on some of the basic themes of social life" (Horne 2006, 4). The mediatization of sports has reshaped the discourse surrounding the social construction of sport, noted Varda Burstyn in her 1999 book, *The Rites of Men: Manhood, Politics, and the Culture of Sport.* This discourse has shifted from one once characterized as local, active, and participatory to one marked by commercialization, commodification, and controlled behavior (quoted in Horne 2006). Following these critical lines of argument allows for a more nuanced understanding of the always-contested terrain of sports media as a patriarchal capitalist structure.

This chapter takes up Jhally's (1989) merged application of Stuart Hall's (1980) encoding/decoding model in tandem with Richard Johnson's (1986) similar "circuit of culture" model. The latter model, insisted Jhally, augments Hall's examination of preferred, negotiated, and oppositional reading positions with a closer understanding of the lived cultures within which these reading positions are shaped and out of which further cultural production occurs. The "circuit of culture" model specifically describes production processes (or encoding), textual codes, audience readings (or decoding), and the broader cultural frame. Sport media research in each of these areas was sparse through the 1980s (Jhally 1989). Researchers and cultural critics did not turn any significant attention to the sports-media relationship until the 1970s (Real 2005), well after televised spectator sports had become a staple in American households. As a result, any application of this model to specifically parse out the baby boom generation's hand in the sports/media complex must necessarily rely on some extrapolation from the present-day context in combination with sometimes disparate research on the evolution of the sport industry and the place of television in a particular period of American life.

A BRIEF HISTORY: MODERN SPORT AND MASS MEDIA

The first challenge to understanding the sports television revolution of the late 1960s and early 1970s (McChesney 1989) and its long-term implications is to recognize the historical context out of which that revolution grew. Sport itself has a long and diverse history but what contemporary audiences recognize as sport is of comparatively recent origin (Rowe 1999). The "spectacular rise in the popularity of sport" (McChesney 1989, 50) and the critical developments in the history of the sport-media relationship are complex issues inextricably tied to the forces of industrialization, capitalism, the rise of mass consumption and the commodification of leisure, and developments in technologies of mass communication. The backdrop to modern sport's development includes department stores, retail chains, and wider circulation of magazines and newspapers (Horne 2006). This symbiotic relationship of sport and mass media in the United States (Jhally 1989; McChesney 1989; Sage 1998; Falk 2005; Real 2005; Horne 2006) therefore dates to the 1830s at least and has been shaped by the forces of capitalism since. "The linkage between sport and media did not await the arrival of television" (Rowe 1999, 30).

The origins of modern sport can be traced to Victorian England (Rowe 1999; Real 2005; Horne 2006), where both elite and religious groups were wracked by changes in social organization that "made control and surveillance of 'popular amusements' more difficult" (Rowe 1999, 15). This moral panic brought pressure for these groups to find ways of maintaining control over, or containing, working-class activities. The solution was found in organized sport and compulsory physical education (Rowe 1999), which were distinguished from earlier notions of "sport" such as field sports (hunting or fishing, for example) or bull fighting (Horne 2006).

Alongside this moral element, however, were the promises of capital and profit. Nineteenth-century entrepreneurs were giddy over the opportunities presented by maturing industrialist societies; the entertainment industry was booming. The greater division of labor and the rationalization of work and leisure nurtured conditions ripe for new kinds of leisure pursuits, including sports, to emerge as profitable business prospects (Rowe 1999). Promises of profit became the line drawn in the sand between amateur and professional sports, and the development of professional sports was integral to the development of a sports market.

The sporting press of the mid-19th century actively worked to "legitimate sport as a cultural institution" (McChesney 1989, 52). To accomplish this task, sports journalism emerged as a distinct genre between 1880 and 1900, and Pulitzer's *New York World* established its first sports department in 1883. Such efforts began to redraw the boundaries of meaning around sport (Horne 2006). Additionally, the telegraph was bringing sports information to journalists' desks regardless of space and time, which, combined with other developments in transportation, communication, and social mobility, resulted in the "nationalization" of sport (McChesney 1989, 54) by 1910.

By the 1920s, professional sports had staunchly embraced the mass production principle of making as much of the same thing as cheaply as possible, rendering sport spectatorship an especially attractive leisure pursuit among working-class men (Rowe 1999); professional sports had become the cornerstone of American culture and sports writing entered its golden age (McChesney 1989, 55). In effect, "sport sold newspapers and newspapers sold sport" (Horne 2006, 41). American households also welcomed radio in the 1920s, and by the end of the 1930s stations had begun contracting broadcast rights with baseball teams. Radio brought the games to a hitherto untapped audience, opening up "new vistas for millions who had never had access to a major sporting event in the past" (McChesney 1989, 59).

But an even bigger revolution was to come.

TELEVISION CHANGES THE PLAYING FIELD

The sports television revolution of the late 1960s and early 1970s rested on the foundation established by more than 100 years of sport-media symbiosis. Even in the early years of television (1940s to mid-1960s), all three major communication media—print (encompassing magazines and newspapers), radio, and television—were still sorting through their roles in this sport-media relationship. For sport and television, each relied on the other to help establish their respective positions in the world of mass entertainment (Falk 2005; Whannel 2009). The future of television depended on the sale of sets first and foremost (Baran 1997). Of the four major networks in the late 1940s, three (NBC, CBS, and DuMont) made and sold receiver sets. Sports were attractive to broadcasters for a number of reasons; they not only could be relatively cheap to produce because there are no origination costs but sport could also keep the viewer in front of the television for long periods of time (Skornia 1965). Baran (1997) argued that television set sales were at least in part a function of televised sports, noting that the number of sets in use jumped from 190,000 in 1948 to 10.5 million in 1950.

Boxing and wrestling, sports confined to enclosed spaces, were the most easily initiated to the world of televised sport (Rader 1984). Baseball, "America's pastime," was too fast and required too big a space for the small screen and limited technology (Guttmann 1986). However, in the early 1960s, television became a true mass medium, infiltrating most American homes with the significant help of sports programming (McChesney 1989; Whannel 2009). Soon, the inevitable improvements in the technology—including color and instant replay—allowed television to more easily capture the experience of outdoor team sports as well (Rader 1984). Improvements in the technology expanded the list of sports television would be suited to broadcast. *Channels* writer Julie Talen noted that "all sports are not created equal. The most popular sports on TV are those best served by the medium's limitations" (quoted in Baran 1997).

Professional football was the first to jump on the bandwagon of these developments in the early 1960s, and within a decade it had become the leading spectator sport. Before television, interest in football had been primarily situated in the college realm—a remote phenomenon for the many who had never attended college. Television brought football to the masses, educated and uneducated alike (Falk 2005). Humphreys and Ruseski (2008) noted that the National Football League (NFL) remains the most watched professional sport. In their estimation of the total television viewing audiences for professional sports in 2005, they found that more than one in three Americans watch professional football. A 2011 Harris Interactive poll of 2,374 U.S. adults, aged 18 years and older, found that 31 percent of men watch 6–10 hours of football a week during the NFL season, with another 16 percent watching at least 16 hours a week (Statista 2012).

Cable television, widely adopted in the 1980s, and the big three networks of ABC, NBC, and CBS entered into a frenzy of competition for the millions of new spectators brought into the fold by television: "within a decade, the hours of network television devoted to sports doubled" (Rader 1984, 5). McChesney (1989) reported that during the 1970s, the annual network hours devoted to sports jumped from 787 to 1,356; by 1985, the networks were broadcasting 1,700 hours of sports annually. That number jumped to more than 2,100 hours of television sports on the four major networks (now including Fox) by the mid-1990s (Sage 1998). On cable television, ESPN, which went on the air in 1979, has broadcast multiple versions of its flagship program, *SportsCenter*, every day, celebrating its 25,000th episode in 2002 (Mittell 2010, 20). The network reaches at least 70 percent of American homes and broadcasts more than 8,000 hours of live sports each year (Sage 1998).

Television sport represents one of the most powerful entertainment genres (Gitlin 2000). Michael Real (2005) suggested that the combination of television and sports is not just powerful but "even, if you will, imperial" (338). This power is economic, social, cultural, and ideological. Some media corporations, including Walt Disney, Time Warner, and Comcast, even have ownership in professional teams. Today's popular sports and media institutions alike arose amid a context of well-established patriarchy and racial discrimination. Sports had long been primarily white and male by the time television came on the scene, and the commercialization of sport through its relationship with television (where network executives were also primarily white and male) reinforced wealthy, male involvement in the sports industry. The ensuing decades "have witnessed a long struggle for gender parity, racial justice, and class egalitarianism in televised sports" (Real 2005, 346).

The Production Logic of Sports Television

Television and commercial sponsorship have left their lasting imprint on sport, changing its rules, presentation, and cultural form (Whannel 2009) to increase appeal and accommodate programming needs (Sage 1998). Jhally (1989) argued that the overall logic of television sports is dominated by a concern for the circulation of commodities; *professional* sports have always been based in commercial relations. In the early 1960s, television stations began to buy broadcast rights from professional teams and leagues and then sell time on each telecast to advertisers. By the mid-1980s, the three networks combined sold more than $1 billion in advertising for sports programming (McChesney 1989, 63). By 2005, the economic size of the sports industry was estimated to be approximately $117 billion (Humphreys and Ruseski 2008). This figure encompasses both the supply and demand side of goods and services in the three main components of the industry: participation, attendance, and following via the media.

According to Jason Mittell (2010), sports television is "a leader in commercial infiltration" (62); almost every facet of the broadcast has been "colonized" by brand names (McChesney 1989, 65). The real product of sport in the sports/media complex, however, is the consumer. As far as advertisers are concerned, sports fans are a reliable and desirable commodity, as is the less-committed audience that still flocks to the major sports spectacles (Rowe 1999). Advertisers are particularly wild about the adult male demographic whose expendable income is extensive (Horne 2006; Real 2005) and who "most commercially driven media organizations otherwise find difficult to reach" (Horne 2006, 43). In this case, audience composition (18- to 49-year-old men) is more important than audience size (Baran 1997). Consumers in this market can be sold a range of goods, from typical blue-collar items like beer to big-ticket purchases like automobiles (McChesney 1989).

Robert McChesney (1989) argued that a television contract essentially means everything to the survival of any sports league. Broadcasters might be interested in sports programming, but not if the ratings are poor. Sport only constitutes important content for television so long as it generates sufficiently large, wealthy, and/or otherwise hard-to-reach audiences (Horne 2006). In a vicious cycle, the most-watched sports on television are also the most read about in newspapers; therefore, they also receive the most sponsorship. Poor ratings mean minimal commercial exploitation, which in turn results in minimal attention. Thus, despite the explosion in women's athletics for the later baby boomers and Generation X as a result of Title IX, women's sports go underreported (McChesney 1989; Real 2005). At the same time, games have been increasingly structured to fit broadcast needs, especially for commercial time. For example, Michael Real, in his 1977 book, *Mass-Mediated Culture*, indicated that according to his own stopwatch, the football moved for a mere 7 minutes in the 1974 Super Bowl broadcast (quoted in Gitlin 2000, 583). Thirty-five years later, the *Wall Street Journal* found that during a regular season NFL game, the ball is in play for an average of 11 minutes, while an average of 60 minutes is given to commercials (Biderman 2010).

The process of production is not solely situated within commercial relations. It also has a discursive aspect as it mediates, or encodes, any sporting event. To encode a sporting event is to use "*codes* (technical, organizational, social, cultural, and political) to produce a *meaningful discourse*" (Jhally 1989, 83; italics in original). As a cultural forum (Newcomb and Hirsch 2000), television presents a multiplicity of meanings for the audience to work through; values, attitudes, and cultural meanings can be tested and contested with and within the discourse encoded by the production process. Commodity logic and gender ideologies both provide dominant codes by which the text of the televised sporting event is encoded.

The Genre—and Gender—of the Sports Television Text

As important as profit is to the production of sports content, economic decisions don't tell the entire story. There also exists a cultural economy of sport (Rowe 1999), which deals in images, ideas, symbolic value, and ideology. Sport taps into the affective power of loyalties to produce all kinds of audience loyalties—to teams, players, and coaches; to region (city, state, nation, etc.); to media; and to products and sponsors (Rowe 1999). A televised sports event accomplishes these loyalties predominantly through a narrativized construction that shapes sport as a mesmerizing, flashy spectacle with a human element (Fiske 1987; Rowe 1999; Real 2005).

Narratives are structured according to the formal devices of genre, which can "[tell] us something about popular moods" (Gitlin 2000, 581). According to Todd Gitlin (2000), the ways in which television consistently frames professional sporting events reveal the hegemonic impositions of dominant American values, and the power of these stories on television can be greater than the live event itself; television sports "provide [stories] in intensified, vivid forms" (Real 2005, 343), relying on the same values that guide the broadcasting of news and other genres of entertainment.

Television is visual, and sports are visually active; their narrative modes are well-suited to each other. Through close-ups, anecdotes, statistics, and instant replays, television personalizes the competition. These production conventions routinely frame the broadcast's subjects as heroes and villains (Mittell 2010), arbitrarily defined protagonists and antagonists who "engage in direct conflict issuing in victory and defeat" (Real 2005, 342). The genre of sports television is therefore intertextual, combining the physical or violent elements of action dramas with emotions and detailed characterizations (Rowe 1999).

The television industry considered the apparatus to be gendered from the beginning (McCarthy 2000). Using conventions of genre, television genders its audience along a continuum between masculine and feminine ideals (Fiske 1987; Mittell 2010). Soap operas, for example, are usually linked with feminine ideals, sports programming with masculine. The television text

> copes with, and helps to produce, a crucial categorization of its viewers into masculine and feminine subjects. Mellencamp . . . traces this back to the 1950s, where she finds the origin of the "gender base" of television, with sport and news shows for men, cooking and fashion shows for women, and "kidvid" for children. (Fiske 1987, 179)

The unequal gender order in sports television relies on narrative devices of character, conflict, and resolution to represent a primarily male world that reinforces traditional ideas embedded in the dichotomies of active/passive and masculine/feminine (Mittell 2010), despite powerful counter-histories from female athletes. Jason Mittell (2010) argued that most television representations reinforce an assumed domesticity/professionalism binary, and the professionalism of sports is framed as male. The authoritative position of sportscaster is usually filled by men, and the active athletes are likewise usually men who embody masculine ideals.

The (usually male) commentators serve to connect the sports action to other cultural phenomena and the larger social context (Rowe 1999). The authority of the commentator, or announcer, is highlighted through a number of devices. Gitlin (2000) identified two devices in particular that work to frame the sports experience according to patriarchal notions of masculinity/femininity and capitalist ideology. First, the announcer's authority is established by virtue of his position as interpreter of the game, even though the viewer can see for himself (or herself) what is going on. The announcer symbolically cues the viewer as to his knowledge of and authority over the game (and, by extension, the world) by rambling off statistics at every turn. "Stats," called up seemingly effortlessly by the announcer, parade as knowledge and meaning at a deeper level that can only be accessed through male professionalism:

> To know the number of megatons in the nuclear arsenal is not to grasp its horror; but we are tempted to bury our fear in the possession of comforting fact. To have made "body counts" in Vietnam was not to be in control of the countryside, but the U.S. Army flattered itself that it looked good. TV sports shows, encouraging the audience to value stats, harmonize with a stats-happy society. (Gitlin 2000, 582)

Second, television sports fuse capitalist and populist dogma by framing the sports text as a string of individual achievements (or failures): "The appeal is to the American tradition of exalting means over ends . . . this is the same spirit . . . that lends itself to the preservation of craft values in a time of assembly-line production, and at the same time distracts interest from any desire to control the goals of the central work process" (Gitlin 2000, 584).

In sum, the television sports text presents a naturalized, ideological version of the world. This version upholds some key values, including militarism, nationalism, fair competition, the capitalist labor process, traditional notions of masculinity/femininity, and "the individual as the prime unit of action" (Jhally 1989, 85). Especially in professional football, hegemonic masculinity is reinforced and women are symbolically annihilated (Sage 1998). The text is linked seamlessly to the culture of consumption through the attendant sponsorship and advertisements. The outcome is that, "*In short, if one were to create from scratch a sport to reflect the sexual, racial, and organizational priorities of the American power structure, it is doubtful that one could improve on football*" (Real 1979, 191; italics in original). Yet the text does not speak in the same ways to all groups across all decoding moments.

Audience Decoding and the Lived Context of Television Sport

For most sports fans most of the time, the experience of spectating at a sporting event is usually mediated through the conventions of television. Different kinds of programming are preferred by different audiences in different kinds of spaces, prompting several questions: What are actual audience readings, and how do they differ across groups? Given that audience readings are not random or infinite, how do these readings constitute a "structure of discourses in dominance?" (Jhally 1989, 89). What are the conditions of attendance in which audience readings take place? Finally, how are these readings integrated into the broader frame of everyday lived experience? These questions help sort through the final two stages of Johnson's "circuit of culture" model, encoding and lived cultures (Jhally 1989); however, the discussion remains necessarily exploratory because of a dearth of ethnographies of sports television viewers, especially in the baby boomer generation.

When it comes to audiences, television navigates two competing needs: the need to appeal to a wide diversity of viewers and "the need to discipline and control those audiences so that they can be reached by a single, industrially-produced cultural commodity" (Fiske 1987, 58). From the early days of the television industry, it was just programming that was gendered; the industry assumed the spaces in which that programming was consumed to be gendered as well (McCarthy 2000). Television's goal, then, was to standardize and supervise different categories of watchers in different kinds of viewing spaces. According to Fiske (1987), however, television never totally achieves this unity in diversity, because audiences take on a diversity of reading positions, ensuring that the hegemonic thrust (Gitlin 2000, 577) of television remains a site of contestation.

Different media forms "create different ways of being a sports consumer" (Horne 2006, 63). Television viewers primarily watch sports in the domestic setting (Horne 2006). The centrality of television's slickly produced text to the spectating experience suggests that consuming the event in the comforts of home has become a *more* satisfying experience than being at the event in person, for even those at the live event check their experience against the Jumbotron (Real 2005; Mittell 2010). Television's assumption of the domestic setting gives it a significant role in the politics of the family (Fiske 1987). The everyday culture of the home is a site of power and resistance as family members undertake the act of watching television and of choosing what to watch. John Fiske (1987) argued that the culture of the home, at least into the 1980s, was generally patriarchal, and so the choice of programming became a form of cultural capital granted particularly to men. The male preference for sport, among other genres such as news, renders these categories of programming "naturally" superior; thus, his viewing preferences are easily imposed on the rest of the family—their "natural" superiority masking the power dynamics at work.

Outside the home, the sports bar is one sphere of public amusement where sports broadcasts were primarily watched by men (Mittell 2010). McCarthy's (2000) historical analysis of American taverns in the late 1940s—the precursors to the modern sports bar—reveals that television viewing spaces were separated along gender and class lines. Industry surveys of the period showed that most viewers, especially sports fans, were in taverns, not at home—a trend that would shift as television infiltrated the American home in the coming decade. In taverns, the predominantly male, working-class viewers preferred news and sports, whereas the home audience was presumed to be predominantly female. Although reality was more complex and diverse than these industry assumptions, according to McCarthy, the tavern was seemingly designated as a center of male recreation and community life. It was a space that early on enclosed the desired male consumer—whoever else it might also include. In this space, the tavern sports fan seemingly had the best of both worlds: the spectacle of the television event as well as the public viewing context akin to the stadium experience (McCarthy 2000).

Ethnographies of sports spectators are sparse, unlike those of audiences for other genres of entertainment, specifically genres considered feminine, such as soap operas (for example, see Hobson 1991; Seiter et al. 1991; Leibes and Katz 1993) or romance novels (Radway 1991). The research has thus far focused on fandom and live spectatorship. For example, Womelsdorf (2008) conducted an ethnography of fan culture at Louisiana State University football games, noting the artifacts, clothing, and cheers that defined the experience and marked attendees as insiders or outsiders to the LSU football culture. Aden (2007) used interviews, questionnaires, and e-mail correspondence conducted with 500 Nebraska Cornhusker fans to understand how devotion to the football team—performed at stadiums and at "watch parties" in homes or bars—constituted a "communitas" intimately linked to the history, geography, and culture of Nebraska. Research in this vein is a relatively recent phenomenon, slow to answer Jhally's (1989) call for critical cultural studies to take the imperative step toward audience research in relation to sports: "An ethnography of sports viewing and the manner in which media messages are a *part* of the process through which meaning is constituted have to be included in the future of critical cultural studies" (Jhally 1989, 88; italics in original). Moreover, the lived cultures of the baby boomers within which mediated sports meanings were signified and put into practice went largely overlooked. It remains for historical analyses to piece together answers to some of Jhally's burning questions:

> For example, why is sports so important as a form of nationalism, and what is its ideological and cultural link to the military/industrial

complex? Also, in addition to the linking of sports discourses to the naturalizing of the commodity-form, the language of sports has also been used in other spheres. (Jhally 1989, 91)

CONTAINING GENDER: ATHLETICS VERSUS FITNESS ON TELEVISION

There are two sides to the coin of media sport—one side is economic, the other is ideological (Sage 1998). The sports/media complex clearly marks sport ideology as masculine. Eileen Fischer and Brenda Gainer, in their 1994 essay, "Masculinity and the Consumption of Organized Sports," argued that watching, following, or participating in sport endure as

> deeply associated with defining what is masculine and, concurrently, what is not feminine. It has been noted that participating in and watching sports lead to a range of masculinities, and each of them relies for its definition on being distinct from femininity. (quoted in Horne 2006, 152)

Although women's sports were receiving consistent scheduling on major networks by the end of the 20th century, women in sports, from athletes to representatives of sports and media organizations, remain significantly underrepresented and subject to objectifying and restrictive stereotypes (Real 2005). The conventions of the television sports text, combined with the political economy of sports broadcasting, reinforce the sports/media complex and its ideologies of gender and capitalism as a natural structure. As Real (2005) summarized, "Sports on television contribute to capital accumulation and win consent for a definition of sport that is suited to a capitalist consumer culture" (357), all the while preserving the "male gaze."

Nowhere is this containment of gender made clearer than in the distinction between sports programming and fitness programming on television. Aerobics is a female-dominated athletic conditioning sport that emerged in the 1970s, when more women overall were entering competitive and noncompetitive sports. Attention to women's sports, according to Camacho (2006), has primarily been geared toward less competitive activities, usually those that focus on weight loss, fitness, and "looking good," rather than on athleticism. These activities, such as aerobic exercise classes, are packaged on television as hobbies or advisable pursuits for women to become more sexually attractive and desirable (Camacho 2006) through the jurisdiction of professionals spouting the language of personal liberation (Giulianotti 2005). Camacho (2006) argued that televised exercise routines use production techniques that enhance or emphasize women's appearance; sex appeal as a blatant focus peaked in the 1970s and 1980s, but despite being toned down some, it is still embedded in the overall discourse of workout programs. Her examination of *Denise Austin's Daily Workout* and *Fit & Lite* on the Lifetime Network (a cable network geared specifically toward women) revealed the hegemonic struggle of conflicting media messages. Despite discourses of female empowerment, the programs maintained patriarchal notions of the ideal female body: "firm but shapely, fit but sexy, strong but thin" (Giulianotti 2005, 88).

These same hegemonic patriarchal norms are reproduced in what little coverage is granted to competitive women's sports—the athletes are always attractive (for example, Anna Kournikova), and they are often packaged as spokespeople for perfume or underwear rather than as athletes first and foremost (Giulianotti 2005). In giving more attention to those women athletes who can also be appreciated and exploited for their sex appeal, mass media contain women's sports "safely in the ghetto" (Messner 2005, 88) by downplaying skill and athleticism and "restabiliz[ing] . . . narrow cultural codes of heterosexual femininity that have been restrictive for girls and women" (Messner 2005, 93).

The increasing number of channels and the explosion of female athleticism since the 1970s have undoubtedly nurtured an upsurge in images of women athletes, rendering sports media a continuously contested ideological terrain. According to Messner (2005), the sports media complex has responded in one of two ways: sexualization (often humorous) and silence. On the one hand, the quality of what sparse coverage women in sports receive often constructs their place as on the sidelines, in support roles as sexy spectators, as a pursuer of hobbies for weight loss, and as objects of sexualized humor (especially in pseudo-sports like entertainment wrestling). Femininity and sex appeal still trump athleticism in many instances of sports television.

On the other hand, the sports/media complex has also largely opted to remain silent on the subject of women's sports. Several studies have shown little change over the years as male sporting events continue to dominate television coverage. In the wake of the addition of two professional sports leagues for women (basketball and soccer), Adams and Tuggle (2004) replicated earlier studies of television coverage of women's athletics from the 1990s and found that ESPN's *SportsCenter* reported on 48 male sports stories for every one female story, and male stories received 96.4 percent of the program's time while female sports stories received 2.1 percent, and mixed stories received 1.5 percent. Messner (2005) noted that *SportsCenter* has become "sport's *center*" while only 2.1 percent of its coverage went to women's sports. Christine Brennan, a part-time ESPN commentator, remarked in 2002, "It's a boys club. They don't care" (quoted in Adams and Tuggle 2004, 246).

In college sports media, Huffman, Tuggle, and Rosengard (2004) found that although quality of presentation was similar between male and female sports stories, quantity of presentation remained overwhelmingly lopsided. An exploratory analysis of college television stations indicated that 81.5 percent of the sports stories covered men's athletics, even though 41 percent of college athletes and 56 percent of college students are female. Even though the student journalists grew up with the standards set by Title IX, campus media practices still follow the standards of the professional media. The researchers concluded that the sports/media complex is a self-reinforcing system, still dominated by revenue-producing male sports even for the Title IX generation.

Gender inequality in television sports is still "widespread and deeply rooted" (Sage 1998, 181), despite improvements in representation. Even the proliferation of media outlets by the 21st century has merely relegated respectful coverage of women's sports into small, marginalized outlets, retaining the masculine cultural center of the sports/media complex (Messner 2005). The proliferation of television channels and the explosion of the Internet have not deterred television sport from bringing together millions around the world to share live, exciting viewing experiences, while other programming genres face fragmentation of the audience and domestic leisure (Whannel 2009). The baby boomer's legacy to modern sport is an international economic and cultural machine in the service of patriarchal hegemonic ideals of gender relations and capitalist consumer culture. Further critical cultural studies on the implications of this legacy, two generations later, should undertake ethnographies of television sports audiences and further analysis of athletics versus fitness in the encoding and decoding of television sports texts.

REFERENCES

Adams, Terry, and C. A. Tuggle. 2004. "ESPN's *SportsCenter* and Coverage of Women's Athletics: 'It's a Boy's Club.'" *Mass Communication & Society* 7 (2): 237–248.

Aden, Roger C. 2007. *Huskerville: A Story of Nebraska Football, Fans, and the Power of Place*. Jefferson, NC: McFarland.

Baran, Stanley J. 1997. "Sports and Television." In *Encyclopedia of Television*, edited by Horace Newcomb. http://www.museum.tv/archives/etv.

Biderman, David. 2010. "11 Minutes of Action." *Wall Street Journal*. January 15. http://online.wsj.com.

Camacho, Melissa. 2006. "Television and Aerobic Sport: Empowerment and Patriarchy in 'Denise Austin's Daily Workouts.'" In *Sport, Rhetoric, and Gender: Historical Perspectives and Media Representations*, edited by Linda Fuller, 145–157. New York: Palgrave Macmillan.

Falk, Gerhard. 2005. *Football and American Identity*. New York: Haworth Press.

Fiske, John. 1987. *Television Culture*. New York: Routledge.

Frank, Thomas. 1987. *The Conquest of Cool*. Chicago: University of Chicago Press.

Gitlin, Todd. 2000. "Prime Time Ideology: The Hegemonic Process in Television Entertainment." In *Television: The Critical View*, 6th ed., edited by Horace Newcomb, 574–594. New York: Oxford University Press.

Giulianotti, Richard. 2005. *Sport: A Critical Sociology*. Malden, MA: Polity Press.

Guttmann, Allen. 1986. *Sports Spectators*. New York: Columbia University Press.

Hall, Stuart. 1980. "Encoding and Decoding." In *Culture, Media, Language*, edited by Stuart Hall, Dorothy Hobson, Andrew Lowe, and Paul Williss, 128–138. London: Hutchinson.

Hobson, Dorothy. 1991. "Soap Operas at Work." In *Remote Control: Television, Audiences & Cultural Power*, edited by Ellen Seiter, Hans Borchers, Gabriele Kreutzner, and Eva-Maria Warth, 150–167. New York: Routledge.

Horne, John. 2006. *Sport in Consumer Culture*. New York: Palgrave Macmillan.

Huffman, Suzanne, C. A. Tuggle, and Dana Scott Rosengard. 2004. "How Campus Media Cover Sports: The Gender-Equity Issue, One Generation Later." *Mass Communication & Society* 7 (4): 475–489.

Humphreys, Brad R., and Jane E. Ruseski. 2008. "Estimates of the Size of the Sports Industry in the United States." Presented at the 10th Annual International Association of Sports Economists Conference, Gijon, Spain. http://college .holycross.edu/RePEc/spe/HumphreysRuseski_SportsIndustry.pdf.

Jhally, Sut. 1989. "Cultural Studies and the Sports/Media Complex." In *Media, Sports, & Society*, edited by Lawrence A. Wenner, 70–93. Newbury Park, CA: Sage.

Johnson, Richard. 1986. "What Is Cultural Studies Anyway?" *Social Text* 16: 38–80.

Liebes, Tamar, and Elihu Katz. 1993. *The Export of Meaning: Cross-cultural Readings of "Dallas."* 2nd ed. Cambridge, UK: Polity Press.

May, Elaine Tyler. 1988. *Homeward Bound: American Families in the Cold War Era*. New York: Basic Books. Retrieved from http://ez.hamilton.edu:2096/2027/heb.01654.

McCarthy, Anna. 2000. "'The Front Row Is Reserved for Scotch Drinkers': Early Television's Tavern Audience." In *Television: The Critical View*, 6th ed., edited by Horace Newcomb, 451–469. New York: Oxford University Press.

McChesney, Robert W. 1989. "Media Made Sport: A History of Sports Coverage in the United States." In *Media, Sports, & Society*, edited by Lawrence A. Wenner, 49–69. Newbury Park, CA: Sage.

Messner, Michael A. 2005. "Center of Attention: The Gender of Sports Media." In *Sport in Contemporary Society: An Anthology*, edited by D. Stanley Eitzen, 87–97. Boulder, CO: Paradigm Publishers.

Mittell, Jason. 2010. *Television and American Culture*. New York: Oxford University Press.

Newcomb, Horace, and Paul M. Hirsch. 2000. "Television as a Cultural Forum." In *Television: The Critical View*, 6th ed., edited by Horace Newcomb, 561–573. New York: Oxford University Press.

Puente, Maria. 2011. "Boomers Rocked the Culture, Turning TV, Pop Music into Art." *USA Today*, January 3. http://www.usatoday.com.

Rader, Benjamin G. 1984. *In Its Own Image: How Television Has Transformed Sports*. New York: Free Press.

Radway, Janice A. 1991. *Reading the Romance: Women, Patriarchy, and Popular Literature*. Chapel Hill: University of North Carolina Press.

Real, Michael R. 1979. "The Super Bowl: Mythic Spectacle." In *Television: The Critical View*, edited by Horace Newcomb, 170–203. New York: Oxford University Press.

Real, Michael R. 2005. "Television and Sports." In *A Companion to Television*, edited by J. Wasko, 337–360. Malden, MA: Blackwell.

Rowe, David. 1999. *Sport, Culture and the Media*. Philadelphia: Open University Press.

Sage, George Harvey. 1998. *Power and Ideology in American Sport: A Critical Perspective*. 2nd ed. Champaign, IL: Human Kinetics.

Seiter, Ellen, Hans Borchers, Gabriele Kreutzner, and Eva-Maria Warth. 1991. "'Don't Treat Us Like We're So Stupid and Naïve': Towards an Ethnography of Soap Opera Viewers." In *Remote Control: Television, Audiences & Cultural Power*, edited by Ellen Seiter, Hans Borchers, Gabriele Kreutzner, and Eva-Maria Warth, 223–247. New York: Routledge.

Skornia, Harry Jay. 1965. *Television and Society: An Inquest and Agenda for Improvement*. New York: McGraw Hill.

Statista. 2012. "Time Spent Watching NFL Football on TV 2011." Data bar graph. http://www.statista.com/statistics/205941/nfl-football-tv-viewing-time-of-us-adults/.

Whannel, Garry. 2009. "Television and the Transformation of Sport." *Annals of the American Academy of Political and Social Science* 625: 205–221. doi: 10.1177/0002716209339144.

Womelsdorf, Charles. 2008. "Welcome Home: An Ethnographic Journey into the Tigers' Death Valley." In *Proceedings of the International Communication Association (ICA)*. Washington, DC: International Communication Association 2008.

7

"And Now Bringing You the Good Life—A Word from Our Sponsors": The Changing Face of Television Advertising from the Sixties to the Present Day

Rebecca Kern

The 1960s brought many changes, not the least of which included a television in nearly every American household. In turn, this new medium offered a venue for advertisers to show products in an innovative way. Television commercials, unlike radio commercials, were visual, and unlike print had motion. They offered the best of all worlds and promised a captive audience, something that over time was guaranteed to change as the digital world expanded.

By the 1960s, at least two-thirds of all American households had at least one television (Cohen 2003; Leiss et al. 2005), and televisions were enjoyed by all of the children coming of age during this era, better known today as the "boomers." Those born from 1946 to 1964—almost 80 million in the United States alone—are post–World War II babies, children of the prosperous, commercial 1950s and the sociopolitical 1960s. They may have first been introduced to broadcasting through the radio but became quickly enamored of television as it became a staple in the American home. It is this generational group who would have a major impact on consumption and economic growth of goods and services in the next few decades (Leiss et al. 2005).

Television flourished as a medium, and advertisers quickly discovered that they could reach many audiences at different times of the day to sell all sorts of products. Advertising agencies like Ted Bates Inc., Young & Rubicam, and DDB (Doyle Dane Bernbach) started television buying and planning departments. In an effort to capitalize on brand recognition, television programs provided a platform for delivery. The shows were entertainment, but they could not exist without the advertisers buying in. First, it began with sponsorships of programs by various brands, just as had been the case with radio in decades prior with companies like Procter & Gamble and General Mills. Later, the commercials became a form of entertainment as well. One- to two-minute commercials were all that separated one show from the next and became mini shows unto themselves.

The boomers—young, impressionable children at this point— were repeatedly shown brand after brand and any number of products with which to make their lives more enjoyable (Schudson 1984; Leiss et al. 2005). Their parents were introduced to new household technologies that would save time—washing machines; new transportation technologies that would get them from point to point faster—electric trains and faster airlines; and new media that provided faster forms of information—the television. All of these items were goods that were assumed to be necessities for boomer children. They did not know a life without them as their parents had, and because of these products and the many others that were sold through television advertising, they were on a new journey of mass consumption as no generation of such number had been before.

Television advertising ignited a new social consciousness: a new generation of mass consumers. The boomers have the greatest spending power of any generation (Nielsen Research 2012) and are passing along this consumer mentality to their children, the millennials. The present chapter explores the growth of television technology and its effect on the advertising and consumer industries, specifically focusing on the economic, psychological, and sociocultural relevance this generation has played in the commodity market and the construction of the good life in America.

GROWTH OF TECHNOLOGY

The advent of the television and its growth in American households came quickly after the end of World War II. Antitrust actions by the federal government disintegrated the motion picture industry's control of motion picture houses. At the same time, the Federal Communications Commission (FCC) began licensing television stations on VHF bands. Although its initial start was in the late 1930s, within a decade the FCC had granted licenses to 10 additional commercial broadcasters (Allen 1983; Leiss et al. 2005). As another decade went by, most of the United States was covered by a television signal from some television market; there were 63 markets in 1952 and by 1957 television had 97 percent coverage[1] (Leiss et al. 2005). In addition to increased coverage, the 1950s also saw many changes to the broadcast day as daytime and weekend programs were introduced to reach women and children and were a complement to primetime family viewing hours. By 1960, "daytime broadcast hours more than quadrupled, and weekend hours increased tenfold" (Alexander et al. 1998, 2).

Not surprisingly, the demand for television sets quickly increased, and with this increase the ways in which Americans interacted with television also changed. American television, particularly in the early years before cable, saw great economic success, especially between the 1950s and 1970s (Boddy 2004). Much of this was due to increased advertising spending—$128 million in 1951 up from $12.3 million two years prior (Alexander et al. 1998), despite worries by radio and advertising executives that television would cause women to get less done around the house and cause men to become sedentary. Where Americans' lives had once revolved around the radio as a way to obtain news and entertainment, the television took over the role. The television set became a focus of living rooms, much like fireplaces previously. It provided a completeness, a sensory experience of touch, not just sound, that was a replacement for personal interaction like no other medium before. The medium was indeed very much the message.

Television, as McLuhan (1964) argues, offered a sense of unification and utopian imagination, or "synesthesia" (274), which had been sought after by culturists for decades prior. It is the great equalizer, at least in the minds of Americans, as television seemingly bridged the gap between races, sexes, and classes. The world was not the dangerous or economically starved place it had been, rather a new environment full of promise. Commercial television's most important role was, as Lipsitz (2003) argues, as "an instrument of legitimation for transformations in values initiated by the new economic imperatives of postwar America" (105). The pastoral existence portrayed on television was not only necessary as an escape from the atrocities and loss of war and the economic strife of the Great Depression but it also conveyed a sense of hope and change (Lipsitz 2003; Buckingham 2011).

Television content in the 1960s shifted only in that life was also portrayed as glamorous. This was perhaps ironic as the 1960s were also rife with social change for many marginalized societal groups, including African Americans and women, as well as being a politically charged time due to the Vietnam War and President Kennedy's assassination. None of this, however, was seen in television programming (outside of news), and advertising continued to maintain the status quo set forth in the 1950s. Presidents Kennedy and Johnson both implemented new stimulus programs to keep the economy flourishing, mostly through tax cuts. In 1964, Johnson signed the Revenue Act, meant to give American families more money to spend by decreasing income taxes and increasing take-home pay (Cohen 2003). The result gave the consumer economy another boost and opened the door for further changes.

NEW ECONOMY AND NEW MEDIA = THE GOOD LIFE

Economic growth in the form of new communities, growing businesses, and newly available products made Americans desire a new life. This new life included buying homes, living in suburbia, shopping in newly created malls (Cohen 2003), forming the nuclear family, traveling via automobile out of cities and sightseeing throughout the United States on newly constructed highway systems. The government needed to encourage spending in the postwar economy by 30 to 50 percent (Lipsitz 2003), and they did this through homeowner and vehicle stimulus programs as well as tax incentives for manufacturers, including those that made television sets.

In addition, there was a push for increasing consumption of products to make life easier. It was at this time that the term "keeping up with the Joneses" was born (Leiss et al. 2005), implying that Americans not only sought the good life but also desired to compete for visible status with friends, family, and neighbors. Advertising was a major catalyst in increasing desire, suggesting that consumption was the only way to be better and show others success. Advertising, as Ewen (1976) noted, had to reflect the inadequacies of the population because profit could only be gained when people saw what they did not have, but could. Particular products and brands equaled status, and hence the "middle class" took on a new meaning. These were just some of the initial factors that influenced the mind-set and behavioral characteristics of the boomer generation.

During the radio era, program content was controlled by the sponsor of the show. The concept of soap operas arose because of afternoon serial dramas sponsored by Procter & Gamble and their detergent products. This was an ideal situation for advertisers as they had a noncompetitive message and a captive audience. Alternatively, this was not a lucrative business for growing media, especially television, as they were creating content across many genres: drama, soaps, game shows, and vaudeville and variety. One advertiser per show did not warrant enough profit, as programming production was very expensive; thus, it was inevitable that the advertising industry would need to change.[2]

The new model television networks used to gain revenue included switching to multiple advertisers per show. Sponsorship of programs worked for radio, but television networks found that they could have more control over revenues (Cohen 2003) if they created programming that appealed to "the lowest common denominator" (Meehan 2003, 74), making television a mass market medium. Nielsen ratings for 1955 showed that the average American home had the television on for "5 hours and 28 minutes a day or 38 hours a week" (Spring 2011, 128). It brought millions of people together for a specified moment in time and was an efficient platform for marketing products. Targeted programming, which was part of this new programming model, took off in the 1950s and allowed for networks to sell commercial time for specific products that related to the audience watching.

Advertising from the 1950s into the 1960s focused on the growing medium and gaining national advertisers who could present their product in what Leiss et al. (2005) describe as a combination of "design and cultural symbolism" (157), something radio could not do. Product messages reflected programming content of the 1950s—idyllic, family oriented, and pastoral. It is what Leiss et al. (2005) explain as the stage of personalization, or the third stage in the development of advertising. Goods were embedded with feelings, so instead of a simple use value, goods had psychological value; they were a sign that was interpersonal. The sign as a lingual articulation and the signified as a conceptual visualization indicated by a verbal signifier define the sign (Barthes 1968), but a sign does not necessarily require a verbal indicator. The visual and audio medium of television created the perfect platform for technological linguistic growth. Products were signs that held psychological value but could only be made so if they made a connection and had meaning.

Codes of symbolism were necessary as some could be universally applied and some were meant for particular audiences. When products and brands integrate into everyday sociocultural spheres, they become a part of popular culture and carry cultural meaning. Advertising points to a preferred reading, one that is meant to be understood specifically by a particular audience in a particular moment. It is because of preferred readings that products promise social membership, and the advertising of products is a method of achieving social membership (Schudson 1984). Social membership is identifiable through the symbols and signs that a target group personally promotes through consumption and use. Often commodities are emblematic of social class and status, yet increasingly commodities are "visible symbols of inner worth" and "provide people with some sense of identity and continuity in their lives" (Schudson 1984, 156-157). Through personalization and lifestyle connections, advertising speaks to larger social groups on an interpersonal level.

Products could not only make life easier but could also promise aspirations to a new life, a different life (Schudson 1984). They were, however, as Gitlin (2002) reminded, "broken promises ever renewed" (79), as the consumer was forever in a state of searching for a product that would fulfill a new desire. Ewen (1976) discusses advertising at the time as a reminder of the loss of a simpler time and the start of a more modern era, one that many in society feared would create a loss of independence. In turn, advertising "offered mass produced visions of individualism" and a way to "put that unhappiness to work in the name of society" (45). Ultimately, as Ewen (1976) and others argue, advertising encourages the consumption of things we do not need and powerfully shapes social reliance on commodities.

Schudson (1984) and Jhally (2003) would partially disagree, as advertising can only promise so much, other socioeconomic messages are negotiated along with the advertising message, and it is really part of a larger system, one that Jhally (2003) calls the "commodity image-system" (252). Commodities, as Jhally notes, are related to the achievement of happiness, but not directly; advertising simply helps to make that connection. He further argues that the problem lies within "the institutional structure of a market society that propels definition of satisfaction *through* the commodity/image system" (251). In other words, changes in media technology, economics, and sociocultural experiences are important elements in a market society and affect the persuasive messaging of advertising. So although goods may not be needed as utilities, and instead are laden with symbolic meaning and persuasive messages of desire, this is achieved in tandem with other market forces.

Leiss et al. (2005) point to the growth of advertising during the 1940s and through the 1960s as particularly important in the development of symbolism attached to goods, more specifically as they reflected the inner desires and personality of the people who consumed them. Essentially, advertising promoted symbolism by integrating the referent of the product with sociocultural practice. These three decades shifted the ways in which consumers looked at goods as utilitarian, and paved the way for an expansion of the interpersonal consumer message, one which looked to groups or segments of population and the ways in which products could reidentify individuality at a subcultural level. Identified as "totems" by Leiss et al. (2005), products subsumed with symbolic meaning are reworked to have various meanings depending on who is being targeted.

TARGETING AUDIENCES

One of the biggest and most important changes in the 1960s was the targeting of specific consumer audiences through targeted programming and the increased use of psychoanalysis by advertising agencies. In general, television programming during primetime hours still maintained a level of homogenization, aimed at the entire family as that was who was watching. The themes focused on family values, such as in shows like *Leave It to Beaver* and *Father Knows Best*, and networks also "presented programs rooted in historical experiences and aspirations of diverse working-class traditions" (Lipsitz 2003, 108), such as *The Honeymooners* and *I Love Lucy*. The former showed happy families consuming products that would increase their comfort and happiness. The latter was necessary to encourage Depression and war-era adults to consume the new medium of television and, ultimately, to consume more goods and services. They also reinforced the ethic that if you work hard you can achieve the American dream. Lipsitz (2003) pulls from Habermas's theory of capitalistic legitimation and media, as media continually reinforce family as "centers of consumption and leisure" (127) and work is necessary to provide for the family. The America dream is then a circular arrangement prompted by mediated reminders of how to live, who is important, and what is necessary to achieve a status recognized within society.

Programming during other hours was aimed more at individual population segments: women during the day and children in the afternoons and on weekends. Targeting women during the day was a concern for networks as they worried that women would be less likely to stop and watch a program while taking care of their daily home duties, something that was not a concern with radio media (Boddy 2004). This proved to be less of a concern as more products meant to make life easier became everyday items all middle-class homes had (Cohen 2003)—washers and dryers, vacuum cleaners, and dishwashers. Women now had more time in their day to watch and not just listen. Television also needed to cater to children as they were the next generation of media consumers. Hence, television manufacturers worked to encourage families to purchase a television as a benefit for their children, as children were seen as having important "symbolic status" (Buckingham 2011, 187). Television programming for children emerged quite quickly; animated programs filled Saturday mornings, and children were seen as a significant cohort of future loyal consumers (Spring 2011). Advertisers, like television networks, knew they could further diversify revenues by targeting segments of the population. This was not coincidental by any means. Networks encouraged it to gain revenue, and agencies saw an equally profitable opportunity.

Synethesia, or homogenization, was a concern of scholars in the 1950s (Leiss et al. 2005; McLuhan 1964), as it encouraged a loss of individuality and increased consumption of unneeded products and unnecessary lifestyles. Advertising based on sociological models, however, saw an opportunity to embrace social and lifestyle difference and to use this as a way to increase advertiser revenues and their own profits. Instead of focusing on class differences, as in previous decades, primarily from the 1920s to the 1950s, advertisers were more interested in how and where people lived and on their life stage (Cohen 2003; Leiss et al. 2005) in an effort to combat the uniformity of previous decades. The meaning of middle class expanded even further, and as Cohen (2003) explains:

One marketer predicted in the 1960s that with "New" money having climbed within the last generation to the top of the financial structure, integration with "Old" money would only be a matter of time because its children were increasingly sharing the same lifestyles as the old elite. (313)

This is particularly poignant as these children of old and new money became known as the boomers and were affected by their parents' loss of money and the lifestyle changes they had to make during the Depression and World War II. In other words, their parents wanted their children to have what they did not, or at least to do better than they had.

The focus on children as a marketing segment was an important force in shaping boomer consumer attitudes and behaviors. Many scholars have noted that an understanding of consumption begins in childhood (Schudson 1984; Roberts and Manolis 2000; Buckingham 2011). Advertising agencies saw that they could mold future consumers for their clients, ensuring loyal customers for years to come. Outside of the increased focus on women as the primary household purchasers and new life-stage segmentations, like newlyweds and full nesters (Cohen 2003), children and especially teenagers were seen as a highly profitable market. They had specific product desires, such as clothing, music, and small electronics, and often they were also influential in prompting larger-item purchases made by their parents (Buckingham 2011).

Children as television consumers were captivated by the moving image in their living rooms in a different way than their parents. McLuhan (1964) describes this as "synesthetic" and said that child viewers experience "the world in a spirit antithetic to literacy" (291). Literate society focuses on the print and oral word found previously in magazines and radio, but television takes the semiotic value even further by creating a deeper technological involvement with the iconic. In other words, signs take on greater meaning, and the child viewers of the 1950s and 1960s were consumed by these images, perhaps before they could become part of a literate, non-televisual society. This is not to say that later generations have not encountered the same situation; it has just involved different technology. This is precisely why television advertising worked, and continues to work, so well at engaging children. They are less literate, especially as it pertains to important information, making print advertising less influential, and they do not easily discriminate between programming and commercial time (Schudson 1984). A study conducted by Alexander et al. (1998) of 1950s commercials aimed at children concluded that three primary devices were used to engage with children. Spots, or those commercials separate from programming, made up half of the commercials they analyzed, but the other half were commercials that were integrated into programming or that linked show segments together, making product pitches indistinguishable from program content. Again, emphasis was placed on integrating the product as a sign of happiness, fun, and an exciting future, which hooked the children of the 1950s and 1960s and became the norm for generations to come.

Examples of how children became engaged with advertising and programming were examined by Barfield (2008) in an ethnographic study on television viewing from the 1950s to the 1970s. These studies provide an interesting insight into the impact television had on the young boomer generations and the ways in which these images may have shaped their consumptive future. For one, television was an "escape from my parents' crumbling marriage" (113). Others stated that "most of my fantasy life and play revolved around things I saw on television" and that "TV was my very best friend [. . .] and being an only child it was just me and my best friend" (112). One interviewee stated: "School gave us the tools we had to have. TV suggested places we could go with them" (118). Television, as Barfield notes (2008), taught family values, socioeconomic class behaviors, and community. Advertising on television linked these themes together, and kids waited in anticipation for commercials just as they did for their favorite programming. "Mostly, everyone loved what was on. The medium was so fascinating that no one turned his or her nose up at anything. Even the commercials were popular" (73). Speaking about her childhood watching, Elizabeth Blakely states:

> Very few commercials had an impact on us in terms of purchases, but I recall enjoying the Coke and Cheerios commercials and once convincing my mom that I would eat a bigger breakfast if it were Lucky Charms instead of Shredded Wheat. (74)

So although commercials, and programming, perhaps had less of an influence on parents of boomers, they clearly affected boomers, as they saw a multitude of new products, shown in new ways, and offered new opportunities.

BOOMERS AND THE FUTURE ECONOMY

The children of the 1950s and 1960s have always been collectively called the baby boomers, or the boomers, as they were all children of wartime parents. The boomers, however, are actually best described in two groups: the baby boomers, who were born between 1946 and 1954 and came of age between 1963 and 1972, and "Generation Jones," who were born between 1955 and 1965 and came of age between 1973 and 1983. The reason for the split is that each group had significantly different life experiences (Schroer 2013) and each were children of parents with different experiences. The former experienced much greater economic stability than generations prior and saw great potential for American postwar growth. The latter, due to economic and political struggles such as Watergate, the Iranian conflict, and oil embargoes, were less optimistic but, as Schroer (2013) notes, were more "narcissistic" and had an "I'm in it for me" attitude. This is significant as advertising in the late 1950s and early 1960s focused on how products could serve as emblems of personal and familial status. In other words, the focus was on the self and what the product could do for the individual rather than simply on its utility. The boomers were raised with advertising that later shaped how they viewed the world. Although television advertising cannot be singled out as the only cause, it did play a significant role as commercials signified how products could create a lifestyle. Commercials aimed at boomers' parents, and at families in general, encouraged the purchasing of products to help the economy and to provide their children with commodities and pleasures they never had. Commercials aimed at boomer children showed how products could make life better and more fun, ultimately prepping them to be narcissistic adult consumers. Though the two boomer groups are opposite in many ways in terms of their attitude about American prosperity, they did in fact share similar traits in buying habits as both desired products that would fulfill their familial or personal needs.

As previously discussed, early boomers were born during the advent of TV, and both boomer groups came of age during some of television's most important growth points. Generation Jones, in particular, continues to be one of television's largest viewing groups, watching 174 hours a month. This generation is second only to their parents and the baby boomers, who watch 205 hours a month on average (Nielsen Research 2012). This is particularly important to advertising. As television and marketing grew, there was a push for increased consumption of the bevy of new products available and, in turn, the possibilities for new lifestyles. The "me" generation sought the opportunity to stand apart from their parents, to not be a part of the masses, but to also find a way to be included in society. The advertising images were emblematic of the synesthesia discussed by McLuhan (1964) but still promised individuality, which has been deemed important to both boomer groups, but more significantly to Generation Jones (Ewen 1976; Roberts and Manolis 2000; Schroer 2013). The children growing up during this era were not concerned about what was lost, as they only knew what they could have, and for many the economic growth of the revived middle class gave them ample opportunities.

Interestingly, for all of the advertising targeting in their youth, many boomers spent some period rejecting consumerism. Boomers, whose parents are known as the "establishment" generation, snubbed the life their parents wanted them to have and snubbed the idea that products could make life better. By the 1960s, as the United States entered a stage of social volatility, these boomers were teens or were entering college, decided they would not follow in their parents' footsteps as major consumers, and fought against the persuasion in advertising messages (Roberts and Manolis 2000). By the 1980s, these same people became yuppies, "preoccupied with money and material possessions" (Roberts and Manolis 2000, 3). As the boomers matured, they carried their love of products and quest for the good life with them.

This segment of the population has been, and should continue to be, important to marketers for a number of reasons. As Nielsen Research (2012) states, "On the day that the first Baby Boomer turned 18 in 1964, their generation officially became part of Madison Avenue's fashionable 18–49 target audience" (1). In other words, they were targeted as children and teens in the 1950s, as target market segmentation within advertising and television was just beginning, and by the 1960s they were seen as a highly profitable market, despite their backlash against advertising's messaging. Baby boomers and Generation Jones, who are now in the 50+ age segments, amount to more than 100 million consumers in the United States and are expected to grow 34 percent by 2030 (Nielsen Research 2012). Their affluence also continues to grow; they have succeeded far more than their parents (Rice 1988; Nielsen Research 2012) and are very interested in consuming products that will help them achieve the good life they were conditioned to want. In fact, they account for 50 percent of all consumer packaged goods spending and "dominate 119 of 123 consumer packaged goods categories" (Nielsen Research 2012, 13). Yet ironically, as many have noted (Brown 2001; Reisenwitz and Iyer 2007; Nielsen Research 2012), these two generations are often left behind by marketers as they no longer belong to the coveted 18- to 49-year-old target audience. So although they earn more than previous generations and generations since, spend more, and are conditioned to be drawn by television commercials, they are not viewed as desirable by marketers and advertisers despite research stating otherwise.

Yet they are the current and future economy and are ushering their children—"Generation Y" or the "Millennials"—into this quest for a certain lifestyle as they use money and products as rewards (Roberts and Manolis 2000). Because, as previously noted, learning about consumption starts in childhood, it is no surprise that boomer children will follow suit. The millennials want what their parents have, because they, like their parents, were brought up with heavy consumption and desire the same lifestyles with which they were raised.

CONCLUSION

The boomer and Generation Jones children, raised by their parents who lived through wars and the Depression, were reprogrammed through government and advertiser interventions to engage and grow with the economy. Conditioned in their youth to be avid consumers, through the advent of television and subsequently targeted advertising, they grew to desire a life that their parents had only begun to embrace. These two influential groups have played an important role in the current economy as not only one of the largest generational groups in history but also one with an enormous amount of spending power.

Boomers were born as television entered American homes, and although their parents reluctantly embraced this new medium, boomer children were raised with it and by it. Almost every American home had a television by the early 1960s, and advertising recognized the importance of reaching American consumers through this medium. It was a means to reach the masses in a way that no medium, other than perhaps radio, had achieved before. Unlike radio, however, it could visually show the product, its uses, and the way it could enhance sociocultural and socioeconomic identities. Commercials offered the perfect platform to create totems (Leiss et al. 2005) as the visual signifiers paired with audio and a strong persuasive message expanded the way consumers understood products. No longer was it only about use-value but about psychological and symbolic value (Schudson 1984; Jhally 2003; Leiss et al. 2005). While, as some have argued, these messages and symbolism may have encouraged the purchase of unneeded items (Ewen 1976), and made promises that could never be fulfilled without constant consumption (Gitlin 2002), their symbolic value was necessary to build economic stability.

The influence of advertising on children, although a potential ethical concern, is important to advertisers, as it begins a lifelong commitment to a product. Boomer children were schooled in consumerism by television and were targeted early on during Saturday morning programming in the 1950s; thus, by the time the earliest boomers reached the age of 18 in the 1960s, they were coveted as a primary advertising audience. Thus what makes boomers so important is the ways in which they were targeted, the fact that they strove to be individuals at the beginning of mass marketing, and how they negotiated the maintenance of their individuality while also belonging to social classes. Their desires for the good life have continued for decades, and now they have passed on those same desires to their millennial children. From an economic perspective this appears to ensure a strong commodity system going forward; unfortunately, however, no generational group has ever had the same economic stability as the boomers.

NOTES

1. Coverage refers to the percentage of the United States that is able to receive a television signal from at least one market.

2. The second factor that influenced this change was fraud in the form of fixed winners on game shows, notably $64,000 *Question*.

REFERENCES

Alexander, Alison, Louise Benjamin, Keisha Hoerrner, and Darrell Roe. 1998. "'We'll Be Back in a Moment': A Content Analysis of Advertisements in Children's Television in the 1950s." *Journal of Advertising* 27 (3): 1-9.

Allen, Jeanne. 1983. "The Social Matrix of Television: Invention in the United States." In *Regarding Television*, edited by E. A. Kaplan, 109-119, Los Angeles, University Publications of America.

Barfield, Ray. 2008. *A Word from Our Viewers: Reflections from Early Television Audiences*. Westport, CT: Praeger.

Barthes, Roland. 1968. *Elements of Semiology*. Translated by A. Lavess and C. Smith. New York: Hill and Wang.

Boddy, William. 2004. *New Media and Popular Imagination: Launching Radio, Television, and Digital Media in the United States*. Oxford: Oxford University Press.

Brown, Pete. 2001. "Are the Forties the New Thirties?" *Brand Strategy* 153 (November): 26.

Buckingham, David. 2011. *The Material Child: Growing Up in Consumer Culture*. Cambridge, UK: Polity Press.

Cohen, Lizabeth. 2003. *A Consumers' Republic: The Politics of Mass Consumption in Postwar America*. New York: Vintage Books.

Ewen, Stuart. 1976. *Captains of Consciousness: Advertising and the Social Roots of the Consumer Culture*. New York: Perseus.

Gitlin, Todd. 2002. *Media Unlimited: How the Torrent of Images and Sounds Overwhelms Our Lives*. New York: Henry Holt and Company.

Jhally, Sut. 2003. "Image-Based Culture: Advertising and Popular Culture." In *Gender, Race, and Class in Media: A Text-Reader*, edited by G. Dines and J. Humez, 249-257. Thousand Oaks, CA: Sage.

Leiss, William, Stephen Kline, Sut Jhally, and Jacqueline Botterill. 2005. *Social Communication in Advertising: Consumption in the Mediated Marketplace*. 3rd ed. New York: Routledge.

Lipsitz, George. 1981. *Class and Culture in Cold War America*. Westport, CT: Greenwood.

Lipsitz, George. 2003. "The Meaning of Memory: Family, Class, and Ethnicity in Early Network Television Programs." In *Connections: A Broadcast History Reader*, edited by M. Hilmes, 101-133. Toronto: Wadsworth.

McLuhan, Marshall. 1964. *Understanding Media: The Extensions of Man*. New York: Signet Books.

Meehan, Eileen. 2003. "Why We Don't Count: The Commodity Audience." In *Connections: A Broadcast History Reader*, edited by M. Hilmes, 63-82. Toronto: Wadsworth.

Nielsen Research. 2012. *Nielsen BoomAgers*. New York: Nielsen Company & BoomAgers LLC.

Reisenwitz, Timothy, and Rajesh Iyer. 2007. "A Comparison of Younger and Older Baby Boomers: Investigating the Viability of Cohort Segmentation." *Journal of Consumer Marketing* 24 (4): 202-213.

Rice, Faye. 1988. "Wooing Aging Baby-Boomers." *Fortune*, February 1, 68-73.

Roberts, James, and Chris Manolis. 2000. "Baby Boomers and Busters: An Exploratory Investigation of Attitudes toward Marketing, Advertising and Consumerism." *Journal of Consumer Marketing* 17 (6): 481–499.

Schroer, William. 2013. "Generational Progress. "March 25." The Social Librarian, Center for Media Research. www.socialmarketing.org/newsletter/features/generation1.html

Schudson, Michael. 1984. *Advertising: The Uneasy Persuasion.* New York: Basic.

Spring, Dawn. 2011. *Advertising in the Age of Persuasion: Building Brand America, 1941–1961.* New York: Palgrave Macmillan.

8

Moving with the Pictures: Film Viewing across the Boomer Era

Sheila J. Nayar

Outside the invention of film as a medium for mass entertainment and of sound for that medium, all the major technical developments and platforms for film—from the shift from black-and-white to color, widescreen, television, and Netflix—have occurred within the baby boomer generation. Or should we say, *generations*, given that the period covers almost two decades (1946-1964), such that a boomer born in 1946 could have given birth to a "shadow-boomer" daughter in 1964.[1] Between said mother and daughter—not to mention, ensuing grandchildren—"going to the movies" has meant many things, not all of them splendored, and some not even readily discerned.

For instance, most people probably don't think about the importance of air-conditioning to theatrical filmgoing. But until well into the 1950s, "Movie theatres were one of the few public institutions in which the middle-class and poor citizens of the United States could indulge in cool, dehumidified comfort" (Gomery 1992, 76). In fact, that's how summer became a prime moviegoing season in the United States (Gomery 1992, 67). Still, if one were asked to choose a single word or feature that might encompass or illuminate the migratory journey of film viewing most effectively and succinctly, that word would probably have to be "housing."

IF YOU LEAVE, THEY WILL FOLLOW: THE DRIVE-IN

Many people understandably assume that the decline in movie viewing after World War II was due to the advent of television. However, movie viewing's decline was in progress well before television emerged as competition.[2] Preceding the proliferation of that small black-and-white wonder into homes was the relocation of those homes. Suburbanization, it turns out, was the initial foe. The 1944 GI bill had rendered the suburbs financially accessible to the middle class (Gillon 2004, 140), so families moved away from the city centers and into houses on parcels of what had, until recently, been farmland. By 1950, one in four people resided in suburbia (Gillon 2004, 141)—a domestic migration comparable with the 1907 landing of Europeans on American shores (Gomery 1992, 85). Those young adults who had before been "the most loyal of movie fans" now concentrated their energies on raising families (Gomery 1992, 83). And so came the boom of babies, with the more typical two-child family giving way to families of four and five children. That massive 1950s migration (and baby making) is depicted in the film *Revolutionary Road* (2008), which has a decidedly somber edge, and the older *Rebel Without a Cause* (1955), which portrays suburban middle-class life as spawning confused, directionless youth.

The postwar drop in workweek hours (from a six-day workweek of 48 hours to a five-day one of 40 hours) and the innovation of the paid one- or two-week vacation (Belton 2005, 306)—accompanied by a rise in disposable income[3]—might lead one to assume an increase in moviegoing. Instead, the young homeowners invested their time and money into other recreational activities: camping, gardening, boating, golfing, and even "puttering around the house, working on do-it yourself home repair projects" (306).

Of course, commuting to the city (where the greater part of employment still existed) necessitated urban rail transportation, freeways, and, most importantly, cars. And so, it was thanks to a vehicle that entrepreneurs[4] found a cheap and expedient solution to the hurdle of having to construct suburban theaters: the drive-in (Belton 2005, 308). More fields were paved over, and massive screens, projection booths, and sound systems constructed, so that movie fans—often as families—could watch from their vehicles *en* pseudo-*plein air* (Gomery 1992, 191). These theaters were so convenient that, by 1958, the 554 auto theaters across the nation in 1947 had become 4,700 (Belton 2005, 308). In fact, in the early 1950s, the public spent more money at drive-ins "than at live theatre, opera, and professional and college football combined" (Gomery 1992, 91). And by this time, some drive-ins had grown profitably deluxe, with space for 2,000+ cars; service via carhops; cafeterias offering pizza, hot dogs, french fries, ice cream, popcorn; and even playgrounds and the occasional petting zoo to entertain those boomer children (Gomery 1992, 92, 82). This sedan-'n'-screening culture is foregrounded in the movie musical *Grease* (1978), with one scene and song plaintively devoted to being "Alone at a Drive-In Movie." Meanwhile, many B-grade horror and slasher flicks from the 1970s and 1980s, such as *He Knows You're Alone* (1980), took advantage of the inexpensive, culturally resonant—and potentially creepy—setting of the drive-in.

BECOMING LESS SQUARE: THE WIDESCREEN

Although there had been limited television broadcasting even before World War II, it wasn't until the early 1950s that it began its shift—and then, by the mid-1950s, its surge—toward becoming a mass entertainment (Gomery 1992, 83–84). As former NBC head Brandon Tartikoff has remarked, "Television itself is a baby boomer," and "The baby-boom generation has never known a living environment in which there wasn't a television" (quoted in Gillon 2004, 8). *The Man in the Gray Flannel Suit* (1956), a drama about postwar adjustment to white-collar life, is punctuated by scenes of Gregory Peck's three boomer children glued to the tiny set with its perpetual play of gunslinging cowboy adventures.

Thus, over the span of a mere 20 years, from 1948 to 1968—right during the period that most boomers had learned to walk and talk, endured adolescence, and come of voting age—Hollywood "lost three-quarters of its audience and the nature of moviegoing in America . . . evolved from the status of ingrained habit to infrequent diversion" (Belton 2005, 304). Hollywood did what many a corporate body does upon finding itself moribund: it worked to redefine itself, pursuing various means—some successful, others not—by which to lure spectators back to theaters. Indeed, it did what theatrical film in the postmillennial era is currently doing: concentrating on bigger, more technologically advanced, more visually startling products.

In the case of the 1950s, the thinking was that these techno-upgrades would eclipse the tiny, staticky, monochromatic programming emanating from the televisions of so many American homes (9 out of 10 by 1960 [Gillon 2004, 8]). So, the industry set about producing fewer, but more expensive and more sensational, films that would draw audiences back (Belton 2005, 309)—spectaculars, in a word: biblical ones like *David and Bathsheba* (1951) and *The Ten Commandments* (1956); musical ones like *Oklahoma!* (1955) and *The Sound of Music* (1965); and semihistorical extravaganzas like *Ben-Hur* (1959), *Lawrence of Arabia* (1962), and *Cleopatra* (1963). They would be widescreen; they would be in color. They would be 3D—70 mm—with magnetic sound tracks for stereo sound—no, with Sensurround. In other words, a veritable race for the optimal means (technically, but also financially) by which to make film viewing distinct had begun. Consider how the aforementioned *The Man in the Gray Flannel Suit* proudly declares in its opening credits that its drama (about a man working for a television network, no less) is filmed in DeLuxe color and CinemaScope. Meanwhile, *Oklahoma!* used the Todd-AO widescreen system (70 mm film, single projector, deeply curved screen) and *Spartacus* (1960) used Super Technirama (a 70 mm version of Technirama, which relied on an anamorphic lens) (Gomery 1992, 242–243).

This technological race, this "widescreen revolution" (Belton 2005, 309), had begun with 1952's *This Is Cinerama*, a two-hour travelogue that used a special widescreen process that relied on synchronizing projectors. Although not financially optimal for wide installation, the film initiated a wave of experiments with curved screens and with anamorphic lenses that could squeeze a wide-angle view of the world into a more standard film stock or camera. In this way, a screen that had "remained more or less square for over 60 years, from 1889 to 1952–1953" (Belton 2005, 309) was transformed to such a degree that, by the winter of 1953, "every major studio—save Paramount with its VistaVision process—had jumped on the CinemaScope bandwagon"; by late 1954, "nearly half the existing theatres in the United States had facilities to show CinemaScope" (Gomery 1992, 242). (CinemaScope, which premiered with Twentieth Century-Fox's *The Robe* in September 1953 [Gomery 1992, 242], was eventually replaced by Panavision [Belton 2005, 315].) As for color, let us just say that, by the 1960s, virtually *all* Hollywood films were going that direction, such that, when Peter Bogdanovich premiered his two-toned *The Last Picture Show* in 1971, he was "hailed for his 'throwback' to the old days, to the Hollywood masters of the past" (Gomery 1992, 237).[5] True, Hollywood continued to release cheap black-and-white films—at least until the 1960s, when American television would become available in full color (Gomery 1992, 237).

The "special-event widescreen spectacles" did manage, albeit in limited fashion, to bring 1950s audiences back to the theaters (Belton 2005, 304–305) and to resuscitate movie-palace culture. Other theaters managed to do so, interestingly enough, by screening art films, which the millions of post–G.I.-bill college students had come to embrace.[6] But bringing spectators back to the physical space of the theaters also brought the slow demise of the drive-in, which, with its seasonal limitations; lack of (fantasy-inducing) privacy; tinny, unreliable (TV-like?) sound system; less-comfortable-than-one's-living-room seating; and noisy reserves of "wild teens" (whose primary interest was often *not* the movie) could hardly compete. Besides, the mushrooming nature of suburban development (by 1990, one of every two people would be suburbanites [Gillon 2004, 141]) meant that the land was now too valuable to accommodate a plethora of carefreely sprawling drive-ins (Gomery 1992, 92–93).

Of course, the technological bases of many of these perceived innovations were not actually new.[7] But the industry was now in a continued state of needing to find means to boost its ailing movie-theater profits through exciting, exhilarating, color-saturated, high-fidelity, engulfing means of differentiating itself from TV.[8] And so, like many other films of the era that were trying to distinguish themselves from TV, *House of Wax* (1953) advertised itself as "3-D Action! 3-D Color! 3-D Sound!" (quoted in Gomery 1992, 227). Still, magnetic sound tracks were expensive and had a relatively short shelf life (227). Only in 1970, thanks to Dolby, would theatergoers experience a "clear, lifelike reproduction of the entire musical range and accurate reproduction of the volume range" (227)—responsible, no doubt, for the spate of lavish musicals produced during that decade, including several innovative takes on the genre, such as the rock opera *Tommy* (1975), *Nashville* (1975), and the disco classic *Saturday Night Fever* (1977).

Not only sound but also location shooting—in England, Italy, Spain, and the South Sea Islands—may have been one of the creative responses to the boxlike television, whose broadcasts were typically crude studio productions (Gomery 1992, 182–183). Besides, faster film stocks and more portable recording equipment often made it more economical now to shoot on location—and simultaneously to offer spectators another form of colorful engulfment, this time as part of an exhilarating cultural enchantment (183). Later, this would permit such avant-garde, on-the-road movies as *Easy Rider* (1969) and *Bonnie and Clyde* (1967), not to mention "the hugely expensive cycle of top-grossing disaster movies," such as *Airport* (1970) and *The Poseidon Adventure* (1972) (Krämer 1999, 96).

BECOMING MORE SQUARE: FILM *ON* TELEVISION

The paradox in the film-viewing experience being forever recast and remodeled in order to distinguish it from that of TV is that soon those movies were *on* TV. By the early 1960s, feature-film showings had become one of television's dominant forms of programming (Gomery 1992, 247). In fact, thanks to regular, and oft repeated, broadcasts, Americans were soon watching *more* movies than at any other time in film's history (xxii). This was a spatial transition especially salient for African Americans, who, before 1965, were frequently "not welcome in mainstream movie theatres" (155).[9]

But how did theatrical films make their way onto that square, archrivalrous box? In short, what had started as a series of smaller, British studios unable to break into the American market renting their films to TV (e.g., Ealing, Korda) ended up becoming a veritable spate of small studios—including American ones—delivering thousands of titles to TV (Gomery 1992, 247). Often these were B westerns or "thrill-a-minute serials" like Flash Gordon (247); but soon the major Hollywood studios were agreeing to rent, and sometimes even sell, their libraries of films to television—and to make tidy profits in the millions at that. (It was those profits, in fact, that helped subsidize the studios' forays into widescreen technology [Gomery 1992, 247–248].) Those studios also began to produce their own weekly programs, such as *Warner Bros. Presents*, *M-G-M Parade*, *Disneyland*, and *Twentieth Century-Fox Theatre* (Belton 2005, 316). At first these broadcasts consisted of pre-1948 titles, for which no residuals needed to be paid to performers or craft unions (Gomery 1992, 248). And so, boomer children more likely feasted on Hollywood classics like *King Kong* (1933) and *Casablanca* (1942) via television than from within a theater. But then came color television, and with that, the three television networks yearned to fill the "lucrative, attractive, prime-time slots" with movies in color (Gomery 1992, 249). As a result, the weekly TV program-producing studios secured royalty agreements that would enable them to release more recent films for television (Belton 2005, 316). As a result, in 1961, 1953's *How to Marry a Millionaire*, starring Marilyn Monroe, aired on NBC's *Saturday Night at the Movies* (Gomery 1992, 249; Belton 2005, 316), and black-and-white films were eventually relegated to late—and late, late—shows, or to independent stations.

Ironically, the movies that eventually fueled television's hunger for films—such as *Gone with the Wind* (1939), which drew in half the nation's TV owners in 1976 (Gomery 1992, 250)—were often visually crippled by the very technology that had distinguished them from television: widescreen.[10] *How to Marry a Millionaire*, for instance, with its wide shots highlighting the stars' lavish apartment—not to mention Monroe's recumbent, wide-as-the-screen legs—had to be readjusted to conform to TV's boxy shape. Thus was born "panning and scanning," a technique whereby a camera panned and scanned the widescreen film, focusing attention on the action in the shot and cropping the remainder of the image (Belton 2005, 317). Few baby boomers perchance realize that they spent their youth watching movies whose shots were literally half what their originals had been.

But the number of those youths was considerable, enough to spawn a veritable youth frenzy in the 1960s. With $14 billion in purchasing power—$1.5 billion of which was spent on entertainment (Gillon 2004, 73)—those teenagers no doubt helped to facilitate "the Coppola-Altman-Penn-Nichols-Bogdanovich-Ashby decade" of filmmaking (Harris 2011). Moreover, they could now see in theaters what they could *not* see on television—that is, edgy, violent, offbeat films, and films that were satirical, realistic, surrealistic, avant-garde, New Hollywood, New Wave influenced, and even R and sometimes X rated. The films became evermore targeted toward, and representative of, young men. Consider *The Dirty Dozen* (1967), *Butch Cassidy and the Sundance Kid* (1969), *MASH* (1970), *Dirty Harry* (1971), *The Godfather* (1972), and even the James Bond series (Krämer 1999, 96). Women, meanwhile, were progressively shifted onto television, such that entire genres, like the "weepies," or the once reputable genre of the "women's picture," largely disappeared from theatrical venues.

To be sure, this content shift was precipitated by the 1968 replacement of the Production Code with a movie ratings system that "regulat[ed] access to individual films according to the age of the movie-goer" (Krämer 1999, 97). Thus, X-rated films like *Midnight Cowboy* (1969) and *Rosemary's Baby* (1968) "signalled the industry's willingness to abandon the notion of inoffensive entertainment for everybody, and instead to appeal strongly and specifically to some audience segments, especially young males" (97). Theaters continued to capitalize on more inoffensive entertainment, however, especially in the form of musicals, which could still bring in families eager for amicably engulfing sights and sounds: box-office hits like *Oliver!* (1968), *Funny Girl* (1968), *Love Story* (1970), and *Fiddler on the Roof* (1971). Nevertheless, a film like *Midnight Cowboy* narratively intimated that it was no longer safe for women to go to the movies, depicting the theater as a venue in front of which johns were picked up or inside of which the homeless slept, stole coats, or engaged in illicit sex. (The movie presciently begins with a shot of an eerily abandoned Texas drive-in—a landscape that Jon Voight [as wannabe rodeo hustler Joe Buck] has left for seedy Times Square with its midnight showings. Then again, many mainstream movie houses in urban centers *had* grown dilapidated and noticeably insanitary, often because of their "proximity to porn cinemas" [Krämer 1999, 97].) One wonders if the spate of artistically cutting-edge, R-rated films in the late 1960s to the 1980s—of which *Easy Rider* and *Bonnie and Clyde* might qualify—were in part attractive to moviegoers because of the sort of violence and sexual mores that could not yet be witnessed on television, but that captured something of the post-JFK assassination zeitgeist and, after that, the Vietnam War zeitgeist.

In concentrating on a predominantly young male audience, the industry increasingly ignored the majority of the population: those over 25. It also more willingly accepted the tenet that younger children will watch whatever older children express interest in and girls will watch whatever boys are interested in, and, so, to catch the greatest audience, one is wisest to hone in on 19-year-old males (Krämer 1999, 97). (This, incidentally, had been the doctrine underpinning the successful marketing of 1950s exploitation cinema [97].) It was a doctrine perhaps most fully realized in the original summer blockbusters of boomer directors Steven Spielberg (who released *Jaws* in 1975) and George Lucas (who released *Star Wars* in 1977). Such decidedly male-hero movies were joined by film of a similar ilk, including such top-grossers as "Sylvester Stallone's string of hits with the *Rocky* and *Rambo* series from 1976 onwards; Burt Reynolds's action comedies, starting with *Smokey and the Bandit* (1976); . . . rogue cop movies . . . ; combat movies . . . ; and Arnold Schwarzenegger's 'serious' action films" (Krämer 1999, 97–98).

As for what was happening filmically on television, one new development was saturation advertising, the promotion via TV commercials of films that were being released in theaters. Beginning with Spielberg's *Jaws*, this trend, which continues today, would eventually lead, even if only indirectly, to promotional shows like Paramount's *Entertainment Tonight* and to programs devoted to the critical reviews of films, such as the long-running *Siskel & Ebert* (Gomery 1992, 295). Directors, meanwhile, got wise to the cramped, cropped, weirdly jumbled nature of re-cut images that panning and scanning produced, such that, by the mid-1980s, most cinematographers were framing a movie's action to accommodate both the theater's widescreen *and* the limited frame of the TV (Gomery 1992, 259). Still, mishaps continued, "such as the diner scene in David Lynch's *Blue Velvet* (Panavision, 1986) in which Laura Dern's nose listens attentively to Kyle MacLachlan's explanation of what he discovered in Isabella Rossellini's apartment" (Belton 2005, 318). Screening letterbox versions of the films—that is, reducing the size of their images so that their full width could be seen (Belton 2005, 318)—was apparently not an option, if only because distributors were adamant that consumers preferred cropped movies that expanded out to their TV's perimeter (Belton 2005, 318).

Eventually, there were too many slots for movie showings on TV and too little new product to fill them—not to mention too-high prices being demanded by Hollywood, which had grown savvy to the needs of television programmers. When the asking price for hit or award-winning films entered the million-dollar range, TV executives originated a new genre: the made-for-television movie (Gomery 1992, 251). By the 1970s, made-for-TV movies had become broadcast mainstays, with millions upon millions tuning in for *Women in Chains* (1972); *The Thanksgiving Story* (1973), based on the TV show *The Waltons*; and *A Case of Rape* (1974) (252). Perhaps the movie signaling the genre's having come of age was *Brian's Song* (1971), for which one-third of American households tuned in (252). Often, made-for-TV movies outdrew even the biggest theatrical films broadcast during that era—films like 1961's *West Side Story* and 1964's *Goldfinger* (both with TV premieres in 1972), and 1967's *The Graduate* (which premiered on TV in 1973) (252). Even as late as 1983, the post–nuclear holocaust drama *The Day After* would attract nearly half the nation's television-possessing homes (257).

Most boomers who had "entered their prime movie-going age (16–24) in the late 1960s and early 1970s" and who constituted the bulk of that period's cinema audience, were, by 1980, in the 25- to 34-year-old age range (Krämer 1999, 98). *Variety* urged Hollywood to retain that generation as its target audience in order to preempt the typical drop in theatergoing that occurred after age 15 (Krämer 1999, 98). Besides, new platforms for theatrical film viewing were making inroads. Movie and entertainment television channels were blurring the distinction even further between theatrical audiences (who paid at a ticket window) and home audiences (who paid a monthly bill by mail) (Krämer 1999, 98). The biggest complaint viewers had had about televised movies was that they were interminably interrupted by advertisements or edited down, sometimes crudely so, to fit a 90-minute slot (Gomery 1992, 261). The cable network HBO, which televised "uncut, uninterrupted movies a few months after they had disappeared from theatres" initiated a new growth in film-viewing that proved nothing less than spectacular—spectacular enough that it was joined by rival Showtime in 1976, with both channels pursuing exclusive agreements with studios in "an effort to catch a future hit" (Gomery 1992, 264–265). Soon, other emerging independent television networks began, with a few snips and a notice advising parental discretion, to show R-rated films practically in their entirety—films like *Taxi Driver* (1976) and *The Texas Chainsaw Massacre* (1974) (255). Increasingly these channels came to target specific audiences, such as the all-movie channel Cinemax, which oriented itself toward yuppies, and the Disney channel (267), which served the echo-boomer babies of the boomers (Allen 1999, 110).

Just as important was the arrival in the late 1980s of cable networks like Turner Network Television (TNT) and the film buff–oriented American Movie Channel (AMC), which were unaffiliated with other network channels (Gomery 1992, 269). These continued the expansion of the film-on-television viewing audience—as did, too, the arrival of pay-per-view television, or PPV. Slowly, then, as film itself was reaching its centenary, platforms like these were bringing to its knees the notion that films were something to be seen, in the words of Sandy Flitterman-Lewis, "in large, silent, darkened theaters" and that enforced an "anonymous collectivity of the audience" (quoted in Bolter and Grusin 2000, 186).[11] Then again, even the darkened theaters had metamorphosed. By the mid-1980s, boomers, who had become responsible for 50 percent of all personal income in the United States, had also produced a boom in the suburban housing market (Gillon 2004, 117)— alongside which came a boom in the construction of shopping malls. Soon, motion pictures followed, which is to say, they migrated even further out of downtown theaters, paving over (sometimes quite literally) many of the suburban drive-ins before settling into multiplex theaters and mall cinemas. By 1980, going to the movies had come to mean for most Americans "going to the mall"—in one of the 22,000 malls across the United States (Gillon 2004, 93–94).[12] Moviegoing in this way progressively mutated from being perceived as an isolated activity to being one of a series of activities identified with leisure: shopping in that mall, eating in its climate-controlled environs, catching that movie, and so on. If this seems overplayed, know that, by the late 1970s, "reports claimed that Americans spent more time in shopping malls than anywhere outside their jobs or homes" (Gomery 1992, 94–95)—a cultural pastime well represented in the film *Smooth Talk* (1986), with its restlessly troubled teenage protagonist who escapes nuclear-family life by cruising the mall with her friends.[13] The multiple theaters, with their staggered show times, conveniently accommodated consumers' schedules.

Of course this physical arrangement often meant that many of the screens were small, the theaters were cramped, and the improved Dolby sound systems permitted thudding battle sounds from the adjacent theater to pour through the walls (Gomery 1992, 100). Moviegoing had also become somewhat self-service, as few ushers were around, and the settings were far removed from the architectural splendor of the palaces of old (100). And so, with too many sticky floors, too many noisy patrons (see the gremlins in *Gremlins* [1984] who disruptively engage in popcorn-related antics while singing along to *Snow White and the Seven Dwarfs*), and because of too many films seemingly cut from the same cloth, boomers stopped attending the movies regularly (101). Besides, new technological foes were arising to disorient—if not, at times, outright displace—how movies could be watched; and, once again, central to that displacement was housing.

Film-Viewing Gone Viral: The Video, DVD, and Digital Eras

Home video—which initially entailed cassettes and a videocassette recorder (VCR) to play them on one's television—transformed film viewing forever; or, to quote the trade paper *Variety*, the coming of the VCR was "the biggest boon to the movie biz since the advent of celluloid" (quoted in Gomery 1992, 287). Although only 1 percent of homes possessed VCRs in 1978— and these were used to record television (Gomery 1992, 279)—with time and the movie studios transferring their archives to tape, soon one could filmically watch *what* one wanted, *when* one wanted, and in the convenience of one's own home. Even better, one could do so comparatively cheaply.[14] No wonder, then, that, in 1984, the term "media center" entered the popular lexicon; and in the ensuing decades, middle-class moviegoers would reconfigure their living space in an even more pronounced fashion "around an expanding array of audio-visual technologies: the VCR, CD player, video-game console, personal computer, satellite receiver and television monitor" (Allen 1999, 112). No longer did one need to be Howard Hughes—see Leonardo DiCaprio in *The Aviator* (2004)—in order to afford lounging in one's private screening room. Choice, compounded by "home economics," resulted in video penetrating households at such a rapid rate that, by 1990, two-thirds of American homes had adopted the VCR (Gomery 1992, 279).

Video rental stores, which had started off as adjuncts to mom-and-pop stores and from which one could rent a movie for little more than a dollar, understandably proliferated. Of course people like Jack Valenti, head of the Motion Picture Association of America, feared that the VCR would kill moviegoing, not to mention Hollywood's ability to make worthwhile movies (ironic, in some sense, considering that movies were now being watched in record numbers) (Gomery 1992, 280). Then again, more than half of films rented were X-rated (282)—a detail humorously depicted in the indie film *Clerks* (1994), in which a video manager orders a string of films over the phone, all but one bearing decidedly pornographic titles. Not so with the video-rental superstores that eventually emerged, however—like Blockbuster, with its 1,000+ stores nationwide. They stocked their shelves with non-X-rated inventory: "classics, art films, children's films, and all sorts of Hollywood features" (Gomery 1992, 282). Meanwhile, studios were now selling copies of films on tape directly to consumers at prices low enough to tap into a mass market—and make boomer directors and the studios even wealthier. During Christmas 1988, for instance, copies of *E.T.* were strategically sold through direct sale to the tune of $200 million (Allen 1999, 113).[15] Soon, discount mass retail stores like Kmart, Target, and Walmart were handling as much as 50 percent of the sale of videos (113); to capitalize on this market, studios shortened the post-theatrical release of films (from what had sometimes been years) to as little as a few months (Gomery 1992, 284). Despite the initial anxiety on the part of "theater owners and film producers that VCRs would detract from their box-office receipts," 1980s "movie-goers attended in record numbers and still rented videos" (Friedberg 2010, 273).[16]

Alas, the same was not the case for repertory theaters (recall *Annie Hall* [1977], in which Woody Allen, while waiting to see *The Sorrow and the Pity*, handily produces Marshall McLuhan, who then proceeds to castigate the loud-mouthed, McLuhan-misinterpreting media-studies professor standing in line with Allen).[17] Nor was it the case for art-house theaters, which, because of home video, dwindled even further in number (Gomery 1992, 195). The same needs be said for the porno theaters for which home video proved a veritable death knell. Those interested in X-rated material—$400 million dollars' worth of tapes at the wholesale level by the late 1980s—were much happier engaging with it in the privacy of their homes (Gomery 1992, 289). And so, far less likely was it now for a man to accompany his date to a Swedish sex film, as Travis Bickle does in *Taxi Driver* (1976) with disastrous results. As for the mainstream industry, in order to fully exploit the profit potential of a home market, Hollywood increasingly developed cross-generational family films: cute, domestic-friendly films like *Look Who's Talking* (1989) and *Home Alone* (1990)—as well as their sequels—which were not only cheaper to produce but procured additional profits from merchandising, product placement, and promotional tie-ins with fast-food chains (Allen 1999, 113).[18] In some sense, then, boomer executives were reaping profits by cornering their own offspring as a market. But it worked. As Robert Allen waxes, "the post-twenties baby-boomers and their 'echo boom' children . . . joined together in the industry's imagination around the glowing (video) hearth of the middle-class home," and they emerged "as 'the family' audience that would drive the video industry and transform the film business in the early 1990s" (Allen 1999, 118).

And so, movies on tape had, much as Gomery proclaimed in 1992, joined the ranks of the nickelodeon in terms of their extent in shaping movie-watching habits. Of course Gomery had also proclaimed that the "franchising of home video rental operations on a national basis—in the manner of McDonald's—promise[d] to be the wave of the future" (Gomery 1992, 283). He could hardly have anticipated the relative disappearance of video franchises from the commercial landscape. This was not because of the slender digital video discs (DVDs) and games, which, in time, replaced all those chunky plastic videotapes. After all, Blockbuster, much like its customers, switched readily in the 1990s to this new mode of recording[19]—not to mention to playing their discs on widescreen TVs. In fact, DVDs revitalized the industry, with available titles shooting up from 600 in 1997 to 20,000 by 2002 (with rental and purchase revenues of $22 billion) (Belton 2005, 318). That same year, 2002, theatrical box office receipts likewise "hit an all-time high of $9.5 billion" (318). What, then, proved the downfall for Blockbuster and its franchise cousins? It was the swift emergence of new film-distribution mechanisms, ones that operated by mail, Internet, or even, physically speaking, via one's grocery store (in the form of DVD-rental vending machines). In the spectrum of businesses, Blockbuster's legacy was very short-lived, less than 30 years in span—which is to say, less than the drive-in's.

Perhaps the greatest irony with respect to film viewing in the boomer era, however, has been the disappearance of, well, film. Celluloid, the very medium that gave films their name, has slowly been giving way to digital technologies. "Who would have dreamed film would die so quickly?" bemoaned Roger Ebert in 2011. "Was it only a few years ago that I was patiently explaining how video would never win over the ancient and familiar method of light projected through celluloid? And now Eastman Kodak, which seemed invulnerable, is in financial difficulties" (Ebert 2011). Alas, Eastman has since gone bankrupt, and three major motion-picture camera brands have ceased "production of celluloid based cameras . . . in favour of their digital counterparts . . . [H]arsh economic times and the affordability of digital media is successfully pushing film to the side in independent and major motion pictures" (Gilbert 2012). The digitization of cinema had begun much earlier, of course—in the 1980s, particularly in the "realm of special effects" (Belton 2005, 405), with digital editing supplanting postproduction video editing by the early 1990s (405). At the turn of the millennium—as if to herald that turn[20]—George Lucas began using digital cameras and, with the 1999 release of his *Star Wars Episode I: The Phantom Menace*, "spearheaded the advent of digital projection in motion picture theaters. In fact, 2002's *Star Wars Episode II: The Attack of the Clones* was filmed entirely with digital technology" (405).

Lucas has optimistically envisioned this transition to digital as widening the film "creator's palette" (quoted in Belton 2010, 285), akin to earlier technological revolutions in cinema, such as the introduction of sound, color, or CinemaScope (Belton 2010, 285). On the other hand, that the Hollywood digital revolution is "driven by the lucrative home entertainment market" leads scholars like Belton to highlight the peril of its spawning "an all-fantasy cinema" overly oriented toward animation (2010, 283, 287).[21] Then again, given that the number of U.S. teenagers was at a historical all-time high in 2010—these being the children and grandchildren of the baby-boom generation—perhaps these films needed to distinguish themselves in such exhibitionistic ways, given the variety of platforms now competing with theatrical releases. The children of the drive-in have given way to children accustomed to watching film on computers and portable DVD players, on iPhones and iPads via instant streaming, on planes, in hotels, and even from the rear seat of their parents' SUVs.[22] Once again, then, perhaps these films need to be sufficiently sensorily and auditorily appealing—astonishing enough, magical enough, pleasurably vertiginous enough[23]—in order to get audiences *into* the theaters (Allen 1999, 123). Studios have increasingly concentrated, after all, on "selling theatrical film-viewing in terms of physical size, sensory intensity and phenomenal scale . . . resurrect[ing] dinosaurs, cataclysmic natural disasters, nuclear-mutated monsters, doomed luxury liners, [and] atomic Armageddon" (123)— and often via 3D or stories-high IMAX screens capable of magnifying the experience even further. Hence the focus now not on multiplexes but on *mega*plexes, on "postmodern Xanadus of pleasure" built with patrons' comforts in mind (Gomery 1992, 113). Although megaplexes began emerging in the 1990s, expansive auditoriums and screen sizes—as well as clearer sound systems, better food choices, and the ability to host private parties (Acland 2003, 85)—have served well in this more spectacle-oriented digital era. But that is not to say that more artistically inclined film directors, like Ang Lee (*Life of Pi*, 2012) and Martin Scorsese (*Hugo*, 2011), are not also making the foray into digital 3D cinema-making—and often to innovatively magical and narratively rich ends.

We continue thus to witness not only a reformulation of what it means to go to the cinema, but a wholesale reconfiguration of the very practice of cinema going (Acland 2003, 59). Consider, after all, that today's boomer can—thanks to having more leisure time (Barnes and Cieply 2011)[24]—take a grandchild to a screening of the latest animated fantasy film; or, if enamored with the lush, widescreen films of his youth, curl up in bed with a good movie via the iPad.

Cries about the "death of cinema" and of moving-image consumption as a public experience continue relatively unabated (Harris 2011), to be sure, as do laments over increased piracy and declining moviegoing etiquette (Jacobson, Paredes, and Hanson 2007, 5). But as Jacobson, Paredes, and Hanson (2007) wisely caution, these are only the latest in a "series of *petits morts* associated with technological change: from the introduction of sound to developments in color to the emergence of television to the proliferation of video and digital technologies, each instance of media change has been the occasion of a new (or the same old) cinematic 'death'" (5–6). Perhaps, then, as a concluding moral, we are best to remember that the first headline to scream "the death of film" appeared in 1957, as a commentary on the arrival of color TV (Acland 2003, 222–223).[25]

NOTES

1. Here, I am following Gillon, who considers boomers that nationally influential group of individuals "born between 1945 and 1957. . . . 'Shadow boomers' are those born between 1958 and 1964, maintaining the momentum of the Boomers but not changing its impact" (Gillon 2004, 14).

2. As Belton notes, "Weekly motion picture attendance, which hit a high of 95 million in 1929, had averaged 85 million during the war years and climbed to 90 million in the immediate postwar period of 1945–1948. But attendance fell off dramatically thereafter, sinking to 60 million per week in 1950 and then to 46 million in 1953" (Belton 2005, 304).

3. "Disposable personal income rose from $76.1 billion in 1940 to $207.1 billion in 1950, and then to $350 billion in 1960" (Belton 2005, 306).

4. This opening in the theater business was due in no small measure to the "[b]reakup of the Big Five circuits," those major Hollywood studios of MGM, Paramount, RKO, Twentieth Century-Fox, and Warner Bros. (Gomery 1992, 91).

5. Technicolor, which had initially had a monopoly on Hollywood productions in color, soon lost its dominance when, in the mid-1950s, Eastman Kodak developed a negative that could be used in a standard black-and-white camera, as opposed to in special technicolor equipment (Geomery 1992, 237).

6. By 1956, "the number of art cinemas had reached two hundred; ten years later it was five hundred; by the late 1960s (including film societies presenting the best of the European art cinema) the total exceeded one thousand" (Gomery 1992, 181). Still, it has been pointed out that the art-house movement "suffered during Hollywood's experiments with 3-D, CinemaScope, and VistaVision" (188).

7. Henri Chrétien had been working in France in the 1920s on an anamorphic lens process (Gomery 1992, 242); and 3-D, which would have a briefly spectacular life in the 1950s before succumbing to technological problems and the specter of its association with B-grade and exploitation films (Belton 2005, 311), had also been around since the 20s (Gomery 1992, 239).

8. There was even some intention of developing celluloid "smellies" (Gomery 1992, 230).

9. Indeed, such separation of audiences continued afterward in the form of "de facto segregation by neighborhood" (Gomery 1992, 164). Bitterly ironic is that, when the urban riots of the 1960s reached Tampa, Florida, resulting in the closing of its downtown African American theater (Gomery 1992, 168), the film playing there was *To Kill a Mockingbird* (1962), "a sympathetic tale of a southern jury's racism" (Gomery 1992, 168–169).

10. The same was true of these films' stereo sound (Belton 2005, 316).

11, Italics removed.

12. Again, however, there was geographical unevenness. For instance, "for two decades prior to 1986 there were no first-run theaters in Harlem. It was only with the efforts of the Harlem Urban Development Corporation that a five-screen multiplex opened in December 1986" (Acland 2003, 89).

13. By the late 1970s and 1980s, theatrical films had witnessed a "moderate comeback" of female genres and stars, and several more domestic dramas became

box-office hits—films like *Annie Hall* (1977), *Kramer vs. Kramer* (1979), and *Ordinary People* (1980). Clearly the boomers had tapped into their own generation's family dynamics for artistic fodder, dealing as many of these movies did with relatively new, or at least increasingly common, sorts of problems and crises: divorce, child custody battles, extramarital relations, alternative sexualities, psychotherapy, and so forth.

14. Interestingly, the arguably superior Sony Betamax lost out to the VHS cassette, in part because the former could only record for an hour, whereas the VHS could do so for two hours; and, because the recorders "were first used primarily for recording broadcast feature films, the two-hour cassette made a difference in the competitive market" (Friedberg 2010, 273).

15. According to Gomery, the "sales of *E.T.* videotapes proved so extraordinary that one in five U.S. households reportedly owned the video" (1992, 286).

16. Nevertheless, by 1986 receipts "for rentals and sales of prerecorded tapes (principally movies) for the first time exceeded the box-office take in the United States. As the 1980s drew to a close, there were a record twenty-five thousand movie theatres in the United States, but an astonishing one hundred thousand outlets renting video tapes of films" (Gomery 1992, 283–284).

17. Today's youth, who are said to expect theatrical film viewing to entail an *event*, are not so far removed, then, from their boomer parents and grandparents, whose midnight visits to repertory theaters—especially for cult screenings of films like *The Rocky Horror Picture Show* (1975)—involved dressing up as characters and "dialoguing" with the screen via a varied assortment of lines, gestures, dance steps, and props.

18. As Allen (1999) notes, *Variety* made it clear, by 1995, "who the real stars were in Hollywood: McDonald's, Burger King and Pepsi. Executives from these and other companies contemplating tie-in arrangements with particular films now routinely review scripts before they go into production to make sure that the film under consideration is consonant with the image the company wishes to project for its soft drink, fast food or other product line" (120). Consider that, by the 1990s, "George Lucas was in the product licencing business as much as he was in the film-making business, with the *Star Wars*™ films functioning as part of a complex corporate strategy, the goal of which is to keep the licence viable indefinitely as a merchandising asset" (121).

19. It took only five years for the number of DVD players to jump in sales from 320,000 in 1997 to more than 25 million by 2002 (Belton 2005, 318).

20. As Belton remarks, "Strategically, it was the perfect moment to introduce the new technology, since the popular media was looking for symbolic events to mark the advent of the new millennium" (2010, 285).

21. Here, he is following—admittedly so—in the analytical footsteps of Lev Manovich.

22. Gillon (2004) notes that "[b]etween 1982 and 2000 the U.S. population grew by 20 percent, but the amount of time Americans spent in traffic increased by a staggering 236 percent" (292).

23. This I take from Gunning, who writes, "This vertiginous experience of the frailty of our knowledge of the world before the power of visual illusion produced

that mixture of pleasure and anxiety which the purveyors of popular art had labelled sensations and thrills and on which they founded a new aesthetic of attractions" (quoted in Bolter and Grusin 2000, 156).

24. In 2008, "Robert Bucksbaum, president of Reel Source, which tracks the box office and polls moviegoers, said boomers account[ed] for about a third of moviegoers, up from about 25 percent five years [before]" ("Baby Boomers Go Hollywood" 2009). Boomers also watch more DVDs at home now than they used to ("Baby Boomer Generation" 2012).

25. It was published in *Variety*.

REFERENCES

Acland, Charles R. 2003. *Screen Traffic: Movies, Multiplexes, and Global Culture.* Durham, NC: Duke University Press.

Allen, Robert C. 1999. "Home Alone Together: Hollywood and the 'Family Film.'" In *Identifying Hollywood's Audiences: Cultural Identity and the Movies*, edited by Melvyn Stokes and Richard Maltby, 109–134. London: bfi Publishing.

"Baby Boomer Generation Likes Convenience of Online DVD Movie Rentals." 2012. BabyBoomer-Magazine.com, June 26. www.babyboomer-magazine.com/news/.

"Baby Boomers Go Hollywood." 2009. CBS News. February 13. www.cbsnews.com.

Barnes, Brooks, and Michael Cieply. 2011. "Graying Audience Returns to Movies." *New York Times*, February 25. www.nytimes.com/2011/02/26/ business/media/.

Belton, John. 2005. *American Cinema/American Culture.* 2nd ed. Boston: McGraw Hill.

Belton, John. 2010. "Digital Cinema: A False Revolution." In *The Film Theory Reader: Debates and Arguments*, edited by Marc Furstenau, 282–294. London: Routledge.

Bolter, Jay David, and Richard Grusin. 2000. *Remediation: Understanding New Media.* Cambridge, MA: MIT Press.

Ebert, Roger. 2011. "The Sudden Death of Film." Roger Ebert's Journal. November 2, 2011. http://blogs.suntimes/ebert/2011/.

Friedberg, Anne. 2010. "The End of Cinema: Multimedia and Technological Change." In *The Film Theory Reader: Debates and Arguments*, edited by Marc Furstenau, 270–281. London: Routledge.

Gilbert, Andrew. 2012. "The Death of Film and the Hollywood Response." *Senses of Cinema* 62. (April). http://sensesofcinema.com/2012/feature-articles/.

Gillon, Steve. 2004. *Boomer Nation: The Largest and Richest Generation Ever and How It Changed America.* New York: Free Press.

Gomery, Douglas. 1992. *Shared Pleasures: A History of Movie Presentation in the United States.* Madison: University of Wisconsin Press.

Harris, Mark. 2011. "The Day the Movies Died." GQ. February. www.gq.com/entertainment/movies-and-tv/.

Jacobson, Brian, Veronic Paredes, and Christopher Hanson. 2007. "Deaths of Cinema: Introduction." *Spectator* 27 (supplement): 5–8.

Krämer, Peter. 1999. "A Powerful Cinema-Going Force? Hollywood and Female Audiences since the 1960s." In *Identifying Hollywood's Audiences: Cultural Identity and the Movies*, edited by Melvyn Stokes and Richard Maltby, 93–108. London: bfi Publishing, 1999.

9

Chilling to *The Big Chill*: Representations of Boomers in Movies*

Robert Hensley-King

Baby boomers are often characterized as knowing what they reject more than what they want. This chapter examines how the idealistic dreams and hopes of a generation were forgotten as the events and reality of life overtook them. It considers how the baby boomers who once rejected (or at least flinched at) the idea that hard work could buy comfort, and laughed at the shallowness of the domestic bliss of 1950s pro–American dream Cold War propaganda in television and film, became hungry, greedy, and even lost.[1] The methodology of the chapter is a historical reading of the baby boomers' culture and influences, with a focus on film culture. In particular, it presents case studies of three different yet important baby boomer films from the materialist 1980s. As discussed here, the case studies reflect the influence of the coming-of-age films enjoyed by the older baby boomers. The ways the case-study films differ from films constructed to offer positive portrayals of materialism provide insightful glimpses through dark humor to the identity crises of the lost person of Reagan's America. These films examine the tantalizing corruption of "greed being good" in *Wall Street* (1987), the fragmented lives and dreams of friends in *The Big Chill* (1983), and the misadventures of a wanderer trying to find his way home in *After Hours* (1985).

The baby boomers belong to the demographic of people born between 1946 and 1964. They were born into a period of postwar economic transformation and grew up during the emergence of a new, prosperous middle-class suburban America. The potential prosperity for domestic bliss with a plethora of home appliances to proclaim one's success reflected a new manifestation of the American dream. Middle-class children were raised having the

---

* The author of this chapter dedicates it to the memory of his late father, Michael Hensley King, a baby boomer who died while he was writing it.

opportunity of a good education and a path to success in the footsteps of their parents.[2] Older baby boomers came to be influenced by popular culture in the form of music, literature, and film, in which those born before or during World War II challenged the hegemonic construction of a successful man providing for his family.

Such developments reflect how American artists reclaimed diverse forms of popular culture from European artists. As the Europeans had been politicized and had adapted their art to question the place of individuals in relation to their respective societies, Americans applied the same critique to their own cultural contexts. The Europeans had, in turn, often been inspired by the styles and structures of American popular culture, especially in music and cinema. This cross-continental development is a post–World War II phenomena and is of particular importance to this chapter in that Hollywood film antiheroes increasingly reflected trends in music and literature and encouraged the young to question and rebel against the lives prepared for them by society.[3] Such antiheroes embodied and expanded the rebellion-generated angst in the songs of such bands as the Rolling Stones and the Beatles and in the American beat literature inspired by such European existentialists as Albert Camus and Jean-Paul Sartre in a way that transformed American cinema. Moreover, this transformation presented the angst of a generation whose financial freedom afforded them the luxury of being able to fret about the meaning of their existence. Such a transformation reflected how the baby boomers enjoyed greater work and educational opportunities, in contrast to the concerns of financial instability that had preoccupied the previous generation. This is especially evident in Benjamin Braddock's rejection of a future in plastics in *The Graduate* (1967, directed by Mike Nichols). This generation might have known what they didn't want, but they could not articulate exactly what they did want. Shaun Karli's study of Jack Nicholson as an auteur supports the assertion that Nicholson's frequent portrayal of antiheroes spoke to a younger generation of boomers who found much to protest against but little to embrace.[4] Karli argues that Nicholson is an auteur because of the dislocation technique he uses when acting, so that he always remains Nicholson for the audience while performing each character. The many antiheroes portrayed by Nicholson reflect a spectrum of masculinities, but each still challenges the perceived wisdom of a hegemony that imposes the unrealistic burden of expectation. In doing so, Nicholson reflects the gender imbalance of popular media that expects young men to behave in particular ways and demonstrates how that perception slips into public consciousness.

The angst of the existentialist antiheroes resonated with baby boomers during a turbulent time in the United States. If the domestic bliss of the 1950s served to reflect American values in the face of Soviet austerity during the Cold War period,[5] the existentialist antiheroes spoke to a generation who campaigned against the Vietnam War, and especially to the young men who feared the draft.[6] In addition to concerns about the war, film took a lead in exploring the dark world of politics, in particular that surrounding President Nixon's espionage and subsequent exposure in Watergate.[7] Likewise, it is important to consider that at this time many Americans continued to struggle with coming to terms with the assassinations of President Kennedy (1963), Dr. Martin Luther King (1968), and Robert F. Kennedy (1968).[8]

For many baby boomers the 1970s were a transformative decade that served as a period of existentialist transition from the idealism of the 1960s toward a new optimism in the 1980s. The New Hollywood cinema of the late 1960s and early 1970s spoke to baby boomers and presented them with wounded and angst-ridden antiheroes in contrast to the strong individuals typified in roles played by Clint Eastwood.[9] Cinema during the 1980s is particularly interesting because it juxtaposes and at times combines weakness and strength through antiheroes who reflect what happened to the dreams and hopes of the one-time idealists.

Robin Wood offers an insightful study of the transformation of film from the troubled 1970s to the triumphant reassertion of American values and might as reflected in the films of the Reagan era.[10] This chapter, however, presents a reading of three innovative films that challenge the Reaganite ideology of 1980s cinema. The films are discussed with regard to how they reflect that many baby boomers reassessed, and even rejected, greed and economic comfort to continue their search for meaning. This is especially evident in how the films' protagonists respond to the challenges and changes in their material circumstances that force them to stop and reconsider the directions their lives are taking.

Before concentrating on the case studies it is important to consider the trend toward reinventing the American image in the films of the 1980s, especially because the films challenge much about Reagan's America. In his electoral campaign against President Carter, Reagan drew on his reputation as an actor to promise a return to the image of prosperity for the hardworking and enterprising people common to 1950s films.[11] Reagan argued that because Carter was weak he had failed to deliver his own election promise to revitalize the United States.[12] Reagan's campaign was helped by the fact that people increasingly considered Carter a hen-pecked husband, and Reagan offered a manifesto of re-masculinization that the electorate and subsequently Hollywood soon embraced.[13]

After Reagan's election, Hollywood started to reflect the ideology of the revitalized American dream through films that showed how people could and should work hard to succeed financially. Likewise, Reagan's efforts to present himself as a president more interested in people than government bureaucracy were reflected in maverick protagonists with exceptional personal resolve and power.[14] This is strongly evident in the transformation of the John Rambo (Sylvester Stallone) character from an emotionally and psychologically damaged Vietnam veteran in *First Blood* (1982; directed by Ted Kotcheff) to a warrior hero capable of defeating the Vietcong on his own terms in *Rambo: First Blood II* (1985; directed by George P. Cosmatos). The character not only asked the question, "Are we allowed to win this time?"[15] but Reagan himself also mused publically about how Rambo could have helped with the Beirut hostage crisis in 1985: "Boy, after seeing Rambo [*First Blood II*] last night, I know what I should do next time this happens."[16]

CASE STUDIES

The films discussed in this chapter offer alternative insights to 1980s America through their use of dark humor to challenge the theme of greed in the pursuit of happiness and the triumph of the industrious individual. They show that enough of the spirit of New Hollywood remained to challenge, albeit subtly, ideology through the mainstream medium of Hollywood films. The films challenge the zeitgeist of greed and the individual of the 1980s. However, they nonetheless reflect the individual in relation to society and in response to the material realities of his or her circumstances. The films are of particular interest to this chapter in that they offer a spectrum within an age of binaries. At a time when the film culture of the 1980s drew on the binary of the Cold War tensions between the communist East and the democratic West, when wealth and might came to symbolize a successful person, the case-study films offered something innovative: the central protagonists are skillfully constructed to both combine and, at times, juxtapose popular ideas of strength and weakness. Unlike the dichotomy between the angst-ridden and the mighty antiheroes of the 1970s, these characters show both sides while remaining existentialist in how they react to circumstances and situations beyond their control.

In the wider context of film history this can be read as much more than a transition from the broken protagonists of the 1970s to the "cool" characters of postmodern cinema in the 1990s. Instead, these heroes show interesting layers of character complexity; likewise, the films themselves offer an astute social critique in a decade noted for its shallowness and artificiality.

Wall Street

Wall Street, directed by Oliver Stone, has become the iconic film of the age of greed in the 1980s. Gordon Gekko's (Michael Douglas) egocentric one-liners and extended speeches reflect the perceived wisdom of the day that "greed is good," and the work ethic that "lunch is for wimps." Moreover, the quotes have become infamous as crude reminders of the 1980s race to make lots of money and aptly capture the zeitgeist of a decade that inspired numerous self-help books. Such books are themselves a proselytizing rant against the weak, authored by the strong, and each selling the dream that people can increase their fortunes by casting aside inhibition in the pursuit of success. *Wall Street* tells the story of what happens when the pursuit of wealth becomes conflated with the pursuit of happiness. From the opening shots to the ambiguous ending, Oliver Stone narrates the journey of how Bud, an ambitious everyman, embraces and then rejects the individualism of the age to address the tensions between his idealistic and his excessively materialistic sides. The reasons for its inclusion in this chapter are obvious, especially as numerous scholars have researched and written on various aspects of the film. This case-study analysis strengthens the concept of the baby boomers as a generation struggling to find meaning, which is presented in this chapter.

The film opens with shots of Bud Fox (Charlie Sheen) arriving in the financial district of Manhattan juxtaposed with Frank Sinatra's rendition of "Fly Me to the Moon"—a song that is an aspirational anthem about transcending one's humble setting to climb to the dizzy heights of greatness. Such an opening is very much in keeping with the classic Hollywood technique of introducing the protagonist as an everyman primed for an adventure. However, the shots increasingly focus on Bud, singling him out as the person at the center of the narrative of the film. In this way, it facilitates an exploration of individualism and greed, rather than the usual heroic adventures of classic Hollywood, or the antiheroic dichotomy of might and despair in New Hollywood.

In the workplace, Bud is shown to be an ambitious underdog, heavily in debt, who longs for a shot at success and pesters Gordon's secretary for an opportunity to impress. The shallowness of Bud's aspiration is painfully evident when he determinedly leaves a woman in his bed to work on executing his plan to present Gordon with expensive Cuban cigars, in the hope of gaining a few minutes of his time. In doing so he sets aside both the human decency demanded of a sexual relationship and the lustful desires of a young man interested in sex to put his mission to make money first. The plan works, and in his efforts to impress, Bud crosses the first of many lines: later giving Gordon insider information about his father's airline and making money through questionable means by trading on information given to him by Gordon. In this way, Bud simultaneously moves toward his aspiration, compromises himself, and sets himself up as a child torn between two very different father figures. The father figures and Bud's need to impress them both are discussed later.

The tension shown in *Wall Street* is interesting for many reasons, not least as a metaphor for the tension experienced by many baby boomers during the 1980s. Those who once held lofty ideas of rejecting the hegemonic and ready-made roles of a boy becoming like his father now found themselves even greedier than their parents, of whom they once disapproved. As a filmmaker commenting on the age, Stone uses the character of Bud to show a young man trying desperately hard to impress both his real and his surrogate father. Furthermore, it is interesting in that Carl Fox (Bud's father) is played by Charlie Sheen's own father Martin Sheen. The complexities of a real father-and-son relationship strengthen the overall performances of the two characters. This is significant, especially because Martin Sheen is politically similar to the character he plays.

Carl Fox is a trade unionist and an obvious and dichotic opposite to Gordon. In particular, Carl has fought hard to ensure and protect workers' rights throughout his career. Bud's love for his father is never really in question, even when he attempts to justify his actions with an angry tirade that his father puts his work before him. Indeed, there is even a visible tension as Bud tries to resist passing on his father's comment about the airline's court case to Gordon as information useful for insider dealing. In fact, it is not until Bud is reminded that he is already compromised that he fully engages in insider dealing and begins to enjoy the riches his conduct brings.

Once Bud finds himself on the slippery slope of the road to profit at any cost, he very much feels an adopted son of Gordon and his aggressively capitalistic gospel of making money with no thought for emotional attachment. This reaches a climatic head when he is naive enough to think Gordon will place the interests of the airline company and the employee stakeholders over management. However, the realization becomes a pivotal moment for Bud to have his "baby boomer turned bad" moment of crisis.

Bud's journey toward greed is certainly more exaggerated than in any of the other films used here as case studies. Yet, it is a compelling narrative of a man realizing his corruption and resolving to fix it. Like all of the baby boomers in this chapter, Bud has to ask himself how he managed to grow so distant from his youthful hopes and ambitions of being different from his father but nonetheless still a good man and a person of integrity like him. To become a hero, Bud was confronted by two opposing ideals, and he chose to put the good of others before his own pursuit of wealth. In doing so he reconciled his personal struggle for meaning and purpose.

The Big Chill

The Big Chill, directed by Lawrence Kasdan, is an innovative film, not least for its audacious inclusion of seven (arguably eight) protagonists, who serve to illustrate the gulf between youthful college idealism and the realities of life. A group of college friends, now in their thirties, reunite to mourn the suicide of a friend whom they had gradually lost touch with. As they struggle to come to terms with their collective and individual grief, the friends are forced to reflect on how they have become wealthy and lost sight of the issues that once mattered to them. To this effect Alex, the deceased friend, is introduced as a free spirit; at the funeral, the minister's blunt eulogy opens with the line that Alex was "a brilliant physics student at the University of Michigan, who paradoxically chose to turn his back on science and taste life through a seemingly random series of occupations," and concludes by asking, "Where did Alex's hope go?" This is further emphasized when Alex's young girlfriend tells Nick that she first met Alex when she "told him that he was wasting his life."

Alex was clearly the linchpin that first brought the group of friends together, and the exchange of looks between the friends at the funeral reveals much unresolved tension. The discussion in this section shows how issues and tensions are resolved and addressed.

A brief introduction to the characters will help with the analysis of this film. Sam Weber (Tom Berenger) now plays the lead character in a television detective drama with an opening sequence that suggests a similarity with the program *Magnum, P.I.* (1980–1988). Sarah Cooper (Glenn Close) loved Alex but, in spite of their extramarital affair, settled for the stability of married life with Harold Cooper (Kevin Kline), who spoke at Alex's funeral and clearly knows about his wife's compromise. Michael Gold (Jeff Goldblum) is a successful writer for *People* magazine who questions the integrity of his profession. Meg Jones (Mary Kay Place) is a lawyer who is increasingly aware of her ticking biological clock and wants one of her friends to father her a child without the commitment (or burden) of a relationship. Karen Bowens is hurt and frustrated by her unhappy marriage. Finally, of the friends, Nick Carlton (William Hurt) is the one whose life was changed by being drafted to fight in Vietnam.

As a character, Nick performs the role of troubled Vietnam vet well, and in doing so he successfully reminds the audience of the concerns the young friends had when they were college students during those troubled times. In particular, he is a reminder of its cost in terms of body count and budget, and of the clarion call for change from various protest groups of the late 1960s and early 1970s. However, Nick is interesting in that he is the one who ultimately forces the group to confront their displaced guilt. This is particularly interesting in light of the fact that the Vietnam War psychologically silenced articulate men who faced the draft and feared dying. As footnoted earlier, the psychologist Carol Gilligan has drawn on her experiences of the time and her subsequent scholarship of the period to explain how male silence about the war was indicative of their feeling vulnerable. For many, their fears were rooted in and experienced through a series of relationships with people they loved and didn't want to hurt.[17] Interestingly, Nick finds himself at odds with the group as someone who has numerous unresolved issues relating to his experiences of war and his subsequent return to civilian life. This is particularly evident in his spat with a police officer (Ken Place). After Harold intervenes to resolve the situation, Nick quips that his mediation with the officer shows how much he has sold out to "authority." Although Harold is quick to point out that Nick needs to grow up, it is ultimately Nick's speaking up that reminds the friends that they have all grown up and that life has changed.

The film presents the friends as middle class and comfortable in their lives. Reference is made to their sense of being radical in their political stances and various protests when they were college students. However, the group members are very much archetypal WASPs in their thirties. More importantly, they are almost oblivious to their having become the older generation they once rejected as the established class who perpetuated the American dream of hard work being rewarded with success.

In confronting their suppressed feelings the group members recognize the compromises they have made and the simple fact that they have each put their own material comfort and safety first. This is played out through the rivalries, sexual tensions, jealousies, and other unresolved issues repeating themselves. Again, this is brought to a head by Nick's curt questions about the actual value and validity of their friendships as he dares to ask whether they really know and understand each other.

The climatic long night of confrontations and reconciliations results in a process of resolution by honesty for each of the protagonists. During his honest conversation with Sarah about changing his life, Michael's intuition leads him to believe that he's not alone facing the truth. He is "almost certain that there's sex going on around here," that is, by members of the group in different rooms and parts of the house. This night of vented passion between members of the group effects a healing that resolves the unspoken tension between Harold and Sarah through an attempt to impregnate Meg. It also sees how Sam and Karen's plan to find happiness together in Hollywood is replaced by her decision to return to her husband; and finally, it brings Nick and Chloe together under the protection of Harold and Sarah to heal each other.

After Hours

Another film that illustrates a dissenting voice within the zeitgeist of greed in the 1980s cinema is *After Hours*, an interesting and often overlooked film in the filmography of Martin Scorsese. As a director, Scorsese came to prominence by his ability to explore masculinity through marginal and liminal characters.[18] In *After Hours* he inverts his preference for traditional blue-collar and fringe gangster protagonists to offer the story of Paul Hackett, played by Griffin Dunne, as a man trapped in a lower-middle-class existence as a computer programmer in a information technology company, which serves as a metaphor for the factories of the 1980s and beyond. Paul is introduced at first as an everyman, but then more closely as a man who is both bored with his work and lonely outside of it. Again, this is representative of the enduring quest for meaning that typifies the screen portrayal of so many baby boomers. This is evident in his induction of a new recruit into the company and in his conversation with Marcy Franklin (Rosanna Arquette) in a diner. The diner scene highlights Paul's loneliness in how he is drawn from the safe world of reading a favorite novel into conversation with Marcy, and his subsequent over-reading of her interest in him. The scene of Paul alone in his apartment after the encounter shows how a desire for adventure is sparked in a man who is suddenly aware of his loneliness. The viewer is invited to grab his or her jacket to share in Paul's nocturnal journey from his world into a series of challenging experiences, which ultimately show Paul how unhip and dislocated he is, how he is a cog in the wheel of the contemporary technological industry. In this way Paul is forced to ask what happened to his hopes and dreams.

Paul's journey begins with the intriguing fusion of the image of a man about town juxtaposed against the image of someone stupid enough to leave a twenty-dollar banknote, his only banknote, where it could be blown out of the window in an accelerated journey downtown. On arrival at Marcy's apartment he is shown to be completely out of his comfort zone through a painfully awkward combination of scenes. The man who was introduced as a worker finds himself in the completely different reality of a bohemian world of a changing downtown.

Through a series of episodic misadventures and misunderstandings Paul becomes lost and also unwittingly moves from someone who is alienated to someone who causes pain. Eventually, he becomes wanted after being mistaken for a burglar. Throughout the journey Paul longs to simply go home. His eventual safe return to his work world places Paul back in a surrounding where his identity makes sense. Whether he has learned anything from his roam around town is quite another matter.

Scorsese is noted for constructing existentialist antiheroes who are forced to adapt to their material situations. Unlike the creators of other existentialist protagonists, Scorsese prefers to leave his characters stuck in the reality of the world. Paul's ambiguous return to his workplace shows that although he might not have learned any life-changing lessons, he has certainly come to discover that he is trapped in his world. His inability to step into another world is much more than a metaphor; instead, Paul walks and ultimately runs toward his unexpected journey to ask when he became just another cog in the industrial wheel.

CONCLUSION

This chapter has examined the ways in which baby boomers are characterized as existentialists, especially in films that challenge the zeitgeist of their era, for knowing what they reject more than for knowing what they want. In doing so the chapter provides insight into the baby boomers as the lost dreamers of the 1980s through the prism of film. This is different from the constructed heroes of each era who aspire to the American dream of hard work resulting in success. The case studies show how the baby boomers have taken inspiration from the film antiheroes of their own youth to reject in turn the perceived wisdom of the 1980s. Just as the ambiguous New Hollywood antiheroes played by Dustin Hoffman and Jack Nicholson, among others, rejected the restraints the world prepared for them, the case study films narrate a diverse mix of baby boomer protagonists who taste and then reject a world of greed in favor of an existentialist search. In doing so, the chapter presents their cultural formation through the good times and bad to juxtapose their own inevitable hunger to succeed against the values they once held close. In short, the chapter shows how some of those once inspired by the left-leaning antiheroes, who reflected the angst of vulnerable and struggling America, have become greedy and lost in their own antiheroic selfishness. Although the films represent something lost, they show that the questioning baby boomer is capable of recognizing selfishness.

NOTES

1. For further discussion, see Wilber W. Caldwell, *Cynicism and the Evolution of the American Dream* (Washington, DC: Potomac Books, 2008), 101–115.

2. For further discussion, see Andrea Press, "Gender and Family in Television's Golden Age and Beyond," *Annals of the American Academy of Political and Social Sciences* 625, no. 1 (2009): 139–150.

3. For further discussion, see Ian Scott, *American Politics in Hollywood Film* (Edinburgh: Edinburgh University Press, 2000).

4. For further discussion, see Shaun R. Karli, *Becoming Jack Nicholson: The Masculine Persona from* Easy Rider *to* The Shining (Lanham, MD: Scarecrow Press, 2012).

5. For further discussion, see Andrea Press, "Gender and Family in Television's Golden Age and Beyond," *Annals of the American Academy of Political and Social Sciences* 625, no. 1 (2009): 139–150.

6. For further discussion on the fears that silenced a politicized generation, see Carol Gilligan, "Looking Back to Look Forward: Revisiting in a Different Voice," *Classics@* Issue 9 (2011). http://nrs.harvard.edu/urn-3:hul.ebook:CHS_Classicsat.

7. For further discussion, see Geoff King, *New Hollywood Cinema: An Introduction* (New York: I.B. Tauris Publishers, 2005).

8. For further discussion, see Michael Allen, *Contemporary US Cinema* (Harlow, UK: Pearson Education Limited, 2003).

9. For further discussion, see David A. Cook, "Auteur Cinema and the 'Film Generation' in 1970s Hollywood," in *The New American Cinema*, ed. Jon Lewis (Durham, NC: Duke University Press, 1999), 11–37; and Mark Shiel, "American Cinema, 1970–75," in *Contemporary American Cinema*, ed. Linda Ruth Williams and Michael Hammond (New York: Open University Press, 2006), 124–163.

10. For further discussion, see Robin Wood, *From Vietnam to Reagan . . . And Beyond* (New York: Columbia University Press, 2003).

11. A good example of how Reagan drew on his film career is how he paraphrased Al Jolson's first spoken line from *The Jazz Singer* (1927, directed by Alan Crosland), "You ain't seen nothing yet" in his inauguration speech for his second term. During the same speech he even described Jolson as his old friend from Warner Bros. Throughout his reelection campaign, with its theme of "Morning in America," Reagan claimed that a return to valuing the individual was essential for a continued renaissance of confidence.

12. For further discussion, see Allen Rostron, "Mr. Carter Goes to Washington," *Journal of Popular Film and Television* 25, no. 2 (summer 1997): 57–67.

13. For further discussion, see Susan Jeffords, *Hard Bodies: Hollywood Masculinity in the Reagan Era* (New Brunswick, NJ: Rutgers University Press, 1994).

14. For further discussion, see Andrew Britton, "Blissing Out the Politics of Reaganite Entertainment," in *Britton on Film*, ed. Barry Keith Grant (Detroit: Wayne State University Press, 2008), 97–154.

15. For further discussion, see Rick Berg, "Losing Vietnam: Covering the War in an Age of Technology," *Cultural Critique* xx, no. 3 (Spring 1996), 92–125.

16. "Reagan Gets Idea from 'Rambo' for Next Time," *LA Times*, July 1, 1985.

17. Cf. Gilligan, 2011.

18. For further discussion, see Paul A. Woods, *Martin Scorsese: A Journey Through the American Psyche* (London: Plexus Publishing Ltd., 2008).

REFERENCES

Allen, Michael. *Contemporary US Cinema*. Harlow, UK: Pearson Education Limited, 2003.

Berg, Rick. "Losing Vietnam: Covering the War in an Age of Technology." *Cultural Critique* xx, vol. 3 (Spring 1986): 92–125.

Britton, Andrew "Blissing Out the Politics of Reaganite Entertainment." In *Britton on Film*, edited by Barry Keith Grant, 97–154. Detroit: Wayne State University Press, 2008.

Caldwell, Wilbur W. *Cynicism and the Evolution of the American Dream*. Washington, DC: Potomac Books, 2008: 101–115.

Cook, David A. "Auteur Cinema and the 'Film Generation' in 1970s Hollywood." In *The New American Cinema*, edited by Jon Lewis, 11–37. Durham: Duke University Press, 1999.

Gilligan, Carol. "Looking Back to Look Forward: Revisiting in a Different Voice." *Classics@* Issue 9 (2011).

Jeffords, Susan. *Hard Bodies: Hollywood Masculinity in the Reagan Era.* New Brunswick, NJ: Rutgers University Press, 1994.

Karli, Shaun R. *Becoming Jack Nicholson: The Masculine Persona from Easy Rider to The Shining.* Lanham, MD: Scarecrow Press, 2012.

King, Geoff. *New Hollywood Cinema: An Introduction.* New York: I.B. Tauris Publishers, 2005.

Press, Andrea. "Gender and Family in Television's Golden Age and Beyond." *Annals of the American Academy of Political and Social Sciences* 625, no. 1 (2009): 139–150.

Rostron, Allen. "Mr. Carter Goes to Washington." *Journal of Popular Film and Television* 25, no. 2 (Summer 1997): 57–67.

Scott, Ian. *American Politics in Hollywood Film.* Edinburgh: Edinburgh University Press, 2000.

Shiel, Mark. "American Cinema, 1970–75." In *Contemporary American Cinema,* edited by Linda Ruth Williams and Michael Hammond, 124–163. New York: Open University Press, 2006.

Wood, Robin. *From Vietnam to Reagan . . . And Beyond.* New York: Columbia University Press, 2003.

Woods, Paul A. *Martin Scorsese: A Journey Through the American Psyche.* London: Plexus Publishing, 2008.

10

The New Horror Movie

Todd K. Platts

In 1957, Screen Gems, a subdivision of Columbia Pictures, signed a 10-year lease for 550 films in Universal-International's pre-1948 catalog for a sum of $20 million. The company divided the acquisition into several thematic blocks of films to sell to the booming television syndication market. One of the packages, simply called "Shock!," contained 52 pictures from Universal's classic era of horror. For television affiliates who broadcast the collection of old fright flicks it became a smashing success in the Friday and Saturday after 10 p.m. time slot. Other firms followed the Screen Gems lead and began offering their own classic horror film packages. Soon enough, virtually every town in America had its own rendition of *Chiller Theater*, often introduced by local hosts camped out in vampire, mad scientist, or zombie garb.[1]

Using over-the-top gothic shtick, characters like Ghoulardi and Zacherle introduced countless young baby boomers to horror cinema. Their wit and puns mimicked that of the EC Comics (1950–1955) emcees from just a few years earlier. Boomers ate it all up. So much so that in the early-1960s Aurora Plastics introduced plastic model sets of Dracula, Frankenstein's monster, the Wolf Man, and other now-beloved creatures. Numerous genre fan magazines started popping up as well, Forrest J. Ackerman's *Famous Monsters of Filmland* being the most notable. According to David J. Skal, this early consumption of horror provided baby boomers with both a mechanism to deal with the confusing passage into adulthood, "disturbing physical transformations, nocturnal visitations/emissions, and moon-driven 'curses' were part of the appeal of Monster Culture to young Americans tottering on puberty's abyss" as well as a tension release to the ever-present threat of nuclear annihilation because the films offered "an image of survival, however distorted or grotesque."[2]

In this chapter I will argue that where horror films initially offered boomers glimmers of hope and comfort during their childhood, the same genre would effectively capture the nightmares of their young adulthood—particularly the nightmares of those boomers who identified with the leftist political movements of the 1960s and 1970s. Using 1968 as my point of departure, I will demonstrate how horror began taking a dark and twisted turn by directly commenting, increasingly critically, on contemporary American life and institutions and locating the monstrous as within us rather than away from us. These films, among them, *Night of the Living Dead, Rosemary's Baby* (both 1968), *The Last House on the Left* (1972), *The Exorcist* (1973), and *The Texas Chainsaw Massacre* (1974), evoked outrage and controversy in their day and, in the process, established new thresholds of violence for cinematic horror as well as new blueprints for subsequent productions.[3] I will delve into the context, meaning, and legacy of these films—films I collectively refer to as "new horror movies."

I will develop the meaning of the new horror movie as my argument progresses, but, for now, I will loosely define the term as those horror films produced between 1968 and 1985. The dates bookend the films mentioned earlier and, fittingly enough, *Day of the Dead* (1985), the conclusion of George Romero's original living dead trilogy. The common thread of New horror films is their critiques of the current state of affairs[4] and their refusal to provide reassuring narrative closure,[5] but the dates are by no means exact. Films bearing the hallmarks of new horror both predate (e.g., *The Birds* [1963]) and postdate (e.g., *The Purge* [2013]) the time frame. Likewise, despite prominent scholars characterizing the period as possessing a progressive bent, numerous films produced within the period contain reactionary elements (e.g. *The Exorcist, Halloween* [1978], *Dressed to Kill* [1980]). It is by the mid-1980s, though, that most scholars agree the horror genre took a decidedly conservative turn[6] and began to appeal to another group of youths;[7] it will, therefore, signal the conclusion of my analysis.

My central claim is that the horror films produced between 1968 and 1985 can be seen as a witness to, and acculturation of, the era's social movements and trauma, including the feminist, civil rights, environmentalist, peace, student, and countercultural movements. Rather than arguing that these films reflected the turmoil of their time, like Michael Ryan and Douglas Kellner, I maintain that they transcoded it. That is, they translated political discourse and social life into meaningful cinematic narratives.[8] Taken together, the films explored in this chapter signaled a radical shift in horror aesthetics that profoundly shaped the genre in the years to come. To understand how this was possible, I will first consider the industrial conditions that laid the groundwork for the new horror movie before analyzing the films themselves.

INDUSTRIAL CONTEXT

Though the sociopolitical unrest of a given era strongly imprints itself into popular culture, it is a mistake to assume that such forces unilaterally influence the culture industries and the creative personnel responsible for generating entertainment-based ephemera such as horror films.[9] The zeitgeist must, inescapably, pass through the mediating structures of industry practice, which, in film, includes, but is not limited to the interorganizational personnel governing the production, financing, and distribution of films; censorship standards governing acceptable levels of violence, sex, and other potentially offensive themes; conventions conscribing storytelling poetics; budgetary constraints inherent in individual film projects; and the technological limitations of filmmaking's creative tools (e.g., cameras, editing equipment, special effects). In the case of new horror movies, in addition to ever-present social strife, their subversive and disturbing content was also made possible by a combination of industrial shifts that affected the film industry writ large. In other words, the new horror movie was not only underwritten by the tumultuous changes taking place in American culture but also by general changes in the logic of film production.

Most importantly, in the late 1960s, changes in content regulations afforded filmmakers greater artistic license in tackling previously forbidden topics, with Stephen Prince going so far as to argue that the new rules governing filmmaking "actually provided [filmmakers] with incentives to transgress social mores."[10] Specifically, September 1966 saw Hollywood revise its inhibiting Production Code to allow for franker treatments of violence, sex, religion, and other themes once deemed too touchy. By 1967, there was a noticeable trend in sanguinary cinema with *Bonnie and Clyde*, *A Fistful of Dollars*, and *The Dirty Dozen* (all 1967) hitting box-office pay dirt. Motion Picture Association of America (MPAA) president Jack Valenti even defended this violent turn, juxtaposing the real-life horrors aired on the nightly news against the contrived situations of film.[11] In November 1968, the MPAA instituted the Classification and Ratings Administration and its age-specific rating categories of G, M, R, and X (now G, PG, PG-13, R, and NC-17). With few exceptions, the horror film was quickly institutionalized as an R-rated genre.[12] The new rating allowed for and arguably legitimated the depiction of gory and unsettling violence that has since characterized cinematic horror, argues Gregory Waller.[13]

The loosening of content restrictions was strongly related to industry polling and assessments of the cinematic marketplace. The major studios discovered that baby boomers, many of them now between the ages of 16 and 24, constituted a majority of the filmgoing public.[14] Industry research also indicated that this young audience was responsive to socially conscious, politically challenging, and otherwise innovative films.[15] Studio brass reacted by handing over an unprecedented amount of creative power to a group of young, politically minded, film-school–trained directors in the hopes of capturing the fancy of cine-literate boomers.[16] Concurrently, from 1969 to 1974, Hollywood suffered a deep fiscal crisis, and the major studios accrued

$600 million in losses. The crisis resulted from a flooding of the market with expensive musicals like *Doctor Dolittle* (1967) and *Hello, Dolly!* (1969).[17] Spurred by the successes of *The Godfather* (1972), *The Exorcist*, *Jaws* (1975), and *Star Wars* (1977), Hollywood embarked on a blockbuster strategy of film-making wherein studios sank more funds into the films thought to have the broadest appeal.[18] This would eventually halt the industry's brief experiment with politically challenging films. Crucially, however, because regional exhi-bition remained vibrant from the late-1960s through the mid-1980s, the major studio's retrenchment practices allowed for independent filmmakers with paltry resources to enter the market—many of whom specialized in the surefire horror market.[19]

Collectively, these industry developments facilitated the production of the more socially critical and transgressive new horror movie. Likewise, these historically specific conditions opened an opportunity space for a group of filmmakers to experiment with and fundamentally challenge the conventions of the horror genre. As I shall show, the creators of new horror films, who were just slightly older than baby boomers, latched onto subject matter that strongly resonated with issues prescient to boomers.

THE MOVIES OF THE NEW HORROR GENRE

Because companies and individual filmmakers invest tremendous amounts of capital in researching, producing, and marketing new films, cinematic expressions provide a particularly ripe indicator of the historical periods that played a part in their gestation. In contrast to other genres, the primary aim of horror cinema is to elicit fear, shock, or disgust in viewers. As Brigid Cherry observes, the creators behind horror films often achieve the genre's task by drawing upon contemporaneous "social upheaval[s], anx-ieties about natural and manmade disasters, conflicts and wars, crime and violence."[20] In this sense, the genre can be seen as an index to and com-mentary on an era's "collective nightmares"[21] or the nightmares of a specific social group.[22] The period of the new horror movie transcodes a culture in despair, trying to come to terms with severe political and social crises, the assassinations of progressive leaders, and the failure of the counterculture movement that had started with such high hopes.

The new horror film refers to an extraordinarily diverse group of texts, encompassing a myriad of cycles and trends as well as curious oddities (e.g., *Let's Scare Jessica to Death* [1971], *Barn of the Naked Dead* [1975], *Frozen Scream* [1975], *Blood Sucking Freaks* [1976]). My analysis will focus on three major trends of the new horror film: what I call apocalyptic horror films, which are characterized by downbeat brutality and wherein normative order fails to be restored in the narrative's denouement; occult and supernatural horror films, which include demonic children, possessed women, and haunted dwellings and wherein changes in sexual mores and family structures are metaphorically grappled with; and revenge of nature horror films, which feature the revolt of mutated or encroached-upon wildlife and wherein humans' negative impact on the environment is brought to the fore. My conclusion will briefly consider the infamous slasher cycle, which has been read as a reactionary response to women's rights and a conservative eulogy to the sexual permissiveness of the 1970s.[23] The categories are meant to be instructive, not rigid constructions. Admittedly, the categories easily blend into each other at times.

This account of the new horror movie will be necessarily selective and neglect numerous key works, variants, and diversions of the film type that would merit discussion in a more rigorous survey.[24] Specifically, I will skip over blaxploitation horror films, such as *Blacula* (1972) and *Sugar Hill* (1974),[25] and the countless horror films produced by exploitation independent filmmakers.[26] Finally, my analysis will exclusively focus on horror films produced for the American market. Because I argue that the new horror film began in earnest in 1968 and that new horror films transcoded the social upheaval of the time, I will set the historical stage of the new horror film in the remainder of this section by highlighting the key events of that year.

The year 1968 has gone down as one of the most infamous years in American history; numerous tensions that had been building in the preceding years erupted in violence and horrifying bloodshed. Once more, for many young baby boomers, there was no happy ending—all hope seemed lost. The year kicked off with the Tet Offensive, one of the deadliest campaigns in the increasingly unpopular Vietnam War. Back home domestic tensions seemingly teetered on the brink of civil war. Numerous progressive figures, including Martin Luther King Jr. and the antiwar Robert F. Kennedy, were gunned down in cold blood. The assassination of King sparked race riots throughout the United States; the assassination of Kennedy evoked stunned apathy. In August, Chicago police beat and gassed peaceful demonstrators outside the Democratic National Convention, effectively turning peaceful protests into life-threatening events. Together with a torrent of disturbing images coming from home and abroad, dreams of peace and love faded into a spirit of violence and pessimism. Then, in November 1968, Richard Nixon's "silent majority" swept him into office. Meanwhile, segregationist candidate George Wallace carried much of the Deep South. For boomers on the political left, the apocalypse had arrived. Horror films are particularly useful in sorting through these and other monumental changes because, to quote Ryan and Kellner, "it is in the horror genre that some of the crucial anxieties, tensions, and fears generated by these changes, especially by feminism, economic crisis, and political liberalism, are played out."[27]

THE APOCALYPTIC NEW HORROR MOVIE

Apocalyptic new horror movies thematically centralize violence in order to horrify and shock their intended audience.[28] Such films typically thrived in and often catered to urban grindhouses (theaters specializing in exploitation fare) and rural southern drive-ins circuits, usually eking out wafer-thin profits on cut-price budgets.[29] At their best they use violence and gore to make provocative social statements; at their worst they devolve to the level of gratuitousness and the politically retrograde. Unfortunately, the bottom of the barrel is quite wide here, containing countless exploitation schlock films such as *Flesh Feast* (1970), *Torture Dungeon* (1970), *The Wizard of Gore* (1970), and *The Corpse Grinders* (1971) that rise to little more than a diarrheic spectacle of subpar stage blood, patently fake severed limbs, and misogynistic sadism. In the hands of capable filmmakers like George Romero (*Night of the Living Dead, Dawn of the Dead* [1979] and *Day of the Dead*), Wes Craven (*Last House on the Left* and *The Hills Have Eyes* [1977]), and Tobe Hooper (*Texas Chainsaw Massacre*), however, apocalyptic horror can spotlight the monstrous aspects of quotidian American life and expose the moral conflicts in all of us (not just the so-called monsters). Moreover, in the denial of reassuring closure, the films position dominant institutions and authorities as primary sources for a variety of social ills.

Night of the Living Dead's narrative, though mostly completed before the events of that year and not widely viewed until 1970, resonated with dire character 1968. The film focuses on a septet of uncooperative survivors who attempt to board themselves into an abandoned farmhouse in order to protect themselves from a marauding horde of flesh-hungry ghouls. With its bickering brother and sister tandem, its strained nuclear family that devours itself, its charred teenage couple, its black hero who is senselessly shot dead by an all-white posse, and its indictment of a flawed media and government response to the situation, the film has been read as a "thoroughgoing critique of American institutions and values"[30] with the zombies representing, according to *Sight and Sound* critic Elliot Stein, Nixon's "moral majority."[31] In many ways, its violent critique without solution was an obituary for the ambitions of counterculture boomers. As Kendall Phillips observes, "its audience consisted of many of those students, intellectuals, and African Americans who had been, and some who still were, involved in the youth revolution of the late-1960s"[32] and who were still trying to figure out what happened. The intensity of *Night of the Living Dead*'s message was actually bolstered by its limitations: the black-and-white film stock hid the shortcomings of its visual effects, which, combined with its use of handheld cameras for action sequences, gave it a cinema vérité style that strongly resembled news reports about Vietnam and police attacks against civil rights protestors.[33]

Throughout Romero's living dead trilogy, the zombies gain a different tenor in relation to their historical context. In *Dawn of the Dead*, zombies become metaphors for many boomers' turn toward conspicuous consumption.[34] That zombies, in a brain-dead state, should instinctually return to a mall is a commentary that virtually anyone can get. By *Day of the Dead*, zombies begin to resemble victims as they are morbidly experimented upon by the deranged Dr. Logan. Produced when many boomers had turned their backs on progressive ideals,[35] the film serves as a broadside against militarism and conservative rollbacks to democratic gains. The military guards represent the reactionary patriarchal underbelly of society: brashly intolerant, uncivil, outright racist, and chauvinistically sexist. As Robin Wood puts it, "what Romero captures, magnificently, is the hysteria of contemporary masculinity, the very excesses of which testify to an anxiety, a terror."[36]

In addition to triggering cash-ins like *Garden of the Dead* (1972), *Children Shouldn't Play with Dead Things* (1973), and a slew of straight-to-video titles in the 1980s, *Night of the Living Dead* set the mold for critically engaged low-budget horror films.[37] Wes Craven recalls how Romero's opus, "more than anything else I can think of, liberated me to make *Last House on the Left*, because I knew that after that there was a whole new kind of film blossoming in American cinema."[38] Craven's contributions to the apocalyptic new horror movie, *The Last House on the Left* and *The Hills Have Eyes*, subvert the family as the moral centerpiece of American social life. Both films humanize the "monsters," and "monstrosize" the heroes, thereby corroding conventional barriers between good and evil. In *The Last House on the Left*, two teenage girls on their way to a concert are ruthlessly raped and murdered by a criminal trio. By happenstance, the killers find shelter with one of the girl's parents, who learn of their daughter's fate. The parents proceed to exact a grisly revenge on the killers, stooping to the same gruesome lows as the killers. In *The Hills Have Eyes* a vacationing middle-class family sees their recreational vehicle break down on an isolated stretch of desert highway. A family of cannibals soon kills the patriarch of the bourgeois family. The film turns into a fight for survival where no one wins in the conclusion. The tit-for-tat brutality between the monster family and the normal family exposes the patriarchal violence at the heart of American domestic life.[39] *Texas Chainsaw Massacre* takes the apocalyptic family in a different direction. This time a tight-knit, though dysfunctional, family of unemployed slaughterhouse workers lays waste to a van full of youngsters. The desperation of their situation reflects that of those who managed to slip through the American social safety net at a time when many were losing trust in the government. The Sawyers, as they are called in *Texas Chainsaw Massacre 2* (1986), put a grotesque face to the damaging impact of forced unemployment as many in the United States wallowed in a recessionary economy.

Taken together, apocalyptic new horror movies fracture the utopian myths of the civilizing process and any idea of moral superiority. Unlike the science fiction genre, these films are often set in a postapocalyptic wasteland not of the future or in a parallel universe. The desolation is in often rural,[40] contemporary America, and the situation is inescapable. Tobe Hooper recalls what led to *Texas Chainsaw Massacre*'s gloom: "Times were turbulent, we were all low on fuel and the outlook was bleak."[41] For his part, Wes Craven likened *The Last House on the Left* to "a howl of anger and pain."[42] Informed by such heartache, the real fear in these films "is that there is nothing we can do that will make any difference at all,"[43] a message that profoundly hit home for many distraught boomers.

The Occult and Supernatural New Horror Film

The occult and supernatural new horror movie represents the most diverse category in this survey. It includes films like *Rosemary's Baby*, *The Exorcist* (its sequels), *It's Alive* (1974) (its sequels), *Carrie* (1976), *The Omen* (1976) (its sequels), *Amityville Horror* (1979) (its sequels), *The Shining* (1980), *Poltergeist* (1982) (its sequels), and *Firestarter* (1984) to name a few. The breadth of this film set traces back to the staggering box-office draws of *Rosemary's Baby* and *The Exorcist*,[44] which invariably encouraged a number of carpet-bagging derivatives. Such films use either possession or spectral hauntings to explore gender relations in the midst of changing socio-sexual and socio-gender dynamics. More often than not, possession themes deal with aspects of femininity such as pregnancy and sexual liberation while spectral hauntings focus on aspects of masculinity such as the decline of middle-class patriarchal authority. In contrast to apocalyptic new horror movies, occult and supernatural new horror films sported comparatively higher budgets (an aspect that jeopardized the bitingness of their critique), contained big name actors, were geared toward wider audiences, and often started out as novels; although a fair share of these films emanated from the low-budget and exploitation sector (e.g. *Abby*, *Angel Above–The Devil Below* [1974], *The Premonition* [1976], and *Nurse Sherri* [1978]).

Occult and supernatural new horror movies emerged at the intersection of several historical events from the late 1960s through the 1970s that redefined understandings of gender and sexuality. Starting in the late 1960s divorce rates started increasing as birthrates began declining. This coincided with widespread access to birth control and, in 1973, legal access to a professionally supervised abortion. The former trend, in particular, underscored the sexual revolution of the 1960s and 1970s as women could now separate coital sex from reproduction.[45] Of course, guardians of moral culture decried the advances in sexual expressiveness, but one of the sources propelling the movement, contraceptive drugs to be exact, came with its own horrific concerns. As appropriate medical dosages for birth control were still being worked out, numerous scientific studies found links between the drugs and blood clotting, which sometimes resulted in death.[46] Furthermore, the thalidomide scare from a few years earlier was still fresh on everyone's mind. All these issues, to one extent or another, were transcoded into occult movies.

Amid the hailstorm of the birth control controversy several texts emerged to turn expectant motherhood and parenthood into a horrifying ordeal.[47] *Rosemary's Baby* inaugurated the film type. Its narrative depicts the titular Rosemary, a hopeful mother-to-be, getting demonically raped in a dream after her husband made a deal with the devil in order to further his acting career. Rosemary carries the pregnancy to term despite gestating the son of the devil. Larry Cohen's *It's Alive* (1974) puts the monstrous pregnancy angle into overdrive by turning newborns into mutated vicious killers. The idea is carried into absurdity in its sequels—*It Lives Again* (1978) and *It's Alive III: Island of the Alive* (1987). The killer baby trilogy may also be related to the revenge of nature film type as the plotlines suggest that pesticide-treated foods and pollution in the environment may be contributing to the mutations. Where some occult films cast a shadow in the womb, others unsheathe fears about women's liberation and female sexuality. In possession films, the perceived wantonness of feminine sexuality turns violent and aggressive when not kept in check by Judeo-Christian patriarchy.[48] *The Exorcist*, for example, shows a fatherless girl, Regan, becoming demonically possessed. Her possession heightens her sexual bravado to the point of lewdly taunting the exorcising priests and even masturbating with a crucifix. Regan is brought under control when tied to the bed, a symbolic act of patriarchal fantasies regarding female submissiveness. The process of the exorcism itself is tantamount to beating the young girl back into the acceptable bounds of prepubescent femininity: sweet, submissive, and seemingly innocent.[49] The films transcend a simplistic explanation. They did, no doubt, transcode very heady changes in women's socio-reproductive status that had accelerated in the late 1960s and early 1970s.[50]

Spectral haunting films take the battleground of horror from women's bodies to the patriarchal sanctuary of the bourgeois home. Films like *The Amityville Horror* (1979), *The Shining* (1980), and *Poltergeist* (1982), in particular, see the home itself become a monstrosizing force on contemporary manhood/fatherhood. Each film, more or less, sees its patriarch turn mad "under pressure from his corrupt and demanding dream house in a period of economic recession," and, in turn, starts "terroriz[ing] his children."[51] The narratives capture the decline of paternal power in the wake of stagnating middle-class wages.[52] In this environment, when many younger boomers were becoming parents, the home was no longer a man's castle but a nightmarish burden—an edifice "in a cold and bleak economic landscape."[53]

Vivian Sobchack makes the point succinctly, "rather than serving bourgeois patriarchy as a place of refuge from the social upheavals of [the 1970s and 1980s], the family has become the site of them."[54]

THE REVENGE OF NATURE NEW HORROR FILM

Revenge of nature new horror movies are the offspring of radioactive monster films from the 1950s (e.g., *Them!* [1954], *Tarantula* [1955], and *The Deadly Mantis* [1957]) brought up to date for the ecological concerns of the late 1960s and early 1970s—concerns that led to the institution of the Environmental Protection Agency in 1970. Their appearance coincided with heightened awareness regarding ecological catastrophe such as the proliferation of nuclear power, toxic waste, and pesticide poisoning.[55] Nuclear radiation remains a mutating force on nature, but it is supplemented by unfettered capitalist expansion in these films. Many of the films concern the creation of monsters that result from industrial pollution or scientific or military experiments gone awry. In the words of Maurice Yacowar, they "provide a frightening reversal of the chain of being, attributing will, mind, and collective power to creatures usually considered to be safely without these qualities."[56] Sometimes titles give the focus of the film away as in *Frogs* (1972), *Grizzly* (1976), *Kingdom of the Spiders* (1977), and *Piranha* (1978). Other times titles were less than revealing, such as *Night of the Lepus* (1972), a film featuring aggressive gigantic rabbits; *The Food of the Gods* (1976), in which any animal ingesting a mysterious foodstuff balloons to amazing size; and *Prophecy* (1979), wherein a mutated bear cub runs amok. Budgets in this category vary quite considerably: *Squirm* (1976) cost an estimated $470,000 to produce and *Prophecy* carried a price tag of $12 million.

Revenge of nature new horror movies trace their lineage back to 1962 with the publication of Rachel Carson's *Silent Spring*, a book that made environmental issues a matter of public debate.[57] In the early 1970s, when many of these films went into production, public discourse was beset by the prospect of ecological disaster from a variety of angles: "overpopulation was joined by numerous other ecological concerns including a new ice age, planetary drying, and global warming as Americans became increasingly concerned about the fragility of life upon the planet."[58] The films transcode the fear that meddling with nature could lead to retaliation from the natural world. *Day of the Animals* (1977), for example, shows how a hole in the ozone layer turns all animals above the 5,000 foot altitude into frothing killers. Frogs and other woodland critters band together to exact vengeance on a wheelchair-bound polluting industrialist and his family in *Frogs*. *The Hellstrom Chronicle* (1971) plays itself as a documentary (it actually won the 1972 Academy Award for Best Feature Documentary) and warns of insects' eventual reign over humanity. *Jaws* emerges as the most successful revenge of nature horror film ever produced, but its success transcends the category. Although not as well remembered as the other categories, the revenge of nature new horror movies dovetailed into "fears of social collapse that were apparent in the 1970s" insofar as the films "mixed apocalyptic despair with an emerging environmental awareness."[59]

CONCLUSION

The era of the new horror film covered in this chapter saw an unprecedented influx of diverse and innovative films. Despite the abundant differences in the films mentioned here and those I was unable to discuss, they are all "seemingly related to the prevalent temper of insecurity, distrust, and lack of confidence" that pervaded much of the late 1960s through the mid-1980s. To remain fresh, however, horror films must change to meet the demands of their primary audience. By the late 1970s many boomers were aging out of the genre, a genre that has historically catered to teenagers and young adults.[60] Starting with the success of *Carrie* (1976), an increasing number of filmmakers began tailoring horror films for the youth market. The practice, Richard Nowell argues, led to the advent of the teen slasher film, or films involving a lone psychopathic murderer stalking and killing (usually) youthful victims.[61] Vera Dika locates the emergence of slasher films to a transitional period in American history, a time that saw the complete reversal of the countercultural ideals that *Night of the Living Dead* first grappled with.[62] Teen slashers, with their violence against women, are seen as punishment for female sexual promiscuity in the 1970s, but this claim has recently been challenged.[63] Regardless, the 1980s brought with it "a sea change in American politics and culture," a time of "renewed optimism and a return to 'traditional' American values,"[64] and slasher films carried the horror genre through the 1980s and into the 1990s.[65]

Though slashers ran with the horror baton for approximately 15 years, the new horror movie left a powerful legacy. Remnants of new horror, especially *Night of the Living Dead* and *Texas Chainsaw Massacre*, helped initiate the body horror film, or those films focusing on the frailties of the human body, which included such films as *The Fly* (1986) and *Hellraiser* (1987).[66] Similarly, *Dawn of the Dead* helped sire the "splatstick" horror film, or horror films that use gore and violence for comedic effect, which included films along the lines of *The Evil Dead* (1981) and *Dead Alive* (1992).[67] New horror films also provided blueprints for what has come to be called the postmodern horror film; these are characterized by the complete collapse of conventional normative boundaries.[68] Moreover, countless new horror movies have been remade in the 21st century (e.g., *Texas Chainsaw Massacre* [2003],

Dawn of the Dead [2004], *Amityville Horror* [2005], *The Hills Have Eyes* [2006], and *The Last House on the Left* [2009] to name a few). Relatedly, let us not forget that the visions of George Romero have served to undergird the current crop of zombie films. Finally, *Night of the Living Dead*, *The Exorcist*, and *Halloween* have been preserved by the National Film Registry as "culturally, historically, or aesthetically significant films." Importantly, for many of the baby boomers who first saw these films, the new horror movie provided a safe seat from which to consider the tumultuous social changes taking place outside the confines of the movie theater. The new horror movie projected their nightmares on the silver screen.

NOTES

1. Kevin Heffernan, *Ghouls, Gimmicks, and Gold: Horror Films and the American Movie Business, 1953–1968* (Durham, NC: Duke University Press, 2004), 155–179, 229–261.

2. David J. Skal, *The Monster Show: A Cultural History of Horror* (New York: Faber and Faber, 2001), 277, 278.

3. Wheeler Winston Dixon, *A History of Horror* (New Brunswick, NJ: Rutgers University Press, 2010), 123–124; Kim Newman, *Nightmare Movies: Horror on Screen Since the 1960s* (London: Bloomsbury, 2011), 10–25; Kendall R. Phillips, *Dark Directions: Romero, Craven, Carpenter, and the Modern Horror Film* (Carbondale: Southern Illinois University Press, 2012), 1–15; Gregory A. Waller, "Introduction," in *American Horrors: Essays on the Modern American Horror Film*, ed. Gregory A. Waller (Urbana: University of Illinois Press, 1987), 4–6.

4. These critiques focused on a welter of social issues, including capitalism, patriarchy, the environment, and racism.

5. Dana B. Polan, "Eros and Syphilization: The Contemporary Horror Film," in *Planks of Reason: Essays on the Horror Film*, ed. Barry Keith Grant and Christopher Sharrett (Lanham, MD: Scarecrow Press, 2004), 142–152; Robin Wood, "An Introduction to the American Horror Film," in *Planks of Reason: Essays on the Horror Film*, ed. Barry Keith Grant and Christopher Sharrett (Lanham, MD: Scarecrow Press, 2004), 107–141.

6. Phillips, *Dark Directions*, 169–173; Michael Ryan and Douglas Kellner, *Camera Politica: The Politics and Ideology of Contemporary Hollywood Film* (Bloomington: Indiana University Press, 1988), 185–193; Christopher Sharrett, "The Horror Film in Neoconservative Culture," *Journal of Popular Film and Television* 21, no. 3 (1993): 100–110.

7. Richard Nowell, "'Between Dreams and Reality': Genre Personae, Brand Elm Street, and Repackaging the American Teen Slasher Film," *Iluminace* 24, no. 3 (2012): 69–101.

8. Ryan and Kellner, *Camera Politica*, 12–13.

9. Stephen Prince, *Visions of Empire: Political Imagery in Contemporary American Film* (Westport, CT: Praeger, 1992), 2–8, 49–79.

10. Stephen Prince, "The Hemorrhaging of American Cinema: *Bonnie and Clyde*'s Legacy of Cinematic Violence," in *Arthur Penn's* Bonnie and Clyde, ed. Lester D. Friedman (New York: Cambridge University Press, 2000), 132.

11. "'Brutal Films Pale Before Televised Vietnam'—Valenti," *Variety*, February 21, 1968, 2, 26.

12. David A. Cook, *Lost Illusions: American Cinema in the Shadow of Watergate and Vietnam, 1970–1979* (Berkeley: University of California Press, 2000), 222–226; Richard Nowell, *Blood Money: A History of the First Teen Slasher Film Cycle* (New York: Continuum, 2011), 24–41.

13. Waller, "Introduction," 5.

14. Cook, *Lost Illusions*, 398–399.

15. Aniko Bodroghkozy, "Reel Revolutionaries: An Examination of Hollywood's Cycle of 1960s Youth Rebellion Films," *Cinema Journal* 41, no. 3 (2002): 38–58.

16. Cook, *Lost Illusions*, 67–72.

17. Ibid., 25–26.

18. Cook, *Lost Illusions*, 26–68; Thomas Schatz, "The New Hollywood," in *Film Theory Goes to the Movies*, ed. Jim Collins, Hilary Radner, and Ava Preacher Collins (New York: Routledge, 1993), 17–25.

19. Stephen Thrower, *Nightmare USA: The Untold Story of the Exploitation Independents* (Surrey, UK: FAB Press, 2007), 11-48.

20. Brigid Cherry, *Horror* (New York: Routledge, 2009), 11.

21. Wood, "An Introduction to the American Horror Film," 117.

22. Matt Becker, "A Point of Little Hope: Hippie Horror Films and the Politics of Ambivalence," *Velvet Light Trap* 57 (2006): 42–59.

23. Vera Dika, "The Stalker Film, 1978-81," in *American Horrors: Essays on the Modern American Horror Film*, ed. Gregory A. Waller (Urbana: University of Illinois Press, 1987), 98–99; Fred Molitor and Barry S. Sapolsky, "Sex, Violence and Victimization in Slasher Films," *Journal of Broadcasting and Electronic Media* 37. no. 2 (1993): 233–242; Kendall R. Phillips, *Projected Fears: Horror Films and American Culture* (Westport, CT: Praeger, 2005), 129–132; Ryan and Kellner, *Camera Politica*, 185–193.

24. It should be mentioned that virtually any film that attained any modicum of success, however parochial, spawned a flurry of mostly uninspired imitators. For a more complete survey of the trends discussed in this chapter, see Newman, *Nightmare Movies*, 10–25, 43–140, 177–250, 270–293.

25. Robin R. Means Coleman, *Horror Noire: Blacks in American Horror Films from the 1890s to Present* (New York: Routledge, 2011), 118–144.

26. Thrower, *Nightmare USA*, passim.

27. Ryan and Kellner, *Camera Politica*, 169.

28. Ibid., 169-170.

29. Ed Lowry, "Dimension Pictures: Portrait of a 1970s' Independent," in *Contemporary American Independent Film: From Margins to the Mainstream*, ed. Chris Holmlund and Justin Wyatt (New York: Routledge, 2005), 42–43; Thrower, *Nightmare USA*, passim.

30. Waller, "Introduction," 4.

31. Elliot Stein, "*Night of the Living Dead.*" *Sight and Sound* (Spring 1970): 105.

32. Phillips, *Projected Fears*, 92.

33. It is important to note that Romero has both embraced and denied any political commentary in the narrative of *Night of the Living Dead*; see interviews reprinted in Tony Williams, *George A. Romero Interviews* (Jackson: University of Mississippi Press, 2011).

34. Christopher Lasch, *The Culture of Narcissism: American Life in an Age of Diminishing Expectations* (New York: W.W. Norton, 1991), passim.

35. Peter Collier and David Horowitz, "Lefties for Reagan," *Washington Post Magazine*, March 17, 1985, 8.

36. Robin Wood, *Hollywood from Vietnam to Reagan . . . and Beyond* (New York: Columbia University Press, 2003), 290.

37. Cook, *Lost Illusions*, 222–223; Ryan and Kellner, *Camera Politica*, 182; Waller, "Introduction," 4.

38. Joe Kane, Night of the Living Dead: *Behind the Scenes of the Most Terrifying Zombie Movie Ever* (New York: Citadel Press, 2010), xvi.

39. D. N. Rodowick, "The Enemy within: The Economy of Violence in *The Hills Have Eyes*," in *Planks of Reason: Essays on the Horror Film*, ed. Barry Keith Grant and Christopher Sharrett (Lanham, MD: Scarecrow Press, 2004), 347.

40. David Bell, "Anti-Idyll: Rural Horror," in *Contested Countryside Cultures: Otherness, Marginalization and Rurality*, ed. Paul Cloke and Jo Little (New York: Routledge, 1997), 94–108.

41. Quoted in Becker, "A Point of Little Hope," 58.

42. Ibid.

43. R. H. W. Dillard, "*Nightmare of the Dead*: It's Not Like Just a Wind That's Passing Through," in *American Horrors: Essays on the Modern American Horror Film*, ed. Gregory A. Waller (Urbana: University of Illinois Press, 1987), 28. Though writing on *Night of the Living Dead* specifically, Dillard's comments can be applied to the films discussed in this section.

44. In their year of release, *Rosemary's Baby* was the seventh highest grossing film in 1968; *The Exorcist* came in second in 1974. See "Big Rental Films of 1968," *Variety*, January 8, 1969, 15; "Big Rental Films of 1974," *Variety*, January 8, 1975, 24, 75.

45. Andrew J. Cherlin, *The Marriage-Go-Round: The State of Marriage and the Family in America Today* (New York: Alfred A. Knopf, 2009), 90–97.

46. Skal, *Monster Show*, 288.

47. Ibid., 387–305.

48. Phillips, *Projected Fears*, 118; Ryan and Kellner, *Camera Politica*, 58.

49. Ryan and Kellner, *Camera Politica*, 58.

50. Skal, *Monster Show*, 302–304.

51. Vivian Sobchack, "Bringing It All Back Home: Family Economy and Generic Exchange," in *American Horrors: Essays on the Modern American Horror Film*, ed. Gregory A. Waller (Urbana: University of Illinois Press, 1987), 184.

52. Ibid., 184–188.

53. Ryan and Kellner, *Camera Politica*, 174.

54. Sobchack, "Bringing It All Back Home," 178.

55. Ryan and Kellner, *Camera Politica*, 179.

56. Maurice Yacowar, "The Bug in the Rug: Notes on the Disaster Genre," in *Film Genre Reader IV*, ed. Barry Keith Grant (Austin: University of Texas Press, 2012), 314.

57. Ralph H. Lutts, "Chemical Fallout: Rachel Carson's *Silent Spring*, Radioactive Fallout, and the Environmental Movement," *Environmental Review* 9, no. 3 (1985): 210–225.

58. Phillips, *Dark Projections*, 110.

59. Peter Hutchings, *The A to Z of Horror Cinema* (Lanham, MD: Scarecrow, 2008), 263.

60. Richard Nowell, "'There's More Than One Way to Lose Your Heart': The American Film Industry, Early Teen Slasher Films, and Female Youth," *Cinema Journal* 51, no. 1 (2011): 118–122.

61. Nowell, *Blood Money*, passim.

62. Dika, "The Stalker Film, 1978-81," 97.

63. Nowell, *Blood Money*, 1–7.

64. Phillips, *Dark Visions*, 169.

65. Rick Worland, *The Horror Film: An Introduction* (New York: Blackwell, 2008), 104–112.

66. Michael Grant, "Body Horror," in *The Cinema Book*, 3rd ed., ed. Pam Cook (London: British Film Institute, 2007), 355–360.

67. Kyle William Bishop, *American Zombie Gothic: The Rise and Fall (and Rise) of the Walking Dead in Popular Culture* (Jefferson, NC: McFarland, 2010), 15–16.

68. Isabel Cristina Pinedo, *Recreational Terror: Women and the Pleasures of Horror Film Viewing* (Albany: State University of New York Press, 1997), 9–50.

REFERENCES

Becker, Matt "A Point of Little Hope: Hippie Horror Films and the Politics of Ambivalence." *Velvet Light Trap* 57 (2006): 42–59.

Bell, David. "Anti-Idyll: Rural Horror," In *Contested Countryside Cultures: Otherness, Marginalization and Rurality*, edited by Paul Cloke and Jo Little, 94–108. New York: Routledge, 1997.

"Big Rental Films of 1968." *Variety*, January 8, 1969, 15.

"Big Rental Films of 1974." *Variety*, January 8, 1975, 24, 75.

Bishop, Kyle William. *American Zombie Gothic: The Rise and Fall (and Rise) of the Walking Dead in Popular Culture*. Jefferson, NC: McFarland, 2010.

Bodroghkozy, Aniko. "Reel Revolutionaries: An Examination of Hollywood's Cycle of 1960s Youth Rebellion Films." *Cinema Journal* 41 (2002): 38–58.

"'Brutal Films Pale Before Televised Vietnam'—Valenti." *Variety*, February 21, 1968, 2, 26.

Cherlin, Andrew J. *The Marriage-Go-Round: The State of Marriage and the Family in America Today*. New York: Alfred A. Knopf, 2009.

Cherry, Brigid. *Horror*. New York: Routledge, 2009.

Collier, Peter, and David Horowitz. "Lefties for Reagan." *Washington Post Magazine*, March 17, 1985, 8.

Cook, David A. *Lost Illusions: American Cinema in the Shadow of Watergate and Vietnam, 1970–1979*. Berkeley: University of California Press, 2000.

Dika, Vera. "The Stalker Film, 1978-81." In *American Horrors: Essays on the Modern American Horror Film*, edited by Gregory A. Waller, 85–101. Urbana: University of Illinois Press, 1987.

Dillard, R. H. W. "*Nightmare of the Dead:* It's Not Like Just a Wind That's Passing Through." In *American Horrors: Essays on the Modern American Horror Film*, edited by Gregory A. Waller, 14–29. Urbana: University of Illinois Press, 1987.

Dixon, Wheeler Winston. *A History of Horror.* New Brunswick, NJ: Rutgers University Press, 2010.

Grant, Michael. "Body Horror." In *The Cinema Book*, 3rd ed., edited by Pam Cook, 355–360. London: British Film Institute, 2007.

Heffernan, Kevin. *Ghouls, Gimmicks, and Gold: Horror Films and the American Movie Business, 1953–1968.* Durham, NC: Duke University Press, 2004.

Hutchings, Peter. *The A to Z of Horror Cinema.* Lanham, MD: Scarecrow Press, 2008.

Kane, Joe. *Night of the Living Dead: Behind the Scenes of the Most Terrifying Zombie Movie Ever.* New York: Citadel Press, 2010

Lasch, Christopher. *The Culture of Narcissism: American Life in an Age of Diminishing Expectations.* New York: W. W. Norton, 1991.

Lowry, Ed. "Dimension Pictures: Portrait of a 1970s' Independent." In *Contemporary American Independent Film: From Margins to the Mainstream*, edited by Chris Holmlund and Justin Wyatt, 41–52. New York: Routledge, 2005

Lutts, Ralph H. "Chemical Fallout: Rachel Carson's *Silent Spring*, Radioactive Fallout, and the Environmental Movement." *Environmental Review* 9 (1985): 210–225.

Means Coleman, Robin R. *Horror Noire: Blacks in American Horror Films from the 1890s to Present.* New York: Routledge, 2011.

Molitor, Fred, and Barry S. Sapolsky. "Sex, Violence and Victimization in Slasher Films." *Journal of Broadcasting and Electronic Media* 37 (1993): 233–242.

Newman, Kim. *Nightmare Movies: Horror on Screen since the 1960s.* London: Bloomsbury, 2011.

Nowell, Richard. *Blood Money: A History of the First Teen Slasher Film Cycle.* New York: Continuum, 2011.

Nowell, Richard. "'The Ambitions of Most Independent Filmmakers': Indie Production, the Majors, and *Friday the 13th* (1980)." *Journal of Film and Video* 63 (2011): 28–44.

Nowell, Richard. "'Between Dreams and Reality': Genre Personae, Brand Elm Street, and Repackaging the American Teen Slasher Film." *Iluminace* 24 (2012): 69–101.

Phillips, Kendall R. *Projected Fears: Horror Films and American Culture.* Westport, CT: Praeger, 2005.

Phillips, Kendall R. *Dark Directions: Romero, Craven, Carpenter, and the Modern Horror Film.* Carbondale: Southern Illinois University Press, 2012.

Pinedo, Isabel Cristina. *Recreation Terror: Women and the Pleasures of Horror Film Viewing.* Albany: State University of New York Press, 1997.

Polan, Dana B. "Eros and Syphilization: The Contemporary Horror Film." In *Planks of Reason: Essays on the Horror Film*, edited by Barry Keith Grant and Christopher Sharrett, 142–152. Lanham, MD: Scarecrow Press, 2004.

Prince, Stephen. *Visions of Empire: Political Imagery in Contemporary American Film.* Westport, CT: Praeger, 1992.

Prince, Stephen. "The Hemorrhaging of American Cinema: *Bonnie and Clyde*'s Legacy of Cinematic Violence." In *Penn's* Bonnie and Clyde, edited by Lester D. Friedman, 127–147. New York: Cambridge University Press, 2000.

Rodowick, D. N. "The Enemy within: The Economy of Violence in *The Hills Have Eyes*." In *Planks of Reason: Essays on the Horror Film*, edited by Barry Keith Grant and Christopher Sharrett, 346–355. Lanham, MD: Scarecrow Press, 2004.

Ryan, Michael, and Douglas Kellner. *Camera Politica: The Politics and Ideology of Contemporary Hollywood Film*. Bloomington: Indiana University Press, 1988.

Schatz, Thomas. "The New Hollywood." In *Film Theory Goes to the Movies*, edited by Jim Collins, Ava Preacher Collins, and Hilary Radner, 8–36. New York: Routledge, 1993.

Sharrett, Christopher. "The Horror Film in Neoconservative Culture." *Journal of Popular Film and Television* 21 (1993): 100–110.

Skal, David J. *The Monster Show: A Cultural History of Horror*. New York: Faber and Faber, 2001.

Sobchack, Vivian. "Bringing It All Back Home: Family Economy and Generic Exchange." In *American Horrors: Essays on the Modern American Horror Film*, edited by Gregory A. Waller, 174–194. Urbana: University of Illinois Press, 1987.

Stein, Elliot. "*Night of the Living Dead*." *Sight and Sound* (Spring 1970): 105.

Thrower, Stephen. *Nightmare USA: The Untold Story of the Exploitation Independents*. Surrey, UK: FAB Press, 2007.

Waller, Gregory A. "Introduction." In *American Horrors: Essays on the Modern American Horror Film*, edited by Gregory A. Waller, 1–13. Urbana: University of Illinois Press, 1987.

Williams, Tony, ed. *George A. Romero: Interviews*. Jackson, MS: University Press of Mississippi, 2011.

Wood, Robin. *Hollywood from Vietnam to Reagan . . . and Beyond*. New York: Columbia University Press, 2003.

Wood, Robin. "An Introduction to the American Horror Film." In *Planks of Reason: Essays on the Horror Film*, edited by Barry Keith Grant and Christopher Sharrett, 107–141. Lanham, MD: Scarecrow Press, 2004.

Worland, Rick. *The Horror Film: An Introduction*. New York: Blackwell, 2008.

Yacowar, Maurice. "The Bug in the Rug: Notes on the Disaster Genre." In *Film Genre Reader IV*, edited by Barry Keith Grant, 313–331. Austin: University of Texas Press, 2012.

11

Rock Music on Film: A Selective Chronology

Sarah Boslaugh

(Editors' note: If it can be argued that the baby boomers had a soundtrack, most of that soundtrack would comprise rock and roll, but rock and roll was not merely an auditory phenomenon; there was always a visual aspect to it as well. In this chronology, author Sarah Boslaugh annotates key moments in movie representations of rock and roll from its inception until the present day.)

1956 *Rock Around the Clock* features the hit single of the same name, performed by Bill Haley & the Comets, and performances by the Platters, Freddie Bell and the Bellboys, and a pre-scandal Alan Freed.

1956 Frank Tashlin's leering live-action cartoon, *The Girl Can't Help It*, is enlivened by the performances of, among others, Little Richard, Gene Vincent, and Fats Domino.

1957 Elvis Presley's third film, *Jailhouse Rock*, signals the ascendancy of bad-boy rock and roll, as exemplified by the music of Presley's character Vince Everett, over the sweet but sadly passé country sound of his musical cellmate Hunk Houghton (Mickey Shaughnessy).

1958 Elvis Presley stars in the Michael Curtiz film *King Creole*, playing a high school student who hopes his vocal talents will be enough to raise his family out of poverty. Reportedly Presley's favorite among all his films, it is well regarded by critics as well.

1963 Ann-Margret stars in the musical comedy *Bye Bye Birdie*, directed by George Sidney, as the high school girl chosen to give the last kiss to teen heartthrob Conrad Birdie (a character based on Elvis Presley) before he is inducted into the army.

1964   Albert and David Maysles's *What's Happening! The Beatles in the U.S.A.* documents the Beatles' first U.S. visit; the footage is later reedited for the 1991 film *The Beatles: The First U.S. Visit.*

1964   Elvis Presley and Ann-Margret costar as a racecar driver and a swimming instructor in *Viva Las Vegas*, one of Presley's better-regarded films.

1964   Richard Lester's *A Hard Day's Night* showcases the musical talents of the Beatles and helps cement their images as likable young lads trying their best to cope with their newfound fame; the film's screenplay and score are both nominated for Academy Awards.

1965   The Beatles' music carries the day in *Help!*, Lester's follow-up to *A Hard Day's Night*, helping viewers overlook an elaborately silly (and potentially offensive) plot involving a mysterious Eastern cult whose members are played primarily by white actors in dark makeup.

1966   Andy Warhol's documentary *The Velvet Underground and Nico: A Symphony of Sound*, filmed in black-and-white, presents the band rehearsing until the police arrive, ostensibly because of a noise complaint.

1966   The television documentary *The Beatles at Shea Stadium*, focused on the band's 1965 concert in New York City, first airs on the BBC; in the United States, it is first seen on ABC in 1967.

1967   Bob Dylan flashes plenty of surly attitude in D. A. Pennebaker's documentary *Dont Look Back* [sic], shot during Dylan's 1965 concert tour of the United Kingdom; the film includes performances by Dylan and Joan Baez and opens with a proto-music video of Bob Dylan's "Subterranean Homesick Blues."

1967   The Beatles' television film, *Magical Mystery Tour*, airs on the BBC to poor response from critics and the public alike; it is released in U.S. theaters in 1974.

1967   Sex and drugs (LSD) occupy most of the plot in Roger Corman's *The Trip*, but music by the blues-rock group the American Music Band is also key to the film's experience.

1968   In *Sympathy for the Devil*, Jean-Luc Godard juxtaposes footage of the Rolling Stones writing and recording their hit song of the same name with shots of, among other things, the Black Panthers and Anne Wiazemsky (then Godard's wife) playing a character identified only as "Eve Democracy."

1968 The made-for-TV band the Monkees stars in the comedy film *Head*, a critical and commercial failure that has since acquired something of a cult following.

1968 The animated film *Yellow Submarine* features a Beatles soundtrack drawn from their *Revolver* and *Sgt. Pepper's Lonely Hearts Club Band* albums, plus some original songs, and a plot in which their cartoon avatars must free an undersea paradise, Pepperiarel, from the Blue Meanies.

1969 The open road has never looked more alluring (particularly to disaffected youth) than in Dennis Hopper's *Easy Rider*, as Hopper, Peter Fonda, and Jack Nicholson traverse the country on choppers accompanied by a soundtrack including Jimi Hendrix, the Byrds, Bob Dylan, and the Band.

1969 Arlo Guthrie stars as a bohemian draft dodger in Arthur Penn's *Alice's Restaurant*, a love letter to the counterculture based on the musical monologue "Alice's Restaurant Massacree" released in 1967 on Guthrie's album *Alice's Restaurant*.

1969 Elvis Presley's movie career fizzles out with his final feature film, *Change of Habit*, which stars Presley as an inner-city physician who falls in love with a nun (played by Mary Tyler Moore) who works at his medical clinic.

1968 Despite the title, many rock performers are featured in *Monterey Pop*, a documentary of the 1967 Monterey Pop Festival; among those appearing are Eric Burdon and the Animals, Jimi Hendrix, Janis Joplin, Big Brother and the Holding Company, and the Who.

1970 Michael Wadleigh's documentary *Woodstock* captures not only the music but also the communal experience of the legendary festival; featured performers include Joan Baez; the Who; Crosby, Stills & Nash; Jefferson Airplane; Santana; Janis Joplin; and Jimi Hendrix.

1970 The darker side of rock culture is explored in *Gimme Shelter*, directed by Albert and David Maysles and Charlotte Zwerlin, which centers on a Rolling Stones' concert at Altamont Speedway in California. During the concert, a disorderly crowd member was stabbed to death by members of the Hells Angels motorcycle club who had been hired to provide security.

1970 The Beatles rehearse and record their final album and rehearse for a concert that never happened in Michael Lindsay-Hogg's documentary *Let It Be*. The film captures their legendary and final live unannounced performance on the roof of the Apple Records studio in London.

1971   Many luminaries of the folk rock scene appear in the concert film *Celebration at Big Sur*, directed by Baird Bryant and Joanna Demetrakas, including Joan Baez, Joni Mitchell, and Crosby, Stills, Nash & Young.

1971   The film *200 Motels*, written and directed by Frank Zappa and Tony Palmer, offers a surreal view of life as a touring band and features performances by the Mothers of Invention, Ringo Starr, and Theo Bikel.

1972   *Concert for Bangladesh*, directed by Saul Swimmer, documents the 1971 concerts organized by Ravi Shankar and George Harrison to raise money for those affected by the Bangladesh Liberation War; Eric Clapton, Bob Dylan, Leon Russell, Ringo Starr, Shankar, and Harrison are among the many performers who appear in this film.

1972   In *Fillmore*, Richard T. Heffron captures the last concert at the historic Fillmore West concert venue in San Francisco; performers include the Grateful Dead, Jefferson Airplane, Santana, and Elvin Bishop.

1972   Adrian Maben's concert film *Pink Floyd: Live at Pompeii* features the band performing, without an audience, at an ancient Roman amphitheater.

1972   John Lennon and Yoko Ono star in their self-directed, self-produced film *Imagine*, which includes home movies and TV clips as well as performances by John, Yoko, and the Plastic Ono Band.

1972   Reggae is introduced to a wide audience on the soundtrack of *The Harder They Come*, directed by Perry Henzell and featuring the singer Jimmy Cliff as a young Jamaican musician who becomes involved in crime after he can't get a fair shake in the music business.

1973   The Andrew Lloyd Webber and Tim Rice hit musical *Jesus Christ Superstar*, based on a concept album and Broadway musical of the same name, is brought to film by Norman Jewison with mixed success.

1973   The weirdness of David Bowie's glam-rock years is captured in D. A. Pennebaker's *Ziggy Stardust and the Spiders from Mars*, which revolves around Bowie's final concert in that persona.

1973   A contemporary Madison Square Garden concert forms the centerpiece of Robert Abel and Sid Levin's documentary *Let the Good Times Roll*, which also includes interviews and archival footage of performances from the 1950s; performers include Chuck Berry, Bo Diddley, Little Richard, and Chubby Checker.

1974   Harry Nilsson provides the music and stars in the title role in Freddie Francis's *Son of Dracula,* produced by Ringo Starr, who also appears in the film as Merlin the magician.

1975   Jim Sharman's film version of the stage musical *The Rocky Horror Picture Show* overcomes so-so critical response to become one of the most popular cult films ever, with audience participation becoming more or less mandatory at midnight showings.

1975   A film of the rock opera *Tommy,* directed by Ken Russell and based on the double album of the same name released by the Who in 1969, features performances by, among others, Pete Townshend, Roger Daltrey, Ann-Margret, Tina Turner, Elton John, and Eric Clapton.

1976   Lonette McKee, Irene Cara, and Dawn Smith star as a girl group with problems in Sam O'Steen's *Sparkle,* which is also notable for a soundtrack by Curtis Mayfield.

1976   The Led Zeppelin concert film *The Song Remains the Same,* directed by Peter Clifton and Joe Massot, combines footage from several 1973 concerts plus additional shots captured in the studio.

1977   John Travolta rockets to stardom as the best (white, nongay) male dancer most people know in *Saturday Night Fever,* while director John Badham captures a sense of the central role played by disco in the social life of contemporary teenagers. The soundtrack features the music of the Bee Gees.

1977   Country musician Earl Scruggs is the central focus in Richard Abramson and Michael Varhol's documentary *Banjoman,* but he is joined in concert by some luminaries of the folk rock scene, including Joan Baez and the Byrds.

1978   *All You Need Is Cash,* written by Eric Idle and Neil Innes and directed by Eric Idle and Gary Weis, stars the parody group the Rutles (Eric Idle, John Halsey, Ricky Fataar, Neil Innes) and generally spoofs the Beatles' music and films.

1978   The original, satirical tone of Warren Casey and Jim Jacob's stage musical *Grease* is all but lost in the film version, directed by Randal Kleiser and starring John Travolta and Olivia Newton-John as a 1950s-era greaser and his lady love, but adoring audiences hardly seem to notice.

1978   Martin Scorsese's *The Last Waltz* documents the final (1976) concert of the Band, which also features performances from numerous guest stars, including Bob Dylan, Eric Clapton, Van Morrison, Dr. John, and Joni Mitchell.

1979   First-time director and long-time fan Jeff Stein's documentary about the Who, *The Kids Are Alright*, captures the band's spirit and style, as well as their music, through well-combined interviews and performance clips.

1979   The groundbreaking rock musical *Hair*, which opened in New York City in 1967, is brought to film by the Czech director Milos Forman. Although some (including the musical's creators Gerome Ragni, James Rado, and Galt MacDermot) feel the film misses the countercultural message of the stage musical, it is generally a critical and popular success.

1979   Bette Midler shows off her acting and singing talents in *The Rose*, playing a troubled singer bearing more than a little resemblance to Janis Joplin; the film is nominated for four Oscars, and the title song becomes a hit single.

1979   Teenage angst of the British, early 1960s variety, seethes throughout *Quadrophenia*, a nonmusical film loosely based on the rock opera of the same name by the Who. Forget the remake of *Brighton Rock*—if you want the low-down on the 1964 clashes between the mods and rockers in Brighton, this is the film to see. Added attraction: Sting plays a mod known as "Ace Face."

1980   If you can take John Landis's *The Blues Brothers* as a satire (how come so many great African American musicians are working at other jobs?), this will free you up to enjoy the performances of Aretha Franklin, Ray Charles, James Brown, and Cab Calloway, among others; otherwise, it's just another film about white people co-opting African American music.

1980   Paul McCartney and Wings are the featured performers in the concert film *Rockshow*, which includes parts of four concerts during their 1976 tour of North America.

1980   In *Divine Madness*, Michael Ritchie captures the energy and the music (and general outrageousness) of Bette Midler's live stage show; songs include "The Rose," "You Can't Always Get What You Want," and "Leader of the Pack."

1980   Robert Kaylor's *Carny* stars Robbie Robertson, former lead guitarist of the Band, as co-operator (with Gary Busey) of a low-rent traveling carnival; Robertson also co-wrote and produced the film. Not a musical, but close in spirit.

1980   The kitschy *Can't Stop the Music*, directed by Nancy Walker, pairs Olympic decathlon champion Bruce Jenner with the disco group the Village People in a film that is notable as the first winner of the Golden Raspberry for Worst Picture.

1980   Paul Simon plays the central character, a musician/father who's lost his way, in *One Trick Pony*, but the real appeal are musical performances by Simon, the Lovin' Spoonful, and Sam and Dave, among others.

1982   Alan Parker's *Pink Floyd–The Wall*, based on the 1979 Pink Floyd album *The Wall*, mixes live action and animation to tell a densely symbolic story about a young man named Pink (played by Bob Geldof) who's having a tough go of it.

1984   Jonathan Demme's concert film *Stop Making Sense* captures the Talking Heads performing over three nights at the Pantages Theater in Los Angeles; notably, it features long takes of performances on stage rather than quick cuts, and it seldom cuts to the audience, thus reproducing something of the feel of being at one of the performances.

1984   Rob Reiner's mockumentary *This Is Spinal Tap*, starring Christopher Guest, Michael McKean, and Harry Shearer, captures the many absurdities of the metal scene and of touring band life in general. "This goes go to eleven!"

1984   Before Prince's name became an unpronounceable symbol, he starred as "The Kid" in *Purple Rain*, by director Albert Magnoli, which included three hit singles—"When Doves Cry," "Let's Go Crazy" and "Purple Rain"—and won an Academy Award for Best Original Song Score.

1985   Madonna stars as the mysterious Susan Thomas in Susan Seidelman's feature film *Desperately Seeking Susan*, which also stars Rosanna Arquette and Aidan Quinn.

1988   You're not likely to find *Superstar: The Karen Carpenter Story* at any legitimate movie theater or rental house because director Todd Haynes didn't bother getting permission to use either the Carpenters' music or Mattel's trademarked Ken and Barbie dolls. Still, it's more than worth seeking out, as Haynes artfully skewers the pretensions of the Carpenters' squeaky-clean image and the many absurdities of 1970s culture. Not a full length feature, but a pivotal indie film.

1988   Leave it to John Waters to imagine a world in which rock and roll can defeat racism, big girls have more fun, and the best woman for the role may be a man. It all happens in the original film of *Hairspray*, featuring Ricki Lake, Sonny Bono, Deborah Harry, and Divine.

1991   According to Alan Parker's comedy *The Commitments*, the Irish are the blacks of Europe, a premise he sells pretty well in this feature about a group of working class young people who form a soul band in Dublin. The soundtrack includes many hit songs, including "Chain of Fools," "Mustang Sally," "Try a Little Tenderness," and "In the Midnight Hour."

1991   Madonna's "Blond Ambition" tour is the focus of Alek Keshishian's film *Madonna: Truth or Dare*, one of the most financially successful documentaries of all time. Notably, *Truth or Dare* is shot primarily in black-and-white; only the concert sequences are presented in color.

2002   Paul Justman's documentary *Standing in the Shadows of Motown* brings recognition to the house musicians (they call themselves "the Funk Brothers") at the Motown recording studio; the soundtrack won two Grammy Awards in 2004, and the Funk Brothers were presented with a Grammy for lifetime achievement in 2004.

2004   *Metallica: Some Kind of Monster*, directed by Joe Berlinger and Bruce Sinofsky, documents the heavy-metal band at a time of crisis, as one member quits the band and another leaves to undergo rehabilitation for alcoholism. Notably, Berlinger and Sinofsky previously used Metallica's music as a key feature in their 1994 documentary *Paradise Lost*, focused on the trial of the West Memphis Three.

2006   *The U.S. vs. John Lennon*, a documentary directed by David Leaf and John Scheinfeld, focuses on John Lennon's battles with the U.S. government in the 1960s and early 1970s.

2008   The life and work of punk-rock poet and musician Patti Smith, a fixture on the New York City arts scene since the 1960s, are the focus of Stephen Sebring's documentary *Patti Smith: Dream of Life*.

Part 3

Popular Music

12

"It's Only Rock-'n'-Roll": The Rise of the Contemporary Popular Music Industry as a Defining Factor in the Creation of Boomer Culture

Thom Gencarelli

The birth and growth of the popular music industry from the middle to the latter part of the 20th century maps the birth and rise of baby boomer culture. Not only do the two happen concomitantly with one another but modern, rock-based popular music is also a key defining feature with respect to boomer identity and cultural production.

Of course, it can be said that *two* mass media developments define boomer culture in the United States more than any other cultural developments. The other is television, in that the advent and evolution of the television industry after World War II also parallels the rise of the boomer generation; that television programming during its early years (the 1950s and 1960s) was mostly produced for and targeted toward the white, suburban populace of the postwar boon years and the Great Society; and that boomers were the first generation to be raised with television in their lives and who would never know a world without it. The sole difference between television and music, however, with respect to boomer culture and identity is that music has always been *cool*. Most of the people within the demographic with which this collection is concerned have always proudly and emphatically identified with music that was *theirs* as they came of age. In the case of television, however, there has always been a certain ambivalence, which former Federal Communications Commission (FCC) chair Newton

Minow spoke to in 1961 when he described so much of the television programming from the turn of the 1950s into the 1960s as a "vast wasteland."

It is also important to note that popular music and the popular music industry, as opposed to television, existed before the postwar years and that music itself of course has existed for the greater part of the civilized history of our species. However, just like the birth and growth of the television industry, the growth of what we have come to recognize and understand as the *modern* popular music industry—even at the present moment in time when its fortunes and even its very existence seem to be imperiled—did not happen until after World War II.

This chapter seeks to fulfill three purposes. The first is to explain the development of the modern popular music industry as a postwar development, and thus as an industry that arose concurrent with the rise of the baby boomer generation. Following from this, a second, more significant, purpose is to tell this story in such a way as to illuminate how the stars aligned with respect to the creation and explosion of popular music and its place as a defining factor in boomer culture. This story is one about: (a) the technologies for music creation and production, (b) the history of media in the 20th century, and (c) the evolution of the music itself. As a result, the structure of the chapter is based on the telling of this story. Finally, the third purpose is to argue and justify the argument that rock-based popular music is not merely *as* important to boomer culture as television but that it is, in significant and essential ways, *more* important.

To achieve these purposes, the chapter is divided into four sections. The first examines the technological developments that allowed popular music to be created, recorded, and distributed in ways that greatly expanded upon the possibilities and practices for the popular or mass culture music produced and marketed before World War II. The second section addresses how the onset of the television industry and the transformational impact of the introduction of television on American culture also affected the radio business in ways that set the table for the music and the music industry to come. The third section looks at the innovations in and extensions of music composition, performance, and sound that brought about the era of rock-based popular music. Finally, the fourth section builds on the arguments from these first three sections to make the summary case for popular music as a central, defining component of boomer culture and the life's world of the boomer generation.

TECHNOLOGICAL ROOTS

The popular music of the second half of the 20th century grew out of two distinct sets of technological roots. The first were inventions in musical instrumentation; that is to say, inventions by which people create music. The second set of roots was a matter of inventions and innovations in the machinery via which music recordings are produced, stored and retrieved, and disseminated.

The two most important inventions in musical instrumentation were the development of sound reinforcement/amplification and the drum set or kit or trap set. Of course, these inventions were fully conceived and formed before World War II, and each has its own unique history of discovery and improvement before and leading up to the boomer age. However, not only is each a necessary precursor to the boomers' music but the evolution and impact of their combined use also establishes the very foundations for the music to come.

The history of the inventions by which electrical energy is used to amplify sound is a complex one and includes Samuel Morse's telegraph, in that the only means to convert the pulses of electronic signal sent through a wire into perceptible phenomena is by transducing them into sound energy, and Alexander Graham Bell's telephone, which transduces sound waves into electrical energy and back. Amplification itself, however, encompasses two related but distinct inventions: the microphone by which the voice is amplified and the contact microphone, or "pick up," by which a musical instrument is amplified. The most significant among these instruments is the electrification of the guitar and bass guitar.

Emile Berliner's invention of the carbon button microphone (circa 1877) as an improvement on Bell's voice transmitter for his telephone device is generally considered the root of the invention of the microphone. Notably, however, Berliner's "patent didn't survive a legal challenge, which resulted in an 1892 ruling by the U.S. Supreme Court ruling that gave the credit to Thomas Edison."[1] (In fact, neither inventor can lay rightful claim to either the idea *or* the invention as, in reality, they both extended previous experiments with and discoveries in the technology.) Further development of the microphone was also spurred by other inventions in media technology that would become important to the story of 20th-century mass media and music. The most important of these were Edison's invention of the phonograph, also introduced in 1877, and the experiments and inventions in radio beginning with the work of Reginald Fessenden and Lee DeForest in 1906. By the time the radio broadcasting industry came into being after World War I and during the 1920s, and once the early recording industry was already in full swing, "microphone singing"[2] began to become the norm.

The history of electrical and electronic instruments is generally understood to begin with Thaddeus Cahill's invention of his Telharmonium in 1897. The Telharmonium was a kind of electronic organ, the sounds of which "were generated by enormous electromagnetic tone-wheels mounted on a set of shafts driven by a single motor."[3] Following on the heels of this rather large and unwieldy instrument, most of the other early inventions in electronic instruments were also keyboard-based and synthesizer-like, such as the theremin. However, a quantum leap in the electrification of musical instruments came in 1931 with the invention of a different and much more portable kind of instrument: the Hawaiian lap steel-style "frying pan" electric guitar. The invention and design of this first electric guitar is credited to George Beauchamp of the National Guitar Corporation, and the instrument was commercially produced and brought to market a year later via a partnership of Beauchamp, Paul Barth, and Adolph Rickenbacker.[4] Their company would come to be known as the Electro String Instrument Corporation. In the meantime, the electrification of the guitar also became necessary as guitarists sought to be heard within the context of big bands and orchestras.

The drum set, or trap set was also designed to meet the needs of dance bands and orchestras. However, with drums, the problem to be solved was not a matter of needing to be heard but of space issues on small stages and because of large ensembles. Until this time drums were played by hand, and by a section of percussion musicians. The drum set, in turn, enables a single musician to play multiple drums simultaneously, using both the hands *and* the feet. This also brought about a completely new style of playing and a new form of musicianship, as the one musician plays polyrhythmically, with each appendage performing a unique part and rhythm and with all four parts arranged and/or orchestrated on the fly. In addition, the individual innovations that culminated in this ultimate innovation came from drummers themselves, most notably in the jazz tradition and beginning in New Orleans, as well as from the foot pedal, in particular the bass drum pedal, a critical invention developed by two brothers, Theobald and William Ludwig. The brothers would go on to found the Ludwig & Ludwig Company in 1909.

It is the sum total of these inventions and further innovations in their use that led, in the 1950s, to a sonic style that was louder, brasher, and more powerful than any previous musical form. Moreover, the physical styles musicians developed to perform on these instruments—for instance, playing the guitar in a standing position using a strap, and thus being able to move around—allowed for the kind of free movement that contributed to the decision to televise Elvis Presley from the waist up on *The Ed Sullivan Show*. It presaged the physicality associated with most of the music that evolved out of the original moment of rock and roll. This physicality also came to affect both sides of the musical transaction—performer *and* audience—as audience members were prompted to move in response to the power and intensity of the new rhythms and the resonant, loud, and low frequencies of the electric bass guitar and bass drum. Thus, it is not that there was no dance-oriented popular music before this time but that the sonic intensity arising from the combination of these new instruments was more sexually charged and suggestive, and thus resulted in a more sensual physical experience, than any musical form that came before.

Changes in recording technology, as well as in the hardware and software for music consumption, also came about at this time and set the table for the new, contemporary music industry after World War II. The first of these was the groundbreaking development of audiotape recording by the German company AEG and the manufacturing of audiotape by the German company BASF during the war. Before these inventions, sound could only be recorded directly to an acetate disc, a costly process for all but the most gifted and trained musicians because the acetate could not be re-cut. It had to be discarded if a significant mistake was made or a technical problem arose during the recording, and the process would need to begin from scratch. The invention of audiotape therefore meant that not only was there a reusable medium for sound recording, as tape can be erased and used over and over again, but also that a less practiced and/or schooled musician could now make a record without the anxiety and pressure of needing to put forth a perfect performance. (Certainly such concerns are a factor that can impede the nature and quality of performance.) Les Paul's innovations in multitrack, or sound-on-sound recording, would come soon after this in the 1950s.

Shortly after World War II, in 1948, the Radio Corporation of America (RCA) also developed two new technologies for the consumption of music: the 45 rpm single record and the 33 1/3 rpm long-playing, or LP record, along with the devices on which to play these new forms of musical software. The 45 rpm format caught on and became important within a decade as an inexpensive, disposable format that was attractive and easily available to teenagers. In the postwar boom years of the 1950s, middle-class teenagers began, on a mass scale, to accumulate disposable income through babysitting jobs, newspaper routes, and the like and, as a result and for the first time, became a market to be targeted and exploited by various consumer industries. According to Steven Gillon—citing Eugene Gilbert, who referred to himself as the "Pied Piper of Youth Marketing" and "whose syndicated column, 'What Young People are Thinking' ran in more than 300 newspapers in the late 1950s"—toward the end of the decade "the average teenager had $10 a week to spend" and together "they spent more than $75 million on pop records" annually.[5]

In this context, then, a single record was an easily affordable cultural product and one worth obtaining once musical content arrived on the scene to make it worthwhile. The 33 1/3 rpm format, on the other hand, did not catch on right away, but became important only later on, during the mid- to late 1960s, as the purely popular in music began to make way for creators of music with artistic aspirations and for music that can be said to *be* art. Up until this time, an album was just a collection of songs. After this time, artists, groups, and producers extended the form in ways that made the songs cohere, and even created coherent song cycles, turning the album into an extended art form in and of itself.

THE RADIO INDUSTRY IS RECONFIGURED IN RESPONSE TO THE CULTURAL CATACLYSM OF TELEVISION

After World War II, the moment of television also arrived, and the television industry began its unstoppable transformation of American popular culture—quickly becoming the most ubiquitous, prominent, and powerful medium of the time. The invention of electronic television technology clearly dates back before the war, to the 1930s, and the medium was first introduced to the American public at the 1939 World's Fair in New York as a part of RCA's World of Tomorrow pavilion. However, in 1948, as the wartime economy wound down and government and commerce-based priorities shifted back to a peacetime economy, the television industry truly began to take flight. This was true with respect to the sudden growth in the number of stations on air, the number of cities served by stations, the number of sets owned and in use, the number of programming hours offered, and, most importantly, the laying of the coaxial cable infrastructure that made national network television possible and the beginnings of an exodus of national advertisers away from network radio and into network television.[6]

It is the latter fact that matters most with respect to the story told in this chapter. National advertisers quickly came to see television as the superior medium for advertising because the visual dimension afforded them greater and more powerful possibilities to design and construct their messages and therein make them more appealing and effective to consumers. In the meantime, the all but immediate abandonment of radio by these advertisers sounded the death knell for the national network radio business that, until this time, had constituted the primary business of broadcasting. Of course, network radio did not completely collapse, and vestiges of it still exist today. Nonetheless, it would never again be as important as it was from the beginning of broadcasting in the 1920s until this time of transition.

The radio industry underwent an almost complete reconfiguration in the face of the competition of television. No longer would radio be a mass medium for national and long-form programming sponsored by advertisers. Instead, it became a local-station and local-market medium that would rely mainly on the short-form programming of music—again, once a musical content arrived on the scene that could draw and hold the attention of a sufficient number of listeners and thus draw enough revenue for the industry to survive and even thrive. This shift is also the root factor in broadcasting's general switch from program sponsorship to short-form commercials between and during the programming that is the reason listeners tune in in the first place. Network television would also adopt the use of short-form commercials within a decade.

In the context of this transition a new type of radio personality came into being, who would come to be known as a "disc jockey," or "DJ." The disc jockeys of the early to mid-1950s, such as Bill Randle, Alan Freed, Wolfman Jack, Jocko Henderson, and Casey Kasem, became extremely influential players within the nascent music industry. (This is of course before program directors, before the payola scandal of the late 1950s, and before the phoenix-like rise of FM radio—prompted by the FCC's nonduplication rule in 1965—brought about an entire subindustry of radio consultants.) These men became largely responsible for the discovery, promotion, and ultimately even the success of new artists and music. However, it must be acknowledged that their charismatic, showman personalities and self-promotion would not have mattered much or had the same impact had it not been for a new and exciting form of music that came on the scene for them to champion.

A final factor with respect to changes that affected the radio industry and, as a result, popular music is yet another technological development. The invention in 1947 of the transistor, or miniaturized circuit, by a team of Bell Labs physicists led by William Shockley, led to the production of transistor radios beginning in the mid-1950s. In contrast to the furniture-sized console radio receivers found in people's living rooms up to this time, the transistor radio made the mass medium of radio portable. In turn, this portability contributed to teenagers' ability to share their music, to listen to it in public and gathering places outside of their homes, and thus, to break free from the bonds of the generation gap that separated them and their parents. That is to say, the schism that arose between the youth culture of the mid-1950s and the culture of their parents—a schism brought into sharp relief by music more than anything else—created the very foundation and launching pad for boomer culture. The first boomers were not yet teenagers in the mid-1950s. However, they would be greatly influenced by their older and cooler teenage siblings, and the transistor radio would serve as a catalyst in defining, enabling, and bringing to prominence their new culture and a burgeoning awareness of the cultural shift taking place.

THE MUSIC AT THE CENTER OF IT ALL

In 1948, the war was over, the U.S. economy had begun the transition from a wartime to a peacetime economy, the television industry had begun, the radio industry was facing the question of its future in response to television, and the baby boom was into its third year. In the same year, *Billboard* magazine, which had been the music industry's primary trade publication since the end of the 19th century and the formative days of Tin Pan Alley, tracked the sales and success of popular music recordings in three categories. The first, the long-standing "Best Sellers in Stores" category, charted the most popular records overall, eventually evolving into the "Hot 100" and then the "Top 100" chart. The second category, added in 1948, charted the "Best Selling Retail Folk Records." This chart would soon become the "Country & Western" chart and, in the early 1960s, "Hot Country." The third category was known until 1949 as "Race Records." This chart was renamed "Rhythm and Blues" in 1949 and would undergo numerous name changes up to the present day.

All of this matters as an introduction to the evolution of and developments in popular music in the 1950s because of a certain pattern that developed in the 20th century, wherein young white audiences would discover and become fans of music created by blacks, and the music industry, as part of the whole of our "culture industries," would exploit this phenomenon by producing supposedly safer and less exotic versions of such music to market it and make it more palatable to a white majority audience. Of course, mass culture critic Theodor Adorno would argue that those working within the music industry never consciously or deliberately did anything of the sort—that it was never anyone's intent to make music that was safer. To Adorno, culture industries like the music industry simply seek to create a least objectionable form of content by attenuating out all of the outlying and extreme elements, so as to not alienate anyone in the heterogeneous mass audience by going against or offending their tastes.[7]

Adorno notwithstanding, this pattern first arose with respect to big band dance music. The original big bands from the 1920s grew out of a jazz tradition that had roots in the ragtime of the late 19th century, epitomized in the music of Scott Joplin, and then in New Orleans after the turn of the century in the music of Jelly Roll Morton and, later, Louis Armstrong. The big bands that arose out of this tradition in the 1920s, however, were primarily white musicians and bandleaders. Then, toward the end of the 1920s, a new strain of big band music evolved, this one hewing more closely to the improvisational tradition of jazz. It included such bands as Duke Ellington and his Cotton Club Orchestra, and was the first brand of popular music to be categorized as "race music." (This is because jazz cannot accurately be characterized as popular music.) After this, the big bands that came onto the scene in the 1930s and 1940s featured such white musician/bandleaders as Benny Goodman and Glenn Miller. It is also significant to point out that these latter bands rose to prominence during the so-called golden age of radio—a time when the radio and recording industries truly began to work together for their mutual benefit. For instance, in 1939, the music licensing agency Broadcast Music Inc. (BMI) was established to better address music licensing for radio, and to provide a competitor to the American Society of Composers, Authors and Publishers (Ascap), which had been established in 1914.[8]

This same pattern occurred in the early 1950s. The origin of the term "rock and roll" is of course a euphemism for sexual intercourse—"rockin' and rollin'"—and was immortalized in the words to Etta James's 1955 hit, "The Wallflower," when she sang "You've got to roll with me, Henry." This song, sometimes referred to as "Dance With Me, Henry," was written by Hank Ballard and Johnny Otis (with writer's credit also given to James) and was a reworking of Ballard's earlier song "Work With Me, Annie," the lyrics to which were not merely suggestive but overtly sexual. Part of the reason for the reworking is that white teenagers had begun to gravitate toward and listen to what was coming to be known as rhythm and blues, but which was still widely and worrisomely referred to as race music by adults in the white majority, to the point that the FCC began to put pressure on radio stations to refrain from playing such records.

An earlier rhythm and blues record, "Rocket 88," written and recorded by Ike Turner (of Ike and Tina Turner fame) in 1951, is often credited as the first rock and roll record. The genesis, or at least the lore of this song is that it was penned by Turner in the backseat of an Oldsmobile Delta 88 while he was on his way to a recording session for which he needed a song. The song reached number one on *Billboard*'s Rhythm and Blues chart in 1951, credited to Jackie Brenston and his Delta Cats.

James W. Chesebro and his colleagues, however, make the case for 1955 as the year the popular music industry as we know it truly began. As they write: "For all practical purposes, popular music—as a viable market, economic, and mass culture entity—began in 1955."[9] They explain that when "adjustments for annual costs of living and annual growth rates are accounted for, record sales during 1954 were actually slightly less than those of 1948," but that "from 1955 to 1959, the record industry experienced an explosive growth rate of 261%."[10] In addition, they note that the "conversion from 78 RPM records to the 45 and LP format, the drastic shift in popular tastes of record purchasers from the Bing Crosby-Dinah Shore era to the Bill Haley-Elvis Presley era, and changing market concentrations within the record industry" clearly influenced this growth.[11]

However, a significant event with respect to the music is widely regarded as the pivotal moment for this newly ascendant industry in 1955: the release of *Blackboard Jungle*, a motion picture about an inner-city high school starring Glenn Ford and Sidney Poitier. The movie's opening credits feature the song "Rock Around the Clock," recorded and released in 1954 by a white musical act, Bill Haley and the Comets. Although Turner's "Rocket 88" is considered the first rock and roll song sonically and stylistically, "Rock Around the Clock" is typically considered to be the groundbreaking record in rock and roll history. It is accorded this status because it stands at the juncture between race music by blacks and the same music performed by whites. That the artists (and the song itself) received their break as the result of the song's placement in a movie about disenfranchisement and the black and African American experience in the United States in the 1950s speaks even more emphatically, and with great semiotic coherence, to this watershed moment in our history. This is so whether one views these events as a matter of cultural exploitation and appropriation or as an important and even necessary breakthrough in our culture, in both senses of the term "culture."

Nonetheless, if there is truly a watershed moment in which everything changes for popular music, the music industry, and the place of music in the life's world of our popular culture, it comes down to a choice between two. The first of these moments took place late at night on July 5, 1954, at Memphis Recording Service, a storefront recording studio in Memphis, Tennessee. Sam Phillips, an engineer and the owner of Sun Records (an independent label that produced blues and race records) was overseeing an initial recording session with a 19-year-old white singer, originally from East Tupelo, Mississippi, who had a decent voice and who fancied himself a balladeer. The session was not going well; it was quite late on a Monday/ work night, and everyone decided to take a break. During the break, the singer began fooling around with an old blues number by Arthur "Big Boy" Crudup titled "That's All Right (Mama)." The other musicians joined in the fun. Phillips, in the meantime, recognized the song, was surprised that the singer knew it given the kinds of songs they had been trying to record, and came out of the control room to ask what they were doing. The performance, the looseness, the sudden, surprising uniqueness of its sound, and the realization/discovery by Phillips, resulted in singer Elvis Presley's first record, effectively released when Dewey Phillips played it (at least seven times) on his radio show on Memphis's WDIA on July 8, 1954.[12]

The second moment came three weeks later, on July 30, 1954, when Elvis was booked as an opening act for hillbilly singer Slim Whitman at an outdoor amphitheater in Memphis's Overton Park, in front of an audience of thousands, all of whom were fans of hillbilly music.[13] Elvis's trio, featuring Scotty Moore on guitar and Bill Black on bass, performed "That's All Right (Mama)" along with the record's flip side, a version of "Blue Moon of Kentucky" by bluegrass mandolin virtuoso Bill Monroe. The crowd responded with an abandon that no one could have anticipated, even though the record had been receiving the same response from listeners of popular, folk, *and* race record radio programs.[14] The audience called the group back for an encore: a rarity for opening acts at popular music concerts to this day. All they could do, since they knew only two songs at the time, was offer a reprise of "Blue Moon of Kentucky."

The cliché of Elvis's story is that he was a white boy, and a bit of a hillbilly himself, who sounded black, and who was therefore exploited by the culture industry as the first crossover artist of this new musical age. (As a footnote to this cliché, it was Elvis, and not Bill Haley, who struck this gold because Elvis was the younger, more handsome, and more sexually charged of the two men.) This is, however, a cliché; an oversimplification. The fact is that Elvis's second song, "Blue Moon of Kentucky," was originally a bluegrass song and that Elvis (and company) made that song his own as much as he appropriated a race song and made it more acceptable to a white majority audience.

Thus, three points must be made to clarify the significance of Elvis and this moment in popular music history. The first is that the crossover went both ways. The moment of rock and roll was never simply a matter of white musicians and a white industry appropriating black music. Rather, the two strains of music, race/rhythm and blues and hillbilly/country/Appalachian, had for a long time crossed and influenced one another all up and down the Mississippi River and throughout the American south. The mid-1950s was simply the time when a series of developments in technology, instrumentation, industry, media, and music all coalesced to allow and enable a young white man to be anointed "king." Elvis was lucky enough to become that man: to be in the right place at the right time and to have all of the tools and skills (including the right look). The second point is to note the extent of his impact as a sociocultural phenomenon: in 1956, Elvis had three songs on *Billboard*'s Top 10 Best Sellers in Stores for the year, three songs in the Top 10 from the Top 100 chart, and five songs in the Top 40 in both categories. The third and most important point, however, is that the music the baby boomers identify with from this time on, and which is identified with them and their culture—that is to say, everything about rock-based popular music—is derivative of this moment.

CONCLUSION

It is important of course to emphasize that Elvis does not and never did belong to the baby boomers. In 1956, when "Don't Be Cruel," with its flip side of "Hound Dog" was released and both songs made it into *Billboard*'s Top 10, the first boomers, who were born in 1946, were only 10 years old. It is, then, the music that is derivative of this moment that becomes the music of the boomer generation. The Beatles and the Rolling Stones, along with the rest of the British invasion, were the initial vanguard of the boomers' music, as Beatlemania and the Beatles themselves first arrived on U.S. shores in the winter of 1964, just as the oldest boomers were turning 18 years old (and as the youngest ones were being born). It is also important to note the influence of American rhythm and blues artists like Chuck Berry and Little Richard on the Beatles, and the influence of early 20th-century American blues artists such as Howlin' Wolf and Muddy Waters on the Rolling Stones. Bob Dylan, too, is part of this first wave, except that his music arises from the other side of the equation: the white Appalachian tradition of folk music. Nonetheless, and without oversimplifying the matter, by 1965 Dylan had gone electric at the Newport Folk Festival and the Beatles released the album *Rubber Soul*, which clearly manifests Dylan's influence on them, both musically and lyrically. (The Beatles met Dylan in 1964, when they discovered and were listening to his music just like everyone else; Dylan turned them on to marijuana.)

Moreover, this was still a time of 45 rpm single records and the Top 40, which is to say that it was before the modern, complex, and consultant-driven radio industry began to impose stratification in music listening by establishing music radio formats that allow stations to aurally position themselves in local markets served by many stations, AM and FM. This is important up through the mid-1960s because it resulted—for approximately, but only, a decade's time—in most of popular music being color blind. Berry Gordy's Detroit-based Motown label was a powerfully important player in the industry during this time, and such Motown artists as Diana Ross and the Supremes and Smokey Robinson and the Miracles were not only listened to by everyone but a song like the Four Tops' "I Can't Help Myself (Sugar Pie, Honey Bunch)," the number two song in 1965, could be followed on the radio by the Rolling Stones' "(I Can't Get No) Satisfaction," the number three song in that year.

With the release of the Beatles' 1966 album *Revolver*, and the Beach Boys' album *Pet Sounds* in the same year, the 33 rpm long-playing album began its evolution into its own art form. The pinnacle achievement in this evolution is widely regarded to be the Beatles' album *Sgt. Pepper's Lonely Hearts Club Band* in 1967 (which Paul McCartney himself admitted was influenced by a bout of creative competitiveness after he listened to *Pet Sounds*.[15]) An equally important and influential album in this tradition is the Who's double-album rock opera *Tommy*, released in 1969.

By the time of *Tommy*'s release, however, 1967's Summer of Love had passed, and the Who went on to perform the opera at 1969's Woodstock Festival, which is typically regarded as the quintessential event that defines 1960s music and youth culture and the figurative end of the 1960s as a decade of sometimes positive, sometimes idealistic, and sometimes naive social movement and change. Shortly afterward, in December 1969, the Rolling Stones' free concert at the Altamont Speedway, with its tragic end immortalized in the documentary film *Gimme Shelter*, marks a door closing on the ideals of the 1960s as a decade of peace and love. Six months later, on May 4, 1970, the fatal shooting by National Guardsmen of four Kent

State University students who were protesting the war in Vietnam becomes the other door that forever closes on those ideals.

The trajectory of popular music after the 1960s, however, in particular with respect to what came to be known in radio-industry parlance as "album-oriented rock," continued in ways that are artful and sincere but also, and alternatively, blatantly crass, vapid, and bombastic. Largely in response to the artistic pretensions of the progressive rock of mostly British bands, the punk movement began in Great Britain and the United States as a return to the fun and simplicity of a three-chord song and to expression rather than musical prowess and virtuosity. That the punk movement arose concurrently with the onset of disco, the musical soundtrack to the 1970s' "me generation," only served to amplify its underlying message and the reaction to it.

However, yet another form of music arose out of the mid-1970s, lagging only slightly behind the introductions of punk and disco. Evolving out of an amalgam of cultural practices, including the hiring of DJs to spin records at parties (live bands were often too impractical, too expensive, or too unreliable in terms of quality), the game of insults known as "the dozens," and innovations in dance known as "break dancing," hip-hop culture and rap music first appeared in and grew out of block parties that took place in the New York City borough of the Bronx.

This music represented the end of the boomers' music and its place at the apex of popular music culture in the United States. Rap/hip-hop music is *not* played with electric guitars and drum sets, and therefore, is not derivative of that moment of rock and roll in the 1950s. It is music that was first performed with turntables as instruments and later with digital "samplers" and a combination of turntables and samplers. As such, it became a unique new form and innovation in its own right. It also marks the juncture at which the oldest of the baby boomers turn into their parents, disparaging music that is too loud emanating out of boom boxes and car radios and dismissing it all as "a bunch of noise."

The oldest boomers were 33 years old when the Sugarhill Gang's seminal rap record, "Rapper's Delight," came out in 1979. The youngest boomers had just turned 15. It is little wonder, then, that when the classic rock radio format was first introduced in the early 1980s, to target the substantial, increasingly affluent, and then almost middle-aged demographic of baby boomers, the youngest boomers—who were at the very least young adults at the time and therefore still at an age at which one might have expected them to be open to and interested in new music—became the secondary but unanticipated crossover audience that made the classic rock format so successful. Yet it is also not surprising that, a short time later, during the ascendancy of rap and hip-hop culture, white teenage boys would predictably follow the pattern established earlier in the 20th century and turn to black culture for their musical entertainments.

NOTES

1. Matthew Shechmeister, "Birth of the Microphone: How Sound Became Signal." *Wired*, January 11, 2011, http://www.wired.com/rawfile/2011/01/birth-of-the-microphone/.

2. Paula Lockheart, "A History of Early Microphone Singing, 1925–1939: American Mainstream Popular Singing at the Advent of Electronic Microphone Amplification," *Popular Music and Society* 26, no. 3 (2003): 367–370.

3. Hugh Davies, "Electronic Instruments," *Grove Music Online*, http://www.oxfordmusiconline.com/subscriber/article/grove/music/08694pg3#S08694.3.

4. André Millard, "Inventing the Electric Guitar." In *The Electric Guitar*, ed. André Millard (Baltimore: Johns Hopkins University Press, 2004), 44.

5. Steven Gillon, *Boomer Nation: The Largest and Richest Generation Ever and How It Changed America*. (New York: Free Press, 2004, 5).

6. Erik Barnouw, *The Golden Web: A History of Broadcasting in the United States: 1933 to 1953*, vol. 2 (New York: Oxford University Press, 1968).

7. Theodor W. Adorno and Max Horkheimer, *Dialectic of Enlightenment: Philosophical Fragments*, translated by Edmund Jephcott (1944; repr., Palo Alto, CA: Stanford University Press, 2002), 94–96.

8. Ben Sisario, "Pandora Suit May Upend Century-Old Royalty Plan," *New York Times*, February 13, 2014, http://www.nytimes.com/2014/02/14/business/media/pandora-suit-may-upend-century-old-royalty-plan.html?hp.

9. James W. Chesebro, Davis A. Foulger, Jay E. Nachman, and Andrew Yannelli, "Popular Music as a Mode of Communication, 1955–1982," *Critical Studies in Mass Communication* 2, no. 2 (1985): 115.

10. Ibid., 115.

11. Ibid.

12. Peter Guralnick, *Last Train to Memphis: The Rise of Elvis Presley* (Boston: Little, Brown and Company, 1994), 94–95.

13. Ibid., 109–111.

14. Ibid., 108.

15. Geoff Emerick and Howard Massey, *Here, There & Everywhere: My Life Recording the Music of the Beatles* (New York: Gotham Books, 2007), 142.

REFERENCES

Adorno, Theodor W., and Max Horkheimer. *Dialectic of Enlightenment: Philosophical Fragments*. Translated by Edmund Jephcott. 1944. Reprint. Palo Alto: Stanford University Press, 2002.

Barnouw, E. *The Golden Web: A History of Broadcasting in the United States: 1933 to 1953*. Vol. 2. New York: Oxford University Press, 1968.

Chesebro, James W., Davis A. Foulger, Jay E. Nachman, and Andrew Yannelli. "Popular Music as a Mode of Communication, 1955–1982." *Critical Studies in Mass Communication* 2 no. 2 (1985): 115–135.

Davies, Hugh. "Electronic Instruments §III: 1895–1945." *Grove Music Online*. *Oxford Music Online*. http://www.oxfordmusiconline.com/subscriber/article/grove/music/ 08694pg3#S08694.3.

Emerick, Geoff, and Howard Massey. *Here, There & Everywhere: My Life Recording the Music of the Beatles*. New York: Gotham Books, 2007.

Gillon, Steven. *Boomer Nation: The Largest and Richest Generation Ever and How It Changed America*. New York: Free Press, 2004.

Guralnick, Peter. *Last Train to Memphis: The Rise of Elvis Presley*. Boston: Little, Brown and Company, 1994.

Lockheart, Paula. "A History of Early Microphone Singing, 1925–1939: American Mainstream Popular Singing at the Advent of Electronic Microphone Amplification." *Popular Music and Society* 26, no. 3 (2003): 367–385.

Millard, André. "Inventing the Electric Guitar." In *The Electric Guitar*, edited by André Millard, 41–62. Baltimore: Johns Hopkins University Press, 2004.

Shechmeister, Matthew. "Birth of the Microphone: How Sound Became Signal." *Wired*. January 11, 2011. http://www.wired.com/rawfile/2011/01/birth-of-the-microphone/.

Sisario, Ben. "Pandora Suit May Upend Century-Old Royalty Plan." *New York Times*. February 13, 2014. http://www.nytimes.com/2014/02/14/business/media/pandora-suit-may-upend-century-old-royalty-plan.html?hp.

13

"In My Life": The Transformative Power of Music and Media during the Rebellions of the 1960s

Robert Albrecht

The rebellions of the 1960s, massive and at times ferocious, continue to echo in the present day. The advances made in the areas of racial equality, women's rights, civil rights, gay rights, environmental advocacy, and so on are hard to imagine without the profound changes in consciousness and political action that evolved during the 1960s. Erupting from a rather complacent post-World War II America, the revolts of the sixties could not have been anticipated a decade earlier when a newly gained affluence and widespread fears about national security had suffocated critical thought and political action. In this chapter, I wish to explore the role that changes in music and media played in effecting a shift in consciousness that motivated this unexpected rebellion throughout the country.

But why then? Why the 1960s? What is to account for the sudden explosion that pried a complacent generation from a consumer-driven ethos to a sustained confrontation with powerful political, military, cultural, and economic institutions? Certainly there had been issues of poverty, racial oppression, and militarism before then, just as these same challenges continue to persist in the present day. In this chapter, I will argue that music was an essential motivating force—not just a sonic wallpaper—behind the rebellions of the period and that the power of that force was largely a consequence of fundamental changes in the media environment. No longer background, no longer mere entertainment or diversion, music came downstage and out front, providing inspiration and direction to a bewildered generation no longer mindlessly obedient to the leadership and guidance of adult authority whether it be parental, scholastic, military, or political.

But music, as much as we like particular songs, styles, and musicians, cannot exist without the mediation of some form of technique or technology.

There is no such thing as music alone. All forms of music, from the most rudimentary to the most complex, from the rhythmic clapping of hands to the digital wizardry of a modern recording studio, depend on various techniques and technologies for their mediation. Each new development in the evolution of media creates new music environments that determine what music is and can be. As I have argued elsewhere:

> There could not have been a "Beethoven" in the tenth century because Beethoven's instrument and his compositional materials—the piano, the symphonic orchestra of finely tuned instruments, and an accurate form of musical notation that allowed music to be worked out on paper beforehand—had yet to be invented. For the same reason, there could not have been a "Frank Sinatra" before there was a microphone to croon to, a "Jimi Hendrix" before there were electric guitars and megawatt amplifiers to amplify and distort sound, nor an "Elvis" had there not been photographs, magazines, and television to publicize his good looks and provocative gyrations. (Albrecht 2004, 54)

Music, therefore, in its conceptualization, creation, performance, recording, transmission, and mode of reception, depends on a changing set of techniques and technologies that alter not only the music itself but also our understanding and appreciation of it.

As we entered the 1960s, the United States was crossing a technological Rubicon from which there would be no turning back. It wasn't that the electronic revolution didn't exist before then—it did—but now the oral and literate culture that once tempered its advance was being pushed aside in a way that caught the adult world flat-footed and baffled. Starting with the invention of photography and telegraphy in the 19th century, communication technology had been steadily advancing with every wave of the magic wand: the telephone, electric light, phonograph, cinema, wireless telegraph, radio, tape recorder, television, and so on. The oral/literate dam that had restrained some of the more extravagant changes in patterns of perception and behavior engendered by electronic culture was cracking under such enormous pressure, and, by the 1960s, the dam broke open.

The youth of the period, not yet fully acculturated to the old patterns and therefore more susceptible to the seductive influence of the new were, as a consequence, more easily swept away in this gush of technological novelty. The much talked about generation gap—adults on one side, adolescents on the other—is primarily the result of this divide between one generation born into a rather stable oral/literate environment and one coming of age in an electronic one. The political and social conflicts that came to a head at this time were all experienced and played out through this technological divide—"don't trust anyone over 30"—and music became the flag, the bugle, and the light that led the charge.

Although every form of communication—from art, theater, fashion, and speech to photography, motion pictures, radio, and TV—was rocked by the changes, it seems indisputable that music was the central component in sustaining the massive emotional energy necessary to make visible that which had been hidden and to challenge that which had been thought immutable. Virtually every political or cultural issue that came to a boil during the decade was expressed and energized through song. In short, to take a page from Neil Postman (1985) and reapply it in a way not originally intended, music became both the metaphor and the epistemology for the generation of the 1960s. More than just a soundtrack to the sweet bird of youth, music mediated and thereby structured the systems of knowledge and the rebellious spirit of the times, pushing everything forward at a frantic pace: challenging, confronting, and igniting a culture much too comfortable with war, much too complacent about racial injustice, and too much at home with a consumerism gone wild.

"In My Life," the title of this chapter, more than just a clever reference to the song by John Lennon, is an attempt to tell the story of a generation's struggle to challenge and change deeply embedded social and psychological patterns. In essence, it is the story of a change in attitude, perception, and orientation. My argument is that music and media, more than just being reflective of these changes, were factors that greatly energized and sustained a fundamental change in consciousness. By charting my own experience as I journeyed through this decade, I will attempt to add to our knowledge of the impact of music and media on society by simply recounting the life of one person swept up in the changes of the day.

It didn't happen overnight, however. In my life, as the 1960s began, I found myself nailed to a seat in the sixth grade at St. Mary's Grammar School in Rahway, New Jersey. There were 60 or 70 of us crowded into that room, arranged in straight rows, boys on one side, girls on the other, with Christ on the Cross in the middle. The icons we worshipped—the American flag in one corner, a statue of the Virgin Mary in another—were honored daily with pledges, prayers, and flowers of devotion. On the left side of the blackboard, Sister kept a running tally—boys in one column, girls in the other—that recorded how much money we had raised to save pagan babies in China. If I'm not mistaken, pagan babies went for $5 each, and every month or so we had accumulated enough to save another soul from communism.

It was a medieval-like pedagogy we mostly endured. Much of what we learned was through dictation, the copying of texts, rote memorization, and frequent prayer that marked the passage of the day and the seasons of the year. Movies, TV, phonograph records, slide shows, and photography were a rarity in the classroom, and videotape, of course, did not yet exist. Our pedagogical materials were oral or literary in nature, that is, memorization and recitation, pen and paper, blackboards and chalk, notebooks that we did our lessons in, and textbooks that we covered with brown paper so as to protect the books for those who would use them next. Above the board, running left to right, the alphabet was written in perfect cursive letters for us to emulate in our penmanship exercises. We wrote only with fountain pens—never with pencils or (God forbid) ballpoint pens—and could never cross out our errors but had to start our work anew with every mistake committed to paper.

All our instruction was done by nuns, and all the nuns at that time wore habits. Discipline was strict, and physical punishment was freely administered and unquestioningly tolerated by ourselves and our parents. We stood and prayed four times a day: once in the morning before we began, once before lunch, once after lunch, and once more at dismissal. On Friday afternoons during Lent, we were led into the church for the Stations of the Cross, and throughout the month of May the entire school assembled outside on the playground to say the rosary in honor of the Virgin. The praying was tedious and certainly not something I looked forward to but, in retrospect, it did bring the class together in regular assembly, reminding us that we were a group. More importantly, there is a poetic cadence to prayer, a heightened language that, collectively recited and regularly repeated, works its way down into one's soul. I sometimes wonder if the musical sense of rhythm, alliteration, and lyrical flow I inherited from childhood was as much from these prayers as it was from any of the songs I listened to on the radio or heard on TV.

Sister Eugenia was a tough old Irish nun from Boston —she must have been in her 80s—who had the habit of taking tea every morning at 10 accompanied by a couple of girls privileged enough to leave the room with her. During her absence, we were kept busy with arithmetic drills, diagramming sentences, or copying questions and answers from our catechism books. Not a sound was heard in the room and only the bold and the brave dared to move from their seats. As a native of Massachusetts, Sister would often rhapsodize at length about this glorious family called "the Kennedys." We lived in New Jersey and had no idea who she was talking about but, in her eyes, the Kennedys were God's gift to America. I imagined them as something like one of those perfect families we all saw on TV—handsome, affluent, pleasant, soft-spoken, understanding, and wise—except that they were Irish and Catholic, went to Mass and were a bit more like the people around us. Sister said that one of them was a senator who might be president one day and that our parents (as if they took political advice from us) should vote for him when the time came. That spring, she cut out a circular picture of the smiling senator and scotch taped it to the clock at the back of the room. As a result, whenever we snuck a glance at the time, we saw the face of "Jack" grinning back at us. It was an annoying but effective piece of propaganda.

I guess you could say the 1960s began for me with that picture of Kennedy on the clock, but I didn't really get the spirit of the times until we went down South that summer to visit my sister. Marilyn and her husband, Tommy, had moved to Florida the year before to better their situation but, as far as I could tell, it only got worse. He went from being a truck driver in New Jersey to a laborer in Florida where he worked harder, sweat more profusely, and got paid a whole lot less. My sister still worked as a waitress but now the tips and wages were even more meager, all the diners were racially segregated, and she was separated from her family for the first time in her life. They moved back to the old neighborhood the following year, and I don't remember them ever talking about the South again.

As for me, I was just happy to be out of New Jersey. Rahway is a small town along the industrial corridor that connects Jersey City, Newark, Elizabeth, Linden, and Carteret. Other than an occasional suicide, car accident, polio outbreak, or petty robbery, not much ever happened there. We merrily breathed in the toxic air of the nearby oil refineries along the New Jersey Turnpike and played in streets devoid of traffic, broken glass, or violence. As the summer approached, I was elated to be going down South. Besides the fact that the farthest south I had ever been was Seaside Heights, New Jersey, I had grown up on a pop culture rich with southern references: Davy Crockett, Tom Sawyer, Fats Domino, and Elvis Presley. Anything that smelled of the South, therefore, excited my nose and tickled my imagination. All the way there, the car radio repeatedly played Roy Orbison ("Only the Lonely"), the Everly Brothers ("Cathy's Clown"), Brenda Lee ("I'm Sorry"), Fats Domino ("Walking to New Orleans"), and Elvis ("It's Now or Never") while our '57 Ford zoomed across a strange new landscape. It was ungodly hot that August—even the heavy winds blowing through the open windows didn't help—and sometimes we passed stretches of trees covered with a ghostlike moss that fascinated me. Mile after mile, billboards relentlessly announced a tourist trap called "South of the Border," watermelons stacked high were sold 10 for a dollar at roadside stands, people in rags sat idly on the steps of dilapidated shacks, signs pointed the way to segregated restaurants, and here and there, like a bad scene in an old movie, I saw white men with guns guarding black men with chains. While all of this was novel to me and therefore interesting, a chain gang and a string of segregated restaurants is a strange thing to see for the first time having grown up on *Leave It to Beaver* and *My Little Margie*.

As the fates would have it, a new song by Sam Cooke was starting to get airplay on the AM radio in my father's Ford. The musical grunts, the rhythmic clangs of metal on metal, and the compassionate commentary of the lyrics, set it apart from the other songs we heard on that trip. But as we got deeper and deeper into the southland, I began to notice how well the song accompanied the view outside my window. "Chain Gang" is an excellent example of music's power to stir the soul of the listener and to point at things and say, "SEE!" "PAY ATTENTION!" "HERE'S WHAT I THINK ABOUT THIS. HOW ABOUT YOU?" At times certain songs intersect with and affirm feelings we are experiencing and help us to put them into an understandable framework. More than just a soundtrack for that trip down South, "Chain Gang" was a revelation, an epiphany, a moment that changed a little boy's life.

In November 1960, Kennedy was elected president, just as Sister Eugenia had said, and now the decade could begin in earnest. Right off the bat, there was a new spirit emanating from the White House. In his inaugural address Kennedy famously challenged "ask not what your country can do for you, ask what you can do for your country" and we listened and took note. Today, in more jaded times, these words may sound like the empty rhetoric of a scripted politician, but at that time, these words were taken very seriously. College students—both black and white—were already getting involved with the civil rights struggle and risking their teeth, skulls, and lives in the South. Others were going up into the mountains of Appalachia to work with the rural poor, others were serving in urban soup kitchens, and others were tutoring inner-city children. When the Peace Corps was first introduced in 1961, young people signed up to volunteer in foreign countries, to live and work in shantytowns, slums, and remote rural areas, all hoping to make a difference in the lives of the poor. Suze Rotolo (2008), the young woman who appears on Bob Dylan's arm in the iconic photograph on the cover of *The Freewheelin' Bob Dylan* (1963), expresses the spirit of the times in her penetrating memoir:

> Today "What's in it for me?" is the question most often asked. To acknowledge that we are in this together, to ask what would be better for the community, or to lend support to someone else's request for improvement or change helps everyone in the long run. The sixties were an era that spoke a language of inquiry and curiosity and rebelliousness against the stifling and repressive political and social culture of the decade that preceded it. The new generation causing all the fuss was not driven by the market: we had something to say, not something to sell. (367)

Like the adults all around me, I immediately felt the new enthusiasm and the vigor that the Kennedys brought to the national stage. Magazines, newspapers, and TVs were jammed with flattering images of the Kennedys on vacation, the Kennedys boating, the Kennedys playing touch football, the Kennedys on Cape Cod, little Caroline wearing mommy's shoes and

John Jr. hiding under daddy's desk, and family picnics attended by scores of cousins with toothy Kennedy grins. Women copied Jackie's coiffeur, and her every outfit became a fashion statement. Men started to comb their hair à la JFK, and stories about the Kennedy clan were shared at the dinner table and on the blanket at the beach as if they were part of our own family. On TV, Dick Van Dyke and Mary Tyler Moore became cardboard cutouts of the first couple playing out their lovable foibles in the intimacy of our living rooms. Meanwhile, comedians lined up on every channel to poke fun at the Kennedys in an affectionate way. Kennedy impersonators such as Vaughn Meader gently parodied the life of the Kennedy clan, and his album *The First Family* became the fastest-selling album in America at that time. McAleer (1996) writes that "the album broke existing records by selling over three million copies in its first month—not surprisingly it went on to earn a handful of Grammy awards" (81). Bits and pieces of the album were played repeatedly on the radio, along with Jimmy Dean's recording "P.T. 109," which recounted the president's heroism in World War II. Little Jo Ann took on the persona of the president's daughter, Caroline, and sang a very successful cornball ditty, "My Daddy is President." The historians and the pundits called the Kennedy administration "Camelot"; America now had a royal family.

The optimistic and idealistic spirit of the times was also reflected quite vividly in the Hollywood western *The Magnificent Seven* (directed by John Sturges) which was released the same year Kennedy was elected. After two expert gunmen (Yul Brynner and Steve McQueen) engage in some fancy shooting and risk their lives to make sure a black corpse is buried with white corpses in a segregated cemetery, the film tells the tale of how they accept the invitation of Mexican peasants to organize, arm, train, and defend their village against the repeated pillaging of a coldhearted villain (Eli Wallach) and his band of (literally) 40 thieves. Answering the call of justice, Brynner and McQueen recruit five other gunslingers (thus, the "magnificent seven") who, against all odds, heroically take on the bandits, much to the admiration and gratitude of the villagers. At the conclusion of the film, satisfied that their work is done and their contribution to justice has been served, Brynner and McQueen ride off into the sunset.

Based on the 1954 Japanese classic film *Seven Samurai* (directed by Akira Kurosawa), *The Magnificent Seven* worked well in its translation to the 19th-century American West. What is particularly relevant here is how well the film unconsciously reveals the glories and perils of the self-righteous sense of mission the United States had in 1960. Kennedy initiatives—the promotion of civil rights legislation, the Alliance for Progress, Vista, the Peace Corps, and other social programs—reflect the idealism that motivated the best hearts and minds of the period and foreshadow the dangerous attitude that led the United States so blindly into the quagmire that was

Vietnam. It was all so simple. The good guys had come to save the poor guys from the bad guys.

The new energy at the White House was paralleled by a new energy in the pop music culture. Although it was obvious to no one then, three key musical styles that would ignite the decade and get the ball rolling were beginning to make themselves felt around this time. The twist, a new dance introduced without much attention by Hank Ballard and the Midnighters in 1959, was rerecorded and massively popularized in 1960 by a one-time chicken plucker named Chubby Checker. It was one of those moments when a fad spreads like wildfire, and no one can ignore its presence or escape its influence. The dance was based on a simple pivot and twisting motion easy enough that almost anyone could do it. After its initial success in 1960, the twist rebounded and came back even stronger the following year when the society set picked up on it. At one point (March 1962), there were five songs in the Top 20 with "twist" in the title. The twist rapidly became a world phenomenon and fleet-footed entrepreneurs scrambled frantically to cash in on the craze by providing an almost endless stream of songs ("Soul Twist," "Slow Twistin'," "Twistin' the Night Away," "Twist Señora," "Dear Lady Twist," "Twist It Up," "Let's Twist Again," "Twist and Shout," "The Peppermint Twist," "Merry Christmas Twist"), albums (*Chuck Berry Twist, Twistin' Round the World, For Twisters Only, For Teen Twisters*), shows (*Murray the K's Twist Party*), and movies (*Twist Around the Clock, Don't Knock the Twist*) with "twist" in the title.

Unlike swing dancing and the fox-trot of the 1930s and 1940s, or the lindy hop in the 1950s, with the twist partners danced apart from one another and were allowed a more individualized experience on the dance floor. White people, who had long repressed the rhythmic rolling of their hips, were now eager to learn and enjoy the benefits. It was exhilarating. The always affable Chubby Checker was everywhere on TV, singing, dancing, and even giving twist lessons for those calcified stiffs who still hadn't gotten the hang of it yet. "It was Chubby Checker's mission," Black Panther Eldridge Cleaver (1968) wryly observed, "bearing the Twist as *good news*, to teach whites, whom history had taught to forget, how to shake their asses again" (177). And shake our asses we did. The phenomenal success of the twist was followed by similar dances (the mashed potato, pony, watusi, swim, fly, jerk, monkey, etc.), all of which were built around the separation of partners. By the end of the decade dancing would evolve into a total free form, allowing each person enough space to interpret and respond to the music in unencumbered abandonment. In fact, in many instances by the late 1960s, dancers no longer even had a partner.

A second major trend emerging around this time was one that would accompany the rise of the black power movement and would soon spawn the soul music phenomenon. By the onset of the 1960s, African Americans had long been successful as entertainers within the music business but not yet as entrepreneurs or in positions of real authority. The lucrative end of the business was still a Jim Crow club that controlled production, artist development, audio engineering, public relations, writing, distribution, all legal considerations, and, most importantly, the divvying up of royalties. African American songwriter Berry Gordy Jr. soon figured out that he was getting the short end of the royalty stick and set out to create a business and a label of his own. Hanging a large placard outside his home in Detroit that read "Hitsville USA," Gordy sought to develop a successful business model that would cross-market black music to a mass audience while creating an enterprise built entirely around African American talent from top to bottom. In his drive to capture the white teenage market, all of Gordy's artists were meticulously groomed and expertly choreographed with a repertoire of songs that were catchy, smooth, well produced and devoid of sexual innuendo. For the remainder of the 1960s, Berry Gordy and his stable of artists (Smokey Robinson and the Miracles, Mary Wells, the Marvelettes, Martha and the Vandellas, the Supremes, the Temptations, the Four Tops, Marvin Gaye, Stevie Wonder, and, by the end of the decade, the Jackson Five) always had a few songs on the charts. "By 1965," write Hardy and Laing (1995), "Tamla, Motown and other Gordy labels had achieved forty-five Top Twenty hits and in 1966 seventy-five percent of Motown singles reached the charts" (376). Motown had become, just as Gordy always bragged it would, a "hit factory."

Yet a third musical trend making its presence felt at this time was the folk revival movement. After a couple of decades of laying low during World War II, McCarthyism, and Cold War hysteria, folk music started brewing again in the coffee shops of Greenwich Village. Submerging its roots in the labor struggles of the 1930s, Communist Party summer camps in the Catskills, and the socially conscious compositions of Woody Guthrie, Pete Seeger, and multiple others who had been blacklisted from radio and TV, the folk revival made its way slowly into the mainstream with songs that carefully avoided explicit political or social commentary. Clean-cut groups like the Kingston Trio, the Limeliters, the Highwaymen, the Chad Mitchell Trio, the Rooftop Singers, and the Brothers Four had huge hits with songs that worked in the folk idiom but managed to stay clear of controversial subject matter. A gradual transition to a more socially committed music came with Peter, Paul and Mary, whose melodious voices, masterful arrangements, and manicured bohemian look opened the door to a more critical and vibrant musical culture. Although most of the folk or folk-like music on radio was rather tame—"The M.T.A.," "Puff the Magic Dragon," "Michael," "The Lion Sleeps Tonight"—Peter, Paul and Mary's recordings of "If I Had a Hammer," written by Pete Seeger and Lee Hays, and Bob Dylan's "Blowin' in the Wind" managed to slip under the door and announce that there was going to be a change in the weather.

Because of the seriousness of its message and its impact on the decade that followed, "Blowin' in the Wind" deserves special attention. The song's deceptively simple refrain—"the answer my friend is blowin' in the wind"—is easily memorized, easily sung, and easily played on a guitar. Through a string of rhetorical questions, Dylan announced the central themes of the decade to come while conjuring up a romantic image that was at once introspective and pensive and yet resonated with a sense of solidarity and social commitment. Softened somewhat by the soothing harmonies of Peter, Paul and Mary and made slightly oblique by Dylan's use of poetic metaphor, the song marked a clear break with the stifling political climate of 1950s music and invited a younger generation to enter the 1960s by choosing a new path that embraced liberation, commitment, and compassion, as opposed to hate, fear, and aggression.

In its commitment to social causes, "Blowin' in the Wind" and the entire folk revival were greatly influenced by the music of the civil rights movement, which had grown by leaps and bounds since the initial act of defiance by Rosa Parks in 1955 and the ensuing Montgomery bus boycott. Pete Seeger, Bob Dylan, Phil Ochs, Joan Baez, and scores of other musicians made their way south to participate in the protests and brought back images, words, songs, and a strong sense of belonging to something bigger than themselves. The civil rights movement used music like no other political movement in the history of the United States to build solidarity and inspire the tenacious spirit that such an undertaking demanded. Musicians and their audiences who were now being exposed to this music for the first time—either through recordings, interpersonal experiences with friends, or singalong public performances known as "hootenannies"—were also being moved by something much deeper and more powerful than anything they had known before.

The music on Top 40 radio—on the stations we tuned in to regularly—reflected these emerging trends, of course, but there was much more going on. A key characteristic of radio programming at that time was its diversity, incorporating a great motley of styles, cultures, and generations: Frank Sinatra and the Isley Brothers, Dinah Washington and the Singing Nun, the Shirelles and Alan Sherman, Conway Twitty and Kyu Sakamoto, Lawrence Welk and Ray Charles, Annette Funicello and Jackie Wilson, Henry Mancini and Johnny Horton, the Drifters and the Ray Conniff Singers, "The Girl From Ipanema" and "The Eve of Destruction." We didn't like all of it but, since it was in steady rotation on the stations we tuned in to, we listened and absorbed much of it. Although his audience comprised adolescents almost exclusively, even New York's top rock and roll DJ, Murray the K ("and his Swinging Soiree"), opened his show every evening with a Frank Sinatra recording. The most obvious TV corollary to this variety, of course, was *The Ed Sullivan Show*, but many other TV shows of the time

(*The Steve Allen Show*, *The Perry Como Show*) were also very broad in their programming.

In the fall of 1962, as all of these trends were beginning to heat up, I entered high school. Although many look back on their high school years as the best years of their lives, for me they were the worst. I was caught between two worlds and didn't really belong to either. My neighborhood was populated by working-class guys whose fathers worked as truck drivers, firemen, sheet metal workers, bartenders, and boiler-room workers, while their mothers waitressed, did factory work, or mostly just took care of the home. When it came time for high school, they all went to the local public high school without much in the way of dreams or aspirations other than passing to the next grade, playing football, lifting weights, and meeting girls. College and a career were not a part of the plan.

My father, however, who had only an eighth-grade education and hoped that his son would do better, insisted that I take my best shot and attend a Catholic high school in a nearby suburban town. I hated the idea of being separated from my friends and the neighborhood but there was no arguing with my old man once he had his mind made up. At the Catholic high school, we were forced to wear sport coats and ties every day, which immediately set me apart from the guys back on my block and made me the magnet of ridicule when I returned home at the end of the day lugging a great big green and white bag filled with books. I got plenty of homework; was forced to read books at night, on the weekends, and during the summer; and had to type up the many papers I was assigned. My classmates in high school were by no means wealthy but they were definitely a cut above what I was used to back home on the block. It was assumed that they would all be going to college; they would all get professional jobs and would go further and higher than their parents.

Although the 1960s were starting to spill out all around me and beginning to take root with my high school classmates, the inherent conservatism of working-class street-corner culture restrained experimentation back in the neighborhood. "The twist? Are you kidding?" "Puff the Magic Dragon? Give me a break!" "The Beach Boys? What are you nuts?" The only new music that penetrated the walls of the neighborhood was Motown, probably because it grew out of the doo-wop of the 1950s and therefore was already familiar and accepted. There is a great irony here because, as a white working-class neighborhood, we were segregated to the core and steeped in a racist lexicon and philosophy that I'd be ashamed to repeat today. And yet, the musicians and the style of dress we most admired were black. Why should this be so? Why should an ethnic group so openly despised and ridiculed also be the object of admiration and emulation? I've often thought about this and have come to the conclusion that this was an instance where class trumped race. The folk music, the surf music, and the mainstream pop music represented not only a different kind of music but it appeared to be the music of a different class. The acceptance of this music, therefore, was not simply a question of taste but one of loyalty. To embrace it was to be a traitor to our class.

It was around this time that the guys in the neighborhood formed a gang we called "the Majestics." We hung out on the corner, wore black jackets with "Majestics" on the back, and, before long, were singing the doo-wop that we loved. At first we sang in simple unison. but after encountering a girl group from another neighborhood, we started working out the harmonies that are the heart and soul of doo-wop. This isn't folk music, of course, but it did serve to retrieve oral participation within the emerging realm of electronic culture. I guess for the grandchildren of families dislocated by the Industrial Revolution and immigration, it was the closest we ever got to having a folk music of our own. Not really from the Old World, not really from the New, we orally absorbed the doo-wop repertoire (just as our parents had orally absorbed the tunes of Tin Pan Alley), which provided a generation of people from diverse and uprooted ethnicities with an ersatz culture that allowed us to harmonize and bond as a community.

In the fall of '63, as I was starting my sophomore year, the call went out for a talent show at the movie theater in downtown Rahway. We auditioned in the men's room of the theater because the acoustics were better there, and now we were on the bill for our first public performance. We rehearsed, told our families and friends, and argued over steps, what clothes to wear, who was going to sing lead, and what songs to sing. We decided to go with "Little Star," a song made popular back in the '50s by the Elegants, copying the original version word for word, note for note. I'm almost surprised we didn't copy the ever-present hisses and scratches that were on the record. It was an exciting couple of weeks.

Around noontime on the Friday of the performance, while I was anxiously waiting out the clock in sixth-period English class, we received the first reports over the school's intercom that President Kennedy had been shot in Dallas. How could this be? Things like that just didn't happen in the United States of America. About an hour later, Brother Claude, the principal, came in to tell us that the president had just died. No one knew how to respond; there was a hush in the room. Mr. Malia, my history teacher, who also doubled as the basketball coach, began to cry. We were dismissed early. The hallways were eerily silent for the only time I can recall as we went to our lockers to close up for the weekend.

On the way home, people were crying on the public busses, sniffling into their handkerchiefs, and clinging tightly to the transistor radios that they held close to their ears. The streets were empty, stores were silent, and those who were out and about spoke quietly in muted tones. All television programming was dedicated to the assassination; every conversation was focused on this one event. When the Majestics finally got together later that day, we thought for sure that the show would be cancelled. But this is America! The show must go on! The promoter, who had already rented the theater for that night and didn't want to lose his investment, announced that the program would proceed as scheduled. When we finally did get on stage before a packed house, they had placed the amplifiers directly behind us so that there was a confusion of sound. As a result, we couldn't hear each other or even the key very clearly, and I remember Joey's last line of "Little Star"—"There you are little star!"—echoing as flat as a pancake off the ceiling and walls of that old movie palace. It wasn't his fault; it was the situation of a group accustomed to sing acoustically defeated by its first meeting with electronic mediation. In short, the Majestics bombed on the same day that Kennedy died.

Right after that, Joey—or maybe it was his Uncle Mickey—won a guitar at a chance wheel on the boardwalk at Seaside Heights, and then a neighbor who saw us singing on the corner gave me an old guitar her husband had left behind when he took off for greener pastures. We continued to work in the doo-wop idiom but, with the benefit of a guitar to guide us and keep us on key, the singing improved greatly. Gradually we upgraded to electric guitars, and the a cappella group on the corner became a band in Johnny's cellar that got louder and louder but never much better. Common sense more than humility caused us to turn down the few opportunities for gigs that came along, so that when Mrs. Genovese, an Italian lady whose son Carmine was being drafted into the army, offered us $50 (a lot of money for us back then when we were all working at Chicken Delight or Ducoff's Candy store for $1 an hour) to play at his going away party, we prudently turned down her generous offer. Mamma was very proud of her son who was going to become a soldier and make his contribution to America. Her son went away all right but he never came back. The issue of the war was starting to come home. A couple of years later I rewrote the words to "When Johnny Comes Marching Home Again" thinking of that night:

> When Johnny went off to war again, hurrah, hurrah
> When Johnny went off to war again, hurrah, hurrah
> We gave him a party with plenty of beer
> Every one of his friends was here
> And we all felt proud when Johnny went off to war.

Then the culture broke open with the arrival of the Beatles. Coming on the heels of the Kennedy assassination of November 22, 1963, the Beatles were the opening act for the so-called "British Invasion," which was not just a change in music but a whole ideological shift in what music was and could be. Right from the opening note, there was an exhilarating joy embodied in everything they did. "At the beginning of 1964," Carl Belz (1972) notes, "the

American public was experiencing a lingering gloom over the assassination of John Kennedy. It is hard to substantiate, but it can be suggested that the Beatles' arrival provided an escape from that gloom" (128).

From the very outset, from their very first song, the Beatles and all the British bands were different. They were giving back to us, in imitation and homage, something we had given to them but had then discarded as outdated and obsolete. Whereas by 1964, we had pretty much dismissed most of the great performers of the 1950s—Elvis Presley, Carl Perkins, Jerry Lee Lewis, Little Richard, Buddy Holly, Chuck Berry, and the rest—the British bands adored them. Whereas we were for the most part totally ignorant of the blues and its importance to the music we loved, the British bands looked upon Robert Johnson, Howlin' Wolf, Muddy Waters, and Willie Dixon as the granddaddies and true geniuses of the genre. Although England is a million miles from the Mississippi Delta, phonograph records allowed young Brits to absorb the roots of rock and roll much better than their American cousins. Foreigners were teaching us our own culture.

But that was just the beginning. With the arrival of British bands into our musical diets, there was also a different inflection: they looked different; they dressed different; and they thought, spoke, and sang different. It was like discovering a different part of yourself you didn't know you had. But "the special significance of the Beatles," Belz (1972) adds, "is not simply a matter of their Britishness . . . the Beatles brought an atmosphere of fun and happiness to a rock style that had previously been filled with mourning and self-pity" (126). And yeah, yeah, yeah, you want to know what all the screaming was about? It was a cry of liberation. For the girls, it was a break with the repressed roles they were forced to play, restraining their personalities and restricting their possibilities. For me, it was a break with that working-class corral leading me and my friends from pasture to slaughterhouse: hang out on the corner, lackadaisical about school and career, accept unquestioningly the inevitable draft into the military when the time came, hope you didn't get killed or lose a leg, get out of the military as soon as you can, get a job, get a car, get married, have kids, buy a house, watch TV, and work 'til you drop. Doo-wop, an unchained melody of four chords repeated endlessly in three-part harmony accompanied by falsetto and bass, was a perfect metaphor for this most circumscribed and dead-end life.

And the Beatles, as audacious and outspoken as they were talented, quickly reshaped what it meant to be a pop star. John Lennon was particularly frank in his comments. At first his remarks were cute but soon his wit began to cut. In a performance before Queen Elizabeth and other royals in 1963, he announced to the audience: "Those in the cheap seats can clap your hands. The rest of you can just rattle your jewelry" (Friedlander 2006, 82). In 1966, Lennon made another remark that sparked quite a controversy: "Christianity will go. It will vanish and shrink . . . We're more popular than Jesus now—I don't know which will go first, rock 'n' roll or Christianity" (Norman 2003, 297). This last comment, while ignored in England as adolescent bombast when it was first uttered, created an uproar when it was reported in the United States. Some stations banned the Beatles from the airwaves while others burned their records in public ceremonies.

The Beatles were from a different world but technology brought them into mine: the movies brought them into my town, the television into my living room, radio and records into my bedroom, and the guitar into my soul. Suddenly, everyone was learning how to play the guitar and writing their own songs. It was also around this time that the first Xerox machines were showing their magic, and the fathers of high school friends would photocopy sheet music in their offices, which their sons then sold at school. More commonly, friends wrote out lyrics with chord diagrams, each song a revelation that challenged my fingers to stretch into strange new configurations. Whereas doo-wop was constrained in its form and subject matter, the Beatles' songs were varied, frequently modulating back and forth from major to minor keys, using unusual chords and unusual chord changes, and introducing novel lyrical ideas. Anthony Scaduto (1973) quotes Bob Dylan's reaction to the Beatles:

> They were doing things nobody else was doing. Their chords were outrageous, and their harmonies made it all valid . . . But I kept it to myself that I really dug them. Everybody else thought they were for the teenyboppers that they were going to pass right away. But it was obvious to me that they had staying power. I knew they were pointing the direction where music had to go . . . in my head, the Beatles were *it*. (203–204)

The lyrics, even when simple and straightforward, were intelligent and meaningful. And perhaps most of all, the songs they recorded were incredibly varied and challenged the listener to be open to different styles. Beginning with their first album and continuing to their last, the Beatles were all over the musical map: traditional rock and roll, old-time British music hall, blues, show tunes, pop tunes, chamber music ensembles, Motown, sitar music, experimental and atonal compositions, parodies, the use of different languages, country and western covers, and so on. In short, the Beatles were the very soundtrack to the global village that Marshall McLuhan (1964) was talking about. Later, when I went to Latin America at the end of the decade, I was to learn just how deeply the Beatles were admired there as well. In fact, is there any more compelling illustration of the optimism expressed in the phrase "global village" than the Beatles' performance of "All You Need Is Love" to 500 million people in 31 countries via the first satellite broadcast in human history (Norman 2003, 335)? Like McLuhan, the Beatles weren't ahead of their time: they were right on time, with British punctuality, front and center in 1967, the antennae of the race.

Another major figure who absorbed and then transformed the inherited musical ideology of the period was Bob Dylan. Like the Beatles, he was both a synthesizer and an innovator, someone who borrowed and pillaged from the past at the same time that he blended everything in a totally unique way. Laced together in Dylan, one finds the Old and New Testament, Woody Guthrie and Allen Ginsberg, country blues and rock and roll, surrealistic art and American corn. Marqusee (2005) writes that

> Between late 1964 and the summer of 1966, Dylan created a body of work that remains unique. Drawing on folk, blues, country, R&B, rock'n'roll, gospel, British beat, symbolist, modernist and Beat poetry, surrealism and Dada, advertising jargon and social commentary, Fellini and *Mad* magazine, he forged a coherent and original artistic voice and vision. (139)

The Beatles and Bob Dylan were like twin pipers who led me through a portal into a world I never knew existed. Dylan spoke in skipping reels of rhyme that I didn't quite understand but that tickled my ear and inspired the poet that was dormant in my soul. The Beatles were more like good friends, not quite the banshee that Dylan was, but companions of the road with whom I was exploring the world, listening, learning, seeing, and taking more daring chances at every turn. Soon, like so many others of the time, I was writing songs that either imitated Dylan and the Beatles or were influenced by them. No longer locked into the four chords of doo-wop and the adolescent conceits of pop, I began to explore with different musical structures and different themes—humorous, grotesque, satirical, tragic, and political—things about which the inherited musical culture had been thunderously mute.

By the time I was finishing my senior year of high school, the neighborhood was beginning to disappear. One by one the Majestics enlisted in the Navy to avoid the draft, and now I was left alone to explore new possibilities. Neighborhoods, reformulations of village life and bastions of orality, are great places to grow up in but are also cages for those in search of something different. With everyone gone, I started to branch out and explore the world beyond the walls of the street corner. I made new friends, joined new clubs, expanded my listening habits, visited new places like the Catholic Worker in the Bowery, and played new songs on my guitar. I was walking in a new land and enjoying every inch of it.

Next stop was college. Unlike high school, college was a grand liberation for me. Although only 15 miles from my hometown, St. Peter's College in Jersey City was yet a further step away from my family and the old neighborhood. After commuting by train for the first semester, I found a room at Mrs. V's rooming house on Highland Avenue for just $10 a week. It was a three-story wood-frame building in the middle of the block with faux brick shingles covering the exterior walls and a conical turret crowning the top. Mrs. V lived with her husband and soon-to-be-married daughter on the first floor while renting out rooms on the second and third floors to students from the college just a block away.

On the Sunday night I first arrived there, I met the other students as they returned one by one from the Christmas break. Once my parents left and all the niceties were over, two of the boarders—Joe Del and Jim—got into a heated argument, which, I was to learn, was something they did on a regular basis, each one provoking and taunting the other. They bounced all over the place, trading insults and polemics, mostly about God, religion, law, the war in Vietnam, poverty, civil rights, drugs, sexual liberation, feminism, and of course, music. Jim defended Motown and doo-wop, which, in his view, was clear evidence that changes in attitudes regarding race were coming about gradually and peacefully. Steven Van Zandt, rhythm guitarist for Bruce Springsteen and the actor who played Silvio Dante on *The Sopranos*, expressed it this way: "You're dancing to the Temptations, and you're watching Jackie Robinson or whoever it is play sports. How much of a racist can you continue to be?" (quoted in Luscombe 2013, 54).

Joe, however, attacked Motown as banal music—slick, shallow, and silly—that danced around the social issues of the day without ever engaging them. Rather, he gravitated toward the British bands, the Beatles, the emerging American rock bands, and, in particular, to a new group that he was to champion, the Doors. I sided with Jim mostly—the neighborhood within me stubbornly persisted—who seemed to be the voice of reason confronting a radical vision I was not comfortable with. Weren't all these bands with the long hair, flamboyant clothes, and funny eyeglasses just trying to cash in on the novelty inspired by the Beatles? But, as the semester went on and the arguments continued going round after round, my smug self-assuredness began to wither away. Maybe there was more.

As it turned out, the polemic that Jim and Joe Del had created by contrasting black pop music with the emerging rock music proved to be a false opposition. Like a Hegelian dialectic, the two forms began to merge and create an exciting synthesis. Artists such as Sam and Dave, Wilson Pickett, Aretha Franklin, and Otis Redding broke through to white audiences who, although exposed to black music through rock and roll, doo-wop, and Motown, had never before experienced the profound power and glory of soul music. At the same time, white performers like Janis Joplin tried to channel the grittiness and intensity of the blues for audiences unaccustomed to such raw expression, especially from a woman. British musicians, of course, such as the Rolling Stones, the Animals, Cream, John Mayall and the Bluesbreakers, and many others had long ago tuned to the blues and were spreading their passion to teenagers around the world.

Even the polemic of folk music (as "authentic") versus rock (as "crass commercialism") was blurred by the arrival of one of the bands defended by Joe in those ongoing discussions. The Byrds were especially important for their ability to translate the headiness of the folk revival into a more accessible rock medium without destroying the integrity of the original. "The Byrds," writes Robert Shelton (1986) "who in 1965 cut 'Mr. Tambourine Man,' one of the decade's most successful singles, assisted Dylan's entry into rock" (208). Tom Gannon (personal communication, December 14, 2012) adds quite correctly that the importance of the Byrds is that "they made Dylan palatable to the American masses." The influence of the Beatles was also a part of this emerging mix. Roger McGuinn (founder of the Byrds) stated that he "saw a niche, a place where the two of them [The Beatles and Dylan] blended together. If you took Lennon and Dylan and mixed them together, that was something that hadn't been done" (Szatmary 2000, 96). The British group the Animals did much of the same with their moving interpretation of a song ("The House of the Rising Sun") that had been unearthed and popularized in folk circles by Dave Van Ronk and then recorded by Dylan on his first album in 1962. It would seem that this hybridization of styles was not an aberration of the period but its central characteristic.

And finally, Dylan himself made the transition from folk into the world of rock with heavily amplified electric guitars and bass, drum kits and organs, and lyrics that explored themes untouched in the folk revival. Szatmary (2000) recalls the oft-told tale of the day Dylan crossed over into the world of rock:

> On July 25, 1965, at the Newport Folk Festival, Dylan unveiled his new electric sound and brand of songwriting to the folk community. Behind the stage, some of the folk performers tried to prevent Dylan from playing his electric music with the Paul Butterfield Blues Band. "On one side you had Pete Seeger, [concert organizer] George Wein, the old guard," remembers Paul Rothchild, who mixed the Dylan set and had recently recorded the Butterfield band. "Pete is backstage, pacifist Pete, with an ax saying, 'I'm going to cut the fucking cables if that act goes onstage.' Eventually Seeger dashed to his "car and rolled up the windows, his hands over his ears." When Dylan unleashed the electrified "Maggie's Farm," recalled Elektra Records owner Jac Holzman, "suddenly we heard booing, like pockets of wartime flak." ... "People were just horrified," Peter Yarrow later related. "It was as if it was a capitulation to the enemy—as if all of a sudden you saw Martin Luther King Jr. doing a cigarette ad." (93–94)

This blend of opposing worlds—the folk revival within the rock, soul music within a white teenage context—was more than just a synthesis of styles but of ideology as well. The folk revival, with deep roots in social struggle and leftist politics, helped to extend the commitment to civil rights, racial justice, and the pursuit of peace to the masses through the influence of rock. The black performers were no longer the "coons, bucks, minstrels and clowns" that a racist America had once cast them as but artists admired and emulated by the masses of white youth. David Chase, creator of *The Sopranos* and *Not Fade Away*, a film set in the 1960s, holds the view that

> For some reason at that time, white teenagers made common cause with African-American adults. And part of it was through music, because that music had its roots in the African American experience. What happened to pop music gave birth to marches on Washington, especially the antiwar part of it. It was all tied up with race and identity politics, and music hasn't done that since then. (quoted in Luscombe 2013, 54)

Such respect for African American musicians and the things they were singing about demanded white audiences to at least consider, and for white artists to comment on, the nature of ethnic prejudice in America. Not only did black artists like Curtis Mayfield ("People Get Ready," "Movin' on Up"), Aretha Franklin ("Respect"), Sly and the Family Stone ("Everyday People," "Don't Call Me Nigger, Whitey"), and James Brown ("Say It Loud") write and record songs raising awareness about racial oppression and the move toward liberation but so did several white performers as well (the Young Rascals, "People Got To Be Free"; the Youngbloods, "Get Together"). And even Dion DiMucci, that one-time doo-wopper from the Bronx, chimed in with a very moving lament ("Abraham, Martin and John") after the assassinations of Dr. Martin Luther King and Robert Kennedy in 1968.

Sometime during the winter of 1967, Joe dragged me to see a folk singer named Phil Ochs at Hunter College. Ochs was very much part of a line of politically committed folk singers extending back through Joe Hill, Woody Guthrie, Cisco Houston, Josh White, Pete Seeger, and others who had allied themselves with the dispossessed and the downtrodden, who understood music as a potent weapon of social change. Ochs is not much remembered these days, and even then in 1967, one seldom heard his name on the radio or in conversation and never on TV. Not the poet that Dylan was nor the musician that the Beatles were, Ochs nonetheless deserves special mention for his promotion of a political critique into a culture not accustomed to having its assumptions questioned. Songs such as "Draft Dodger Rag," "Cops of the World," and "I Ain't A-Marching Anymore" became the battle cry for many who not only opposed the war in Vietnam but who were also in some instances considering acts of civil disobedience—burning draft cards, refusing induction, going to jail, or fleeing across the border to Canada—as the only sane response to an insane policy.

Ochs is also noteworthy in his attempt to marry the oral and literate tradition to the electronic environment that was erupting all around us at that time. From the oral tradition, he maintained an acoustic, low-tech performance style with an interpersonal directness. Whereas other musicians fought to move into the spotlight of stardom, Ochs seemed to exhibit a strong commitment to community and grassroots simplicity above the call of celebrity and the temptations of wealth. Ochs had honed his performance and songwriting skills as part of the community of folk singers (Judy Collins, Bob Dylan, Dave Van Ronk, Tom Paxton, Fred Neil, Richie Havens, etc.) who had migrated to Greenwich Village in the late 1950s and early 1960s, where they lived in proximity, hung out together, crashed at each other's apartments, and regularly shared ideas, stories, opinions, and songs via face-to-face communication. They performed acoustically in small neighborhood coffee shops without access to microphones or amplification for their instruments or their voices and lived off the donations patrons put in the baskets they passed around after performing (Dylan 2004, 17). Suze Rotolo (2008) remembers that "Folk venues were small and informal places that didn't pay; performers passed around a basket for tips—hence the term *basket houses*" (113).

At the same time, as a onetime journalism major at Ohio State and a news junkie, Ochs exuded a highly intellectualized and rational perspective that underscored his very literate approach to music. The Village itself at that time was a highly intellectualized neighborhood filled with bookshops and scores of people willing to discuss at length literate ideas and the works that they were reading. In this vein, Bob Dylan (2004) spends a great deal of time in his memoir describing the contents of the library in the apartment he crashed in upon first arriving to New York in 1961. Ochs is very much representative of this literate mind-set, and his songs can be construed as a series of political essays set to music, political pamphlets put to rhythm and rhyme. His first album—*All the News That's Fit to Sing*—was an ironic rephrasing of the motto used by *The New York Times* and reflected the degree to which his songs were characteristically responses to stories he had read in the newspaper. He was also adept at placing literature in musical settings, as he did with the poem "The Bells" by Edgar Allan Poe. One could say that the songs Ochs wrote were not only very literate but that they even demanded a highly literate audience to appreciate what it was he was singing about. His public persona may have been "everyman" (his second album showed him dressed in a Navy pea coat, sitting against a leaflet-covered wall on a littered New York City sidewalk in winter, with a hole in the sole of his shoe) but his art appealed to the educated and deeply literate, not the hoi polloi.

The stage that night at Hunter College was simple—one mike for the guitar, one mike for the voice, one light for the performer—and I remember Phil kept tuning and retuning his guitar, leisurely conversing with the audience as he did so, complaining that he had just changed the strings. His songs relentlessly attacked American foreign policy, imperialism, the obsession with waging war, hypocritical politicians and a whole litany of social ills. For a working-class child of the Cold War, his songs were a tough pill to swallow. While the crowd hung on every word of every song, I was disturbed at hearing my version of America being lanced by this cocky young man with a guitar. Joe and I argued long and hard in the days and weeks that followed but, by the summer of '67, I knew that all I believed in was going through a reevaluation and a vast revision. I began, for the first time in my life, to question.

As the war in Vietnam escalated, so did the movement against it. The media environment became saturated with the sights and sounds of the mounting opposition to the war while those who still supported it seemed lame and out of step. The nightly images of war on the evening news, the video coverage of antiwar protests, and the music that questioned and condemned American foreign policy were becoming inescapable. In a working-class environment like Jersey City, however, steeped in the symbols and rhetoric of patriotism, change came very slowly, but on college campuses elsewhere in the country, opposition to the war was growing exponentially. "Between 1965 and 1967," Todd Gitlin (1993) writes, "as American troops doubled and re-doubled twice more, most antiwar movers and shakers shook off their leftover faith in negotiations and endorsed immediate withdrawal" (261). In this spirit, a small chapter of Students for a Democratic Society (SDS) formed at St. Peter's to raise awareness about the war, though at first it wasn't very vocal or very visible. Initiated by one of the most academically brilliant students on campus, the SDS at St. Peter's promoted an overly intellectualized critique of American foreign policy based on critical reading and reasoned argument. They were forever handing out literature that few took the time to read and organizing teach-ins that frequently turned into screaming matches among the self-righteous. To speak out against the war at that time was, in itself, a courageous act in Jersey City, for not to support the war was understood as an act of treason and a betrayal of sons, brothers, friends, and cousins who were now in Vietnam or shortly on their way.

It seemed to me, at least initially, that most of those who openly opposed the war at St. Peter's were not, in fact, from Jersey City or Hudson County but transplants like Joe and myself who rented apartments for about $95 a month near the college and lived away from their home environments. At that time it was difficult, almost impossible, for students who lived at home and commuted to school to rebel against not only their parents but also against their extended families, neighbors, and lifelong friends. Such

is the stabilizing power of orality. The antiwar protests of the period, therefore, that were going on around the nation were much more likely to take
place on campuses where students boarded and were living outside their
accustomed social milieu, where the bonds of kinship and tradition did not
prevail with the same degree of weight. For the most part, therefore, the
SDS at St. Peter's was an isolated group on campus who, even if they hadn't
opposed the war, would have been considered outsiders by virtue of their
dress, ideas, lifestyle, intellect, and town of origin. I distinctly remember that
at the New Year's Eve party welcoming in 1968, the head of SDS played Phil
Ochs and Joan Baez records in her apartment while people stood around
eating corn chips and discussing politics. There was barely a whiff of the
bacchanal that was about to begin.

Meanwhile, the counterculture upheavals sweeping east from California
were beginning to promote an alternative vision of living, thinking, and
being that went far beyond the reasoned left-brain political critique that was
SDS at St. Peter's in 1967. As questions about the war in Vietnam (teach-
ins, informal discussions) turned into opposition (antiwar demonstrations)
and opposition turned into civil disobedience (the burning of draft cards,
the refusal to pay taxes, the participation in sit-ins and seizures of university buildings), the music pushed forward perspectives that encouraged such
actions. Whereas Sam Cooke in the aforementioned "Chain Gang" was
asking for mercy a few years earlier, the new music was promoting rebellion
and resistance, often speaking in the language of insurrection and civil disobedience ("Street Fighting Man," by the Rolling Stones; "Alice's Restaurant," by Arlo Guthrie, son of Woody; "I Feel Like I'm Fixin' to Die Rag,"
by Country Joe and the Fish; "The Unknown Soldier," by the Doors).

Just as important as the politicized expression of the music, the growing
prominence of hallucinogenic drugs was influencing ways of seeing and
understanding. Drugs slowly made a surreptitious appearance on campus
and Joe, after getting beat a couple of times with the purchase of nickel bags
of oregano from winos in Washington Square, was among the first to experiment with reefer. Politics were still very much a part of his discourse but
now talk of "mind expansion" and "tuning in, turning on, and dropping
out" increasingly entered his conversation. On the door to his room, Joe
hung the words of Jean Jacques Rousseau to express his new turn of mind:
"Man is born free, and everywhere he is chains." At the same time, buying,
selling, and using illegal substances wasn't just being rebellious, it was being
criminal, and, for young people, the outlaw persona became an exciting and
dangerous one to don.

With the widespread use of hallucinogenic drugs, musicians were stimulated to express themselves in compositions that were much longer, louder,
more hypnotic, and markedly more Dionysian in spirit. Although AM radio
shied away from playing this more controversial music (many AM stations,

for example, mistook the Byrds' "Eight Miles High" as referring to a drug high and refused to play it), FM radio, emerging as a music forum targeting college students, embraced it. James Monaco (1978) writes, "if there was a medium that characterized the 1960s, it wasn't film, it wasn't television, it wasn't even records; it was FM radio, especially as it flourished in union with 'progressive rock' . . . [whereas] AM radio consisted of simplistic two minute popular singles and news . . . FM helped to define the counterculture" (173).

Students identified themselves not only by which station they tuned in to but also whether they listened to AM or FM. The AM radio stations followed the tried, the true, and the safe, featuring babbling DJs with a scripted playlist of short noncontroversial songs. Topics such as the war, racial oppression, drugs, and sexual liberation—in short, all the things that mattered most to many college students at that time—were steadfastly ignored. Chapple and Garofalo (1978) note that

> [U]nlike AM disc jockeys, who were told what to play . . . DJs on the new progressive FM stations had near total freedom to play whatever they wanted . . . [Moreover] to handle audience response, FM stations established switchboards that provided listeners with rides, addresses of places to spend the night, and news of concerts and demonstrations . . . Many FMs built radical news departments that did not simply "rip and read" the wire service releases as AM did, but gathered their own news from a variety of sources . . . Even commercially, the original stations, especially the non-chain independents, were often responsive to the anti-materialism of the youth communities. Many progressive FMs, like WBCN, refused to advertise cigarettes, or the products of particularly conspicuous war-making corporations. In the aftermath of the burning of the Santa Barbara Bank of America branch, KZAP, among others, turned down Bank of America ads. (176–178)

At the same time, improvements in music technology were placing a whole new set of tools in the hands of musicians, who were now experimenting with synthesizers, wa-wa pedals, and fuzz boxes; the use of vibrato, reverb and delay, and innovative recording and playback devices; advancements in amplification; and so on. Moreover, the surge in volume meant that music wasn't only something one listened to but, quite literally, it was now something that one could feel as a vibration resonating throughout the body. People danced with or without partners, in total abandon and unrestrained by form or social norms. Clothing became more flamboyant, face and body paint became common, designs were painted on cars, shoes and sometimes even clothing were discarded, strobe lights and black lights disoriented perception, wall posters presented mystical visions or called for radical actions, and incense soaked the environment along with the pungent smell of marijuana. The five senses were reunified and collectively stimulated in ways that hadn't been experienced since our Paleolithic past.

Alternative or underground newspapers (*The Berkeley Barb*, *The East Village Other*, *The Oracle*, *The Bugle American*), magazines (*Ramparts*, *The Realist*), and comic books (Robert Crumb's *Mr. Natural*, Gilbert Shelton's *The Fabulous Furry Freak Brothers*) creatively celebrated and promoted the new culture. Alternative movie theaters, societies, and clubs brought in the best of foreign movies rarely exhibited in commercial houses (Fellini, Antonioni, Truffaut, Godard, Kurosawa, Bergman, Buñuel, etc.). Experimental theater groups introduced avant garde methods of breaking through the fourth wall and involved the audience more directly in the performance. Guerrilla theater brought performances to the streets and to public places, and groups such as the San Francisco Mime Troupe politicized plays in a way that Broadway never dared. Bread and Puppet Theater used huge puppets to bring attention to social causes. Artists of every medium were admired and emulated, and it seemed that everyone wanted to be an artist or at least considered to be artistic; business and the military were widely disdained and deplored as dishonorable professions. Things have changed quite a bit since then.

Parents and neighbors were horrified by the radical changes in behavior, taste, and appearance of their children, but teenagers were in their glory. Music, more than just a background sound, became a badge of identity and an assembly point that not only separated the youth from their parents but also the "freaks" (those on board with the new culture) from the "straights" (those still clinging to the old culture). "I'm gonna wave my freak flag high!" Hendrix exclaimed in his song "If 6 Was 9," and now even the eggheads from SDS felt marginalized by this "revolution in the revolution" that was pushing them—the "people's vanguard"—unceremoniously aside.

In March 1968, Joe and I went to a new place that had just opened up on 2nd Avenue in the East Village called the Fillmore East. Founded by early rock impresario Bill Graham, the New York City venue was the offshoot of an earlier auditorium in San Francisco that was key in launching and sustaining the rock revolution. Always a controversial and confrontational figure, Graham did much to keep the costs of rock shows down while he boldly mixed acts—rock groups with blues, jazz, and Latin musicians—in a way that had never been done before. Ironically, we drove into the city that night in that same '57 Ford that had once taken me down South as a child to witness chain gangs and segregation with my own eyes. Only this time, the music on radio was different, and I was in the driver's seat on my way to see the Doors. Joe was especially excited about this concert for there was no other group—not even the Beatles—that he admired more than the Doors. Because he was such a big fan (he would constantly quote from their music and had a big Doors poster on the wall above his bed), Joe insisted that we spring the $5 for the most expensive seats (the cheapest were $3).

At the open, the stage was dressed in a dark blue light and only silhouettes could be seen on stage. As sounds of a repetitious blues vamp in a minor key hypnotized the crowd, Jim Morrison suddenly leaped out, screamed a primordial cry, and then broke into "When the Music's Over." The Doors represented perhaps the best and certainly the most controversial of the West Coast groups. Taking their name from a line of William Blake's poetry ("If the doors of perception were cleansed everything would appear to man as it is, Infinite") that had also formed the title of Aldous Huxley's 1954 book *The Doors of Perception,* the Doors were a band determined to open those doors and break on through to the other side. "If my poetry aims to achieve anything," Morrison stated, "it's to deliver people from the limited ways in which they see and feel" (quoted in Hopkins and Sugarman 2006, xv). Hopkins and Sugarman add that: "Here was a band whose unexpressed goal was nothing short of musical alchemy—they intended to wed rock music unlike any heard before with poetry and that hybrid with theater and drama" (viii).

The personnel that formed the band were the perfect group to effect this desired unification of poetry, music, theater, and drama. Both the keyboardist (Ray Manzarek) and the guitarist (Robby Krieger) had studied classical technique and were able to translate their training into creating mesmerizing musical settings for Morrison's poetry. Moreover, the members of the band—Manzarek, Krieger, and John Densmore (drums)—had all met while students of yoga and devotees of the Maharishi Mahesh Yogi, which helps to explain the meditative drone and transcendental quality of the music behind Morrison.

The net result of this hybridization of music, poetry, theater, and drama was nothing less than the reunification of something quite ancient: more than performance or a catchy tune, music became ritual. As the evening progressed, the "Joshua Light Show," with its colorful projections of amorphous, slowly moving, liquid shapes, added to the theatricality of the performance. At one point, Morrison screened a movie he had made (both Morrison and Manzarek had studied film at UCLA) to accompany his composition "The Unknown Soldier." It was truly a multimedia, multisensory experience.

With poetic lyrics and musicians who had studied classical music, the Doors were bringing literate elements into the electronic world. Jim Morrison, Lester Bangs (1976) points out, "wanted to be a literary figure . . . [and years later in 1971] headed for Paris, home of the French Symbolist poets, birthplace of the Surrealist movement, Céline's misanthropic ellipses . . . He probably had some vague idea, like Hemingway and Fitzgerald before him, of finding literary sustenance in that atmosphere" (262–263).

But Jim Morrison also symbolized the rabid narcissism and self-destructive tendencies of the 1960s. Electric technology not only increased the notoriety of musicians but it also fanned the flames of their egos. They were no longer mere performers or even glitzy superstars but transcendental shamans with special powers presiding over the tribes gathered there for communion with the gods. There was talk of "re-tribalization," and concerts took on the aura of ritual where musicians donned the persona of priests and priestesses who channeled the magic that energized the assembled. Morrison embraced this calling, grew a poet's beard (or was it the beard of an Old Testament prophet or an Eastern mystic?) and began to refer to himself as the "Lizard King." But the price of such self-aggrandizement and ego inflation is sanity itself. Bangs (1976) goes on to describe Morrison as "a clown" and "a cartoon," who was getting "drunker and fatter," becoming more outrageous and ridiculous by the minute. The music of the Doors, so powerful at first, lost aesthetic direction and "not only failed to live up to their original promise—they had (Morrison had) turned what they represented into a joke" (262).

The disintegration of Morrison was paralleled by the disintegration of others who were wasted most of the time and given to behavior that was more and more erratic and out of control. Hendrix, the most brilliant guitarist of his generation, destroyed his instrument and equipment on stage as part of his performance. In fits of rage, Pete Townshend of the Who did the same. Janis Joplin drank Southern Comfort right out of the bottle as she screeched on stage to an audience cheering her self-destruction. Others—John Lennon, Jim Morrison, Eric Clapton, Lou Reed, and Keith Richards among others—became addicted to heroin. Without boundaries and guideposts, and dismissing all forms of self-restraint, the shamans and the stars and the audiences that adored them drove wildly to the edge and then over the cliff. The Woodstock Festival, "An Aquarian Exposition of 3 days of Music and Peace" in August 1969, grandiose and spectacular, can perhaps best be understood as the going away party for the best and the worst that was the 1960s. With a few notable exceptions (the Beatles, the Rolling Stones, Bob Dylan), it seemed that anybody who was somebody was performing there. Despite the huge crowds, the poor planning, the drugged-out audience, the continual rain, and the lack of facilities, the concert managed to fly by the seat of its pants and made its way into the folklore of American culture.

After Woodstock, however, it went downhill fast. In December 1969, the Rolling Stones tried to repeat the success of Woodstock with an outdoor concert at Altamont in California. In an attempt to out-hip the East Coast extravaganza, the Stones turned security concerns over to the Hells Angels and paid them with beer. Bad decision. By the end of the day, several people had been severely beaten and four were dead. "Amidst the violence," writes

Carl Belz (1972), "the rock world lost much of the respect it had gained at Woodstock" (219).

And then, one by one, all the cards began to fall. In April 1970, the Beatles broke up, and it was like I lost the arrow on my compass. In September, Jimi Hendrix died, choking on his own vomit in London, and, in October, Janis Joplin died of a heroin overdose in California. And then in 1971, just a few months after the deaths of Janis Joplin and Jimi Hendrix, the Lizard King died a mysterious death, à la Marat, in a Parisian bathtub. Many of their fans had also driven themselves too hard, too fast, and too far. Some were strung out on drugs, some were suddenly lost not knowing where to go, and some were just plain exhausted. The bands kept on playing but the party was over. Time to go home.

If Allen Ginsberg could howl that he saw the best minds of his generation destroyed by madness, what could I say about mine?

DISCUSSION AND CONCLUSION

"Great events are great events," writes the historian Samuel Hand (1984), "because they deeply influence the lives of countless persons" (53). As insignificant and miniscule as we may sometimes feel, we are nonetheless participants, witnesses, recorders and carriers of the times in which we are tossed. Coming of age during a time of rebellion, I was exposed to a great deal that both extended what I learned as a child and challenged the contradictions I was being asked to ingest as an adolescent. Although the tale I have told here is mine and no one else's, there is no doubt in my mind that music and changes in media are core to the stories of all who experienced this period during their youth.

Todd Gitlin (1993) justifiably ridicules the simplistic notion of discussing history in terms of decades. "No sooner do we enter a year whose digit is nine than the great machinery of the media is flooding us with phrases to sum up the previous ten years and characterize the next" (xiii). And yet, as the title of Gitlin's book (The Sixties) testifies, there is something self-contained about a decade that began with the election of Kennedy and ended with the breakup of the Beatles and the deaths of Janis Joplin, Jimi Hendrix, and Jim Morrison. The idealism, once so abundant, was dead. The rebelliousness was gone as well, and the new music that came to replace the innovative experiments of the 1960s was more flamboyant and flimsy, more akin to rococo than to rock. A decade that had begun full of vigor, vitality, and high hopes was coming to its conclusion on a disco dance floor or, worse yet, in a flop house on desolation row. The exploratory challenge "tune in, turn on, and drop out" had been replaced by the hedonistic "sex, drugs, and rock and roll."

If *The Magnificent Seven* (1960) acted as a cinematic metaphor for the decade at its outset, perhaps *Butch Cassidy and the Sundance Kid* (George Roy Hill, 1969) can be said to provide a fitting one for its demise. Lovable out-laws—not really bad, just rebellious and free-spirited—are relentlessly tracked by the repressive forces of law and order and then, vastly outnumbered and outgunned, Butch (Paul Newman) and Sundance (Robert Redford) are mas-sacred by the military. The traditional good guys of Hollywood (those repre-senting law and order) had become the villains, and the traditional villains (bank robbers and bandits) had become the heroes. More importantly for our purposes, there is a significant shift in the music that accompanied both these films. The theme song to *The Magnificent Seven* (composed by Elmer Bernstein) is expansive, majestic, powerfully optimistic, and heroic. The theme song to *Butch Cassidy and the Sundance Kid* ("Raindrops Keep Falling On My Head," composed by Burt Bacharach and Hal David), in contrast, is pleasant enough but wimpy and frail: the starch has been washed out of it. A decade that began with dreams for a better tomorrow was ending up feel-ing trapped and defeated. The *federales* had us surrounded and we knew it.

More than a time, however, the 1960s were a place—a battleground even—where a well-entrenched oral and literate culture was confronted and routed by a newly emerging electronic one. Electronic media were flooding Amer-ican homes, and the novelty of these multiple devices endowed them with a miraculous aura that such devices lack today now that they have become the mundane machinery of our daily routine. For adults, more fully social-ized into the old oral/literate culture, the impact of this electronic invasion was more distanced and less immediate. For adolescents, however, the elec-tronic media separated them from their families socially, psychologically, culturally, and physically and brought with them a tsunami of change.

The decade was the scene of a great rebellion, and it is this fact that also sets the period apart from others and gives its music a particular impor-tance. There were scores of race riots, hundreds of sit-ins, and thousands of demonstrations protesting the war in Vietnam, racial injustice, and various other issues, great and small, that affected local communities across the country. It was a time of deep involvement and fearless action. Many young men refused military induction and were sent to jail or escaped across the border into Canada. Others burned draft cards, took over college campuses, refused to pay taxes used to support the war effort, or engaged in other acts of civil disobedience. Students were reading and quoting Henry David Tho-reau, Herbert Marcuse, Ché Guevara, and Eldridge Cleaver, and attending fiery speeches delivered by Stokely Carmichael, Dick Gregory, Jane Jacobs, Ralph Nader, and Daniel and Philip Berrigan. The women's movement, the environmental movement, the New Age movement, and others that demanded new ways of thinking and behaving were being born at this time, and today, as mature and established movements, continue to challenge and change the status quo. The Black Panthers, the Young Lords, the American Indian Movement, the Weathermen, and various other groups openly defied the authorities and, by the end of the 1960s, there were instances of public buildings being bombed, numerous race riots, sniper shootings of police officers from the rooftops of housing projects, and bold confrontations with the military. The revolution so often talked about never came, of course, but there's no denying that rebellion was in full swing.

The importance of the music of the 1960s is that it affirmed this rebellion while creating the gathering point that cemented it together—an alternative culture—where young people assembled and to which they devoted every ounce of creative energy that their young bodies could muster. Contesting the establishment, young people took it upon themselves to explore new possibilities—spiritual, political, economic, sexual, and cultural—that opened the doors of consciousness and the pathways of being to a new way of thinking, feeling, and living in the world. To rebel—to question all the assumptions of the society into which one is born and to openly defy convention, tradition, and law, to endanger one's present situation, and to jeopardize one's future livelihood—requires a sustained courage and a tenacity of spirit that the music of the time fortified and made resolute. The music, then, was not so much a background beat or a soundtrack to the glories of youth as it was a powerful force pushing everyone and everything forward and then assuring us that we were righteous in our rebellion, confident that victory was ours, and that there could be no turning back.

This thunderous clash of cultures was less about generations than it was about media. During the 1960s, the entrenched oral/literate consensus was being challenged by an electronic onslaught that stimulated the youth to rebel against the restrictions of the old. By abandoning the oral contract with our families and our government, which demanded blind acceptance of inherited responsibilities, and abandoning the literate contract with our schools and universities, which demanded adherence to the hierarchies of learning and the acceptance of a script that no longer made sense to us, we entered the newly arrived electronic environment where music was both the message and the massage. Dylan challenged ("How many times can a man turn his head and pretend that he just doesn't see?"), the Beatles inspired ("There's nothing you can do that can't be done"), Frank Zappa tormented ("TV dinners by the pool/I'm so glad I finished school"), and the Doors commanded ("Break on through to the other side"). Without the powerful force of music expressing and inducing the emotions necessary for such insights, the rebellion would never have had advanced as far or as widely as it did.

It was Marshall McLuhan who boldly went where no academic had gone before and launched a series of probes exploring the psychological and social changes brought about by electronic media. McLuhan emphasized that centuries-old habits and ways of being formed by oral and literate communication were being challenged by the onslaught of electronic media. McLuhan (1964) writes that "the interplay among media is only another name for this 'civil war' that rages in our society and psyches alike" (57). But this civil war provoked by changes in the media environment is also an opportunity pregnant with great possibility. McLuhan concludes his chapter on hybrid energy with the observation that "The hybrid or the meeting place of two media is a moment of truth and revelation from which new form is born . . . The moment of the meeting of media is a moment of freedom and release from the ordinary trance and numbness imposed by them on our senses" (63).

The musical hybridization that synchronized so powerfully during the decade took place on several different levels. First of all, electronic media—especially recording and playback technology, the enhanced amplification of sound, and the extensions of radio, television, and cinema—brought many diverse cultures and cultural styles into one's daily existence and, ultimately, into one's own being. The parochial character of orality and the detachment that literacy cultivates were suddenly challenged by the onslaught of an expansive new culture made possible through electronic communication. On top of this, the recent availability of commercial jet air travel made it possible for people to move about in ways heretofore impossible. The global village was afoot. Suddenly the world was at our fingertips, vibrating before our eyes, pounding in our ears, and transforming our hearts and our minds. There was, so to speak, an ontological shift, that is, a profound change in what it meant to be human. No longer limited to the four walls of our physical environment, our sensorium was stretched and our beings were able to wander into other worlds transported on the vicarious wings of technologies increasingly available.

Second, there was also a powerful hybridization of oral and literate culture with the sudden surge of electronic culture that had not, as of yet, established itself with the hegemonic force it enjoys today. In other words, although we were suddenly swamped with new electronic technologies, we had also grown up in families, neighborhoods, and schools profoundly marked by the rhythms, relationships, and habits of orality and literacy. Although we fell in love with this energizing electronic environment and were seduced by every new gadget it provided, we were immigrants to this new world, certainly not natives. Everything was newly available to the youth: FM radio, miniature transistor radios, stereos, component sound systems, color TV, portable TV, headphones, posters on the walls of the bedroom, tape recorders, etc. And yet, kids on the corner still sang, played games, and jumped rope. Families still ate dinner together and shared stories, adults read newspapers after dinner, neighbors hung out on the front stoop in the evening, and life moved about at a much slower pace.

Face-to-face, interpersonal relationships still prevailed while strict rules governed the use of language, dress, forms of address, public demeanor, sexual behavior, and so on. At the same time, schools were structured with the decorum, orderliness, and quietude that literacy demands. Discipline was much less of a problem for the simple reason that children arrived to school already socialized to these rules of conduct. All of this, of course, would be challenged over the course of the decade and, by the onset of the 1970s, significant changes to the oral/literate stasis had spread across the entire spectrum of American society. Orality and literacy had undoubtedly been weakened by the advance of electronic technology and the oral/literate/electronic balance that gave birth to the 1960s was fading fast. You can never go home again, and the cultural conservatives of the present day who preach about the good ol' days do so through the rearview mirrors of their SUVs while talking a mile a minute on their cell phones.

Third, explorations with drugs, especially marijuana and LSD, opened (in the words of Aldous Huxley) "the doors of perception" for a youth inclined to experiment with these newfound agents that effectively stimulated aural, visual, and tactile sense organs. All of the arts responded accordingly, but music did so most voluptuously. Artwork decorated album covers and light shows accompanied concerts. The widespread use of hallucinogens encouraged musicians to express themselves more poetically and required audiences to do the same. The music became louder, the dancing freer, the hair longer, and the clothing more flamboyant. Face and body paint became common, and incense soaked the environment as much as did the distinctive aroma of marijuana. The sensorium was flooded with stimulation while musicians channeled the magic that energized the crowd. The regimentation of the post–World War II era and the avaricious consumerism and paranoia of the Cold War were understood in this new light and no longer made sense. "What if they gave a war and nobody came?"

As a result of these multiple levels of hybridization, the decade's music took the youth on a wild roller coaster ride that not only produced a great body of work that remains influential to this day but also an irresistible force that propelled a social rebellion forward. Exposed to an avalanche of influences, excited by the existence of new technologies, and stimulated by mind-altering drugs, the new music seized control of the wheels of culture with an intensity and a purpose it never had before and has not had since.

To return where we started at the top of this chapter, there are places I'll remember all my life, and certainly the 1960s is one of them. More than just a shoebox of old photographs or a bundle of perfumed letters, however, the 1960s were a time that forever marked me and radically altered who I was and who I was to become. Although it is certainly true that music from the past is commonly used to invoke nostalgia, sell automobiles, promote political candidates, or become a collector's fetish, in my life the music of the 1960s will always be identified with the rebellion I experienced and the changes I was forced to make within an intense period of 10 short years. The distanced traveled from Sister Eugenia's sixth-grade classroom to the psychedelic ambiance of the Fillmore East in New York City, from chain gangs in Georgia to mass demonstrations against the war, was an enormous one. Along the way there were powerful images, voices, movies, and words that guided my footsteps, but the constant and indispensable companion on this journey was the music. Take away the music and the rebellion of the era falls on its face. The civil rights movement was sustained by the music of the southern African American church just as the antiwar movement was energized and affirmed by the dissident sounds of rock. When a political or social movement attempts to state its case with words alone, it crumbles; it has no heart; it has no soul. Music was the fire beneath the pot that boiled over during the 1960s.

The music described in this chapter, what it was and what it is still, vibrates within me yet. In my life, music shook the earth.

REFERENCES

Albrecht, Robert. 2004. *Mediating the Muse: A Communications Approach to Music, Media and Culture Change.* Cresskill, NJ: Hampton.

Bangs, Lester. 1976. "The Doors." In *The Rolling Stone Illustrated History of Rock & Roll,* edited by Jim Miller, 262–263. New York: Random House.

Belz, Carl. 1972. *The Story of Rock.* New York: Oxford University Press.

Chapple, Steve, and Robert Garofalo. 1978. "The Rise and Fall of FM Rock." In *Media Culture,* edited by James Monaco, 173–185. New York: Delta.

Cleaver, Eldridge. 1968. *Soul on Ice.* New York: Dell.

Dylan, Bob. 2004. *Chronicles: Volume One.* New York: Simon and Schuster.

Friedlander, Paul. 2006. *Rock and Roll: A Social History.* Cambridge, MA: Westview.

Gitlin, Todd. 1993. *The Sixties: Years of Hope, Days of Rage.* New York: Bantam.

Hand, Samuel. 1984. "Some Words on Oral Histories." In *Oral History: An Interdisciplinary Anthology,* edited by David Dunaway and Willa Baum, 51–63. Nashville, TN: American Association for State and Local History.

Hardy, Phil, and Dave Laing. 1995. *The Da Capo Companion to 20th Century Popular Music.* New York: Da Capo Press.

Hopkins, Jerry, and Danny Sugerman. 2006. *No One Here Gets Out Alive.* New York: Grand Central Publishing.

Luscombe, Belinda. 2013. "Getting the Band Back Together." *Time Magazine,* January 14, 52–54.

Marqusee, Mike. 2005. *Wicked Messenger: Bob Dylan and the 1960s.* New York: Seven Stories Press.

McAleer, Dave. 1996. *The All Music Book of Hit Singles.* London: Carlton Books.

McLuhan, Marshall. 1964. *Understanding Media.* New York: McGraw-Hill.

Monaco, James. 1978. *Media Culture.* New York: Delta.

Norman, Philip. 2003. *Shout!* New York: Simon & Schuster.

Postman, Neil. 1985. *Amusing Ourselves to Death: Public Discourse in the Age of Show Business.* New York: Penguin Books.

Rotolo, Suze. 2008. *A Freewheelin' Time: A Memoir of Greenwich Village in the 1960s.* New York: Random House.

Scaduto, Anthony. 1973. *Bob Dylan: An Intimate Biography.* New York: Signet.

Shelton, Robert. 1986. *No Direction Home.* New York: Beech Tree Books.

Szatmary, David. 2000. *Rockin' in Time: A Social History of Rock 'n' Roll.* Upper Saddle River, NJ: Prentice-Hall.

14

"Love Is All You Need": Why There Will Never Be Another Beatles

Phil Rose

Notwithstanding the widely varying perspectives of what constitutes a baby boomer—both in technical or cultural terms, and within or across regions—it is generally agreed that a certain generation of people represent a significant demographic bulge that helped massively to reshape Western societies in the immediate aftermath of World War II. The boomers continue to remodel society as they now approach their senior years. With most being born within a roughly 20-year period of seemingly endless economic expansion and unprecedented affluence in the United States (1946–1964), the boomers were and remain the wealthiest and most privileged generation history has seen. When they were young, North America—living through a period of tremendous cultural change—was marked by what demographer David Foot (1998) calls a "cult of youth." Frequently, those most influential among this generation were people born just ahead of the boom, like Allen Ginsberg, Jack Kerouac, Bob Dylan, the Rolling Stones, and, of course, the Beatles. It is with the latter that rock music becomes art and explodes into the 1960s, dovetailing with all the upheaval that characterized that decade. Here, I trace the enduring prevalence of the Beatles as boomer cultural icons in relation to a number of elements, including the influence of the band's exceptional artistry, its drug use, its spirituality, and its politics. I will also probe what these elements continue to signify in relation to boomer identity and what they mean for what the generation bequeaths to its successors. Ultimately, I maintain that it is the group's relationship to the counterculture and the towering influence of John Lennon's political outspokenness that provide the singular most important facets of this legacy.

ANOTHER BEATLES?

Toward the end of the documentary film *Imagine: John Lennon* (1988), the Beatles perform on the rooftop of their Apple offices in London in what was to be their final performance. On the street below, English girls around 20 years of age are questioned by an interviewer. "There could never be another Beatles," one says, seemingly a meaningless or absurd statement. The poignancy of her comment becomes readily apparent, however, when she and her friend go on to explain: "We grew up with them" (quoted in *Imagine: John Lennon*, 1988).

It isn't difficult to apprehend how profoundly the Beatles moved their boomer audience—from the crazed teenage girls associated with early Beatlemania to more sober reflections like that just articulated. For fans of any age, it is difficult not to feel a great deal of sympathetic resonance. The Beatles saturated boomer culture with rich webs of cultural significance, each in its own way representing one more reason why there can never be another Beatles. First, as Allan Moore (1997) reminds us, it is highly significant that the Beatles were among the world's first teenagers, a new category of identity "bound up with electronics." This new teenager developed in tandem with the appearance of what Foot (1998) denotes "the cult of youth." Observing that adolescents belong to the world of the book (representing artifacts of print culture or the typographic age), Marshall McLuhan (1960)—whom John Lennon and Yoko Ono met with when they visited Toronto in 1969—elucidates Moore's observation of how teenagers correspond to life in the electronic era. Adolescents know they are not adults, as McLuhan suggests, but are merely dwelling in an enclosed "world within a world," or in the "waiting room" of life, which only properly begins with adulthood. Teenagers, on the other hand, know they are adults and act like adults, says McLuhan, who explains how this new breed of young person wants "the complete package" and wants it immediately. As teenagers have never been isolated in the ways adolescents once were they know no innocence, according to McLuhan, because they have never lived in anything but an adult world:

> any child today can grab a big chunk of adult life just by turning on the TV set, or going to a film, or leafing through a magazine. He can enter at the push of a button, the whole spectrum of adult life . . . from its most sordid to its most idealistic. They have one partner like adults . . . going steady. They think of security, of their careers, the way adults are supposed to; they want the full charge of religion and spiritual values. (McLuhan 1960, xxviii)

Of course, the same year that McLuhan recorded these observations another transformative technology entered Western culture—that is, the birth control pill, which soon helped to thrust teenagers even further into an adult world.

As Moore makes clear, "because this new teenager was not only different, but separate, its social identity could not be found within established structures, but had to be created anew" (1997, 5). In accordance with this reality, the business community and communications media offered up much with which the baby boomers and their immediate predecessors were able to perform this important identity work. Their music—namely rock and roll, became one of the key expressions of this new generational identity. The newfound affluence of these young people also permitted them to access this primary acculturation resource in most places they went, especially by way of the recently developed transistor radio.

The term "rock and roll" was originally an African American euphemism for sex, and the medium was rebellious from the very first. Alongside other white Memphis kids, Elvis Presley had taken advantage of the nonsegregated airwaves, listening intently to the sounds emanating from America's first black radio station in 1948, then assimilating these musical influences, incorporating them into his own performances. In reference to his blending of blues, country, and Tin Pan Alley styles, John Shepherd (2012) suggests that Presley was able intuitively to identify and give musical expression to many of the numerous contradictions apparent in the United States at that time, citing, particularly, those "between black and white communities, rural and urban life, men and women, working and middle classes, young and old, the South and the North" (78).

On the other side of the Atlantic Ocean, meanwhile, John Lennon, as one of the first children of the television generation, recalls seeing Elvis at home on TV and thinking to himself, "now that's a good job"—especially upon hearing the reception that Presley enjoyed from the females in his audience. Similarly, after the Beatles' 1964 invasion of America, young men would see the hysterical response of the Beatles' female fans and immediately respond by putting together their own rock groups, even if they were not the least bit musical. As John Ryan and Richard Peterson (2001) recount: "Between 1940 and 1959 guitar sales doubled. By 1964 they had doubled again, and by 1970 they had more than doubled yet again" (101). Rock and roll was evidently in the air, and although the Beatles certainly troubled some parents with their long hair, they soon won over practically everyone else with their charismatic charm.

The group initiated what was to become known in the United States as the "British Invasion," paving the way for a series of British rock/pop performers who experienced continuing American success during the mid-1960s. Moore (1997) gives us a sense of the suddenness of this development, when he notes how the 1963 U.S. charts featured only one UK success, whereas, come 1964, there were 32. This so-called invasion got its launch with the Beatles' appearance on *The Ed Sullivan Show*, for which it was estimated a mass audience of more than 73 million Americans—or 45 percent of those watching television that night—viewed their performance (Leopold 2004). This is surely another reason that there could never be another Beatles, given that those were the days when there were only three national television networks and a handful of broadcast channels, long before the hundredfold array of specialty channels that later became available with the onset of cable and satellite services. Likewise, this was considerably before subsequent innovations made it easy for people to watch programs at a time other than when they were originally aired, a development that obsolesced the requirement for masses of viewers to tune in simultaneously to a broadcast. This massive cultural focus greatly contributed to the Beatles' yet unparalleled feat of holding the top five spots on the *Billboard* Hot 100 chart (accomplished April 4, 1964).

In descending order these songs were "Please Please Me," "I Want to Hold Your Hand," "She Loves You," "Twist and Shout," and "Can't Buy Me Love." Four were original compositions, penned under the new songwriting partnership that Lennon had established with Paul McCartney, and many have observed the healthy rivalry that existed between the two and fed their enormous creative output. The band's first five albums—*Please Please Me* (1963), *With the Beatles* (1963), *A Hard Day's Night* (1964), *Beatles for Sale* (1964), and *Help!* (1965)[1]—comprise mostly songs credited to Lennon and McCartney, with the occasional piece by George Harrison, but they also include a selection of cover versions of early rock, rockabilly, girl-group R&B, country soul, and other styles. This early material tended to be cleverly crafted and strikingly well-performed, and, in October 1965, the enormous influence they were having was to be acknowledged in Great Britain when the government of Harold Wilson made them Members of the Most Excellent Order of the British Empire (MBE).

Just as musicologists and cultural theorists talk about an early, middle, and late period with regard to the work of figures like Ludwig von Beethoven or other creative people, we can also effectively speak in such terms when considering the biography of the Beatles. The band's early period included five straight years of recording, touring, and filmmaking. Their late period, on the other hand, is usually said to begin with the group's resolution to give up live performance and touring upon the conclusion of their last world tour in August 1966 in North America, and to conclude in 1970 with the band's final dissolution. The middle period, meanwhile, spans roughly one full year before the beginning of the late period and can be said to begin when the band "started to get weird"—to borrow the formulation of a childhood boomer neighbor of mine, who reported being a fan during the years of Beatlemania but became estranged from the group shortly thereafter.

I have since surmised that "getting weird" consisted largely of exactly those iconic elements I wish to focus upon here—the band's increasing artistic maturity and concomitant move away from straight-ahead pop music; their growing incorporation of non-Western, avant-garde, and other musical influences; and their experimentation with drugs and increasing identification with the counterculture; and their increasing political activism, particularly, as I have suggested, that of John Lennon. These elements are highly interconnected, of course, but I shall now attempt to address each in turn, beginning with the Beatles' trajectory of artistic maturity, which put into effect rock music's transformation into an art form.

LET THERE BE ART

The album *Help!* is predominantly representative of the Beatles' first period, most of its songs being pop oriented. But the album revealed some more introspective musical statements as well, and some observers attribute this to their increasing use of cannabis, which Bob Dylan famously introduced them to in 1964 upon their first meeting with the then folk singer. This trend was evident in songs like "You've Got to Hide Your Love Away" and "Yesterday" (included on the British version of the album), and continued into the next album *Rubber Soul* (1965), especially in songs like "Nowhere Man" and "In My Life." With its use of a string quartet, "Yesterday" represented a further broadening of musical influence, a tendency that was enhanced yet again with George Harrison's use of sitar on "Norwegian Wood (This Bird Has Flown)"—generally recognized as the conduit for that instrument's introduction to Western listeners. Examples of continued incorporation of different musical influences was also apparent in songs like "Michelle" and "Girl."

By 1966, with their third and last world tour, the Beatles had started to become less interested in touring and performing. Not only did they find they could no longer hear themselves play over the screaming young female voices but that summer they also became entangled in scandal, first in the Philippines, where they unintentionally snubbed the nation's first lady, and then in the U.S. South, where conservative groups, including the Ku Klux Klan, organized demonstrations against the band. At these events, young people were encouraged to burn their Beatles records and other paraphernalia in response to the U.S. publication of Lennon's decontextualized comments pertaining to how the Beatles were now more popular than Jesus Christ among contemporary young people—comments that had appeared in Great Britain six months earlier to no reaction. Their music was also becoming increasingly difficult to perform, because, as Ian MacDonald (2005) observed, by the time the band members were working on *Revolver*

(1966), which came out in the midst of all of the backlash, they were "no longer interested in simulating their live sound under studio conditions, instead creating a new sonic environment in each successive track" (202).[2]

Like Glenn Gould before them, they were now to concentrate their efforts predominantly on recording, and one cannot, in this regard, overestimate the contribution of the band's producer George Martin to their subsequent musical development. With his extensive formal musical training and technical expertise in the studio, Martin became increasingly central to turning the Beatles' musical ideas into action, as they sought ever-new sounds to use and musical styles to incorporate. Having already employed the first use of recorded guitar feedback on their early single "I Feel Fine" (1964), sometimes these exotic sounds consisted of orchestral strings, as with the octet in "Eleanor Rigby," the nonet with harp in "She's Leaving Home" from *Sgt. Pepper's Lonely Hearts Club Band* (1967), or the cellos, mellotron, and trumpets of "Strawberry Fields Forever," which saw release the same year as *Magical Mystery Tour* (1967). Alternatively, these sounds were made manifest in the full brass of "Got to Get You Into My Life," the clarinets and chimes of "When I'm Sixty-Four," or the flute, oboe, and piccolo trumpet of "Penny Lane."

Even more exotically, we could talk about the use of tabla, sitar, and tambura on the track "Love You To"; or the use of this ensemble with added dilrubas and svarmandal for "Within You Without You"; or mention the shehnai, sarod, pakavaj, and harmonium heard on "The Inner Light." The group, moreover, started to experiment with what tape itself could do, as with the use of tape loops in songs like "Tomorrow Never Knows" and "Being for the Benefit of Mr. Kite," the tape-reversed drumming on "Strawberry Fields," or the speeded-up imitation of a shehnai on "Baby You're a Rich Man." Incorporating these techniques from the musical avant-garde, particularly by way of Karlheinz Stockhausen, the Beatles did likewise with those of musique concrete, or recorded sound effects, most notably on *Sgt. Pepper* and on the track "Revolution 9" from "the White Album"—or what was officially titled *The Beatles* (1968). They were to do the same with compositional techniques of indeterminacy, most famously represented in the two orchestral crescendi found in "A Day in the Life."

"Since 1965, the major British and American pop acts had been waging a friendly competition to come up with the most extraordinary music," writes MacDonald, and, as far as the Beatles were concerned, their competition was primarily the Beach Boys. The LP, or long-playing record, provided the focus for this competition, and over 1966–1967, as MacDonald further observes, this produced a significant structural change in the music business. "The hit-and-miss turnover of mass produced 'artistes,'" he suggests, "suddenly gave way to a more stable scene based on self-determining 'artists' no longer manipulated by record companies" (2005, 213). The period allowed for an unprecedented amount of creative freedom for artists in the studio, but Moore (1997) points out how such freedom was rather short-lived (except in the relatively rare exception). As Moore suggests, record labels during that time were in a position to invest significantly in their artists, but as Bill Bruford, the drummer of Yes, aptly put it: "Those were fertile times for musicians. They were allowed to develop something. . . . And record companies were run by people who liked records" (quoted in Anderton 2010, 423).

In the Beatles' case, it was equally helpful that EMI, their record company throughout most of their career, also owned Abbey Road Studios, where they had always done the lion's share of their recording. Given the expensive character of studio time, this was a good thing; for, whereas the first Beatles LP was recorded live off the floor over a period of 10 hours, the song "Strawberry Fields Forever" itself required an unprecedented 50 hours of studio time (MacDonald 2005, 219), and the *Sgt. Pepper* album took 700 hours to complete (Durant 1984, 213). The latter's release was also the first time that an LP included printed song lyrics, which, aside from helping to draw attention more closely to the words, also gave the songs a sense of larger coherence, embedding them within the album form. This sense of cohesion was further reinforced by other novel techniques that were soon to become important for the new rock "concept albums." Along with its reprise of the title song, the recording fuses many of the album's songs together, so that their continuity lends itself to the perception that they are not wholly separate entities but, instead, belong to what David Montgomery (2002) refers to as an "extended work for rock"—a practice the Beatles were to adopt in an even more ambitious way two years later with the second side of their LP *Abbey Road* (1969). Of course, the loose concept of *Sgt. Pepper* was that it presented a live performance by a surrogate band that in reality had just given up touring.

The concept-album form became associated with progressive or art rock, a genre in which the Beatles were highly influential pioneers, given their intense musical experimentation and the fact that, as Moore (1997) suggests, their "sheer versatility far outstretched any of their rivals" (47). This movement toward being considered as art was felt profoundly in the celebrated reception of *Sgt. Pepper*, with the wide-ranging reports of special listening parties being organized around the new album or of Jimi Hendrix incorporating its title track into his live set at a concert three days after its release. Rock acquired even further aesthetic weight with the development of serious rock criticism, first through the 1967 advent of *Rolling Stone* magazine, followed closely by other publications such as *Creem*, *New Musical Express*, and *Melody Maker*. Rock was transforming into a music that had primarily comprised dance compositions into one composed expressly for listening. And its expanded ideational content, no doubt, at least in part, reflected the significantly extended exposure to advanced education that typified the boomers, who were their primary audience.

In a study of different top 100 album lists of all time, Ralf Von Appen and André Doehring (2006) attempted to deduce whether a popular music canon could be identified. They determined that the golden age of rock music was 1965–1969, when 40 percent of the top 100 albums were released. In their cumulative top 100 album list (compiled from a total of 38 international lists from the years 1985–2004), four of the top 10 records belonged to the Beatles, who had seven albums in total on the list. Moreover, the researchers found that the band's ranking had significantly increased over the last five years of lists at which they looked, and, thus, that their classic status had not only been maintained but enhanced, in contrast to that of other monumental artists of the time, such as Bob Dylan, the Rolling Stones, or Jimi Hendrix.

THE PSYCHEDELIC EXPERIENCE

From *Revolver* onward, the Beatles were also central to what became known as "psychedelic rock." The word *psychedelic*, as MacDonald pointed out, was coined by Dr. Humphrey Osmond in a 1956 letter to Aldous Huxley and was typically defined as "mind expanding"; it came "from the Greek *psyche*, mind or soul, and *delos*, to reveal or manifest" (2005, 186). Psychedelic music attempted to recreate or enhance the effects of mind-expanding drugs, and the drug of choice at this time was LSD. "*Sgt. Pepper* was produced," Moore writes, "within a drug culture, to the extent that Lennon was regularly using LSD and marijuana by 1966, with the other Beatles to a lesser extent" (1997, 60). With lyrics such as "I get high with a little help from my friends," the Beatles helped to bring drug use to the fore, testing the boundaries of expression; as a result, the BBC initially banned "A Day in the Life" for its provocative line "I'd love to turn you on," and the public broadcaster maintained that this was tantamount to encouraging the use of drugs. Although he was the last of the Beatles to try LSD, McCartney was the first to be asked by a journalist whether he had taken the drug. Admitting that he had, McCartney made clear his preference for keeping that information private and insisted on the media's culpability should it not be, which, of course, it was not. Both McCartney and Harrison had been to California to the Haight-Ashbury district of San Francisco, and the latter articulated, much later in *The Beatles Anthology* (1995) documentary series, that the apparent hub of the American countercultural scene appeared more to resemble a kind of "alcoholism" rather than a spiritual awakening.

Lennon had earlier turned to Harvard psychologists Timothy Leary and Richard Alpert and their mind expansion manual *The Psychedelic Experience*

(1964). MacDonald (2005) explained the underlying spiritual significance of the work:

> Wishing to give the unpredictable acid "trip" a frame of reference comparable with the mystical systems of Catholicism and Islam, Leary and Alpert had selected *The Tibetan Book of the Dead*, an ancient tome designed to be whispered to the dying so as to steer them through the delusory states which, according to Tibetan Buddhism, hold sway between incarnations. Leary and Alpert chose this holy book because they believed LSD to be a "sacramental chemical" capable of inducing spiritual revelations. Leary had met Aldous Huxley, another Lennon fancy, in 1960 and been struck by his prediction that the drug would make mystical experience available to the masses and produce a "revival of religion which will be at the same time a revolution." (185)

In 1967, their quests for meaning led the Beatles to take up meditation with the Maharishi Mahesh Yogi—the Hindu tradition being the British counterculture's model of renewal, in contrast to the Native American one of North American hippies. In this regard, MacDonald credits George Harrison with being more responsible than anyone else for popularizing Hindu thought in the West; and as with the American counterculture, whose opposition to materialism had gotten a strong boost through its resonance with the stance of the earlier Beat generation, the British counterculture, and the Beatles as iconic elements of it, also sought to transcend these cultural conditions. They did so particularly through such Harrison tracks as "Within You Without You," "Piggies," and the last song that the Beatles were ever to record together, and which appeared on *Let it Be* (1970), "I Me Mine"—a track, according to Harrison, about "the ego problem," or "the soul's identification with the personal self to the exclusion of the universal Self, the 'I' that is God or Love" (quoted in MacDonald 2005, 368).

As Theodore Roszak observes in his book *Technocracy's Children* (1969), "what the counterculture offers us . . . is a remarkable defection from the long-standing tradition of skeptical, secular intellectuality" (quoted in Moore 1997, 77). With their respect for the traditional worldview, their pioneering focus on ecology, and their emphasis on flower power, the hippies came very much to resemble a revival of the 19th-century counter-Enlightenment force of Romanticism. The Romantics represented an artistic and literary movement associated with such poets as Blake, Wordsworth, Coleridge, Byron, Shelley, and Goethe; with such composers as Beethoven, Liszt, and Wagner; and, in the American context, with such literary figures as Poe, Melville, Emerson, and Thoreau. Drugs played a similarly prominent part in the Romantic creative experience, most famously in the case of Coleridge and Poe. As Chris Anderton writes, "there is a consonance between Romantic

ideals and the mysticism, pantheism, surrealism and boundary-breaking of
the psychedelic era," and there is, likewise, a general consensus identifying
the foundational Romantic belief in the idea "that nature, intuition, imagination and human feeling/experience were more important than the ratio-
nalisation and industrialisation of capitalist entrepreneurialism" (424–425).
Responding to the feelings of alienation and isolation engendered by the
technological and social changes of their respective eras, both cultural waves
advocated for notions of less complicated, more authentic modes of living.
Paramount, however, was the insight Neil Postman (1999) sought to remind
us about, and that Shelley articulates in his famous defense of poetry—"It is
only through love, tenderness, and beauty . . . that the mind is made recep-
tive to moral decency" (32). Rearticulating this message and becoming part
of world culture in a novel way, on June 25, 1967, the Beatles performed
their anthemic "All You Need is Love" as representatives of Great Britain for
Our World, a TV special that was broadcast to more than 500 million people
by satellite as the first live global television link (Lewisohn 1992, 259).

REALIZING OUR IDEALS

Usually portrayed as having rejected traditional values, or at least as having redefined them, only a small minority of young boomers were actually
involved in radical politics or the hippie movement. "Boomer big shots occu-
pying 'expensive corner offices' in the late 1990s haven't abandoned their
youthful radicalism" notes David Foot, because "most of them had none
to abandon" (1998, 5). Importantly, as he goes on to observe, a small percentage of a huge number is still a lot; and this fraction of the baby boomer
generation clearly very much made its mark on how the 1960s are perceived.
By and large a white, middle-class phenomenon characterized by its robust
internationalism, the youth counterculture was galvanized by its shared pro-
fundity of experience with the "generation gap," a phrase that, as Moore
(1997) points out, was coined only in 1967. The counterculture likewise
bonded internationally through shared values and sensibilities, particularly
as these manifested themselves in opposition to the ongoing U.S. war in Vietnam. Given that members of the Beatles, and especially Lennon, had been
publicly opposing the Vietnam War since 1966, John Platoff (2005) noted
that "[they] were widely seen by young people as cultural leaders, setting the
direction for social change and showing others where to follow" (263–264).

Platoff (2005) outlines how the social foment among the students and
youth at the time spread from U.S. college campuses, and, then, in 1968–
1969, to most countries of Europe—especially Italy, France, Germany, and
Greece. Events took the form of campus occupations, sit-ins, civil disruptions,
and street demonstrations. Frequently, underground psychedelic rock scenes

would follow such events around, and these were sometimes connected with other happenings, festivals, clubs, or magazines. As Platoff details:

> In February 1968, thousands of students demonstrated in West Berlin; a month later a protest at the American embassy in London culminated in "a pitched battle between police and 100,000 antiwar marchers." Students at Columbia University in New York seized campus buildings to protest both the war and the university's proposed expansion into local neighborhoods, and were attacked by New York policemen, resulting in hundreds of injuries. May saw the start of a lengthy and at times violent student uprising in France, which largely paralyzed much of the country for weeks. President Charles de Gaulle had to dissolve the National Assembly and call for new national elections. In August, troops from the Soviet Union suddenly invaded Czechoslovakia "to snuff out the freedom and democracy movement heralded in the West as the Prague Spring. (241)

Toward the end of August, this stream of activity was to reach a disturbing climax for white, middle-class Americans at the Democratic national convention, with its televisually amplified spectacle of Chicago police indiscriminately beating not only antiwar protestors but journalists and party delegates as well—a spectacle to which demonstrators memorably chanted "the whole world is watching." Again, Platoff (2005) recounts:

> Mass protests organized both by the Yippies, led by Abbie Hoffman and Jerry Rubin, and by a variety of anti-Vietnam-war groups provoked a devastating overreaction on the part of Mayor Richard Daley's police. Several nights of violence, including many police attacks on nonviolent demonstrators and innocent bystanders, were reported in newspapers and shown on television across the country. Following the end of the convention Tom Hayden, a leader of anti-war protests, spoke for many when he said that "it may be that the era of organized, peaceful and orderly demonstrations is coming to an end, and that other methods will be needed." (244)

Platoff (2005) further notes how the first day of the convention just so happened to correspond with the Beatles' release of Lennon's song "Revolution." And in his analysis of the counterculture's complex reception of the song's two considerably different versions (the acoustic one from the White album contains the line "but if you talk about destruction, don't you know that you can count me out, in"), Platoff details the schism that arose between two strains of antiestablishment thinking in the late 1960s, and the way Lennon was eventually to situate himself in relation to them:

The New Left were the political activists, whose rhetoric had sharpened and whose willingness to become involved in violent confrontation had increased as the decade had progressed. The "psychedelic Left" were the hippies, the social drop-outs and commune-organizers. They were the people who felt that the appropriate response to social and political oppression was a personal transcendence, a search for a purer and less compromised way of living. In "Revolution" Lennon clearly aligns himself with the latter ("change your head," "free your mind instead"); small wonder that those in the New Left, the politically militant side, screamed in outrage, especially because they had been convinced up to that point that he was one of them. (265–266)

Lennon was similarly to align himself with the psychedelic left when he wrote "Come Together" for Timothy Leary's 1969 gubernatorial campaign in California. He did so in an even bigger way, moreover, when he and Yoko Ono staged their famous Dadaish events for peace, as a means of celebrating their marriage, in March that same year. "What we had in common was love," suggested Lennon, "and from love came peace . . . so we decided to work for world peace" (quoted in Ono 2008). Their first "bed-in"—a word they derived from "sit-in"—took place in Amsterdam, where they invited the world's media to visit them every day between 9 a.m. and 9 p.m. for a week. Having just released their album *Two Virgins* (1968), with its frontal and rear views of Lennon and Ono standing fully nude, reporters purportedly were half anticipating some sort of sexual element but instead found the newlyweds dressed in their white pajamas, promoting and discussing peace. At the end of that week, Lennon and Ono held a press conference in Vienna, at which they introduced their idea of "bagism," or what they referred to as "total communication." Appearing entirely covered in bags, so as to amplify the verbal content of their message, they were simultaneously satirizing prejudice and stereotyping based on aspects of outward appearance, including such things as hair length, age, skin color, and the like. These events were recounted in "The Ballad of John and Yoko," a track that was hurriedly recorded with Lennon and McCartney playing all of the instruments because Harrison and Ringo Starr were otherwise unavailable, and Lennon had wanted to get the track released right away.

Two months later, the Canadian city of Montreal became the site of Lennon and Ono's second week-long bed-in after the couple was disallowed entry to the United States on account of Lennon's 1968 charges for possession of cannabis in the United Kingdom. Among a number of other people, the couple invited Timothy Leary and Tommy Smothers to visit, and during this time, they sang and recorded "Give Peace a Chance," a song that was soon to become a paean for the antiwar movement. The month prior, the Beatles had begun to work on *Abbey Road*, which was to be released the following September, around the same time that Lennon and Ono's new group, the Plastic Ono Band, performed at the Toronto Rock and Roll Revival, a performance that was recorded and then released as *Live Peace in Toronto 1969*. November saw Lennon return his MBE to Queen Elizabeth to protest the British involvement in the Nigerian civil war and its support of the American war in Vietnam. Toward the end of the year, the couple launched the next celebrated stage of their campaign for peace in 11 major cities, including Montréal, Toronto, New York, Los Angeles, Hollywood, London, Paris, Berlin, Rome, Athens, and Tokyo. Following up Ono's idea to plaster posters reading "WAR IS OVER! (If You Want It) Happy Christmas from John and Yoko" around these cities, Lennon had the further idea of extending the campaign to large billboards, in reference to which Ono later pointed out that "his arena of communication was much bigger than mine" (quoted in LENNONYC 2010). As Lennon was to say, in relation to these techniques:

> We do it by the advertising method. We believe that in today's society, advertising is the thing that politicians use, commercial companies use, the Beatles use it, and John and Yoko should use it. Our product is peace. Less war and more peace. The only way to do it is Gandhi's way. And that's nonviolence, passive, positive or whatever you call it. We are selling it, like soap, you know, and you have got to sell, sell, until the housewife thinks "there's peace or war, but the true product is peace"— peace in your mind, peace at work, peace on earth, peace in the home, peace in the world. It's to try and get people oriented to think peace, eat for peace, breathe for peace, dance for peace, and make love for peace. Just have the peace, going like a mantra round and round in your head. (quoted in Ono 2008)

However, just as the hopes of the Romantics for social transformation faded in the wake of the failed revolutions of 1848, the end of the 1960s saw the souring of the countercultural dream, as a general sense of powerlessness emerged in its wake, along with the disappointing realization that changing society was not nearly as easy as the counterculture had made it out to be. As MacDonald (2005) notes, in a 1970 interview with *Rolling Stone*, Lennon "dismissed the preceding years of social upheaval and countercultural revolt as little more than a clothes show: 'Everyone dressed up but nothing changed'" (2). This notwithstanding, at the rally for John Sinclair, which took place toward the end of 1971, he optimistically acknowledged to the crowd: "So flower power didn't work—let's start again," referring also to the ongoing necessity for blocking "the war machine" (quoted in LENNONYC 2010). For all their efforts, Lennon and Ono's activities were heavily surveilled not simply by the Federal Bureau of Investigation (FBI), but also by the Royal Canadian Mounted Police (RCMP); and it is well known that, for four years in the early 1970s, the former Beatle was forced to fight the Nixon administration's ongoing and politically motivated effort to deport him, until he was finally granted permanent U.S. residency in 1976.

The couple's activities inspired many of their own generation, among whom we can include the Pakistani born Tariq Ali, one of the New Left's most influential voices in the United Kingdom, as well as the British progressive rock band Yes, with their quotation of the line "all we are saying is give peace a chance" in their song "I've Seen All Good People" (1971). Meanwhile, Led Zeppelin's Robert Plant, a bona fide baby boomer, also remarked in the 1970s:

> I admire John Lennon tremendously because he advocates peace. He is trying to introduce a bit of sanity into the world. Ironically, to present his sane message he had to use eccentric means and many people laughed at him. But what is laughable about someone who wants everyone to love each other? When Jesus Christ presented His case He was crucified. The same thing happened to Lennon. The majority of people crucified his character. But as long as even a few people dig what he was trying to say, he has won. (Kendall 1981, 125)

Another boomer, often considered the heir of Lennon's political activism, U2's Bono, was to suggest in 2007 that without Lennon he would not have "dared to dream so loudly, to risk such foolishness, and never to fear ridicule" (quoted in Bono 2010). Similarly, Roger Waters once mentioned to me how Lennon was one of his great heroes, and, in this relation, the recording of Lennon's other peace anthem "Imagine" (1971) was played before the ex-leader of Pink Floyd's 2012 performances of *The Wall* (itself a work concerned with the detranscendentalization of war). Though not himself a boomer, for these performances Waters's audiences—who enthusiastically applauded after Lennon's recorded performance—comprised not only boomers but also their progeny.

Four months after Lennon and Ono launched their billboard/poster campaign, McCartney announced on April 10, 1970—in the press release for his eponymously titled first album—that the Beatles were no more. Having "grown up," and now possessing families of their own, all were pulled in alternate directions. Although he cited creative and business differences as the primary reasons for the band's breakup, a quarter century later McCartney mused with great pride, at the conclusion of *The Beatles Anthology* documentary series, about how the activities of the group had been "all about love, peace, and understanding," and was much pleased that there had been "a very good spirit behind it all."

Alas, there will never be another Beatles, and—as the narrator observes at the end of the documentary film *The Compleat Beatles* (1982)—the group was to remain a phenomenon of the 1960s, while the 1970s and beyond "were only to feel their influence." This extraordinary influence continues to encompass not only their ongoing musical legacy but that, too, of their drug use, their role as conduits for Eastern philosophical and artistic forms, and their function as countercultural icons who articulated the aspirations and ambitions of the 1960s generation. Lennon's political efforts have had continued saliency with elements of the late 1990s international antiglobalization protests, which were derailed with the post-9/11 crackdown, but his influence continued to be felt in the largest global demonstrations ever held against the Iraq war in 2002. The mass demonstrations of the 1990s resurfaced as the Occupy movement in 2011, and we can only hope, as it further unfolds, that the world will remember the position John Lennon espoused and rearticulated, in relation to the song "Revolution," in the final interview he gave before a deranged fan assassinated him in New York City on December 8, 1980: "The lyrics stand today. They're still my feeling about politics: I want to see the plan. Count me out if it's for violence. Don't expect me on the barricades unless it is with flowers" (quoted in Platoff 2005, 266). Similarly, in relation to the future well-being of the world, it is worth noting too the words of the chief justice of the U.S. Court of Appeals, who wrote the following in the decision that granted Lennon his final victory of permanent residency in the United States: "If in our two hundred years of independence we have in some measure realized our ideals, it is in large part because we have always found a place for those committed to the spirit of liberty and willing to help implement it. Lennon's four-year battle to remain in our country is testimony to his faith in this American dream" (quoted in LENNONYC 2010).

NOTES

1. The UK releases became the definitive ones with adoption of compact disc technology in the 1980s, with the exception of the U.S. release of *Magical Mystery Tour* (1967).

2. For a discussion on the character of such environments in the Beatles' late period see MacFarlane (2013).

REFERENCES

Anderton, Chris. "A Many Headed Beast: Progressive Rock as European Meta-Genre." *Popular Music* 29, no. 3 (2010): 417–435.

Appen, Ralf von, and André Doehring. "Nevermind the Beatles, Here's Exile 61 and Nico: 'The Top 100 Records of all Time' —A Canon of Pop and Rock Albums from a Sociological and an Aesthetic Perspective." *Popular Music* 25, no. 1 (2006): 21–39.

The Beatles Anthology. Directed by Geoff Wonfor and Bob Smeaton. London: EMI, 1995.

Bono. "Lennon and Me." *Q Magazine*, November 2010.

The Compleat Beatles. Directed by Patrick Montgomery. MGM, 1982.

Durant, Alan. *Conditions of Music*. London: MacMillan, 1984.

Foot, David, with Daniel Stoffman. *Boom, Bust, and Echo 2000*. Toronto: Macfarlane Walter and Ross, 1998.

Imagine: John Lennon. Directed by Andrew Solt. London: Warner Bros, 1988.

LENNONYC. Directed by Michael Epstein. American Masters, 2010.

Leopold, Todd. "When the Beatles Hit America." *CNN.com*. February 10, 2004.

Lewisohn, Mark. *The Complete Beatles Chronicle*. New York: Harmony Books, 1992.

MacDonald, Ian. *Revolution in the Head: The Beatles' Records and the Sixties*. London: Pimlico, 2005.

MacFarlane, Thomas. *The Beatles and McLuhan: Understanding the Electric Age*. Lanham, MD: Scarecrow Press, 2013.

McLuhan, Marshall. *Project in Understanding New Media*. Toronto, Canada: National Association of Educational Broadcasters; U.S. Department of Health, Education, and Welfare, 1960.

Moore, Allan. *The Beatles: Sergeant Peppers Lonely Hearts Club Band*. Cambridge: Cambridge University Press, 1997.

Ono, Yoko. "John Lennon & Yoko Ono: WAR IS OVER! (If You Want It)." http://www.youtube.com/watch?v=CbKsgaXQy2k, 2008.

Platoff, John. "John Lennon, 'Revolution', and the Politics of Reception." *The Journal of Musicology* 22, no. 2 (2005): 241-267.

Postman, Neil. *Building a Bridge to the Eighteenth Century*. New York: Alfred A. Knopf, 1999.

Ryan, John, and Richard Peterson. "The Guitar as Artifact and Icon: Identity Construction in the Baby Boom Generation." In *Guitar Culture*, edited by Andy Bennett, 89–116. London: Berg, 2001.

Shepherd, John. "Music and Social Categories." In *The Cultural Study of Music: A Critical Introduction*, 2nd ed., edited by Martin Clayton, Trevor Herbert, and Richard Middleton, 239–248. New York: Routledge, 2012.

15

Bob Dylan and Spectacle Culture: Yesterday and Today

Salvatore J. Fallica

Never trust the artist. Trust the tale.
—D. H. Lawrence, *Studies in Classic American Literature*, 1923

MEDITATIONS ON THE ARTIST IN SPECTACLE CULTURE

After six decades of performing all over the world, Bob Dylan is no stranger to the culture of the spectacle. At the time of this writing, Dylan is in his seventies, a professional performer since his late teens who became a bona fide star in his early twenties and has continued to create and perform in a variety of ways, embellishing an already mythic career. At this point in Dylan's career he is as he ever was: a mercurial artist, unreceptive in his work to musical or aesthetic taxonomy, although scholars and critics have continued to try.[1] Decades ago he (or the narrator he embodied) sang to an erstwhile lover in the song "All I Really Want to Do," an ode to relationship equality if there ever was one, that he would not classify, analyze, categorize, define, or confine the object of his desire. Dylan could have been asking for that same flexibility in apprehending his art and his persona from critical and audience categories and expectations. So perhaps it is, in the words of Jonathan Crary, "the imposition of an illusory unity"[2] to make the case for understanding the performance artist we know as Bob Dylan as a cultural spectacle, a shape shifting force within the media spectacle[3] of contemporary culture.

Although the Bob Dylan spectacle was formed, nurtured, and expanded in the 1960s, there were several major additions to the Dylan spectacle in the first decade of the 21st century that resulted in new interest—academic as well as commercial—in Dylan's work. For example, in 2004, Dylan published a critically acclaimed yet somewhat disappointing memoir that stayed on the *New York Times* best seller list for 19 weeks.[4] In 2006, Martin Scorsese created a landmark music documentary with *No Direction Home: Bob Dylan*, placing Dylan's work in a larger context of American culture, using unseen performance film footage from the Dylan archives and interviews with many of American music's icons[5] from the 1960s, including extensive commentary from Dylan himself. The documentary premiered on PBS's award-winning *American Masters* series and was also broadcast in England on the BBC. Then, in 2007, the director Todd Haynes created an imaginative cinematic biography of Dylan, *I'm Not There*,[6] based on Dylan's life and legend. In fact, "Inspired by the music and many lives of Bob Dylan" appears on the screen at the beginning of the film. The film had generally good reviews and was nominated for a number of awards. It was also distinctive in that the director had six actors play the elusive star, including film stars Christian Bale, Cate Blanchett, Richard Gere, Heath Ledger, and Ben Winshaw and a 13-year-old African American newcomer, Marcus Carl Franklin.

For a short period in the life of the latter Dylan spectacle, this was quite a spate of creative output, and it is fitting, for Dylan's own creative output over the decades is daunting by any standard. His contributions to American—and global—culture includes more than 500 songs,[7] 35 studio albums, 58 singles, 11 live albums, and 30 compilation albums,[8] including official and unofficial bootlegs,[9] assorted music videos, live performances for more than 50 years,[10] documentaries, many television performances, and lead roles in two feature-length films. There are two best-selling books so far,[11] three children's books based on his songs,[12] poetry published in scattered places, and a huge number of interviews, so many in fact that there are two books of compilations,[13] and although most of these interviews are authentic, some are not;[14] some are remarkably informative, some are not. Over the years Dylan has also exhibited artwork in various galleries and museums, and there are several published volumes of his artworks, drawings and paintings, and collages.[15] He had a three-year stint as a radio host,[16] which allowed him to showcase his extraordinary familiarity with American and European musical genres, including pop music, folk, country, rhythm and blues, and even classical. Finally, and perhaps what might be his most enduring legacy, he has engaged in a continuous worldwide touring schedule for almost 30 years.

Contributing to this mosaic-like output is the Dylan para-textual material, although when contemplating such things in spectacle culture, it is sometimes difficult to know where the "textual" ends and the "para-textual" items begin. For example, one could argue that Dylan's many interviews as noted earlier should be listed as para-textual because those events usually occurred when Dylan had a new album or tour project to promote. So this category, if indeed it is a category, would include those interviews already mentioned as well as the music programs and advertising from the various concerts and tours, liner notes to albums (sometimes written by him), cover art for various albums, posters, and art catalogs. There are more than a few biographies,[17] scores of photo books,[18] along with countless compilations of professional photos taken at various stages of his career—some of him performing, some strictly publicity photos, and some alleged photos of his private life. There are literally thousands of feature stories and concert reviews in newspapers and magazines, thousands of websites (including the official one), countless tumblr sites, an official twitter account (@bobdylan) along with several fan twitter accounts, and an extensive presence on YouTube with, of course, a Bob Dylan channel (and almost 10 millions views), along with thousands of fan uploads, mashups, and covers.

Moreover, there is an overabundance of academic scholarship, including hundreds of articles in a variety of learned journals that inspect and examine and explicate his lyrics, songs, and performances, and, recently, his art work.[19] Some of this academic commentary has emerged from scholarly conferences and symposia dedicated to Dylan's lyrics. For example, in 2004 a conference discussing Dylan's spiritualism as manifested in his lyrics took place at the evangelical institution Messiah College. And just a few years ago, in 2011, a conference presented by Touro Law School and Fordham University's law and ethics center featured legal scholars discussing the criminal justice system and the judicial fiascos as seen in some of his major songs, such as "Hurricane" and "The Lonesome Death of Hattie Carroll."[20] Other conference sites that included presentations, seminars, and panel inquiries or just individual papers on Dylan's lyrics, themes, performances, and vocal styles included those held at Dartmouth University, the College of the Holy Cross, the University of Missouri-St. Louis, and many others.[21]

While these conferences might suggest that scholarly and academic interest in Dylan seems to be on the rise,[22] culture critics and the professoriate have been paying attention to Dylan, his lyrics, and his performances for quite a while—actually from the beginning. One of the earliest was *Bob Dylan: A Retrospective*,[23] published in 1972, which included commentary, some of Dylan's earliest interviews, and performance analyses. Then came what seems like a deluge of academic and cultural commentary; some of the standouts include Betsy Bowden's analysis of Dylan's work in *Performed Literature: the Words and Music of Bob Dylan*,[24] first published in 1982, an exegesis of his songs that avoids the usual focus on his lyrics and analyzes the music and vocals as well. Another milestone of criticism, especially in regard to Dylan's lyrics, and by one of the major textual critics of our time, Christopher Ricks, focuses solely on Dylan's lyrics and "reads" them as he would Keats or Shakespeare or Donne or any other major poet, in his palpably poetic tome, *Dylan's Vision of Sin*.[25] In a discussion with a reporter, Professor

Ricks defended the seriousness he visits on Dylan's work, claiming that Dylan has "a Shakespearean size and ambition in the themes he explores and what he achieves." Another writer would sum up all of this academic interest in Dylan by saying that "few, if any, pop-culture figures have been as thoroughly embraced by intellectuals and critics as Bob Dylan."[26]

Besides this sort of scholarship that provides Dylan with a certain kind of fame and legitimacy, the Bob Dylan spectacle continues with what I call Dylan's journey through pseudo event culture—his tours of the awards show circuit, an integral part of spectacle and celebrity culture. Part of the noise machine of spectacle culture, where the rhetoric of overweening piety and spurious gravitas harbors unmatched and where competitive drama is easily manufactured, is the entertainment industry's awards show, a genre of programming that seems to metastasize ad infinitum. This part of the entertainment spectacle, and its cousin the entertainment competition show, constructed by networks, producers, agents, and others in the entertainment industry's publicity machinery, fits neatly into Daniel Boorstin's famous if somewhat awkwardly worded concept of the "pseudo event." Boorstin explained that a "pseudo event" is not a spontaneous event; it is planned for the purpose of being reported or reproduced in as many media iterations as possible, thereby functioning as a form of advertising for the participants and the sponsors; the pseudo event also has an ambiguous relationship to the reality of the situation; that is to say, its "reality" or "truth" is secondary to the event's ability to gain and hold public attention; and finally, the pseudo event is intended as having a self-fulfilling prophecy.[27] This last point is worth discussing—the awards show gives, say, a lifetime achievement award or an award for best performer to a lucky and talented performer or performers and, lo and behold, as if by magic, the concept is physically realized in that singer or band through a vote of certain industry authorities (whoever they might be). So, representatives of the industry have elevated that performer based on whatever criteria they find compelling.

Now that Dylan is in the latter stages of his career, he seems to be on course for almost all the obtainable honors and awards. In 2013, he received the French Legion of Honor Award, France's highest cultural award. In 2012, he received the Presidential Medal of Freedom from President Barack Obama. In 2010, he was awarded the National Medal of Arts (Dylan was not in attendance for the ceremony), but two weeks before that event, he had been to the White House to perform in a concert commemorating Black History month and the music of the civil rights era, and performed "The Times They Are A'Changin'."[28] The Obama administration, which has paid tribute to Dylan twice, is not the first—in 1997 Dylan received the Kennedy Center Lifetime Award, presented to him by President Bill Clinton. The nationally televised ceremony had performances of some of his major songs by several major artists, among them Bruce Springsteen. But while these awards[29] come as he enters the final phase (or one of them) of his long and winding career, it should be noted that Dylan, from the very beginning of his career, has always been the recipient of tributes and awards, mostly within the entertainment industry, but now, as we have seen, also outside of the industry, as the French award and the presidential medals attest.

The reasons for these awards—whether to Dylan or to Madonna or to any star—vary: nations and governments do want to award and recognize what they feel are artists' cultural achievements and contributions as they directly or indirectly bring cultural prestige and honor to the state. In some cases, bestowing an award on Dylan might suggest the desire of that government or organization to align themselves with *his* significance and *his* audiences, a form of capital that he and his organization have built over time. State governments as well as cultural organizations want to take advantage of his global reach as a musical icon and lend themselves a patina of authenticity and legitimacy while they ostensibly honor him. This, I think, was the case with Dylan's Academy Award in 2001, which I discuss in more detail later, and it was most certainly the thinking behind one of his very first awards, the Tom Paine Award, which he received from the National Emergency Civil Liberties Committee at their annual Bill of Rights Dinner in December 1963.

Dylan, in 1963, was at the apex of the folk scene; he was the preeminent topical songwriter[30] and a somewhat socially unsophisticated 22-year-old. According to almost all reports, Dylan drank too much during the reception, and as he accepted the award, he proceeded to provide the audience with a rambling, insulting monologue. The audience, which was made up of mostly older progressives and radicals (well, Dylan was 22), were told that he wished he were talking to people with "hair on their head[s]."[31] Apparently, that was Dylan's lame attempt at humor, if indeed it was humor. More awkward insults followed, but the pièce de résistance of Dylan's remarks came when he started discussing the recent Kennedy assassination, which was less than four weeks old and still raw in everyone's emotions. Dylan turned to the topic of Lee Harvey Oswald and said cryptically that he "saw some of myself in him."[32] Dylan was booed from the dais and had to leave the room, so the dinner and awards ceremony was by all accounts a disaster. Dylan later apologized by sending a long conciliatory poem to the director of the organization, Corliss Lamont, who in turn also apologized to his membership as he shared Dylan's poem with them. But Lamont's apology to the members of the organization allows us to see how some award shows are conceptualized. Lamont writes to the "attendees of the dinner":

> Whether we approve or not, Bob Dylan has become the idol of the progressive youngsters of today, regardless of their political factions. He is speaking to them in terms of protest that they understand and

applaud. . . . E.C.L.C. feels that it is urgent to recognize the protest of youth today and to help make it understood by the older generation. Walt Whitman and Woody Guthrie, the culture (sic) antecedents of Bob Dylan, were not appreciated by their society until they were very old. We think it would be better to make the effort now to comprehend what Bob Dylan is saying to and for the youth.[33]

These days political and cultural progressives probably pine for the days when such an organization[34] was a normal part of the public sphere and could make headlines simply by hosting its own pseudo event, in this case, an awards dinner, with a major music star. In the early 1960s the ECLC, made, as noted by Lamont's words, a somewhat calculated move: by honoring Bob Dylan, they were really honoring and hoping to get attention from—and to their credit, the director of the organization is pretty up front about it—the generation that looked up to Dylan. Part of this cohort was that irascible group known as baby boomers, and I will have more to say about them, and their relationship to Dylan, later. Now, this is not to say that the ECLC was not a serious organization, simply interested in publicity. This organization's work and its members certainly were very serious in the pursuit of civil liberties, a code word then for civil rights, and the previous year it had feted the very serious Bertrand Russell, the philosopher and social critic. So Dylan was in excellent company, even if he himself was not, at the time, very good company.

Political and social organizations sort of left Dylan alone after this debacle, except, of course, to hound him for contributions and donations, but the entertainment and recording industry was not about to ignore this rising star, even if they were not as honest or as open about their reasons for providing Dylan with their awards as the ECLC was. Although the Tom Paine Award was an unmitigated disaster, Dylan did apologize and everyone moved on, especially Dylan himself, and some 25 years later, after an envious career path through the decades, he was inducted into the Rock and Roll Hall of Fame. So within a 25-year span, a blip in the history of the world but several lifetimes in the world of popular music, things had changed. By now, the entertainment industry had also moved on and in the process did what the entertainment industry does best: publicize itself by making the awards show a major genre of mass mediated culture.

The awards presented to Dylan at the various music industry awards shows over his career were the usual markers of a star performer and added to Dylan's and the industry's profile in spectacle culture. In 1963, the year of Dylan's Tom Paine Award disaster, he was also nominated for Best Folk Recording for his first album, *Bob Dylan (1962)*—this was also, incidentally, the year he released his second album, *The Freewheelin' Bob Dylan*, the one with the now famous album cover of Dylan with his then girlfriend Suze

Rotolo as archetypes of sixties' folkies. Fast-forward almost 40 years, to 2010, when Dylan releases not one but three albums, all three historical compilations meant for the collectors and to broaden his legacy, as if that were necessary, and we note that between those two events, Dylan received 37 major music industry awards. Some of Dylan's musical awards will also shock the casual fan: in 2004, with his voice teetering between a growl and a scratchy shout, Dylan wins the Best Male Rock Vocal Performance award for "Down in the Flood." And it's not the first time, as many Dylan aficionados must know: he won that award before in 1996 for a live version of "Knockin' On Heaven's Door."

Dylan has also been recognized, if not lionized, in other areas as well. In some cases the award or medal he received actually made the sponsor look good, as noted with the ECLC, but I am thinking of the Oscar he won for Best Original Song, the evocative "Things Have Changed," which closes the film *Wonder Boys*.[35] Actually there were three other Dylan songs in the film score, but this new song fit the category of Best Original Song. The song appears as a postscript to the narrative and seems to comment on the "wonder boy" theme as presented in the film, which depicts an artist who suffers from extraordinary early success—not unlike the composer of the song. But did the Academy members who voted for "Things Have Changed" want some of Dylan's authentic artistry, his reputation and image as an uncompromising artist, to rub off on the film industry in general and the Academy in particular? Dylan, who proudly displays the Oscar at almost all of his concerts, was effusive in his acceptance remarks, saying, "Oh good God, this is amazing . . . I'd like to thank the members of the Academy who were bold enough to give me this award for this song."[36] Bold? The Academy of Motion Picture Arts and Sciences? I think in this instance the Academy gained more from giving the award to him than Dylan actually "gained" in receiving it.

Very often, Dylan makes his presence at award shows seem like existential errands—you never quite know what he will do or what will happen. Appearances have ranged from the sardonically comic to the solemn. For example, in 1998 his album *Time Out of Mind* was nominated for and ultimately won a Grammy for Album of the Year. Dylan was scheduled to perform a single from the album, "Love Sick," his take on the wasteland of love, the narrator walking through the dead streets of the contemporary world, musing on a type of "love" that makes him "sick." It's a remarkable lyric, in which he references both T. S. Eliot and Hank Williams. In the Grammy production, there were dancers and assorted hip young people arrayed behind Dylan and his band, and this addition to the proceedings proved to be interesting as one of the dancers was actually performance artist Michael Portnoy. After a few minutes of Dylan's performance, Portnoy moved to center stage a few feet from Dylan (who carried on with his usual world-weary aplomb) and started dancing violently, flailing his arms somewhat comically, with a message "Soy Bomb" (more about that later) written on his bare chest. Now, according to *Entertainment Weekly*, the background group of dancers and young people were hired by Dylan's production company,[37] and I'm thinking that someone had to know that the group included this noted performance artist. Portnoy's dance lasted for several minutes, and during the musical break in the song, security guards dragged him offstage.

What made this event seem dangerous was that it really appeared to be spontaneous, unscripted, something that should not happen in the middle of the music industry's major pseudo event. However, one of the characteristics about spectacle culture is that spontaneity can be faked. So what actually happened here? We will never know for sure, but Portnoy's message "Soy Bomb" was explained by the dancer in interviews later on the next day's news shows and in industry news venues. He told reporters that "Soy . . . represents dense nutritional life. Bomb is, obviously, an explosive destructive force. So, soy bomb is what I think art should be: dense, transformational, explosive life."[38] Portnoy became one of those accidental celebrities—although just how accidental remains in question. What is also interesting is that the statement made by this performance artist[39] could be a reflection of the thinking of another performance artist, the one he tried to interrupt on that memorable Grammy evening, the one known as Bob Dylan.

Of all the awards, however, that Dylan has received, the one that usually stands out as part of his legacy of turning awards shows into theater of the absurd, an award show that was as remarkably awkward as it was telling, is his Grammy for Lifetime Achievement in 1991. The award came during a time that Dylan, as David Yaffe puts it, "appeared to be crumbling in public" and "seemed to be defacing his own icon."[40] What Yaffe is referring to are a series of artless and casual performances that year along with the release of albums that were pedestrian in terms of arrangements and content, with his voice assuming a phlegmatic blur. But this awards show seems to be a turning point of sorts. The Grammy award show was held during the first days of the first Gulf War, and for those who thought that Dylan had abandoned politics (well, at least overtly), he did make a kind of political statement by performing a blistering punk but muffled version of "Masters of War." For the most part his enunciation of the lyrics were barely comprehensible, although, in retrospective viewings on YouTube, they seem intelligible enough, and it appears from my perspective that the audience in the theater that evening (who knows about those watching at home on television) knew exactly what he was singing and its significance.

But if his performance was a roaring and boisterous (and vocally problematic) affair, it was what happened afterward that that was as theatrical as anything Dylan has ever done, and perhaps as inexplicable. I say "perhaps" because with a little examination—as several scholars have done—his acceptance speech on this night contributed to his overall artistic project of challenging and making audiences uncomfortable. At the show Dylan was presented the award by Jack Nicholson, whose speech was in the tradition of Grammy Award speeches, mawkish, worshipful, almost religious in its reverence, putting Dylan on a plane with the traditional cultural elite.[41] And then Dylan proceeded to make one of the most awkward yet remarkable acceptance speeches. Dylan, who is a better actor than most give him credit for, came out seeming to stumble, seemingly drunk, and dressed, as Yaffe puts it, like "a Steinbeck character," and said:

> Well my daddy, he didn't leave me much, you know he was a very simple man, but what he did tell me this [a long pause followed by uncomfortable laughter . . .]. He said so many things, you know. He did say, son, he said, 'you know it's possible to become so defiled in this world that your own father and mother will abandon you and if that happens, God will always believe in your ability to mend your ways.[42]

As scholars have noted, Dylan's remarks seemed to be a reworking of the 19th-century German rabbi Shimson Rafael Hirsch who wrote, "Even if I were so depraved that my own mother and father would abandon me to my own devices, God would still gather me up and believe in my ability to mend my way."[43] Was this a commentary on the music industry? His own career? The morality of these awards shows? His relations to people who used to be his friends and colleagues? Or, perhaps, something too serious to think about while all of the glitter and glamor of the American musical spectacle tells audiences all is right with the world, that these are lives and values worth paying attention to? Dylan's commentary suggests a dark side to the glitter, a haunting affirmation that the world is not as comfortable as an awards show.

All of this material in all of these media formats should lead us to see the performance artist we call "Bob Dylan" as a noteworthy, indeed an ongoing, presence in contemporary spectacle culture. The question remains how to corral this artist into a genre of contemporary culture usually reserved for media events such as the Super Bowl or the World Cup, as the word "spectacle" suggests? The word usually refers to excessive visual display and performance, but spectacle is also a term that identifies a form of public speech and a particular production of culture, as well as a way of talking about a media event or a series of media events. In this sense, spectacle not only refers to a genre of our mass mediated culture but also to a way of comprehending and critiquing products and events of the mass media and its now abetting crony, social media.

Spectacles have been created by such powerful institutions as the film industry, the sports industry, the Roman Catholic Church,[44] various political parties and factions, and, of course, the state as a technique of control and propaganda. Think of Nazi Germany and the use of spectacle for social and political power: the rallies, parades, posters, films, and book-burning ceremonies, a variety of events and artifacts all devotedly reported and repurposed through Nazi-controlled media. For another example of the modern spectacle think of the American presidential debates, which have become, especially with their institutionalization[45] in 1988, a recurring spectacle of the American political system.

The spectacle as concept and event has a long history in Western culture. However, in 1968, Guy Debord, in *Society of the Spectacle* brought new attention to the term as he alerted us to the modern situation: given the explosion of manufactured imagery, what Daniel Boorstin has called the "graphic revolution," our social and political life has been reduced to various forms of "representation."[46] Debord has also suggested that the society of the spectacle came to modern prominence in the late 1920s with the development of sound in motion pictures, the rise of fascism (in Germany and Italy), and the technological completion of television,[47] all contributing to the development and use of the modern spectacle for entertainment and politics. While Debord uses "spectacle" to point to the prominence and privilege of the image in all facets of our culture as a critique of capitalism, other scholars, notably Douglas Kellner, have built on his concept and see the spectacle as a way of understanding and critiquing the society in which the spectacle occurs. As Debord points out in his Thesis #4, the spectacle is "not just a collection of images," but allows us to see a "social relationship between people that is mediated by images."[48] This concept of the spectacle, then, allows social and media critics first to identify significant media events in the culture and second to examine such phenomena or a closely related range of phenomena, the social and political and gender relations as exhibited in those events and performances mediated through mass media and social media.[49]

A good example of an American spectacle would be the Super Bowl. While this one game has become a major media event across the world, it is also the result of an entire season of football games, the narratives of many teams with their trials and successes, the immense number of feature stories, interviews, commentaries, and, of course, images—indeed, a universe of imagery—and, finally, at the end of the season, two top teams remain. Then, after another two weeks worth of hyper-publicity and promotion,[50] these two teams play on Super Bowl Sunday, a media event that, while it does not have more than one television channel broadcasting it, dominates the television viewing audience, social media, and social discourse. The overarching spectacle of the Super Bowl includes the advertising spectacle as well;

commercials during the game take on a special interest and have their own publicity machinery. Advertising agencies, along with their clients, put enormous efforts into getting—and then maintaining—the attention of the spectators. Even the half-time show becomes a celebrated event, also a spectacle in itself—whether it is Beyoncé or Madonna or Paul McCartney performing. Everything connected with the Super Bowl becomes part of an organized and manufactured pattern of imagery and pseudo event that works in part as social propaganda but can also be an occasion for social critique.[51]

Another example of spectacle culture would be any presidential campaign. Douglas Kellner, for example, examines the 2008 campaign in his chapter "Barack Obama, the Power Elite, and Media Spectacle"[52] and finds that "the spectacle . . . promoted the candidacy of Barack Obama." He describes how "Obama (and his political organization) has become the master of the political spectacle and a global celebrity of the first rank."[53] Candidate Obama did this with all of the spectacle tools at his command: televised speeches and other campaign pseudo events, an extensive social media campaign, political advertising, interviews and, of course, the many candidate debates. These particular spectacles began first as part of the primary system where he debated the other celebrity of the Democratic Party, Senator Hillary Rodham Clinton, but second in the presidential debates against the Republican nominee, Senator John McCain. Kellner examines this package of mass mediated imagery, media events, and the attendant discourse as "the Obama campaign spectacle," which he afterward unpacks, discussing the various elements of the spectacle through a critical theory lens.

Of course, the Dylan spectacle is different from either the Super Bowl or the Obama political spectacles, and not just because the Super Bowl is a sporting event and the Obama campaign was, well, a different type of sporting event, one with certainly more serious social and political consequences. Whereas the theme of the Obama spectacle has been one of "hope and change," and the Super Bowl an orgy of excess and commodity fetishism, the theme that tends to carry the Dylan spectacle—from his recordings, writings, interviews, and tours—is usually evocative of ambiguity, despair, loss, and mortality, a voice—and not a genteel one—noting life's contradictions, ironies, and trade-offs. Dylan's uneasy and sometimes haunting spectacle over the length of his career challenges audiences and critics, and indeed, his musical contemporaries, providing audiences with performative themes that examine human and social change, the fragile nature of identity and relationships, the vicissitudes of the human condition, and the problematic nature of reality. Finally, the theme of the Dylan spectacle, which I attribute to the entire Dylan oeuvre, no matter its individual form—album, live performance, song, artwork, interview, et al.—has to do with these essential themes and the presentation of his work.

MEDITATIONS ON THE ARTIST AT FIRST LIGHT

Perhaps the spectacle of Bob Dylan begins to come to light with his relationship to the generation most closely identified with the 1960s, the baby
boomers.[54] It is a formidable cohort, one that references the dramatic spurt
in population growth that accompanied the end of World War II. Seen at
first as a statistical anomaly on the population grid, it then grew and developed and went on to enhance and transform almost all aspects of American
life, from the concept of adolescence to the popular culture, redefining the
music industry, higher education, political and social activism, and sexual
culture along the way. Now as baby boomers retire, they are sure to alter the
codes of retirement and health care. It is a group that has contributed by
participation, attendance, and, in some cases, initiation, to the spectacle of
politics and entertainment of the 20th century.

But while all generations might have their particular social, academic,
media, and scientific characteristics, successes, and failures, it was this baby
boomer generation that found itself with something that previous generations did not have, and it was probably due to an accident of economic
history: spending power (now a feature of the many middle-class and upper-
class generations that have followed). Because of this economic ability, the
boomers became the darlings of mass marketers and transformed fashion,
recreation, and, of course, music. In a sense, the baby boomer generation
and their immediate predecessors helped to create the modern music industry that exploded in the 1960s and 1970s, just as the digitalized generations
(many of whom were the boomers' children) have helped to revolutionize
the industry through downloading and file sharing, leading to another, certainly more dramatic, reconfiguration of the music and recording industry.

Dylan and the baby boomer generation will always be indissolubly linked,
as noted by many journalists and scholars.[55] Dylan's early songs and performances touched the hearts and minds of the generation that would call the
1960s and most of the 1970s their own, but Dylan is demographically distant enough from being one of them, born about five years before that first
wave of boomers entered history at the end of World War II. And in pop
culture history, those five years are not meaningless; Dylan grew up with different cultural and entertainment reference points than the baby boomers.
Dylan might have written songs with boomer politics and personal angst in
mind, but many of these songs can and do relate to other generations and
to other political and social contexts as well. Perhaps because it makes for a
neat musical and sociological connection, many journalists and music critics have tried to keep this tenuous affiliation alive, branding Dylan a major
voice of the baby boomers or a spokesman for the '60s generation.

Dylan being characterized as the spokesman for a generation was common parlance in various media discourses in the 1960s. Today we would say

it was a meme that more or less went out of control. It can still be found in so many places it is usually taken for fact.[56] And even though Dylan took pains to reject such a label, going so far to say so in various places, including in his memoir *Chronicles*[57] and in an interview on *60 Minutes*[58] with broadcast journalist Ed Bradley, it is understandable how such a label would stick. For what the public mind knows of Dylan is that he came to fame in the 1960s, and for many, scholars, journalists, fans, and critics included, he also came to his most accomplished artistic successes during that period. Of course, this is an impoverished way to look at his body of work, but such is the reality in a sound-bite, headline-focused culture. The boomers also came to their historical distinctiveness at the time as well; but that is where the correlation begins to fade. The boomers can claim him; they can (and apparently do) attend his concerts along with fans from other generations; and the critics and the pundits can label him as "the voice of the '60s" or whatever suits the story of the moment; but it's not going to do any good. Dylan was always beyond their command.

What does not usually take place in this discussion is that there are meritorious arguments to credit Dylan with a title as grandiose as the spokesman of a generation, or the "voice of the '60s," and when such phrases are uttered, it is taken for granted that it means the spokesman for the baby boomers. First, Dylan did come up as a performer in the early sixties, just as that first tier of boomers was flowering into adolescence, searching for a variety of social and political expressions with which to annoy their elders and to differentiate themselves culturally. They found it in the folk revival and Dylan was, as noted previously, the rising star of that revival. But as preteens, boomers saw—or perhaps felt—how Elvis could shake up that command establishment and that set a template, and Dylan seemed to be in the right place at the right time. Of course, in American popular culture history, these sorts of phenomena—singers and musicians creating a tumult among a young generation of fans—was a pretty old story, as old in fact as the past century, going back to Rudy Vallee and the development of the microphone.[59] The changes in technology allowed for musical presentation for the mass mediated audience, each generation seeing and hearing and appreciating and fawning over a figure or group that they thought represented them and entertained them at the same time. And like the boomers who "rebelled" against an older generation, usually seen as their parents or the political establishment, Dylan would "rebel" against the generation that had this tenuous jurisdiction over the folk music scene of his day and then proceeded over the next decade to transform the mainstream recording industry as well.[60]

But Dylan may have unwittingly cemented his baby boomer bona fides with his 1960s songwriting and performances. He composed one of the major anthems of the 1960s, and certainly as a hybrid, a folk song that became a pop song, had enormous influence on the sensibilities of a generation that moved through time with all the indelicacies the 1960s offered. "Blowin' in the Wind" was a song that became one of the major anthems of the civil rights movement and that was covered by many '60s performers, from the folk trio Peter, Paul and Mary to the rhythm and blues artist Sam Cooke and to such mainstream artists as Stevie Wonder. If Dylan had done nothing else, written or performed nothing else, he would still be a wealthy man from the royalties of this song and a cultural contributor of enormous proportions. Indeed, "Blowin' in the Wind," practically typifies Dylan's art—as it is a composition in the truest sense—a pastiche of gospel, blues, and folk song structure with a lexicon that sounds as if it came out of the 19th century; a notable remix of musical ideas and phrases.

It may seem, in retrospect, that Dylan's rise to the highest levels of his chosen profession was "destined" because it appeared seamless and apparently swift, just as "Blowin' in the Wind" became a standard song of the times in a breathtakingly short period of time. His rise to stardom was, in fact, by no means ordained, but it did seem like an inevitable story. In the early days of the folk revival in Greenwich Village (1959–1964) there were all the obvious obstacles to his success. When Dylan arrived in Greenwich Village, he joined a burgeoning folk scene in New York City that had been developing in fits and starts since the early 1950s, when the Weavers[61]—performers from the 1930s and 1940s—came on the scene and performed at the famed Village Vanguard for several months and were a hit, extremely popular with the bohemian crowd. However, the Weavers' insurgent music[62] came to an almost immediate public halt when Pete Seeger, one of the founding members of the group (along with Lee Hays, Ronnie Gilbert, Fred Hellerman, and at times Woody Guthrie), became a target of the House Un-American Activities Committee (HUAC). Seeger refused to testify, while Hays took the Fifth Amendment. These setbacks caused the group to disband even though they had sold millions of records during their time and played to sold-out clubs.

And so the development of folk music as a significant part of the pop music industry was temporarily stalled for a few years. In the late 1950s, folk music again saw a revival, and Greenwich Village again became one of the national centers of the folk scene.[63] This time the revival would stick, as it were. The political atmosphere became somewhat less toxic, and there was a broad and talented group of performers, some young and some who had been around for a while: The Chad Mitchell Trio, the Kingston Trio, and the Limelighters—groups who had fostered the revival on college campuses and on the pop charts.[64]

More importantly, there was also a growing audience of young people, and some not so young, who were disappointed with the pop music of the day. And these disaffected young people were drawn to the talents of a new generation of folk performers who brought a modern sensibility to the genre and its audiences. This included Joan Baez, who was an actual star in those days, and who introduced Dylan to her audiences with great success; Peter, Paul and Mary, who made folk music palatable beyond the small circle of Village friends (they were a somewhat hipper version of the Kingston Trio and the Chad Mitchell Trio); Dave Van Ronk, who was a performer and mentor to many young folk singers (including Dylan); Richie Havens; Judy Collins; Tom Paxton; Tim Hardin; Phil Ochs; Eric Anderson; and many others too numerous to mention here. These were the artists who were part of the changing of the guard, bringing folk music to college students and the Village denizens, and ultimately to the masses. Even so, the old guard of folk singers and musicians was still around performing, including the aforementioned Pete Seeger and the Weavers, whose members sometimes worked as arrangers and producers, and Bob Gibson, mentor to Joan Baez; and Ramblin' Jack Elliot. The elder statesman of this group, Woody Guthrie, was by this time in the hospital wasting away with Huntington's disease.

The folk community of Greenwich Village provided a congenial space for Dylan's talent, and ultimately his particular genius was able to shine. By the time Dylan was 22, around the age many young people graduate college, he had put in several years of performing and arranging traditional songs, but he had also written several other protest songs[65] that would become standards of the 1960s American folk songbook—and beyond—songs that the public would come to identify as the mind-set of a generation; songs that became part of the repertoire of artists more famous than he (at the time). In the process, and over a relatively short amount of time compared with other performers, he became a star performer.

One of those early songs that became part of the American musical spectacle, and ultimately helped launch the Dylan spectacle, was "Blowin' in the Wind," a simple folk melody, a variation on a slave lament, with the striking structure of nine rhetorical questions, influenced by biblical imagery, and a refrain reprising the title that was ambiguous enough to allow audiences to provide their own meanings as to what the "answer" is. With this song, a very young Bob Dylan captured the imagination of the folk community, his peers, certainly his audiences, and a generation bent on questioning everything, and this put him on a trajectory for fame and stardom. Perhaps it is with this unvarnished and underproduced song,[66] "Blowin' in the Wind," that Dylan's spectacle begins.

The song's origins are somewhat humble, and even Dylan has been quoted as saying he wrote the song in 10 minutes based on a melody from the slave lament "No More Auction Block for Me," a song associated with Odetta and the Carter Family, versions that Dylan was familiar with when he was starting out in Minnesota,[67] and Dylan had performed "No More

Auction Block for Me" in some of his early shows.[68] The actual performing history of "Blowin' in the Wind" begins one night at Gerde's Folk City, when Dylan brought the song (after working on it with David Blue) to Gil Turner, who had a job at Gerde's introducing the performers and making judgments as to their ability and popularity with audiences. Dylan sang the song for Turner who was, to put it mildly, extremely impressed and realized this was an extraordinary opportunity and demanded that Dylan teach him the song so he could perform it that very evening. Robbie Woliver reports[69] that when Turner performed the song—and because he had not as yet learned the words, he had a sheet with the verses on it taped to the microphone—he received a standing ovation. According to Woliver, Dylan was in the back by the bar observing his handiwork.

There is, of course, a more colorful story about this song told by Robert Cohen,[70] a friend of Dylan's from those Greenwich Village days, and also a performer of some note. Cohen was part of a folk group called the New World Singers, which included Dolores Dixon, Gil Turner (the aforementioned emcee), Happy Traum, and Cohen. During their performances, Delores Dixon would take a solo turn and sing "No More Auction Block for Me," and Dylan was more than likely in the audience many times to hear her version of the song. But the song, as I noted earlier, which had been made popular by Odetta, was covered by many folk singers at the time; in fact, Dylan performed it regularly at the Gaslight, so it must have already been in his repertoire. The performances at the Gaslight were duly recorded by Terry Thal (who was married to Dave Van Ronk), and while bootlegs were around among the Dylan collectors for many years, it was only released by Dylan's record company on a compact disc in 2005 entitled *Live at the Gaslight*.[71]

"Blowin' in the Wind" was a huge success in a variety of ways—it put Dylan on the map as a songwriter and provided him with income so that he could pursue his art. The song was covered by hundreds of artists disseminating the song—and its lyrics, if not its message—to such a variety of audiences that it is no wonder the song more or less seems to be authorless and simply part of the culture. The rhetoric of the song helps this idea because it has, as with almost all of Dylan's work, a kind of biblical flavor to the syntax and symbolism. But the artists who covered this song—and this is not a complete list—are a remarkably eclectic lot, ranging from Stan Getz, who did it as an instrumental in 1964, to Marlene Dietrich, who sort of talks her way through the verses, also in 1964. Of course the standard versions that most of the public recognizes are from Peter, Paul and Mary and Stevie Wonder, both of whom had top 10 hits with the song. The list of other artists who covered this song seems like a who's who in American music and includes the folk singer Judy Collins, country artist Chet Atkins, pop singer Bobby Darin, and soul singers Sam Cooke and Etta James. Elvis Presley may have recorded "Blowin'" in 1966, but it was released on an album entitled *In a Private Moment* 20 years after Presley died.[72] What would have happened in this country had the Presley version been released as a single in 1966?

MEDITATIONS ON THE ARTIST IN TWILIGHT

Apparently, Bob Dylan has performed almost everywhere, and if his current touring schedule remains remotely the same as it has for the past 25 years or so, Dylan will probably be appearing at a theater, state fair, stadium, airplane hangar, minor league ball park, military academy, college gym, racetrack, or casino near you. His tours usually include international performances, and so Dylan has appeared in European, South American, and Asian venues, and as I write this, Dylan has just begun the European leg of his summer 2013 tour. He performs live more than any of his contemporaries who are in the same star strata (e.g., Paul Simon, Eric Clapton, the Rolling Stones, Billy Joel) mostly out of will and partly because he has outlived and outlasted some of them, but more importantly, because he still commands major audiences for his live shows. "To those who know him well, it is clear there is nothing else he wants to do,"[73] claims Dylan biographer Howard Sounes. Indeed, Dylan's touring has become, like many of his major songs, and even his name, part of the pop culture firmament. Dylan's traveling show has been called "The Never Ending Tour"[74] by music journalists, a term later disputed by Dylan, of course; but whatever it is called, since 1988, or thereabouts, Dylan has been on the road, "heading to another joint," as he sings in "Tangled Up in Blue," performing about a 100 shows a year.[75]

When he does perform, Dylan presents an eclectic mix from his own rather extensive songbook, a body of work that contains his visions of life (and death), identity, love, loss, and implicit, if not explicit, social commentary. For example, the lines from the song "High Water (For Charley Patton)," on *Love and Theft* (2001) may not refer to any one particular event, but rather the overall condition of the nation, and such was the case during the Bush administration. His work contains refrains, images, and melodies from the American folk and gospel songbook, with cadences and catchphrases of the American rhythm and blues traditions as well as the folk and pop traditions. His songs allude to or respond to or rework lyrics and melodies from these genres, which is to say, traditional songs, songs in the public domain, songs associated with the likes of Sonny Boy Williamson, Muddy Waters, Charley Patton, Sleepy John Estes, Lightnin' Hopkins, and others, all of whom can be seen as contributing to his art as much as, say, Woody Guthrie, the Bentley Boys, and Odetta.[76] His lyrics are mixed with quotations and appropriations, references and images from the Bible, as well as the works of F. Scott Fitzgerald, the French Symbolists, Civil War poets Henry Timrod[77] and Sidney Lanier, Jack Kerouac and Allen Ginsberg, and other American Beats, Walt Whitman, American film noir, and whoever and whatever else he's been listening to, watching or reading.

Dylan's interests in these artists as well as his remarkable curiosity with ancient and sometimes anonymous texts of American music, those ballads and folk tunes, what Greil Marcus has called that "old weird America,"[78] emerges more overtly in his tours and recordings from the mid-1980s through the 1990s.[79] Of course, the previous few years, known as his Gospel period, were nothing if not a period of appropriation, as Dylan explored one of the richest songbooks and styles in American culture, African American gospel music, complete with backup singers who had serious gospel credentials.[80] During the tours from the late 1980s through the 1990s and indeed up until about 2002,[81] audiences were treated to some remarkable songs that had fallen by the wayside in a world obsessed with the new: the classic, "Shake a Hand,"[82] versions of "Barbara Allen" and "The Wagoner's Lad," versions of "Dixie" (yes, that "Dixie," which he played seven times during 1990; and there is an intense performance as well in the film *Masked and Anonymous*), "Pretty Peggy O," "Rock of Ages," "The White Dove," "Hallelujah, I'm Ready To Go," and "Are You Ready"—were all given the Dylan treatment.

This aspect of his live show came into prominence during the period starting with *Down in the Groove* (1988), an album of collaborations with an enormous number of artists ranging from Full Force, Clydie King, and Carolyn Dennis, who provided background vocals; Robert Hunter, one of the Grateful Dead lyricists; along with Jerry Garcia, Mark Knopfler, Eric Clapton, and Ron Wood, who all contributed their own particular musical artistry. The trend continued with *Good as I Been to You* (1992) and *World Gone Wrong* (1993); both albums are compilations of folk and blues standards that are arranged and performed by a solo Dylan. Dylan seemed to have come back to his starting point since the productions were similar to his very first acoustic albums. In a sense, these albums and tours are other versions of *Self Portrait* (1970), which I discuss later, as they are a mixture of traditional music and standard songs with Dylan's arrangements that seem uncannily to touch on themes and musical concepts that he has explored his entire career. Covering other artists' material and performing traditional songs on his tours, say after 2010, has generally stopped, but who knows what he will do on future tours.

But even though Dylan has the reputation as one of popular music's major and most respected songwriters, covering other songwriters and arranging traditional folk ballads and blues tunes had been the *raison d'être* of Dylan's performance art since he first stepped onto the stages of Greenwich Village. His first album, *Bob Dylan* (1962), was indeed a compilation of traditional songs[83] from the repertoire of the likes of Bukka White, Jesse Fuller, and Blind Lemon Jefferson. It is worth noting that the predominant theme of that first album seems to be about death, and, as Michael Gray puts it, the songs are "performed without gentility and with a voice that, far from suggesting a soul-mate for Peter, Paul and Mary suggested some black octogenarian singing personal blues."[84]

Eight years and eight[85] albums later, the remarkably misunderstood *Self Portrait* (1971) was released. This album was seen as a document of artistic transition and redirection, so the rationale of Dylan's many observers went, because no artist could maintain the kind of whirlwind of significant originality that he had developed in the previous decade. But looked at again, the album is a melding of old songs, standards of another era, with new material that gives the impression of being old. This seems integral to Dylan's aesthetic. Dylan came to the recording sessions for *Self Portrait* with a number of songs, songs that were traditional, pop songs, country songs, a contemporary song or two, and some of his own songs; to paraphrase Robbie Robertson's characterization of *The Basement Tapes*[86] sessions, no one, not the musicians, the arrangers, or the recording people could tell if these songs "were his or not." [87] That same sentiment—were these Dylan songs or traditional songs?—could well describe the release in 2013's *Another Self Portrait*, an album of all the unreleased, ancillary, and discarded material from those recording sessions. While the original was greeted with jeers and disappointments and disenchantment, this 2013 addition, even though it had inferior and underproduced performances, allowed music critics to justify their respect for Dylan's overall work and to reaffirm his place in the American music pantheon.

Nowadays, such mixed up confusion, albeit of another sort, is experienced at Dylan concerts. Here the confusion concerns not so much the question of whether Dylan wrote the song but what song is he *performing*. Yes, these days even Dylan aficionados turn to each other at shows to ask, what song is this? Many refuse to even ask that question, basking in the high musical technique and aura on stage. Actually, for those who have followed this artist in his live shows, this has been going on for a while. Dylan now sets his songs into musical structures that have become over the years as complicated as they are diverse. Reviewers of Dylan's concerts always note that he "changes" his songs around, "confusing" some in attendance who don't know the new arrangements, and therefore cannot apparently recognize the songs. This is part of Dylan's long standing reputation as an artist who is never interested in doing the same thing twice. In conversation with author Jonathan Lethem in 2006, Dylan comments on this accepted truism of the constantly changing arrangements and after a long discussion he emphatically tells Lethem that "the arrangements don't change night after night. The rhythmic structures are different, that's all. You can't change the arrangement night after night—it's impossible."[88] Of course, for most of us, this is a distinction without a difference. Nevertheless, part of the "Dylan experience," which is to say, attending one of his concerts over the past 10 years or so, is figuring out what he's actually playing, since Dylan does not introduce anything, much less talk to the audience, except, of course, to introduce his band around encore time.[89]

Audiences at contemporary Dylan shows are in a somewhat peculiar place psychologically—they are out of their comfort zone, and have to work for some sort of understanding of what is being performed. One of the aspects of pop culture that is most appealing is that genres are recognizable with conventions that are familiar and accessible, sometimes even comforting. This is one of the differences in attending a Dylan show than almost any other contemporary popular music act, and it is not to everyone's taste. Most contemporary rock and pop and folk performers try to commit themselves in live performance to what they did on record. Dylan seems to work the other way. For most of his career, Dylan has treated the recording studio as a laboratory ("I don't like to make records"[90]) where he develops his songs and creates the frames for his performances, but those songs are only fully *composed* in live performance. Just consider the song that he has played more than any other song over the past 25 years or so, "All Along the Watchtower."[91] This song began its long life in American music as a simple (in terms of presentation), spiritually infused, acoustic folk song on *John Wesley Harding* (1967). But in performance, thanks to the killer version by Jimi Hendrix (1968), an arrangement that Dylan has very rarely varied from in his own shows, it has become an audience favorite, an anthem to the role of art, the artist, and value in society as well as to the notion of the coming cataclysm. The song also plays with chronological time, as Christopher Ricks points out, that as the bare narrative ends, it seems to begin again.[92] But the theme of the song is carried not just by the words as much by the dramatic musical performance, especially the guitar solos. What this means for audiences is that you have to listen carefully to the music being played, and live rock concerts do not usually and have not generally required nor rewarded such thoughtful behavior.

For some in the contemporary Dylan audience not used to this type of listening, this was not included in the price of their tickets. Dylan's new renditions of older songs can sometimes change a song's original conception and mar the memories. But these new versions can also introduce new musical genres and styles, such as a New Orleans shuffle, rockabilly rhythms, boogie woogie, Texas swing and cowboy tunes, gospel chord structures and ornamentations, classic rock, the blues shouts of Joe Turner, the rasps of Mississippi John Hurt, the bluegrass pickings of Ralph Stanley, and, recently, at least during some of the 2012 and 2013 tours I attended, Dylan seems to be channeling the crooning styles of Bing Crosby.[93] When you are at a Dylan concert, you get quite an inventory of American popular music. Considering the sources of his lyrics, his nuanced visions of life and death, as well as his reworking of his songs, it is no wonder why Dylan the performance artist is a favorite among the professors[94]: there is just so much to deconstruct.

But what do you see when you see Bob Dylan perform? Well, that has become the never-ending question. Some music journalists are mostly content to review the legend, with the usual particulars, and so the story becomes the indomitable artist still performing after all these years. And that approach goes over well and serves various media narratives, especially the narrative that boomer culture still matters. Other music journalists see a contemporary Dylan concert, with the different arrangements, and with the growing vulnerability of his voice, performing songs they and perhaps many in the audience do not really know well, and they see an opportunity to trash the legend and to attack what they see as the indulgence of a star. They can show their readers/viewers that they are brave enough and critical enough and honest enough to go against the grain, to dismiss this star in the twilight of his career.[95] Both of these approaches seem to me to be an impoverished way to deal with this artist; but such critical views may be more of an indication of the problematic nature of popular culture criticism in general, especially as so much of the music commentary in the mainstream media is provided by publicity agents or writers working for publications that have interests in promoting the industry and, as such, much of what passes for commentary and reviews that we are exposed to borders on advertising. Or, the commentary travels the dead-end road of stark opinion. But as far as music journalism goes, given the tools and the procedures that it has, it may be an impossible task to provide a review of a Dylan concert without descending to these practices or variations on these practices.

Dylan tours—and the concerts that are part of them—are like chapters in the long and unfolding narrative of Dylan's work. So, at a Dylan concert you see many Dylans: you see someone who was not yet 21 singing Woody Guthrie songs to Woody Guthrie himself; someone who wrote and sang "Only a Pawn in Their Game," a song about Medgar Evers, the murdered civil rights worker who was a few feet from Martin Luther King Jr. on the day King delivered his "I Have a Dream" speech. At a Dylan concert you see a performer who in 1963, as a young and upcoming and ambitious artist, refused to perform on the *Ed Sullivan Show* because the producers wanted to change what he wanted to sing, a humorous "talking blues" about the John Birch Society, called "Talkin' John Birch Paranoid Blues."[96]

When you attend a Dylan concert you see someone who in a moment of casual inspiration wrote "Blowin' in the Wind" (and decades later saw that song's refrain discussed by a pope[97]), a performer who reinvigorated the singer songwriter genre, a singer who challenged and continues to challenge the conventions of vocal presentation. When you attend a Dylan concert you see a performer who unceremoniously and indelicately extricated him-self from the folk revival, even though he had brought it significance and vitality in the early 1960s, and yet is one of several artists today who con-tinue to practice that particular musical tradition, the folk process, on a larger scale. At a Dylan concert you see a recording artist who changed the length of the "single" record played on mainstream radio (when radio was the major distribution medium for pop music) with his song "Like a Rolling Stone," which comes in at a blistering 6 minutes and 13 seconds (in the stereo version), and because of the demands of radio listeners usually had to be played in its entirety.

These are just some of the many pixels that contribute to Dylan's never-ending story. And noting an artist's historical profile—as incomplete as mine was—might not be on the agenda of audiences these days. However, Dylan's contributions were clearly on the mind of Bruce Springsteen as spoke at Dylan's induction into the Rock and Roll Hall of Fame. At the end of his remarks, Springsteen said that Dylan "freed your mind, and showed us that because the music was physical did not mean it was anti-intellect. He had the vision and talent to make a pop song so that it contained the whole world. He invented a new way a pop singer could sound, broke through the limitations of what a recording could achieve, and he changed the face of rock 'n roll for ever."[98]

Of course, who really knows what the various audiences, fans, fanatics, or those just passing by actually see and hear at a Dylan show? To answer that empirically demands a different type of study than the one that is here. But those who have attended his concerts over the past 10 years or so, and who have not followed his career closely, and think they are going to relive the 1960s or see a major signifier of that time (and Dylan pretty much cre-ated the soundtrack of the 1960s) are going to be bewildered if not bitterly disappointed, maybe even angry. Perhaps it is Dylan's way of puncturing the spectacle of his own iconic status or undermining the nostalgia that seems to infect generations as they move into pop culture irrelevance: the Dylan voice they hear today bears no relation to the seemingly drug-addled yet arresting vocals on, say, "Desolation Row," the righteous anger of "The Lonesome Death of Hattie Carroll," the sneering tone in the "How does it feel" chorus from "Like a Rolling Stone," or the country crooner in "New Morning." They will notice, however, and maybe even with alarm, that these days Dylan barely picks up a guitar, preferring piano and harmonica as he directs his band from a keyboard ensemble. Perhaps during that evening's show they will see Dylan come center stage with just the microphone and his harmonica and talk them through the drama of "Ballad of a Thin Man," the narrator calling attention to our fragile understanding of reality, some-thing is happening but we don't know what it is—which is as much the sub-ject of his lyric as it is a commentary on his performance art.

For those who came to Dylan late in his career, say in the late 1990s when he started to embody the guise of the old blues troubadour, the funereal persona observing the contemporary emaciated moral landscape, when he began a series of successful albums, *Time Out of Mind*, (1997), *The Bootleg Series 1966* (1998), *Love and Theft* (2000), and *Modern Times* (2006), which brought him new critical recognition, his voice in concert was already a rasp and a squall, and becoming something more like the scratching of used sandpaper. Well, the rasps and squalls are now deeper and even more strained. And those curious souls who might have just walked into the casino, state fair, or campground, having some vague idea as to who Dylan is, or more precisely, who Dylan was, and he has played enough of these venues so that this actually happens, might repeat inadvertently the famous first sentence of the Greil Marcus review of *Self Portrait* (1971), in *Rolling Stone* many decades ago: "What is this shit?" The consternation for these individuals, of course, is real because Dylan's voice now comes out of what Yeats called "the foul-and-rag bone shop of the heart."[99] Dylan's voice, which has always been a point of discussion, even when he was in his twenties, and which over the years has taken on several iterations,[100] was astutely described by Christophe Lebold as "a complex sign that the artist uses for pathos, self-parody, and/or to enhance his fatalistic and stoic vision of a fallen world in which 'everything is broken.'"[101] Dylan's voice is just one of his signifiers of mortality and ruin—of the social unraveling that he sees—and perhaps epitomizes in and of itself the haunting spectacle of Bob Dylan.

In performance these days (circa 2015), the uneasy spectacle that Dylan has created in a career that spans more than half a century, with no sense of an ending, takes on a different dimension. While he is an elder statesman of contemporary popular music, he presents himself as ages older. In fact, as Dylan ages he becomes more and more the embodiment of the history of popular music. And this "of the ages" aura comes through with the elaborate introductions to his shows. For almost a decade, beginning in 2001[102] or so, most Dylan shows have started with selections from the orchestral music of Aaron Copland, the "Hoe-Down," "Fanfare for the Common Man," and, at times, "Appalachian Spring." Using Copland's music in this way, as part of his introduction to audiences might seem out of place at a rock concert, but at a Dylan show this music seems perfectly natural. The link between Copland and Dylan is examined closely by Sean Wilentz in *Bob Dylan in America*,[103] where in a lengthy section, Wilentz shows how Copland's creative work—his process of quoting and reworking American folk melodies, themes, and other aspects of Americana in orchestral form—parallels Dylan's own work with the folk music tradition and rock and roll. In this perhaps too subtle way, Dylan is framing himself and his work, since music reviewers rarely comment on this part of the show.

In conjunction with the Copland music, and starting around 2001 as well, and ending just a few tours ago, there was also an oral introduction that set the evening's theme, a set piece welcoming everyone to the show usually recited with fervor (or was it irony? or both?) by Al Santos, a member of Dylan's stage crew:

> Ladies and gentleman, please welcome the poet laureate of rock and roll. The voice of the promise of the '60s counterculture. The guy who forced folk into bed with rock. Who donned makeup in the '70s and disappeared in a haze of substance abuse. Who emerged to find Jesus. Who was written off as a has been by the end of the '80s, and who suddenly shifted gears releasing some of the strongest music of his career in the late '90s. Ladies and gentleman—Columbia recording artist, Bob Dylan! [104]

There is so much that is slippery in this preamble to Dylan's performance. There is so much that needs to be explained or at least added to such a monologue that some Dylan fans became annoyed into silence. The actual words spoken by Santos come from a concert review by a Buffalo music critic, slightly revised, but there is so much here that could be questioned, that needs to be contextualized and examined. Although no one usually disputes that first descriptor, naming Dylan as the "poet laureate of rock and roll," except those who might want to discuss the question as to whether or not song writing is the same as poetry writing,[105] all the rest of the statements need at least a chapter of explication, evidence, and context. At the various concerts I have attended, I can see members of the audience that I know actually wince or smile wanly or chuckle (sometimes loudly) as Santos delivers these words, especially when he intones "the promise of the '60s counterculture," or "the guy who forced folk into bed with rock," or "who emerged to find Jesus" (after which there is usually a noticeable pause). These phrases point to various historical periods in Dylan's career, but all of these phrases are historically problematic. Here I will point out only that describing Dylan as "the promise of the '60s counterculture," is pretty meaningless. How is the term "counterculture" being used? Or for that matter "promise"? Dylan was never an overtly political activist of any sort (as Joan Baez most certainly was), although as noted earlier he was given the Tom Paine Award from the Emergency Civil Liberties Committee in 1963 and wrote songs that inspired student activists and civil rights workers, who would claim, "he sang for us"[106] and whose lyrics would be quoted by several presidents and major politicians.[107] And while he demurred on the political activities of the New Left, no one was more critical, no one was more hostile to the activities of the so-called counterculture and that entire lifestyle than Dylan.[108]

And maybe that's the point—this "Dylan through the decades" introduction was so general, so wide ranging as to epitomize (and sanitize?) a significant part of musical folklore for the past 50 years or more. Sort of like a bad Wikipedia entry? What this introduction did in a fevered 86 words is to summarize and mythologize, to make palatable, perhaps too palatable for many Dylan fans, Dylan's performing career, the words racing through the decades and genres without any of the subtlety of time or place, making him part of the pop culture landscape. Making him, dare I say it, ordinary? This version of the Dylan story in about a minute seems perfectly timed for audiences in tune to a sound bite culture. As these words are invoked at the beginning of each show, they perform a kind of pop culture origins story, a desiccated history of a complex artist who has lived through some transformative times, and so this wily introduction also seemed like Dylan's ultimate revenge on those who would categorize him or understand him too quickly, or try to comprehend him at all. These opening remarks are sort of legendary shorthand, a skeletal transcription of history that provides a mirror to the misunderstandings—willful or otherwise—that has dogged Dylan's career. As introductions go, it's pretty much typical stage business, the outline of a myth, a coat of many colors that tries to cover us with a simplistic context for the performance art at hand. After a career of defying labels, at this point he seems to be embracing the labels. For Dylan followers it is immense irony; but, as the title of his 2000 Oscar-winning song says, "Things Have Changed."

More recently (at this writing), the Copland music and the Santos speech have given way to a variety of blues riffs, usually played by Stu Kimball, providing audiences with "another shift in his self-presentation."[109] Perhaps these traditional blues chords, which could bring to life any number of lyrics, work as another type of fanfare, announcing the presence of an older, traditional blues man who has come to town.

As the instrumental begins to fade, the lights are turned down, and the venue is bathed in darkness, the impatient cheering begins accompanied by the usual flashing and circulating spotlights, eyes straining to see and then cheer as Dylan walks onstage with his band. After the blues riff comes to an end, there is no chatter, no banter, no show biz patter. There is no "Hello New York!" The only words that will emanate from the stage now will be those spoken or sung with instrumentation. The lights go up, the cheering and acclamation soar excitedly and hungrily and earnestly; a collective effervescence sets in among the crowd;[110] the band, already at their marks, are like thoroughbreds champing at the bit eager to start their race through our musical past and present; their introductory notes, chords, and riffs, held in check with only nodding obbligatos as the stage is wrapped in darkness, now become decisive and forceful and dramatic; the crowd's cheers continue to escalate, and Dylan, these days standing at a piano, in perfect timing as the lights come on to shatter that darkness, bends down to the microphone and with his band now in full stride, starts performing.

NOTES

1. Lee Marshall, *Bob Dylan: The Never Ending Star* (New York: Polity, 2007), 92. Here Marshall argues that Dylan's "earlier stardom (in the folk revival of the 1960s) and his electrified output in the 1960s . . . became the hallmark of rock culture."

2. Jonathan Crary, "Spectacle, Attention, Counter-Memory," *October* 50 (Autumn 1989): 96.

3. Douglas Kellner expands Guy Debord's concept of the spectacle, explaining that the media spectacle includes phenomena of media culture, politics, sports, and entertainment. See Kellner, *Media Spectacle* (New York: Routledge, 2003), 2.

4. Bob Dylan, *Chronicles: Volume One* (New York: Simon and Schuster, 2004). The memoir was nominated for the National Book Critics' Circle Award in the Biography/Autobiography category. At the same time, the memoir was disappointing to many Dylan fans and cultural historians because he barely spent three chapters on his arrival in Greenwich Village in 1961, ignored the mid-1960s, the period of his rise to stardom, and then jumped to discuss his recollections of recording *New Morning* and *Oh, Mercy*.

5. *No Direction Home* was produced for American television as part of the American Masters Series (PBS) and directed by Martin Scorsese. Dylan's production company provided many hours of historical film footage for the time period covered in this documentary. This includes a damaged recording of Dylan's high school band, a screen test for an Andy Warhol interview, and footage from Dylan's famous Manchester concert in 1966 where a fan called him "Judas" for leaving "folk music." This footage was found in 2004 in Dylan's vault. About 20 figures active in the 1960s and beyond were interviewed, including Joan Baez, Dave Van Ronk, Allen Ginsberg, Maria Muldaur, Bruce Langhorne, Suze Rotolo, Pete Seeger, Mavis Staples, and Peter Yarrow.

6. *I'm Not There*, 2007, directed by Todd Haynes, written by Todd Haynes and Oren Moverman, and produced by Christine Vachon.

7. David Yaffe, *Bob Dylan: Like a Complete Unknown* (New Haven, CT: Yale University Press, 2011), 129. But there is some dispute. Discographers make distinctions among songs that have been written, recorded, and/or released. *The Definitive Bob Dylan Song Book*, edited by Ed Lozano and Don Giller (Milwaukee, WI: Music Sales of America) listed 329 released and recorded songs as of 2003; bobdylan.com, the official Dylan website lists 458 total songs as of 2012; a major fan site, http://expect ingrain.com/discussions/viewtopic.php?p=1148954&sid=9dcf1b27f98af851eb 0559578ba006f4, has a convoluted discussion, but the number 458 does show up there as well and refers to released songs.

8. For a complete listing of Dylan's discography see www.bobdylan.com/us/ albums/chronological.

9. Dylan is one of the most bootlegged musicians ever; bootlegs (unofficial recordings sold in various places) are extremely popular and profitable, but not to

the artist, and so in an attempt to stem the monetary bleeding from these bootlegs, Dylan and his record company decided in 1991 to start a series of official releases called the Bootleg Series, which includes outtakes, alternative versions, unreleased songs, and selected live performances.

10. Robert Zimmerman began performing as Bob Dylan in 1959 at the Ten O'Clock Scholar, a coffee house in downtown Minneapolis when he was supposed to be attending the University of Minnesota. He was 19 years old, and during this time, Dylan became an active participant in what was called the Dinkytown folk scene. See Robert Shelton, *No Direction Home: The Life and Music of Bob Dylan* (New York: De Capo Press, 2011), 65–68.

11. Bob Dylan, *Tarantula* (New York: Macmillan and Scribner, 1966); this was a collection of experimental poetry in the style of the Beats, with Allen Ginsberg, William Burroughs, and Jack Kerouac as major influences; and Dylan, 2004.

12. Bob Dylan and Scott Campbell, *If Dogs Run Free* (New York: Atheneum Books for Young Readers, 2013); Bob Dylan and Jim Arnosky, *Man Gave Names to All the Animals* (New York: Sterling, 2010); Bob Dylan and Paul Rogers, *Forever Young* (New York: Atheneum Books for Young Readers, 2008).

13. Dylan has given so many interviews that there are now compilations; see *Younger Than That Now: The Collected Interviews With Bob Dylan*, ed. Jim Ellison (New York: Da Capo Press, 2004); *Bob Dylan: The Essential Interviews*, ed. Jonathan Cott (New York: Wenner Press, 2006).

14. Here I am referring to the infamous San Francisco Press Conference in 1965, where an apparently stoned Dylan (or Dylan acting like he's stoned) chain-smokes his way through some banal questions, where his responses point to the inanity of the press and the whole procedure. See and enjoy the entire event at http://youtu. be/q7wzPtdqm_o.

15. Dylan has always drawn and painted, and recently, he has been working in sculpture. In November 2013 he had his first exhibit of iron sculptures at the Halcyon Gallery in London, England. See www.bbc.co.uk/news/entertainment-arts-24955933. Some of his drawings have ended up on his albums, for example, the cover of *Self Portrait* (1972). Collections of his artwork, some of which have appeared in galleries around the world have been published and include *Bob Dylan: Face Value: Character Sketches* (National Portrait Gallery, 2013); *The Asia Series Catalogue*, 2011; *Bob Dylan: the Drawn Blank Series: Water Colors and Gauache*, which can be viewed at bobdylan.com/art; and *Revisionist Art: Thirty Works by Bob Dylan*, with an introduction by Luc Santé and an essay on the history of revisionist art by B. Clevery. See the video of the installation of Dylan's artwork at the Gagosian Gallery, New York City here: http://youtu.be/3tcOekhCCII.

16. Dylan hosted the *Theme Time Radio Hour* on XM Satellite Radio, now called Sirius XM Radio, from May 2006 to April 2009. The show centered on various themes such as "Coffee," "Baseball," and "Goodbye" (which was the theme of the final show), which was not unlike his own concerts. His shows included recordings of artists as diverse as Patti Page, Frank Sinatra, Little Milton, the Stanley Brothers, Mahalia Jackson, and the Dixie Hummingbirds. For a history of Dylan's *Theme Time Radio Hour*, see http://leeabrams.blogspot.com/2006/04/dylan-diary-part -one.html.

17. See Perry Meisel, *The Myth of Popular Culture: From Dante to Dylan* (New York: Wiley Blackwell, 2007), who discusses many of the biographies.

18. Images of Dylan abound on the Internet and in books and photo exhibitions. Some major texts include Douglas R. Gilbert and Dave Marsh,*Forever Young: Photographs of Bob Dylan* (Boston: Da Capo Press, 2006); Bob Dylan, *The Bob Dylan Scrapbook* (New York: Simon and Schuster, 2005) (personal photos of Dylan, friends, and family); Essential Works, *Bob Dylan: Inspirations* (Riverside, NJ: Arthur McMeel Publishing, 2005); *Dylan: 100 Songs and Pictures*, ed. Peter Doggett, Chris Charlesworth, Anne Barkway, Andy Neil (London: Omnibus Press, 2009); and too many others to list here.

19. For a website that chronicles scholarly interest in Dylan since the 1960s, see *Twenty Pounds of Headlines* at http://public.wsu.edu/~scales/dylan/. This website contains many gems of scholarship, but it is a work of love rather than the product of a scholarly institution; the site's author claims it to be comprehensive but not complete, and it contains an extensive bibliography of periodical articles about Dylan since 1962. You will find citations of articles, abstracts, and links to many full-text articles and essays.

20. Both of these songs deal with the issue of justice and to what extent the legal system can provide justice for the poor and the marginalized. They also raised legal issues in terms of their overall accuracy, not exactly Dylan's intention. "Hurricane," cowritten with Jacques Levy, was released in 1975 on *Desire*, after some legal disputes questioned some of the material in the lyric. "The Lonesome Death of Hattie Carroll" also had some legal issues; it was released in 1964 on Dylan's *The Times They Are A'Changin'* album. There are too many songs to list here that reference a "judge" or "judgment," but notably, there is the extraordinary "Seven Curses," recorded in 1963 but inexplicably left off Dylan's third studio album, *The Times They Are A'Changin*. See www.bobdylan.com/us/songs.

21. Messiah College's symposium was on the topic of Christianity and Popular Culture; Dylan's concert there on November 6, 2004, was the capstone to a week of events on this topic, one of which was a presentation by Scott Marshall, coauthor along with Marcia Ford of *Restless Pilgrim: The Spiritual Journey of Bob Dylan* (Winter Park, FL: Relevant Books, 2002). At the 2013 academic conference at the College of the Holy Cross, Rebecca Castellani delivered a paper on the "The Masks of T.S. Eliot and Bob Dylan"; also in 2013, the University of Missouri-St. Louis sponsored a conference entitled "Bob Dylan: Immigrants, Wanderers, Exiles and Hard Travelers in the Poems, Songs and Culture of Ancient Greece and Modern America," and scholars and guest speakers discussed the oral tradition, songs of the traveler in the work of Bob Dylan, as well as his early life as Robert Zimmerman who grew up in the immigrant communities of Minnesota. Bristol University held a conference entitled "The Seven Ages of Dylan" in 2011. There has been quite a tradition of academics discussing Dylan, going back to at least 1998 at Stanford, where scholars discussed Dylan's legacy and whether Dylan's lyrics should be considered literature. In 2012, in Germany, the International Conference for Political Science Students at the University of Bremen paraphrased a Dylan song as their conference was titled, "The States They Are A-Changing," a conference that had nothing to do with music but rather with the changing nature of modern European nation states, their economies and citizenry.

22. In 2010–2011 three major academic texts on Dylan appeared: David Yaffe's *Bob Dylan: Like a Complete Unknown* (New Haven, CT: Yale University Press, 2011); Daniel Mark Epstein's *The Ballad of Bob Dylan* (New York: Harper Collins, 2011); and, Greil Marcus's *Bob Dylan by Greil Marcus: Writings 1968–2010* (New York: Public Affairs, 2010). Many more appeared in 2012, Dylan's 70th year.

23. *Bob Dylan: A Retrospective*, ed. Craig McGregor (New York: W. Morrow, 1972). Reprinted with a new preface by Nat Hentoff in 1990 and retitled *Bob Dylan: the Early Years: A Retrospective* (New York: William Morrow and Co).

24. See Betsy Bowden, *Performed Literature: Words and Music By Bob Dylan* (Bloomington: Indiana University Press, 1982). This is an academic treatise that examines Dylan's performed art, his live performances. Bowden develops a method for a close reading of what audiences hear. Originally, this was a doctoral dissertation, and she was one of the first scholars to note Dylan as a performing artist and not a poet in the traditional sense.

25. Christopher Ricks, *Dylan's Vision of Sin* (New York: Harper Perrennial, 2005). The precursor to Rick's close reading of Dylan's lyrics was Aiden Day's *Jokerman: Reading the Lyrics of Bob Dylan* (New York: Blackwell Publishers, 1988).

26. Evan R. Goldstein, "Dylan and the Intellectuals," *Chronicle of Higher Education*, September 5, 2010. http://chronicle.com/article/Dylanthe-Intellectuals/124218/.

27. Daniel Boorstin, *The Image: A Guide to Pseudo Events in America* (New York: Vintage Books, 1961).

28. You can see Dylan's White House performance here: http://youtu.be/sGMSyFde7F8.

29. Lists of Dylan's awards can be found on the Web; see chronologies here: www.aceshowbiz.com/celebrity/bob_dylan/awards.html and www.imdb.com/name/nm0001168/awards.

30. By 1963 Dylan had written "Blowin' in the Wind," "Only a Pawn in Their Game," "Masters of War," "Who Killed Davey Moore," "Oxford Town," and "A Hard Rains A' Gonna Fall."

31. For a detailed summary of the evening, see Howard Sounes, *Down the Highway: The Life of Bob Dylan* (New York: Grove Press, 2001), 144. For a transcript of Dylan's remarks, and his later apology, along with the evening's program and the apology of Corliss Lamont to the attendees of the ceremony and dinner, see www.corliss-lamont.org/dylan.htm.

32. Sounes, 2001, 144.

33. See www.corliss-lamont.org/dylan.htm.

34. In 1998, the NECLC merged with the Center for Constitutional Law.

35. The music video of the song was directed by the director of the film and includes Dylan interacting with characters from the film, giving viewers of the video the impression that Dylan is in the movie.

36. See http://aaspeechesdb.oscars.org/link/073-15/.

37. Rob Brunner, "Bombs Away," *Entertainment Weekly*, March 13, 1998, 14.

38. Brunner, 1998, 14.

39. For more information on Michael Portnoy, see Derek Yip, "Michael Portnoy AKA Soy Bomb: Upstart Pissing on the Contemporary Mix," *A Journal of Performance and Art* 61, no. 1 (1999): 36–44 (originally *Performance Arts Journal*). See Michael Portnoy's website: www.strangergames.com/Michael_Portnoy.html.

40. Yaffe, 2011, 91.

41. You can see the performance here: http://youtu.be/Zeq3NG8lcjQ. Dylan's acceptance speech is here: http://youtu.be/AeBzvgewgsc .

42. Yaffe, 2011, 109.

43. Yaffe, 2011, 109.

44. The Roman Catholic daily mass can be considered a spectacle of sorts; certainly the liturgical rituals from the high holy days, such as Christmas Eve or Easter Sunday, have ceremonies that can be considered spectacles, at least for those who attend. But this version of the spectacle, the Mass, is part of the prehistory of the modern spectacle as developed by Debord and others and is more about relationships, ceremony, and imagery and not the spectacle as a mediatized event. Today, the church's contribution to spectacle culture usually has to do with the choosing of a new pope, which becomes a media event of some note, commanding the attention of huge global audiences and the dutiful coverage by mass media news agencies and part of the overall public commentary.

45. The year 1960 was the year of first presidential debate on television, and it was sponsored by the networks; there were no presidential debates for 16 years, after which they were usually sponsored by the League of Women Voters and the networks; in 1987, the Republican and Democratic Parties established the Commission on Presidential Debates which would subsequently sponsor the debates with both campaigns' input and make them a media event in every presidential campaign.

46. Guy Debord, *Society of the Spectacle* (Detroit, MI: Black and Read, 1983), Thesis # 1.

47. Crary, 1989.

48. Debord, 1983, thesis # 4.

49. Douglas Kellner, *Media Spectacle*, 2003, 2.

50. There have been many scholarly analyses of the Super Bowl, but one of the first to see how the game and the sport itself was a form of enculturation and spectacle was Michael Real's "Super Bowl: Mythic Spectacle," *Journal of Communication* 25, no. 1 (1975): 31–43. Also see an extended version of the article in Michael Real, *Mass Mediated Culture* (Upper Saddle River, NJ, Prentice Hall College Division), 1977.

51. See for example, Mark Axelrod, "Popular Culture and the Rituals of American Football," *Comparative Literature and Culture* 3 (2002) http://docs.lib.purdue.edu/clcweb/vol3/iss1/ and Gene Michaud, "Patriot Games: a Ritual Analysis of Super Bowl XXXVI," in *Communication and Social Change*, ed. Henna Barthel and Kevin Carragee (St. Ingbert, Germany: Röhrig University Press, 2004).

52. Douglas Kellner, "Barack Obama, the Power Elite, and Media Spectacle," in *Media Spectacle and Insurrection, 2011: From Arab Uprisings to Occupy Everywhere* (New York: Bloomsbury, 2012), 11–44.

53. Kellner, 2012, 3.

54. Most scholars on the matter define the baby boomer generation as all those born in the United States between 1946 and 1964. See Diane J. Macunovich, "The Baby Boomers," *Macmillan Encyclopedia of Aging*, ed. Daniel Ekerdt, 1.

55. Marshall 2007; Yaffe 2011.

56. See the *New York Times* compilation of reviews and articles on this theme: http://topics.nytimes.com/top/reference/timestopics/people/d/bob_dylan/index.html.

57. Dylan, *Chronicles*, 2004.

58. See portions of the interview here: www.youtube.com/watch?v=X2geiziu ASg&feature=share&list=PLB9B663C9AB309E40&index=2.

59. Simon Frith and Andrew Goodman, *On Record: Rock, Pop and the Written Word* (New York : Routledge, 2000), 373.

60. Marshall, 2007, 98.

61. The Weavers were an American folk-singing group who, through their music, personnel, and political outspokenness, shaped the folk revival of the late 1950s and 1960s. Their personnel included Pete Seeger, Lee Hays, Ronnie Gilbert, and Fred Hellerman. Seeger left the group in 1958 because of a disagreement over the use of the group's vocals for a cigarette commercial. The group suffered a lack of bookings in the early 1950s because they were blacklisted because of their political beliefs, and so disbanded temporarily. Seeger refused to testify before the House Un-American Activities Committee and Lee Hays had taken the Fifth Amendment. The history of the Weavers is told in a documentary film entitled *Wasn't That a Time*, released in 1982.

62. The Weavers' music was socially conscious and they performed folk music from various parts of the United States as well as from around the world. They sang pro-labor and pro-union songs, blues and gospel songs, as well as children's songs, and provided the American public with an alternative, less obtrusively produced sound.

63. Boston, Chicago, and San Francisco being the other major areas; but almost every major city had a folk scene in the late 1950s—including Minneapolis, where Robert Zimmerman began performing in folks clubs as "Bob Dylan."

64. The Kingston Trio had a major hit with "Tom Dooley" in 1958, reaching No. 1 on the Billboard charts, as well as the country music charts, ultimately selling more than 4 million copies. The song and the group and their influence on the folk revival are explained in great detail in Robert Cantwell's magisterial study *When We Were Good: The Folk Revival* (Boston: Harvard University Press, 1997).

65. "Blowin' in the Wind" (1962) and "The Times They Are A'Changin'" (1963) were songs that became anthems of the 1960s generation and the civil rights and peace movements, and were covered by countless artists; other "finger pointing" or topical songs include "Masters of War" (1963), "Oxford Town" (1963), "A Hard Rain's A Gonna Fall" (1963), "The Lonesome Death of Hattie Carroll" (1963); "With God on Our Side" (1964); "Chimes of Freedom" (1964); "Only a Pawn in Their Game" (1963), "The Ballad of Emmett Till" (1962), "Talkin' John Birch Society Blues" (1963), and "Who Killed Davey Moore" (1963). After the 1960s, Dylan wrote fewer "protest" songs but several did surface: "George Jackson" (1971), "Hurricane" (1975), "License to Kill" (1983), and "Clean Cut Kid" (1984).

66. Here I'm referring to the recording of the song on *The Freewheelin' Bob Dylan*, 1962.

67. Yaffe, 2011, 100.

68. You can find a set list here: www.bjorner.com/DSN00150%201962 .htm#DSN00265. Dylan's performance of "No More Auction Block" was recorded at the Gaslight Café in October 1962 and first appeared on *The Bootleg Series Volumes 1–3 (Rare & Unreleased) 1961–1991*. Various performances at the Gaslight were released on compact disc, as noted in the text, in 2005.

69. Robbie Woliver, *Hoot! A Twenty-Five Year History of the Greenwich Village Music Scene* (New York: St. Martin's Press, 1994), 83–84.

70. See www.americansongwriter.com/2009/05/the-greatest-bob-dylan-songs-of -all-time-1/ for a complete history as recalled by Robert Cohen.

71. See note 8.

72. See www.spirit-of-rock.com/album-groupe-Elvis_Presley-nom_album-In_a_ Private_Moment-l-en.html. For more cover history, see Joel Whitburn, 2002, "Top Adult Contemporary: 1961-2001," *Record Research*, 192. See also Jasper Rees, 1993, "Lives of the Great Songs" at www.independent.co.uk/arts-entertainment/ lives-of-the-great-songs-blowin-this-way-and-that-blowin-in-the-wind-it-was-a-protest -song-but-not-everyone-seemed-to-notice-jasper-rees-traces-the-career-of-bob-dylans -first-classic-1461263.html.

73. Howard Sounes, 2001, *Down the Highway: The Life of Bob Dylan* (New York: Grove Press), 441.

74. The Never Ending Tour (NET) is the name that is usually associated with Dylan's constant touring schedule; however, it was a term first used by music journalist Adrian Deevoy in an interview with Dylan in *Q Magazine*, December 1989. See Michael Gray, *The Bob Dylan Encyclopedia* (New York: Continuum, 2006), 174. Dylan rejects the term, and in his liner notes to his *World Gone Wrong* album, he explains that each tour has its "own character and design." For an examination of the NET from 1988 to 2000, see Andrew Muir, *Razor's Edge: Bob Dylan & the Never Ending Tour* (London: Helter Skelter Publishing, 2001).

75. Two major websites update and archive the dates, venues, and set lists of Dylan's tours: http://expectingrain.com/, which is not connected to the official website, and www.bobdylan.com/us/, which also archives and updates his tours.

76. There are so many influences on Dylan's work that I must apologize for not including more, but it would be impossible. He most certainly heard the Bentley Boys sing "Penny's Farm" on the Harry Smith *Anthology of American Folk Music* (Folkways, 1952), which he reworked into "Maggie's Farm," on *Bringing It All Back Home*, 1965; and Odetta, as legend would have it, made him trade in his electric guitar for an acoustic one. See David Yaffe, 2011, 66.

77. For a discussion of Dylan's appropriation of Timrod's work, see Robert Polito, "Bob Dylan: Henry Timrod Revisited," at the Poetry Foundation, www .poetryfoundation.org/article/178703. Thanks to Professor Robert H. Cataliotti, personal correspondence.

78. This is from the title of Greil Marcus's *The Old, Weird America: The World of Bob Dylan's Basement Tapes* (London: Picador, 2011); it is a reworked version of Marcus's *Invisible Republic: Bob Dylan's Basement Tapes* (New York: Henry Holt & Co).

79. See www.bobdylan.com for archival material of the tours and the set lists. What I'm referring to here are traditional songs, gospel songs and, for example, "Rock of Ages," and songs by others, notably Townes Van Zandt, Paul Simon, and Buddy Holly.

80. Dylan's backup singers on the gospel tours and on his albums included Regina McCrary Brown (now Regina Havis), Carolyn Dennis, Mona Lisa Young, Helena Springs, Clydie King, and Madeline Quebec (mother of Carolyn Dennis).

81. For all set lists, see the Bob Dylan official website under the section tours, www.bobdylan.com/us/events.

82. Ruth Brown had covered this classic, originally recorded by Faye Adams.

83. *Bob Dylan* contains only two original songs, one dedicated to Woody Guthrie, "Song to Woody," and the other "Talkin' New York," a "talking blues" monologue that has roots in cowboy songs beyond Guthrie's time.

84. Michael Gray, 2008, 69.

85. Here I'm not counting *Bob Dylan's Greatest Hits*, 1967.

86. *The Basement Tapes* album was officially released in 1975. It is Dylan's 17th album, probably the most bootleggedbootleg of all time; the material is performed by Dylan and the Crackers (the Band) in Woodstock in 1967. The original sessions included an enormous amount of traditional material. These sessions have become the subject of *Invisible Republic*, by Greil Marcus.

87. For Robertson's original remarks see Greil Marcus, liner notes to *Another Self Portrait* (2013).

88. Jonathan Lethem, "The Genius of Bob Dylan," *Rolling Stone*, September 7, 2006.

89. There are, however, several exceptions. I recall a concert at the State University of New York at Stony Brook, when Dylan said something about cameras, and introduced a song by saying, and of course I'm paraphrasing, "Here's a sad song that will make some of you happy." Dylan spoke to the audience around election time 2008. He was introducing his band, and when he came to Tony Garnier, who he usually introduces last, on this occasion said "Tony Garnier, wearin' the Obama button—[applause] alright! Tony likes to think it's a brand new time right now. An age of light. Me, I was born in 1941—that's the year they bombed Pearl Harbor. Well, I been livin' in a world of darkness ever since. But it looks like things are going to change now." See Yaffe, 2011, 92.

90. Lethem, 2006.

91. According to www.bobdylan.com/us/songs, "All Along the Watchtower" has been played publically 2,167 times since 1974. Now, since Dylan has toured since then, that number has gone up.

92. Ricks, 2003, 359.

93. Professor Robert H. Cataliotti, music critic and historian, remarked at a Dylan show at Lehigh University in Bethlehem, Pennsylvania, that Dylan seemed to be channeling Jimmy Durante. Personal correspondence.

94. See *'Do You, Mr. Jones': Dylan and the Professors*, ed. Neil Corcoran (New York: Random House, 2003) for a series of essays by notable literary scholars who examine Dylan's work in a variety of contexts. Dylan famously dismisses intellectuals in many places, certainly in his songs, mainly because he would rather not be categorized in any academic way.

95. There are so many reviews critical, even hostile, toward Dylan, and they are worth a study in themselves. I am not decrying them, just pointing out how they fit a pattern. The most famous is Greil Marcus's review of *Self Portrait*. One critic urges Dylan to stop touring; see Mike Conklin in *The L Magazine* www.thelmagazine. com/TheMeasure/archives/2010/07/06/brit; others include Marcus Hondro, "Bob Dylan Mumbles Songs, Tour May Be Hitting Rock Bottom," http://digitaljournal .com/article/336974; Wade Tatangelo, "Bob Dylan Disappoints in Tampa," *Herald Tribune*, June 28, 2013, http://www.ticketsarasota.com/2013/06/28/review-bob

-dylan-distressing-at-midflorida-amphitheatre-tampa-wilco-my-morning-jacket-america narama/; Marty Clear, *Bradenton Herald*, "Herald's Bob Dylan Review Draws Heated Response," July 7, 2013, www.bradenton.com/2013/07/07/4597251/heralds-bob-dylan-review-draws.html.

96. This song was written in 1962 and was part of Dylan's early performance history; it was finally released on *The Bootleg Series Vol. 1–3 Rare and Unreleased, 1961–1991* in 1991. It was last performed in public in 1965. See www.bobdylan.com/us/songs.

97. In 1997, Dylan performed at the World Eucharistic Conference in Bologna in front of the Pope and 300,000 people; the Pope greeted him with the words, "You say the answer is blowing in the wind, my friend. So it is; but it is not the wind that blows things away" (www.songfacts.com/detail.php?id=1669).

98. From Bruce Springsteen's remarks inducting Dylan into the Rock and Roll Hall of Fame, http://rockhall.com/inductees/bob-dylan/transcript/bruce-springsteen-on-dylan/.

99. W. B. Yeats, "The Circus Animals' Desertion," from *The Collected Poems of W.B. Yeats* (New York: Scribner, 1996).

100. Dylan aficionados might remember his crooning style on "New Morning" as well as "Self Portrait."

101. Lebold, Christophe, "A Face Like a Mask and a Voice That Croaks: An Integrated Poetics of Bob Dylan's Voice, Personae, and Lyrics," *Oral Tradition* 22, no. 1 (2007): 57–70.

102. This introductory music is no longer played; it was usually absent when Dylan was on the bill with other acts. In the summer 2013 tour, when touring with Wilco and My Morning Jacket, on what was called the Americanarama tour, this introduction was not heard.

103. Wilentz, 2010. The title of Wilentz's book is a conscious reference to a well-known book in literary circles examining the work of Allen Ginsberg, entitled *Allen Ginsberg in America*, by the Beat Generation historian, Jane Kramer.

104. This quote comes from the Jeff Miers article in *The Buffalo News* in August 2002. According to Julie Bender; "Dylan liked this quick summation of his life so much, he now uses it as his introduction at every concert he performs" (www.ndsmcobserver.com/2.2755/bob-dylan-shines-in-chicago-1.269389#.Ud3JTWJJ7z4).

105. This discussion is pretty old by now, but briefly: One reason we don't have such a "criticism" is because it is hard to achieve one that "does full justice to both lyrics and music." See Corcoran 2002. Other reasons, as proposed by Lebold 2007, are "first, the fact that the historical affinity with the lyrical mode makes songs the ideal vehicle for complacent, second-rate romantic poetry; second, that songs are not meant for the page and therefore, their literary potential is restrained by the corset of a traditional poetical system (stanza-rhyme-meter) that can be easily put to music; and finally, that as a performer, the songwriter establishes no clear barrier between "entertainment" and "art"—his potential audience is therefore far too extensive " (58). For a more contemporary discussion of this issue, and whether or not Dylan's work is poetry, see two essays under the title "Bob Dylan: Musician or Poet?" by Dana Stevens and Francine Prose, *New York Times Book Review*, December 22, 2013, 27.

106. Todd Gitlin, *The Sixties: Years of Hope, Days of Rage* (New York: Bantam Books, 1987), 197–198.

107. Presidential candidate Jimmy Carter used the line "He that's not busy bein' born is busy dying," from "It's Alright Ma, I'm Only Bleeding," as he accepted the Democratic presidential nomination. In the 2000 presidential campaign, the Democratic nominee for Vice President, Al Gorel, also used that line, saying it was one of his favorite quotes.

108. Dylan, *Chronicles*, 2004, 115–117.

109. Robert H. Cataliotti, personal correspondence.

110. Unfortunately, this phrase and the concept behind it are not original with me. Coined by Emile Durkheim in *The Elementary Forms of Religious Life* (New Free Press, 1995), he uses it to describe an occasion when the "tribe" convenes on a momentous or sacred occasion, and describes the strong emotions and joy felt among the members of the tribe. Seeing Dylan in concert for many of his fans is just such an experience. See pages 216–218.

REFERENCES

Axelrod, Mark. "Popular Culture and the Rituals of American Football." *Comparative Literature and Culture* 3, no. 1 (March 1975): 31–43.

Boorstin, Daniel. *The Image: A Guide to Pseudo Events in America*. New York: Vintage Books, 1961.

Bowden, Betsy. *Performed Literature: Words and Music by Bob Dylan*. Bloomington: Indiana University Press, 1982.

Brunner, Bob. "Bombs Away." *Entertainment Weekly*. March 13, 1998, 14.

Corcoran, Neil, ed. *'Do You, Mr. Jones': Dylan and the Professors*. New York: Random House, 2003.

Cott, Jonathan, ed. *Bob Dylan: The Essential Interviews*. New York: Wenner Press, 2006.

Crary, Jonathan. "Spectacle, Attention and Counter-Memory." *October* 50 (Autumn 1989): 96–107.

Day, Aiden. *Jokerman: Reading the Lyrics of Bob Dylan*. Oxford: Blackwell, 1988.

Dogget, Charlesworth, and Neil Bankway. *Dylan: 100 Songs and Pictures*. Oxford: Omnibus Press, 2009.

Durkheim, Emile. *The Elementary Forms of Religious Life*. Translated by Karen Fields. New York: Free Press, 1995.

Dylan, Bob. *Tarantula*. New York: Macmillan and Scribner, 1971.

Dylan, Bob. *Chronicles, Volume One*. New York: Simon and Schuster, 2004.

Dylan, Bob. *The Bob Dylan Scrapbook*. New York: Simon & Schuster, 2005.

Debord, Guy. *Society of the Spectacle*. Detroit: Black and Red, 1983.

Ellison, Jim, ed. *Younger Than That Now: The Collected Interviews with Bob Dylan*. Boston: Da Capo Press, 2004.

Epstein, Daniel Mark. *The Ballad of Bob Dylan: A Portrait*. New York: Harper Collins, 2011.

Frith, Simon, and Andrew Goodman. *On Record: Rock, Pop and the Written Word*. New York: Routledge, 2000.

Gilbert. Douglas R., and Dave Marsh. *Forever Young: Photographs of Bob Dylan*. Boston: Da Capo Press, 2006.

Gilmour, Michael J. *The Gospel According to Bob Dylan: The Old, Old Story of Modern Times*. Louisville, KY: Westminster John Knox Press, 2011.

Gitlin, Todd. *The Sixties: Years of Hope, Days of Rage*. New York: Bantam Books, 1987.

Goldstein, Evan."Dylan and the Intellectuals." *Chronicle of Higher Education*, September 5, 2010.

Gray, Michael. *The Bob Dylan Encyclopedia*. New York: Continuum, 2006.

Hadju, David. *Positively Fourth Street: The Lives and Times of Joan Baez, Bob Dylan, Mimi Baez Farina and Richard Farina*. New York: North Point Press, 2002.

Heylin, Clinton. *A Life in Stolen Moments, Day by Day 1941–1995*. New York: Schirmer Books, 1996.

Heylin, Clinton. *Behind the Shades Revisited*. New York: Harper Entertainment, 2003.

Kellner, Douglas. *Media Spectacle*. New York: Routledge, 2003.

Kellner, Douglas. "Barack Obama, the Power Elite, and the Media Spectacle." In *Media Spectacle and Insurrection, 2011: From Arab Uprisings to Occupy Everywhere*. New York: Bloomsbury Academic, 2012, 11–44.

Lawrence, D.H. *Studies in Classic American Literature*, 1923.

Lebold, Christophe. "A Face Like a Mask and a Voice That Croaks: An Integrated Poetics of Bob Dylan's Voice, Personae, and Lyrics." *Oral Tradition* 22, no. 1 (2007): 57–70.

Lethem, Jonathan."The Genius of Bob Dylan." *Rolling Stone*, September 7, 2006, 74–80, 128.

Marcus, Greil. *Invisible Republic: Bob Dylan's Basement Tapes*. New York: Henry Holt & Co., 1997.

Marcus, Greil. *Like a Rolling Stone: Bob Dylan at the Crossroads*. New York: PublicAffairs, 2006.

Marcus, Greil. "Liner Notes," *Another Self Portrait*. Columbia Records, 2013.

Marcus, Greil. *The Old, Weird America: The World of Bob Dylan's Basement Tapes*. New York: Picador, 2011.

Marqusee, Mike. *Wicked Messenger: Bob Dylan and the 1960s (Chimes of Freedom Revisited)*. New York: Seven Stories Press, 2005.

Marshall, Lee. *Bob Dylan: The Never Ending Star*. Cambridge, UK: Polity, 2007.

Meisel, Perry. *The Myth of Popular Culture: From Dante to Dylan*. New York: Wiley Blackwell, 2007.

Michaud, Gene. "Patriot Games: A Ritual Analysis of Super Bowl XXXVI." In *Communication and Social Change*, edited by Henna Barthel and Kevin Carragee. St. Ingbert, Germany: Röhrig University Press, 2004, 243–257.

Muir, Andrew. *Razor's Edge: Bob Dylan and the Never Ending Tour*. London: Helter Skelter, 2001.

Pichaske, David. *Song of the North Country: A Midwest Framework to the Songs of Bob Dylan*. New York: Continuum, 2010.

Polito, Robert. "Bob Dylan: Henry Timrod Revisited." *Poetry Foundation*. Accessed December 6, 2013. http://www.poetryfoundation.org/article/178703

Real, Michael. "Super Bowl: Mythic Spectacle." *Journal of Communication* 25, no. 1 (March 1975): 31–43.

Real, Michael. *Mass Mediated Culture.* Upper Saddle River, NJ: Prentice Hall College Division, 1977.

Ricks, Christopher. *Dylan's Visions of Sin.* New York: Harper Perennial, 2005.

Shelton, Robert. *No Direction Home: The Life and Music of Bob Dylan.* Boston: Da Capo Press, 1987.

Scaduto, Anthony. *Bob Dylan: An Intimate Biography.* New York: Grosset and Dunlap, 1971.

Scobie, Stephen. *Alias Bob Dylan: Revisited.* Markham, ON: Red Deer Press, 2003.

Sounes, Howard. *Down the Highway: The Life of Bob Dylan.* New York: Grove Press, 2001.

Spitz, Bob. *Dylan: A Biography.* New York: W. W. Norton and Company, 1991.

Wilentz, Sean. *Bob Dylan Inspirations.* Riverside, NJ: Arthur McMeel Publishing, 2005.

Wilentz, Sean. *Bob Dylan in America.* New York: Doubleday, 2010.

Williams, Paul. *Bob Dylan Performing Artist I: The Early Years, 1960–1973.* New York: Omnibus Press, 1994.

Williams, Paul. *Bob Dylan: Watching the River Flow, Observations on His Art-in-Progress, 1966–1995.* New York: Omnibus Press, 1996.

Williams, Paul. *Bob Dylan, Performing Artist: The Middle Years, 1974–1986.* 2nd ed. New York: Omnibus Press, 2004.

Williams, Paul. *Bob Dylan: Mind Out of Time–Performing Artist 1986–1990 and Beyond.* New York: Omnibus Press, 2005.

Woliver, Robbie. *Hoot! A Twenty-Five Year History of the Greenwich Village Music Scene.* New York: St. Martin's Press, 1994.

Yaffe, David. *Bob Dylan: Like a Complete Unknown.* New Haven, CT: Yale University Press, 2011.

Yeats, W.B. "The Circus Animals Desertation." In *The Collected Poems of W.B. Yeats.* New York: Scribner, 1996, 346–347.

Yip, Derek. "Michael Portnoy AKA Soy Bomb: Upstart Pissing on the Contemporary Mix." *A Journal of Performance and Art* 61, no. 1 (1999): 36–44.

16

"Come See about Me": Why the Baby Boomers Liked Stax but Loved Motown

Gary Kenton

Ethnomusicologists and anthropologists Steve Feld and Charles Keli studied how meanings are reconstituted when music moves from indigenous communities to a global market. They argue that you cannot separate music from the social identity of the people who make it (Feld and Keil 1994). A 2012 documentary on the making of Paul Simon's 1986 *Graceland* album, *Under African Skies*, deals with this same theme, showing how thin the line can be between tribute and appropriation, cultural appreciation, and imperialism. Among the first to raise these issues was LeRoi Jones (who later changed his name to Amiri Baraka), in his seminal *Blues People*, who put forth the maxim that music cannot be separated from the history of the people who make it. "The music," he says, referring to the blues, "was the score . . . to those actual, lived lives" (Jones [1963] 2002, ix).

The field of musicology in the United States has been dominated by a fascination with roots. Alan Lomax, Richard Waterman, Charles Hamm, and others have used this approach to trace the process through which the quintessentially American musical genres of gospel, jazz, rhythm and blues, and rock were derived from various African and European influences. Anthropologist Melville Herskovitz summed up this scholarship with the term "syncretism," the means by which a new synthesis is created from elements derived from divergent cultural sources.

In addition to providing insight into the ways in which music is created, appropriated, and disseminated by musicians, this framework can be usefully applied to the ways in which music is received by audiences. The basic idea is that the meaning of a given text cannot be defined wholly by the text itself but must be considered a collaboration between the originator of the message(s) and the receiver in meaning-making. Citing Roman Ingarden, Robert C. Allen (1992, 104) describes the original text as "a schemata, a skeletal structure of meaning possibilities waiting realization" by the audience. This is closely aligned to the concept of acculturation, which Merriam-Webster defines as "cultural modification of an individual, group, or people by adapting to or borrowing traits from another culture."

These ideas have been widely applied in reader-oriented criticism in literature and audience-oriented criticism in television but will be used in this chapter to frame an examination of the output of two prominent independent record companies specializing in rhythm and blues—Motown and Stax—focusing less on what the music can tell us about the people who made it than on the meanings it conveyed to a particular audience at a particular time: the baby boomers in the 1960s. It is important to note that, as used here, the term "boomers" will assume whiteness. Although the word could certainly be applied more inclusively, the historical context and the demographic makeup of 1960s music audiences justify this usage.

The baby boomers of the 1960s were pampered in many ways, not least of which was that these young people became the focus of national attention. The entire orientation of popular culture, which had historically subordinated the interests of young people to those of adults, shifted toward them. The activities and proclivities of young people came to dominate the media; the boomers became the obsession and the target of what Theodor Adorno and Max Horkheimer (2002) had previously identified as the "Culture Industry." Marketing experts who gained prominence in the business world of the 1950s recognized boomers as the most coveted prize, both because of their sheer numbers—the proverbial pig moving through the python of society—and their growing influence on consumer trends. They also seized upon music as one of the most effective conduits to reach them.

The antipathy expressed toward rock and roll in the mainstream media did not prevent the beat from seeping into and burrowing under all aspects of life, especially advertising, but it did require that the most virulent, transgressive elements of the music had to be watered-down and suppressed. Perhaps the most obvious manifestation of this process was the transformation of rock and roll, under the tutelage of Dick Clark on ABC's *American Bandstand*, from the province of such progenitors as Bo Diddley, Jerry Lee Lewis, and Hank Ballard to the pimple-cream pabulum of Frankie Avalon, Connie Francis, and Chubby Checker. So even as rock and roll was providing the soundtrack of a cultural revolution, beginning in the 1950s and erupting in the 1960s, it was being co-opted and transformed into something less threatening. Rhythm and blues provided an alternative score.

In the 1940s and 1950s, independent labels such as King, Chess, Modern, Vee-Jay, Savoy, Specialty, Sun, Duke, and Atlantic made history by recording the American roots music that major labels ignored. However, Berry Gordy, the founder of Motown Records, was not interested in making what had been, until 1949, called "race records," even if the indies had demonstrated that black artists from New Orleans, Memphis, Chicago, and elsewhere could find a national audience and turn a profit. He didn't want a niche, and he wasn't satisfied with the occasional hit that would cross over from the R&B to the pop charts—he wanted to be at the front and center of the music business. And so he was.

Even as the Beatles and their British co-invaders came to dominate the charts and media in the mid-1960s, no label rivaled Motown in numbers of hit records and acts, *averaging* 11 Top Ten hits a year throughout the decade. No single label has ever duplicated this dominance of the pop music market-place. One explanation for this phenomenon is simple: it's in the grooves. No critique can cast a pall on the brilliance of "Dancing in the Street" (Martha and the Vandellas), "My Girl" (the Temptations), or "Tears of a Clown" (Smokey Robinson and the Miracles), to name three iconic Motown hits. To the casual listener, these records may reflect what Adorno and Horkheim-ner (2002) saw (heard) as the "ruthless unity" of the culture industry, but they also transcend it, carrying listeners beyond considerations of culture, time, and space. There is more to be teased out of Motown's success than an appreciation of the "smooth gospel-pop fusion with irresistible, melodies and widely appealing romantic lyrics" (Ray Allen 1996, 142). The musical formula, by itself, cannot adequately explain Gordy's inordinate success in connecting with the baby boomer audience he so coveted. Others have writ-ten comprehensively about the musical aspects of the Motown oeuvre and the compelling personalities involved; the focus here is on the cultural and communication factors that helped the Motown message to resonate, how it differed from the sensibility at Stax, and what that can tell us about rela-tionship of the music to the baby boomers.

The sum—the genius of Motown artistry—was certainly greater than the total of the parts, but it was the parts that Gordy sought to control, creat-ing the musical equivalent to the auto industry assembly line (on which more than a few Motown employees put in time). In the most comprehen-sive example of vertical integration ever achieved in the music industry, all aspects of production were controlled in-house, with each area of spe-cialization—writers, arrangers, musicians, singers, and producers—applying their craft before pushing the song further down the line. The famous Studio A, where most of the Motown hits were recorded (it was called "the snakepit" with mixed affection) was located in a house on West Grand Boulevard, which Gordy dubbed "Hitsville," and was open 24 hours a day, seven days a week, from 1959 until 1972. Although union rules pro-hibited more than four songs being recorded in one session, Motown's legendary in-house band (the Funk Brothers, the subject of the 2002 doc-umentary *Standing in the Shadows of Motown*) was always on call, and union rules were often ignored. From 1969 to 1972, arrangement, production, and composition credits on many Motown songs were ascribed to "the Corporation." While the measure of acceptability at Stax generally meant digging deeper into a groove, at Motown it was more a matter of what manufacturers would call "quality control." The question wasn't whether a musical epiphany could be reached but rather whether the customer would be satisfied.

Stax was more artist oriented and spoke to change. Many of the Stax artists were composers, and nearly all were engaged in the process of choosing which songs to record. And, although most Stax artists used in-house musicians and the label developed a sound nearly as identifiable as that of Motown, they were given considerable latitude in the studio. To paraphrase Chicago producer Carl Davis, Motown manufactured a picture frame and put artists in the frame, while other R&B labels fitted the frame to the artist (Hoekstra 2012).

When Berry Gordy named his company, he was clearly referencing Detroit, but the motto he adopted, "the Sound of Young America," reflected ambitions that went beyond the Motor City and the African American community. Stax, meanwhile, referred to itself as "Soulsville U.S.A.," and the audience was envisioned as an extension of the African American community that spawned and supported the label in Memphis. The echoes of the church were equally prominent in the Motown and Stax sounds, but Stax retained the minority outsider's longing for acceptance and redemption, whereas Motown never lost its ties to the movement led by the National Association for the Advancement of Colored People (NAACP) to "recreate the public image of African-Americans" (Ramsey 2003, 44), to be freed of the burdens of the outsider and to be full participants in the American middle class. Most boomers could readily identify with the urbanized Motown sound, but there was still something exotic in the backwoods rawness of Otis Redding or the church-sanctified soul of Aretha Franklin; Motown was acculturation made simple. Gordy laid his music in the laps of white kids, who could embrace it without having to make the cultural leap that Stax required. Evan Eisenberg (1987) described the Motown sound as appealing "both to blacks who aspired to suburbia and whites who wanted to escape it." Stax may have been integrated in the studio, but Motown was integrated at the level of its DNA.

It is more than ironic that, whereas Stax was *actually* integrated, both in the front office (co-founders Jim Stewart and Estelle Axton were white, and co-owner Al Bell was black) *and* in the studio (Booker T and the MGs, which provided many of the basic tracks for hits by Sam and Dave, Otis Redding, Carla Thomas, Wilson Pickett, and others, consisted of two blacks, keyboardist Booker T. Jones and drummer Al Jackson Jr., and two whites, guitarist Steve Cropper and bassist Donald "Duck" Dunn), few white people worked or played at Motown. Anyone with the musical chops could make music at Stax, but the label generally focused on its black audience, as if the market were still segregated, and, for all its commercial success, the label seldom shed its identification with the African American community or its underdog status.

The records made in Stax's McLemore Avenue studios were the fruits of a true musical miscegenation, but the sound remained relatively exotic to many white listeners. Admittedly, the distinction between the experience of, say, Sam and Dave's "Hold On I'm Comin'" and the Four Tops' "Reach Out (I'll Be There)," which were both big hits in 1966, may seem fine. But one can discern in the Sam and Dave song, written by Isaac Hayes and David Porter with recurring references to a "river of trouble," the subtext of the generalized suffering of African Americans, while the Four Tops song, a Holland-Dozier-Holland (Lamont Dozier and Brian and Eddie Holland) composition with its emphasis on "love and comfort," is more difficult to read in other than romantic terms. A much clearer difference can be seen in the comparison of the two artists most closely associated with the labels: the rough-hewn Otis Redding at Stax and the high-heeled Diana Ross at Motown.

Redding, the son of a Georgia farmer whose first recordings were in the shout mode of fellow-Georgian Little Richard, forged a powerful sound equally rooted in gospel and country blues, exemplified by the ballad "I've Been Loving You Too Long" and by "Respect," the up-tempo song he wrote that would become an anthem for Aretha Franklin. It is not demeaning the protean contributions of Smokey Robinson, David Ruffin, Martha Reeves, and Levi Stubbs to say that Diana Ross is the artist who most fully represents the Motown ethos. This can be explained less by sounds than by images, less by grooves than glamour. As Betrock succinctly explained, "at Motown, style always won out over soul" (1982, 156). This was no coincidence.

Although the singers occupied central stage, Gordy wouldn't turn on the spotlight until his Artists Development Department had made sure that the performers were ready for prime time. It functioned as a kind of finishing school that "provided the veneer, with wigs, gowns, and lessons in etiquette" (Hirshey 1984), the Artists Development Department established a rigid set of guidelines for fashion and deportment to which all Motown artists had to adhere. This effort, modeled after the Hollywood studio system that worked so well for the movie moguls from the 1920s to the 1950s, can be seen not only as a marketing strategy but as part of a larger campaign of cultural uplift and assimilation for African Americans. The ultimate barometer for achievement in the Motown orbit seemed to be a booking at the Copacabana nightclub, a nominally integrated New York venue often associated with Frank Sinatra, Dean Martin, and the Rat Pack. Stax made music to satisfy its own ethnocentric impulses, but Motown was always aimed at the broadest possible market.

There is no question that Ross was Gordy's pet project, a fact that became evident in 1967 when the Supremes, with a dozen Top Ten hits already to their credit, were official renamed Diana Ross and the Supremes. She embodied the poise and sophistication that Gordy wanted people to associate with Motown. Although she came from a decidedly working-class background in Detroit, Ross had had aspirations in fashion design as a teenager and seemed to burst on the scene with waving hair and long eyelashes intact. Ross was more significant as a symbol of class and as a diva than as a singer or performer. In the early years, the image of Motown was predominantly male, focused on the Miracles, the Temptations, and the Four Tops with their matching suits and synchronized dance routines. The female groups, led by Martha Reeves and the Vandellas and the Marvelettes, followed a similar formula. But Ross brought a high-tone elegance and female sexuality into the mix that was in keeping with mainstream (white) norms. She brought the game uptown. Gordy had numerous reasons for moving the label from Detroit to Los Angeles in 1972, but significant among them was a greater emphasis on the visual (film and TV) and a campaign to turn Ross into a movie, as well as a recording, star.

The same accessibility and de-culturalization that provided white teenagers with a direct experience with the "soul" of African America without all the sociocultural baggage, also made Motown ideal for the most important medium for popular music in the early and mid-1960s: AM radio. Radio was the lifeblood of the baby boom generation and, as Marshall McLuhan noted, served as "the tribal drum . . . to the teenager, radio gives privacy, and at the same time it provides the tight tribal bond of the world of the common market, of song, and of resonance" ([1964] 1994, 405). Not until the later 1960s did long-playing records, played at home or on FM radio stations, become the focal point for the baby boomers. Before that, the 45 rpm single dominated, serving the dual purpose of promotional tool and commodity. Although disc jockeys (DJs) enjoyed more discretion in the 1950s, before Top 40 and other formats came to dominate the airwaves, they generally chose among singles—those songs designated by the record company "for airplay." Following suit, teenagers generally bought singles that they were exposed to on the radio.

Although radio was in the process of being displaced by television as the media centerpiece of American culture, radio stations retrenched and focused on music (and talk) as their strongest domain. This was a great boon to the music industry as a whole, especially for makers of rock and roll and rhythm and blues who had previously had difficulty getting exposure to a mainstream audience. But it also created a powerful pull to the mainstream middle, and of all the independent labels, Motown, with a production process engineered to meet the specifications of the marketplace, was uniquely positioned to benefit. In addition to increasing efficiency and controlling costs, the great advantage of the Motown factory model was standardization.

Reducing unpredictability was especially important to the AM radio stations, especially as they became increasingly formatted in the mid- and late 1960s. Where the focus at Stax remained on the execution of songs, which they hoped would gain, Motown self-consciously produced records ready-made for station program managers.

One common accomplishment of Motown and Stax (along with Atlantic, Chess, and other rhythm and blues independents) was to curtail the industry emphasis on cover songs. Although the practice of rerecording a song by another artist to capitalize on its popularity had been used widely for decades, in the 1950s the tactic was generally used to supplant rhythm and blues songs with versions by white artists. Poet Langston Hughes referred to this as "highway robbery across the color line" (1955, 10). The indie labels not only succeeded in getting their own records onto playlists and into stores but also whetted the appetite of boomers for greater authenticity. They came to believe, as the Marvin Gaye/Tammi Terrell title suggests, there "Ain't Nothing Like the Real Thing." Again, the Motown sound was advantaged by meeting the baby boomers halfway by offering this authenticity in easy-to-swallow nuggets.

Toward the end of the 1960s and into the 1970s, as a more politicized black consciousness emerged, Motown was often accused of pandering or, in a phrase common at the time, "selling out." But if one of the most poignant aspects of the African American experience has been the underlying desire on the part of the great majority of ex-slaves to gain acceptance, to become fully American, then Motown surely represents one fulfillment of that aspiration. The ambiguity inherent in the demand for equal rights on one hand and the desire to belong on the other has played out in black communities throughout the history of the country. For many African Americans in the 1960s, the relevance of Motown was more symbolic than musical. The label may have been part of the vanguard in socioeconomic terms, but in the musical arena, the cutting edge was defined by the cool jazz of Miles Davis on the one hand and the avant-garde bebop of Charlie Parker and John Coltrane on the other. For the black audience, Motown the company epitomized upward mobility, but the music itself represented the transformation of rhythm and blues into pop. As Simon Frith points out, this fits Marx's definition of alienation, when "something human is taken from us and returned in the form of a commodity" (1998, 12). The experience was almost exactly the opposite for the baby boomers, for whom questions of identity and assimilation were obviously not at issue. For them, Motown was pure joy—an unalloyed, often unconscious, affirmation of Martin Luther King's promise of a color-blind world.

The innocent pleasure of Motown, unaffected by cultural and political considerations, became an increasingly difficult proposition for many black listeners in the 1960s. LeRoi Jones ([1963] 2002, 219) identifies the dichotomy that came into sharp focus at this time in the African American community between "cool," exemplified by the detached jazz style of Lester Young and Miles Davis, and the emergent "soul brother," the black man seeking "to recast the social order in his own image." The ultimate soul man, of course, was James Brown, whose 1968 "Say It Loud, I'm Black and I'm Proud" was a hit on the pop charts, topping out at No. 10, but an anthem that remained No. 1 on the R&B charts for weeks. As Brown defined the subgenre and earned the undisputed mantle of "Soul Brother Number One," the reverberations could be felt in almost every song coming from Stax. The effects were less obvious and far more diffuse at Motown. From the standpoint of the burgeoning black nationalist movement, Motown was anathema, having become inextricably linked with the incrementalism of the NAACP and the accommodationist policies supported by many black leaders.

Although the civil rights movement certainly did not end with King's assassination in 1968, the black power movement was in ascendance. The very enterprise of integration was brought into question by Malcolm X and others. No longer satisfied with an accrual of legal rights, the black nationalists saw integration as a process of capitulation and perpetual minority status that tended to bring greater benefit to the white community than the black. For the many liberal, middle-class, white people in the 1960s, integration seemed an overdue remedy for segregation, the most obvious manifestation of a society belatedly coming to grips with its history of slavery and Jim Crow. But for many African Americans who had, either out of separatist ideology or a lack of economic and social alternatives, built their own communities—schools, stores, churches, and other institutions—integration often marked the end of self-sufficiency and self-determination.

In the wake of the 1960s riots, the strategy of white elites shifted from one of direct confrontation to one of cooptation, and, for the most part, it proved remarkably effective. The floodgates of competition for all kinds of products and services were opened. Given a choice, many black consumers abandoned shops in their own community, gravitating to better-stocked white-owned stores. The circulation rates of most black newspapers began a precipitous drop. Many segregated African American schools, which had provided education and nurturance to two or three generations of students (despite underfunding), were either closed or subsumed by large, white-dominated school districts. The impact, which might be called the downside of upward mobility, was felt in every facet of African American life, and on black identity itself. As one minister put it, "integration fell on our community."

The music business does not provide a perfect parallel, but the end of the "race" charts coincided with the decline of many independent record companies that had championed rhythm and blues, gospel, and jazz; the closing of many black-owned clubs; and the assimilation of black booking, publishing, and promotion businesses into larger, white-owned companies. What Nelson George (1988) refers to as "the death of rhythm and blues" was not just about a loss of connection between a genre of music and its audience. In broader sociopolitical terms, it was a manifestation of the disembowelment of predominantly black neighborhoods that had figured out how to thrive under a separate (and rarely equal) regime. Many in those communities had tacitly, if not overtly, accepted Marcus Garvey's conclusion that equality was probably unattainable for blacks in the United States. The debate between separation and assimilation was, of course, not new, having been demarcated in the early years of the 20th century between Booker T. Washington and W. E .B. Du Bois, one of the founders of the NAACP, who espoused compromise. This dialectic may have reached its apotheosis in the 1960s when Malcolm X held up the goal of self-sufficiency as a better bet for black communities than Martin Luther King's more utopian promise of a world where his children would "not be judged by the color of their skin but by the content of their character." Placed within this ongoing conflict, Motown would clearly belong in the Booker T. Washington/Martin Luther King Jr. camp, whereas Stax is more likely to be aligned with the W. E. B. Du Bois/Malcolm X camp. (In the last months of his life, when he foregrounded economic justice in his agenda, King gravitated to the plight of the sanitation workers in Memphis. The sound of Stax was no doubt in the air when he was assassinated there in 1968.)

This is not to suggest that Motown did not shift with the times, but the risks were calculated. As LeRoi Jones observes, "The middle class reacted to the growing 'nationalism' among poorer Negroes and the intelligentsia by adopting a milder kind of nationalism themselves" ([1963] 2002, 135). This was reflected in a heightened race consciousness in the songs of the Temptations, Stevie Wonder, and Marvin Gaye, and in a younger generation of Motown stars, including Lionel Richie, the Commodores, Rick James, Teena Marie, and DeBarge. But even into the 1970s, when the Temptations were addressing social issues in songs like "Papa Was a Rollin' Stone" and Marvin Gaye was talking about ecology and singing the "Inner City Blues (Make Me Wanna Holler)," the label was most closely identified with Diana Ross and the assiduously apolitical Michael Jackson (who left the label in 1975). In the 1970s, Motown (along with a significant portion of its white audience) struggled with the shift from the slicker, cooler rhythm and blues the label exemplified to the rougher, hotter soul music. Stax, riding the "hot-buttered soul" of Isaac Hayes and the politico-cultural relevance of the Staple Singers, thrived. In response to the race riots that had been touched off in cities across the country where significant black populations had been ghettoized, Stax produced Wattstax, a 1972 concert that drew more than 100,000 to the L.A. Coliseum, a combination of music and political activism that featured nearly every artist on the Stax roster (performing for free) along with such luminaries such as Jesse Jackson Sr. and Richard Pryor. By comparison, Motown was a music industry bystander.

Coming a decade later, the Motown equivalent of Wattstax was the altogether self-congratulatory (and perhaps wishful) "Motown 25: Yesterday, Today, Forever," which was performed live at the Pasadena Civic Auditorium in March 1983 and broadcast nationally on NBC on May 16 of that year. Michael Jackson came back to the fold, at least for an evening, and proved to the television audience, much as Elvis Presley had done on his 1968 "Comeback Special," why he was the King of Pop. (Even as attention shifts to the Internet, television remains the national platform on which such "proof" can be instantly made to the masses.) From an audience analysis point of view, the highlight of the show came when Jackson went into one of his signature glides across the stage in front of a huge screen on which his younger self danced with the Jackson 5. This is a prime (time) example of remediation, where content from one medium is transposed and presented through another, resulting in an effective layering of associations for older and newer, black and white audiences. There is no one who does not belong under the big tent that is Motown.

One might say that the baby boomer generation came of age along with Motown, learning to make the compromises and concessions necessary to survive and succeed. The move to Los Angeles was as inevitable for Motown as the imperative faced by the many boomers who identified with the hippie counterculture to conform and make peace with the mainstream. Their lives became as seamless and orderly as a song by DeBarge or the latter-day Smokey Robinson, who, as of this writing, is still cranking out beautiful, romantic, unthreatening records. Motown could no more maintain its independence than most of the boomers could. Since 1988, the label has been bought and sold several times, first to MCA and Polygram and most recently to Universal and its Island Def Jam division. Stax has undergone its own industry misadventures but always exhibited a clear ambivalence toward corporatization; it now enjoys considerable autonomy under the ownership of the Concord Music Group.

When it comes to the baby boomers, the classic Holland-Dozier-Holland question looms: where did our love go? One can still catch many of the 1960s Motown acts at packaged oldies shows, with some of the original artists still trotting out their hits, but the numbers of white people attending these shows has been decreasing. Perhaps the label is coming full circle, relying more heavily on the loyalty of its original black middle-class audience. But Berry Gordy still counts on nostalgia and the power of the old hits to strike a universal emotional chord. In February 2011, he was featured prominently in a Public Television extravaganza called "The Motown Sound: In Performance at the White House," hosted by (yes) the president of the United States, with help from First Lady Michelle Obama and Jamie Foxx. Interestingly, few of the artists who performed (including John Legend, Gloriana, Nick Jonas, and Seal) were actually connected to Motown at the time, Smokey Robinson being the notable exception. So it felt more like a celebration of old-school rhythm and blues, with Motown as exemplar, than a springboard onto the contemporary musical landscape. But, in addition to airing on PBS stations nationally, the show was streamed via the Internet by PBS and the White House, so it was certainly a media coup. Even if all Gordy can hope to do is mine the Motown catalog, his ambition remains grandiose. He brought *Motown: The Musical* to a Broadway theater in 2013.[1] Perhaps the message is that once you've connected with the largest and most influential generation of Americans, all you have to do is maintain a presence in the media firmament and keep repackaging the hits. Even if "the Sound of Young America" is now "old school," and the baby boomers are going into retirement, the shared meaning between text and audience remains. Perhaps the ongoing legacy of Motown is that, when it comes to music, relevance is irrelevant.

NOTE

1. Motown has previously been represented on Broadway in the form of Michael Bennett's *Dreamgirls*, a thinly veiled account of the career of Diana Ross and the Supremes. It is interesting to note that, before he gained fame for his choreography for the hit show *A Chorus Line*, Bennett had been one of the dancers on the TV show *Hullabaloo* when the Supremes performed in 1965.

REFERENCES

Adorno, Theodor, and Max Horkheimer. 2002. *Dialectic of Enlightenment*. Stanford: Stanford University Press.

Allen, Ray. 1996. "Unifying the Disunity: A Multicultural Approach to Teaching American Music." *American Studies* 37 (1): 135–147.

Allen, Robert C. 1992. "Audience-Oriented Criticism and Television." In *Channels of Discourse, Reassembled*, 2nd ed., edited by Robert C. Allen, 101–137. Chapel Hill: University of North Carolina Press.

Betrock, Alan. 1982. *Girl Groups: The Story of a Sound*. New York: Delilah Books.

Campbell, Richard, Christopher R. Martin, and Bettina Fabos. 2013. *Media & Culture*, 8th Ed. Boston: Beford St. Martin's.

Eisenberg, Evan. 1987. *The Recording Angel*. New York: Penguin Books.

Feld, Steven, and Charles Keil. 1994. *Music Grooves*. Chicago: University of Chicago Press.

Frith, Simon. 1988. *Music for Pleasure*. London: Routledge.

George, Nelson. 1988. *The Death of Rhythm & Blues*. New York: Pantheon Books.

Hansen, Drew D. 2003. *The Dream: Martin Luther King, Jr., and the Speech that Inspired a Nation*. New York: Harper Collins.

Herskovitz, Melville. 1966. *The New World Negro: Selected Papers in Afroamerican Studies*. Bloomington: Indiana University Press.

Hirshey, Gerri. 1984. *Nowhere to Run: The Story of Soul Music*. New York: Times Books.

Hoekstra, Dave. 2012. "Producer Carl Davis, Architect of 'the Chicago Sound,' Dies at 77." August 9. *Chicago Sun Times*. www.suntimes.com/news/obituaries/14373356-418/soul-music-producer-carl-davis-architect-of-the-chicago-sound-dies-at-77.html.

Hughes, Langston. 1955. "Highway Robbery Across the Color Line." *Chicago Defender*, July 2:10.

Jones, LeRoi (Baraka, Amiri). (1963) 2002. *Blues People*. New York: Harper Collins.

McLuhan, Marshall. (1964) 1994. *Understanding Media*. Corte Madera, CA: Gingko Press.

Ramsey, Guthrie P., Jr. 2003. *Race Music*. Berkeley: University of California Press.

Tate, Greg, ed. 2003. *Everything but the Burden*. New York: Broadway Books.

Part 4

Literature

17

Reading the Boomers' Reading: What Did They Read? Who Did They Read? Who Wrote about Them?

David Linton

If we consider Todd Gitlin's memoir-like take on the 1960s, which might have been titled "L'60s et moi," it would seem that baby boomers read very little and what they did was written in previous decades. Rather, they went to the movies and listened to a lot of music. Which, of course, they did. But the boomer era was more—far more—than the "years of hope and days of rage" that Gitlin refers to in his book's subtitle.[1]

During the coming of age phase, the early years of the boomer generation—let's say 1960 to 1973—they were reading widely among authors brought to their attention or assigned by older adults who were of the World War II and Korean War generations, Europeans authors who lived and published quite a few years earlier: Thomas Mann (1875-1955), *The Magic Mountain* (1924) and *Death in Venice* (1912); Hermann Hesse (1877-1962), *Steppenwolf* (1927) and *Siddhartha* (1922); Albert Camus (1913-1960), *The Plague* (1947) and *The Stranger* (1942); and Jean-Paul Sartre (1905-1980) *Nausea* (1938). Though old or dead and "foreign," these typically existential explorations resonated with the sense of social and psychological angst that was infusing the culture. A number of overlapping developments— second-wave feminism, the civil rights movement, sexual liberation, the counterculture, the breakdown of traditional family structures, changes in the media environment, and, eventually, the anti–Vietnam War protest movement, somehow found expression through the voices of those dead or aged European writers. Even the beatnik era's Allen Ginsberg (1926-1997) and Jack Kerouac (1922-1969), though their presence was felt, published nothing of note beyond the mid-1950s, and Kerouac's *On the Road* (1957) felt quaint compared with Ken Kesey's acid-dropping Merry Pranksters while J. D. Salinger's fame seemed to run on perpetually based on his single novel from 1951, *The Catcher in the Rye*, which drove the high sales of his later short story collections. Meanwhile, in America a new generation of writers was emerging—post Hemingway, Faulkner, Salinger, Lewis, Mailer, Wolfe, et al.—who, though born before World War II, spoke more directly to the emerging postwar generation about the circumstances from which it emerged and in which it found itself. Though many authors fit this description, there are four in particular who not only chronicled where the boomers came from but also what they were dealing with and where they might be headed. In addition, their careers paralleled the boomer cohort for the next five decades, observing its developments, successes, failures, challenges, ripening, and decay.

Though too young to be identified with the World War II generation, and too old to be birth peers of the boomers, these novelists were writing to and for the boomers, sending them a message: "Here's where you've come from; here's the world that the not-so-greatest generation has left you; here's what you've been bequeathed, with all its messy sexual demands and broken gender and family rules, all its twisted racial conflicts and injustices, and all its cultural and geographic dislocations. NOW YOU DEAL WITH IT!"

These four novelists are among the most celebrated, influential, and prolific authors of their times. And from 1960 to the early 1970s they produced a set of novels that addressed salient issues while producing a series of portraits of both the boomers and the forbears who produced them, embraced them, and sometimes rejected them. Together, the works of Toni Morrison, Joyce Carol Oates, Philip Roth, and John Updike embody Walt Whitman's grand vision in his 1871 essay "Democratic Vistas" of a *divine literateur*, a species of prose and poetry that would capture and advance the glory of democracy.[2] From 1960 to 1973 this foursome penned 10 novels of lasting significance, novels that explored the circumstances that shaped the new generation and addressed the circumstances of their new lives. While there are obviously many other books and authors worthy of inclusion in any recounting of the era under examination, taken together, these works can be read as trusty representatives. Furthermore, the writers, aging along with the cohort, chronicled its adventures over 50 years and, in the case of Updike, created a single story line that followed one character through five novels from his early 20s to his death and haunting presence afterward—a span of more than 40 years. There had been recurring characters before—Sherlock Holmes, James Bond, Nancy Drew, not to mention those on radio and television soap operas and plenty of others—but there were none whose life seemed to unfold in an approximation of real time in what came to be a massive saga worthy of Tolstoy or Proust but written and published in episodes separated by decades.

Here are the books we'll consider:

John Updike
> *Rabbit, Run* (1960)
> *Rabbit Redux* (1971)

Philip Roth
> *Goodbye, Columbus* (1960; National Book Award)
> *Portnoy's Complaint* (1967)

Joyce Carol Oates
> *A Garden of Earthly Delights* (1966)
> *Expensive People* (1968)
> *them* (1969; National Book Award 1970)
> *Wonderland* (1971)

Toni Morrison
> *The Bluest Eye* (1970)
> *Sula* (1973)

It's not just for convenience and the tyranny of the calendar that we identify 1960 as the start of the new era. In fact, in literary terms, 1960 was really
quite momentous. The decade opened with what might be seen as many
harbingers, omens, and last gasps. In the latter category, the 1961 Pulitzer
Prize went to the 1960 publication, *To Kill a Mockingbird*, a novel that deified
the noble white man, Atticus Finch, who, despite the benighted Southern
society he lives in, stands up for his physically and mentally impaired neighbor, a wayward orphan, and a wrongly accused, poor black man, all the while
raising two children as a single parent. White liberal guilt is assuaged by Atticus's heroics ("We'd all stand up like him if we had to!"), and the Southern
white bigot is vividly portrayed in all his two-dimensional hatefulness. And
to wrap up the stereotypes, the black housekeeper, Calpurnia, is the idealized
black mammy. It's no wonder that the novel and later film adaptation have
remained favorites in high school classes, though I suspect that its use in the
South has always been limited. But while the heroics of Atticus were making
white folks feel proud, the appearance of Updike's *Rabbit Run* and Philip
Roth's National Book Award winner, *Goodbye Columbus*, the same year told
a different story, one of instability and impending disaster. Though Atticus
was a single parent, his family life and community relations were solid. Such
was not the case for the Angstroms in Updike's version of white, Protestant,
working-class Pennsylvania or for Roth's struggling Jewish family in Newark, New Jersey. And not many years later there would arrive tales of similar
upheaval in Morrison's rural Ohio and Oates's Detroit and Midwest.

Perhaps the theme that is most common and most troublesome to these
writers is the precarious state of the nuclear family in American life. In

these 10 novels all of the characters are involved in one form or another of familial distress.

Within 10 pages of the opening of *Rabbit Run*, Harry Angstrom, a former high school basketball star known as "Rabbit," ditches his drunken, pregnant wife, Janice, and his son, Nelson, and drives south toward some unidentifiable better life. But, in only two days he runs out of steam and returns to shack up with a woman named Ruth until Janice has her baby and he returns to live with her, leaving Ruth pregnant with a daughter who is not seen again until four novels and four decades later when, years after Harry's death, she suddenly appears on Janice's doorstep and strikes up a friendship with her half-brother Nelson, Harry and Janice's son. However, his return to Janice is not a peaceful one as a few months later, while in a drunken fog, Janice accidentally drowns her new baby in the bathtub.

Updike has been taken to task—thoroughly thrashed might better describe it—by the likes of David Foster Wallace who called him, along with Mailer and Roth, one of the "Great Male Narcissists," claiming that women in particular find Updike offensive and don't read his books. Wallace claims that women have described Updike to him as "Just a penis with a thesaurus," and say that he "Makes misogyny seem literary."[3] Yet Updike's uncompromising descriptions of the emptiness of the lives of Rabbit's wife, Janice, his mother, and his lover, Ruth, are strikingly similar to those that Betty Friedan chronicled in *The Feminine Mystique* in 1963, just three years later. And men fare no better in Updike as readers are given a stark picture of the many reasons why the emerging generation found cause to reject the circumstances into which they were born. Although Rabbit may be Updike's protagonist, he's no hero, no Atticus Finch, no one to emulate.

By the second "Rabbit" novel, *Rabbit Redux* (1971), Harry is again separated from Janice, who has moved in with another man and left Harry with 11-year-old Nelson in a suburban tract home into which Harry brings Skeeter, an angry African American antiwar protester, and Jill, a rich runaway hippie girl from Connecticut, an arrangement that so outrages the neighbors that they eventually set the house on fire, killing Skeeter and Jill.

Family arrangements are not much better, though less lethal, for Philip Roth's Jewish families in the Newark vicinity where *Goodbye, Columbus* is set. Neil Klugman, who works in a dead-end job in the Newark library and lives with an aunt who hovers over every tiny detail of his life as an obsessed enforcer of her notion of Jewish decorum and practice, falls in love with Brenda Patimkin, the daughter of a prosperous manufacturer of sinks. Neil and Brenda struggle to get out from under the stifling pressure of the older generation's insistence on ethnic, religious, and sexual orthodoxy while surrounded by signs of racial, economic, and sexual upheaval.

The family themes laid out by Updike and Roth will continue to haunt their characters in even more amplified fashion in ensuing works while finding related yet unique expression in the novels of Oates and Morrison just a few years later.

Joyce Carol Oates may be the darkest literary novelist of the past 50 years. Nearly all of her many stories depict victims of deranged families whose lives play out in the midst of economic strain and abject misery with large doses of alienation and even insane outbursts of violence and depravity. The foundation for this pattern was laid in the four novels that have come to be known as "The Wonderland Quartet," published between 1967 and 1971. Space limitations do not allow a full account of the wide range of family dysfunction described in these lengthy books. One, titled *Wonderland*, opens with a father taking a shotgun and murdering his wife and two of his children while another, Jesse, escapes. Later, Jesse is adopted by a severely narcissistic doctor who eventually disowns him, which leads Jesse to become a respected physician himself. Jesse enters into a tortured marriage and troubled family; his runaway daughter becomes a sex slave to a character who appears to have been modeled after Charles Manson. Along the way Jesse mutilates himself with a razor at the moment he is about to consummate a relationship with a woman he has loved for years. The novel ends with him clutching his dying daughter in his arms shortly after rescuing her from the man who had been abusing and pimping her for drug money.

This sort of darkness is typical of Oates's view of the condition of American families in the 1960s, though she prefers to focus on the social and political commentary embedded in the stories. In 1999, Oates commented on her work of this period as, "a set of novels exploring the inner lives of representative young Americans from the perspective of 'class war'—a taboo subject in supposedly apolitical literary quarters" and a look "into the yet-uncharted, apocalyptic America of the late Vietnam War period when the idealism of antiwar sentiment had turned to cynicism and the counterculture fantasy of egalitarianism and 'love' had self-destructed."[4]

Most of her tales of this period begin years earlier, providing extensive backstories about sharecropping or Depression conditions or displacement from rural settings to city slums. People are always running away or being thrown out of their homes, their social instability finding expression in emotional misery and often physical abuse, obesity, sexual exploitation, drug or alcohol abuse, suicide, and general alienation. Even when, by the end of the novel, characters have reached some degree of economic stability, their lives have been so twisted by adversity that they are commonly left spiritually broken and psychologically maimed.

The family circumstances in Toni Morrison's characters' lives are not much better. Her two novels of the boomer era, *The Bluest Eye* (1970) and *Sula* (1973), set in rural Ohio towns, explore the world through the stories of women who are followed from childhood well into their adult years—in Sula's case to her lonely death, and in Pecola's to a state of emotional

derangement and the status of social pariah. She has become the community scapegoat upon whom all fears of inadequacy are piled:

> The birdlike gestures are worn away to a mere picking and plucking
> her way between the tire rims and the sunflowers, between Coke
> bottles and milkweed, among all the waste and beauty of the world—
> which is what she herself was. All of our waste which we dumped on
> her and which she absorbed. . . . We were so beautiful when we stood
> astride her ugliness. . . . Her inarticulateness made us believe we were
> eloquent. Her poverty kept us generous.[5]

These words are from the last page of *The Bluest Eye*, but to get there the
reader must traverse an odyssey of small-town nastiness and racial despair.
Perhaps the most illustrative element in the story is the description of the
relationship between Pecola's parents, Cholly, who rapes and impregnates
his daughter, and Mrs. Pauline Breedlove, her ironically named mother. It
is in the bosom of the family that all of the self-loathing, internalized racism
finds expression as the couple, unable to act against their victim status or
even articulate it, take out their rage on their daughter and on each other.
Their fights, often triggered by Cholly's drinking binges, are brutally violent
though they satisfy morbid needs:

> They relieved the tiresomeness of poverty. . . . In these violent breaks
> in routine that were themselves routine, [Mrs. Breedlove] could dis-
> play the style and imagination of what she believed to be her own true
> self. To deprive her of these fights was to deprive her of all the zest and
> reasonableness of life. Cholly, by his habitual drunkenness and orneri-
> ness, provided them both with the material they needed to make their
> lives tolerable. . . . If Cholly had stopped drinking, she would never
> have forgiven Jesus. She needed Cholly's sins desperately. . . . No less
> did Cholly need her. She was one of the few things abhorrent to him
> that he could touch and therefore hurt.[6]

Elsewhere in the book Morrison explores the nuances of the construction
of race: black-white distinctions as well as formulations of skin-color variations from the perspective of the black community. Her insights into both
phenomena reflected clearly the issues bedeviling two significant elements
of the American community at the time: liberal white desire to understand
and rectify the damage wrought by the history of racial injustice; and militant black desire to exorcise and expunge the debilitating heritage of bigotry
and internalized self-negation. In the case of responses to notions of white
racial superiority, the range of attitudes is illustrated by the responses of the

two primary girl characters to being given white, blue-eyed baby dolls. Claudia, the narrator of the story, says:

> I had only one desire: to dismember it. To see of what it was made, to discover the dearness, to find the beauty, the desirability that had escaped me, but apparently only me. . . . I could not love it. But I could examine it to see what it was that all the world said was lovable. Break off the tiny fingers, bend the flat feet, loosen the hair, twist the head around.[7]

Although Claudia is working through her emerging race consciousness, a reflection of what is happening within the civil rights movement and every other constituent of the larger society including the judicial, educational, political, and media systems, Morrison presents, by contrast, Pecola, a little girl who has so internalized race stigma that she is obsessed by the thought that if she could just change her eye color to the pretty blue of the baby dolls she would become beautiful and loved, even going so far as to give money to a man claiming to have the magic power to grant her wish.

A more nuanced treatment of skin-tone politics is offered in descriptions of another little girl, Maureen Peal, a "high-yellow dream child with long brown hair braided into two lynch ropes,"[8] and in a scene when Pecola is being taunted by other black children for the darkness of her skin. The narrator observes, "It was their contempt for their own blackness that gave the . . . insult its teeth."[9] At its most extreme the internal racial conflict is expressed by the aspiring mother of a young boy in semantic terms: "his mother did not like him to play with niggers. She had explained to him the difference between colored people and niggers. They were easily identifiable. Colored people were neat and quiet; niggers were dirty and loud."[10] These passages are the literary embodiment of the insights expressed in other venues, such as in the lyrics of a James Brown anthem, "I'm black and I'm proud!," Muhammad Ali's defiant claim, "No Viet Cong ever called me nigger," and the radical postures of Rap Brown, Angela Davis, Stokely Carmichael, and leaders of the Black Panther Party.

Though white, Oates, Updike, and Roth were not indifferent to the racial tensions of their communities and make laudable efforts to address them. For example, Roth's description of a young black boy who comes to the Newark library to sit in the stacks and stare at prints of Gauguin's Tahiti is two dimensional and risky in its attempt to capture the boy's deep accent, but it does offer a glimpse of the undercurrents of race-based suspicions ever present just beneath the surface of black-white interactions. And the protagonist's efforts to help the boy satisfy his curiosity and hunger for escape through art and the library, though feeble and ultimately unsuccessful, offer other like-minded readers a glance at a different way of relating across racial lines from that of the earlier generation. Neil Klugman is no Atticus Finch, but he represents a newly emerging white sensibility.

Updike's Harry Angstrom is quite a different kind of white man. Unlike Roth's hero, whose social conscious is molded by his awareness of the outsider status of his own minority Jewish background, Updike's character has no social or ethnic reason to feel kinship across the racial lines of demarcation. In fact, his family and community are fully imbued with the garden-variety bigotry of their place and time. Yet somehow, Harry's inchoate discomfort with the status quo—the character trait that accounts for his running away, his sexual impulsivity, his perpetual dissatisfaction despite the surface appearance of middle-class conventionality—draws him to a rebellious, radical black man from "the Negro side" of town. It is the same gesture that, nearly 40 years later, prompts him, despite a serious heart condition, to challenge a young black kid to a one-on-one basketball game on the Florida playground where he will have the heart attack that ends his life. Harry is no liberal, yet his failed, and ultimately fatal, attempts to live in the emerging world of integrated and conflict-ridden American society of the 1960s more fully expresses the complexity of race relations within mainstream white America than many seemingly more progressive representations.

Given their shared racial and class backgrounds, it is not surprising that Oates's and Updike's characters express similar values, though Oates's are usually darker or rawer. Racial animus is especially strong in *them* (lower case intended), with its focus on poor whites dislocated from their rural southern roots who find themselves in the slums of Detroit in 1966. Maureen, one of the children of the central family, is openly racist, but her brother perceives his privilege and exploits it, "Actually he was immensely grateful for being white. In Detroit being white struck him as a special gift, a blessing."[11] What's more, in one of the few overt references any of the novelists make to organized political action or resistance, Jules, the featured son in the family, cynically joins a radical group modeled after Students for a Democratic Society even while he is exploiting a young girl acting as her pimp. As a sign of his manipulative character and the author's skepticism regarding political activism he is last seen heading for California as a follower of a charismatic but callow radical organizer.

While Oates was chronicling the dark side of white life in and around Detroit, Toni Morrison was contributing to the literature of race and family as well, and her vantage point on the lives of black women provided an important perspective in the midst of the second-wave feminist movement that was dominated by white activists and writers. *Sula*, published in 1973, just three years after *The Bluest Eye*, presents the title character as one who is immersed in a black community and dealing with the taint of racism and the changes in race relations that occurred from 1919 when the novel begins to its conclusion in 1965. Within her community, Sula exhibits many of the qualities that were then associated with militant white feminists who were garnering the bulk of mainstream public attention. Not only is Sula socially emancipated from any sense of second-class status based on gender, but her sex life is as unfettered as that of any man in the community. As a child she witnessed her mother's casual couplings with random men and learned to appreciate sexual pleasure as a natural right: "Seeing her step so easily into the pantry and emerge looking precisely as she did when she entered, only happier, taught Sula that sex was pleasant and frequent, but otherwise unremarkable."[12]

As an adult, Sula follows her mother's example with similar outcomes. Although she enjoys the physical sensation of sex, she is indifferent to nearly every man whose attentions she momentarily received. And, as was the case with her mother, her ubiquitous sexual availability makes her a threat to the rest of the community and so thoroughly isolated that even at her death, only one of her race is willing to lift a finger to arrange for her funeral or even attend her burial. The most vivid depiction of her complete outcast status is told in racial terms. Sula is found dead in her home but left unattended until, "It was Nel who finally called the hospital, then the mortuary, then the police, who were the ones to come. So the white people took over . . . The white people had to wash her, dress her, prepare her and finally lower her."[13]

Nel is the only member of the black community to attend the funeral, and it is the complexity of her lifelong relationship with Nel that is the core of the novel. It is finally through Nel's eyes that the reader sees what has become of community, of family, and of life's details both large and small over the 46-year span of the story. And it is not an unambiguous vision. The final chapter begins this way, "Things were so much better in 1965. Or so it seemed."[14] And the chapter ends with Nel walking away from a visit to Sula's grave and breaking down in inconsolable grief, not just over the loss of the person she loved most in her life but over the collapse of a way of life: "It was a fine cry—loud and long—but it had no bottom and it had no top, just circles and circles of sorrow."[15] Though their individual lives frequently diverge, Nel and Sula are drawn together even after years of separation through their shared formative experiences and repressed sexual attraction to each other. As is the case in every one of the 10 novels discussed here, there is a haunting sense of the inescapable nature of personal, class, and racial history held up in contrast to the struggle to make a new self in defiance of the shaping forces. This is, after all, a common theme of much of the American literary canon. Nowhere is this conflict more evident than in the representation of sexual behavior and attitudes in boomer literature.

It is not the least hyperbolic to refer to the events of the era as a sexual revolution, for revolutionary it surely was. Once again, 1960 is the year that marks the inception of the sexual revolution for it was on May 9, 1960, that the U.S. Food and Drug Administration granted approval to G. D. Searle Company for the sale of Enovid-10, the first birth-control pill, a decision whose ripples are still spreading in ever new and unanticipated ways. Yet the variety of other developments that changed the social/sexual ecology and thereby the literary climate is much richer. Between the earliest novels of Updike and Roth and their next forays, and while Morrison and Oates were making their literary débuts, over a mere 13 years, America entered a new world of sexual expression marked by the following key moments:

1960 D. H. Lawrence's *Lady Chatterley's Lover* is published in England 32 years after its completion; the delay was due to censorship

1961 Henry Miller's *Tropic of Cancer* in the United States; in 1964 the Supreme Court rules that it is not obscene.

1961 Lenny Bruce performs in Carnegie Hall and is later arrested in San Francisco for saying "cocksucker" on stage.

1963 *Fanny Hill* is published 215 years after its original limited edition; the delay was due to censorship restrictions.

1964 Lenny Bruce is convicted of obscenity in New York State (he was posthumously pardoned by Republican governor George Pataki 37 years later).

1965 Lenny Bruce publishes his book *How to Talk Dirty and Influence People* serially in *Playboy* magazine.

1966 Masters and Johnson's clinical study of human sexual response is published.

1967 *I Am Curious, Yellow*, a Swedish film with explicit erotic scenes is released in art houses.

1969 Gloria Steinem's coverage of abortion activism is published in *New York Magazine*.

1971 *Our Bodies, Our Selves* is published by the Boston Women's Health Book Collective.

1971 *Playboy* magazine publishes photos that show women's pubic hair.

1972 George Carlin records "Seven Dirty Words You Can Never Say on Television."

1972 *Deep Throat*, an explicit pornographic film, is released and receives wide distribution.

In 1967, in the midst of this cornucopia of sexual release, along came Philip Roth's *Portnoy's Complaint*, a flagrantly DIRTY BOOK! Roth took full advantage of the unbridled license allowed by court decisions, shifts in sexual mores, and the public's liberalized tastes in reading, filmgoing, and other entertainment. Whereas in *Goodbye, Columbus* the sexual content was limited to having the young protagonist sleep with his girlfriend and persuade her to get fitted for a diaphragm, just seven years later in *Portnoy's Complaint* Roth completely discards euphemism and propriety. Lest anyone miss how thoroughly he has embraced the colloquial semantics of sex, he even goes so far as to intersperse the text with several large type, all cap headlines, just in case the reader missed the nonstop raciness throughout:

"CUNT CRAZY"

"WHACKING OFF"

Even the title of the book is an effort to express both the sexual confusion Roth sees as pervasive in American society and a slap at the prevalence of Freudian explanations for every personal and social malady. Before the narrative begins, there is an academic-sounding definition of the title's meaning:

> Portnoy's Complaint . . . n. [after Alexander Portnoy (1933–)] A disorder in which strongly-felt ethical and altruistic impulses are perpetually warring with extreme sexual longings, often of a perverse nature. . . . It is believed by Spielvogel that many of the symptoms can be traced to the bonds in the mother-child relationship.[16]

As is common with Roth, he makes sly references to himself in even this mock-dictionary definition as the birth year assigned to Portnoy is the same as his own.

Alex Portnoy's obsession as well as his guilt and anxiety embody well the sexual zeitgeist that is far from resolved by the end of the novel, as suits the larger social situation. Roth's characters, here and throughout the dozens of novels to follow, are the mirror image of that other avatar of libidinal license, the sexual *flaneur* Hugh Hefner.

In their ways Joyce Carol Oates and Toni Morrison also chronicle boomer sexuality. But while the men who occupy the worlds of Roth and Updike are perpetually seeking pleasure despite their hang-ups, and Morrison's Sula is bent on self-satisfaction, Oates commonly portrays women as victims, sometimes captives of their own unsatisfied yearnings, more often of the predations of crude, narcissistic, indifferent men. Clara, the protagonist of *A Garden of Earthly Delights*, uses her attractiveness to climb out of the poverty of share cropping only to have her beloved son shoot himself in the head in front of her. Natasha, in *Expensive People*, the beautiful daughter of poor emigrants, passes herself off as a descendent of royalty but, her son, the narrator of the novel describes her in a way that Portnoy would recognize: "Mothers who cringe and beg for love get nothing, and they deserve nothing, but mothers like Nada who are always backing out of the driveway draw every drop of love out of us."[17] These are her son's reflections a few years after he has murdered her. The women of *them* fare no better. The young

Maureen is beaten into a coma by her stepfather when he discovers she has become a prostitute. In *Wonderland* Jesse's wife is sexually unresponsive and wishes to abort each of her pregnancies; Jesse's daughter becomes a drug whore and he ends up buying her from a pimp for $500 only to have her die in his arms a few hours later.

Given the lightheartedness, even goofiness, that is often associated with the boomer era and images of Woodstock, hippies, free love, pot smoking, psychedelic rock concerts, and idealistic political optimism, it is noteworthy that the most prolific and long-lasting of the novelists of the time paid little attention to those occasionally joyful experiences. Perhaps it is because the writers were just a half-generation older than the boomer celebrants or because they discerned a side of the times that prompted dark foreboding. And perhaps it is because they chose to maintain a critical distance from their subjects that their renderings are still in print and still shed light on the lives and times they were observing.

NOTES

1. Todd Gitlin, *The Sixties: Years of Hope, Days of Rage* (New York: Bantam Books, 1987), 1.

2. Walt Whitman, *Democratic Vistas*. 1871. http://xroads.virginia.edu/~DRBR2/whitman.html.

3. Quoted in Elaine Blair, "American Male Novelists: The New Deal," *New York Review of Books*, July 12, 2012, 20.

4. Joyce Carol Oates, "Afterword," in *them* (New York: Modern Library, 2006), 540-541.

5. Toni Morrison, *The Bluest Eye* (New York: Washington Square Press, 1970), 159.

6. Ibid., 36-37.

7. Ibid., 20.

8. Ibid., 52.

9. Ibid., 55.

10. Ibid., 71.

11. Joyce Carol Oates, *them* (New York: Modern Library, 2006), 360.

12. Toni Morrison, *Sula* (New York: New American Library, 1973), 44.

13. Ibid., 173.

14. Ibid., 163.

15. Ibid., 174.

16. Philip Roth, *Portnoy's Complaint* (New York: Vintage Books, 1967), frontpiece, unpaginated.

17. Joyce Carol Oates, *Expensive People* (Princeton, NJ: Ontario Review Press, 1968), 165.

18

Equipment for Living: The Popularity and Use of Second-Wave Feminist Literature among Baby Boomers

Kim Trager Bohley

I first read The Women's Room *when it came out in 1977. I was a sopho- more in college, and I held babysitting jobs to make extra money. One of the women that I babysat for was a young single mother, and she was the one that put me on to it because she was tired of the wife and mother business. I thought she was pretty neat doing what she was doing—hiring a sitter for her kids so she could go back to school and get her degree. Anyway, she was the one who got me to read it, and I am so glad she did because it really changed the way I thought about relationships.*

—Meg, 55, librarian

One book I want to bring up is The Women's Room *by Marilyn French, which I think is one of the most sexist books ever written. I read it because it was one of those books people said you must read.* Rubyfruit Jungle *also had a very strident tone, but it as opposed to the Women's Room presented issues in a way that made you say, yea, this is hard to read, but yes Molly [Bolt] has an issue here and Molly has a right to have this issue with society. Whereas French portrayed all men across the board as jerks, Brown painted a more complex picture.*

—Tom, 62, graphic designer

During the 1960s and 1970s, feminist writings such as Marilyn French's *The Women's Room* and Rita Mae Brown's *Rubyfruit Jungle* played a significant role in the personal and collective formation of baby boomers like Meg and Tom. Importantly, works by Gwendolyn Brooks, Maya Angelou, Alice Walker, and Audre Lorde brought the oppression of minority women and lesbians to the forefront and provided an "aha!" moment for Tom about the everyday heterosexism that permeated his world. Meg and Tom's auto-biographical memories highlight an important aspect of the cultural act of reading. Readers, even those of the same generation, often have different experiences with and interpretations of the same texts. Certainly, gender, race, class and other social factors can play a role in reading reception. Despite these differences, though, the intense popularity and use of feminist texts among baby boomers during this period point to a shared desire for social change and cultural interrogation.

Baby boomers, who were born between 1946 and 1964, viewed feminist texts as both a mirror and a hammer, reflecting, shaping, and intertwining with their increasingly politically charged world marked by the Vietnam War and the civil rights movement— two important collective frameworks in which the aforementioned writings were read, discussed, and incorporated into their lives. For historians of reading, literary critics, and media scholars, this formative function of books is probably not surprising. As Ana Garner points out, "The idea that what we read influences who we are and how we negotiate our positions within our culture is not new."[1] Yet, the relationship between baby boomers, books, and reading was special in at least one important way. Of this, cultural critic Malcolm Jones said, "The noteworthy distinction with boomer books was the missionary zeal with which readers pressed their favorites on other readers."[2] And so was the case with Meg. After she learned about *The Women's Room* from her female employer, she went on to tell "everyone who would listen" about it, including the man she was dating.

> *Meg:* I said, if you want to understand what makes me tick, read this book. And he actually got something out of it, even though he was of a slightly older generation.

Meg's experience with *The Women's Room* highlights the importance of intergenerational book-sharing and discussions in the dissemination of second-wave feminist literature. Several baby boomers interviewed for this project contend that it was through these social book practices that they connected with other boomers.

Drawing on qualitative research, including interviews and online analyses of selected posts from goodreads.com (a site for readers and book recommendations), this chapter examines the social motivations, uses, and lasting effects that underlie the reading of seminal second-wave feminist works by everyday readers who came of age in the 1960s and 1970s. Through this exploration, the chapter also revisits some classic feminist texts (e.g., Virginia Woolf's *A Room of One's Own*, Charlotte Perkins Gilman's *The Yellow Wallpaper*, Kate Chopin's *The Awakening*, Jane Austen's *Pride and Prejudice*, and Charlotte Brontë's *Jane Eyre*) that were frequently mentioned by boomer readers and writers. Autobiographical reflections by baby boomers in this study provide many vivid examples of the ways in which feminist texts became "equipment for living," to use a term by literary theorist Kenneth Burke, who was interested in the functions of literature.[3] More specifically, this chapter argues that second-wave feminist writings, which intersected with television, film, music, and classic feminist texts, were used by baby boomers as (1) life markers, (2) social signifiers, (3) alternative targets for identification, and occasionally, (4) action triggers.

It should be noted that all the baby boomers I interviewed or with whom I corresponded for this project described themselves as avid readers, though they didn't always have easy access to books. In general, their parents or caregivers supported (or at least didn't interfere with) their childhood reading. Of the 25 participants in this project, most were educated, white, middle-class, persons in their fifties or sixties, and more women than men participated in this project. The interviewees were given pseudonyms. However, the names that were attached to goodread.com posts appear as they did online. Before explicitly digging into the use of second-wave feminist writings by baby boomers, a discussion of the nature, qualities, and sociohistorical context of these texts seems in order.

SECOND-WAVE FEMINIST LITERATURE: A SOCIOHISTORICAL CONTEXT

What Is Feminist Literature?

What the heck is feminist literature? I know there is academic feminism. I don't think of academics and literature in the same sentence, frankly [laughter]. See, I never thought of the things that we have talked about as feminist. I don't think that was an important box for me, as far as I can remember.

—Kay, 56, writer

Perhaps the question Kay asked during my interview with her should begin our discussion: What the heck is feminist literature? The quick response to her question is that feminist literature refers to writings that are informed and inspired by feminist thinking. Literary critic Heather Blaha notes that "although the majority of what is considered feminist literature was written after the 1960s, early feminists and their writings were just as crucial a starting point, even though their impact may not have instantly been quite as strong."[4] Significantly, first-wave writers such as Virginia Woolf kept writing about gender inequality (between Shakespeare and his sister

Judith in the gender-bending *A Room of One's Own*) even after the ratification of the Nineteenth Amendment in 1920, a period that witnessed a dramatic reduction in feminist discourse. Their writings would provide a baseline for second wavers like Marilyn French and Elizabeth Hardwick whose major works—*The Women's Room* and *A View of My Own: Essays in Literature and Society*—respectively, evoke and engage with Virginia Woolf's *A Room of One's Own*, a title that still serves as a compelling metaphor and actual precondition for some of the baby boomers whom I interviewed. Consider these autobiographical memories by Dee, who was born in 1944 and grew up in east-central Ohio, and Lou Ann, who was born in 1950 and lives in Beachwood, Ohio.

> *Dee:* As I read more, and I read a wider range, I fell in love with Woolf's *A Room of One's Own*, and I read another book that was obviously influenced by it—in it the wife actually goes out for a walk and spots a small cottage for sale—later it turns out she has bought that cottage and is spending her time there rather than in her home with her family. I remember nothing else of how the book ended or what she did. Just that one fact has stuck in my memory. I often fantasize what it would be like to have a room of my own, to do such a thing, but instead I look for breathing space within my home.

> *Lou Ann:* Working with single women, seeing their independence, made me long for some of my own, a room of my own, so to speak. So the extremely direct message in *The Women's Room* gave me the confirmation and support I needed to begin my new journey.

Today, most literary scholars view feminist texts, including novels, poetry, confessionals, autobiographies, personal essays, journalistic writings, and other nonfiction works, as texts that understand and position gender as a social construct that, importantly, can be reconstructed.[5] Feminist writers view language as a means to challenge and alter male dominance and gender inequality. In regards to this, Caribbean-American writer and poet Audre Lorde writes, "We share a commitment to language and to the power of language, and to the reclaiming of that language which has been made to work against us."[6] Of course, what is deemed as male dominance and gender inequality changes through the decades as society sets new standards of acceptance and rejection. Similarly, what is considered important and relevant in feminist literature changes and evolves (or in some cases regresses) as society and the segments within it change. In *Changing the Story: Feminist Fiction and Tradition* Gayle Greene said, "Change is an exciting and often excruciating thing for feminist writers—and a central fact of existence."[7]

The nebulous nature of feminist literature and the shifting standards that assess it are evident on goodreads.com in which classic second-wave texts that were viewed as path breaking by baby boomers are frequently considered outdated or less poignant by younger readers. When the paperback copy of Erica Jong's *Fear of Flying* came out, it caused a national sensation; selling three million copies in just three months.[8] The story's protagonist, Isadora Wing, shocked many boomers and others with her uninhibited discussions and fantasies of the "zipless fuck." Although this sex manifesto, as some have called it, is appreciated and liked by many generation X readers, it is not seen as provocative to them as it was to boomers. The following goodreads.com post captures this change:

Kirk: My mother and Erica Jong are roughly the same age, so over the past 35 years as I remember sneaking into the basement paperback stack to peruse this cult classic [*Fear of Flying*], my responses become deeply Oedipal. In the end, this book deserves respect for what it accomplished in the mid-70s: it gave many women who didn't identify with the feminist generation a story to identify with and to rethink what they had previously been taught about feminine sexuality (which, for many of them, was nothing). If the book no longer packs the provocative punch that it once did, it's because we have changed, not it.

While Erica Jong, Adrienne Rich, Marilyn French, Gloria Steinem, and Germaine Greer all embraced or at least accepted the feminist label attached to their work, a large number of women writers, including Edith Wharton, Willa Cather, Flannery O'Connor, Margaret Drabble, and Joan Didion, whose works have all been anthologized widely in feminist/women studies primers, have balked at such gender classifications. In an interview, Annie Dillard, author of *Pilgrim at Tinker Creek*, said, "I want to divorce myself from the notion of the female writer right away and not elaborate."[9] Nobel Prize–winner Doris Lessing, who was enthusiastically adopted by feminist critics and readers after the publication of *The Golden Notebook* and the Martha Quest novels, vehemently rejected the feminist labels attached to her work:

What the feminists want of me is something they haven't examined because it comes from religion. They want me to bear witness. What they would really like me to say is, "Ha, sisters, I stand with you side by side in your struggle toward the golden dawn where all those beastly men are no more." Do they really want people to make oversimplified statements about men and women? In fact, they do. I've come with great regret to this conclusion.[10]

Lessing's comments are especially intriguing to me given the fact that several baby boomers interviewed for this project cited her work as highly influential to them because of its thoughtful analysis of the female condition and consciousness. For example, Elsa, who was born in 1952 and grew up in Inwood, a small neighborhood above Washington Heights in Manhattan, suggested that Doris Lessing's *The Golden Notebook* played an important role in her shift from reading male-centered authors to exclusively women-centered authors.

> *Elsa:* As the daughter of a working class family (not particularly sexist for the time), Lessing's book came close to literally changing my life—or at least my perception of it. I went from reading almost exclusively male authors to women (first Victorian and then, later, 20th century). [This] was a major shift in my life and my consciousness.

Interestingly, two male participants in this study, Frank, 56, and Tom, 62, agree with Lessing's assessment that feminist labels limit the scope of *The Golden Notebook.*

> *Frank:* It is unfair to reduce this epic [*The Golden Notebook*] into a feminist text. There is much more than that in it. I liked the way Lessing pictured the dilemma of intellectuals who find themselves politically committed, as well as her insightful explorations of free sex. A masterpiece no doubt.

> *Tom:* I did not think of *The Golden Notebook* as a text on women's liberation. First of all, it had been written in '62 or '63, right? So, I am reading it [in] '73, '74 maybe '75. So as I look at the publication date of this book I can say that this was not written for the women's lib movement. It is a book about understanding the human condition that specifically deals with male-female relationships. There is a difference.

Other study participants also spoke with me about the problems attached to the feminist literature label. Even though genre labels inherently lead to the simplification of complex works, many feminist writers, critics, and readers point to their importance in bringing awareness and organization to bodies of literature that have been silenced and/or disparaged by dominant society. Most of my interviewees seemed to have a pretty good understanding of what second-wave feminist literature meant to them. For example, Sue, 56, a former professor, summed it up the best: "These are all books that stretched my idea of how both women and men could live."

Landmark Second-Wave Feminist Texts and Their Intersection with Popular Culture

The problem lay buried, unspoken, for many years in the minds of American women . . . As she made the beds, . . . matched slipcover material, . . . chauffeured Cub Scouts and Brownies, lay beside her husband at night–she was afraid to ask even of herself–the silent question–"Is this all?"

—Betty Friedan[11]

The year 1963 was marked by several historical events, including the assassination of President Kennedy, the march on Washington, and the publication of Betty Friedan's *The Feminine Mystique*, hailed by many, including the mainstream press and antifeminist pundits, as the founding text of second-wave feminism and the book that "launched," "sparked," or "led to" the women's liberation movement.[12] This work challenged the postwar ideology of the happy housewife and examined the origins of the depression, anxiety, self-doubt, and boredom that marked the lives of many white, middle-class wives and daughters of "the greatest generation," who were caught between feminism's first and second waves.

In a Strange Stirring: The Feminine Mystique and American Women at the Dawn of the 1960s, social historian Stephanie Coontz analyzes interview data from more than 200 women who recalled the first time they read *The Feminine Mystique*. "Half a century after they read the book, many of the women I talked to could still recall the desperation they had felt in the late 1950s and early 1960s, and their wave of relief when Friedan told them they were not alone and they were not crazy," Coontz said.[13] Since its publication, cultural critics of different stripes, including Coontz, have challenged and demystified simplified cause-effect stories that position *The Feminine Mystique* as the origin point of contemporary feminism.[14] *The Feminine Mystique* has also been criticized by bell hooks (Gloria Watkins) and other feminists for its classism, racism, and heterosexism. Despite its flaws, *The Feminine Mystique* must be given credit for providing thousands of women and men trapped in or affected by an unrealistic and harmful feminist ideal with a source of inspiration.

It is important to point out that baby boomers were just entering high school or college when *The Feminine Mystique* was published. Most of them would not read this book until years, in some cases many years, later. Though a large number of my informants asserted that *The Feminine Mystique* was an "important," "landmark," "pioneering" book when I asked them about it, their memories of it were often vague ("I'm pretty sure I read it"; "I must have read it") compared with other second-wave texts, such as Simone de Beauvoir's *The Second Sex*, which informed *The Feminine Mystique*, even though Friedan did not directly attribute this work or its French existentialist author. My participants' reflections on *The Feminine Mystique* jibe with Coontz's assertion that "For the younger women who energized the early 1970s women's movement, *The Feminine Mystique* was less likely to provide a 'click moment' than it was for the slightly older group of women who first discovered it."[15] After reading *The Feminine Mystique*, a couple of baby boomers I interviewed remembered being puzzled by "all the hoopla" surrounding the book.

> *Connie:* I cannot remember when I read *Feminine Mystique*, but I will say that by the time I read it [the book] seemed so old hat. I thought why are people so excited about this. I just don't get it. I mean, I have known this forever. So I kinda don't think I read it until grad school. It may have been late in college, but I thought it was a pretty low level analysis of what I already knew.

For Connie, *The Feminine Mystique* didn't have the shock value that characterized much of the second-wave literature that was published in the late sixties and the seventies, a period defined by its heighted social and political activism. In regards to the politicization of feminist literature, Phyllis Rose noted that writings by women and other minorities "took on a new edge" as readers and authors gained an increase awareness that work published by "those outside the mainstream constituted a political statement."[16] At this time, feminist writings also increasingly crossed national boundaries. Feminist writers such as Germaine Greer from Australia, Margaret Atwood from Canada, Margaret Drabble from England, and Ruth Prawer Jhabvala who moved back and forth between India and the United States, were frequently discussed by baby boomers interviewed for this project.

The dawn of the seventies witnessed a boom in published fiction and nonfiction by and about women. Independent, feminist, underground, and academic presses during this era found and published hundreds of lost, banned, and out-of-print books by women. For example, in the early 1970s, the Feminist Press reprinted Rebecca Harding's *Life in the Iron Mills*, which was originally published anonymously in 1861, and Charlotte Perkins Gilman's *The Yellow Wallpaper*, which was originally published in 1892. Alice Walker's "In search of Zora Neale Hurston," which was published in *Ms. Magazine* in 1975, helped lead to the popular reception of this now revered author's work. Interestingly, three male baby boomers whom I interviewed or who posted on goodreads.com expressed their preference for these classic feminist texts over second-wave literature.

> *Bruce:* Even though this book [*The Awakening*] is known for its controversial feminist posture, scandalous in 1899, I had forgotten how

beautifully written and how observant and insightful Chopin is. (I'll take the 19th century feminists over the 1970s baby boomer versions any day of the week.)

Certainly, one of the most celebrated mainstream publication events in second-wave feminist literature history was Kate Millet's pioneering *Sexual Politics*, which was published in the late summer of 1970, close in time to the Women's Strike for Equality in New York City. The sensational market-ability of *Sexual Politics*, along with other best-selling women-centered books such as *The Female Eunuch* and *The Dialectic of Sex: The Case for Feminist Revolution*, prompted mainstream publishers to take an interest in feminist authors. In 1972, William Jovanovich, the then chairman of Harcourt Brace Jovanovich Inc., told *The New York Times*, "There's no question that publishers are aware that the whole society is thinking about women in a new way, and a good book about or by a woman is looked at with keener interest than it would have been 10 years ago."[17]

Feminist literary critic Gayle Greene notes that the early seventies also ushered in a new literary genre—feminist metafiction—in which "the protagonist looks to the literary tradition for answers about the present . . . [and] seeks 'freedom' from the plots of the past."[18] Greene cites Margaret Drabble's *The Realms of Gold*, Margaret Atwood's *Surfacing*, Margaret Laurence's *The Diviners*, and Gail Godwin's *The Odd Woman* as representative of this new genre. Several of my informants, such as Donna, who was born in Shaker Heights, Ohio, remembered the influx of this form of feminist writing with glee. Like the protagonists of feminist metaficition, Donna turned to reading for self-validation and answers.

Donna: By the late '70s there was so much more literary fiction by women. I can remember being involved with a man back then who observed: "God you seem to read a lot of books by women." And I remember thinking, I do. It hadn't occurred to me before his comment. I hadn't thought of it that way. But by then those were the books that were speaking to me. Alice Munro, her collection *The Beggar Maid* [*The Beggar Maid: Stories of Flo and Rose* (1977)]. Margaret Drabble's work also comes to mind. Those were the writers who could tell me something.

In keeping with the times, several of my informants first learned about (or learned more about) second-wave feminists texts and writers through the mainstream media that was increasingly covering the women's liberation movement and spotlighting a few token feminist writers such as Betty Friedan, who was also founder of NOW (the National Organization for Women); Gloria Steinem, cofounder of *Ms. Magazine*; and Germaine Greer,

author of *The Female Eunuch*. Helynne's post on goodreads.com offers one
such example:

> *Helynne:* I remember shortly after [*The Female Eunuch*] was published,
> Greer was a guest on William F. Buckley's TV interview show. He
> apparently felt so threatened by her as a strong (but sophisticated, low-
> key, and well-mannered) feminist that he attacked her at every turn,
> and would not even allow her to finish a sentence.

While television, popular magazines, and newspapers helped turn some
key second-wave concepts (e.g., the female eunuch, the personal is political,
sisterhood is powerful, the second sex, sexual politics, male chauvinism, and
patriarchy) into catchphrases dropped at dinner parties, they also, at times,
distorted important messages in classic feminist texts of this era.[19] Moreover,
they held the power to anoint and then publicly dethrone some feminist
writers (e.g., Kate Millet) who were viewed as less "palatable" for the press
and public than the attractive Gloria Steinem.[20] Of this, Susan Douglas
asserts, "the most important legacy of the media coverage was its carving up
of the women's movement into legitimate and illegitimate feminism."[21] In
an effort to self-define, some radical feminists (e.g., Radicalesbians) decided
to establish their own publications (e.g., *Ain't I a Woman?*, *It Ain't Me Babe*,
and *Off Our Backs*), while Friedan, Steinem, and others chose to continue
working within the mainstream media. An estimated 560 radical feminist
publications circulated between 1968 and 1973.[22] Not surprisingly, these
alternative outlets often devoted a substantial amount of ink to literature
reviews and critiques of feminist poetry, novels, autobiographies, and other
writings. Memories by my informants highlight the intertexuality of second-wave feminist literature with the mainstream news as well as alternative
publications and international media. During our interview, Connie, who
was born in 1945 and spent much of her professional life in a midwestern
college town, urged me to stress the intermingling of feminist books with
other media.

> *Connie:* You have to acknowledge that these books that we are dis-
> cussing are working hand in hand with the other cultural forms. I
> feel like if you ever do a bigger project movies have to be a part of it.
> For me, the French New Wave was really important. Movies like *Jules
> and Jim* [1962]. Those were films that were showing men and women
> in different types of relationships from the conventional American
> ones. These books mixed with film and music. For example, I think of
> Joan Baez as an important feminist figure . . . [She was] a very strong
> woman whom I heard first in college when I began reading some of
> these books.

AUTOBIOGRAPHICAL READING MEMORIES OF BABY BOOMERS: FEMINIST LITERATURE AS "EQUIPMENT FOR LIVING" FOR BABY BOOMERS' LIFE MARKERS

Through my analysis of baby boomers' autobiographical memories, I discovered several functions that feminist literature performed; these writings, then, served as "equipment for living." This section of the chapter focuses on how boomers "used" feminist texts on a conscious and/or unconscious level to accomplish certain ends.

First, for example, autobiographical memories of baby boomers spotlighted the ways that readers used feminist writings as "life markers." Deaths, divorces, mental breakdowns, and sexual encounters were often linked with particular books. In this way, books and other literary works performed an important mnemonic function for boomer readers, as Donna and Meg's memories compellingly reveal.

Donna: Well, it wasn't until my late 20s that I had a breakdown, and I struggled with depression for many years . . . I was seeing a therapist, and I was really trying to explore what was wrong, you know? And I was looking for wisdom anywhere I could find it. And I remember just so vividly sitting there in my little apartment on West 11th Street and reading an essay in the *Village Voice* by Karen Durbin about a woman who was going through some of the same pain I had gone through and was going through. And it was describing it in a way that spoke to me. [The article] was called "On Being a Woman Alone." I remember [Durbin] talking about feeling like she was drowning. And it was at a time when all my dreams seemed to be filled with water. It was sort of a metaphor that spoke to me so explicitly that it felt really meaningful.

Meg: Okay, I know why I reread *The Women's Room.* [It was] because my second husband had asked me for a divorce, and I was furious. And I needed to read something that was just affirming to women. So it is very personal.

The coupling of important life events to particular feminist writings helps explain why some boomers are still so emotionally invested in and attached to these works. Frequently, boomers' reflections of these important "life marking" texts were colored by significant news events and social trends of the day, such as the Kent State shootings, the National Women's Strike for Equality in New York City, and the sexual revolution of the 1970s. Consequently, personal memories of reading became intertwined with public events that thousands of other baby boomers also experienced.

This interconnection is important to keep in mind when considering the following autobiographical accounts by Tom, Dee, and Connie.

Tom: It was just one of those things that if you were at all attuned as a guy in Madison, Wisconsin, if you weren't a Luddite or ignorant to the women's movement, you were hearing things and reading things so you could understand something that maybe you didn't understand. And I am sure that is where I was when I read *The Golden Notebook* the first time. You need to understand I was in Madison from [1968 to 1972], as an undergraduate. My freshman year we had the National Guard on campus because [of] black studies demonstrations. We had the National Guard on campus the year before I came to Madison because of the Dow demonstrations. We had the National Guard on campus my sophomore year because of Kent State. There was a lot to be engaged with. The women's movement to a certain extent was part of that whole mix of change.

Dee: I think the basic reason for [my] interest in these books was because I was at the university in the last half of the sixties and a young married woman with small children in the early seventies. They [feminist writings] gave me a look at what was happening with the women's movement. The student protests over the Vietnam War clouded the era also. Having not been a part of that but seeing what happened there influenced me. Take as an example what happened at KSU [Kent State University] on May 4, 1970, which was only four years after I graduated from Kent and while people I knew were still there, including my brother-in-law. It may well be that all of this combined started a search for answers. French's [*The Women's Room*] was definitely the catalyst for further feminist reading.

Connie: I remember reading the book *Open Marriage* in the '70s, and that was really important to me. I'm sure it was basically about the confinement of marriage. It was just the times. They were awful because of the assassinations in the late '60s. They were really awful. But then, along about that time, we also had this opening up of culture, which also came from movies. And books such as *Open Marriage* were a part of this. I would say for me the issue of sex and marriage and freedom was very important and that it was a generational issue, not just for women. I feel like for me the feminist strand was just part of the liberation of the late '60s early '70s. It was a cultural liberation and a lot of it was sexual liberation.

While the collective memories of second-wave feminist literature by Tom, Dee, Connie, and other baby boomers are not unified, a large number of these readers, especially those from the same cohort and region, were reading these works through shared cultural frameworks. In many cases, these collective cultural frameworks have become almost intrinsically linked to the memory of the books themselves. Connie, for example, said it was difficult to discuss her interpretations of Nena O'Neill and George O'Neill's *Open Marriage* without connecting the book to the sexually liberating environment in which she read it. Significantly, thousands of other baby boomers were reading and evaluating this text, which was on the *New York Times* best-seller list for 40 weeks, through the same lens around the same time. This sort of collective reception prompted many baby boomers to interpret a particular text, such as *Open Marriage*, as a "sign of its time," and it also served as a vehicle for collective identity construction.[23]

Autobiographical memories by Dee and other boomers highlight the ways that social reading practices, such as book suggestions and borrowing, also facilitated a sense of belonging among members of this generation.

> *Dee:* What would happen is my across-the-street-neighbor would set up her lawn chair and get her drink and settle in and one by one anywhere from two to five others would come over and either bring their own drink or she would fix a pitcher of Bloody Marys or open a box of wine. We talked about everyday goings on in our lives, and those who were readers would mention books if they thought someone else would be interested . . . I think *The Women's Room* stirred the most controversy . . . I know the French book had us talking about the various factions of the women's movement and the pros and cons of each. It was fun, yes, but I believe we learned a great deal as well from sharing our thoughts on the deeper topics from time to time.

Social Signifiers

Dee's recollection of her neighbor's informal book and drink gatherings captures the shared passion and sociability that was often attached to second-wave feminist literature. Although Dee's "reading group" was informal and social, other boomers belonged to more serious women-centered book clubs and conscious-raising groups. Several baby boomers whom I interviewed or corresponded with noted that they didn't initially seek out second-wave feminist literature but read such works because these texts were "in the air" and "being carried around by" a lot of people during their formative years. The following memories by Jane, Bruce, and Tom illuminate the fact that selecting and reading second-wave feminist texts were, in part, cultural activities, influenced by the social climate and actors of the day.

Jane: No one in particular has ever encouraged me to read feminist texts, but when I was growing up feminism was "in the air" and naturally I imbibed the atmosphere, and picked up on the new wave of feminist writers.

Bruce: When this book [*The Women's Room*] was current, late 1970s, when I was just past college age, it seems every woman in my age group was carrying this book around.

Tom: Sometimes things are just sort of in the air. You hear something and you go "that is something everybody is reading and if I consider myself open-minded on this issue I should take a crack at it."

Tom's comment, in particular, illustrates the way that second-wave texts were sometimes viewed as social signifiers of certain traits, such as open-mindedness. Two male informants that I interviewed confided that they thought their success in relationships with "progressive women" depended, in part, on their having "at least some knowledge" of these books. Reflections by other baby boomers suggested that, at times, they had felt internal and/or external pressure to read and like certain second-wave books and writers. The following comment by May, 55, who was born and raised in Troy, New York, suggests that she felt some sort of internal force or expectation to appreciate influential feminist writers: "I wanted to like Audre Lord [*sic*] and Adrienne Rich, but I didn't. I found their writing strident." Multiple boomers made similar types of comments (e.g., "There was a lot of buzz about [*The Second Sex*]. So I thought I would like it and wanted to, but didn't"). A few boomers even suggested that they felt external pressure to read certain second-wave texts as a sign of their allegiance with feminism. Consider this comment posted on goodreads.com about Margaret Atwood's *The Edible Woman*, a novel that initially received lackluster reviews but is now commonly viewed as a heralding second-wave novel.

Anneke: I must be the only woman to have read this book [*The Edible Woman*] and hated it . . . Perhaps because at the time I read it, we were all expected to be Feminists and that as women, we had to read *The Edible Woman* and find meaning in it . . . Not that I wasn't a Feminist, or at least didn't agree whole-heartedly that women could do anything and be anything they chose to do. I just objected to the rationale that if I didn't like *The Edible Woman* there was something wrong with me.

In contrast, Sophia, who was born in 1966 and currently lives in Canada, wrote to me that she has never felt pressure to read women-centered books and that she didn't think *The Edible Woman* or other books by Atwood "pushed" feminist issues.

> *Sophia:* For me, *The Edible Woman* is a gentle parody of the modern issues of the couple; *Alias Grace* is a parody of the sensational literature (so appreciated in 19th century) and *The Handmaid's Tale* a parody of the future, in Huxley/Orwell style. Are there remarkable heroines in every one of them? Definitely, but they don't fight to affirm their feminist rights, nor are they created to illustrate them. [T]his would be a too narrow interpretation [of her work].

Alternative Targets for Identification

In addition to signaling group identification or distance, autobiographical memories elicited from interviews and collected on goodreads.com reveal that many boomers have used feminist texts throughout their lives in the construction and renegotiation of their individual identities. Feminist writings (fiction and nonfiction) have offered some boomers "alternative targets for identification when they experienced division within their environment," as Ana Garner would say.[24] This literary function was particularly important for the female participants of my study who were often aware of the social constraints placed on them at a young age and sought other models of what could be. For example, Sarah, who was born in Williamston, North Carolina, in 1948, resented the gendered regulations that her parents and others placed on her social activities. In the literary heroine Nancy Drew, Sarah found an intelligent, curious young girl whose behaviors and interests didn't conform to prescribed gender roles.

> *Sarah:* When I was a girl, I knew that boys had much more freedom and felt it was very unfair. I wanted to play Little League, but was told I couldn't because I was a girl; I wanted a paper route, but was told I couldn't because I was a girl; I climbed trees and was told "Don't do that" and I did it anyway. I jumped fences and was told the same thing, and did it anyway. I twirled on tree branches and was told to quit, and when I didn't, they cut down the tree branch. So I have a lot of personal experience with being treated unfairly because of my gender. I liked Nancy Drew. She was a girl and had an impact on her world.

As children, the most popular fictional heroines mentioned by female baby boomers were Nancy Drew, created by Edward Stratemeyer; Ann Shirley of Lucy Maud Montgomery's *Anne of Green Gables* series; and Jo March of Louisa May Alcott's *Little Women*. These heroines were perceived to possess traits that boomers respected and admired as children.

Connie: As a child I read *Anne of Green Gables*. She would be a very early heroine . . . She was so independent and spirited and didn't do what she was supposed to do. A grown up in a way at a very young age because she had been an orphan. And she had a very imaginative life she was full of imagination, very lovable though.

Dee: Much of what I loved and read from early on had a feminist slant— Louisa May Alcott's works with their strong young girls encouraged by their elders, male or female, to be independent and not simply to marry and be dependent upon their spouse. Montgomery's independent *Anne of Green Gables*.

Significant to several boomers of this study were heroines such as Anne Shirley who "didn't do what she was supposed to do," as noted by Connie. Consequently, Anne provided these readers with an alternative model of living that departed from the cultural norm. As teenagers and young adults, baby boomers often found fictional heroines in 19th-century classics. Here Charlotte Brontë's *Jane Eyre* and Jane Austen's *Pride and Prejudice* were the two most frequently mentioned. Several men who participated in this study voiced their "respect" and "admiration" for these particular heroines, too, though they didn't list them as their personal heroines. As boomers became adults, they often sought fictional heroines or autobiographical/biographical subjects who dared to live authentic lives.

Donna: Oh God, of course I love Jane Austen, but I also love *Jane Eyre*. And I adore, I just adore the Alice Munro character Rose in the *Beggar Maid*. Any of Alice Munroe's single woman characters are fabulous . . . They are females who are seekers who are looking for their lives, who want something. They don't always know what it is. And it involves trying to separate themselves from their families. They dare to walk outside of the family. And [by] family I mean hometown, all the cultural and social glue that still sticks to them and what to draw them back to that safe place, which isn't always so safe. But they feel like they have to change or die. I have felt this way.

In rereading and/or reevaluating classic and second-wave feminist texts over a period of years, some boomers began to interrogate the ideas and values of their youth. As a consequence, they develop a new or renegotiated understanding of an idea or value. Rhonda's post on goodreads.com seems to capture this process. While Rhonda "the college student" appears to have wholeheartedly agreed with Greer's ideas on gender relationships, Rhonda "the adult" challenges some of Greer's assertions about motherhood and comes to the more complex conclusion that all theories and schools of thought are inherently partial in their explanatory powers.

Rhonda: This book was hugely influential on me and my girlfriends when we read it as college girls in the 1970s. Greer was a scholarly and entertaining writer, and we were all excited to find out how much we were hated just for being females. Over the years I began to question some of her assertions that had seemed so convincing: e.g., it would be better for children to be raised by Italian peasants so their educated, ambitious, free-wheeling mothers could do important things, for instance, and go visit the children once in a while, since children are more attached to places than people. At least that's how I remember it . . . I didn't realize then how utterly Greer's thinking was influenced by Marxism . . . I wish her well, but no one strain of feminist thought, or any political thought, seems to explain the universe totally.

ACTION TRIGGERS

Not surprisingly, the overall influence and affect that second-wave writings had on baby boomers varied. As mentioned earlier, several boomers clearly credited one or two "stand out" texts or writers that triggered a change in their thoughts, attitudes, or outlook. For other baby boomers, there wasn't necessarily one book or writer that "produced a click moment," to borrow a term from Stephanie Coontz. Rather, they cited several works that collectively shifted their outlook. Lou Ann's comment is representative of this type of response.

Lou Ann: Our Bodies, Ourselves, The Women's Room, and most importantly, *Ms. Magazine* were all important [to me]. Above all, they showed me that there was a world out there that I had a place in. It might not be recognized by the men that inhabited it, but I still had a place and it was up to me to make sure that I filled it to the best of my ability.

Though less rare, some baby boomers discussed books that spurred them into action. For example, Susan, who was born in Santa Monica, California, in 1950, asserted that her reading of *The Golden Notebook* prompted her to engage in the same sort of reflexive, ambitious journaling that preoccupied Anna, the book's protagonist.

Susan: Even though I read this book [*The Golden Notebook*] over 30 years ago, I remember how affected I was by its writer protagonist, and her various notebooks. I was a single mom, working and going to junior college, and Lessing's book was one I read in my first "Feminist Lit" course. It inspired me to try writing in various journals: I named one "Rage & Anger," another one "Dreams & Visions," and another "Magic & Madness." There were others, but I eventually went back to one journal when all those spirals were filled.

While Lessing's *The Golden Notebook* seems to have ignited a direct, deliberative response from Susan, Lessing's *The Four Gated City* informed Connie's actions in a more complicated, indirect way.

Connie: *The Four Gated City* had a big impact on me. I would say her [Doris Lessing's] work in general helped contribute to my divorce, thank God. You know, I got married at 21. Shouldn't have. Should have gotten unmarried as quickly as possible but didn't and stuck with it for seven years. But I didn't just read *The Four Gated City* and say: "Okay, I am out of here." It took time. But I did read it and started having affairs.

CONCLUSION

In a 2010 blog post for *Ms. Magazine*, Michele Kort began with the following autobiographical information and confession:

I'm your classic Second Waver—I came to feminism reading this familiar canon: *The Feminine Mystique, Sisterhood is Powerful, The Female Eunuch, Lesbian Nation, The Second Sex, Against Our Will, Women and Madness, Sexual Politics, Towards a Recognition of Androgyny, Ms.* magazine (I especially loved Jo Freeman's essay "The Tyranny of Structurelessness"), *Chrysalis* and *Heresies* magazines, and anything Gloria Steinem wrote. But since those days, I've gotten way behind in feminist theory. Aside from *Ms.*, Steinem's books, and Susan Faludi's *Backlash*, I garnered my feminism through experience, conversation, and popular media rather than going to primary sources.[25]

Like Kort, many of the baby boomer participants in this project were familiar with and at one time avid readers of second-wave feminist writings. Today, however, only a handful of these boomers seek out new or old writings explicitly informed by feminist theory, though several boomers did say they still seek out books with strong literary heroines. Brianna's post on goodreads.com is representative of this trend:

Brianna: I do read much literature centered on woman protagonists, but literature such as *The Golden Notebook* purposely exploring feminist themes is part of my past. I am definitely a baby boomer. I remember clearly those days of *Ms.* Magazine and self-discovery, but now I am a woman concerned with family, career, and trying to find time for myself.

In the 1980s, literary critics, journalists, publishers, and others started to recognize a decline in the popularity and production of feminist writings that coincided with a larger backlash on feminism. Indeed, Elinor Langer wrote an article for *The New York Times* in 1984 in which she asks, "Where are the partisans of yesteryear—the housewives-in-transition of Marilyn French's *The Women's Room*, the rebellious feminists of Alix Kates Shulman's *Burning Questions*, the questioning communards of Marge Piercy's *Small Changes?*"[26] These fiery novels (and ones like it) no longer seem to attract the large number of zealous readers that they once did. In regards to this, some boomers said that their once focused interest on feminist writings had been "somewhat eclipsed" or de-centered by writings that explore issues that are of interest to them now. For example, Donna said, "Right now, all I want to read about is aging. All I am interested in is somebody dealing with aging at the stage of life that I am at." Though boomers' reading patterns and taste have shifted throughout the decades, most boomers from this study agree that the "ideas and lessons" they learned from second-wave feminist writings have not disappeared from their thinking.

NOTES

1. Ana Garner, "Negotiating our Positions in Culture: Popular Adolescent Fiction and the Self-Constructions of Women," *Women's Studies in Communication* 22, no. 1 (1999): 85–111.

2. Malcolm Jones, "Baby Boomers and Their Books: A Love Affair with Literature," *Newsweek*, March 18, 2007, http://www.newsweek.com/baby-boomers-and-books-love-affair-literature-95719.

3. Kenneth Burke, *The Philosophy of Literary Form: Studies in Symbolic Action* (Baton Rouge: Louisiana State University Press, 1967).

4. Heather Blaha, "Feminist Literature" Confessional Writing Beyond National Boundaries," *Undergraduate Review* 10, no.1 article 8. http://digitalcommons.iwu.edu/cgi/viewcontent.cgi?article=1091&context=rev.

5. Gayle Greene, *Changing the Story: Feminist Fiction and the Tradition* (Bloomington: Indiana University Press, 1991), 2.

6. Quoted in Rita Felski, *Beyond Feminist Aesthetics* (Cambridge, MA: Harvard University Press, 1989), 100.

7. Greene, *Changing the Story*, 36.

8. David Bowman, "The Sex Woman," *Salon*, June 14, 2003. http://salon.com/.

9. Quoted in Frank Magill, ed., *Masterpieces of Women's Literature* (New York: Harper Collins, 1996), 401.

10. Quoted in Lesley Hazelton,"Doris Lessing on Feminism, Communism and Space Fiction," *New York Times Book Review*, July 25, 1982.

11. Betty Friedan, *The Feminine Mystique* (New York: W.W. Norton, 1963), 1.

12. Kathryn Cady, "Labor and Women's Liberation: Popular Readings of the Feminine Mystique," *Women's Studies in Communication* 32, no. 3 (2009): 359.

13. Stephanie Coontz, Foreword to *In a Strange Stirring: The Feminine Mystique and American Women at the Dawn of the 1960s* (New York: Basic Books, 2011), xx.

14. Arlie Russell Hochschild, "The Woman with the Flying Hair," *St. Petersburg Times*, April 7, 1991, sec. D.

15. Coontz, *In a Strange Stirring*, 157.

16. Phyllis Rose, *The Penguin Book of Women's Lives* (New York: Vintage Books, 1993), 15.

17. Eric Pace, "New Book Crop Is Full of Novels," *New York Times*, September 5, 1972, http://newyorktimes.com/.

18. Greene, *Changing the Story*, 7.

19. Kristan Poirot, "Mediating a Movement, Authorizing Discourse: Kate Millet, Sexual Politics, and Feminism's Second Wave," *Women's Studies in Communication* 27, no. 2 (2004): 204–235.

20. Ibid.

21. Susan Douglas, *Where the Girls Are: Growing Up Female with the Mass Media* (New York: Random House, 1994).

22. Kristan Poirot, "Domesticating the Liberation Woman: Containment Rhetorics of Second Wave Radical/Lesbian Feminism," *Women's Studies in Communication* 32, no. 3 (2009): 272.

23. José van Dijck, "Record and Hold: Popular Music Between Personal and Collective Memory," *Critical Studies in Media Communication* 23, no. 5 (2006): 358.

24. Ana Garner, "Negotiating Our Positions in Culture: Popular Adolescent Fiction and the Self-Construction of Women," *Women's Studies in Communication* 22, no. 1 (1999): 85.

25. Michele Kort, "Catching up on Feminist Theory: bell hooks" *Ms. blog Magazine*, Last modified September 12, 2010, http://msmagazine.com/blog/2010/09/12/catching-up-on-feminist-theory-1-bell-hooks/.

26. Elinor Langer, "Whatever Happened to Feminist Fiction?" *New York Times Book Review*, March 4, 1984.

REFERENCES

Alcott, Louisa May. *Little Women*. Boston: Little, Brown, 1968.
Atwood, Margaret. *The Edible Woman*. Toronto: McClelland & Stewart, 1969.
Austen, Jane. *Pride and Prejudice*. New York: Longman, 2003.

Beauvoir, Simone de. *The Second Sex*. New York: Knopf, 1953.

Blaha, Heather. "Feminist Literature: Confessional Writing Beyond National Boundaries." *Undergraduate Review* 10, no.1 (1997): article 8. http://digital commons.iwu.edu/cgi/viewcontent.cgi?article=1091&context=rev.

Boston Women's Health Book Collective. *Our Bodies, Ourselves: A Book by and for Women*. New York: Simon & Schuster, 1971.

Bowman, David. "The 'Sex' Woman." *Salon*. June 14, 2003. http://www.salon.com/.

Brontë, Charlotte. *Jane Eyre*. New York: Random House, 1943.

Brown, Rita Mae. *Rubyfruit Jungle*. Plainfield, VT: Daughters, 1973.

Burke, Kenneth. *The Philosophy of Literary Form: Studies in Symbolic Action*. Baton Rouge: Louisiana State University Press, 1967.

Cady, Kathryn. "Labor and Women's Liberation: Popular Readings of *The Feminine Mystique*." *Women's Studies in Communication* 32, no.3 (2009): 348–379.

Chopin, Kate. *The Awakening*. New York: Bantam Classic, 1981.

Coontz, Stephanie. *In a Strange Stirring: The Feminine Mystique and American Women at the Dawn of the 1960s*. New York: Basic Books, 2011.

Dillard, Annie. *Pilgrim at Tinker Creek*. New York: Harper's Magazine Press, 1974.

Dow, Bonnie. "Reading the Second Wave." *Quarterly Journal of Speech* 91 (2005): 89–107.

Douglas, Susan. *Where the Girls Are: Growing up Female with the Mass Media*. New York: Random House, 1994.

Drabble, Margaret. *The Realms of Gold*. New York: Knopf, 1975.

Durbin, Karen. "On Being a Woman Alone." *Village Voice*, August 30, 1976.

Faludi, Susan. *Backlash: The Undeclared War against American Women*. New York: Crown, 1991.

Felski, Rita. *Beyond Feminist Aesthetics*. Cambridge, MA: Harvard University Press, 1989.

Firestone, Shulamith. *The Dialectic of Sex: The Case for Feminist Revolution*. New York: Morrow, 1970.

Freeman, Jo. "The Tyranny of Structurelessness." *Ms.*, July 1973, 76–78, 86–89.

French, Marilyn. *The Women's Room*. New York: Summit Books, 1977.

Friedan, Betty. *The Feminine Mystique*. New York: W. W. Norton, 1963.

Garner, Ana. "Negotiating Our Positions in Culture: Popular Adolescent Fiction and the Self-constructions of Women." *Women's Studies in Communication* 22, no.1 (1999): 85–111.

Gillman, Charlotte Perkins. "The Yellow Wallpaper." *New England Magazine* 5 (1892): 647–656.

Godwin, Gail. *The Odd Woman*. New York: Knopf, 1974.

Greene, Gayle. *Changing the Story: Feminist Fiction and the Tradition*. Bloomington: Indiana University Press, 1991.

Greer, Germaine. *The Female Eunuch*. New York: McGraw-Hill, 1971.

Harding, Rebecca. *Life in the Iron Mills*. Boston: Ticknor and Fields, 1861.

Hardwick, Elizabeth. *A View of My Own: Essays in Literature and Society*. New York: Farrar, Straus and Cudahy, 1962.

Hazelton, Lesley. "Doris Lessing on Feminism, Communism and Space Fiction." *New York Times*, July 25, 1982. http://www.newyorktimes.com.

Hochschild, Arlie Russell. "The Woman with the Flying Hair." *St. Petersburg Times*, April 7, 1991, sec D.

Jones, Malcolm. "Baby Boomers and Their Books: A Love Affair with Literature." *Newsweek*, March 18, 2007. http://www.newsweek.com/baby-boomers-and -books-love-affair-literature-95719.

Jong, Erica. *Fear of Flying*. New York: Holt, Rinehart and Winston, 1973.

Kort, Michele. "Catching up on Feminist Theory, 1: bell hooks." *Ms. Blog Magazine*. Last modified on September 12, 2010. http://msmagazine.com/blog/2010/ 09/12/catching-up-on-feminist-theory-1-bell-hooks/.

Langer, Elinor. "Whatever Happened to Feminist Fiction?" *New York Times Book Review*, March 4, 1984: 35–36.

Laurence, Margaret. *The Diviners*. New York: Knopf, 1974.

Lessing, Doris. *The Four Gated City*. New York: Knopf, 1969.

Lessing, Doris. *The Golden Notebook*. London: Michael Joseph, 1974.

Magill, Frank, ed. *Masterpieces of Women's Literature*. New York: Harper Collins, 1996.

Millet, Kate. *Sexual Politics*. New York: Ballantine, 1970.

Montgomery, Lucy Maud. *Anne of Green Gables*. Peterborough, ON: Broadview Press, (2004) [1908].

Munro, Alice. *The Beggar Maid: Stories of Flo and Rose*. New York: Knopf, 1979.

O'Neill, Nena, and George O'Neill. *Open Marriage: A New Lifestyle for Couples*. New York: M. Evans, 1972.

Pace, Eric. "New Book Crop is Full of Novels." *New York Times*, September 5, 1972. http://newyorktimes.com/.

Piercy, Marge. *Small Changes*. New York: Doubleday, 1973.

Poirot, Kristan. "Mediating a Movement, Authorizing Discourse: Kate Millet, *Sexual Politics*, and Feminism's Second Wave." *Women's Studies in Communication* 27, no. 2 (2004): 204–235.

Poirot, Kristan. "Domesticating the Liberation Woman: Containment Rhetorics of Second Wave Radical/Lesbian Feminism." *Women's Studies in Communication* 32, no. 3 (2009): 263–291.

Rose, Phyllis. *The Penguin Book of Women's Lives*. New York: Vintage Books, 1993.

Sarton, May. *Journal of a Solitude*. New York: Norton, 1973.

Shulman, Alix Kates. *Burning Questions*. New York: Knopf, 1978.

van Dijck, José. "Record and Hold: Popular Music between Personal and Collective Memory." *Critical Studies in Media Communication* 23, no. 5 (2006) 357–374.

Walker, Alice. "In Search of Zora Neale Hurston." *Ms.*, March 3, 1975, 74–79, 85–89.

Woolf, Virginia. *A Room of One's Own*. New York: Harcourt Brace & Co., 1989.

19

"After *Life*, the Magazine, the Splintering of the Categories: Boomers as a Target Audience" (including "Mau-Mau-ing the Press: The Rise of 'New' Journalism," "*Rolling Stone*: The Magazine That Marked a Generation," and "Tom Wolfe, Gay Talese, and the 'New Journalism' as Literature")

Brian Cogan

This chapter addresses the quantum shift in the magazine (and to a lesser extent book) industry in the 1960s that occurred largely as a result of the introduction of television and how a new form of journalism replaced the need for the photojournalism of such magazines as *Life* and *Look* and their digested version of the news for people who tended not to read newspapers regularly. As television brought in a new form of journalism, one that ultimately valued entertainment over traditional reporting, the nature of magazine journalism gradually adapted to the new visual-based environment of televised journalism by reinventing itself into something new, a new form of storytelling that mimicked, in some ways, the dramatic effects of television and film. The chapter also examines as cultural touchstones the genres of feature writing (including Hunter S. Thompson's gonzo journalism and the New Journalism movement) that came to prominence in the magazines of the 1960s—particularly in that quintessential boomer magazine, *Rolling Stone*.

Although the term "New Journalism" (capitalized herein when referring specifically to the movement as opposed to a catch-all for any kind of updated news reporting) indicates a radical shift from what came before, in reality the New Journalism took its cue not only from the rapid ascent of television as the principal mode of visual journalism (*Life*, perhaps the premier

photojournalism magazine of its time, seemed rather stodgy in comparison
to televised news, especially after the advent of color, and eventually ceased
publication as a weekly in 1972) but also from a new, almost documentary
approach to news filled with well-drawn versions of real people, where vivid
movie-like scenes dominated profiles and the author of the piece frequently
occurred as a character.

In the early 1960s a new kind of journalist was emerging, one who
tackled not just long-form pieces in general but who, inspired by the Beat
generation and the muckrakers of yore, also wanted to find a new way
of writing, and one who could still tell a news story, but a new kind of
news story, one that was conceptually structured more toward the form of
a novel or television script than was accepted in journalistic circles at the
time. In the early sixties, writers such as Hunter S. Thompson, Gay Talese,
Jimmy Breslin, and especially Tom Wolfe, were soon seen as the vanguard
of this new kind of journalism. Wolfe in particular was soon seen as the
face of New Journalism when he took some of his long-form pieces and
published them in book form as *The Kandy-Kolored Tangerine-Flake Streamline Baby* in 1965. These long-form pieces, many of them originally published in *Esquire*, took their title from the more cumbersome original title
of one of Wolfe's pieces (on custom cars) in 1963, "There Goes (Varoom!
Varoom!) That Kandy-Kolored (Thphhhhhh!) Tangerine-Flake Streamline
Baby (Rahghhh!) Around the Bend (Brummmmmmmmmmmmmmmm)
. . ." This new stylistic mash-up that favored stream of consciousness as
well as dramatic changes in punctuation and style (often within the same
paragraph) was startling to many, who simply could not understand how
Wolfe's work could be considered traditional journalism. Wolfe described
what he was attempting as follows:

> It was a garage sale, that piece . . . vignettes, odds and ends of scholar-
> ship, bits of memoirs, short bursts of sociology, apostrophes, epithets,
> moans, cackles, anything that came into my head, much of it thrown
> together in a rough and awkward way. Its virtue was precisely in show-
> ing me the possibility of there being something "new" in journalism.
> What interested me was not simply the discovery that it was possible
> to write accurate non-fiction with techniques usually associated with
> novels and short stories. It was that plus. It was the discovery that it was
> possible in non-fiction, in journalism, to use any literary device, from
> the traditional dialogisms of the essay to stream-of-consciousness, and
> to use many different kinds simultaneously, or within a relatively short
> space . . . to excite the reader both intellectually and emotionally. I
> am not laying all those gladiolas on that rather curious first article of
> mine, you understand. I'm only talking about what it suggested to me.
> (Wolfe 1972)

Many who analyzed Wolfe's New Journalism, such as Robert Boynton (2005), thought that it "was a truly avant garde movement that expanded journalism's rhetorical and literary scope by placing the author at the center of the story, channeling a character's thoughts, using nonstandard punctuation and exploding traditional narrative forms." In his view the New Journalism was more akin to the script of a movie than a traditional news piece, as it proceeds "scene by scene, much as in a movie; incorporates varying points of view rather than telling a story solely from the perspective of the narrator; and pays close attention to status details about the appearance and behavior of its characters" (Boynton 2005).

However, the historiography behind any literary or journalistic movement is always contentious, and in a public literary scuffle in the pages of the *Chronicle of Higher Education*, Boynton took pains to point out that Wolfe (and Talese and others) had not invented the New Journalism but had merely revived an important tendency sometimes forgotten in American journalism history. In a *New York Times* summary of the feud, Kathleen Q. Seelye (2005) noted, "The real primogenitors of these writers, Mr. Boynton suggested, were muckrakers like Lincoln Steffens and Jacob Riis." Although earlier journalists had stretched the boundaries of journalistic practice, many of the New Journalists in the 1960s thought the movement was an indicator of a specific time and place where the emerging counterculture led to more freedom for creative long-form journalism. Apparently, Wolfe could not resist firing a shot back across the bow and responded in a letter to the *Chronicle* in which he argued that Boynton was not just wrong but "wildly gibber-gibber ape-shrieking off the wall" (Seelye 2005).

The rejoinder almost read as a parody of vintage Wolfe, but both authors made valid points. Though the New Journalism of the sixties was part and parcel of a new, freer, more experimental style of writing, it did have an ancestry in the muckrakers so beloved by the journalism establishment. As Helen Rounds (2002, 226) put it, "The new journalism of the sixties was sometimes even called 'modern muckraking.'" She also noted how the New Journalism reporter "focused on uncovering corruption and establishment ills in much the same manner as the muckrakers of the progressive era had done" (226) albeit in a new, hipper more free-form style than the writings of Riis and Upton Sinclair. Not all critics were pleased with the new stylistic freedom, and one of the more eminent critics of low and high culture, Dwight MacDonald, wrote about the New Journalism in highly critical terms, noting, "It is a bastard form, having it both ways, exploiting the factual authority of journalism and the atmospheric license of fiction. Entertainment rather than information is the aim of its producers, and the hopes of its consumers" (1974, 223).

Most of the practitioners of the New Journalism were quite aware of what they were doing, however, and argued that they were not debasing journalism but saving it from becoming calcified and stagnant. Gay Talese, one of the earliest writers to adopt the style, defended the New Journalism by noting that "the new journalism, though often reading like fiction is not fiction. It is, or should be, as reliable as the most reliable reportage, although it seeks a larger truth than is possible through the mere compilation of verifiable facts, the use of direct quotations and adherence to the rigid organizational style of the older form" (1974, 35).

Many in the establishment were not as quick to catch on to what was swiftly becoming a trend, especially in magazine-based journalism. The *New York Times* does not seem to have paid any attention to the movement until the late sixties, when the first reference appeared in a book review of *Black Is Best: The Riddle of Cassius Clay*. In the review, Robert Daley (1967) notes that there is "a new literary form abroad in the land . . . [and] at its best, it hits the reader with great emotional impact, producing a feeling of awe and the desire to reflect for some time . . . the object of the new journalism is to expose the soul of its subject, and sometimes of its author as well."

One of the founders of the New Journalism was James G. Bellows, who in 1963 helped found a Sunday supplement of the *New York Herald Tribune*, which eventually evolved into *New York* magazine. Nikki Weingartner (2009), in her obituary of Bellows hailed him as "promoting a style that was emotional and truthful." As Weingartner (2009) explains, the four main ideas behind New Journalism were "telling the story using scenes rather than historical narrative as much as possible. Dialogue in full (conversational speech rather than quotations and statements), third person person-point-of-view (present every scene through the eyes of a particular character [and] . . . [r]ecording everyday details such as behavior, possessions, friends and family (which indicate the 'status life' of the character)."

Naturally, in an age when many reporters relied on their notebooks and steno prowess as opposed to a digital tape recorder (although many did use tape recorders), it was easy to question whether the journalists (as Tom Wolfe might have written) "weren't . . . maybe, *making it all up? Or* . . . at least *some* of it?" Although most journalists insisted that what they put in their articles were verbatim reconstructions of real events, others defended the practice as not *literally* journalism per se, but as *literary* journalism.

Wolfe (1972) also saw the potential in the New Journalism for something above and beyond the usual stylistic conventions, noting that "if a new literary style could originate in journalism, then it stood to reason that journalism could aspire to more than mere emulation of those aging giants, the novelists." The New Journalism would not just be journalism; it would take the place of the novel. But novels were not journalism and vice versa. Or were they? Herbert Altschull quoted underground journalist Ray Mungo as defending the liberties taken by New Journalists by saying "facts are less important than truth and the two are far from equivalent . . . for cold facts are nearly always boring and may even distort the truth, but Truth is the highest achievement of human expression" (1984, 203). In creating a new form, the New Journalists were perhaps creating a new way of looking at the function of journalism where tone and style were even more important than checking to see if the published quote was exact or embellished.

No New Journalism writer was better than Marshall McLuhan advocate Tom Wolfe in acknowledging the importance of the medium *and* the message. Wolfe, in his attempt to mimic the complexity of everyday speech, took great pains to put the reader into the emotional heart of the story. In his famous essay "Radical Chic? That Party at Lenny's" Wolfe famously detailed the contradictory scene of a representative, Don Cox of the Black Panther Party, being invited to speak to the hoi polloi of New York City's upper classes at a meeting/dinner party in the luxury apartment of composer and conductor Leonard Bernstein. Wolfe, the unseen reporter narrates how a hushed, mostly older and monochromatic crowd watched the performance of Cox in seeming awe. Wolfe details Cox regaling the crowd with Panther platitudes: "'Right on,' says Cox, softly, raising his left fist a bit, but only as a fraternal gesture—and through every white cortex rushes the flash about how the world here is divided between those that rate that acknowledgment—Right on—and those who don't . . . Right on" (Wolfe 1999, 50). Wolfe, by encapsulating verbatim dialogue and intuiting the internal monologues of the upper-class liberal intelligentsia, juxtaposes revolutionary fervor against banal platitude and creates a compelling scene that figures as a meta-commentary on racial issues. In his article "Mau-Mauing the Flak Catchers," Wolfe (1999) further delves into the racial divide in America, this time going to community organizers on the street as opposed to performances in the penthouses. Wolfe describes how the community organizers use their government contacts' guilt as a bargaining chip, noting, "The word *mau-mauing* was a source of amusement in private. The term mau-mauing said, 'the white man has a voodoo fear of us, because deep down he still thinks we're savages. Right? So, we're going to do that Savage number for him.' It was like a practical joke at the expense of the white man's superstitiousness" (1999, 107). Wolfe's innate sense of style and interclass examination of issues of guilt and performance were a highlight of the New Journalistic style. Wolfe (1972) never apologized for the liberties he took in the name of retaining readers: "I never felt the slightest hesitation about trying any device that might conceivably grab the reader a few seconds longer. I tried to yell right in his ear: *Stick around!* . . . Sunday supplements were no place for diffident souls. That was how I started playing around with the device of point-of-view." Where Wolfe went, others either followed or found out, as in the case of Talese, Thompson, and even Jimmy Breslin, that they were already working in similar directions. These writer's stories might go on for more than 15,000–20,000 words and many became books after they were originally serialized in magazines such as *Esquire* and eventually *Rolling Stone*. The writing was fast and nontraditional, and for the first time gave more than a voice to the people being profiled; it gave them a human dimension absent from journalism up until this point. Wolfe took great pains to describe how the New Journalism was more humanistic in many ways then traditional journalism:

> It was more intense, more detailed, and certainly more time-consuming then anything that newspaper or magazine reporters, including investigative reporters, were accustomed to. We developed the habit of staying with the people we were writing about for days at a time, weeks in some cases. We had to gather all the material the conventional journalist was after and then keep going. It seemed all-important to *be there* when dramatic scenes took place, to get the dialogue, the gestures, the facial expressions, the details of the environment. The idea was to give the full objective description, plus something that readers had always had to go to novels and short stories for: namely, the subjective or emotional life of the characters. (Wolfe 1972)

This does not mean, however, that all could engage in New Journalism successfully, and many just did bad imitations of Talese, Wolfe, Breslin, and others. The style was easily parodied, and soon many major newspapers and mainstream media decided to shy away from the more excessive version of the New Journalism. Also, the stylistic quirks and affectations that made New Journalism so startling at first were seen as old hat after a few decades, and "by the late eighties, the consensus was that the New Journalism was dead" (Boynton 2005). But if the New Journalism was dead by the eighties, apparently no one had informed an upstart music magazine started in San Francisco in the late sixties. For *Rolling Stone*, the gonzo ride was to define the magazine for most of its history.

THE NEW ROCK AND ROLL JOURNALISM

Modern rock criticism especially owes a debt to the New Journalism, especially such noted rock critics as Robert Christgau and Gary Willis. Alternative weekly magazines such as the *Village Voice* had given their writers more freedom to do serious rock and roll criticism, and the emergence of the New Journalism soon solidified rock criticism as a valid genre of music criticism. As Devon Powers noted in her book *Writing the Record, the Village Voice and the Birth of Rock Criticism*, "the challenge Wolfe waged against journalistic convention also inspired Willis and Christgau, as well as other young intellectuals, many of whom were located in New York" (2013, 62).

This was evident as early as the first issue of *Rolling Stone* magazine. In a retrospective piece on the founding of *Rolling Stone* in 1967, Andy Greene (2010) noted that in the first issue Wenner had written, "You're probably wondering what we're trying to do. It's hard to say: sort of a magazine and sort of a newspaper. The name of it is *Rolling Stone*, which comes from the old saying, 'a rolling stone gathers no moss.' Muddy Waters used the name for a song he wrote; the Rolling Stones took their name from Muddy's song, and 'Like a rolling stone' was the title of Bob Dylan's first rock and roll record." This could be taken to mean that, like the magazine itself, there was no clear agenda other than covering the music of the counterculture. But it could also be taken to mean that, like the generation *Rolling Stone* sought to cover, meaning was permeable and the new magazine would not hew to the standards of old-fashioned journalism but instead would seek out writers who wrote in their own style. Many of the finest writers of the New Journalism movement, including Hunter S. Thompson, Lester Bangs, Cameron Crowe, and Greil Marcus, to name but a few, were already working to change the way in which rock music was covered in print.

To understand just how important *Rolling Stone* (and other early rock magazines such as *Crawdaddy*) were, one has to realize that while underground newspapers were featuring cutting-edge rock criticism, and mainstream magazines were publishing groundbreaking pieces of long-form New Journalism, no one source was covering both on a regular basis. As David Weir (1999) wrote, "the idea was unique for its time: Instead of the puff pieces expected from a trade magazine, *Rolling Stone* would cover rock and roll for what it was, the most powerful cultural and political force in a time of wide-spread social tumult" largely because the ever prescient Wenner "recognized that a new social order was forming with music as its binding energy."

The sheer newness of *Rolling Stone* was its brilliance and the idea that in the then-stodgy magazine world one could take rock and roll (considered by many to be a trivial subject) and display for the world that it epitomized the new zeitgeist of youth culture. And in recognizing this zeitgeist, they also realized that they needed journalists who could write in a style that was acceptable to a younger, brasher audience, one that was more than aware of how chemical excess could add new meaning to long-form journalism. Early on, *Rolling Stone* sought out New Journalism writers; in particular, they welcomed to their fold perhaps the most brilliantly unhinged of all the New Journalists, Hunter S. Thompson. Thompson, who was "discovered" after years of writing when his pieces on the Hells Angels were first serialized in *The Nation*, quickly capitalized on the success of the articles to follow the Angels for another year, completing a landmark work of New Journalism that gained him the grudging respect of the literary world. However, Thompson's propensity for drugs and alcohol, and his own outsized legend, made him difficult to work with. As Robert Draper wrote,

"Some assignments worked out; many did not. Editors who enjoyed reading *Hells Angels* were nonetheless unprepared for the writer's hell-bent, semi-hysterical methods" (1990, 162). A rambling, but compelling piece about the Kentucky Derby that followed in *Scanlon's Monthly* was well received, giving credence to Thompson's new style. According to Draper, "The story was labeled 'real gonzo' by fellow writer Bill Cardoso and a new form—Gonzo Journalism—was thus brought yowling into the world" (1990, 163). Writers such as Thompson found their voice at *Rolling Stone* "simply because Jann gave them freedom to do so. Obscene language was allowed; a vicious snubbing or objectivity was encouraged" (Draper 1990,178).

Thompson, and his penchant for finding a story where no such story existed, particularly excited editor-in-chief Jann Wenner. Thompson, like Wolfe, thrust himself into the middle of the story and often into the middle of Middle America, or wherever he saw fit to report about. In one of his most famous long-form pieces for *Rolling Stone* that eventually became an acclaimed book, *Fear and Loathing in Las Vegas*, Thompson "cloaked real events in a mythic realm where the verisimilitude of journalism encounters the juiced-up rhetorical style that had become his trademark. It was journalism as bricolage: he moved around freely in time and space moving from internal acid monologues to brittle cosmic scenes, contrasting the high times in San Francisco to the gold lamé depravity of Vegas, always searching in vain for the American dream" (Weingarten 2005, 234).

Thompson had come upon this style after years of experimentation, and despite what some critics thought, it was not merely a chemically induced trance that led to his peculiar, gonzo style of journalism. In a letter to Tom Wolfe, Thompson wrote about his intention to use the "mind-warp photo technique of instant journalism; one draft, written on the spot at high speed and basically unrevised, edited, chopped, larded etc. for publication" (Weingarten 2005, 236). Thompson churned out brilliant, difficult and challenging pieces for most of the sixties and seventies, until gradually declining and repeating himself in his later years. This accusation was also leveled not just at individual journalists but also at the New Journalism itself, and many wondered if the style had legs. As Marc Weingarten noted, "It got ugly in the 1970s for New Journalism, hastened by the decline of general interest magazines" as well as the increased public reliance on television for information that "tuned celebrity culture into a growth industry" (2005, 276). *Rolling Stone* managed to keep running brilliant long-form stories during this period, but many noticed a general trend away from long-form, hard-hitting pieces and wondered how long the magazine could maintain their audience without adapting to the times.

By the early nineties, many complained that *Rolling Stone* was as contradictory and as apparently apathetic as many in the aging baby boomer demographic. Readership surveys showed the *Rolling Stone* research team that their aging ex-hippie readers had not only drifted away from their previous revolutionary commitments but also "were less involved in community and civic affairs than their parents had been" (Draper 1990, 353). At the same time that, during the nineties and into the next decade, *Rolling Stone* seemed to be publishing more puff pieces and less long-form investigative or New Journalism–influenced pieces, the audience for those pieces seemed to be dwindling as well. As Draper points out somewhat cynically in his (Wenner approved) exposé on *Rolling Stone*, "Jann Wenner understood. Like the vast majority of his generation he neither went to Woodstock nor marched in political rallies" and at the same time that it seemed as though most of the boomers were turning toward materialism rather than activism, *Rolling Stone* was right there with them, aging with style, if not with grace. As Draper notes, "Beliefs could be interesting for a time. They could also get very dull; and if you were Jann Weinner, you moved past your dull beliefs like a feature article that rambled on too long" (1990, 353).

This seems somewhat ironic, as in the very first issue of *Rolling Stone*, Wenner had optimistically declared, "*Rolling Stone's* not just about music, but also about the things and attitudes that the music embraces . . . To describe it any further would be difficult without sounding like Bullshit, and bullshit is like gathering moss." (Please insert your own joke here about *Rolling Stone* gathering no moss before proceeding to the next paragraph.)

The fact that *Rolling Stone* came of age as the New Journalism was becoming more and more the norm demonstrates that, to paraphrase McLuhan, not only was the message ready but the medium was as well. In fact, the freedom *Rolling Stone* allowed its writers and editors led to a new way of writing, not just about rock and culture, and it changed what a magazine was supposed to look like and what it was supposed to cover. To David Weir, *Rolling Stone* was not just an experiment in taking youth culture seriously, but it was a platform for creating a new kind of media. Because most of the *Rolling Stone* editorial staff had good intentions but little experience in the gritty day-to-day business of actually putting out a magazine, Weir (writing in 1999, when the term "new media" was still evolving) compared *Rolling Stone* to computer entrepreneurs, stating that "just like today's web pioneers, this was a new generation creating new media—if we'd had to fit in with what already existed, we wouldn't have been there."

But to say that the New Journalism and *Rolling Stone* are irrelevant is perhaps writing their epitaph too quickly. In June 2010, *Rolling Stone* published a long piece by Michael Hastings on his time embedded with General Stanley McChrystal; the interview captured the general and his staff in a relaxed tipsy state, and the article and its blunt revelations about McChrystal's feelings about his superiors, particularly in the Oval Office, led to McChrystal's being removed from command, an almost unprecedented reaction to a modern magazine article.

The story was almost a fluke because of the fact that the reporter, Michael Hastings, had unprecedented access to McChrystal and his senior staff as they were stuck in Paris during the Icelandic volcano eruption in 2010. As Jon Boone (2010) noted in the *Guardian*, "It was there that the journalist got some of his most explosive material, including McChrystal's anger at having to glad-hand French officialdom and an account of the four star general getting drunk on Bud Light Lime with his men." In the end, it is a strong argument for the continuing relevance of *Rolling Stone* as a source of top-shelf investigative journalism. Although the article may have been more staid than articles by Wolfe or Thompson, it did indicate that an almost movie-like long-form article in which the author is character could still have a genuine impact.

Today, some of the books based on the New Journalism seem almost quaint, a period piece of the sixties excesses in verbiage. The best of them still stand out as masterpieces of literary-style reporting, though, and much of the basic strategy still lingers in the writing of some contemporary journalists. Not only are aspects of the New Journalism accepted as standard parts of modern journalism but the phraseology Wolfe and others developed also lingers in the lexicon to this day. Even conservative columnist Charles Krauthammer (2014) recently used the phrase "radical chic" in describing organizations joining the anti-Israel academic boycotts in 2013.

It could also be argued that long-form journalism is thriving as it has not in a few decades. New versions of the New Journalism, such as Eric Schlosser's *Fast Food Nation* (2001) and Jon Krakauer's *Under the Banner of Heaven* (2003), or even some of the more straightforward work of the late David Foster Wallace, such as *A Supposedly Fun Thing I'll Never do Again* (1997), have the exploratory and visual storytelling aspects of the New Journalism down pat and are certainly groundbreaking in terms of their impact. As Boynton (2005) points out, with the popularity and enduring power of those works, "the New New journalists have revived the tradition of American literary journalism, raising it to a more popular and commercial level than either its 19th- or late 20th-century predecessors ever imagined."

In retrospect, the New Journalism may or may not have been the genesis of something totally brand new, a continuation of the great muckraking tradition, or a combination of both. However, its impact was felt across the landscape starting in the sixties and reverberates to this day. Perhaps it's best to let Tom Wolfe have the last word though: "I have no idea who coined the term the New Journalism or when it was coined. I have never even liked the term. Any movement, group, party, program, philosophy or theory that goes under a name with "new" in it is just begging for trouble, of course. But it is the term that eventually caught on. At the time, the mid-1960s, one was aware that there was some kind of new *artistic* excitement in journalism" (Wolfe 1972).

REFERENCES

Altschull, J. Herbert. 1984. *Agents of Power: The Role of the News Media in Human Affairs*. New York: Longman.

Boone, Jon. 2010. "*Rolling Stone* Man Who Brought Down Stanley McChrystal." *The Guardian*. June 24. http://theguardian.comworld/2010/jun/24/michael-hastings-general.

Boynton, Robert. 2005. "The Roots of the New New Journalism." *Chronicle of Higher Education*. March 4. http://robertboynton.com/articledDisplay.php?article_id=1515.

Daley, Robert. 1967. "Feats of Clay." *New York Times*, February 19. http://query.nytimes.com/mem/archive/pdf?res=F40714F73A58107B93CBA81789D85F438685F9.

Draper, Robert. 1990. *Rolling Stone Magazine: The Uncensored Story*. New York: Doubleday.

Greene, Andy. 2010. "Rolling Stone's First Issue: An Anniversary Flashback." *Rolling Stone*. November 11. http://rollingstone.com/music/news/rolling-stones-first-issue.

Krauthammer, Charles. 2014. "How to Fight Academic Bigotry." *Washington Post*. January 9. http://www.washingtonpost.com/opinions/Krauthammer.

MacDonald, Dwight. 1974. "Parajournalism, or Tom Wolfe and His Magic Writing Machine." In *The Reporters as Artist: A Look at the New Journalism Controversy*, edited by Rand Weber, 223–233. New York: Communication Arts Books.

Powers, Devon. 2013. *Writing the Record: The Village Voice and the Birth of Rock Criticism*. Amherst: University of Massachusetts Press.

Rounds, Helen. 2002. "Reform Journalism, Exposés and Crusading." In *American Journalism: History, Principles, Practices*, edited by David W. Sloan, Ed Mulliken, and Lisa Parcell, 209–228. Jefferson, NC: McFarland & Co.

Seelye, Katherine Q. 2005. "A Stylist and a Professor Clash on Who Invented New Journalism." *New York Times*. May 16. http://www.nytimes.com/2005/05/16/business/16wole.html.

Talese, Gay. 1974. "Authors Note to Fame and Obscurity." In *The Reporters as Artist: A Look at the New Journalism Controversy*, edited by Rand Weber, 35–38. New York: Communication Arts Books,.

Weingarten, Marc. 2005. *Who's Afraid of Tom Wolfe?* London: Aurum.

Weingartner, Nikki. 2009. "New Journalism Movement Promoter Dies at Age 86." *Digital Journal*. March 7. http://www.digitaljournal.com/article/268732.

Weir, David. 1999. "Wenner's World, the Evolution of Jann Wenner: How the Ultimate 60's Rock Groupie Built His Fantasy into a Media Empire." *Salon.com*. April 20. http://www.salon.com/1999/04/20/wenner/.

Wolfe, Tom. 1972. "Tom Wolfe Gives an Eyewitness Report of the Birth of the New Journalism." *New York*. February 14. http://nymag.com/news/media/47353/index10.html.

Wolfe, Tom. 1999. *Radical Chic & Mau-Mauing the Flak Catchers*. New York: Bantam Books.

20

Soul on Ice: The Rise of Minority Literature

Christopher Allen Varlack

In a country where an African American, under the Three-Fifths Compromise, was once considered just three-fifths of a man, the struggle for equality endured by the African American people in the Reconstruction and post-Reconstruction years proved a daily struggle. From the overwhelming fear and agitation rampant in the black community, these days were marked by constant racial tension, stemming in part from the continued dehumanization and mistreatment that blacks faced. The notion of black inferiority that carried across these years thus proved a traveling identity for such figures as Richard Wright, whose perceived social and racial inferiority was foregrounded from the workplace to the streets where he and other blacks faced the constant threat of brutality, every insult and every crushing blow a reminder of the degraded place set aside for blacks. For instance, in his 1940 essay "The Ethics of Living Jim Crow," Wright (2008) recounts:

> Negroes who have lived South know the dread of being caught alone upon the streets in white neighborhoods after the sun has set. In such a simple situation as this the plight of the Negro in America is graphically symbolized. While white strangers may be in these neighborhoods trying to get home, they can pass unmolested. But the color of a Negro's skin makes him easily recognizable, makes him suspect, converts him into a defenseless target. (10)

In these words, Wright expresses the lessons of Jim Crow he was forced to learn as a young child just to survive in a white-dominated society. Taught to always say, "Yes, sir," suppress his ambition, and never rise above his place, Wright "learned to play that dual role which every Negro must play" (13). Wright, however, was not alone in learning what he terms "the ethics of living Jim Crow." The black community at large felt the stinging whip of a different kind of lash in the form of police brutality, inequities in judicial treatment across racial lines, and limited and menial job opportunities—an assortment of new social and political realities that defined the black experience in the land of purported freedom and opportunity.

The stories of such treatment, reported in the speeches and photographs of the era, were soon cemented in the growing body of minority literature—a collection of novels, memoirs, and autobiographies all written to preserve the historical record of the difficult lives African Americans faced. Eldridge Cleaver's 1968 collection of autobiographical and politically charged essays, *Soul on Ice*, is one such text, aimed at responding to the racial tension that developed with the death of the separate-but-equal age. "This controversy," he claims," "awakened me to my position in America and I began to form a concept of what it meant to be black in white America" (Cleaver [1968] 1991, 17). Considered a pivotal work of African American literature, *Soul on Ice* emerges amid the African American struggle for legitimization, equality, and civil rights, offering a necessary glimpse into this time of sociocultural change throughout the United States when the physical and psychological realities of the black experience were in constant flux.

"WE SHALL HAVE OUR MANHOOD": *SOUL ON ICE* AND THE HUNDRED-YEAR STRUGGLE TO GAIN RECOGNITION OF AFRICAN AMERICAN HUMANITY

Through the landmark 1896 *Plessy v. Ferguson* decision, the United States Supreme Court upheld the constitutionality of state laws regarding the doctrine known as "separate but equal"—a ruling that remained the legal and social standard for 58 years. During this time, the Jim Crow culture that Wright experienced eventually became a widespread "way of life, a culture, a code of everyday behavior, a mode of experience, a set of mind for whites as well as blacks" (Dailey 2009, xiii). From the separate schools and public institutions to the multiplicity of unspoken social codes that saw blacks summarily punished for stepping beyond their "place," life in the United States was dictated by what William Edward Burghardt Du Bois has termed the "color line"—the presence of privilege or restriction solely dependent on one's race. This color line was therefore based on a tradition of exclusion: "exclusion from voting booths; from juries; from neighborhoods; from unions and management positions; from higher education; from professions; from hospitals and theaters and hotels," the consequence of which was an African American experience marked by considerable repression—the once vibrant, passionate Negro soul put on ice (Dailey 2009, xiv).

As a result, before the 1950s and the rise of the boomer generation, Eldridge Cleaver argues that "Negroes found it necessary, in order to maintain whatever sanity they could, to remain somewhat aloof and detached from 'the problem'" ([1968] 1991, 17). In the United States, however, that concept of "the problem" was not confined to a single interpretation. For many in the Jim Crow age, the Negro himself was at the heart of the debate, his very presence in American society sparking social and political controversy while intensifying racial tension, at times even hatred, among those who believed the Negro problem threatened their way of life. For others, "the problem" was just that sort of mentality itself—the hesitation to embrace social change in order to preserve an outmoded racial hierarchy never abandoned from the days of slavery. Under this interpretation, the Jim Crow culture became just a combination of social codes and legislation designed "to secure a political and economic order that depended on the disenfranchisement and disempowerment" of blacks (Dailey 2009, xv).

The immediate response that Cleaver embraces is to turn "from America with horror, disgust, and outrage," refusing to remain aloof any longer ([1968] 1991, 17). Discontent with the overall mistreatment of blacks and the unequal partitioning of opportunities to achieve that coveted American dream, he refuses to maintain the image of complacency he perceives as problematic in American society. Here Cleaver writes that "[he] attacked all forms of piety, loyalty, and sentiment: marriage, love, God, patriotism, the Constitution, the founding fathers, law, concepts of right-wrong-good-evil, all forms of ritualized and conventional behavior" (1991, 19). From his point of view, those conventional behaviors and the social norms/expectations upon which they were based were intended to preserve that existing racial order, to strip him of a manhood habitually denied to blacks, and to consistently put his race on ice. For Cleaver, the African American people had been wearing "the mask that grins and lies / [that] hides our cheeks and shades our eyes" for far too long and, as a result, the reality of an African American identity had largely faded away (Dunbar 1997, 1–2).

This is the fundamental flaw that authors such as LeRoi Jones identify in American society and subsequently African American literature at large—their failure to challenge the monologism of American cultural conversation by only expressing the black experience in terms established by the middle class. In his 1966 critical essay, "The Myth of a 'Negro Literature,'" Jones contends that

> Negro reaction to America is as deep a part of America as the root causes of that reaction, and it is impossible to accurately describe that reaction in terms of the American middle class, because for them, the Negro has never really existed, never been glimpsed in anything even approaching the complete reality of his humanity. (Jones 1994, 170)

Instead, the African American was habitually cast in stereotype: the servant or slave, characters such as Zip Coon or Sambo straight from the minstrel stage. In order to develop an authentic and legitimate body of African American literature, black authors, according to Jones, needed to move beyond those limited terms and challenge that consistent denial of African American humanity. In other words, "The Negro writer has to go from where he actually is, completely outside of that conscious white myopia" (Jones 1994, 170).

Soul on Ice, at the core, attempts to achieve this fundamental goal that Jones puts forth, seeking to escape what Cleaver perceives as a master/slave dichotomy in American culture. He first does this by "stepp[ing] outside of the white man's law, which [he] repudiated with scorn and self-satisfaction. [He] became a law unto [him]self" ([1968] 1991, 25). Though physically imprisoned, Cleaver asserts his refusal to remain in the mental and cultural chains crafted for him by American society. By challenging the "white man's law"—a system of rules and values in which the African American people had little to no representation in developing, he seeks to break those chains and assert his freedom. For Cleaver, this perspective is ultimately part of a larger trend. In Soledad State Prison, for instance, black inmates stripped off the grinning, lying masks of their ancestors and instead cursed American culture itself, just as millions of black Americans outside these prison walls were finally coming awake. Here Cleaver observes:

> All respect we may have had for politicians, preachers, lawyers, governors, Presidents, senators, congressmen was utterly destroyed as we watched them temporizing and compromising over right and wrong, over legality and illegality, over constitutionality and unconstitutionality. We knew that in the end what they were clashing over was us, what to do with the blacks, and whether or not to start treating us as human beings. ([1968] 1991, 18)

Through these words, Cleaver reveals the mounting frustration that he experiences from the social and political stagnation of American society. The indignation that reverberates in such passages of *Soul on Ice*—part memoir, part manifesto—is one of the principal reasons why this collection is often heralded as "an authentic voice of black rage in a white-ruled world" where such anger, at least at the time when Cleaver was writing, proves transformative—an extension of the larger struggle for minority rights (Kifner 1998). What Cleaver also acknowledges, however, is his position outside of the white myopia, forging his own distinct existence separate from the terms established by the white middle class.

His later decision to rape white women—a choice that earned him his cell in Folsom State Prison and Quentin State Prison from 1958 to 1966—is what he terms "an insurrectionary act" against those same standards (Cleaver [1968] 1991, 26). Though these scenes are the primary bones of contention in the early criticism of this work (along with his homophobic treatment of James Baldwin), what Cleaver ultimately reveals is a developing trend toward defiance of those crippling social limitations and soon-to-be archaic social norms—a defiance characteristic of minority literature of the mid- to late 1900s. Here Cleaver declares, "It delighted me that I was defying and trampling upon the white man's law, upon his system of values"—the same system of values that institutionalized his dehumanization ([1968] 1991, 26). By raping white women, he sought to regain a sense of power denied him under the existing racial hierarchy while also challenging the undergirding notions of white supremacy and complacency prevalent in American society.

The structure that Cleaver uses in these early passages is particularly important to understanding the rise and development of minority literature. Here Cleaver engages what Gilles Deleuze and Felix Guattari consider one of the most significant aspects of this emerging literary tradition: its "cramped space forces each individual intrigue to connect immediately to politics" (2007, 1778). Under this critical lens, the physical act of rape that Cleaver recounts is less important, though he does later acknowledge that these acts emerge from self-hatred—a realization that directly plays into the spiritual and ideological rebirth he expresses in "On Becoming." Instead, what must be emphasized, as Jones, Deleuze, and Guattari seem to agree, is the related political inquiry that Cleaver offers through those scenes, similar to the social and cultural critique also presented in works by such figures as Malcolm X. These early passages demonstrate Cleaver's commitment to exist outside of terms established by the white, middle-class, and political elite—his commitment to take back his power.

From this example, it is evident that the belles lettres, memoirs, and autobiographies that were authored by African Americans during the boomer generation—works such as Cleaver's *Soul on Ice* or Malcolm X's *The Autobiography of Malcolm X*—are significant in illustrating the struggle of the African American people to obtain acceptance. Together, such works present a resounding message that echoes through every word and every image—a political statement not only directed toward the masses of white Americans trapped in history but also the masses of African American people waiting (often silently) for change. "What the white man must be brought to understand," writes Cleaver, "is that the black man in America today is fully aware of his position, and he does not intend to be tricked again into another hundred-year forfeit of freedom" ([1968] 1991, 118). The tide of social complacency is receding, and in its place is a new wave—a new sense of direction and purpose where the black men arising in America will no longer settle for second-class citizenship, subpar education, or a social code that relegates blacks to the back of the bus. As the literature of the era reveals, the African American people would accept no less than recognition of their humanity, than "their full proportionate share and participation" in American life (Cleaver [1968] 1991, 118).

"NO ONE COULD SAVE ME BUT MYSELF": *SOUL ON ICE* AND THE RECONSTRUCTED IMAGE OF THE BLACK

In this groundbreaking collection of essays, considered to have "had a tremendous impact on an intellectual community radicalized by the civil rights movement, urban riots, the war in Vietnam and campus rebellions," Eldridge Cleaver also steps outside of the myopic white view by present-ing a new standard of beauty—one where black skin does not immediately recall images of the big black Mammy, stripped of sexual allure, or the ingratiating Uncle eager and ready to serve (Kifner 1998). Escaping those prevailing depictions and the history of repression that exists behind them is perhaps the greatest challenge in American society. In his essay "Stranger in the Village," published in 1955, James Baldwin, in response, writes that "people are trapped in history and history is trapped in them" (2012, 167). Overcoming the nightmare of history is, then, the fundamental chal-lenge set for minority literature: to not become burdened by the skewed depictions of a not-so-distant past or the crippling frustration that almost certainly arises when the black community and the degraded black image come face to face.

Cleaver ultimately parallels this notion in *Soul on Ice*, claiming that "a black growing up in America is indoctrinated with the white race's standard of beauty, ... to see the white woman as more beautiful and desirable than [his] own black woman" ([1968] 1991, 23). The result was a trend of rising color consciousness and intraracial color prejudice in the early to mid-1900s, as recounted in such works as George Schuyler's satirical *Black No More* (1931), Wallace Thurman's *The Blacker the Berry*, and Zora Neale Hurston's play *Color Struck* (1925), all works of the ear-lier Harlem Renaissance tradition. In *Soul on Ice*, however, Cleaver seeks to move beyond that internal prejudice and present the black man and black woman as cultural symbols in and of themselves. This characteristic redefinition of long-standing cultural values, after all, is the foundation of the boomer generation's sociocultural critique and the new direction of minority literature at large.

In the final chapter of *Soul on Ice*, titled "To All Black Women, From All Black Men," Cleaver fulfills the expectation of minority literature as Jones defines it. Similar to Baldwin, Jones writes, "If there is ever a Negro litera-ture, it must disengage itself from the weak, heinous elements of the culture that spawned it, and use its very existence as evidence of a more profound America" (1994, 171). In fact, Cleaver devotes much of the chapter to the process of disengagement, calling attention to the history of repression and pervasive stereotypes that African American women once faced in order to move beyond that hindering past. Here he writes:

> In a cowardly stupor, with a palpitating heart and quivering knees, I watched the Slaver's lash of death slash through the opposing air and bite with teeth of fire into your delicate flesh, the black and tender flesh of African Motherhood, forcing the startled Life untimely from your torn and outraged womb, the sacred womb that cradled primal man, the womb that incubated Ethiopia and populated Nubia and gave forth Pharaohs unto Egypt. ([1968] 1991, 190–191)

Cleaver juxtaposes the tragic history of the slave (the master's cracking whip, the deep-set scars dripping with blood) with memories of an illustrious African past (the womb that gave birth to a nation of proud black kings) in order to emphasize what was essentially stolen through slavery, "to recall, that before we could come up from slavery, we had to be pulled down from our throne" (189). Though Cleaver does acknowledge the struggle of the African American people, he does this to disengage the atrocities of the past and, in their place, to foreground the journey upward—the rise of "Queen–Mother–Daughter of Africa" and "Sister of My Soul" (188). In doing so, he replaces the negative images constructed throughout time of the African American woman—images steeped in a tradition of inferiority and servility—with counterimages of her undying strength, more of a soul on fire than a soul on ice.

Later in this same chapter, Cleaver then begins this tedious task of reconstructing the image of the strong black woman as well as the self. For instance, Cleaver writes, "But put on your crown, my Queen, and we will rebuild a New City on these ruins" ([1968] 1991, 192). The revitalized image of the black woman that is presented here is one resurrected from the ruins of slavery and reminiscent of the ancestry in Africa. Once the source of sexual objectification and cultural oppression, she has risen from the ruins of her degraded condition with resilience and strength. As *Soul on Ice* reveals, the direction adopted in minority literature of the boomer generation and beyond is far different from the direction of the preceding years. The plight of the tragic mulatto or the deracinated intellectual once popularized in minority literature is replaced with new images less focused on the African American as a perpetual problem than as a new cultural symbol—a representation of growth and strength.

The redefinition of the image of the black woman, however, is just one component of the larger critique that Cleaver offers in this particular chapter. Equally important is the redefinition of the self—the black man once stripped of his masculinity and castrated by what Cleaver has termed his "impotent silence" ([1968] 1991, 190). Here Cleaver acknowledges the crippling history of the African American man who, for years, listened "to a symphony of sorrows, to your screams for help, anguished pleas of terror that echo still throughout the Universe and through the mind, a million scattered screams across the painful years" (190). Like much of minority literature, these words serve as a veritable mirror to the face of the African American people—a mirror laden with all the distortions built up over the years, from the skewed social perceptions to the equally controversial self-image constructed in the mind. For minority literature, this is just the starting place, however, for these same words hold the promise of a new self-image.

In this regard, Cleaver writes, "I have Returned from the dead. I speak to you now from the Here And Now [though] I have been dead for four hundred years" ([1968] 1991, 188). Similar to his examination of the black woman reimagined, Cleaver uses the tragic past of the African American man as the starting point for his reconstruction. Dead for 400 years, the black man has listened to the suffering of his people, but the focus is neither his "impotent silence" nor the "negated masculinity" that Cleaver perceives (188). The focus instead is on his individual and cultural awakening—that much-awaited return and testament. Cleaver thus filters this chapter through the lens of rebirth. Just as the black woman has risen to build a new city atop the ruins of a torturous past, the black man also rises to life anew, returning to speak where he was once silent, to act where he was once passively waiting for change.

As Joyce Nower (1970) contends, this approach is part of the core spiritual and ideological rebirth that Cleaver offers throughout *Soul on Ice* "based on the understanding that at the seat of human wisdom and compassion is love of the self" (17). For Nower, *Soul on Ice* is therefore "a parable for our times because it is a parable of re-birth from the dehumanizing effects of a racist society" (17). Cleaver and his contemporaries achieve this by turning inward and by reflecting on the politics of race that have shaped life for minorities in the United States. In doing so, they develop a new awareness of self that shatters the skewed image perpetuated in American literature and culture of the past, dating back to works both popular and controversial such as *Swallow Barn, or A Sojourn in the Old Dominion* (1832) by John Pendleton Kennedy and *The Clansman: An Historical Romance of the Ku Klux Klan* (1905) by Thomas Dixon. More importantly, by challenging that inaccurate portrait of minorities and depicting the African American reborn, they essentially mark the true end of the Jim Crow–era disempowered mentality that had plagued African Americans for far too long.

This approach, nonetheless, is not unique to *Soul on Ice*. The image of the black revisited in the belles lettres of the boomer generation is consistent. Black men once castrated (at least in the metaphorical sense) now stand virile at the precipice of change, their souls burning with the passionate fire of a people unwilling to remain suppressed. Embedded within these works is a clear message regarding self-determination—an essential value or principle that Nower (1970) argues the African American needs to develop in order to shed the chains that restrict his humanity. From self-determination "flow diversity, autonomy, personal creativity, a sharpened feeling of brotherhood" all fundamental to the "re-birth of freedom" and the unity of the black community (21). Cleaver develops this self-determination himself; therefore, *Soul on Ice* and the many autobiographies authored by minority authors of his time serve as a message board for black youth under similar circumstances, facing similar oppression, and trying to make sense of the surrounding world.

CONCLUSION

Despites its successes, *Soul on Ice* is criticized at times for what Douglas Taylor (2010) terms a "cultural utopianism" just as flawed as today's "understandings of 'hybridity'" (74). Within *Soul on Ice*, Cleaver does present a heightened sense of the bond between black society and the rising white youth that only finds partial fulfillment off the page. In his 2010 essay, Taylor thus argues: "That white youth were enamored of black culture did not indicate the arrival of the Promised Land. That black people, from 1954–1965, gained a national forum for voicing their grievances over racial segregation in the South did not herald a D'Souzian 'end of racism'" (74–75). While such criticisms are certainly valid, they also miss something valuable about *Soul on Ice* and the lineage of minority literature that it inherently inspires. As Richard Gilman (1969) contends in "White Standards and Negro Writing":

> Black writers make philosophies and fantasias out of their color, use it as weapon and seat of judgment, as strategy and outcry, source of possible rebirth, data for a future existence and agency of revolutionary change. For such men and women, to write is an almost literal means of survival and attack, a means—more radically than we have known it—to *be*. (111)

Minority literature, under this lens, is largely about writing one's own existence—that crucial escape from the chains that have kept its authors enslaved. In the opening chapter of *Soul on Ice*, Cleaver acknowledges that his shattered sense of pride and his diluted sense of self-respect "is why [he] started to write. To save [him]self" and that writing became that indispensable vehicle "to find out who [he is] and what [he] want[s] to be, what type of man [he] should be" ([1968] 1991, 27). The same trend holds true for other works of this bourgeoning tradition. From *The Autobiography of Malcolm X* in 1965 to *Look for Me in the Whirlwind: The Collective Autobiography of the New York 21* in 1971, minority authors tell their own stories, in part giving voice to those once denied the platform to speak, in part correcting the many cultural misrepresentations that, for a long time, became the standard rhetoric of race in American society.

At the same time, minority literature is also about unifying those disaffected masses toward a new vision of society. *Soul on Ice* is at the center of this emerging trend, as it provides valuable insight into the black identity, the conversations of the politics of race, and the direction that minority literature itself must take if black authors are ever to contribute to the realization of the multicultural American dream. Through it, Cleaver helps establish a tradition of black literature whose writers "take their blackness not as a starting point for literature or thought and not as a marshaling ground for a position in the parade of national images and forms, but as absolute theme and necessity" (Gilman 1969, 111). Describing the black experience and the cultural stimuli that have contributed to shaping that experience is thus a core part of the intellectual project that works such as *Soul on Ice* necessarily engage. Connected to a social and political reality, such works are ingrained with a sense of exigency—blackness not just as a form of identity but also as something undeniable and perpetually at stake.

In the end, they are driven to record perspectives on history too often forgotten or ignored, offering critical commentaries in pursuit of active sociopolitical change. These works, always written in the fervent and passionate spirit of its people, serve as notice of their refusal to remain trapped in the cycle of history any longer. And so, in fulfillment of the goal that LeRoi Jones finds largely unfulfilled in literature by African American authors, these works ultimately serve as evidence that the African American has finally found his place at the helm of rebirth and revolutionary change. He has found his seat among leaders and men, activists and policy makers. As a result, "the question of the Negro's place in America, which for a long time could actually be kicked around as a serious question has been decisively resolved," as Cleaver claims. Simply put, "he is here to stay," and that is what minority literature strives to remember (Cleaver [1968] 1991, 110).

REFERENCES

Balagoon, Kuwasi, Joan Bird, Cetewayo, Robert Collier, Dharuba, Richard Harris, Ali Bey Hassan, Jamal, Abayama Katara, Kwando Kinshasa, Baba Odinga, Shaba Ogun Om, Curtis Powell, Afeni Shakur, Lumumba Shakur, and Clark Squire. 1971. *Look for Me in the Whirlwind: The Collective Autobiography of the New York 21*. New York: Random House.

Baldwin, James. (1955) 2012. "Stranger in the Village." In *Notes of a Native Son*. Boston: Beacon.

Cleaver, Eldridge. (1968) 1991. *Soul on Ice*. New York: Dell.

Dailey, Jane. 2009. "Introduction." *The Age of Jim Crow*. New York: Norton, 2009.

Deleuze, Gilles, and Félix Guattari. 2007. "What Is a Minor Literature." In *The Critical Tradition: Classic Texts and Contemporary Trends*, edited by David Richter, 1777–1782. Boston: Bedford/St. Martin's.

Dixon, Thomas. (1905) 1970. *The Clansman: An Historical Romance of the Ku Klux Klan*. Lexington: University of Kentucky Press.

Dunbar, Paul Laurence. 1997. "We Wear the Mask." In *Selected Poems*, edited by Glenn Mott, 17. Mineola, NY: Dover.

Gilman, Richard. 1969. "White Standards and Negro Writing." *Negro American Literature Forum* 3 (4): 111–113.

Hurston, Zora Neale. 2008. *Color Struck*. In *Double-Take: A Revisionist Harlem Renaissance Anthology*, edited by Venetria K. Patton and Maureen Honey, 338–351. New Brunswick, NJ: Rutgers University Press.

Jones, LeRoi. 1994. "The Myth of a 'Negro Literature.'" In *Within the Circle: An Anthology of African American Literary Criticism from the Harlem Renaissance to the Present*, edited by Angelyn Mitchell, 165–171. Durham, NC: Duke University Press.

Kennedy, John Pendleton. (1832) 1977. "The Happy Slaves at Swallow Barn." In *The Minority Presence in American Literature*, edited by Philip Butcher, 259–263. Washington, D.C.: Howard University Press.

Kifner, John. 1998. "Eldridge Cleaver, Black Panther Who Became G.O.P. Conservative, Is Dead at 62." *The New York Times*, May 2.

Nower, Joyce. 1970. "Cleaver's Vision of America and the New White Radical: A Legacy of Malcolm X." *Negro American Literature Forum* 4 (1): 12–21.

Schuyler, George Samuel. (1931) 2011. *Black No More*. Mineola, NY: Dover.

Taylor, Douglas. 2010. "Three Lean Cats in a Hall of Mirrors: James Baldwin, Norman Mailer, and Eldridge Cleaver on Race and Masculinity." *Texas Studies in Literature and Language* 52 (1): 70–101.

Thurman, Wallace. (1929) 2008. *The Blacker the Berry*. Mineola, NY: Dover.

Wright, Richard. 2008. "The Ethics of Living Jim Crow." In *Uncle Tom's Children*. New York: Harper Perennial.

X, Malcolm, and Alex Haley. (1965) 2001. *The Autobiography of Malcolm X*. London: Penguin.

21

The Baby Boom, the Bomb, and Outer Space: Growing Up in a Science Fiction World

Lance Strate

REFLECTIONS OF A BABY BOOMER (AN INTRODUCTION)

I was born well into the baby boom, in 1957, a year in which the United States conducted 30 nuclear weapons tests, the Soviet Union held 16 of their own, and the United Kingdom added eight more. Fifty days before I was born, the International Atomic Energy Agency was established, an organization working in conjunction with the United Nations, dedicated to the prevention of the spread of nuclear weapons and to the peaceful uses of nuclear energy (a notion that at that time went all but unchallenged). It was the atomic age, when children were told to "duck and cover" in the event of a nuclear attack. Growing up in the New York City borough of Queens, I recall that every weekday at noon an air-raid siren would go off—you could set your clocks by it—and of course it was a test, only a test. Most of the apartment buildings in my neighborhood had signs on the outside indicating that they had a fallout shelter, which just meant that they had a basement (my apartment building did not have a basement). In elementary school, in addition to fire drills, we had drills where we lined up in the halls, away from the windows, and drills where we hid underneath our desks, in the event that the attack came with too little notice to get to the hallway (that drill was actually kind of fun).

When I was 10 years old, the 1964 feature film *Fail Safe*, directed by Sidney Lumet, aired on network TV. The story took place before intercontinental ballistic missiles (ICBMs) armed with nuclear warheads were deployed in the United States and Soviet Union, when the main weapon-delivery system was bomber aircraft. An order to drop the bomb on Moscow is accidentally transmitted to a squadron of American bombers, and a fail-safe system prevented them from being recalled before Moscow was obliterated. To prevent an all-out nuclear war, our president orders our own Air Force to destroy

New York City. The movie ends with several scenes of everyday life on city streets, cutting from one motion scene to another, and then back again to the same scenes all in still frames, and then to black. Although this was followed by text assuring the viewer that this could never actually happen, I was thoroughly frightened by this depiction of the destruction of my hometown. For a long time afterward, I had chills whenever a plane flew overhead, even though by then ICBMs had become the delivery system of choice. I remember poring over maps that showed the circle of destruction that would be created if a bomb were dropped on the Empire State Building. If it were an A-bomb, given where we lived in Queens, we would be OK, at least until the fallout came; if it were an H-bomb, not so much.

Like many of my peers, I had nuclear nightmares, but they existed side-by-side with dreams of a more benign nature. Seventeen days after I was born, the Soviet Union rocketed *Sputnik*, the first artificial satellite, into orbit, a feat that many in the United States found both thrilling and terrifying, as it flew over us with impunity, unassailable; this shot heard around the world launched the space race that would culminate with Neil Armstrong setting foot on the moon. This first satellite, or as they referred to it at the time, this first "artificial moon," while doing nothing more than emitting a beeping radio signal at regular intervals, created a ring surrounding the world as it circled the planet, effectively placing the Earth inside an artificial environment, a container of human manufacture, as Marshall McLuhan (1974) observed. He also noted that the orbital loop produced a kind of proscenium arch writ large, and in conjunction with telecommunications technologies, turned the planet into a global stage, and its inhabitants into actors as opposed to mere spectators. More than any astrological phenomenon, the artificial satellite announced that this was the dawning of the age of Aquarius, the New Age associated with the sixties-era youth culture of the baby boomers, and which included new kinds of consciousness and ecological awareness as symbolized by Buckminster Fuller's (1971) famous phrase, "spaceship earth" and McLuhan's (1962, 1974) own "global village" and "global theater."

As much as the dawning of the Aquarian age was a time of change, there was also continuity with the long-standing American belief in progress and technology. Growing up in the sixties, we watched the future unfold on our television sets, as NASA's rocket launches and space missions progressed from the Mercury to the Gemini to the Apollo programs. At the same time, we were exposed to visions of a future that seemed to be just around the corner via programs such as *The Jetsons* (1962–1963), which transplanted contemporary family life into a world of flying cars, moving sidewalks, robot maids, apartments in the clouds, and labor reduced to pushing a button. Like *The Jetsons*, *Lost in Space* (1965–1968) kept the family unit intact as the Robinsons, along with Major West, Dr. Smith, and their faithful robot wandered from a black-and-white world based on fifties B movies in their first season to a universe suddenly shown in living color and dominated by sixties-style camp the following year, encountering a continuing succession of alien beings in their efforts to find their way home. More than anything else, though, it was *Star Trek* (1966–1969) that caught the imagination of my peer group. Almost immediately, the program came to dominate our after-school play (everybody wanting to be Captain Kirk or Mr. Spock), while during school we all were drawing starships in our notebooks (I remember my classmate Yoshi including the caption "starships are everywhere nowadays" with his pictures), and our sixth-grade school play was our own version of a *Star Trek* episode (which our teacher made sure had a suitable emphasis on peaceful conflict resolution and social justice). We knew the series was fictional, but it felt like a reality that was simply not yet manifest, in the same way that we knew summer vacation was not yet here but would arrive eventually.

The future was not only televised, it was also experienced live, for some of us at least, as a taste of things to come could be experienced at the 1964 New York World's Fair, with its monorails, videophones, and computers, not to mention the Hall of Science, the Unisphere and futuristic towers of the New York State Pavilion (featured in Barry Sonenfeld's 1997 science fiction comedy film, *Men in Black*), as well as the "It's a Small World" ride featured at the Pepsi Pavilion, dedicated to UNICEF, and created by Walt Disney (who later moved it to Disneyland and copied it at other Disney theme parks). Perhaps most emblematic of the spirit of the times was the General Electric Pavilion, which included the Carousel of Progress, another attraction created by Disney (and later moved to Disneyland and then the Magic Kingdom), where the theme song ran, "there's a great big beautiful tomorrow, shining at the end of every day." The sense of optimism about the future was pervasive and powerful at that time, and one that we took to be a promise about the world we would live in as adults.

The interaction between imagination and reality was exemplified in 1968, when Stanley Kubrick's brilliant film, *2001: A Space Odyssey* premiered on April 2nd; it featured highly realistic depictions of space travel based on NASA's satellite images and designs for space stations, spacecraft, and other technological advances. Corporations were also present in Kubrick's near-future scenario, where the space station orbiting the earth featured a Howard Johnson's restaurant, a video phone booth operated by Bell Telephone, and passengers arriving via a space plane operated by Pan American World Airways, aka Pan Am. (Optimism about the future has always been a feature of capitalism, and in this instance gave rise to a number of retroactive anachronisms in the film as Pan Am ceased operations in 1991, phone booths were largely displaced by cell phones by the end of the 20th century, and Howard Johnson's dominance of the hospitality industry had begun its steep decline during the seventies.) Nearly nine months after *2001* opened, the astronauts of Apollo 8 became the first human beings to orbit the moon; they toyed with the idea of radioing back to NASA that they had spotted a large black monolith of the sort featured in Kubrick's film on the lunar surface, but decided against making that kind of joke (Clarke 2000). Instead, they read the story of creation from the Book of Genesis as part of a live Christmas Eve television broadcast, the second video transmission from lunar orbit, while transmitting to their audience images of the moon and faraway Earth. Almost immediately after they signed off, Juan Tripple, the founder of Pan Am, announced that his airline would begin to take reservations for the first commercial flight to the moon (another of the leading airlines in the United States, Trans-World Airlines, soon made a similar announcement; TWA, like Pan Am, is no longer in business). I remember being frustrated that I was not able to make a reservation for myself, but took comfort in the expectation that such trips would be commonplace soon enough. What Kubrick showed us was nothing more than a reflection of where we expected to be at the dawn of the 21st century, with a space station in orbit, several permanent moon bases, and commercial space flight.

Peter Thiel, cofounder of PayPal, summed up the disappointment of the baby boom generation with the motto he created for the Founders Fund venture capital firm that he also cofounded: "We wanted flying cars, instead we got 140 characters." (Thiel was born just a few years after the end of the baby boom, in 1967.) The younger generation, born into a world in which new media, the Internet, the Web, and mobile devices, are all taken for granted and seen as second nature, are commonly referred to as "digital natives," in contrast to the "digital immigrants," which include the baby boomers, who have grown up accustomed to now-obsolescent forms of technology (analogical rather than digital) and are now forced to acclimate themselves to the new media environment of the 21st century. But however significant this divide may be, it pales in comparison to the generation gap, as it was called, that separated the baby boomers from the generations that came before, and particularly from what Tom Brokaw dubbed the "greatest generation," the generation that came of age during the Great Depression and World War II. That gap can be attributed to a great many factors, not the least of which was the fact that the baby boomers were the first generation to grow up with television (see McLuhan, 1964, 1969; Meyrowitz, 1985), rendering them television natives and their parents television immigrants. But the baby boomers were also born into a world defined by other new technologies emerging out of World War II, including computers, jets, rockets, and the atomic bomb. McLuhan (1969) was far from the only one to comment on how, in the postwar era, we found ourselves inhabiting a science fiction world, a world in which the future is now, a world characterized by what

Alvin Toffler (1970) referred to as *Future Shock* (see also Postman 1988). I therefore think it would be entirely appropriate to refer to baby boomers as science fiction natives, whereas the older generations were immigrants to this new, science fiction world.

To the immigrants, science fiction was more fantasy than anything else; to us, science fiction was reality, in many ways more real than real, or what Jean Baudrillard (1994) referred to as hyperreal. Science fiction immigrants dismissed the genre as inferior, lacking in the key characteristic associated with elite narrative art, realism, that is, the ability to represent in credible fashion relatively ordinary events and characters living their lives in ways that readers find relatively familiar; this goes hand-in-hand with an emphasis on characterization, on characters that are not all that different from ourselves, more or less mimetic as Northrop Frye (1957) would put it, characters we can relatively easily get to know, identify with, and in the case of 20th-century literature, characters whose consciousness we can inhabit, share, and experience for ourselves. As much as the invention of mimetic characters might sound like science fiction itself (a Frankenstein's monster formed by stitching together printed pages, rather than body parts, along a spine), for the most part characterization was a low priority in the genre, and even plot was secondary in comparison with the scenario; science fiction is more than anything a thought experiment, the answer to a question of *what if?* What if we took a rocketship to the moon? What if we invented robots that developed human-like consciousness? What if intelligent creatures lived on another planet and decided to invade our own? What if radiation caused ordinary animals, plants, and people to mutate into horrible, destructive creatures? What if there was a nuclear war? By way of contrast, science fiction natives, as well as a number of forward-thinking science fiction immigrants, for the most part recognized the social relevance of the genre as a form of popular culture, not to mention its potential for genuine artistic achievement.

SCIENCE FICTION NATIVITY IN POSTWAR AMERICA

As science fiction natives, the baby boomers inherited a set of narratives created over the course of the 19th and early 20th centuries, including the novels and short stories that launched the genre, written by Mary Shelley, Edgar Allan Poe, Arthur Conan Doyle, Robert Louis Stevenson, and especially Jules Verne and H. G. Wells. Through inexpensive paperbacks and even cheaper pulp magazines and digests, such as *Amazing Stories* founded by Hugo Gernsback, readers could encounter the writings of Edgar Rice Burroughs, Robert Heinlein, Arthur C. Clarke, A. E. van Vogt, Theodore Sturgeon, Ray Bradbury, and the most prolific author in the history of the United States, Isaac Asimov. Science fiction narratives were also shared over the medium of radio, in the form of dramatic readings and radio plays (the most famous example being Orson Welles's adaptation of H. G. Wells's *War of the Worlds*, originally broadcast in 1938), and they took the form of newspaper comic strips such as *Flash Gordon* and *Buck Rogers in the 25th Century A.D.*, both of which were later collected and published as comic books and adapted for the screen in the form of juvenile serials shown at the movies on Saturday mornings. Several science fiction feature films were produced before the postwar era, notably Fritz Lang's silent masterpiece, *Metropolis* (1927); David Butler's futuristic musical *Just Imagine* (1930); the well-known screen adaptation of *Frankenstein* (1931) and its sequel *The Bride of Frankenstein* (1935), both directed by James Whale; and *Things to Come* (1936) based on a screenplay by H. G. Wells and directed by William Cameron Menzies.

Baby boomers inherited these and other narratives that were the product of earlier eras, but as science fiction natives inhabiting a science fiction world, they also bore witness to a sudden explosion of such stories native to their own era. Vivian Sobchack (1987) argues that 1950 was a pivotal year, as this was when science fiction suddenly emerged as an American film genre. Science fiction as a literary genre can be traced back to the turn of the 20th century, but science fiction films were few and far between before 1950, and in that sense hardly formed a recognizable genre, whereas a veritable flood of such moving pictures were produced during the fifties, increasing in number as the decade wore on. And even if many baby boomers were too young to see the films in their original release on the silver screen, the movies were later repeatedly broadcast on television (for example, on Saturday afternoons, after the morning cartoons) and, indeed, heavily influenced what would later constitute science fiction as a television genre.

Each medium has its own bias that influences and shapes the content it conveys (McLuhan 1964; Strate 2006), and therefore, each medium recreates the genre in its own image. Science fiction as a literary genre, in keeping with the biases of print media, has tended to emphasize science and technology, but more generally ideas, which is why it has also been recognized as a form of philosophical fiction. Science fiction writers have historically been less concerned with literary poetics than they have with using narrative form didactically to teach readers about scientific theories and methods or as thought experiments to extrapolate and speculate about the future and alien life based on current knowledge and scientific understanding. One of the characteristics of writing and print is specialization (McLuhan 1962, 1964), and science fiction novels and short stories for most of their history have appealed only to a highly specialized, mostly male readership. The cinematic medium, by way of contrast, has tended to appeal more broadly to a general audience, requiring content that is less esoteric than its literary counterpart. As visual media, film and television both are biased toward more concrete forms of content, as opposed to the abstract discussions and digressions that often appear in writing. For this reason, the science fiction film genre has been comparatively weak on science, favoring instead the spectacle, often associated with special effects. As Susan Sontag (1966) explains in the first major analysis of science fiction as a film genre:

> Certainly, compared with the science fiction novels, their film counterparts have unique strengths, one of which is the immediate representation of the extraordinary: physical deformity and mutation, missile and rocket combat, toppling skyscrapers. The movies are, naturally, weak just where the science fiction novels (some of them) are strong—on science. But in place of an intellectual workout, they can supply something the novels can never provide—sensuous elaboration. In the films it is by means of images and sounds, not words that have to be translated by the imagination, that one can participate in the fantasy of living through one's own death and more, the death of cities, the destruction of humanity itself. (212)

Sontag argues that science fiction as a film genre is primarily concerned with disaster, the imagination and aesthetics of disaster. And while this holds true for science fiction films produced before the fifties, a significant change occurs with the first full decade of the postwar era:

> The old science fiction films, and most of the comics, still have an essentially innocent relation to disaster. Mainly they offer new versions of the oldest romance of all—of the strong invulnerable hero with a mysterious lineage come to do battle on behalf of good and against evil. Recent science fiction films have a decided grimness, bolstered by their much greater degree of visual credibility, which contrasts strongly with the older films. Modern historical reality has greatly enlarged the imagination of disaster, and the protagonists—perhaps by the very nature of what is visited upon then—no longer seem wholly innocent. (Sontag 1966, 215)

Loss of innocence became a major theme of the baby boomers' counterculture, and the struggle to somehow reclaim it is in large part a response to what Sontag refers to as the sense "that a mass trauma exists over the use of nuclear weapons and the possibility of future nuclear wars" (1966, 218). Baby boomer rebellion against the mainstream and the authorities that defended the status quo, derisively termed "the establishment," is mirrored by the science fiction genre's expression of fear concerning dehumanization and depersonalization, whether the product of hostile aliens or our own technologies. Sontag also points out that the genre's disaster scenarios are associated with a release from the normal obligations of every-day life, as the extraordinary events and breakdown of civilization lead to a kind of "extreme moral simplification" (215), and here too we can see parallels in the extremes of the counterculture, for example, hippies, yippies, communes, and other forms of dropping out of ordinary society. And there is the utopian fantasy, or as Sontag puts it, the "UN fantasy" (220) of the nations of the Earth uniting in response to alien invasion, a scenario invoked on several occasions during the 1980s by remarks made by our first movie star turned president, Ronald Reagan, notably in an address to the United Nations General Assembly in 1987. As troubling as this may have sounded coming out of the mouth of the leader of the free world in serious situations, baby boomers embraced notions of the global village (McLuhan 1962) and spaceship earth (Fuller 1971) and, more generally, the imagination of utopia, for example, as expressed by the lyrics to John Lennon's song "Imagine" (which describes a one-world utopia that is essentially a poetic rendering of *The Communist Manifesto*).

Sontag concludes that the "imagery of disaster in science fiction [film] is above all the emblem of an *inadequate response* [emphasis in original]" (1966, 224). But this inadequacy is on the part of the adults rather than the baby boomers themselves, on the part of the older generation, the authorities, the establishment, who after all are science fiction immigrants. Inadequate response is a symptom of the generation gap, as it is a common motif in the genre that a child is the only one who recognizes that something is different or wrong, for example in *Invaders from Mars* (1953) directed by William Cameron Menzies; typically, the child's observations and warnings are ignored by the adults until it is almost too late. There is more here than the ingenuous honesty of the main character in "The Emperor's New Clothes," as the child is elevated to heroic status, achieved by virtue of being a science fiction native. A similar oppositional dynamic exists with the emergence of the child as monster, as can be seen in the British film *Village of the Damned* (1960) directed by Wolf Rilla, and in the "It's a Good Life" episode from Rod Serling's *Twilight Zone* television series, in which a child named Anthony terrorizes a small Ohio town, sending away anyone who offends him "to the cornfield." Perhaps the most intimidating image of all is that of the fetal star child seen at the end of *2001: A Space Odyssey*, the next stage of human evolution, power unknown, intent equally obscure.

ALIENS AMONG US

Like the children from *Village of the Damned*, the all-powerful Anthony, and Kubrick's star child, science fiction natives were mutants and aliens in relation to science fiction immigrants, objects of both hope and terror.

Concurrent with the beginnings of the baby boom was a sudden explosion of reports of sightings of unidentified flying objects, most commonly taking the form of flying saucers, spaceships carrying alien visitors. Psychoanalyst Carl Jung (1978), noting that inaccurate statements that he believed in the reality of flying saucers had been widely reported in newspapers all around the world, whereas his own clarifications on the subject were largely ignored, commented in 1958:

> As the behavior of the press is a sort of Gallup test with reference to world opinion, one must draw the conclusion that news affirming the existence of UFOs is welcome, but that skepticism seems to be undesirable. To believe that UFOs are real suits the general opinion, whereas disbelief is to be discouraged. This creates the impression that there is a tendency all over the world to believe in saucers and to want them to be real, unconsciously helped along by a press that otherwise has no sympathy with the phenomenon. (3)

The desire, indeed, the need to believe in aliens suggests a phenomenon distinct from the panic brought on by the 1938 *War of the Worlds* radio broadcast, the eve of World War II being a time of tremendous war jitters in the United States and Europe (Heyer 2003). The idea of alien invasion persisted, of course, along with the more subtle threat of alien abduction, perhaps mirroring the substitution of the Cold War for open hostilities. Indeed, Jung regarded UFO rumors as a kind of collective response involving psychological projection that was brought on by the emotional tension of the Cold War and the threat of nuclear war:

> The recent atomic explosions on the earth, it was conjectured, had aroused the attention of these so very much more advanced dwellers on Mars or Venus, who were worried about possible chain-reactions and the consequent destruction of our planet. Since such a possibility would constitute a catastrophic threat to our neighboring planets, their inhabitants felt compelled to observe how things were developing on earth, fully aware of the tremendous cataclysm our clumsy nuclear experiments might unleash. The fact that the UFOs neither land on earth nor show the least inclination to get into communication with human beings is met by the explanation that these visitors, despite their superior knowledge, are not at all certain of being well received on earth, for which reason they carefully avoid all intelligent contact with humans. But because they, as befits superior beings, conduct themselves quite inoffensively, they would do the earth no harm and are satisfied with an objective inspection of airfields and atomic installations. (1978, 15)

This new, more benign image of our other worldly visitors coexisted with more traditional paranoid themes about alien invasion in forming what Jung referred to as a modern myth of flying saucers and UFOs. More than benign, the aliens, whose visual appearance was sometimes associated with characteristics common to young children (short stature, large heads, large eyes), might even be here to help us out of our difficulties:

> According to the rumor, the occupants are about three feet high and look like human beings or, conversely, are utterly unlike us. Other reports speak of giants fifteen feet high. They are beings who are carrying out a cautious survey of the earth and considerately avoid all encounters with men or, more menacingly, are spying out landing places with a view to settling the population of a planet that has got into difficulties and colonizing the earth by force. Uncertainty in regard to the physical conditions on earth and their fear of unknown sources of infection have held them back temporarily from drastic encounters and even from attempted landings, although they possess frightful weapons which would enable them to exterminate the human race. In addition to their obviously superior technology they are credited with superior wisdom and moral goodness which would, on the other hand, enable them to save humanity. (Jung 1978, 11)

In this last variation, rather than being the source of disaster, the aliens are seen as the answer to the problem of humanity's inability to respond adequately to self-inflicted catastrophe. In the quintessential baby boomer film of 1969, Dennis Hopper's *Easy Rider*, the character of George Hanson, played by Jack Nicholson, conveys this version of the myth:

> They've got bases all over the world now, you know. They've been coming here ever since 1946, when scientists first started bouncing radar beams off the moon. And they have been living and working among us in vast quantities ever since. The government knows all about them.

Hanson then goes on to explain:

> Well, they are people, just like us, from within our own solar system. Except that their society is more highly evolved. I mean, they don't have no wars. They got no monetary system. They don't have any leaders. Because, I mean, each man is a leader. I mean, each man, because of their technology, they are able to feed, clothe, house and transport themselves equally, and with no effort.

And when Hanson is asked why the aliens remain hidden from humanity, he answers:

Why don't they reveal themselves to us is because if they did it would cause a general panic. Now, I mean, we still have leaders upon whom we rely for the release of this information. These leaders have decided to repress this information because of the tremendous shock that it would cause to our antiquated systems. Now, the result of this has been that the Venusians have contacted people at all walks of life, all walks of life . . . It would be a devastating blow to our antiquated systems. So now Venusians are meeting with people in all walks of life in an advisory capacity. For once, man will have a godlike control over his own destiny. He will have a chance to transcend and to evolve with some equality for all.

Clearly, what Hanson is expressing here is a religious quality to his belief in UFOs, an imagination of transcendence if you will, an actual aspect of the UFO myth that Jung (1978) acknowledges, noting

In the threatening situation of the world today, when people are beginning to see that everything is at stake, the projection-creating fantasy soars beyond the realm of earthly organizations and powers into the heavens, into interstellar space, where the rulers of human fate, the gods, once had their abode in the planets. . . . Eye-witnesses of unimpeachable honesty announce the "signs in the heavens" which they have seen "with their own eyes," and the marvelous things they have experienced which pass human understanding. (14–15)

Jung notes that the flying saucer in particular is a manifestation of the mandala archetype, a symbol of the collective unconscious that represents totality, order, psychic unity, and the divine. And the vision of a savior from the skies associated with UFO sightings was reflected early in the history of the science fiction film genre, in the 1951 film *The Day the Earth Stood Still*, directed by Robert Wise. The visitor, Klaatu, appears otherworldly and frightening when he first emerges from his flying saucer after landing on a baseball field in Washington, DC. But we soon learn that his alien appearance is only due to his space helmet, and once it is removed, he looks just like an ordinary human being, the sort of person who, back in the fifties, would be dubbed an "everyman." That he hails from a world more technologically advanced than our own is evident from his spacecraft, the featureless and voiceless robot Gort that accompanies him, the heat ray that the robot emits when threatened, the device Klaatu brought with him as a gift for the president that would enable him to study life on other planets (which was destroyed when a trigger-happy soldier shot at Klaatu soon after he emerged from the saucer), the advanced state of their medical technology (Klaatu is 78 but has the body of a 35-year-old, and toward the end of the film is brought back to life shortly after being killed), a remark Klaatu makes to the young boy Bobby whom he befriends about trains that run without tracks, and Klaatu's ability to solve an equation that was still being worked out by Professor Barnhardt, a character modeled after Albert Einstein and identified as the smartest person on the planet. And of course there is the event that gives the film its title, when Klaatu demonstrates his power by turning off all of the earth's electricity, bringing all technological activity to a halt; the benign quality of the alien is also shown in that an exception was made in any instance where powering down devices would harm people, for example, in hospitals and planes in flight.

But the film goes beyond science, drawing on the religious themes associated with the UFO mythos and themes familiar from religious allegory. Klaatu is presented as Christ-like in his descent from the heavens to walk among human beings as an ordinary man, while being hunted and persecuted by the authorities. Adopting a human alias associated with Jesus of Nazareth's earthly vocation, Klaatu takes the name of Carpenter, performing miracles, including the worldwide power shutdown. Professor Barnhardt takes on the role of John the Baptist, clearing the way for Klaatu to deliver his message to the world, while Helen Benson, a widow, is Klaatu's Mary Magdalene, assisting him and functioning as a companion, albeit in a way that is subtle and implicit, and ultimately unconsummated. Her boyfriend, Tom Stevens, turns out to be the film's Judas Iscariot, as he betrays the alien to the authorities, leading to Klaatu's death and subsequent resurrection. While Klaatu takes pains to distinguish between the advanced medical science that restores him to life as opposed to true divine power, the narrative still follows the New Testament's narrative structure, as Klaatu explains that he is only restored for a short time, delivers his message, and then ascends back into the heavens. His message, however, is political in nature rather than spiritual:

> I am leaving soon, and you will forgive me if I speak bluntly. The universe grows smaller every day, and the threat of aggression by any group, anywhere, can no longer be tolerated. There must be security for all, or no one is secure. Now this does not mean giving up any freedom, except the freedom to act irresponsibly. Your ancestors knew this when they made laws to govern themselves, and hired policemen to enforce them. We of the other planets have long accepted this principle. We have an organization for the mutual protection of all planets and for the complete elimination of aggression. The test of any such

higher authority is, of course, the police force that supports it. For our policemen, we created a race of robots. Their function is to patrol the planets in spaceships like this one, and preserve the peace. In matters of aggression, we have given them absolute power over us. This power cannot be revoked. At the first sign of violence they act automatically against the aggressor. The penalty for provoking their action is too terrible to risk. The result is we live in peace, without arms or armies, secure in the knowledge that we are free from aggression and war, free to pursue more profitable enterprises. Now, we do not pretend to have achieved perfection, but we do have a system, and it works. I came here to give you these facts. It is no concern of ours how you run your own planet, but if you threaten to extend your violence, this Earth of yours will be reduced to a burned-out cinder. Your choice is simple: Join us and live in peace, or pursue your present course and face obliteration. We shall be waiting for your answer. The decision rests with you.

Although the message is directed at all of the nations of the world, with the United States at best the lesser of the many evils, Klaatu's warning accurately reflects American foreign policy of that time, affirming the values of individual freedom, peace, and security, along with the belief that societies ought to determine their own internal affairs but cannot be allowed to threaten others. Klaatu's interplanetary organization mirrors the United Nations, still seen as an extension of American democracy, while the robots represent the threat of military force, their heat ray in particular symbolic of the bomb. The fact that the robots are referred to as police is significant, in that the Korean War that the United States had entered into in 1950 under the auspices of the UN was referred to as a "police action." The invasion of South Korea by the communist regime of North Korea was seen by the north as a civil war and a bid for forceful reunification, but the United States viewed what was known as international communism as an external force subverting the self-determination of various peoples around the world, and this was reinforced when communist China entered the war in support of the north, staving off a victory on the part of America and its allies. It is worth noting that General Douglas MacArthur advocated for the use of nuclear weapons against the communist forces before he was relieved of command in 1951.

Klaatu's warning is strict but not uncaring, and the fact that he becomes parental and paternalistic underscores the films subtle theme of the absent father figure, as expressed through the interaction between Klaatu and Helen's son, Bobby. Helen is a single, working mother, not by choice but by necessity, and they live in a boarding house, suggesting a difficult financial and social situation. Her desperation to provide Bobby with a father, and the financial security a husband would bring, has driven her to accept

Tom Stevens as a boyfriend; she seriously consider his marriage proposal, her facial expressions giving away the fact that she has mixed emotions, at best, about him. That he is a poor choice is borne out by the fact that he encourages Helen to allow Bobby to show Mr. Carpenter, aka Klaatu, a relative stranger, around the city, so as not to spoil their dating plans when there is no one to watch Bobby; this of course occurs long before concerns about child abuse and abduction become commonplace but still demonstrates a cavalier and selfish attitude on Tom's part. Any doubts about Tom's character are dispelled when he learns Carpenter's true identity and betrays him, bragging about how big a man he is going to be as a result. Before the betrayal, Bobby takes Carpenter to Arlington Cemetery, and confides that his father is buried there, a casualty of World War II, a truly poignant moment. The growing bond between Carpenter and Bobby and the yearning for the absent father on a personal level are abandoned in the last part of the film, however, as the concluding scenes shift the emphasis to Klaatu as a father figure for humanity as a whole. But Bobby as the young person who is the first in the boarding house to believe the reports about the UFO, and the first to recognize that Carpenter is not of this world, becomes an easy point of identification for baby boomers viewing the film, and the situation of the single-parent family is one that baby boomers were able to relate to with increasingly greater ease over the ensuing years.

It is rather remarkable to note the similarities and differences between *The Day the Earth Stood Still* and another science fiction film from 1951, *The Thing from Another World*, directed by Christian Nyby and produced by Howard Hawks. Both reflect the postwar fascination with UFOs and concern about alien visitors. But whereas *The Day the Earth Stood Still* gives us an alien messiah, *The Thing from Another World* features an alien monster, not unlike the monsters of horror movies of the thirties and forties. Whereas Klaatu descends from the heavens and in the end returns to the celestial sphere, the unnamed "thing" is found in a saucer that crashed and became buried under the ice near the North Pole; it is defeated in the end by being electrocuted and burned to ashes. The government and the military are portrayed in a negative light in *The Day the Earth Stood Still*, but the heroes of *The Thing* are a small group of Air Force servicemen. The scientist, Professor Barnhardt, is a benign figure in *The Day the Earth Stood Still*, whereas Dr. Carrington is at best misguided, and arguably a traitor to the human race in *The Thing*. The meaning of all of the major science fiction icons common to the two films, the flying saucer, the alien, the military, and the scientist, are completely reversed, demonstrating the utter plasticity of the genre's conventions; as Sobchack (1987) explains, in the place of set meanings, the genre instead juxtaposes the alien (or unknown) and the familiar. Thus, Klaatu at first appears alien, but is rapidly revealed to be a familiar, everyman type, a more advanced version of ourselves, with alien quality displaced onto his technology, especially the robot Gort. The alien quality of the thing, on the other hand, is heightened as it is revealed to be markedly biological, in being a form of intelligent plant life, and as the monstrous visitor repeatedly attacks his human hosts.

The chaste, spiritual quality of *The Day the Earth Stood Still* stands in stark contrast to the emphasis on reproduction in *The Thing*. Although the thing is asexual in nature, Dr. Carrington takes on the feminine role in helping it to reproduce, nursing the seedling with human blood. In this sense, the scientist exhibits a form of what would be considered deviant sexuality, clearly presented as immoral and threatening within the context of the narrative, but given expression nonetheless, and open to other interpretations (as celebrated in Jim Sharman's 1975 comedy, *The Rocky Horror Picture Show*). Carrington expresses his admiration for the alien, referring to "the superiority of its brain," and noting that "its development was not handicapped by emotional or sexual factors." Carrington refers to "the neat and unconfused reproductive technique of vegetation," which can proceed with great rapidity and, as he describes the alien form of life: "No pain or pleasure as we know it. No emotions. No heart. Our superior. Our superior in every way." In this decidedly elitist fashion, the scientist elucidates what it is that makes us human, while the heroes of the film, Captain Hendry and Nikki Nicholson, illustrate the typical confusion of human courtship and signify the model of appropriate sexuality, which presumably will involve marriage soon after the close of the film.

As noted, *The Day the Earth Stood Still* reflects American foreign policy circa 1951, but specifically the internationalist foreign policy of the Democratic Truman administration, the same policy espoused by Democratic presidential candidate Adlai Stevenson during the campaign that took place the following year. *The Thing from Another World*, on the other hand, reflects the more conservative, isolationist policy of the Republican Party and their victorious 1952 candidate, General Dwight D. Eisenhower. The difference is encapsulated in the most memorable lines from each film. *The Day the Earth Stood Still* gave us the first alien language ever heard in a motion picture, "Gort, Klaatu barada nikto," the words Helen was instructed to say to the robot to keep him from destroying the planet and that direct him to revive Klaatu. *The Thing* closed with the reporter Scotty radioing his account of the successful defense against the alien, and admonishing his listeners to "keep watching the skies!" That *The Thing* went on to spawn an entire subgenre of alien invasion films that dominated the fifties science fiction scene, while *The Day the Earth Stood Still* stood alone as the only film of its type, the alien messiah theme (Ruppersberg 1987) being virtually ignored for the next quarter century, mirrors Eisenhower's defeat of Stevenson in 1952 and 1956. Moreover, *The Thing* assumes an audience that can relate to military service as a milieu, true for the greatest generation that fought in World

War II, and the silent generation that followed them and experienced the Korean War, but unfamiliar to most baby boomers, who opposed and/or tried to evade military service and the Vietnam War. Science fiction natives could therefore view this film with more sympathy for Dr. Carrington and the alien than science fiction immigrants.

The Thing from Another World is based on a novella by John W. Campbell, in which the alien is able to disguise itself in human form, impersonating whomever it kills. This plot element was left out of the 1951 film (it was restored in the 1982 and 2011 versions) but was included in subsequent alien invasion films, notably 1956's *Invasion of the Body Snatchers*, adapted from a novel by Jack Finney and directed by Don Siegel. Here too, the aliens are a form of plant life, their invasive reproduction placed in contrast to the failed marriages of the main characters, the physician Miles Bennell and his former girlfriend Becky Driscoll. (That both are divorced is revealed through an oblique reference to having taken a trip to Reno, most adults being aware of the fact that Nevada has the most lenient divorce laws in the United States.) The attraction between the two divorcés is readily apparent, reflecting the simmering sexuality of the decade that gave us Marilyn Monroe, *Playboy* magazine, and Elvis "the Pelvis" Presley. Their failure to come together, unlike the main characters of *The Thing*, is in line with *Invasion*'s more pessimistic ending, which despite the studio's addition of a postproduction framing sequence meant to reassure audiences that the authorities were aware of the invasion and ready to take the necessary steps to counter it, ends with a measure of ambiguity and doubt about the eventual outcome. While in one sense embodying right-wing paranoia regarding communist subversion, *Invasion* can also be viewed as a warning about 1950s-era conformity and the dangers of McCarthyism, in both instances upholding the American value of individual freedom that was very much a part of baby boomer rebellion and counterculture.

The same year that gave us the claustrophobic film noir classic *Invasion of the Body Snatchers*, in which familiar, everyday small town/suburban life is shown to be increasingly more alien, also saw the release of the more expansive *Forbidden Planet*, directed by Fred McLeod Wilcox, a relatively big budget movie, filmed in Cinemascope and color, with reasonably good special effects for its time, and loosely based on Shakespeare's *The Tempest*. Set in the 23rd century, *Forbidden Planet* followed *The Thing* in featuring male bonding among a group of military men, this time patterned after the Navy. And like *The Thing*, this film assigns a negative value to science and scientists, although the person who functions as a scientist, Dr. Morbius, actually explains that he is a philologist, that is, a scholar of language and literature. His background enabled him to decipher the writings of the now-extinct alien race, the Krell, and identify a kind of "educational" technology with the ability to permanently increase an individual's mental capacity. Having a very high IQ, Morbius survived the treatment, just barely, and went on to utilize the rest of the Krell's advanced technology, while his captain, whose IQ was significantly lower, tried to use the machine to enhance his intelligence and died. The strain of anti-intellectualism, a common theme in American popular arts, reflecting our democratic and egalitarian culture, is apparent here in the fact that, however unintended it may be, Morbius, like Carrington, plays the role of villain. The two are similar in appearance as well, as both sport beards, as opposed to the clean-cut military men who are the heroes of the two movies, and whose style baby boomers rebelled against. The film's antielitism extends to the United Planets ship's physician, Dr. Ostrow, who, having been identified as also having a high IQ, uses the brain booster to uncover the secret of the Krell and survives long enough to relate it to Commander Adams before succumbing to the effects of the machine. Ostrow's sacrifice is heroic, however, as opposed to the hubris of the tragic figure of Morbius, who brings about his own doom in giving himself the ability to turn thought into reality, by not taking into account the activity of his unconscious mind, "the monsters from the id," as Ostrow puts it.

Every member of the expedition that came to Altair IV aboard the spaceship Bellerophon had been killed by a mysterious force (i.e., the monsters from Morbius's id), either on the planet or as they tried to escape aboard their ship, with the exception of Morbius and his wife, who died after giving birth to their daughter, Altaira. Beautiful, young, and virginal, Altaira is the subject of intense interest on the part of the interstellar sailors, interest that she returns in kind, not entirely understanding the implications due to her innocence. In this respect, the film bears some resemblance to the beach party film genre that originates with the Paul Wendkos film *Gidget* in 1959 and can be seen as a precursor to the much more explicit adventures of the innocent, but sexually active heroine of Roger Vadim's 1968 film *Barbarella*. Altaira is the youngest character in the film, presumably past her 18th birthday, but not by much. As an innocent, she is talked into experimenting with kissing, an activity new to her, by Lieutenant Farman. Before they can progress too far, the aptly named Farman is chased off by Commander Adams. Both paternalistic and puritanical, Adams chastises Altaira for wearing clothing that is too revealing, and letting Farman take advantage of her. Defending herself, she explains, using Farman's own words, that they "were just trying to get some healthy stimulation from hugging and kissing, that's all," which prompts the commander to respond: "Oh, that's all? It's so easy for you, isn't it? There's no feelings, no emotions. Nothing human would ever enter your mind." Compare this to *Invasion of the Body Snatchers*, where the pod people who replace their human counterparts are said to have "no need for love," "no emotion," "only the instinct to survive," explaining: "Love, desire, ambition, faith, without them, life's so simple." And although

Altaira's humanity is never really called into doubt, the unspoken fact is that she is the only living character in the film who was not born on Earth, who is in that sense truly an alien, whose very name places her in an identity relationship with the alien planet. This can be understood in gendered terms as the female being an alien from a male point of view, a common interpretation of this science fiction motif. But it can also be viewed in generational terms, as Altaira is the sole teenager in the film, leading to the conclusion that baby boomers are aliens in the eyes of the older generations.

Interestingly, when Adams explains to Morbius that all of the killing that has taken place on the planet is the product not of an alien monster but of Morbius's own unconscious imagination, that he has made the same mistake as the Krell, whose brain-boost technology led to their own extinction, Adams says: "Like you, the Krell forgot one deadly danger: Their own subconscious hate and lust for destruction." The use of the term "lust" here is peculiar and significant, as the word is normally associated with sexual desire, rather than aggression and violence. From a psychoanalytic perspective, it is not surprising that Morbius might harbor an unconscious sexual desire for his daughter, his sole companion on the alien planet, and wish to eliminate any rivals for her affections that might appear. Of course, any overt reference to such psychodynamics would not be possible in a fifties film, but this element adds to the underlying theme of simmering sexuality that presages the sexual revolution associated with the baby boomer generation. However, for the actual baby boomers at the time of the film's release, the true object of fascination was Robby the robot, invented by Morbius and often accompanying Altaira. While at first glance alien and intimidating, the robot's voice and manner is that of a friendly butler, a character type familiar within popular culture. This stands in contrast to the threateningly impassive mien of Gort, and more so various evil robots such as the often ridiculed gorilla in a diving helmet featured in 1953's *Robot Monster*, directed by Phil Tucker. Robby was particularly noteworthy in that he became the first science fiction film icon to be marketed to children as a toy. Like Altaira, Robby was "born" on Altair IV, and in that sense, as well as being the product of futuristic technology, is a truly alien character.

LOOKING FORWARD TO THE FINAL FRONTIER

Forbidden Planet became the inspiration for two science fiction television series of the 1960s, *Lost in Space*, which also featured a flying saucer as a human spaceship, and *Star Trek*, where the saucer became the leading element of a spacecraft that included a ship-like base, visually emphasizing the naval sensibility of the Star*ship* Enterprise, sometimes referred to as the flagship of Starfleet Command; incorporating the best of both worlds, the starship also featured two rocket-like nacelles. *Star Trek*'s opening reference to space as "the final frontier" was derived from John F. Kennedy's campaign slogan, the "New Frontier," and although the program was launched almost three years after Kennedy's assassination, it reflected the new emphasis on youthfulness and youth culture that he had come to symbolize; JFK was the youngest man ever elected president (at 43 years old), and in the series James T. Kirk was introduced as the youngest officer ever to be made captain of a starship. Gene Roddenberry, the creator and producer of the series, conveyed a clear sense of optimism about the future, one where not only had the planet become united under one government but had also joined with intelligent beings from many other worlds to form the United Federation of Planets (a variation on *Forbidden Planet*'s United Planets, although in the film there is no indication that any of the members are aliens). The federation was truly a reflection of the Great Society envisioned in the rhetoric of Kennedy's successor, Lyndon Johnson, with women accorded relatively (for that time) equal status on the Enterprise, whose crew represented a melting pot, including the African Lt. Uhura, the Asian Lt. Sulu, and the Russian Ensign Chekov, introduced during the second season of the series both to symbolize the desire for a peaceful resolution of the Cold War and to add a somewhat younger officer meant to appeal to teenagers. (His hairstyle was reminiscent of the moptop look of the early Beatles and other British invasion bands, and of their American imitators; the same look was associated with Davy Jones of the TV series *The Monkees*, which aired around the same time as *Star Trek*, from 1966 to 1968.) And then there was Mr. Spock, first officer and science officer, half-human and half-Vulcan, representing the ultimate integration of alien and human both by his presence on board the Enterprise and by his very hybridity. Drawing on characteristics of Jewish culture and more general elements of orientalism, the Vulcan rejection of emotion also reflects the technological nature of postwar society (Ellul 1964; Berger 1976; Postman 1992).

In keeping with the sixties' emphasis on relevance, Roddenberry used the program as a vehicle for addressing issues of the day, such as racism, sexism, overpopulation, war and peace, etc., again generally conforming to the progressive politics favored by the baby boomers. Indeed, *Star Trek* was the first American program to broadcast an interracial kiss (although to play it safe the kiss was attributed to mind control). At the same time, the series reflected the realities of the Cold War, with the militaristic Klingon Empire taking on the role of the Soviet Union, while the Romulan Empire, named after ancient Rome, was the functional equivalent of communist China in *Star Trek*'s counterpart to contemporary geopolitics. And much like *The Day the Earth Stood Still*, Roddenberry's series mirrored the internationalist politics that became Lyndon Johnson's bane, as it led to the escalation of U.S. involvement in the Vietnam War. This was particularly the case in episodes that featured the Prime Directive, which specified that members of the Federation were forbidden to interfere with the natural course of cultural and technological development in the case of alien worlds that had not yet mastered spaceflight. As a plot device, the Prime Directive created conflict in that inevitably Captain Kirk and his crew were forced to interfere in the affairs of other planets, but this interference was typically justified as setting the aliens back on a course of "natural" development after having been interfered with, sometimes by earlier visits from Earth ships, but often due to control by computers or less benign alien races. Reflecting American policy that upheld the right of every people to self-determination, but which viewed communism as outside interference, even if a communist government or revolutionaries were essentially indigenous, this was the logic that led us to enter the Vietnam War and escalate our involvement (Berger 1976; Jewett and Lawrence 1977).

Ironically, as the antiwar movement heated up during the Nixon presidency, baby boomers protesting our involvement and chanting "hell no, we won't go," and "Ho, Ho, Ho Chi Minh, the NLF [National Liberation Front, aka the Vietcong] is gonna win," also tuned into syndicated reruns of *Star Trek* with great enthusiasm. The distancing effect of science fiction allowed baby boomers to have their cake and eat it too, that is, to be countercultural in the here and now and part of the mainstream American culture they grew up with and valued in this imagined future. They could protest the Vietnam War but cheer on the Enterprise's liberation of aliens from mechanized totalitarian control, however benign that control might have been. They could criticize the Cold War but enjoy Captain Kirk's confrontation with the Klingons and Romulans. They could disapprove of nuclear weapons but smile as the Enterprise fired phasers and photon torpedoes. And they could object to the historical treatment of Native Americans and the myth of Manifest Destiny but identify with the starship as an interplanetary sheriff bringing law and order to the wilderness of the final frontier. Although opposed to the mainstream establishment in their attitudes, baby boomers maintained the same long-standing values and beliefs of American culture as the generations that came before them.

Only 80 episodes of *Star Trek* were produced before the series was cancelled after its third year of production. However, especially owing to its long afterlife in syndicated reruns, the program became one of the major touchstones of baby boomer science fiction. Certainly, the brief period during which the program aired, 1966 to 1969, could be considered a major turning point in the history of the genre, as it includes the 1968 release of Kubrick's *2001: A Space Odyssey*. Like *Star Trek*, *2001* promised a future in which humanity was making its way to the stars. Roddenberry's relatively utopian 23rd century was quite different from Kubrick's near future scenario, with its continuation of corporate capitalism, the Cold War, and government secrecy, not to mention its depiction of the dehumanization associated with technological development and the particular requirements of space travel. Kubrick's cynical view of humanity, a species defined by the capacity for murder ever since the dawn of man, is reinforced by the fact that this characteristic is passed on to HAL, the computer shown to be capable of human intelligence and consciousness. But despite its critical stance, 2001 still provides a vision of the aesthetic beauty of outer space, the music and dance of the spheres (and our own space station and spaceships), and, in the finale, the psychedelic explosion of what came to be known as "the ultimate trip," the slogan that the film, on its second run, incorporated into its advertising due to the fact that the last burst of special effects brought to mind LSD-induced hallucinations, and indeed was popular among audience members experimenting with hallucinogens. And 2001 provides a vision of transcendence, not the alien messiah theme of The Day the Earth Stood Still but something much more ambiguous, in that it is never clearly revealed in the film that the mysterious monolith is an alien device as opposed to some supernatural force (although this is spelled out in Arthur C. Clarke's novelization and its sequels). Nor is it established that the monolith and the star child it brings into being are necessarily beneficial to humanity. But the film does favor the concept of evolution and progress, as marked by the beginnings of tool use and space exploration, as well as the transition from ape to human being to the next, neotenous stage of being, once again invoking the archetype of the child so central to the counterculture. In this sense, Kubrick's masterpiece can be seen as a further elaboration of the UFO myth.

The same year as 2001's release saw the distribution in the United States of the French-Italian adaptation from the French comic book series, Barbarella. As something of a parody of Flash Gordon, starring baby boomer icon Jane Fonda, with a screenplay coauthored by Terry Southern, the film is a celebration of the sexual revolution, replete with sixties kitsch, and with the power of love (in all senses of the word) defeating the evil Durand-Durand (from whom the eighties new wave group Duran Duran derived their name, the final "d" being silent in French pronunciation). If Barbarella was a celebration of the free love and jouissance embraced by baby boomer counterculture, 1968 also gave us the misanthropic motion picture Planet of the Apes, directed by Franklin J. Schaffner and based on a screenplay coauthored by Rod Serling. With its topsy-turvy theme of a world in which human beings are treated like animals, and exhibit about as much intelligence, while apes are the dominant species living in a preindustrial society otherwise much like our own, Planet of the Apes uses the distancing effect of science fiction to criticize militarism, the hypocrisies of politicians and religious leaders, the mistreatment of animals, and racism; apes have served as symbols of African Americans, and nonwhites in general, ever since the days of King Kong (1933) and Mighty Joe Young (1949) and, for that matter, the Tarzan series written by Edgar Rice Burroughs, which was seen as a form of science fiction when originally introduced back in 1912. The main character in *Planet of the Apes*, the astronaut named Taylor (played by Charlton Heston), demonstrates a cynicism not usually associated with his vocation, but one very much in keeping with sixties zeitgeist; in his opening monologue, delivered as a log entry before entering suspended animation, noting that thousands of years will pass on earth by the time he and his companions awake, he states that, "I leave the twentieth century with no regrets," and ends with the query directed at the human beings of the future, "Tell me though, does Man, that marvel of the universe, that glorious paradox who sent me to the stars still make war against his brother? Keep his neighbor's children starving?" What he discovers at the end is that the alien planet is in fact his own, that human beings have bombed themselves back into the Stone Age and beyond, that whatever the reason for the evolution of the apes and devolution of humanity, nothing much has changed as the apes appear to be no better than humans at creating a peaceful and just society.

DYSTOPIA AND NOSTALGIA

As science fiction natives, baby boomers grew up with the imagination of disaster, in the form of alien invasions reflecting the older generations' experience of World War II, the Korean War, and the Cold War, as well as the postwar threat of atomic war and nuclear holocaust; with the imagination of transcendence in the form of benign UFOs, alien messiahs, and the possibility of the evolution of the human species itself; and with the imagination of utopia, in the form of progressive future societies based on the American republic and the early promise of the United Nations, such as *Star Trek*'s United Federation of Planets. These motifs reflected the general sense of living in a pivotal moment in history, whether it was the eve of destruction that Barry McGuire sang about in 1965 or the dawning of the age of Aquarius featured in the 1967 musical *Hair*. The sense of being a part of momentous change began to dissipate as the sixties gave way to the seventies, reflecting such events as the election of Richard Nixon to the presidency, the continuation of the Vietnam War, the increasing radicalization of significant segments of the counterculture, the leaking of the Pentagon Papers, the compromises and catastrophic outcome of George McGovern's counterculture-backed campaign as the Democratic challenger to Nixon's reelection, the Watergate scandal and Agnew and Nixon's resignations, the ignominious U.S. withdrawal from South Vietnam and the rapid victory of the communist north, the Arab oil embargo, the Iranian revolution and hostage crisis, and the Soviet invasion of Afghanistan. The increasing sense of negativity was reflected in the increasingly dominant theme of seventies science fiction, the imagination of dystopia. While famously expressed in a number of 20th-century novels, notably Aldous Huxley's *Brave New World* (1932) and George Orwell's *1984* (1949), the updated versions that became a part of baby boomer culture incorporated similar fears regarding the totalitarian potential of modern governments, especially as aided and abetted by technology in the form of the bomb, whether as a postapocalyptic scenario or simply through the threat of such doomsday devices; additionally, there was anxiety concerning the computer as the ultimate mechanization of Big Brother, whether directed by human beings or acting in autonomous fashion. Also, added to the political dimension of dystopian visions was an increasingly more strident critique of late capitalism, in the form of highly ambitious multinational corporations, either working in concert with governments in the form of what Eisenhower referred to as the military-industrial complex, or establishing their own form of oligarchy or corporatocracy.

For example, Kubrick's 1971 follow-up to *2001, A Clockwork Orange*, presents a future society in which the tilt to the left that took place during the sixties resulted in a democratically elected socialist government in the United Kingdom, reflected in the introduction of a number of Russian words into English slang. The children of the baby boomers, rebelling against their parents in the same way that the baby boomers had rebelled against their parents, disdained peace, love, and understanding, opting instead for violence, rape, and murder, while also rejecting rock and roll and embracing classical music. In keeping with sixties liberalism, the future society approached the problem of criminal behavior and evil as a mental health issue, leading the authorities to invent a new form of behavior modification that makes the main character incapable of acting badly, an elimination of free will that is ultimately repudiated. Despite the inherently conservative critique of the counterculture, the essential structure of individualistic rebellion against oppressive authority that was embraced by baby boomers remains intact in this film.

George Lucas made his directing debut in 1971 with the dystopian feature *THX-1138*, in which a computer-controlled society has made drug use mandatory and sex forbidden; the dehumanization of the population is displayed through their unisex look and the use of letter-number combinations in place of names. The narrative follows the title character as he stops taking his medication, falls in love, rebels, and ultimately escapes the underground city within which this society is situated. *Silent Running*, a 1972 film directed by Douglas Trumbull, who had supervised the special effects on *2001*, envisioned a future in which all vegetation on earth had disappeared, the only surviving plants existing in domes out in space. When ordered to jettison and destroy the remaining domes because it would be too expensive to maintain them, one crewman defiantly acts to preserve them. Richard Fleischer's 1973 film *Soylent Green* depicts a future society plagued by overpopulation, famine, euthanasia and the active promotion of suicide, and a corporation that is secretly recycling human bodies as food. Norman Jewison's 1975 movie, *Rollerball*, gives us a future ruled by a cabal of corporations, in which an extremely violent sport keeps the masses enter-tained and distracted, while subtly teaching them that individual effort is futile, a lesson contradicted by the main character, Jonathan. The same year saw the release of Roger Corman's cult classic, *Death Race 2000*, directed by Paul Bartel, featuring a continent-wide car race in which points are awarded for every pedestrian the drivers run over; the race is intended to deflect attention from the totalitarian nature of the future government, which is finally overthrown by one of the drivers, nicknamed Frankenstein. *Logan's Run*, directed by Michael Anderson and released in 1976, depicts a night-mare future derived from the youth culture of the sixties, a decade during which baby boomers often invoked the slogan, "don't trust anyone over 30." In the film's computer-dominated dystopia, the remnants of humanity live in a sealed environment in which everyone over the age of 30 takes part in what they believe to be a ritual of renewal, but in fact they are executed. Anyone who tries to run away to avoid this fate is pursued by enforcers called Sandmen, one of whom, Logan, is prematurely scheduled for renewal and turned into a runner so that he can find the mythical Sanctuary the runners hope to escape to. Although he learns that there is no such place, Logan is able to disrupt the computer's functioning and put an end to the controlled society.

What all of these films have in common is a hero (or antihero) who rebels against the dominant, authoritarian pressures of their societies and rejects their concomitant dehumanization, emerging as a triumphant indi-vidual in keeping with traditional American values and generally restoring some sense of nature and the natural in the face of science and technology gone out of control. Increasingly more emphasis on the economic roots of dystopia, specifically corporate capitalism, can be seen in later films such as Ridley Scott's 1979 horror hybrid *Alien*, in which a corporation regards its employees as expendable as it seeks to obtain an all but unstoppable alien for its weapons division, aided by an android programmed to betray its human companions; along with its sequels, *Alien* reflects the feminist move-ment associated with the counterculture, notably in the fact that the main character and sole survivor at the end of the film is the female Ripley. (This follows the lead of Princess Leia in George Lucas's *Star Wars*, played against type as assertive and combat-ready, and is in turn followed by Sarah Con-nor in James Cameron's *The Terminator* and its sequels, which portrays her character developing from a frivolous young woman to a hardened survival-ist.) *Outland* directed by Peter Hyams, and released in 1981, follows a *High*

Noon-derived narrative, substituting a corporation for the western's gang of outlaws. Ridley Scott's critically acclaimed 1982 film *Blade Runner*, the first of many Philip K. Dick adaptations, shows an environmentally ruined and overpopulated Los Angeles dominated by advertisements encouraging residents to move to Mars, a scenario also reflecting the sudden rise of Japan as an economic force during the eighties; in this dystopia, the Tyrell Corporation rules from a pair of enormous, futuristic versions of Meso-American pyramids, manufacturing artificial human beings, aka replicants, who are sold as technological equivalents of slaves. Another film based on a Dick narrative, *Total Recall*, directed by Paul Verhoeven and released in 1990, shows the extension of capitalism into the commercialization of the air we breathe, and consciousness itself in the form of memory. For baby boomers, the emphasis on capitalism, commercialism, and corporations in these films reflects a fundamental ambivalence, if not dissonance, between the ideals of the counterculture, with its communal ideals, and the realities of entering the workforce and trying to fit into existing organizational structures without entirely abandoning a sense of social conscience.

The dissatisfactions of dystopia lead filmmakers to either abandon the emphasis on outer space entirely, as in *Blade Runner*, or depict the final frontier as an extension of blue-collar and white-collar workplaces, as was the case for much of *Alien*, as well as John Carpenter's 1974 science fiction comedy, *Dark Star*. *Total Recall* does provide a glimpse of machinery left behind by an extinct alien race, reminiscent of the Krell technology of *Forbidden Planet*, but the focus is on a Las Vegas–like district within the Martian colony. Of course, space as a fairytale wonderland was more than adequately depicted in Lucas's 1977 blockbuster, *Star Wars*, and its sequels, *The Empire Strikes Back* in 1981, and *Return of the Jedi* in 1983. Although often labeled "futuristic," what is notably absent from these films is any sense of an actual future that we might aspire to, being set "a long time ago, in a galaxy far, far away." While maintaining an overall positive outlook, these films also reflect the loss of faith in the future and in human progress associated with the dystopian narratives of the seventies. This is not to deny that there is a science fiction motif in which advanced, space-faring civilizations can exist in the past, and perhaps have played a role in the origin of life on earth and/or the development of human civilization (UFO lore includes the possibility of ancient astronauts, while *2001* has the alien monolith playing the role of catalyst in the origin of human consciousness and tool use). But not only is *Star Wars* *not* set in the future, it takes place outside of historical time. How far in the past is the story set, and at what distance from our planet? What relation do the characters and societies depicted bear to our own? Are the human characters actually human beings like us, and if so, are they our ancestors, or do we share common ancestors? These questions are never posed, let alone answered. In *Star Wars*, fantasy serves as the counterpart to dystopia in being a retreat from historical consciousness and the future orientation associated with the modern belief in progress, a point brought home poignantly in Terry Gilliam's 1985 Orwellian comedy, *Brazil*.

The loss of a coherent sense of linear time can also be seen in James Cameron's 1984 film, *The Terminator*, and its sequels. The film draws on older themes of technophobia relating to the development of a hostile artificial consciousness on the part of computers, what might be seen as HAL from *2001* writ large, as the computers initiate a nuclear holocaust with the intent of wiping out human life, the aftermath shown in brief scenes of a postapocalyptic future reminiscent of World War II movie imagery. The terminator, played by Arnold Schwarzenegger, is an all but unstoppable killing machine sent back in time to murder Sarah Connor. Sarah is the mother of the future leader of the resistance, John Connor, who does not actually appear in the film, but whose presence dominates the narrative; his initials, J.C., are indicative of his savior status, not to mention the almost miraculous fact that he is the cause of his own birth. The soldier from the future, Kyle Reese, explains that he was sent back in time by John Connor to save Connor's mother from the terminator. The film implies that John Connor was aware of the fact that Reese is destined to become his father, which is why he supplied Reese with the picture of Sarah that leads Reese to fall in love with her. This story involves a time-loop paradox in which future events cannot occur except for the intervention of time travelers from the future, with no discernible first cause that can be identified (Penley 1986). This is quite distinct from traditional time-travel stories in which it is possible to follow a chain of causes and effects back and forth through time. A similar time loop can be found in Terry Gilliam's *12 Monkeys* from 1995, in which the main character, again a time traveler from a postapocalyptic future, is named James Cole, once again sporting the initials J.C. Based on *La Jetée*, Chris Marker's 1960 experimental short film, *12 Monkeys* portrays its savior as more of a martyr than a John Connor–type leader, but for both the concern is with human survival, not transcendence.

Star Wars offers a vision of transcendence in the form of "the force," as wielded by the Jedi Knights, who are based in part on Japanese samurai warriors, in part on the Jesuit order of the Roman Catholic Church, and in part on the Bene Gesserit of Frank Herbert's *Dune* novels, and Lucas famously drew upon Joseph Campbell's (1968) monomyth structure of separation, initiation, and return in constructing the original *Star Wars* plotlines (Campbell and Moyers 1988). But it is transcendence for a select few who are "strong with the force." Although explained as an energy field, the force is essentially a mystical concept, very much related to the New Age spirituality that evolved out of baby boomer counterculture. In the original film, Darth Vader cautions Admiral Motti in regard to the Death Star: "Don't be too proud of this technological terror you've constructed. The ability to destroy a planet is insignificant next to the power of the Force." Motti responds by characterizing Vader as a sorcerer, and the Jedi Knights as an ancient religion, to which Vader in turn says, "I find your lack of faith disturbing," while telekinetically pinching Motti's windpipe, causing him to choke and gasp for air. The references to sorcery, religion, and faith go hand in hand with the clear contrasts between good and evil in the film that unambiguously situate us in a religious framework, rather than a scientific one; in the *Star Wars* universe, there is no question that it is the Force that is the true source of power, not science and technology. A clear contrast can be made between the modernism of *Star Trek*, in which any seemingly supernatural force or godlike being that is encountered is eventually accorded a scientific explanation, either as a product of advanced technology or higher evolution, in both instances with the promise that humanity can one day reach that level of development (Jewett and Lawrence 1977). There is no magic, mystical energy, or myth in *Star Trek*, whereas the Jedi Knights and the Force are central to *Star Wars*. This goes hand in hand with the postmodern orientation of *Star Wars* as situated outside of historical time, whereas *Star Trek* gives us a clear line of progress from the present to the imagined future.

While *Star Trek*'s characters have familiar ethnicities and ancestries, Captain Kirk for example, being from Iowa, we are expected to take it for granted that Luke Skywalker, Han Solo, Princess Leia, and Obi-Wan Kenobi are people just like us, even though the connection is never explained. And again in contrast to *Star Trek*, where at least some attempt is made to provide a scientific and technological context for every futuristic device and alien encounter, *Star Wars* assumes a familiarity with the icons and tropes of the science fiction genre, to the extent that it is no longer necessary to explain such technologies as spaceships, hyperdrive, tractor beams, force fields, flying cars, jetpacks, blasters, lightsabers, cloning, etc. Famously, *Star Wars* features robots, referred to as "droids," who exhibit intelligence, personality, and, to varying degrees, human consciousness, as if that sort of phenomena was only natural. The existence of alien races, such as Jawas, Wookies, and Ewoks, is also presented as requiring no explanation. In other words, *Star Wars* is arguably the first science film created explicitly for science fiction natives, for an audience that requires no explanation for futuristic technology and discoveries, viewing them as expected rather than extraordinary. In this sense, the alien has become altogether familiar for baby boomers, and in many ways *Star Wars* serves to mitigate the disappointment of the unrealized vision of the future shown to us during the sixties, the future of *2001* and *Star Trek*. *Star Wars* is very much an expression of nostalgia for the visions of the futures from the past, of the *Flash Gordon* and *Buck Rogers* serials that inspired Lucas and that he sought to recreate. As Sontag (1977) notes, nostalgia is associated with discontinuous imagery rather than history's linear narrative, and it is very much connected to contemporary commercialism; this resonates with *Star Wars* being set in an ahistorical fairytale past.

But even the resurrection of *Star Trek* in the form of a series of major motion pictures, beginning with Robert Wise's feature in 1979, while ostensibly grounded in Roddenberry's futurism, was for baby boomer audiences an exercise in nostalgia, rather than a renewed imagination of utopia. The launch of *Star Trek: The Next Generation* television series in 1987, with a new *Enterprise* captained by the much older Jean-Luc Picard, also maintained its nostalgic connection to the original series, as much as it tried to create an independent identity for episodes set almost a century further into the future than the original narratives. Apart from some modest technological advances and, more importantly, the elimination of a number of anachronisms that inevitably crop up as depictions of the future age, *The Next Generation*'s updated version of Roddenberry's progressive vision of the future was wholly given over to political correctness, in keeping with the strong egalitarianism of baby boomer counterculture and the changes it had given rise to in mainstream American society. This had the unfortunate effect of significantly weakening the dramatic elements of the program, missing the sense in which baby boomers defined themselves through their opposition to their parents' generation. The new series also featured a somewhat darker, less utopian image of the Federation and Starfleet, like the dystopian films of the seventies and eighties, reflecting the loss of the optimism and idealism of the sixties. The darker view continued in the series that followed, *Star Trek: Deep Space Nine*, a highly underrated, profoundly psychological program that explored questions of religion and spirituality more deeply than any other version of *Star Trek*; launched in 1993, *Deep Space Nine* also reflected growing concern and conflicts with the Islamic world. *Star Trek: Voyager*, launched in 1995, presented a more compromised image of the future of humanity as well. The steady decline of audiences for these two *Star Trek* series and the prequel that followed, *Star Trek: Enterprise*, launched in 2001 and abruptly canceled after only four seasons, and for the major motion pictures featuring *The Next Generation*'s *Enterprise* crew, are indicative of the loss of faith in the future in 21st-century culture, indeed a loss of an imagination of the future (Strate 2011). This is also apparent in the fact that the franchise has recently resorted to rebooting the original series, an exercise in nostalgic recycling, using time travel to create a darker universe for the characters from the original series to inhabit.

The contrast between *Star Trek* and *Star Wars* represents a shift in baby boomer mind-set from a modernist belief in progress and a future orientation to a postmodernist nostalgia that replaces historical consciousness with a present-centered worldview. And as much as the enormous popularity and financial success of *Star Wars* made 1977 a pivotal year for the science fiction genre, this was reinforced by the release in the same year of

Steven Spielberg's *Close Encounters of the Third Kind*. Returning to the UFO myth that dominated fifties science fiction films, *Close Encounters* draws on the religious and spiritual elements of the alien messiah theme, as the main character, Roy Neary, experiences a close encounter and receives a kind of telepathic summoning to go to the mountain where the aliens will make first contact with humanity. His response is somewhat akin to a religious calling. Roy is seen as insane by his wife, who takes their children and leaves him, and while he is driven to reach the landing site, he meets up with Jillian, whose three-year-old son was abducted by the aliens early in the film. Similarly to *The Day the Earth Stood Still*, the government and military are depicted in a relatively negative light, albeit not as hostile as in the fifties film, but still using secrecy and deception to keep information about the visitations from the public, and actively keeping the people who have been summoned from reaching the landing site. Twelve make it to the vicinity, a number resonant with the 12 sons of Jacob, ancestors of the 12 tribes of Israel, and the 12 apostles of Jesus. Of the 12, only Jillian and Roy make it to the landing site, where Jillian's son is returned to her, the abduction entirely downplayed throughout the movie to maintain the positive image of the aliens, as is the return in the end of various people who had been missing for decades. Roy is chosen to go off with the aliens, and he enters their UFO and flies off with them. There is a return to the imagination of transcendence here, but, as in *Star Wars*, it is transcendence for a select few. Much emphasis is placed on the aliens' use of five tones as a form of communication, which in the end allows for a kind of communion between them and the human scientist, Claude Lacombe. But unacknowledged is the fact that there is an absence of any real communication, in the sense of sharing messages with specific meanings; in postmodern terms, we have style without substance, surface with no depth behind it, signifiers absent any signified, but it does serve to reinforce the mystical sensibility of the film.

Reflecting the realities of baby boomer lifestyles, Roy Neary's home is full of the clutter of consumer products; the children, having been raised by overly permissive parents, are disrespectful if not entirely out of control, and Roy's marriage is disintegrating. That this is not viewed as a tragedy or failure on Roy's part echoes the fact that baby boomers had greatly devalued marriage in comparison to the older generations, rejecting taboos against premarital sex, commonly living together before marriage, sometimes rejecting the idea of marriage altogether while maintaining long-term relationships, and engaging in divorce increasingly more frequently and more readily. The stigma against divorce so apparent in *Invasion of the Body Snatchers* was gone by the mid-seventies, as the first American sitcom to feature a divorced, single-parent household, *One Day at a Time*, premiered at the end of 1975, while the following year a divorced man was for the first time taken seriously as a presidential candidate, Ronald Reagan almost wresting the Republican nomination away from sitting president Gerald Ford (and winning the presidency only four years later, running in large part as the candidate of *family values!*). Although not formally divorced, it is clear in *Close Encounters* that Roy's marriage is over, the fact mitigated by his joining together with Jillian, a single mother, to find the aliens and her abducted son. Even this budding relationship is abandoned as Roy goes off with the aliens, apparently unconcerned about anyone being left behind, certainly not the wife who left him or his three children who may never see their father again. Transcendence here is wedded to a juvenile fantasy of escape from responsibility, and although there is also a genuine sense of spirituality conveyed in the film, the alien messiah theme is unfulfilled in that there is no indication that any significant social change will take place on Earth, certainly no political solution of the sort handed down by Klaatu in *The Day the Earth Stood Still.*

Close Encounters of the Third Kind was overshadowed by Spielberg's 1982 masterpiece, *E.T. the Extra-Terrestrial*, which in many ways is based on *The Day the Earth Stood Still*, albeit one in which the alien is truly alien in appearance, monstrous when first seen, but quickly coming across as childlike and cute. In the film, E.T. displays a variety of miraculous powers, including bringing a dead plant back to life and creating a psychic link with the main character, Elliott, a 10-year-old boy. That the link causes Elliott to rebel against the dissection of frogs in school, disrupting the class and kissing one of the girls, comes across as humorous, and justified in his defense of animal rights. That E.T. mistakenly drinks beer and becomes inebriated, a state that Elliott shares through their link, is also shown as comedic and never called into question within the film. Neither is the much more serious turn of events when E.T. is dying, and Elliott's own health is affected dramatically, until E.T.'s apparent death severs their link. Objectively, we should be horrified by this turn of events, but E.T. and Elliott are so closely identified with each other (note that E and T are the first and last letters of Elliott's name) that audiences generally are not troubled by this plot element, which is soon forgotten when E.T. comes back to life. His resurrection is the greatest of the miracles he is associated with in the film, and unlike Klaatu, he issues no disclaimer about the source of his powers. Indeed, when he first appears after being revived, his heart is glowing red, invoking the image of the Sacred Heart of Jesus commonly depicted in religious art within Catholicism and other branches of Christianity. As in *The Day the Earth Stood Still*, there is an element of persecution by the authorities, who come across as threatening, especially from the childlike point of view of E.T. and Elliott. And after his resurrection, E.T. ascends back up into the heavens at the close of the film (Rushing 1985).

Like *Star Wars* and *Close Encounters*, *E.T.* is a film created for science fiction natives, as Elliott shows the alien his collection of *Star Wars* toys and, in a self-reflexive moment that invariably draws laughter, but violates any sense of historical continuity, E.T. sees a child dressed as Yoda from *The Empire Strikes Back* and reacts with clear excitement and recognition. Perhaps most telling of all is the point toward the end of the film when Elliott is aided by other children, all riding bicycles to elude the authorities, and he explains that E.T. is "from outer space and we're taking him to his spaceship." Another boy, Greg, asks, "can't he just beam up?" and Elliott's reply is, "This is *reality*, Greg!" Another self-reflexive moment guaranteed to get a chuckle out of the audience, this also serves as a subtle repudiation of Roddenberry's modernist science fiction, with its emphasis on rationality, in favor of Spielberg's combination of special effects and special *affects* (Sobchack 1987), the appeal to sentimentality, nostalgia, and joyfulness of youth (as Elliott's brother Michael explains, Elliott does not think E.T.'s thoughts, he *feels* his *feelings*). Indeed, there is an undercurrent of elation in the image of bicycles flying through the air—as McLuhan (1964) noted, the bicycle was the first truly aerodynamic form of transportation, and it is no accident that the Wright brothers were bicycle mechanics. But the film is full of subtle phallic imagery, the bicycles, the frogs, and E.T. himself with his extending neck and head. There is also a hint of both an Oedipal theme here, albeit nowhere near as overt as in the *Star Wars* trilogy where Darth Vader, a Germanic rendering of "dark father," reveals that he is Anakin Skywalker, Luke's father, not to mention *Forbidden Planet*'s unspoken hint of incestuous desire; more mildly, we might see a subtle suggestion of Elliott's sexual awakening in his adventure with E.T.

Even more so than in *Close Encounters*, *E.T.* is about the experience of divorce, so much a part of baby boomers' adult lives and, for a sizable number, their childhoods as well. Elliott's father is entirely absent from the film, having run off to Mexico with a woman named Sally, and like *The Day the Earth Stood Still*, *E.T.* is very much about absent fathers. Early on, we see that Elliott's mother, Mary, is unable to control her children, and her vulnerability is shown by the fact that one of the friends visiting Michael, Elliott's older brother, reaches out to pinch her as she is bending over in the kitchen, his hand slapped away at the last minute by Michael. Later, when Elliott says he saw some kind of creature, and Mary and his siblings seem skeptical, he says that his father would believe him; Mary responds by saying that maybe he should call his father and tell him about it, Elliott says he can't because his father is in Mexico with Sally, and Mary breaks down and leaves the room. We also see that Michael, Elliott, and his younger sister Gertie are latchkey kids, not uncommon at this time, and that Mary is so distracted that she somehow does not notice an alien being living in her home.

The theme of absent fathers is common to alien messiah films, but unlike Klaatu, E.T. is not a substitute father figure, instead connecting to the child's need to escape uncomfortable reality through fantasy. The extra-terrestrial does act as a catalyst, however, in restoring a semblance of family unity, not only as the siblings unite to protect the stranded alien, eventually bringing Mary into their orbit as well, but also in being pursued by one of the film's main characters, a government agent who strangely is never named and not fully seen until the second half of the film. Played by Peter Coyote, the character is known only as "Keys," because he has a large set of keys dangling from his belt. He is only seen from the waist down during the first half of the movie, the focus being on his keys (which also may be regarded as a phallic symbol and a symbol of adulthood and responsibility); the sound of the keys jangling together is given special emphasis in those scenes. Keys and the other government agents who accompany him are portrayed as vaguely threatening at first and, in a great reversal of the alien and familiar dynamic of the genre, E.T. quickly comes to be seen as friendly and familiar, and the authorities suddenly appear in something akin to spacesuits, clearly meant to avoid possible contamination from radiation or alien microbes, but giving them the appearance of aliens as they invade Elliott's home and take E.T. away. This reversal is soon reversed once again as the authorities are shown to be relatively benign in trying to save E.T.'s life, and we finally see the face of Keys, as he speaks with Elliott in a fatherly manner, saying that he has been wishing for someone like E.T. too, ever since he was 10 years old, Elliott's age. After E.T.'s death and resurrection, while government agents in their cars chase after E.T., Elliott, Michael, and their friends as they ride their bicycles, Keys joins Mary, and they arrive together at the site where E.T.'s people come down to earth to take him home. As E.T. leaves, Keys stands together with Mary and the children, visually completing the family unit, and suggesting that this will lead to a fuller healing of their broken home in the future. Elliott and his family, along with Keys, are left with a transcendent experience, signaled at the end by the rainbow left by the departing spacecraft, which was God's sign in the story of Noah. However, the result again is not any change in the world, spiritually or politically, but simply a personal revelation and restoration for Elliott and his family.

This new version of the alien messiah theme initiated by Spielberg and to a lesser extent Lucas can also be found in other films of the eighties. For example, John Carpenter's *Starman*, released in 1984, picks up on Spielberg's emphasis on a bright light associated with alien beings. (Spielberg's signature use of backlighting was inspired by McLuhan and meant to evoke the experience of television natives, who grew up watching moving images projected outward from the rear of the screen on their TV sets, as opposed to the motion picture, which is typically projected onto the front of the movie screen.) *Starman* depicts the title character, an alien, as a being made of light and energy, again conferring a spiritual quality upon the visitor. Coming to Earth after receiving the invitation transmitted via our *Voyager 2* space probe, his ship is shot down by the U.S. government, once more depicted as hostile. He takes human form, utilizing the DNA from a lock of hair from her dead husband kept by widow Jenny Hayden. His incarnation is followed by a series of miracles, such as bringing a dead deer back to life and healing the injuries Jenny sustains as they escape from overzealous police officers. Like E.T., the starman is unable to survive on Earth for very long and must make his way with Jenny's help to the site where his fellow celestial beings will take him home. Although Jenny is initially shocked by the apparent resurrection of her husband by an alien intelligence, the two eventually make love, and before he departs for the heavens, he informs her that she is pregnant, despite the fact that she is infertile, that her baby will be the son of her husband because the DNA was cloned from her husband, and that her son will be a teacher. This invokes the common biblical motif of God making a barren woman able to bear children, as well as invoking the New Testament narrative of Joseph and Mary, the immaculate conception, and Jesus as a rabbi, which translates as teacher. There is, then, some hint of a broader transcendence to come, but within the confines of this film, the miracles are local and personal.

Cocoon, directed by Ron Howard and released in 1985, also posits alien beings composed of light and energy, this time coming to Earth secretly to retrieve cocoons containing other aliens who had been previously left behind on our planet. They store the cocoons in a swimming pool in Florida, where a group of senior citizens sneak in to go for a swim and discover that the cocoons have magical restorative powers, energizing them and reversing the aging process. At the end of the film, most of the seniors leave the planet with the aliens to gain eternal life in the heavens (the only one to stay behind is the one character who is recognizably Jewish, invoking a traditional Christian-centered version of the myth). Again, the imagination of transcendence is a private one and, in this instance, one that is restricted.

FROM OUTER SPACE TO MEDIA SPACE

As the first television generation, baby boomers have also been native to media spaces, even as they looked to outer space for visions of the future and sources of transcendence. And as the promise of Star Trek and 2001 faded, media-related themes began to appear in the genre. Blade Runner is noted for its floating video billboards as well as the main character's use of digital imaging to identify one of the replicants he is chasing. For this reason, and the overall street-level ambience, the film is sometimes considered one of the first examples of the cyberpunk subgenre in film, even though the cyber element is minimal. The replicants themselves, advertised as "more human than human," do invoke Jean Baudrillard's (1994) concept of hyperreal simulation. But a more comprehensive example can be found in the *Star Trek: The Next Generation* series and films, along with *Deep Space Nine* and *Voyager*, in the form of the holodeck, a technology that uses solid light constructs and computer simulations to create the ultimate in fantasy environments (Murray 1997). In keeping with Roddenberry's positive outlook, the holodeck is generally shown to be a benign environment where people can pursue various forms of entertainment, although occasionally the simulations can get out of control. David Cronenberg's *Videodrome* of 1983 offered a much darker vision in which cable television programming that emphasizes sex and violence contains a secret signal designed to affect people's behavior and biology. Significantly, the film features a character named Brian O'Blivion, patterned after sixties media guru and baby boomer icon Marshall McLuhan. *Total Recall* turns memories into media software that can be downloaded directly into the brain, giving new meaning to the concept of vicarious experience. The theme of recording, sharing, and buying and selling memories in the manner of drugs is central to 1995's *Strange Days*, directed by Kathryn Bigelow (Bolter and Grusin 1999). Watching movies and television has frequently been compared to dreaming, and the invasion of dream space is a theme of Joseph Ruben's 1984 film *Dreamscape*, while Wim Wenders posits a device for recording and playing back our dreams in *Until the End of the World*, released in 1991. Despite the apocalyptic title, the threat involves not so much a bang as a whimper as the technology represents a modern form of the Narcissus myth.

As digital immigrants, baby boomers encountered computers as exotic environments that they might be able to visit but could never call home. In 1982, Walt Disney released *TRON*, directed by Steven Lisberger, in which a programmer, Kevin Flynn, is digitized and brought into the computer environment, in which the programs appear to be fashioned in the image of their creators and have a religious belief in the existence of human beings, or users as they are referred to. Battling the evil Master Control Program with the aid of the heroic program Tron, Flynn is able to bring justice to the microworld, and in doing so obtain the proof he was searching for that his own video game programs had been stolen. In a more extreme example, Brett Leonard's *Lawnmower Man* from 1992 depicted virtual reality as a dangerous environment. And a true sense of baby boomer suspicion of cyberspace can be found in *Wild Palms*, a 1993 television miniseries combining science fiction with a soap opera style reminiscent of *Dallas* and *Dynasty*, and produced by Oliver Stone, whose films have dealt with many of the main issues of the sixties and baby boomer culture. Prescient in its vision of a future America in which a terrorist incident results in a major tilt to the right, invoking Eugène Ionesco's theater of the absurd image of the rhinoceros as a symbol of a fascist takeover, *Wild Palms* posits future media that combine the Internet, holograms, television, and hallucinogenic drugs that are also addictive, and which serve the purposes of a conspiracy on the part of corporations, the government, and a Scientology-like religious movement. A similar sense of discomfort with the digital can be found in David Cronenberg's 1999 film, *eXistenZ*, similar to his *Videodrome* in representing the video game space as one that can be quite threatening and dislocating. By way of contrast, consider films that clearly depict the digital natives of the millennial generation, the best known example being *The Matrix*, also from 1999, and directed by the Wachowski siblings, in which the main character, Neo, is completely empowered within the digital environment, turning into a kind of superhero. Although not entirely situated in cyberspace, 1998's *Dark City*, directed by Alex Proyas, similarly depicts the main character as coming to dominate and reshape his artificial environment, in contrast to *TRON*'s Flynn, who merely survives within it. Josef Rusnak's *The Thirteenth Floor* from 1999 presents a virtual reality within a virtual reality and a title character who is the ultimate digital native. More recently, *Avatar*, directed by James Cameron and released in 2009, features a main character who is more comfortable in his telepresence-enabled body than his disabled real one, while Christopher Nolan's *Inception* of 2010 has its characters comfortably moving through other people's virtual reality dreamscapes.

I have somewhat arbitrarily drawn the line here between the baby boomers' experience as science fiction natives and as digital immigrants, as the genre shifted in emphasis from the bomb and outer space to the computer and media spaces. As science fiction natives, baby boomers looked forward to the exploration of outer space, and inner space, the space of consciousness, as depicted in Ken Russell's 1980 film *Altered States*, which invokes a Carlos Castaneda–like sense of tribal mysticism and the use of hallucinogenic drugs to probe the collective unconscious and genetic memory in the service of scientist Eddie Jessup's obsessive search for the true self. Such soul-searching was a powerful theme during the sixties, but this film concludes that there is no *there* there, that at the core all there is is emptiness, and the only reality we can find is in our relationships, in love. More typical of the genre, however, was a film like Paul Verhoeven's *RoboCop* of 1987, in which a dead police officer is turned into a cyborg, his mind a combination of computer technology and the remnants of the living cop's brain, presumably with no recollection of his previous existence. In the face of this radical dehumanization, RoboCop's memories resurface, and he reclaims his humanity. *RoboCop* upholds the idea of a true self, one that can be suppressed but never entirely extinguished, but like *Altered States* also invokes the importance of love and relationships. In many different ways, the science fiction genre has served as a vehicle for the exploration of the self, as we define the human against the alien, the natural against the artificial, the biological against the technological, and the real against the electronically mediated (Rushing and Frentz 1995).

The question of identity has been very much a concern for baby boomers, as the electronic media environment dominated by television undermined the old certainties about the integrated, inner-directed self of print culture. This can be seen as one of the main reasons for the generation gap between baby boomers and the previous generation, as the baby boomers rebelled against and rejected the traditional identity formation of the generations that preceded them. Baby boomers struggled to find themselves, searching for authenticity and the true self, which ultimately meant holding on to key aspects of the heroic individual, without whom rebellion would not have been possible. As forms of popular culture, science fiction films and television programs reflect that quest for identity, as the contrast between the alien and the familiar helped to define what it means to be human. But the counterculture and the rejection of the mainstream establishment also led to the blurring of the distinction between alien and familiar, reflecting the decentered subject, saturated self, and posthuman sensibility of postmodern culture (Poster 1990; Gergen 1991; Hayles 1999). The younger generations of digital natives may be more comfortable with the resultant identity diffusion than baby boomers, but as science fiction natives they were not entirely unprepared for these cultural changes. Indeed, as noted at the beginning of this chapter, the divide between the baby boomers and their children is nowhere near as dramatic as the generation gap that separated them from their parents. Baby boomers and the generations that have followed are all products of the electronic media environment and are all science fiction natives. And as the first generation of science fiction natives, baby boomers grappled with questions that set the agenda for generations to come, as we learn how to adjust to a new environment dominated by nuclear weapons, rockets, and satellites, as well as electric power, information processing, and computers and digital media, and as we contemplate the future of the global village and spaceship earth.

REFERENCES

Baudrillard, Jean. 1994. *Simulacra and Simulation*. Translated by S. F. Glaser. Ann Arbor: University of Michigan Press.

Berger, Arthur Asa. 1976. *The TV-Guided American*. New York: Walker.

Bolter, Jay D., and Richard Grusin. 1999. *Remediation: Understanding New Media*. Cambridge, MA: MIT Press.

Campbell, Joseph. 1968. *The Hero with a Thousand Faces*. 2nd ed. Princeton: Princeton University Press.

Campbell, Joseph, and Bill Moyers. 1988. *The Power of Myth*. New York: Doubleday.

Clarke, Arthur C. 2000. Foreword to the Millennial Edition. In *2001: A Space Odyssey*. New York: New American Library, vii–xvi.

Ellul, Jacques. 1964. *The Technological Society.* Translated by J. Wilkinson. New York: Knopf.

Frye, Northrop. 1957. *Anatomy of Criticism: Four Essays.* Princeton, NJ: Princeton University Press.

Fuller, R. Buckminster. 1971. *Operating Manual for Spaceship Earth.* New York: E. P. Dutton.

Gergen, Kenneth J. 1991. *The Saturated Self.* New York: Basic Books.

Hayles, N. Katherine. 1999. *How We Became Posthuman: Virtual Bodies in Cybernetics, Literature, and Informatics.* Chicago: University of Chicago Press.

Heyer, Paul. 2003. "America under Attack I: A Reassessment of Orson Welles' 1938 War of the Worlds Broadcast." *Canadian Journal of Communication* 28: 149–165.

Huxley, Aldous. 1932. *Brave New World.* New York: HarperPerennial.

Jewett, Robert, and John Shelton Lawrence. 1977. *The American Monomyth.* Garden City, NY: Anchor Press/Doubleday.

Jung, Carl. 1978. *Flying Saucers: A Modern Myth of Things Seen in the Skies.* Translated by R. F. C. Hull. Princeton: Princeton University Press.

McLuhan, Marshall. 1962. *The Gutenberg Galaxy: The Making of Typographic Man.* Toronto: University of Toronto Press.

McLuhan, Marshall. 1964. *Understanding Media: The Extensions of Man.* New York: McGraw Hill.

McLuhan, Marshall. 1969. "Playboy Interview: Marshall McLuhan." *Playboy,* March, 53–74, 158.

McLuhan, Marshall. 1974. "At the Moment of Sputnik the Planet Became a Global Theatre in Which There Are No Spectators but Only Actors." *Journal of Communication* 24 (1): 45–58.

Meyrowitz, Joshua. 1985. *No Sense of Place: The Impact of Electronic Media on Social Behavior.* New York: Oxford University Press.

Murray, Janet H. 1997. *Hamlet on the Holodeck: The Future of Narrative in Cyberspace.* New York: Free Press.

Orwell, George. 1949. *1984.* New York: New American Library.

Penley, Constance. 1986. "Time Travel, Primal Scene, and the Critical Dystopia." *Camera Obscura* 5 (3 15), 66–85.

Poster, Mark. 1990. *The Mode of Information.* Chicago: University of Chicago Press.

Postman, Neil. 1988. *Conscientious Objections: Stirring Up Trouble about Language, Technology, and Education.* New York: Alfred A. Knopf.

Postman, Neil. 1992. *Technopoly: The Surrender of Culture to Technology.* New York: Alfred A. Knopf.

Ruppersberg, Hugh. 1987. "The Alien Messiah in Recent Science Fiction Films." *Journal of Popular Film and TV* 14 (4): 158–166.

Rushing, Janice Hocker. 1985. "E.T. as Rhetorical Transcendence." *Quarterly Journal of Speech* 71 (2): 188–203.

Rushing, J. H., and T. S. Frentz. 1995. *Projecting the Shadow: The Cyborg Hero in American Film.* Chicago: University of Chicago Press.

Sobchack, Vivian. 1987. *Screening Space: The American Science Fiction Film.* New Brunswick, NJ: Rutgers University Press.

Sontag, Susan. 1966. "The Imagination of Disaster." In *Against Interpretation*, 209–225. New York: Farrar Straus Giroux.

Sontag, Susan. 1977. *On Photography*. New York: Farrar, Straus & Giroux.

Strate, Lance. 2006. *Echoes and Reflections: On Media Ecology as a Field of Study*. Cresskill, NJ: Hampton Press.

Strate, Lance. 2011. *On the Binding Biases of Time and Other Essays on General Semantics and Media Ecology*. Fort Worth, TX: Institute of General Semantics.

Toffler, Alvin. 1970. *Future Shock*. New York: Random House.

22

Marshall McLuhan and the Making of a Countercultural Generation

James C. Morrison

This chapter focuses on the ascendancy of Marshall McLuhan as a public intellectual in the 1960s and the symbiotic interactions between his thinking and perceptions and those of the baby boomer generation. His salience in the mind of the public was achieved primarily through his production of a remarkable series of books—*The Gutenberg Galaxy: The Making of Typographic Man* (1962), *Understanding Media: The Extensions of Man* (1964), *The Medium Is the Massage: An Inventory of Effects* (1967), and *War and Peace in the Global Village* (1968). One measure of how times have changed since then is the fact that although McLuhan achieved his ultimate impact through his many appearances in the electronic media, it was possible for him to do so only because he wrote such a stunning series of books.

These books are part and parcel of the sixties, a time that so marked, and was so marked by, the boomer generation. For many boomers, as well as older avant-garde artists, musicians, designers, writers, and academics, McLuhan's sixties books became the bibles of a new consciousness. They were published when television was becoming the defining milieu of American culture. This chapter will therefore speak not only to the media environment of the boomers but also to the influence of McLuhan as the *agent provocateur* who urged and encouraged the whole of our culture to think about and understand media in new ways, and whose ideas resonated with the changes in consciousness fostered by electronic media. McLuhan was both an original thinker and a masterful synthesizer of the intellectual labor of predecessors and colleagues in a comprehensive and unique view of relations that only a mind such as his could present so cogently to a wide public. Those unfamiliar with his work will be presented with perhaps a taste of what it was like to encounter McLuhan's prose and the particular ways in which he "put on" his readership, as he did his listening audiences.[1] All this is in pursuit of demonstrating the central notions of McLuhan's work: that "the medium is the message,"[2] and "[t]he new electronic interdependence recreates the world in the image of a global village."[3]

Herbert Marshall McLuhan was born on July 21, 1911, in Edmonton, Alberta, Canada. He was awarded bachelor's and master's degrees in English literature from the University of Manitoba, and in 1934 he entered Cambridge University at Trinity Hall. He received his baccalaureate in 1936 and was hired as a teaching assistant in the English Department of the University of Wisconsin, where he encountered for the first time students who loved popular culture and were largely ignorant of the high culture that had formed McLuhan's education. In 1937 he converted from Protestantism to Roman Catholicism and was hired to teach English at the Jesuit St. Louis University. He and Corinne Keller Lewis were married in 1939, and they moved back to Cambridge for Marshall to begin research for a PhD. In 1940 they returned to St. Louis University and, when his doctorate was conferred in 1943, he was promoted to assistant professor.

After a brief appointment at Assumption College in Windsor, Ontario, in the spring of 1946, McLuhan moved to the English Department of St. Michael's College of the University of Toronto, which was run, like Assumption, by the Basilian order. With his emphasis on contemporary American culture he soon became an irritant to many of his colleagues, but he was able to turn his series of lectures illustrated with slides of advertisements, comics, newspaper articles, and other cultural objects into *The Mechanical Bride: Folklore of Industrial Man* (1951). The book sold only a few hundred copies and was not widely reviewed, though it did receive an unsympathetic review in *The New York Times*.

In 1953 he and his colleague Edmund S. Carpenter received a grant from the Ford Foundation for a series of multidisciplinary seminars on media and culture. Written contributions from participants were later published in their journal, *Explorations*. In 1959, McLuhan received a grant under the U.S. National Defense Education Act from the National Association of Educational Broadcasters to develop a syllabus in media awareness for high school students. This project eventually led to the writing of *Understanding Media*. McLuhan's fortunes and visibility began rising in 1962 with the publication of *The Gutenberg Galaxy*, which was awarded Canada's Governor General's Award for Non-Fiction and was reviewed in the prestigious journals *The New Statesman* and *Encounter*. This heightened visibility led to an article of his being published in *The Times Literary Supplement* and his being included in another *TLS* article spotlighting avant-garde thinkers. This interest was abetted in no small part by the efforts of two Californian self-styled "genius scouts," Gerald Feigen and Howard Gossage. Feigen and Gossage promoted McLuhan by getting him lucrative corporate speaking engagements and arranging a series of cocktail parties in New York, where he was introduced to prominent publishers of major magazines. Through these latter contacts he met the "New Journalist" Tom Wolfe, who lent his considerable influence to promoting McLuhan. He was subsequently hired as a consultant for *Time, Life,* and *Fortune,* increasing his exposure to broader American publishing and advertising circles.

In November 1965, *New York* magazine published an article by Wolfe profiling McLuhan and his growing influence on denizens of corporate board rooms, titled "What If He Is Right?" The same year, Richard Schickel wrote a generally favorable article in *Harper's* magazine about McLuhan titled "Marshall McLuhan: Canada's Intellectual Comet." Wolfe's article, later republished in *The Pump House Gang,* chronicled the celebrity status McLuhan had gained as a result of the publication of *The Gutenberg Galaxy* and *Understanding Media.* During the 1960s and much of the 1970s, McLuhan achieved the status of a pop icon—his name was on the public's lips and his face and slogans were recognized by the general public, not just the intelligentsia.

McLuhan's fame occurred at a time when television was reaching its peak in defining, promoting, and spreading the pop culture of the baby boom generation. By the time *Understanding Media* was published, television had become the national electronic hearth. Several epochal events had brought huge television audiences together in common, emotionally charged experiences: the appearances of Elvis Presley, the Beatles, the Rolling Stones, and other major pop groups on *The Ed Sullivan Show;* the presidential debates between Vice President Richard M. Nixon and Senator John F. Kennedy; President Kennedy's assassination and funeral; the live, on-screen murder of his suspected assassin, Lee Harvey Oswald, by Jack Ruby; and the civil rights march on Washington led by the Reverend Dr. Martin Luther King, capped by his monumental "I Have a Dream" speech. As a consequence, the concept of an "electronic global village" had become engrained in the national consciousness by the time McLuhan announced it in *The Gutenberg Galaxy* and amplified it in his later works.

Perhaps the apotheosis of his stardom was in Woody Allen's 1977 film *Annie Hall,* when Allen's character, Alvy Singer, pulls McLuhan from behind a poster in a movie theater lobby to settle an argument with a clueless and pretentious Columbia University professor spouting representations of McLuhan's ideas diametrically opposite to what McLuhan meant. McLuhan says to the poseur, "I heard what you were saying! You know nothing of my work! You mean my whole fallacy is wrong. How you got to teach a course in anything is totally amazing!" The sly, self-deprecating redundancy in the third sentence was a put-down McLuhan had devised for hecklers, burlesquing the all-too-common misperceptions of so many of his critics.

Naturally, as McLuhan's star shone, he was bound to attract many critics as well as supporters. Although he was championed by some public intellectuals, his ideas soon drew the scorn of others, and probably drew more disdain than support among the academic establishment. At the University of Toronto in particular, the reaction against McLuhan's celebrity got to the point that he warned his graduate students to erase any trace of his work in their theses and dissertations to avoid reprisals by their review committees.[4] According to his son Eric, "[t]here were at least two concerted efforts (quiet ones, of course) to collect enough signatures to have his tenure revoked."[5] During the 1970s, despite a vigorous publishing output, almost completely in tandem with collaborators, McLuhan receded from our ken. Perhaps his ideas had initially received so much attention and exposure because they appeared so revolutionary, but then eventually they became overexposed and co-opted. His death on the last day of 1980 seemed to occasion reactions more along the lines of "Oh, was he still alive?" than the sense of loss of a contemporary figure. This was, prophetically, the theme of a *New Yorker* cartoon, published in 1970, whose caption read, "Ashley, are you sure it's not too soon to go around parties saying, 'What ever happened to Marshall McLuhan?'"

THE MCLUHAN GALAXY

By the end of the sixties McLuhan had ironically become, despite his learning, a prime example of Daniel Boorstin's definition, in *The Image*, of a celebrity: "a person who is known for his well-knownness."[6] The apogee (or perhaps nadir) of his celebrity occurred when he became the subject of a Henry Gibson poem on *Rowan and Martin's Laugh-In*, the quintessential television program: "Marshall McLuhan, what are you doin'?" The title of his 1969 *Playboy* interview—"Marshall McLuhan: A Candid Conversation with the High Priest of Popcult and Metaphysician of Media"—is emblematic of his elevation into the sixties pop pantheon with such figures as the Beatles, the Maharishi Mahesh Yogi, Peter Max, Mary Quant, Twiggy, Roy Lichtenstein, Andy Warhol, and all the other icons of the age. This was a most ironic position for someone who declared at that time, "I find most pop culture monstrous and sickening. I study it for my own survival."[7]

The McLuhan galaxy was star-crossed and fraught with such irony, for McLuhan is indelibly associated in the popular mind with a medium—television—whose effects he thoroughly mistrusted and even despised. Many, if not the vast majority, of his adulators among the burgeoning baby boom generation, and virtually all his critics, saw him as a television guru, a proselytizer for the electronic faith, whose attitude toward electronic media was akin to that of psychedelic shaman Timothy Leary, with whose philosophy his was sometimes confused: "Turn on, tune in, and drop out." In point of fact, McLuhan was, according to Leary, the source for this slogan:

I was having lunch with him in New York City. He was very much interested in ideas and marketing, and he started singing something like, "Psychedelics hit the spot / Five hundred micrograms, that's a lot," to the tune of a Pepsi commercial. Then he started going, "Tune in, turn on, and drop out."[8]

But when we delve into McLuhan's privately expressed attitudes toward television, his image as a shill for the boob tube is contradictory to his deep distrust of the medium.

One day, while watching television with a colleague and friend from the University of Toronto, McLuhan said, "Do you really want to know what I think of that thing? If you want to save one shred of Hebrao-Greco-Roman-Medieval-Renaissance-Enlightenment-Modern-Western civilization, you'd better get an ax and smash all the sets."[9] And in a 1976 letter advising his son Eric about a grandchild: "Try not to have Emily exposed to hours and hours of TV. It is a vile drug which permeates the nervous system, especially in the young."[10]

Such irony can be attributed, perhaps, to one of the points McLuhan made about media: that the force of the dominant communication medium of any time is ineluctable, despite the best efforts to contravene it:

Earlier it was mentioned how the school drop-out situation will get very much worse because of the frustration of the student need for participation in the learning process. This situation concerns also the problem of "the culturally disadvantaged child." This child exists not only in the slums but increasingly in the suburbs of the upper-income homes. The culturally disadvantaged child is the TV child. For TV has provided a new environment of low visual orientation and high involvement that makes accommodation to our older educational establishment quite difficult. One strategy of cultural response would be to raise the visual level of the TV image to enable the young student to gain access to the old visual world of the classroom and the curriculum. This would be worth trying as a temporary expedient. But TV is only one component of the electric environment of instant circuitry that has succeeded the old world of the wheel and nuts and bolts. We would be foolish not to ease our transition from the fragmented visual world of the existing educational establishment by every possible means.[11]

Of course, it is also true that television was ideally suited to McLuhan's favorite mode of communication—thinking out loud. That is why the clearest and most coherent summaries of McLuhan's ideas are contained in two interviews: the famous one in *Playboy*[12] and the less well-known one in the

critical collection edited by Gerald E. Stearn, *McLuhan: Hot & Cool*.[13] McLuhan understood that the consciousness of the boomer generation had been
irredeemably altered by the television environment, and that there was no
turning back, for better or for worse. The generational revolt of the 1960s
was fostered by this change in consciousness. In 1970, Gil Scott-Heron
released a song/poem titled "The Revolution Will Not Be Televised." He
was right, not only because corporate America would not sponsor it but primarily because television had already achieved a revolution in consciousness
stronger and more lasting than that of any political ideology. To appreciate
what McLuhan meant to the most perceptive of the boomer generation, it
would be useful to explore several propositions.

THE BABY BOOMERS WERE NOT THE FIRST GENERATION MCLUHAN THOUGHT HE HAD TO GET IN TOUCH WITH

The baby boom generation was not the first generation McLuhan thought
he had to get in touch with. It was that of their parents. In 1937, when he
first started teaching, at the University of Wisconsin, he was mystified by
his students' fascination with popular culture and their lack of interest in
the high culture in which he had been educated. Out of self-preservation
he made popcult a cultural artifact for study, using the techniques of practical criticism he learned at Cambridge University from I. A. Richards. In
Practical Criticism,[14] Richards recounts an extensive experiment of stripping
a series of poems in the tradition of English literature of their historical
and biographical information and having Cambridge students record their
reading responses. In his analysis, Richards catalogued and discussed the
students' barriers to understanding and devised counterstrategies for teachers to disabuse students of their misconceptions about poetry and gain a
stronger grasp on how poets achieve their effects on their readers and audiences. McLuhan would dedicate the rest of his career to applying a similar
approach to the effects of media.

But just as we must focus on the form of a poem to understand how it
enacts its content, to understand the effects of media one needs to shift
the focus of attention from their content to their formal characteristics. In
his poem "Ars Poetica," Archibald MacLeish wrote, "A poem should not
mean / But be." McLuhan would later express the corresponding media
relationship in this way: "[T]he 'content' of a medium is like the juicy piece
of meat carried by the burglar to distract the watchdog of the mind."[15] Later,
he added to this percept: "The audience is the content," expanding upon
Sergei Eisenstein's dictum that "the socially useful psychological and emotional effect that excites the audience . . . [is] the content of the film."[16] In

McLuhan's terms, the audience incorporates the content, and the content forms the corporate identity of the audience.

MCLUHAN "GROKKED" THAT THE EXPLOSION OF BOOMER-ORIENTED MEDIA AFTER WORLD WAR II WOULD CREATE A COUNTERCULTURAL GENERATION

In his 1961 book *Stranger in a Strange Land*, Robert A. Heinlein featured the concept of "grokking," which many in the baby boomer generation would adopt as a token of everything about them that separates their state of mind from that of their parents. In this scene (205–206), in a conversation about Martian culture, the Earth-born characters attempt to get their heads around the notion of grokking:

Mahmoud screwed up his face. "'Grok' means 'identically equal.' The human cliché 'This hurts me worse than it does you' has a Martian flavor. The Martians seem to know instinctively what we learned painfully from modern physics, that observer interacts with observed through the process of observation. 'Grok' means to understand so thoroughly that the observer becomes a part of the observed—to merge, blend, intermarry, lose identity in group experience. It means almost everything that we mean by religion, philosophy, and science—and it means as little to us as color means to a blind man." . . .

Mike nodded. "You spoke rightly, my brother Dr. Mahmoud. I am been saying so. Thou are God."

Mahmoud shrugged helplessly. "You see how hopeless it is? All I got was a blasphemy. We don't think in Martian. We *can't*."

"Thou art God," Mike said agreeably. "God groks."[17]

The Vedanta concept of Brahma had been introduced to youth and others in the West by Jack Kerouac's *Dharma Bums* and Gary Snyder's poetry; later, Fritjof Capra, in *The Tao of Physics*, would put the capstone on the growing sense of oneness between East and West that the baby boomers would embrace in their rejection of suburban sleepwalking and *anomie*. McLuhan was fond of quoting the following lines from James Joyce's *Finnegans Wake* to express the similar interface of consciousness fostered by the increase in international and intercultural communication rendered by global electronic communications: "The west shall shake the east awake . . . while ye have the night for morn" (473.22–23).

Heinlein connected with that spirit by providing a counter-environmental alien hero with whom boomers, who already felt themselves as strangers in a strange land, could identify. The Woodstock generation, "[a] generation lost in space," according to Don McLean in the boomer anthem "American Pie," would find its definition in fiction (science and otherwise), on the screens of movie theaters and televisions, and especially in liberated sex, drugs, and rock and roll. McLuhan summed up the age in this way:

> In the electric age, when our central nervous system is technologically extended to involve us in the whole of mankind and to incorporate the whole of mankind in us, we necessarily participate, in depth, in the consequences of our every action. It is no longer possible to adopt the aloof and dissociated role of the literate Westerner.[18]

This culture was the antienvironment to that of the late 1940s and 1950s. John Cage, Andy Warhol, Jackson Pollock, Jack Kerouac, Allen Ginsberg, Herbert Marcuse, Norman O. Brown, Alan Watts, Timothy Leary, Richard Alpert (later Baba Ram Dass), Paul Goodman, William Burroughs, Roger Corman, John Waters, et al. held the dominant culture up to scrutiny, and from all this emerged the boomer-oriented explosion of new media and technologies. McLuhan decided he had to keep up with what was going on or else lose all relevance. In turn, the boomers latched on to his star as a harbinger of the new age, and in the process elevated him to guru status—the Maharishi Mahesh Yogi of media consciousness. Theodore Roszak, teaching at California State College at Hayward, near the epicenter of the tectonic changes in consciousness, observes:

> The easy transition from one wing of the counter culture shows up in the pattern that has come to govern many of the free universities. These dissenting academies usually receive their send-off from campus New Leftists and initially emphasize heavy politics. But gradually the curricula tend to get hip both in content and teaching methods: psychedelics, light shows, multi-media, total theatre, people-heaping, McLuhan, exotic religion, touch and tenderness, ecstatic laboratories. . . . At this point, the project which the beats of the early fifties had taken up—the task of remodeling themselves, their way of life, their perceptions and sensitivities—rapidly takes precedence over the public task of changing institutions or policies.[19]

IN TURN, BOOMERS GROKKED THAT MCLUHAN LINKED TECHNOLOGY WITH FREEDOM OF CONSCIOUSNESS

In *The Greening of America*, another signature book of the sixties, Charles A. Reich posits that a changed attitude toward technology allowed the new generation to see the liberating potential of McLuhan's perspectives on media, in contrast to those of their parents' generation:

> Freedom from imposed consciousness requires freedom from the domination of technology. The new culture is built on the technology of the Corporate State, but not in the same way as the State's own culture is built: in the new culture, it is the technology that is dominated, not the people. The new generation's music makes use of modern electronics; its art (e.g., films) is technically sophisticated; its habits (reading) require affluence; its sexual mores require the pill. But the new generation does not use technology the way the older one does. Consciousness III does not use it for status or conspicuous consumption, not for power over people, or competitive "success." They do not use it to further rationalize society, to make life less challenging, more passive; they do not use it as a substitute for experience. They do not ignore its aesthetic, environmental, and human consequences. In short, instead of letting the technology dictate to them, instead of being the frenetic, driven victims of its demands, they use it as intelligent men and women might, to further their own lives. A key illustration of this is the fact technology is not allowed to rob them of experience.[20]

When baby boomers read in *Understanding Media* that "the medium is the message" (7), they needed no translation, justification, or explanation that McLuhan really didn't mean that the content of media didn't matter. Being the first TV generation, they knew in the fiber of their being that their relationship with electronic media was fundamentally different from that of their parents. In "Media Grammars, Generations, and Media Gaps," Gary Gumpert and Robert Cathcart, building on the work of Walter J. Ong and Edmund S. Carpenter, develop the notion that children born into a particular media environment are separated generationally from their parents (as well as, eventually, from those born after them in new environments), not just by their native expertise with the media they grew up with but also in consciousness and worldview:

> The perspective promulgated here is that media grammar (those rules and conventions based upon the properties which constitute media), and the acquisition of media literacy (the ability to meaningfully process mediated data) are altering social relationships. People develop particular media consciousness because media have different framing conventions and time orientations. That is, persons are influenced by the conventions and orientations peculiar to the media process first acquired and relate more readily to others with a similar media set.

Fifty and sixty year olds, for example, who have learned to process reality in terms of a logically ordered, continuous and linear world produced by a primary print orientation feel linked in rejecting the world view of those whose electronic orientation is to a visual/auditory, discontinuous reality. On the other hand, eighteen to twenty year olds might feel removed from twelve to fourteen year olds because they cannot fully grasp the digitally oriented computer world. . . . While the definition of what constitutes being media literate varies among ages and cultures, one thing is certain: each medium has a unique bias (Carpenter 1960). Thus, the acquisition of media literacy, like a person's native language, produces a particular world perspective which in turn influences social relationships.[21]

TV OR NOT TV—THAT WAS THE QUESTION

In *The Greening of America*, Reich listed many of the old and new technologies that transformed the social and cultural environment of the baby boom generation: electronic music, cinematic art, books, psychedelic drugs, and the Pill. However, he omitted television, the one that was the most influential in how baby boomers formed their self-concept, probably because it was so environmental that it was invisible to him. McLuhan saw all of these technologies as significant in understanding the psychic makeup of the new generation. Of course, Reich did not share with McLuhan a laser-like focus on emergent technologies as agents of social and cultural change. However, Reich's discussion of social, intellectual, aesthetic, and ideational influences on the new generation provides a useful perspective on the gestation of the new consciousness. It is remarkable how Reich and McLuhan came to quite similar impressions about the influences on youth of the day while approaching them from radically different intellectual and cultural stances. While Reich was unstinting in his admiration of the counterculture in transforming the consciousness of the era, hopefully for good, McLuhan, as always, chose not to moralize and withheld from public exposure attitudes and judgments consistent with his conservative cast of mind, which he expressed only in private.

Reich notes that the qualities of inclusiveness, communal sharing, and participation are a major part of the psychic makeup of members of the counterculture (which he is careful to specify as forming only a part of the baby boom generation, though a significant and influential part). He contrasts this tendency with the atomistic and competitive tendencies of their parents' generation. But most significant, it appears, in Reich's mind, was the counterculture's adoption of what Walter J. Ong, in *Orality and Literacy: Technologizing the Word*, terms a "participatory mystique":

At the same time, with telephone, radio, television and various kinds of sound tape, electronic technology has brought us into the age of 'secondary orality'. This new orality has striking resemblances to the old in its participatory mystique, its fostering of a communal sense, its concentration on the present moment, and even its use of formulas (Ong 1971, 284–303; 1977, 16–49, 305–341). . . .

Secondary orality is both remarkably like and remarkably unlike primary orality. Like primary orality, secondary orality has generated a strong group sense, for listening to spoken words forms hearers into a group, a true audience, just as reading written or printed texts turns individuals in on themselves. But secondary orality generates a sense for groups immeasurably larger than those of primary oral culture— McLuhan's 'global village.' Moreover, before writing, oral folk were group-minded because no feasible alternative had presented itself. In our age of secondary orality, we are groupminded self-consciously and programmatically. The individual feels that he or she, as an individual, must be socially sensitive. Unlike members of a primary oral culture, who are turned outward because they have had little occasion to turn inward, we are turned outward because we have turned inward. In a like vein, where primary orality promotes spontaneity because the analytic reflectiveness implemented by writing is unavailable, secondary orality promotes spontaneity because through analytic reflection we have decided that spontaneity is a good thing. We plan our happenings carefully to be sure that they are thoroughly spontaneous.[22]

Hence the appearance of happenings, be-ins, sit-ins, teach-ins, and other manifestations of group solidarity in the sixties and seventies, as well as the flash mobs of the current mobile communications age.

But why should electronic technology, particularly television, foster such a participatory mystique? McLuhan explained this phenomenon by recourse to the formal characteristics of the medium itself, showing why the first generation to be brought up on television, and by television, should be so different in group sense from their parents' and prior generations.

The key to understanding television lies in the distinction McLuhan draws in *Understanding Media* between "hot" and "cool" media:

A cool medium like hieroglyphic or ideogrammatic written characters has very different effects from the hot and explosive medium of the phonetic alphabet. The alphabet, when pushed to a high degree of abstract visual intensity, became typography. The printed word with its specialist intensity burst the bonds of medieval corporate guilds and monasteries, creating extreme individualist patterns of enterprise and monopoly. But the typical reversal occurred when extremes of monopoly brought back the corporation, with its impersonal empire over many lives. The hotting-up of the medium of writing to repeatable print intensity led to nationalism and the religious wars of the sixteenth century. . . .

Similarly, a very much greater speed-up, such as occurs with electricity, may serve to restore a tribal pattern of intense involvement such as took place with the introduction of radio in Europe, and is now tending to happen as a result of TV in America. Specialist technologies detribalize. The nonspecialist electric technology retribalizes.[23]

McLuhan appropriated "hot" and "cool" from jazz argot in the late 1940s and 1950s. A hot medium is one in high definition, providing information in sharply defined packages that flood one particular sense. Similarly, hot jazz consisted of tightly scripted arrangements in which each player had a highly defined part to play, with improvisation restricted to only a few bars in spotlighted solos. By contrast, cool jazz emerged from bebop innovators such as Charlie Parker, Dizzy Gillespie, and Miles Davis. It evolved into a highly participatory style, in which the theme is played briefly at the beginning and recapitulated at the end, but in the middle the players are responsible for mutually creating the work almost entirely through improvisation, with each player having a role in the group composition rather than through a composed part in an arrangement. By parallel, relatively cool media are of lower definition and require greater participation and interactivity to complete the experience; instead of "observers" there are highly involved "participants."

Television is a cooler medium than film, writing, or print, because it requires so much participation on the part of the viewer to complete the image. Like cartoons, early television provided a relatively indistinct and low-definition image, requiring viewers' eyes to constantly explore the contours of the quickly changing image in an attempt to reconstruct it on the fly. Although modern high-definition television provides a vastly sharper image, it does so by increasing the number of pixels and speeding up the refresh rate, thus adding to the viewer's cognitive involvement. As a result, watching television requires a maximal amount of participation in depth in the recreation of its images, erasing the objectified relationship between user and medium fostered by print and, as a consequence, undermining the sense of detachment experienced in reading. Readers have complete control over their pace of scanning, whereas in watching television, the viewer is constantly trying to keep up with the rapid changes in the image.

Ong alludes to McLuhan's "global village," which typically was misunderstood by McLuhan's adherents and critics alike as his version of *Hair*'s "dawning of the Age of Aquarius." Anyone who has lived in a real village, or a city, or any collection of humans, understands that none of these environments is ipso facto an eternal haven of peace, love, and happiness. McLuhan's first published use of the term, in *The Gutenberg Galaxy*, undercuts that notion:

> [T]he electric dilation of our various senses . . . creates what [Teilhard] de Chardin calls the "noosphere" or a technological brain for the world. Instead of tending towards a vast Alexandrian library the world has become a computer, an electronic brain, exactly as in an infantile piece of science fiction. And as our senses have gone outside us, Big Brother goes inside. So, unless aware of this dynamic, we shall at once move into a phase of panic terrors, exactly befitting a small world of tribal drums, total interdependence, and superimposed coexistence.[24]

THE COUNTERCULTURE DIDN'T FADE AWAY—IT BECAME THE COMPUTER COMMUNICATION CULTURE

Since the mid-1990s, with the public's growing consciousness and embrace of the Internet and the World Wide Web, McLuhan's reputation has experienced an astounding upsurge. One possible reason for this revival of interest is that the creation of global television networks and the burgeoning of the Web have manifestly demonstrated the trends he made us aware of 50 years ago. The globalization of consciousness he announced and the cultural effects he spoke of are by now almost taken for granted, and journalists blithely reiterate McLuhan's most revolutionary observations almost daily with no attribution, often, perhaps, because they are unaware of their provenance, so much have McLuhan's ideas been absorbed into the culture. Adopted as the "patron saint" of *Wired* magazine in 1996, he has been the subject of hundreds of publications since then, including several new and updated biographies, websites, online journals, special issues of scholarly print journals, blogs, and on and on.

The enhanced appreciation of his thought has doubtless been reinforced by the World Wide Web's use of hypertext: multilinear associations linking multifaceted, multimediated phenomena that print-oriented consciousness can normally deal with only linearly and one at a time. Although identified in the public mind with television, McLuhan was aware from the beginning of the growth of computer networking and referred to it regularly throughout his work, and only now can we appreciate the fruits of that awareness. As a thinker, McLuhan was both a man of his time and ahead of it—and the complex image he projects demands that we closely examine the intimate interactions between his thinking and that of the baby boom generation.

An intertitle in Jean-Luc Godard's 1966 film, *Masculine Feminine: 15 Specific Events*, reads, "This film could be called *The Children of Marx and*

Coca-Cola." In *Odyssey*, John Sculley's account of his being wooed from Pep-siCo, Inc. to become CEO of Apple Computer, Inc., he recounts the long walking session in New York in which Steve Jobs ultimately persuaded him to join the revolution. Sculley presents this as Jobs's ultimate argument: "Do you want to spend the rest of your life selling sugared water or do you want a chance to change the world?"[25] So it might fairly be said that, in its Apple-driven, consumer-oriented phase, any story of the computer revolution could be called *The Children of McLuhan and Pepsi-Cola.*

Jobs, Steve Wozniak, Guy Kawasaki, Alan Kay, Bill Gates, Steve Ballmer, and other major actors in the Apple–Microsoft wars, not to mention so many others in the rest of the computer industry, were born into or close to the baby boom generation and shared its common mediated experiences. Jobs had the vision to recognize that the research being done at Xerox Palo Alto Research Center on the graphical user interface for personal comput-ers—the marriage between the computer and television—contained the key to the future for computing.

The artists, teachers, designers, academics, typographers, illustrators, architects, and process engineers who had been weaned on McLuhan were the first enthusiastic adopters of the Macintosh, and they and the growing audience of students and other adherents established the groundwork for the rivalry with Microsoft that has defined the era since the first microcom-puters were produced. From Apple I and II through the Macintosh, the NeXT Computer, the iPod, the iPhone, the iPad, and all their imitators, the genius of Steve Jobs and many of his cohort was to recognize the soci-ety-transforming power of the personal computer (combined with what Jobs called the "interpersonal computer")[26] then the mobile, personal commu-nication device: the medium that, no matter what its content, has become the message.

NOTES

1. "He never intended to offer his audience eternal verities, and he was upset when he felt his remarks were taken that way. He was much happier when peo-ple reacted to his provocations by rethinking their own eternal verities. To that end, he would do almost anything to get under their skin. . . . From [the beliefs of Symbolist poets, such as Baudelaire, that poets speak through their readers' reac-tions] McLuhan developed his idea of 'putting on' an audience. The idea was a complicated one. Basically, it meant that McLuhan always tried to avoid a purely didactic role—the role of telling something to others. He rarely went before any group with a prepared text. Armed, at best, with a few headings, he 'put on' the audience by appearing to know something they did not know about the very things they were most certain they knew. (McLuhan believed that speakers who read from

prepared texts put on the texts, not the audience.) He chipped away at the identity of the audience—their assumptions, their expectations. In doing so, he consciously assumed the oracular pose. If the members of the audience were irritated or their sensibilities offended, all the better; chances were good that their awareness, in the end, would be heightened." Philip Marchand, *Marshall McLuhan: The Medium and the Messenger* (Cambridge, MA: MIT Press, 1998), 189–190.

2. Marshall McLuhan, *Understanding Media: The Extensions of Man* (New York: McGraw-Hill, 1964), 7.

3. Marshall McLuhan, *The Gutenberg Galaxy: The Making of Typographic Man* (Toronto: University of Toronto Press, 1962), 31.

4. Bruce Powe, in a comment made during a panel discussion on McLuhan's life at the reThinking McLuhan Conference, York University, North York, Ontario, March 21, 1997.

5. E-mail message to the Media Ecology Association electronic distribution list, August 1998.

6. Daniel J. Boorstin, *The Image: A Guide to Pseudo-Events in America* (New York: Random House Vintage, 1992), 47.

7. "On the Scene," *Playboy*, February 1967, quoted in Philip Marchand, *Marshall McLuhan: The Medium and the Messenger* (Cambridge, MA: MIT Press, 1998), 49.

8. Neil Strauss, *Everyone Loves You When You're Dead: Journeys into Fame and Madness* (New York: HarperCollins, 2011), 337.

9. W. Terrence Gordon, *Marshall McLuhan: Escape into Understanding* (New York: Basic Books, 1997), 301.

10. Gordon, *Marshall McLuhan*, 212.

11. McLuhan, *Understanding Media*, ix.

12. Eric Norden, "*Playboy* Interview: Marshall McLuhan: A Candid Conversation with the High Priest of Popcult and Metaphysician of Media," *Playboy*, March 1969, 53.

13. Gerald E. Stearn and Marshall McLuhan, "A Dialogue: Q & A," in *McLuhan: Hot & Cool*, ed. Gerald E. Stearn (New York: Dial Press, 1967), 266–302.

14. I. A. Richards, *Practical Criticism: A Study of Literary Judgment* (New York: Harcourt, Brace & World, 1956).

15. McLuhan, *Understanding Media*, 18.

16. Quoted in Jim Ellis, *Derek Jarman's Angelic Conversations* (Minneapolis: University of Minnesota Press, 2009), 137.

17. Robert Heinlein, *Stranger in a Strange Land* (New York: Berkley Medallion, 1968), 205–206.

18. McLuhan, *Understanding Media*, 4.

19. Theodore Roszak, *The Making of a Counter Culture: Reflections on the Technocratic Society and Its Youthful Opposition* (New York: Doubleday Anchor, 1969), 63.

20. Charles A. Reich, *The Greening of America* (New York: Random House, 1970), 255–256.

21. Gary Gumpert and Robert Cathcart, "Media Grammars, Generations, and Media Gaps," *Critical Studies in Mass Communication* 2 (1985): 23–24.

22. Walter J. Ong, *Orality and Literacy: Technologizing the Word* (New York: Routledge, 2002), 133–134.

23. McLuhan, *Understanding Media*, 23–24.
24. McLuhan, *The Gutenberg Galaxy*, 32.
25. John Sculley, *Pepsi to Apple . . . A Journey of Adventure, Ideas, and the Future* (New York: Harper & Row, 1987), 90.
26. "Steve Jobs Information: NeXT Computer," http://stevejobsinfo.blogspot .com/p/next-computer.html.

REFERENCES

Boorstin, Daniel J. *The Image: A Guide to Pseudo-Events in America*. New York: Random House Vintage, 1992. First published in 1962 as *The Image or What Happened to the American Dream*. New York: Athenaeum.
Capra, Fritjof. *The Tao of Physics: An Exploration of the Parallels Between Modern Physics and Eastern Mysticism*. 5th ed. Boston: Shambhala, 2010.
Carpenter, Edmund. "The New Languages." In *Explorations In Communication*, edited by Edmund Carpenter and Marshall McLuhan, 162–179. Boston: Beacon Press, 1960.
Ellis, Jim. *Derek Jarman's Angelic Conversations*. Minneapolis: University of Minnesota Press, 2009.
Gordon, W. Terrence. *Marshall McLuhan: Escape into Understanding*. New York: Basic Books, 1997.
Gumpert, Gary, and Robert Cathcart. "Media Grammars, Generations, and Media Gaps." *Critical Studies in Mass Communication* 2 (1985): 23–35.
Heinlein, Robert A. *Stranger in a Strange Land*. New York: Berkley Medallion, 1968.
Joyce, James. *Finnegans Wake*. New York: Viking Compass, 1959.
Kerouac, Jack. *The Dharma Bums*. New York: Viking, 1958.
Marchand, Philip. *Marshall McLuhan: The Medium and the Messenger*. Cambridge, MA: MIT Press, 1998. First published 1989 by Random House of Canada.
McLuhan, Herbert Marshall. *The Mechanical Bride: Folklore of Industrial Man*. New York: Vanguard Press, 1951.
McLuhan, Marshall. *The Gutenberg Galaxy: The Making of Typographic Man*. Toronto: University of Toronto Press, 1962.
McLuhan, Marshall. *Understanding Media: The Extensions of Man*. New York: McGraw-Hill, 1964.
McLuhan, Marshall, and Quentin Fiore (Produced by Jerome Agel). *The Medium Is the Massage: An Inventory of Effects*. New York: Random House, 1967.
McLuhan, Marshall, and Quentin Fiore (Produced by Jerome Agel). (Co-ordinated by Jerome Agel). *War and Peace in the Global Village; An Inventory of Some of the Current Spastic Situations That Could Be Eliminated by More Feedforward*. New York: McGraw-Hill, 1968.
Norden, Eric. "*Playboy* Interview: Marshall McLuhan: A Candid Conversation with the High Priest of Popcult and Metaphysician of Media." *Playboy*, March 1969, 53.
Ong, Walter J. *Rhetoric, Romance, and Technology: Studies in the Interaction of Expression and Culture*. Ithaca, NY: Cornell University Press, 1971.

Ong, Walter J. *Interfaces of the Word: Studies in the Evolution of Consciousness and Culture.* Ithaca, NY: Cornell University Press, 1977.

Ong, Walter J. *Orality and Literacy: Technologizing the Word.* New York: Routledge, 2002.

Reich, Charles A. *The Greening of America.* New York: Random House, 1970.

Richards, I. A. *Practical Criticism; A Study of Literary Judgment.* New York: Harcourt, Brace & World, 1956.

Roszak, Theodore. *The Making of a Counter Culture: Reflections on the Technocratic Society and Its Youthful Opposition.* Garden City, NY: Doubleday Anchor, 1969.

Schickel, Richard. "Marshall McLuhan: Canada's Intellectual Comet." *Harper's,* November 1965, 62.

Sculley, John. *Odyssey: Pepsi to Apple . . . A Journey of Adventure, Ideas, and the Future.* New York: Harper & Row, 1987.

Snyder, Gary. *Riprap.* Ashland, CA: Origin Press, 1959.

Snyder, Gary. *Myths & Texts.* New York: Totem Press, 1960.

Stearn, Gerald Emanuel, ed. *McLuhan: Hot & Cool; A Critical Symposium.* New York: Dial, 1967.

Stearn, Gerald E., and Marshall McLuhan. "A Dialogue: Q & A," in *McLuhan: Hot & Cool,* ed. Gerald E. Stearn. New York: Dial, 1967.

"Steve Jobs Information: NeXT Computer." http://stevejobsinfo.blogspot.com/p/next-computer.html

Strauss, Neil. *Everyone Loves You When You're Dead: Journeys Into Fame and Madness.* New York: HarperCollins, 2011.

Wolfe, Tom. "What If He Is Right?" in *The Pump House Gang.* New York: Bantam, 1969, 135–170.

Index

About the Editors and Contributors

EDITORS

Brian Cogan, PhD, is associate professor and chair in the Department of Communications at Molloy College, Rockville Centre, NY. He is the author, coauthor, and coeditor of numerous books, articles, and anthologies on popular culture, music, and the media. His published work includes Greenwood's *Encyclopedia of Punk Music and Culture*; *Encyclopedia of Politics, the Media, and Popular Culture*; and *Encyclopedia of Heavy Metal Music*; as well as *Mosh the Polls: Youth Voters, Popular Culture, and Democratic Engagement*.

Thom Gencarelli, PhD, is associate professor and the founding chair of the Communication Department at Manhattan College in Riverdale, NY. His published works include articles about media literacy/media education, media ecology, popular media and culture (with an emphasis on popular music), and general semantics. He is currently at work on a book about language acquisition and cognitive development. Gencarelli is also a composer and musician and has two recorded albums to his credit. He holds a doctorate in media ecology from New York University.

CONTRIBUTORS

Robert Albrecht is the author of numerous articles on the relationship of media and culture in Latin America and the United States. He is the recipient of an Organization of American States Fellowship for study in Brazil and the Carlos Vigil Prize for his publications on Latin American popular culture. While a doctoral student in the Media Ecology program at New York University, he served as arts editor to *ETC*. He worked for several years as a music and drama workshop leader with children in Jersey City public schools. He currently serves on the editorial board of several communication journals and teaches theory and media history courses in the Media Arts Department at New Jersey City University in Jersey City. His book, *Mediating the Muse* (Hampton Press, 2004) was the winner of the Dorothy Lee Award for outstanding scholarship in the area of cultural ecology. Robert is also a musician and a songwriter. His most recent CD, *A Tale of Two Cities* (2012), consists of a cycle of songs he composed about people, places, and events in Jersey City. An earlier CD, *Song of the Poet* (2008), is a collection of poems by such authors as Walt Whitman, Edgar Allan Poe, Muhammad Ali, and others that he placed in musical settings. *Song of the Poet* received the John Culkin Award from the Media Ecology Association in 2012.

Sarah Boslaugh is the director of new titles for Golson Media, where she oversees both front-end and back-end operations for multiple reference titles annually. She received her PhD from City University of New York and her MPH from Saint Louis University and worked as a statistician for 20 years, while also developing her writing career, before joining the publishing industry full-time. Her books as an author include *Statistics in a Nutshell* (O'Reilly, 2nd ed., 2012), *Secondary Data Sources for Public Health* (Cambridge University Press, 2007), and *An Intermediate Guide to SPSS Programming* (Sage, 2004), and her works as an editor include *The Encyclopedia of Epidemiology* (Sage, 2007) and *The Encyclopedia of Pharmacology and Society* (Sage, forthcoming).

Cheryl A. Casey is an assistant professor of media communication in the Communication and Creative Media Division at Champlain College in Burlington, Vermont. Among her research interests are the relationship between language and culture, critical media studies, and media history. Casey has presented and published her work in international and national forums and earned several top paper awards. Her most recent project is a media studies textbook, *New Media, Communication, and Society: The Hyper-connected World* (Peter Lang), for which she is a coauthor.

Salvatore J. Fallica teaches in the Department of Media, Culture and Communication at New York University. His fields of interest include social and political propaganda as well as spectacle and celebrity culture. Many years ago, as a teenager, he attended a Joan Baez concert at the Forest Hills Tennis Stadium in Queens, New York. Toward the end of that concert, Ms. Baez performed "Blowin' in the Wind" to great applause and then, to even more applause, introduced the crowd to its author, Bob Dylan.

Michael Grabowski, PhD, is an associate professor in the Communication Department at Manhattan College. He is the editor of *Neuroscience and*

Media: New Understandings and Representations (Routledge). His work on documentaries, feature films, commercials, music videos, and news has played at the Guggenheim, at the Smithsonian, in several film festivals, and on several broadcast and cable networks. He currently is a senior research consultant for Audience Theory, a research firm whose clients include top television networks, producers, and new media companies. His work explores how different forms of mediated communication shape the way people think and act within their symbolic environment.

Robert Hensley-King is a PhD candidate and member of the Centre for Cinema and Media Studies at Ghent University. He has also contributed to the online MSc in history at the University of Edinburgh. His research focuses primarily on the evolution of the antihero in New Hollywood Cinema. His presentations and contracted publications explore the social and historical aspects of screen culture.

Todd Kelshaw is an associate professor in the School of Communication and Media at Montclair State University (New Jersay). His scholarship primarily addresses democratic participation in civic, political, and organizational settings and includes an edited book—*Partnerships for Service-Learning: Impacts on Communities and Students* (Jossey-Bass)—and various articles and book chapters about such topics as public governance meetings, dialogic and deliberative interaction, community organizing, community-based learning, and online democratic communication.

Gary Kenton earned his master's degree in communication from Fordham University. He is an educator who has taught at every level, from Head Start to college. For many years, he specialized in special education, working with students on the autism spectrum. He is currently an adjunct instructor of communication at Marist College and Western Connecticut State University. His writing has been published in *Television Quarterly*, *The Washington Post*, *TV Guide*, and *Rolling Stone* and will appear in the second edition of *The Sitcom Reader*. Gary is also an elected official, serving as a trustee in the village of Rhinebeck, New York, and a member of the Rhinebeck Conservation Advisory Board. He is cohost of *Activist Radio*, a weekly radio show on the public radio station at Vassar College, WVKR (103.1 FM), and on the Web. He is married to Laura R. Linder, PhD.

Rebecca Kern is an associate professor of communication, media studies, and advertising at Manhattan College. Her research interests focus on community and identity discourse and practice; gender studies; critical/cultural studies; and the intersections with television, new media, and advertising formats. Of particular interest is the ways in which media reflects larger cultural values and changes and how media changes the ways community and identity construction are formed. She has published in a number of journals, including: *Sexualities*, *Journal of Homosexuality*, *Telematics and Informatics*, and *First Monday*.

William M. Knoblauch is an assistant professor of history at Finlandia University in Hancock, Michigan. He earned his PhD in American history from Ohio University, where he was also a fellow of the Contemporary History Institute. His research focuses on connections between U.S. foreign policy and popular culture during the Cold War.

Anastacia Kurylo is a communication consultant and former professor who has taught at various colleges, including New York University, Rutgers University, and St. John's University. Her primary research area is the exploration of interpersonally communicated stereotypes, their role in stereotype maintenance, and their consequences for interpersonal, intercultural, and organizational outcomes. Currently, she is president of the New York chapter of the Tri-State Diversity Council and vice president elect of the New York State Communication Association. She has more than 25 publications, including, most recently, *Inter/Cultural Communication: Representation and Construction of Culture* published with SAGE and *The Communicated Stereotype: From Celebrity Vilification to Everyday Talk* published with Lexington Press.

David Linton is professor emeritus of communication arts at Marymount Manhattan College. He received his PhD at New York University in the program in media ecology under the direction of Neil Postman. His research and teaching interests have included Shakespeare's treatment of media, the reading behavior of the Virgin Mary, the Luddite Movement, and, most recently, the social construction of menstruation. He is president of the New York Conference of the American Association of University Professors and editor of the newsletter of the Society for Menstrual Cycle Research.

James C. Morrison teaches in the Communication Department at Boston College and has taught at Harvard University, MIT, Emerson College, and Western Connecticut State University. He has published articles and reviews in *Explorations in Media Ecology {EME}*, the *Proceedings of the Media Ecology Association*, *Counterblast*, *New Dimensions in Communication*, and *Technology and Culture*. He has also contributed chapters to *The Urban Communication Reader* (Hampton Press, 2007), and *Perspectives on Culture, Technology and Communication: The Media Ecology Tradition* (Hampton Press, 2006). A past president of the Media Ecology Association, he has also served as the MEA's historian and Internet officer. He is also a member of the Editorial

Board of *Counterblast: The e-Journal of Culture & Communication*. His research interests focus on the cultural, social, and cognitive impacts of new communication media.

Sheila J. Nayar is a professor of English, communication, and media studies at Greensboro College, Greensboro, NC. She is the author of several books, including *Cinematically Speaking* and *The Sacred and the Cinema* as well as journal publications on a variety of topics, including Bollywood, silent film, film aesthetics, and the politics of the cinematic canon.

Todd K. Platts is a visiting assistant professor of sociology at the University of Southern Mississippi. He has taught courses in introductory sociology, social deviance, marriage and family, and culture and mass media. His publications have explored issues as diverse as race and racism and the sociology of zombies. Among his many current projects is an examination of the industrial conditions that underwrote the (re)emergence of zombie cinema in the 21st century. He is also working on translating his recently completed dissertation on the evolution of zombie cinema into a monograph on the subject.

Phil Rose, PhD, currently teaches in the department of Communication Studies at York University in Toronto and is president of the Media Ecology Association. Among his research and teaching interests are the evolution and history of technology, signal and symbol systems, and communications media (from before the origins of symbolic thought to the most recent technological developments); social and cultural issues related to literacy; concerns pertaining to technology and violence, particularly in relation to the mimetic theory of René Girard; and topics related to popular music and performance. In addition to the Beatles he has also written about Radiohead, and he is author of the forthcoming book *Roger Waters and Pink Floyd: The Concept Albums*, a project to be published by Fairleigh Dickinson University Press for which he extensively interviewed the former creative leader of the classic group.

Lance Strate is professor of communication and media studies at Fordham University. As one of the founders of the Media Ecology Association, he served as the MEA's first president for more than a decade, and continues to serve on the organization's advisory council. He is also a past president of the New York State Communication Association, a trustee and former executive director of the Institute of General Semantics, an editor and partner with NeoPoiesis Press, and the president of Congregation Adas Emuno in Leonia, New Jersey. He is the author of more than 100 articles on media and communication and several books, including *Echoes and Reflections: On Media Ecology as a Field of Study* (Hampton Press, 2006), *On* the *Binding Biases of Time and Other Essays on General Semantics and Media Ecology* (Institute of General Semantics, 2011), *Amazing Ourselves to Death: Neil Postman's Brave New World Revisited* (Peter Lang, 2014), and a poetry collection, *Thunder at Darwin Station* (NeoPoiesis Press, 2014). A former editor of several journals, including *Explorations in Media Ecology*, which he founded, the *Speech Communication Annual*, and the *General Semantics Bulletin*, he has coedited several anthologies, including two editions of *Communication and Cyberspace* with Ron Jacobson and Stephanie Gibson (Hampton Press, 1996, 2003), *Critical Studies in Media Commercialism* with Robin Andersen (Oxford University Press, 2000), *The Legacy of McLuhan* with Edward Wachtel (Hampton Press, 2005), *Korzybski And . . .* with Corey Anton (Institute of General Semantics, 2012), and *The Medium Is the Muse: Channeling Marshall McLuhan* with Adeena Karasick (NeoPoiesis Press, 2014). Translations of his writing have appeared in French, Spanish, Italian, Portuguese, Hungarian, Hebrew, Mandarin, and Quenya. He was a recipient of the Media Ecology Association's 2013 Walter J. Ong Award for Career Achievement in Scholarship and the New York State Communication Association's John F. Wilson Fellow Award for scholarship and service in 1998. In 2002, Denver mayor Wellington E. Webb proclaimed "that February 15, 2002, be known as Dr. Lance Strate Day in the City and County of Denver" in honor of the keynote address he gave for the Rocky Mountain Communication Association.

Kim Trager Bohley is a lecturer at the Institute for American Thought, Indiana University-Purdue University, Indianapolis. Her research interests include the history of the book, media globalization, cultural studies, and ethnographic methods. Her research has been published in a number of academic journals, including *Mass Communication and Society*, *Communication Review*, *Journalism and Mass Communication Educator*, *Participations: International Journal of Audience Research*, and *Asian Journal of Communication*. Kim Trager Bohley received her combined PhD in mass communication and American studies from Indiana University.

Ed Tywoniak is associate professor of communication studies at Saint Mary's College of California where he has served on the faculty in the School of Liberal Arts for more than 35 years. Professor Tywoniak also holds the position of faculty fellow for curriculum and technology and is director of the W. M. Keck Digital Studies Laboratory. He is is the editor of *ETC: A Review of General Semantics*, a member and past chair of the Division for Communication and the Future of the National Communication Association, a member of the board of directors of the Media Ecology Association, and a trustee of the Institute of General Semantics as well as the School of Applied Theology of the Berkeley Graduate Theology Union.

Christopher Allen Varlack is a lecturer in the Department of English and Language Arts at Morgan State University where he teaches courses in freshman composition and humanities. He received his BA in communications from Loyola University Maryland and his MFA in creative writing from the University of Southern Maine. He is also a PhD student at Morgan State University, where he is pursuing a degree in American literature; his research centers on 19th- and 20th-century American literature with an emphasis on race.